C000293751

The Soviet
A Documentary ...story
Volume 2 1939–1991

The Soviet story—the revolution, Lenin, Stalinism, the Great Patriotic
War, the era of Khrushchev, Brezhnev and the Cold War, and the
dramatic collapse under Gorbachev—looms large in history syllabuses
across the world.

This two-volume history casts fresh light on the story by drawing upon
the primary material that has become available since the collapse of communist rule in 1991, much of it not previously published in English.
Combining lucid narrative and analysis and a rich selection of evocative
documents, it provides a lively entrée to current debate over humanity's most
momentous and tragic experiment.

Conceived as a companion to the highly-regarded, best-selling four-
volume *Nazism 1919–1945: A Documentary Reader* by Noakes and Pridham
(also published by University of Exeter Press) Acton and Stableford's documentary history will be a valuable resource for students at all levels.

★ ★ ★

Volume Two is structured chronologically in four parts. It begins with the
Nazi-Soviet pact and the fraught diplomatic and military preamble to the
Nazi invasion, evokes the full horror of the Great Patriotic War, and recounts
in detail the dramas of the Cold War period and the final fracturing of the
USSR along the national faultlines of its 15 Union Republics.

> "Professor Acton engages the reader in every significant debate that has
> emerged. . . This documentary history is interlaced with narrative commen-
> tary which delivers cogent analysis with obvious wholehearted enthusiasm
> and an icy perceptiveness that clarifies and enriches our understanding in
> equal measure."　　　　　　*History Teaching Review Year Book,* 2006

Also available:
The Soviet Union: A Documentary History, Volume 1 1917–1940
paperback 978 0 85989 581 1 / hardback 978 0 85989 715 0

EXETER STUDIES IN HISTORY

General Editors: Jonathan Barry, Tim Rees and T.P. Wiseman

Modern European history titles in this series:

The Civilian in War: The Home Front in Europe, Japan and the USA in World War II edited by Jeremy Noakes (1992)

Nazism 1919–1945

> Volume 1: *The Rise to Power 1919–1934: A Documentary Reader* edited by J. Noakes and G. Pridham (new edition with index, 1998)

> Volume 2: *State, Economy and Society 1933–1939: A Documentary Reader* edited by J. Noakes and G. Pridham (new edition with index, 2000)

> Volume 3: *Foreign Policy, War and Racial Extermination: A Documentary Reader* edited by J. Noakes and G. Pridham (new edition with index, 2001)

> Volume 4: *The German Home Front in World War II: A Documentary Reader* edited by Jeremy Noakes (with index, 1998)

The Last Years of Austria-Hungary: A Multi-National Experiment in Early Twentieth Century Europe edited by Mark Cornwall (revised and expanded edition, 2002)

Nazism, War and Genocide edited by Neil Gregor (2005)

The Soviet Union: A Documentary History, Volume 1 1917–1940 by Edward Acton and Tom Stableford (2005)

The Soviet Union: A Documentary History, Volume 2 1939–1991 by Edward Acton and Tom Stableford (2007)

The Soviet Union
A Documentary History

Volume 2 1939–1991

Edward Acton and Tom Stableford

UNIVERSITY
of
EXETER
PRESS

Paperback cover image: Photograph taken by David King in 1977 at the sixtieth
anniversary celebrations of the October Revolution in Moscow. The banner reads 'Glory
to the Great October Revolution'. (The David King Collection, London)

First published in 2007 by
University of Exeter Press
Reed Hall, Streatham Drive
Exeter EX4 4QR
UK
www.exeterpress.co.uk

© Edward Acton and Tom Stableford 2007

The right of Edward Acton and Tom Stableford to be identified as authors
of this work has been asserted by them in accordance with
the Copyright, Designs and Patents Act 1988.

Maps by András Bereznay, www.historyonmaps.com

British Library Cataloguing in Publication Data
A catalogue record for this book is available
from the British Library.

Hardback ISBN 978 0 85989 716 7
Paperback ISBN 978 0 85989 582 8

Typeset in 11/12½ pt Bembo
by XL Publishing Services, Tiverton

Printed by Gutenberg Press Ltd, Malta

Contents

Part One: Dealing with Hitler (1939–1941)

See pages 463–476 for List of Documents

See pages 463–476 for List of Documents

See pages 463–476 for List of Documents

Part Four: Crisis and Collapse (1985–1991)

See pages 463–476 for List of Documents

See pages 463–476 for List of Documents

Acknowledgements

The first debt which Tom Stableford and I would like to acknowledge is to the team of Russian scholars at the A.M. Gorky Urals State University led by M.E. Glavatsky, who compiled the documentary collection around which both instalments of this two-volume history are built. Robert Lewis of Exeter University made a valuable contribution during the early stages of our work. Our thanks to Peter Gatrell and Steve Smith for their encouragement, to András Bereznay for his fine cartography, and to Simon Baker, Anna Henderson and Tim Rees at University of Exeter Press for their unstinting patience and good counsel. We would also again like to pay tribute to Trish Stableford for her expert proof-reading.

My own greatest debt is to Dr Francis King of the University of East Anglia. Throughout, his expertise and help on every facet of text and documents alike have been indispensable, and he assembled the Biographical Index for both volumes. I am grateful to the British Academy for funding his work on the project, and to the AHRC for funding a period of research leave to enable me to bring the text to completion. Finally, I would like to express my gratitude to Tom Stableford of the Slavonic Division at the Bodleian Library, Oxford. He was the prime mover behind the project. He translated the vast majority of the documents. And he proved the most supportive and considerate of collaborators.

Edward Acton
The University of East Anglia

Note on Transliteration, Russian Words and Acronyms

In producing a volume of this nature, it is always difficult to decide which Russian words, acronyms and concepts to translate, and which to transliterate. In general, we have proceeded as follows:

Acronyms have been left in their Russian form except where there is a well-established English form, such as CPSU and USSR.

Words denoting specifically Russian weights, measures and administrative regions (e.g., *oblasti*) have been transliterated and italicized, and keep their Russian plurals. An exception is the word *rayon*, which corresponds closely enough to the English word 'district' and has therefore been translated. Where Russian words have entered the English language (e.g., 'kulak'), they have been given English plurals and are not italicized. Russian words and acronyms are explained in the glossary.

Transliteration of words and names has been carried out broadly in line with the Taylorian scheme, but we have used the ending '-sky', as in 'Trotsky', for proper names.

Glossary of Russian Words
and Acronyms

artel' (pl. *arteli*) — co-operative association of workmen or peasants.

ASSR — *Avtonomnaya sovetskaya sotsialisticheskaya respublika*, Autonomous Soviet Socialist Republic. Administrative division, denoting an area of a Union republic inhabited by one or more distinct national groups. ASSRs, most of which were in the RSFSR, had a greater degree of autonomy than other administrative divisions on certain legal and cultural matters.

AVP RF — *Arkhiv vneshney politiki Rossiyskoy Federatsii*, Archive of Foreign Policy of the Russian Federation.

CIS (SNG) — Commonwealth of Independent States. Loose grouping of most of the former Soviet states, established after collapse of the USSR.

COMECON (CMEA) — Council for Mutual Economic Assistance. Intergovernmental economic organization based in Moscow. Functioned from 1949 to 1991. Members included Albania (to 1961), Bulgaria, Cuba, Czechoslovakia, GDR, Hungary, Mongolia, Poland, Romania, USSR, Vietnam.

Cominform — Communist Information Bureau. Select group of important communist parties. Functioned from 1947 to 1956. Members included the CPs of Bulgaria, Czechoslovakia, France, Hungary, Italy, Poland, Romania, USSR and Yugoslavia (expelled 1948).

CPCz — Communist Party of Czechoslovakia.

CPSU — Communist Party of the Soviet Union

CzSSR — Czecho-Slovak Socialist Republic.

DRA — Democratic Republic of Afghanistan. State title of Afghanistan after left-wing takeover in 1978.

GARF — *Gosudarstvennyy arkhiv Rossiyskoy Federatsii*, State Archive of the Russian Federation.

GDR — German Democratic Republic.

GKChP — *Gosudarstvennyy komitet po chrezvychaynomu polozheniyu*, State Committee for the State of Emergency. Group of government and party officials which deposed M.S. Gorbachev, 19 August 1991.

GKO — *Gosudarstvennyy komitet oborony*, State Defence Committee. Supreme state body in USSR June 1941 to September 1945.

glasnost — openness. Policy of officially admitting to failings, shortcomings and problems, proclaimed by M.S. Gorbachev in 1986.

Gosplan — *Gosudarstvennaya planovaya komissiya*, State Planning Commission. Established 1921 to devise plans for the entire Soviet economy, including all sectors and regions.

GPU — *Gosudarstvennoe politicheskoe upravlenie*, State Political Administration. Successor to the Cheka as Soviet political police, 1922–23.

GULAG — *Glavnoe upravlenie ispravitel'no-trudovykh lagerey i trudovykh koloniy*, Main Administration of Corrective Labour Camps and Labour Colonies.

HPR — Hungarian People's Republic.

KGB — *Komitet gosudarstvennoy bezopasnosti*, Committee of State Security. Soviet political police from 1954. Subordinate from that date to the USSR Council of Ministers.

kolkhoz — *kollektivnoe khozyaystvo*, collective farm.

Komsomol — *Vsesoyuznyy leninskiy kommunisticheskiy soyuz molodezhi*, All-Union Leninist Communist Union of Youth. Soviet Young Communist League.

korenizatsiya — nativization. CPSU policy aimed at ensuring native participation and leadership in the non-Russian areas of the USSR.

kray (pl. *kraya*) — large-scale administrative and territorial region in USSR after 1920s, usually inhabited by a discrete and compact national group. (See also *oblast'*.)

LDPR — *Liberal'no-demokraticheskaya partiya Rossii*, Liberal–Democratic Party of Russia. Populist–nationalist political grouping founded 1990 by V.V. Zhirinovsky, noted for being neither liberal nor democratic.

MTS — *mashinno-traktornaya stantsiya*, machine-tractor station. Stalin-era rural institutions which rented agricultural machinery to collective farms and collected their produce.

MVD — *Ministerstvo vnutrennikh del*, Ministry of Internal Affairs. Successor to NKVD.

NKGB — *Narodnyy komissariat gosudarstvennoy bezopasnosti*, People's Commissariat of State Security. Took some political police functions from NKVD in 1941 and again 1943–46.

NKVD — *Narodnyy komissariat vnutrennikh del*, People's Commissariat of

Internal Affairs. Largely but not solely concerned with political policing from 1934.

nomenklatura — literally 'schedule'. List of persons deemed suitable by leading party organs to occupy responsible positions in the USSR. Regarded by some as constituting the 'ruling class' in the USSR.

oblast' (pl. *oblasti*) — large-scale administrative and territorial region in USSR after 1920s (see also *kray*).

Orgburo — Organization Bureau of the Central Committee of the CPSU.

perestroika — 'restructuring'. M.S. Gorbachev's policy of political and economic reorganization of the USSR, which immediately preceded its collapse.

Politburo — Political Bureau of the Central Committee of the CPSU. The most powerful political body in the USSR.

PPR — Polish People's Republic.

PRB — People's Republic of Bulgaria.

PRC — People's Republic of China.

pud (pl. *pudy*) — measure of weight, 16.38 kg. or 36 lb.

PUWP (PZPR) — Polish United Workers' Party. Ruling communist party in post-WWII Poland.

RGASPI — *Rossiyskiy gosudarstvennyy arkhiv sotsial'no-politicheskoy istorii*, Russian State Archive of Socio-political History. Formerly the Central Party Archive of the CPSU Central Committee Institute of Marxism–Leninism.

RSFSR — *Rossiyskaya sovetskaya federativnaya sotsialisticheskaya respublika*, Russian Soviet Federative Socialist Republic.

Sajudis — 'Unity'. Lithuanian nationalist independence movement, formed 1988, won elections in Lithuania 1990.

SALT I, II — Strategic Arms Limitation Talks. USSR–US negotiations aimed at slowing the arms race. SALT I — 1969–72; SALT II — 1972–79.

samizdat — 'self-published'. Unauthorized uncensored material produced and circulated unofficially in the USSR.

Sobor — Church Council in Russian Orthodox Church.

Solidarnosc — Solidarity. Polish independent trade union, formed after shipyard strikes in 1980.

Sovnarkom — *Sovet narodnykh komissarov*, Council of People's Commissars. From 1946: Council of Ministers.

stavka (full title *Stavka Verkhovnogo Glavnokomandovaniya*) — General Headquarters of Soviet armed forces in WW2. Headed by Stalin from July 1941.

TASS — *Telegrafnoe agentstvo Sovetskogo Soyuza*, Telegraph Agency of the Soviet Union. The main Soviet state news agency.

troika — three-judge panel presiding over perfunctory legal proceedings.

TsAMO — *Tsentral'nyy arkhiv Ministerstva oborony*, Central Archive of the Ministry of Defence.

TsDOO SO — *Tsentr dokumentatsii obshchestvennykh organizatsii Sverdlovskoy oblasti*, Centre for Documentation of Public Organizations of Sverdlovsk Oblast'. A local archive.

UIA — Ukrainian Insurgent Army. Ukrainian nationalist force, esp. in Western Ukraine, which fought both Red Army and Nazis in WWII.

uskorenie — 'acceleration'. Early policy of M.S. Gorbachev, aimed at a faster pace of economic and technical development.

USSR — Union of Soviet Socialist Republics.

VTsSPS — *Vsesoyuznyy tsentral'nyy sovet professional'nykh soyuzov*, All-Union Central Council of Trade Unions. Soviet trade union confederation.

Zhdanovshchina — post-WWII policy, with strong xenophobic and anti-Semitic undertones, of tighter political control over cultural and artistic expression, associated with A.A. Zhdanov.

Introduction

This is the second instalment of a two-volume documentary history of the Union of Soviet Socialist Republics. The first volume covered the revolution of 1917 and civil war, the consolidation of Bolshevik rule under Lenin and Stalin, and the traumatic industrialization drive of the 1930s. The opening part of this sequel overlaps with Volume 1, beginning with the military–diplomatic dimension of the late 1930s, and then covers the ensuing half-century, which saw the USSR reel under the impact of Nazi invasion, soar to superpower status, enjoy a period of relatively stable socio-economic development, and then in the late 1980s abruptly unravel, fracture along the national fault-lines of its fifteen constituent Union Republics, and in 1991 disappear altogether.

The years since the collapse of communist rule have been exhilarating for scholars specializing on these decades. Those working in Russia and other ex-Soviet republics have been freed from party censorship and the shackles of Marxism–Leninism. For those in the west, the guessing game of 'Kremlinology' has ended: social scientists are no longer compelled to contend with the intense secretiveness of the Soviet regime. For historians, the intellectual stimulus has been particularly strong. Where the Great Patriotic War and Stalin's last years are concerned, the release of new archival material has opened up entirely fresh areas of historical research, sharply revising aspects of conventional wisdom. At the same time, the abrupt collapse of Soviet communism and the disappearance of the Soviet state constituted a structural shift in human affairs so profound that overnight it redrew the normally slow-moving boundary between 'politics and current affairs' and 'history'. Political scientists, sociologists, economists, and military and diplomatic analysts have shifted their attention to issues of 'transition' and post-communist society, and the final Soviet period, including not only the 1950s, 1960s and 1970s under Khrushchev and Brezhnev but the Gorbachev years and the final dénouement, has been swiftly transferred to the province of historians and the history syllabus. Moreover, as the USSR recedes into the past and the Soviet experience ceases to be the uniquely politicized field it was during the long years of the Cold War, historians are gaining a new perspective upon the story as a whole.

The purpose here is to provide those who do not read Russian with a taste of the intellectual feast that is under way. The case for doing so for this later period is no less strong than for the early Soviet decades. Until its dramatic collapse, the USSR constituted a massive political presence and an essential part of the mental furniture of humanity. Its impact was enormous, and the reverberations from its fall are set to continue far into the future. That is manifestly true in terms of the map, make-up and trajectory of the region it once dominated, its six one-time satellites in eastern Europe, and above all the fifteen newly independent states of which it was composed. It is true of the geopolitical and economic framework shaping the wider world, and the position of overwhelming American military dominance bequeathed by its dissolution. And it is true, too, of post-Soviet ideological development. Having defeated Hitler and come to be universally recognized as one of two superpowers in a bipolar world, the USSR succeeded in projecting its ideology, Marxism–Leninism, as the most significant variant of socialism. The result was to ensure that the Soviet collapse gave a tremendous boost to champions of the free market and, in the short term at least, appeared to shift the terms of political debate across Europe and beyond sharply rightward. The 'end of history' was proclaimed and the very word 'socialism', at any rate for the time being, has gone out of fashion.

In short, much about today's world is inexplicable without an understanding of these decades of Soviet history. Students and a wider public need to be given a sense of the primary sources on the basis of which Soviet history is being analysed and rewritten and which convey, as nothing else can, its flavour and smell, the distinctive ethos and culture that was the USSR. Only then will the insights of recent scholarship erase the misconceptions moulded by the Cold War and perpetuated in widely used western textbooks, fiction and journalism—whether about Soviet policy towards the minority nationalities, the scale of the Soviet contribution to Hitler's defeat, the extent to which the ordeal and ultimate triumph of the Great Patriotic War conditioned the rest of Soviet history, the social processes that ultimately destabilized the USSR, or the acute tension between democratic and free-market reform under Gorbachev.

As in Volume 1, the narrative is presented in the form of a commentary woven around and through a sequence of substantial primary sources. The commentary links the documents, sets them in context and draws attention to significant features, supported by a biographical index which provides key details on most of the many hundreds of individuals mentioned. The documents—state and party papers, speeches, letters, newspaper and journal articles, diaries and memoirs—give the narrative weight, texture and nuance. Together they offer a broad entrée to recent debate and current historiographical developments, while the footnotes point to carefully selected secondary studies through which readers without Russian can delve deeper into the issues raised and into specialist work produced in the west, in the former Soviet Union, and, increasingly, by direct collaboration between scholars from both.

The bulk of the documents are drawn from a lively collection published in Russian in the mid-1990s which contains a wealth of material unavailable in English. The second volume of that collection, *Rossiya, kotoruyu my ne znali* [*The Russia We Did Not Know*], *1939–1993* (Chelyabinsk 1995), was compiled at the A.M. Gorky Urals State University under the editorial direction of M.E. Glavatsky. Naturally, it reflects the preoccupations of Russian scholars and citizens in the immediate aftermath of the fall of the USSR. It foregrounds features that had been concealed by the Soviet regime and passed over in silence by official Soviet historiography; rectifies the tendency for Marxist–Leninist accounts to underplay peasant experience and evidence of social protest; gives due attention to religion and repression; ponders the possibility that in 1945 and again in the 1960s Soviet history might have taken a very different turn; and highlights themes that seemed most meaningful in a society undergoing the traumatic political and economic reconstruction of the early 1990s. While the Urals collection provides valuable insight into the regional perspective too often overlooked in the west, its editors somewhat underplayed diplomatic and minority-national issues, and took for granted considerable familiarity with major features of the Soviet story. We have therefore supplemented the collection with a number of additional documents dealing with issues which range from the Soviet mass deportations in western Poland in 1940 to the official Soviet investigation of 1989 into the Nazi–Soviet Pact, and from the 'Novosibirsk Report' of 1983, frankly dissecting the mounting problems facing the USSR, to the inter-ethnic Armenian–Azeri violence of 1988–89. The aim has been to provide an account that is rounded, accessible and freestanding.

Further Reading

This selection of English-language studies provides a guide to the multifaceted reappraisal of later Soviet history under way since the fall of the USSR.

Barber, J., and M. Harrison *The Soviet Home Front 1941–1945* (London 1991)

Beissinger, M.R., *Nationalist Mobilization and the Collapse of the Soviet State* (Cambridge 2002)

Breslauer, G.E., *Gorbachev and Yeltsin as Leaders* (Cambridge 2002)

Brown, A., *The Gorbachev Factor* (Oxford 1996)

Cook, L.J., *The Soviet Social Contract and Why it Failed: Welfare Policy and Workers' Politics from Brezhnev to Yeltsin* (Cambridge, MA, 1994)

English, R., *Russia and the Idea of the West: Gorbachev, Intellectuals and the End of the Cold War* (New York 2000)

Fowkes, B., *The Disintegration of the Soviet Union: A Study in the Rise and Triumph of Nationalism* (Basingstoke 1997)

Gaddis, J.L., *The Cold War* (London 2005)

Galeotti, M., *Afghanistan: The Soviet Union's Last War* (London 1995)

Garthoff, R.L., *The Great Transition: American–Soviet Relations and the End of the Cold War* (Washington, DC, 1994)

Gill, G., *The Collapse of a Single-party System: The Disintegration of the Communist Party of the Soviet Union* (Cambridge 1994)

Glantz, D.M., *When Titans Clashed: How the Red Army Stopped Hitler* (Lawrence, KA, 1995)

Gorodetsky, G., *Grand Delusion: Stalin and the German Invasion of Russia* (New Haven and London 1999)

Hahn, G.M., *Russia's Revolution from Above, 1985–2000: Reform, Transition and Revolution in the Fall of the Soviet Communist Regime* (New Brunswick, NJ, 2002)

Hanson, P., *The Rise and Fall of the Soviet Economy: An Economic History of the USSR from 1945* (London 2003)

Harrison, M., *The Economics of World War II: Six Great Powers in International Comparison* (Cambridge 1998)

Hosking, G., *Russia and the Russians: From Earliest Times to 2001* (London 2001)

Hough, J.F., *Democratization and Revolution in the USSR, 1985–1991* (Washington, DC, 1997)

Kotkin, S., *Armageddon: The Soviet Collapse, 1970–2000* (Oxford 2001)

Naimark, N., and L. Gibianskii (eds), *The Establishment of the Communist Regimes in Eastern Europe, 1944–1949* (Oxford 1997)

Ouimet, M.J., *The Rise and Fall of the Brezhnev Doctrine in Soviet Foreign Policy* (Chapel Hill, NC, 2003)

Overy, R.J. *Russia's War* (London 1999)

Roberts, G., *The Soviet Union and the Origins of the Second World War: Russo–German Relations and the Road to War, 1933–1941* (London 1995)

Rothschild, J., *Return to Diversity: A Political History of East Central Europe since World War II* (Oxford 1994, 2nd edn)

Sandle, M., *A Short History of Soviet Socialism* (London 1999)

Suny, R.G., *The Revenge of the Past: Nationalism, Revolution and the Collapse of the Soviet Union* (Stanford 1993)

Suny, R.G., *The Soviet Experiment: Russia, the USSR and the Successor States* (Oxford 1998)

Taubman, W., *Khrushchev: The Man and His Era* (London 2003)

Thurston, R.W., and B. Bonwetsch, *The People's War: Responses to World War II in the Soviet Union* (Urbana, IL, 2000)

Walker, E.W., *Dissolution: Sovereignty and the Break-up of the Soviet Union* (Lanham, MD, 2003)

Westad, O.A. (ed.), *The Fall of Détente: Soviet–American Relations during the Carter Years* (London 1997)

White, S., *After Gorbachev* (Cambridge 1993)

Zubkova, E.Iu., *Russia after the War: Hopes, Illusions, and Disappointments, 1945–1957* (London 1998)

Maps

Maps by András Bereznay, www.historyonmaps.com

1. Soviet annexations, 1939–40

Legend:
- Frontier of the USSR, June 1941
- Advance of Germany and its allies by the end of 1941
- Annexed by Germany; retaken by Finland/Romania
- Frontiers, 1942
- Front-line, 19 November 1942
- Front-line (where different), at the end of 1943
- Limit of territory held by Germany, 25 October 1944
- Encounter of armies of USSR and its western allies following Germany's surrender

2. The Great Patriotic War, 1941–45

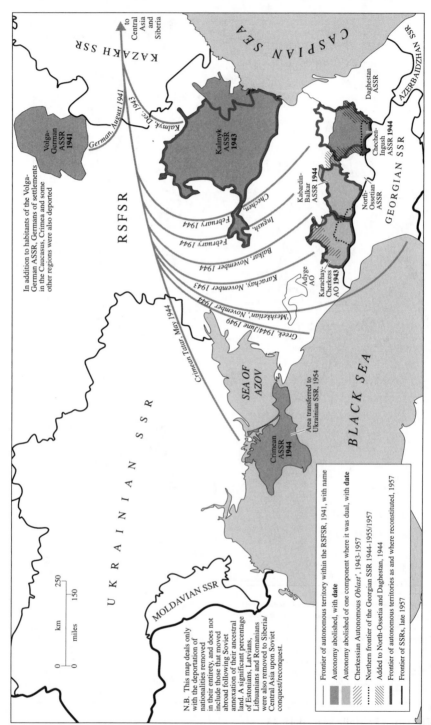

In addition to habitants of the Volga-German ASSR, Germans of settlements in the Caucasus, Crimea and some other regions were also deported

N.B. This map deals only with the deportation of nationalities removed in their entirety, and does not include those that moved abroad following Soviet annexation of their ancestral land. A significant percentage of Estonians, Latvians, Lithuanians and Romanians were also removed to Siberia/Central Asia upon Soviet conquest/reconquest.

Volga-German ASSR 1941

German, August 1941

KAZAKH SSR

to Central Asia and Siberia

Kalmyk, Dec. 1943

CASPIAN SEA

Daghestan ASSR

AZERBAIDZHAN SSR

Kalmyk ASSR 1943

Chechen-Ingush ASSR 1944

Kabardin-Balkar ASSR 1944

North-Ossetian ASSR

GEORGIAN SSR

RSFSR

Chechen, February 1944

Ingush, February 1944

Balkar, November 1944

Karachay, November 1943

Adyge AO

Karachay-Cherkess AO 1943

Meshketian, November 1943

Greek, 1944/June 1949

Crimean Tatar, May 1944

SEA OF AZOV

Area transferred to Ukrainian SSR, 1954

Crimean ASSR 1944

BLACK SEA

U K R A I N I A N   S S R

MOLDAVIAN SSR

0   km   250
0   miles   150

— Frontier of autonomous territory within the RSFSR, 1941, with name
— Autonomy abolished, with **date**
— Autonomy abolished of one component where it was dual, with **date**
····· Cherkessian Autonomous *Oblast'*, 1943-1957
/// Northern frontier of the Georgian SSR 1944-1955/1957
/// Added to North-Ossetia and Daghestan, 1944
— Frontier of autonomous territories as and where reconstituted, 1957
— Frontier of SSRs, late 1957

3. Deportation of minorities

BARENTS
SEA

FINLAND

to USSR,
1945-56
Porkkala

BALTIC SEA

Estonia

Latvia

Lithuania

GERMANY

West
Berlin

GDR
from
1949

POLAND

CZECHOSLOVAKIA

End of all
occupation, 1955

AUSTRIA

HUNGARY

YUGOSLAVIA

ROMANIA

ALBANIA

BULGARIA

Civil war
ended with
defeat of
communist
forces, 1949

GREECE

TURKEY

• Moscow

N

U S S R

SEA OF
AZOV

BLACK SEA

CASPIAN SEA

Kars and
Ardahan

Claim for
area raised
unsuccessfully

Kurdish Republic

'Autonomous
Azerbaidzhan'

IRAN

——— Frontier of the USSR, early 1939

——— New frontier of he USSR by late 1940, where different

\\\\ Annexed by Germany and its allies during the Great Patriotic War

Net gain by the USSR from 1939 to 1945/47

Soviet Zone of Occupation, 1945 (with notes)

Communist state by 1948

- - - Frontier of communist countries, 1948

Communist state defected from Soviet influence late 1948

Failed Soviet attempt to gain territory/control by 1949, with details

Support for separatism
abandoned following
Soviet withdrawal, 1946

0   km   500

0   miles   300

4. **Post-war expansion in Europe**

5. The USSR in the world

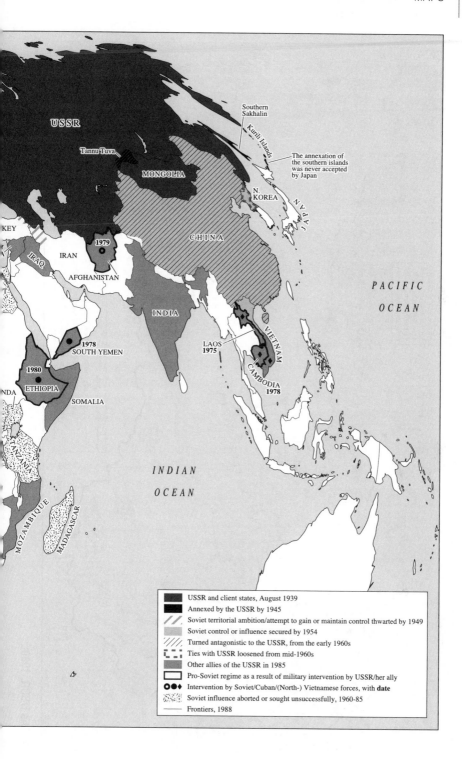

USSR

Southern
Sakhalin

Kunli Islands

Tannu Tuva

MONGOLIA

The annexation of
the southern islands
was never accepted
by Japan

N.
KOREA

JAPAN

KEY

IRAN

IRAQ

1979

CHINA

AFGHANISTAN

INDIA

PACIFIC

OCEAN

1978
SOUTH YEMEN

LAOS
1975

VIETNAM

1980

ETHIOPIA

SOMALIA

NDA

CAMBODIA
1978

TANZANIA

INDIAN

OCEAN

MOZAMBIQUE

MADAGASCAR

USSR and client states, August 1939
Annexed by the USSR by 1945
Soviet territorial ambition/attempt to gain or maintain control thwarted by 1949
Soviet control or influence secured by 1954
Turned antagonistic to the USSR, from the early 1960s
Ties with USSR loosened from mid-1960s
Other allies of the USSR in 1985
Pro-Soviet regime as a result of military intervention by USSR/her ally
Intervention by Soviet/Cuban/(North-) Vietnamese forces, with **date**
Soviet influence aborted or sought unsuccessfully, 1960-85
Frontiers, 1988

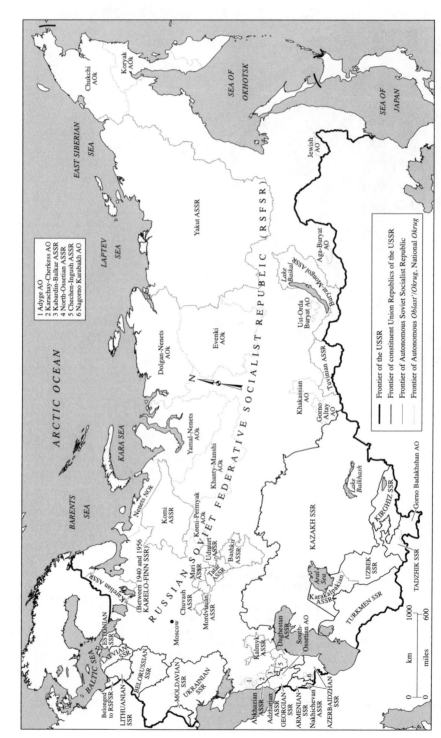

1 Adyge AO
2 Karachay-Cherkess AO
3 Kabardin-Balkar ASSR
4 North-Ossetian ASSR
5 Chechen-Ingush ASSR
6 Nagorno Karabakh AO

———— Frontier of the USSR
———— Frontier of constituent Union Republics of the USSR
———— Frontier of Autonomous Soviet Socialist Republic
·········· Frontier of Autonomous *Oblast'/Okrug*, National *Okrug*

6. The USSR, 1980

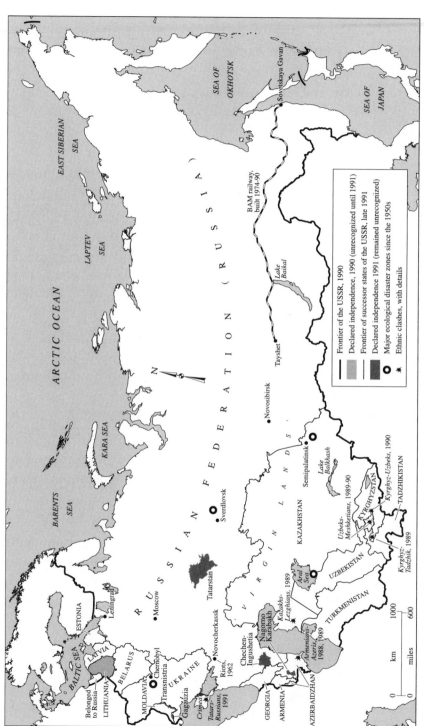

ARCTIC OCEAN

EAST SIBERIAN SEA

LAPTEV SEA

KARA SEA

BARENTS SEA

BALTIC SEA

SEA OF OKHOTSK

SEA OF JAPAN

Sovetskaya Gavan

Lake Baikal

BAM railway, built 1974-90

Tayshet

R U S S I A N   F E D E R A T I O N   (R U S S I A)

Novosibirsk

N

Semipalatinsk

Lake Balkhash

KAZAKHSTAN

V I R G I N   L A N D S

Sverdlovsk

Moscow

Tatarstan

Leningrad

ESTONIA

LATVIA

LITHUANIA

BELARUS

Chernobyl

UKRAINE

MOLDAVIA

Transnistria

Gagauzia

Crimea

Tatars v. Russians, 1991

Novocherkassk

Riots, 1962

Chechen-Ingushetia

Nagorno Karabakh

GEORGIA

ARMENIA

AZERBAIDZHAN

Armenians v. Azeris, 1988, 1989

Lezghians, 1989

Kabards-Lezghians 1989

Aral Sea

TURKMENISTAN

UZBEKISTAN

Uzbeks-Meskhetians, 1989-90

Kyrghyz-Tadzhik, 1989

Kyrghyz-Uzbeks, 1990

KYRGHYZSTAN

TADZHIKISTAN

Belonged to Russia

Frontier of the USSR, 1990

Declared independence, 1990 (unrecognized until 1991)

Frontier of successor states of the USSR, late 1991

Declared independence 1991 (remained unrecognized)

Major ecological disaster zones since the 1950s

Ethnic clashes, with details

km   0   1000

miles 0   600

7. The last decades and the end of the USSR

PART ONE

DEALING WITH HITLER (1939–1941)

In the late 1930s, the Soviet Union's international position became perilous. To the east, Japan vigorously probed Soviet defences; to the west, a resurgent Germany led by Hitler projected its power closer and closer to Soviet borders; the major western powers and most of the USSR's immediate neighbours were deeply hostile. In summer 1939, Stalin's alarm at the risk of facing German aggression alone reached crisis point. Despairing of the prospects of securing a solid defensive alliance with Britain and France, he made a diplomatic about-turn that stunned the other powers. The USSR signed a ten-year non-aggression pact with Nazi Germany. Moreover, when Hitler then invaded Poland, triggering the outbreak of World War II, Stalin colluded in Polish dismemberment and the subordination of the Baltic states. Stalin's attempts to intimidate Finland into accepting Soviet protection and ceding territory close to Leningrad misfired. What followed was the Winter War of 1939/40 in which the Red Army was able to wear down small Finnish forces only after suffering heavy losses. Germany's swift westward drive in 1940, culminating in the abrupt collapse of France in June, intensified Soviet concern to postpone a major military confrontation as long as possible while the country's defences were strengthened. A buffer zone was constructed by annexing outright the Baltic states to the north and the Romanian territories of Bukovina and Bessarabia to the west. But determination to delay war led Stalin to a momentous miscalculation. Though warned that Hitler had resolved to attack the USSR during 1941, he refused to believe it or to prepare for imminent invasion. When German forces swept across the border in the early hours of 22 June 1941, the price the USSR paid was horrendous.

PART ONE

DEALING WITH HITLER
(1930–1945)

1

The Nazi–Soviet Pact

The history of the Soviet Union was from start to finish heavily conditioned by the country's international power and predicament. It was the military potential and sheer size of the fallen Russian Empire that had made it possible for the Bolsheviks' revolutionary regime to consolidate its position at all, to survive the crippling peace terms imposed by Germany in 1918, and then to withstand foreign efforts to destroy it during the civil war (1918–21). Yet the new regime remained perilously isolated thereafter. The challenge it posed to a world dominated by western capitalism found no support from any other government on the globe. During the 1920s, this pariah status fostered the leadership's determination to launch a drastic industrialization drive and attempt to build 'socialism in one country'. In the absence of significant foreign investment or loans, the first Five-Year Plans (1928–32, 1933–37 and the truncated 1938–) were funded by a traumatic and violent squeeze on popular, and above all peasant, living standards. Fear of impending conflict with a hostile west and Japan ensured skewed emphasis on heavy industry and, by the onset of the Third Five-Year Plan (1938), the diversion of massive resources into defence expenditure. The same fear at once encouraged and was used to justify the violent repression of those perceived as actual or potential 'enemies within', a repression that reached its apogee in the Great Terror of 1937–38. And the sequel to the bloody socioeconomic transformation of the 1930s was neither stabilization nor a popular reckoning against Stalin's regime: it was Hitler's invasion of 1941.

The terrible four-year struggle shaped all that followed. It left the country economically devastated and yet, at the same time, victory both conferred on the regime a legitimacy it had never had and catapulted the USSR to the position of a global power in a bipolar world. The result was to lock into place a repressive regime committed to a crude command economy, an open-ended arms race and a hidebound amalgam of the ideas of Marx and Lenin labelled 'Marxism–Leninism'. It was a recipe for rule that proved stable for a generation. But despite delivering rising living standards, it embedded increasing relative backwardness; despite superpower status, ever graver military–diplomatic overstretch; and despite the internal coherence of Marxism–Leninism, a growing disparity between its map of the world and reality. The Great Patriotic War thus cast its shadow right across the later decades of the USSR, up to the dénouement of the Gorbachev years.

Hitler's ability to wreak as much havoc as he did was made possible by the failure of the Soviet Union and western powers to confront him with the two-front alliance that had defeated Germany in 1918. In the 1920s no such alignment had been conceivable. The enmity rooted in the revolution, inflamed in the USSR by foreign support for the Whites in the civil war (1918–21), and in the west by Moscow's creation of the Communist International (Comintern, 1919) dedicated to fomenting revolution, ran too deep. Indeed, the major power with which the USSR reached the smoothest accommodation was Germany. During the mid-1920s, once Comintern had recognized that revolution in the west was not imminent and had moderated its tactics, the Soviet government did secure formal recognition from Britain and France. But from 1928 the efforts of the Foreign Commissariat to improve diplomatic and trading relations with Britain, France and the United States were undercut by Comintern's sharp 'left' turn to extreme militancy. Revolutionary agitation was to be intensified in order both to check the hostile intentions of bourgeois governments and to accelerate what was seen as an incipient crisis of the world capitalist system. Moreover, the policy was upheld through a period of six years during which the onset of the Great Depression drove Japan to alarming expansion in the Far East, and in Germany set rolling the Nazis' virulently anti-Soviet and anti-Slav bandwagon.[1]

Only in 1934, once the notion had been abandoned that fascism in general and Nazism in particular were desperate symptoms of capitalism's crisis and thus of only passing significance, did Soviet policy abruptly change. On the one hand, Comintern demoted revolution far down the agenda and the struggle against fascism took overriding precedence. Other communist parties were instructed to close ranks and co-operate not only with socialists but even with liberal democrats, and in Spain, France and elsewhere communists joined in the formation of anti-fascist 'popular fronts'.[2] On the other hand, the USSR entered the League of Nations, where its voice was

---

1 On Soviet and Comintern foreign policy in the 1930s, see the two volumes by J. Haslam, *Soviet Foreign Policy, 1930–1933: The Impact of Depression* (London 1983) and *The Soviet Union and the Struggle for Collective Security, 1933–1939* (London 1984).

2 On Comintern's volte-face, see E.H. Carr, *Twilight of the Comintern, 1930–1935* (London 1982).

loudest in insisting on the urgency of collective security against aggression from the fascist powers.

Although the following year saw the conclusion of a Franco-Soviet pact, to Soviet disappointment it was not followed up by a firm military understanding. Mutual suspicion remained intense. Soviet support for the Republic in the Spanish Civil War from 1936 aroused acute hostility on the centre and right in Britain and France. Western willingness to align with the USSR was further weakened both by the military purges of 1937 and by concern that to do so would drive the Soviet Union's uneasy neighbours into the arms of Germany. On the Soviet side, the reluctance of the western powers to resist Germany's rearmament, the absorption of Austria and the ultimatum to Czechoslovakia (1938) revived fears of the 1920s that western policy was to turn German aggression eastward. At the Munich conference in September 1938, the USSR was pointedly excluded and its urgent offer to support joint military action to protect Czechoslovakia ignored.

Only when Germany occupied the rump of Czechoslovakia in March 1939 did Britain reluctantly and France more willingly begin to explore seriously an east–west alliance. After guaranteeing the security of Poland, the likely next victim of Germany, the two western governments put out feelers to Moscow. The USSR responded with proposals for a firm triple alliance, and after broad political agreement had been reached in late July, British and French delegations set out for military talks in Moscow. Negotiations, however, were laboured. Soviet doubt that the western powers would commit themselves became near certainty when the British and French proved unable or unwilling to secure Polish or Romanian consent that, in the event of war, Soviet troops would have access across their territory to engage Germany. Berlin, meanwhile, sent out stronger and stronger signals to Moscow that it would welcome an agreement. The terms outlined were that, should Germany take military action against Poland, the USSR would remain neutral in return for Germany's guaranteeing not to go on to attack the USSR, and that they would come to an amicable arrangement over spheres of interest in a reconfigured eastern Europe. As Anglo–French–Soviet talks moved towards deadlock, Moscow responded to the German advances.[3]

The upshot was the Nazi–Soviet Pact set out below. It was signed, under Stalin's watchful eye, by Molotov, who, while remaining chairman of Sovnarkom, had taken over as Foreign Commissar in May from M.M. Litvinov, and by Ribbentrop, the German Foreign Minister and the Pact's most enthusiastic German advocate. It shocked the world as no diplomatic

---

3   For the best treatment of Soviet policy towards Germany immediately before the war, incorporating material made available since the onset of glasnost', see G. Roberts, *The Soviet Union and the Origins of the Second World War: Russo-German Relations and the Road to War, 1933–1941* (London 1995).

revolution has done before or since. For years the Soviet Union had pressed the rest of Europe to unite with it in resisting German expansionism. For years each of the two regimes had depicted the other as its ideological negation and a hate-filled enemy. Suddenly they proclaimed that they had reached an understanding, would resolve any contentious issues by 'a friendly exchange of opinions', and undertook to avoid aggression for a renewable period of ten years. In the text of the Pact, a veil was drawn over the ideological contradictions by sticking closely to the diplomatic vocabulary of an earlier era that both regimes disdained.

Document 1 | *Pravda*'s report of the Molotov–Ribbentrop (Non-aggression) Pact of 23 August 1939

On 23 August at 3.30 p.m., the first meeting between comrade Molotov, chairman of Sovnarkom and USSR People's Commissar for Foreign Affairs, and the German Foreign Minister, Herr von Ribbentrop, on the question of concluding a non-aggression pact took place. The conversation was conducted in the presence of comrade Stalin and the German ambassador, Herr Schulenburg. The meeting lasted about three hours. After a break the meeting resumed at 10 p.m. and concluded with the signing of a non-aggression pact, the text of which follows.

The Non-aggression Pact between Germany and the Soviet Union
Prompted by a desire for tightening the bonds of peace between the USSR and Germany and following on the basic principles of the Neutrality Pact concluded between the USSR and Germany in April 1926, the governments of the USSR and Germany have arrived at the following agreement:

Article 1
Both Contracting Parties agree to refrain from any force, any aggressive act and any attack upon each other both individually or in concert with other powers.

Article 2
Should one of the Contracting Parties be attacked by a third power, the other Contracting Party shall in no way support the latter.

Article 3
The governments of both Contracting Parties shall henceforth remain in contact with each other.

Article 4
Neither of the Contracting Parties shall participate in any alliance of powers which is directly or indirectly aimed against the other Party.

Article 5
Should any conflict arise between the Contracting Parties on any particular question, both sides shall attempt to resolve these disputes or conflicts entirely peacefully,

either by a friendly exchange of opinions or, if necessary, the establishment of a conflict-resolution commission.

Article 6

This Pact is concluded for a period of ten years. Moreover, provided one of the Contracting Parties does not denounce it within a year of expiry, it will be considered to have been automatically renewed for a further five years.

Article 7

This Pact is to be ratified as soon as possible. The exchange of ratification documents shall take place in Berlin. The Pact shall come into force immediately after its signing. Composed in Moscow in both German and Russian languages.

On the authority of the Government of the USSR: V. Molotov
For the Government of Germany: J. Ribbentrop

[Source: *Pravda*, 24 August 1939.]

Alongside the public Pact was a secret protocol. It was to become the most notorious of Stalin's diplomatic commitments. By agreeing on the two powers' respective 'spheres of influence' in north-eastern Europe, it sanctioned the impending German invasion of western Poland and opened the way for the political subordination of the Baltic states and of Bessarabia (now part of Moldova) in Romania to the USSR. This amounted to a depth of collusion with Nazi Germany that Stalin and Molotov knew neither Soviet nor Comintern opinion would be able to stomach. Its terms ran directly counter to the Soviet Union's official stance on international relations. It flouted existing treaties with neighbouring countries, trampled on their sovereignty, and adopted methods and language the USSR had long denounced as hypocritical and imperialist. Unlike the Pact, published the day after its signature and ratified by the Supreme Soviet a week later, the additional protocol remained hidden. It was first mentioned publicly in the west at the Nuremberg trials in 1946, but in the USSR its very existence was officially denied until the Gorbachev era. By then, as we shall see, nationalist movements in Estonia, Latvia and Lithuania, which were to have a momentous impact on the fate of the Soviet Union, had fastened upon it as the ultimate proof that their incorporation into the USSR (1940) was illegal and immoral, and succeeded in compelling Gorbachev's government to acknowledge as much.[4]

---

4 See the report to the Congress of People's Deputies, *On the Political and Legal Assessment of the Soviet–German Non-Aggression Treaty of 1939* (Moscow 1990), and Chapter 21, pp. 414–16 below.

Document 2 | Secret additional protocol

23 August 1939

At the signing of the Non-aggression Pact between Germany and the Union of Soviet Socialist Republics the undersigned representatives of both sides discussed in strict confidence their respective spheres of influence in Eastern Europe. These discussions led to the following outcome:

1. In the event of territorial or political changes to the region making up the Baltic States (Finland, Estonia, Latvia and Lithuania), the northern border of Lithuania constitutes the boundary between the spheres of influence of Germany and the USSR. Moreover, Lithuania's interests with regard to the Wilno region are recognized by both Parties.

2. In the event of territorial or political changes to the region making up the Polish state, the sphere of mutual interests will be roughly represented by a line passing along the Narev, Wisła and San.

The question of whether the continued existence of an independent Polish state is in the interests of both Parties and what the borders of this state should be may ultimately be clarified only by future political developments.

In any case, both governments will resolve this problem by mutual and amicable agreement.

3. Concerning south-eastern Europe the Soviet side emphasizes the USSR's interest in Bessarabia. The German side declares its complete lack of political interest in these areas.

4. This protocol will be kept top secret by both Parties.

On the authority of the Government of the USSR: V. Molotov
For the Government of Germany: J. Ribbentrop

[Source for the Russian version: AVP RF, fond 6, opis' 1, p. 8, delo 77, pp. 1–2.]

The negotiations on the protocol were so hasty and the situation at the time so fluid that it is unlikely that Stalin and Molotov had thought through their precise territorial priorities, or knew exactly how they would exploit the free hand Germany was giving them. Within weeks they would seek to alter the demarcation line. In the Baltic region, they would insist that Lithuania, which had initially been apportioned to the German sphere, be reassigned to the Soviet side. As German forces swept into Poland in September, Lithuania's strategic significance and the fact that it would plainly have by far the longest common border with German-occupied territory became apparent to Moscow. In return, the Soviet side proposed that the line in Poland, which had broadly followed the so-called 'Curzon' line agreed at Versailles before Poland's invasion of Ukraine in 1920, be redrawn, paring back the Soviet sphere to the predominantly Ukrainian and Belorussian areas seized by Poland in 1920. As for the manner in which Soviet 'influence' would be exerted in its sphere—whether it be through tightly drawn military alliances or direct military occupation, and how much if any sovereignty would be retained by the Polish rump and the Baltic states—that too appears to have been undecided in late August. Too much was uncertain.

The dismembering of Poland

Events moved even more quickly than the Soviet government had expected. On 1 September, Hitler launched the invasion of Poland, which marked the outbreak of the Second World War.

Document 3 │ **Hitler's Directive No. 1 for the conduct of the war**

31 August 1939

1. Now that every political possibility has been exhausted for ending by peaceful means the intolerable situation on Germany's eastern frontier, I have determined on a solution by force.
2. The attack on Poland is to be carried out in accordance with the preparations made for *Operation White*, with the alterations, in respect of the Army, resulting from the fact that strategic deployment has now been almost completed.
Assignment of tasks and the operational objective remain unchanged.

      Day of attack   1 September 1939
      Time of attack   4.45 a.m.

The timing also applies for the Gdynia/Gulf of Danzig, and Dirschau Bridge operations.
3. In the west, it is important that the responsibility for the opening of hostilities should be made to rest squarely on Britain and France. Insignificant frontier violations should, for the time being, be opposed by purely local action.

[Source: M. Baumont, M. Lambert and H.M. Smyth, *Documents on German Foreign Policy, 1918–1945* (London 1949), Series D, Vol. VII, pp. 477–78.]

Within days Berlin was urging the Soviet Union to occupy its side of the Polish demarcation line. Briefly Moscow hesitated, anxious to detect how Britain and France, from 3 September officially at war in defence of Poland, would react, and to be sure that Japan would not seize the opportunity to intensify its smouldering conflict with the USSR in the Far East. But the speed with which the Polish army collapsed accelerated Soviet action. In the broadcast announcing Soviet occupation, the justification Molotov used was couched not in class terms, as had been Lenin's justification for counter-invasion of Poland in 1920, but in ethnic terms. Polish foolishness, he said, had placed in jeopardy the Ukrainians and Belorussians over whom they had ruled. There was no expectation, as there had been in 1920, that workers of all nationalities, Poles included, would welcome the Red Army, but there was optimism about the reaction of both these minorities, who had been heavily discriminated against in interwar Poland. The Soviet Union had long sought to arouse popular pressure for incorporation into the Ukrainian and Belorussian Soviet Socialist Republics. Despite intense resentment of Polish treatment, such enthusiasm was severely dampened by what was known of the famine of 1932–33 as well as the Great Terror of 1937–38. Nevertheless, relief at the overthrow of Polish rule and the halt of the German advance initially ensured a measure of welcome for the Red Army.

Document 4 | From a radio broadcast of 17 September 1939 by V. Molotov

This morning the government of the USSR handed a note to the Polish ambassador in Moscow, in which it declared that the Soviet government has instructed the General Headquarters of the Red Army to order troops to cross the border and place the lives and property of the population of Western Ukraine and Western Belorussia under their protection.

The Soviet government also declared in this note that at the same time it intends to take whatever measures are required to extricate the Polish people from the ill-starred war into which they have been dragged by their foolish leaders and enable them to resume normal lives.

At the beginning of September, when there was a partial call-up of reservists in Ukraine, Belorussia and four other military regions, the situation in Poland was unclear and the call-up was undertaken just as a precautionary measure. No one could have imagined that the Polish state would have exhibited such impotence and have collapsed so rapidly, as has now happened throughout Poland. Since, however, this collapse has occurred, and the Polish politicians are utterly bankrupt and incapable of changing the situation in Poland, our Red Army, which has been greatly reinforced by this latest call-up of reservists, must honourably carry out its esteemed task. . .

The Soviet government also wishes to make the following clarification to its citizens. Since the call-up, the urge to hoard food and other industrial goods has been observed among our citizens, for fear that a rationing system will be introduced. The government considers it necessary to declare that it has no intention of introducing rationing of foodstuffs and industrial goods, even if these state measures, brought about by external circumstances, last for a certain period. I fear that the only people to suffer from excessive purchases of food and industrial goods will be the hoarders themselves, in that their hoards are in danger of perishing. Our country has everything it needs and can manage without rationing.

Our task now, the task of every worker, peasant, office worker and intellectual, is to work at their jobs honestly and selflessly and thereby assist the Red Army.

As for the warriors of our glorious Red Army, I have no doubt that they will do their duty towards their Motherland honourably and gloriously. . .

[Source: *Vneshnyaya politika SSSR. Sbornik dokumentov*, Vol. IV (Moscow 1946), p. 447.]

Although the Red Army's mobilization revealed grave weaknesses, within a week scattered Polish resistance had been overcome and almost a quarter of a million Polish troops captured. The new Soviet authorities set about incorporating the territory into the USSR.[5] Wealthier Belorussian and Ukrainian peasants and traders, as well as officials, policemen and politicians, saw their property confiscated and were brutally repressed. The NKVD forces and officials who rapidly moved in to organize the takeover played upon the animosity among both ethnic groups towards the privileged Polish minority. Elections were staged to return two National Assemblies, one in the predominantly Belorussian territory and one in the predominantly Ukrainian territory; the assemblies requested admission to the USSR; and it was formally granted in November. Meanwhile virtually all Poles were under a cloud of suspicion of active or passive support for resistance to Soviet rule and those prominent in any walk of life, nationally or locally, were subject to immediate arrest. Preparations were made for mass deportations to camps and settlements in Siberia and Central Asia. As in the 'ethnic cleansing' of the borderlands in the late 1930s, whole categories of people whose jobs, property, background or affiliations were considered indicators of hostility were uprooted. Between February 1940 and June 1941 wave upon wave of mass deportations in cattle trucks rudimentarily fitted for human occupation were carried out, the total probably exceeding a million.[6] Some idea of the fear and helplessness of the victims is given in the following recollections of Bronisława Chorążyczewska, a teenage Polish schoolgirl at the time. Born in Rovno in 1924, she was attending the Henryk Sienkiewicz School in Sarny during the Soviet invasion. Her friends were caught up in the first

---

5 On the Soviet takeover, see the controversial study by J.T. Gross, *Revolution from Abroad: The Soviet Conquest of Poland's Western Ukraine and Western Belorussia* (Princeton 2002, 2nd edn), which emphasizes the extent to which mutual denunciation by Polish citizens facilitated the spread of Soviet power.
6 For a careful account and summary of conflicting estimates, see K. Sword, *Deportation and Exile: Poles in the Soviet Union, 1939–48* (Basingstoke 1994), ch. 1.

wave, in freezing February temperatures, in which prime targets were ethnic Polish 'settlers' who had moved into this territory, annexed by Poland following its defeat of Bolshevik Russia in 1920.

Document 5 | An excerpt from the wartime diary of Bronisława Chorążyczewska

Saturday, 10 February 1940

I got up early this morning and started my homework. Then I helped Mummy do some cleaning. At midday I went to answer the door. I opened it and saw that it was the Jagodzińskis. I learned that Mr Jagodziński had become head postmaster in Sarny. I was just getting ready for school when Danka Mar came to see me. She said that this morning all the recent settlers had been arrested and taken away with their families, they weren't allowed to take anything, they'd only been given 4 hours and their houses surrounded by policemen (how horrible!). Another classmate brought me the same news. What terrible news! I was in a foul mood all the time at school. I was relieved when lessons ended. Pawlakówna and I decided to go to the Krupskis to try and find out what was going on. I went with her and knocked on the door. Somebody answered in Russian. I asked if Mr Krupski was in, but the voice replied that he and his family had been taken off to Russia today. Who could've expected such a terrible blow? Just yesterday Tereska was at school and was going to go on a skiing trip today. Stasia Pawlakówna and I went to Danka's where we learned that the police had gone to the Krupskis this morning and told them to be ready to leave in 4 hours. One girl saw them leaving with 3 policemen and a 'Bolshevik'. I was too upset to write; I couldn't gather my thoughts; I was really nervous. I couldn't get to sleep for ages. They were taking people away cold and hungry, and it was as if it was freezing almost on purpose.

Sunday, 11 February 1940

I'll never forget that sad, memorable Sunday. You don't forget such times. Happiness has gone for us since Poland perished. This morning I went to Mass, not knowing whether it would be my last. Probably the recent settlers' fate awaits us all, because they're probably going to take all the Poles away to Russia and bring in loads of people, because we expect a referendum, when the riffraff will vote for their 'socialist Fatherland'. After lunch Danka came round and we went to the wagons, where they'd put the recent settlers. We were having a look when somebody called out to us. We looked round and saw it was Wiesia Misztelanka begging us for bread. Danka and I ran home. I got some bread and herb tea, and Mummy and I went to the wagons. There were 7 families in the third one. I gave them what I'd brought, although some 'Bolshevik' shouted, 'Clear off!' (He did let us give it to them eventually.) Wiesia whispered to us, 'Pray for us.' I couldn't hold back the tears burning beneath my eyelids. There were quite a lot of people about. On the way back I met Danka, who was on her way to the wagons. She was carrying some porridge and a little picture she'd put in a bag. I went back home with her. On the way we saw the recent settlers going with buckets to get water, although there were lots of soldiers with fixed bayonets everywhere. We went to the wagons again and Danka managed to give them the porridge because the 'Bolshevik' wasn't looking. We went back home quickly because it was dark, bitterly cold and my legs were freezing in those stockings. I was really tired and upset. I had a headache as well. Holy Mary pray for them and set them free, and may their Catholic faith and Poland's honour give them strength to cope!

[Source: *Kresowe dziewczęta deportowane na Sybir, 1940–1941* / wspomnienia zebrał i opracował Henryk Dąbkowski (Warsaw 2000) pp. 27–28.]

It was in the course of this brutal stamping of Soviet authority on the new territory that one of the most notorious of the crimes proposed by Beria and approved by Stalin was committed. Some 27,000 Poles, a significant proportion of them being officers of the defeated Polish army but including policemen, civil servants and retired men, were massacred by the NKVD. When the Nazis discovered one of the mass graves, in the Katyn' forest near Smolensk in 1943, the Soviet regime furiously denied responsibility and for over four decades stuck resolutely to the claim that it was a Nazi atrocity. Much of the archival evidence appears to have been destroyed in the Khrushchev years, but during the period of glasnost in the late 1980s, a Soviet and Polish commission of historians pieced together enough evidence to put the matter beyond doubt. Subsequently, during Gorbachev's last days in office, the following document was found and handed to him. In his memoirs, he recalls his horror at seeing Beria's recommendation for mass shooting and at its being firmly marked off with the words 'Resolution of the Politburo' written above it in Stalin's blue pencil, along with the signatures of Molotov, Voroshilov and Stalin himself.[7]

Document 6 | Memorandum from Beria to Stalin recommending mass shooting of Polish POWs

NKVD
3 March 1940
No. 794/B
Moscow

CC CPSU
To: Comrade Stalin

In the USSR NKVD prisoner-of-war camps and the prisons of western Ukraine

---

7 M.S. Gorbachev, *Memoirs* (London 1995), p. 481.

and Belorussia, there are at present a large number of former officers of the Polish army, police and security services, members of nationalist counter-revolutionary parties and secret counter-revolutionary insurgent organizations, escapees, et al. They are all sworn enemies of Soviet power, brimming with hatred of the Soviet system. The officers and policemen in these camps are conducting anti-Soviet agitation. Everyone of them is just waiting to be released so that they can get involved in anti-Soviet activity.

In western Ukraine and Belorussia the NKVD has uncovered a number of counter-revolutionary insurgent organizations. These former officers, policemen and gendarmes have been playing an active role in all of them. A significant number of participants in counter-revolutionary espionage and insurgent organizations have been found among the detained escapees and illegal entrants. Excluding common soldiers and NCOs there are in all 14,736 officers, civil servants, landowners, policemen, gendarmes, warders, settlers and agents—97% of them Polish, viz.,

Generals, colonels and lieutenant-colonels	295
Majors and captains	2,080
Lieutenants, second lieutenants and standard-bearers	6,049
Police, border-control and gendarme officers and junior officers	1,030
Policemen, gendarmes, warders and agents	5,138
Civil servants, landowners, priests and settlers	144

In the prisons of western Ukraine and Belorussia there are 18,632 under arrest, 10,685 of them Poles, viz.,

Former officers	1,207
Former policemen, agents and gendarmes	5,141
Spies and saboteurs	347
Former landowners, mill owners and civil servants	465
Members of various counter-revolutionary insurgent organizations, et al.	5,345
Escapees	6,127

Since they are all inveterate and incorrigible enemies of Soviet power, the USSR NKVD believes the following actions to be necessary:

I. The USSR NKVD is to examine as a matter of urgency:

1. The cases of the 14,700 former Polish officers, civil servants, policemen, agents, gendarmes, settlers and warders in prisoner-of-war camps,

2. along with the cases of the 11,000 members of various counter-revolutionary espionage and sabotage organizations, former landowners, mill owners, former Polish officers, civil servants and escapees under arrest in prisons in western Ukraine and Belorussia and impose the maximum penalty on them—shooting.

II. The examination is to be conducted without summoning and charging those

under arrest, and statements concerning the conclusion of proceedings and indictment are to be made as follows:

a. Certificates are to be issued by the prisoner-of-war division of the USSR
NKVD for those in prisoner-of-war camps;

b. Certificates are to be issued by the Ukrainian and Belorussian NKVD for those
under arrest.

III. Examination and implementation are to be the responsibility of a three-man
commission: comrades Merkulov, Kobulov and Bashtakov (Chief of 1st Special
Section of the USSR NKVD).

L. Beria,
People's Commissar for Internal Affairs

[Source: http://katyn.codis.ru/kdocs1.htm.]

The subordination of the Baltic states

When the carving up of Poland began, Baltic anxiety about the next Soviet
move became acute.[8] The Estonian and Latvian governments had little room
for manoeuvre between the great powers, but Lithuania's position seemed
more fluid. As soon as Germany invaded Poland, the Lithuanian regime
considered sending troops to occupy the coveted city of Vilnius/Wilno. It
was briefly encouraged to do so by the Germans, but reluctantly decided
against and on 19 September Soviet troops occupied the city. At this stage,
Hitler intended to take Lithuania: the following draft treaty, composed in
Germany, envisaged binding the country to the German side and establishing
formal protectorate status.

Document 7 | **'Lithuania commits itself to the protection of the Reich'—
draft defence treaty between Germany and Lithuania**

20 September 1939

Mindful of the political situation in Europe as a whole and of the need to safeguard
the interests of both countries, which complement each other in all respects, the
Government of the German Reich and the Government of Lithuania have agreed
on the following:

Article I
Without compromising its independence as a state Lithuania commits itself to the
protection of the German Reich.

---

8 On the prolonged crisis facing the Baltic states, see D. Crowe, *The Baltic States and the
Great Powers: Foreign Relations, 1938–1940* (Boulder, CO, 1993).

Article II
In order that this protection can be realized in practice, Germany and Lithuania are to conclude a military agreement.

Article III
Both governments must immediately commence talks to establish close and all-embracing economic relations between the two countries.

Article IV
The essence of the military agreement is as follows:
1. The size, disposition and equipment of the Lithuanian army must be regularly ascertained with the complete accord of the *Wehrmacht* High Command.
2. A German military commission is to be sent to Kaunas for the practical implementation of point 1.

[Source: *Polpredy soobshchayut. . . Sbornik dokumentov ob otnosheniyakh SSSR s Latviey, Litvoy i Estoniey. Avgust 1939–avgust 1940* (Moscow 1990), p. 52.]

Within days, however, Moscow had made plain to Berlin the priority it placed upon incorporating Lithuania within its sphere of influence. This, and the assignment of Polish territory to the German sphere by way of compensation, was the key point spelled out in a second secret protocol, this one attached to a treaty signed on 28 September agreeing the line dividing the two countries' respective zones in occupied Poland.

Document 8 | *Pravda*'s report of the German–Soviet Friendship and Frontier Treaty

In Moscow on 27–28 September talks took place between the Chairman of the USSR Council of People's Commissars and People's Commissar for Foreign Affairs, Comrade Molotov, and the Minister for Foreign Affairs of Germany, Herr von Ribbentrop, on the question of concluding a German–Soviet Treaty on Friendship and the Frontier between the USSR and Germany.

Comrade Stalin, the Soviet ambassador to Germany Comrade Shkvartsev, and, on the German side, Herr Schulenburg, the German ambassador to the USSR, took part in the discussions. . .

The German–Soviet Treaty on Friendship and the Frontier

28 September 1939

After the collapse of the former Polish state the USSR Government and the Government of Germany consider it their exclusive task to restore peace and order in this territory and guarantee a peaceful existence for the people living there, in accordance with their national characteristics. To this end they have agreed upon the following:

Article I

As a border between the two states' mutual interests in the territory of the former Polish state, the Government of the USSR and the Government of Germany establish a line, shown on the attached map, which will be described in greater detail in a supplementary protocol.

Article II

Both Parties consider the border between their mutual state interests laid down in Article I to be final and will reject any interference from third parties in this decision.

Article III

The necessary state reorganization in the territory to the west of the line indicated in Article I will be carried out by the German Government, and in the territory to the east of that line, by the Government of the USSR.

Article IV

The Government of the USSR and the German Government consider the aforementioned state reorganization to be a firm foundation for the further development of amicable relations between their peoples.

Article V

This treaty is to be ratified. The exchange of documents is to take place in Berlin as soon as possible.

The treaty comes into force the moment it is signed.

Compiled in two originals, in the German and Russian languages.

On the authority of the Government of the USSR
V. Molotov
For the Government of Germany
J. Ribbentrop

[Source: *Pravda*, 29 September 1939.]

Document 9 | Secret additional protocol to the Treaty

28 September 1939

The undersigned plenipotentiaries declare the agreement between the German Government and the Government of the USSR on the following:

The secret additional protocol signed on 23 August 1939 is to be amended in its 1st point to include the territory of the Lithuanian state in the sphere of interest of the

USSR, given that, on the other hand, the province of Lublin and part of Warsaw province are included in the sphere of interest of Germany (see the map attached to the Treaty on Friendship and Frontiers between the USSR and Germany signed today). As soon as the Government of the USSR has taken special measures in Lithuania to safeguard its interests, then in order to establish a natural and simple frontier, the present German–Lithuanian border will be amended so that the territory lying to the south-west of the line shown on the map goes to Germany.

Moreover, it is agreed that the economic agreements between Germany and Lithuania currently in force must not be disrupted by the above-mentioned measures on the part of the Soviet Union.

On the authority of the Government of the USSR
V. Molotov

For the Government of Germany
J. Ribbentrop

[Source: AVP RF, fond 6, opis' 1, p. 8, delo 77, sheet 4.]

During the last week of September and the first days of October, the foreign ministers of all three Baltic states visited Moscow in succession. They were informed by Molotov and Stalin that Soviet security required that each agree to sign a mutual assistance pact with the USSR and accept the establishment of Soviet military bases on their territory. Moscow promised there was no question of altering either the political status or social order of the three countries, and, in the case of Lithuania, the USSR won enthusiastic popular gratitude for transferring Vilnius to the republic.

Contemporary assessments of Soviet action included the following broadcast by Churchill, whom Chamberlain had brought into the British government when war broke out. Churchill put what was, from the British viewpoint, the best possible gloss on Soviet actions, portraying them as an effective veto on further German expansion eastward.

Document 10 | From a radio broadcast by Winston Churchill, London, 1 October 1939

First, Poland has again been overrun by two of the Great Powers which held her in bondage for 150 years, but were unable to quench the spirit of the Polish nation. The heroic defence of Warsaw shows that the soul of Poland is indestructible, and that she will rise again like a rock, which may for a spell be submerged by a tidal wave, but which remains a rock.

What is the second event of this month? It is, of course, the assertion of the power of Russia. Russia has pursued a cold policy of self-interest. We could have wished that Russian armies should be standing on their present line as the friends and allies of Poland instead of as invaders. But that the Russian armies should stand on this line was clearly necessary for the safety of Russia against the Nazi menace. At any rate, the line is there, and an Eastern Front has been created which Nazi Germany does not dare assail. When Herr von Ribbentrop was summoned to Moscow last week, it was to learn the fact, and to accept the fact, that Nazi designs upon the Baltic States and upon the Ukraine must come to a dead stop.

I cannot forecast to you the action of Russia. It is a riddle wrapped in a mystery inside an enigma; but perhaps there is a key. That key is Russian national interest. It cannot be in accordance with the interest or safety of Russia that Germany should plant itself upon the shores of the Black Sea, or that it should overrun the Balkan States and subjugate the Slavonic peoples of south-eastern Europe. That would be contrary to the life-interests of Russia.

[Source: *Churchill Speaks: Winston S. Churchill in Peace and War: Collected Speeches, 1897–1963* (Leicester 1981), p. 694.]

2

The Winter War

The Soviet Union attempted to impose a similar mutual assistance pact on its fourth Baltic neighbour, Finland, and in this case also demanded an exchange of territory.[9] Moscow would cede land in northern Karelia which the Finns had long claimed. In return, Finland must move its border northward to broaden the protective area around Leningrad; cede a number of small islands in the Gulf of Finland; and above all lease the port of Hanko at the entrance to the Gulf, where the Soviet Union would establish a naval base enabling it to close the Gulf, to potential aggressors. In Soviet eyes, as Stalin made plain to a Finnish delegation, such aggression might come from either Germany, with which Finland had been closely aligned during most of the interwar period and which was the preferred ally of much of the Finnish establishment, or Britain, Finland's main trading partner.

The Finns, however, proved resistant. They would not hear of a mutual assistance pact, which would compromise their recent adherence to the Scandinavian policy of neutrality, and they rejected outright the idea that they should lease the port of Hanko. Finnish public opinion was vehemently hostile to accepting the Soviet diktat, and by late October the Soviet Union was drawing up detailed plans to use force to impose its will. On the eve of hostilities, *Pravda* ran an ominous editorial. It reminded the Finns that it was the Soviet government which had recognized the independence which its tsarist predecessors had denied the country; it mocked the prime minister in the vituperative and violent language that had become commonplace during the Great Terror; and, unlike editorials on eastern Poland and the Baltic states, it damned his government in forthright class terms as bourgeois and undemocratic.

---

9   For a recent and detailed analysis of the USSR's diplomatic approach towards Finland, the course of the Winter War, and the conclusions drawn by Stalin and the high command, see C. Van Dyke, *The Soviet Invasion of Finland, 1939–40* (London 1997).

Document 11 | 'A buffoon for Prime Minister'—from a *Pravda* editorial

26 November 1939

The Finnish government is afraid to speak in its own parliament, but Prime Minister Cajander was happy to speak at a concert on 23 November. The Prime Minister spoke as music played. The Finnish bourgeoisie needs distractions in its current difficult situation. Cajander distracted them as best he could. He displayed a remarkable talent for buffoonery. . .

He started by dragging portraits of Russian tsars onto the stage and began bowing low to them. He did this quite seriously, with the touching emotion of a born lackey.

He spoke of the 'sympathy for Finland' in the policies carried out by Alexander I and Alexander II, which 'met with the approval of the whole population of Finland'.

After that, this buffoon stood on his head and made threatening noises at the Soviet Union, which is supposedly encroaching upon Finland's independence. A majestic pose indeed!

Everybody knows that the Russian tsars—both Nicholases and both Alexanders—stifled any attempts at Finnish independence. . . It was Soviet power which gave Finland independence, which the Finnish bourgeoisie has always traded and continues to trade in the imperialist bazaar. . .

This whole pathetic farce is continued just to avoid answering the question the Finnish people keep putting to their confused government of schemers: Why have Latvia, Estonia and Lithuania concluded treaties with the Soviet government which guarantee their independence, peace and undisturbed labour, while the Finnish government has broken off talks, keeping the people on tenterhooks?

A sobbing Cajander replies, 'These three viable Baltic states, which had brilliant futures, have suddenly gone from being independent states to states more or less dependent upon the Soviet Union. This has had a terrible effect on us Finns. . .'

But the Cajanders cannot avoid giving the answer the Finnish people keep demanding ever more insistently, 'Why have you Cajanders broken off talks? The people did not ask you to. Who did, then?'

The Finnish Prime Minister wriggles like a snake. He snivels, wiping tears all over his mucky face, 'Since it was difficult to find common ground in the talks, they have been broken off for the time being. This is a real pity, because Finland sincerely wants to maintain good relations with all its neighbours. . .'

It is hardly surprising that the Cajanders have not found 'common ground' with the Soviet government! This clown turns somersaults on the 'common platform' of militant imperialism, the jazz band blares out, the fifes squeak and the ringmaster's whip cracks.

How long can this political farce last? Not long, we hope. We must hope that the Finnish people will not allow puppets like Cajander to steer Finland's ship of state onto the rocks. . .

[Source: *Pravda*, 26 November 1939.]

That night, Soviet forces manufactured an incident on the Karelian border. The following day Molotov denounced the Finns for ignoring the warnings they had been given of the dangers of placing troops so close to Leningrad, and accused the Finns of an act of aggression.

Document 12 | **V. Molotov: 'The Soviet Government... proposes that the Finnish Government immediately pull back its troops from the border...'—Soviet government note**

26 November 1939

On the evening of 26 November, comrade V.M. Molotov, the USSR People's Commissar for Foreign Affairs, received Mr Yrjö-Koskinen, the Finnish envoy, and handed him a note from the Government of the USSR concerning the provocative firing upon Soviet troops by Finnish military units stationed on the Karelian Isthmus.

On receiving the note, Mr Yrjö-Koskinen declared that he would immediately communicate the matter to his government and give a reply.

The text of the note follows:

Mr Envoy,

According to the General Staff of the Red Army, today, the 26th of November, at 15.45, our troops, stationed near the village of Mainila on the Karelian Isthmus, hard by the Finnish border, were unexpectedly fired upon from Finnish territory by artillery. Seven salvoes were fired, as a result of which three privates and one junior officer were killed, and seven privates and two officers were wounded. Having strict orders not to retaliate against provocation, the Soviet troops refrained from artillery response.

In informing you of this, the Soviet Government wishes to emphasize that during talks with Messrs Tanner and Paasikivi it has already pointed out the potential risk of concentrating a large number of Finnish regulars on the border close to Leningrad. Now, in view of this provocative artillery bombardment from Finnish territory against Soviet troops, the Soviet Government is obliged to state that the concentration of Finnish troops near Leningrad not only constitutes a threat to Leningrad but is also in fact a hostile act against the USSR, which has already led to attacks on Soviet troops and casualties.

The Soviet Government has no intention of exaggerating this disgraceful act of aggression on the part of Finnish army units, which may well have been poorly led by their Finnish commanders. But it does not want any repeat of such disgraceful acts in future.

In view of this the Soviet Government, registering its forceful protest about what has taken place, proposes that the Finnish Government immediately pull back its troops from the border on the Karelian Isthmus by 20–25 kilometres, thereby averting the possibility of repeat provocations.

Respectfully yours,

V. Molotov, USSR People's Commissar for Foreign Affairs

[Source: *Pravda*, 27 November 1939.]

The Finns hurriedly investigated the incident and concluded that Finnish soldiers had fired no guns. They firmly repudiated the Soviet charge, emphasized that their border forces were modestly armed, and, albeit with little expectation that conflict could now be averted, proposed talks about a mutual pullback of forces.

Document 13 | A. Yrjö-Koskinen: 'My government... is ready to embark on talks...'—note in reply to Molotov from the Finnish government

27 November 1939

Mr People's Commissar,

In reply to your letter of the 26th I have the honour, on behalf of my government, to convey the following response:

In connection with the supposed border violation, the Finnish government conducted an immediate investigation. This investigation established that the artillery rounds referred to in your letter did not emanate from the Finnish side. On the contrary, it would appear from the investigation that on the 26th of November, between 15.45 and 16.05 Soviet time, shots were fired from the Soviet side of the border in the vicinity of the aforementioned village of Mainila. On the Finnish side it is even possible to see the place where the shells exploded, as the village of Mainila is only 800 metres from the border, across open fields.

By calculating the speed at which the noise of the seven shots spread, it was possible to conclude that the guns from which the shells were fired were located approximately one and a half to two kilometres south-east of the point where the shells exploded. Observations of these shots were recorded in the logbook of our border guards as soon as they occurred. In such circumstances it seems possible that this was an accident, which occurred during training exercises on the Soviet side, which, according to your letter, resulted in casualties. Consequently, I consider it my duty to reject the protest set out in your letter and state that the hostile act against the USSR of which you speak did not emanate from the Finnish side.

In your letter you also referred to statements made by Messrs Paasikivi and Tanner while in Moscow concerning the danger of concentrating regular troops immediately adjacent to the border, in the vicinity of Leningrad. In relation to this I wish to draw your attention to the fact that on the Finnish side of the border the troops deployed immediately adjacent to it are primarily border guards; there were no guns at all in this area with sufficient range to send shells across the border.

Although there are no valid reasons for pulling troops back from the border zone as you have proposed, my government is nevertheless ready to enter into negotiations on the question of a reciprocal pullback of troops to a given distance from the frontier.

I was pleased to read your statement, in which it is made clear that the government of the USSR does not intend to exaggerate the significance of the border incident alleged in your letter to have occurred. I am happy to have had the opportunity to dispel this misunderstanding the very next day after receiving your proposals. However, in order that there be no further misunderstanding, my government proposes that border commissars from both sides be entrusted jointly to investigate this incident, in accordance with the Convention on Border Commissars concluded on 24 September 1928.

Most respectfully yours,
A.S. Yrjö-Koskinen

[Source: *Pravda*, 29 November 1939.]

Molotov's reply, while reiterating the bogus charge over the incident, also spelled out what was for the Kremlin the key issue, Leningrad's vulnerability, and renounced the existing non-aggression pact.

Document 14 | **V. Molotov: 'The Soviet government... considers itself free of the obligations it took on in the Non-aggression Pact...'— note in response from the Soviet government**

28 November 1939

Mr Envoy,

The Government of Finland's reply to the Soviet Government's note of 26 November is a document which reflects the profound hostility of the Government of Finland towards the Soviet Union and is intended to intensify the crisis in relations between our two sides.

1. The Finnish Government's denial of the fact of the disgraceful artillery shelling by Finnish troops against Soviet troops, causing fatalities, cannot be explained other

than by a desire to delude public opinion and mock the victims of the shelling. Only a lack of feeling of responsibility and a contempt for public opinion could dictate the attempt to explain this outrageous shelling incident—in which Soviet troops came under artillery fire on the very border, in full view of Finnish troops—as a 'training exercise'.

2. The Finnish Government's refusal to withdraw the troops who perpetrated the villainous shelling of Soviet troops, and the demand that Finnish and Soviet troops be pulled back simultaneously, formally based on the principle of equality between the two sides, reveal the hostile desire of the Finnish Government to keep Leningrad under threat. We have here, in fact, not equality in the position of Finnish and Soviet troops, but, on the contrary, an advantageous position for the Finnish troops. Soviet troops do not threaten Finland's main centres of population, as they are hundreds of kilometres away, whereas Finnish troops, stationed thirty-two kilometres from one of the USSR's populated centres, Leningrad, a city of three and a half million, do constitute a direct threat to it. It scarcely needs to be said that there is actually nowhere for Soviet troops to pull back to, since after a pullback of twenty-five kilometres they would end up in the suburbs of Leningrad, which is patently absurd from the point of view of Leningrad's security. The Soviet Government's proposal that Finnish troops pull back twenty-five kilometres is minimal, as its aim would not be to remove this inequality in the positions of Soviet and Finnish troops, but merely to lessen it somewhat. If the Government of Finland rejects even this minimal proposal, then this means that it intends to keep Leningrad under direct threat from its troops.

3. By concentrating a large number of regular troops near Leningrad, and thereby placing a most important centre of population of the USSR under direct threat, the Government of Finland has committed a hostile act against the USSR, incompatible with the Non-Aggression Pact concluded between the two countries. By refusing to pull back even twenty to twenty-five kilometres after the outrageous incident where Soviet troops were shelled by Finnish troops, the Government of Finland has shown that it continues to remain hostile to the USSR, has no intention of complying with the requirements of the Non-aggression Pact and has decided henceforth to keep Leningrad under threat. The Government of the USSR, however, cannot accept a position where one side is violating the Non-aggression Pact while the other is obliged to observe it. In view of this, the Soviet Government feels compelled to declare that from this day forth it considers itself free of the obligations it took on in the Non-aggression Pact concluded between our two countries, which has been systematically violated by the Government of Finland.

Respectfully yours,

V. Molotov, USSR People's Commissar for Foreign Affairs.

[Source: *Pravda*, 29 November 1939.]

The Soviet attack

On 30 November 1939, Soviet troops crossed the border. The following day the Soviet Union announced the formation of a new Finnish government and instead of declaring war portrayed its actions as sanctioned by the country's new authorities. The claim carried very little international credibility. The location of the supposed new government, Terijoki, was a beach resort just six miles north of the Soviet border. Its key figure, Otto Kuusinen, though well known as one of the radical leaders in the Finnish civil war of 1918, had since then become identified as a senior Comintern official rather than a plausible national leader. There was no evidence of popular support for the 'People's Government', even most Finnish communists disowned it, and its puppet status was made plain by its instant proclamation of solidarity with the USSR and agreement to a treaty granting precisely the territorial concessions Moscow sought.

Document 15 | The TASS announcement of the People's Government of Finland

1 December 1939

Leningrad, 1st December (TASS). A new Finnish government—the People's Government of the Finnish Democratic Republic—was formed today in Terijoki by agreement of the representatives of a number of left-wing parties and mutinous Finnish soldiers. It is made up of the following individuals: Otto Kuusinen, Chairman of the Government and Minister of Foreign Affairs. . . The People's Government has issued a declaration setting out its programme.

From the declaration of the People's Government of Finland
(Radio intercept translated from Finnish)

The People's Government of Finland, utterly convinced that the Soviet Union has no designs against the independence of our country, fully endorses and supports the actions of the Red Army on Finnish territory. It regards this as invaluable help to the Finnish people on the part of the Soviet Union, so that by our joint efforts we can liquidate as quickly as possible the most dangerous hotbed of war, created in Finland by the criminal government of war provocateurs. . .

Our state must be a democratic republic serving the interests of the people, unlike the plutocratic republic of Cajander and Erkko, which just served the interests of capitalists and landowners. Nevertheless, our state is not a state of the Soviet type, because the Soviet order cannot be established by the efforts of the government alone without the agreement of all the people, especially the peasantry. . .

The final make-up, powers and actions of the People's Government require the sanction of a Sejm [parliament], elected on the basis of universal, equal and direct suffrage and secret ballot. The People's Government of Finland's first task is to over-throw the government of Finnish White Guards, crush its armed forces, conclude peace and ensure Finland's independence and safety by establishing firm friendly relations with the Soviet Union.

The People's Government of Finland appeals to the Government of the USSR with a proposal to conclude a mutual aid pact between Finland and the Soviet Union and to satisfy the Finnish people's ages-old national aspiration of reuniting with the people of Karelia in a single, independent Finnish state. . .

In its domestic policy, the People's Government of Finland sets itself the following tasks:

1. The establishment of a Finnish People's Army.

2. The establishment of state control over the major private banks and the major industrial enterprises, and measures to assist medium and small businesses.

3. The adoption of measures to liquidate unemployment entirely.

4. The reduction of the working day to eight hours, the guarantee of a two-week summer holiday for workers and rent reductions for manual and office workers.

5. Confiscation of the estates of big landowners without touching the land and property of the peasants, and the transfer of estate lands to peasants with little or no land.

6. The writing-off of tax arrears for peasants.

7. All-round state assistance to poorer peasants to improve their farms, particu-larly by allotting them extra land, pastures and, as far as possible, wood for their domestic needs, from the lands confiscated from the big landowners.

8. The democratization of the state structure, civil service and court procedures.

9. An increase in state subsidies for cultural needs and the reorganization of the school system; guaranteed opportunities for schooling for the children of workers and other poor people; and all-round encouragement for the development of educa-tion, science, literature and art in a progressive spirit. . .

[Source: *Pravda*, 2 December 1939.]

Document 16 | **The Treaty on Mutual Aid and Friendship between the Soviet Union and the Finnish Democratic Republic**

2 December 1939

The Presidium of the Supreme Soviet of the USSR on the one side, and the Government of the Finnish Democratic Republic on the other. . . have deemed it necessary to conclude the following Treaty on Mutual Aid and Friendship between the Soviet Union and the Finnish Democratic Republic and to this end have appointed as plenipotentiaries:

For the Presidium of the Supreme Soviet of the USSR:

V.M. Molotov, Chairman of the Council of People's Commissars and People's

Commissar for Foreign Affairs of the USSR.

For the People's Government of Finland:

O.W. Kuusinen, Chairman of the People's Government and Minister of Foreign Affairs of Finland.

The aforesaid plenipotentiaries, after exchange of credentials which were found to be in due form and good order, have agreed upon the following:

Article I

As a sign of the friendship and profound trust of the Soviet Union in the Finnish Democratic Republic, to meet the national aspirations of the Finnish people for the reunification of the Karelian and Finnish peoples in a single and independent Finnish state, the Soviet Union expresses its willingness to transfer to the Finnish Democratic Republic those regions of northern Karelia with a predominantly Karelian population—some 70,000 square kilometres in total—for inclusion into the state territory of the Finnish Democratic Republic and to establish the state border between the USSR and the Finnish Democratic Republic as indicated on the attached map.

As a sign of the friendship and profound trust of the Finnish Democratic Republic in the Soviet Union, to meet the Soviet Union's desire to strengthen the security of the USSR, especially Leningrad, the Finnish Democratic Republic expresses its willingness to move its border on the Karelian Isthmus in a northerly direction away from Leningrad, thereby transferring to the Soviet Union some 3,970 square kilometres. Moreover, the USSR considers itself obliged to compensate Finland for the value of those railways on the territory of the Karelian Isthmus being transferred to the USSR, to a total of 120 million Finnish marks.

Article II

The Finnish Democratic Republic, in the mutual interests of strengthening the security of both the USSR and Finland, agrees:

a) To lease to the Soviet Union for a period of thirty years the Hanko Peninsula and its territorial waters up to five miles to the south and east and three miles to the north and west, and its adjoining southern and eastern islands, as shown on the attached map, so that a naval base may be established there capable of defending the entrance to the Gulf of Finland against aggression in order to ensure the security both of Finland and the USSR. Moreover, in order to defend the naval base the Soviet Union is granted the right to station there, at its own expense, a limited contingent of land and air forces, the maximum size of which is to be determined by a separate agreement.

b) To sell to the Soviet Union the islands of Suursaari (Gogland), Seiskari, Lavansaari, Tütersaari (Greater and Lesser) and Koivisto, all in the Gulf of Finland, as well as those parts of Rybachiy and Sredniy Peninsulas on the Arctic Ocean belonging to Finland, for an agreed sum of 300 million Finnish marks.

Article III
The Soviet Union and the Finnish Democratic Republic undertake to render all kinds of assistance to each other, including military, in the event of attack or threat of attack on Finland, or in the event of an attack or threat of attack through Finnish territory upon the Soviet Union by any European power.

Article IV
The Contracting Parties undertake not to conclude any treaties or enter into any coalitions directed against one of the Contracting Parties.

Article V
The Contracting Parties have agreed to conclude a trade agreement as soon as possible, and to raise the annual volume of trade between the two countries significantly above the 1927 volume, when it reached a peak of some 800 million Finnish marks.

Article VI
The Soviet Union undertakes to assist the Finnish People's Army with arms and other military materiel at favourable rates.

Article VII
The Articles (III–V) of this Treaty concerning the obligations of mutual assistance between the USSR and the Finnish Democratic Republic are to remain in force for twenty-five years. Moreover, if neither of the Contracting Parties sees fit to denounce those Articles of this Treaty with a fixed term within a year of their expiry, the Articles will be automatically renewed for a further twenty-five years.

Article VIII
The Treaty comes into force the day it is signed, and is subject to subsequent ratification. The exchange of ratification documents will take place as soon as possible in the city of Helsinki.

This Treaty has been drawn up in two originals, in the Russian and Finnish languages, in the city of Moscow, 2nd December 1939.

V. Molotov
O. Kuusinen

[Source: *Izvestiya*, 3 December 1939.]

Moscow's confidence that Finland (population 3.7 million) would buckle as soon as it saw the USSR (population 190.7 million) resort to force proved a grave misjudgement. Despite committing over a million men, and outnumbering Finnish forces by more than five to one, the Red Army's advance rapidly became bogged down. The Finns successfully exploited their superior knowledge of the terrain and encircled and destroyed one division after another. The following series of letters home by M.V. Teterin, a Russian soldier from Petrozavodsk, north-east of Leningrad, conveys the frustration in Soviet ranks at how hard it proved for the Soviet 'elephant' to defeat the Finnish 'ant'.

Document 17 | '... the Finns are so stubborn... '—from the letters home of Soviet soldier M.V. Teterin, killed in action February 1940

24 October 1939

We've moved to new quarters a bit closer to the Finns, so we're about 2.5km apart now, about half an hour away; I don't suppose we'll be staying here very long—only till things have been sorted out. I won't tell you what living conditions are like—you can't say everything in a letter, and anyway there's no point telling you now. I just want to ask you not to worry about me too much. I'll put up with it and get back in one piece...

We'll have to spend the holidays here, of course, but after that can probably start thinking of home. It's not really that long now, and I hope that everything gets sorted out soon. None of us is being given leave at the moment, but some of the lads are getting letters saying that quite a few units have already gone home. Our turn will come and we'll be together again.

10 November 1939

Well, a few words about me. I'm living in virtually the same conditions, if you ignore the current tense situation. Everything's basically all right and I'm alive and well. I spent the holidays in an extremely tense atmosphere, there were no celebrations at all, and we spent the whole time working very hard. On the 5th we moved a bit closer up to the Finns—back to where we started—we can't get any nearer, and we're talking metres apart now, not kilometres. We've been waiting five days now for the order to go into action, it will probably come.

I'm completely calm about all this, not a bit scared, because we've been ready for ages and are used to it now. I've no idea how things'll turn out, but I'm not afraid...

21 November 1939

After the holiday, up until yesterday it was fairly calm, but yesterday there was an official alert and we expected an attack. It's happened again just before a special day—in this case my birthday. I imagine you'll be thinking about me today and there'll be a do in Kezoruch'e. Unfortunately, once again I can't be there with you, and at the moment it's hard even to imagine an early return home. Such is fate, and the Finns are so stubborn.

Never mind, I'm resigned to everything. If I'm destined to return home, then the time will come eventually, but if not, what can you do about it? That's the way things are, but I'm glad you're OK and there is nothing that can disrupt your peaceful life. It's only us who'll have the casualties, but I hope they'll be very low. . .

15 December 1939

I'm writing to you from a foreign country, where I've been for exactly half a month. We crossed the border on the morning of the 30th and are gradually advancing. I got your letter of the 28th—the one with a few words from Lidia and Aunt Nyusha—but haven't had anything else.

There's so much to tell you about myself I don't know where to begin, but I can tell you the main thing is that I'm alive and well. We advanced fairly quickly the first few days after crossing the border, because we met with no resistance from the Finns. All the villages we passed through on the way had already been torched by the Finns, and the population was nowhere to be seen. But for the last few days we've been having to fight our way forwards. Over the last couple of days we have ground to a halt and there's a battle raging, because the Finns are well dug in across the river. . .

24 December 1939

I'm writing in haste, to say I'm still alive and well. I'm on Finnish territory, but we've been stuck here in a front-line trench for 10 days now. There have not been any big battles recently, just occasional artillery fire. We're getting ready for another offensive, because the Finns are fighting back hard. . .

27–28 December

Nothing new to report about myself, but I am, as you can see, alive and well. We still haven't advanced, but are gearing ourselves up for a new offensive. We are hardly doing any fighting, there is just the occasional crackle of machine-gun fire, and every day we send the Finns a little 'present' from our artillery. You probably read all the details in the press on the 24th about how things have gone over the last three weeks in Finland. As you can see, we've lost quite a few men and about 9,000 have been wounded. I bet you've noticed it down in Petrozavodsk, because you, Katya, said in your letter that you're on hospital duty. Never mind, we mustn't get gloomy. We're bound to win—it's the ant against the elephant, after all. I still dream of making it to the Gulf of Finland, getting on the train at Helsinki and coming back home to Petrozavodsk via Leningrad. It won't be soon, though; you may well be basking in the sun by then, but just wait, the time will come. Just have a 'little something' ready for me when I get back—it probably won't go off.

[Source: *Sankt-Peterburgskie vedomosti*, 30 November 1994.]

By late December, Soviet reversals were so serious that major changes were introduced in tactics, materiel and command. Disastrous mass infantry attacks were abandoned; new tanks were committed; and effective command passed from Stalin's loyal but incompetent Defence Commissar, Voroshilov, to Timoshenko. By February, the advance had regathered momentum as Soviet tanks and artillery began to smash their way through Finland's main fortifications and Finnish forces became hopelessly thinly spread. Nevertheless, by the time fighting ceased, Soviet losses far exceeded those of Finland. In the Soviet Union what became known internationally as the 'Winter War' was popularly referred to as the 'inglorious war'.

Document 18 | Casualties in the Soviet–Finnish Winter War

	USSR	Finland
1. Killed, died of injuries or disease	87,506	48,243
2. Missing	39,369	3,273
3. Taken prisoner	5,000	1,100

[Source: *Potery Vooruzhennykh Sil SSSR v voynakh, boevykh deystviyakh i boevykh konfliktakh. Statisticheskoe issledovanie* (Moscow 1993), p. 122.]

The Soviet–Finnish peace treaty

In part what had buoyed Finnish resistance was international reaction to the outbreak of the war. Outrage against Soviet action was worldwide. On 14 December the Soviet Union was expelled from the League of Nations and the Finnish government's hopes were kept aloft by the possibility of Allied intervention. Though in Britain both Chamberlain and Churchill were wary of driving the USSR closer to Germany, the French government, under heavy anti-communist pressure, was more publicly bellicose. It was decided in principle to send Allied forces of 100,000 to aid the Finns, and the French even drew up plans to bomb the massive Baku oilfields in the Caucasus in order both to halt Soviet exports to Germany and to paralyse the Soviet economy. It was in part to avoid the risk of being drawn into conflict with the western powers that, when the Finns began to signal willingness to come to terms, the Soviet government agreed to do so rather than driving home the military superiority the Soviet army had by then at last asserted. While the Soviet Union forced the Finns to cede rather more territory than had been demanded in November, Moscow allowed the country to retain its independence, made no further reference to the abortive 'People's Government' and, instead of imposing a pact of mutual assistance as it had on the Baltic states, acknowledged Finish neutrality.

Document 19 | Peace Treaty between the USSR and the Republic of Finland

12 March 1940

The Presidium of the Supreme Soviet of the USSR, on the one hand, and the President of the Republic of Finland, on the other, guided by a desire to put an end to the hostilities which have arisen between them and establish durable peaceful relations, and convinced that the interests of both Contracting Parties are served by precisely determined mutual security conditions, including the security of Leningrad, Murmansk and the Murmansk railway, to this end deem it necessary to conclude a Peace Treaty and have accordingly appointed as their representatives:

For the Presidium of the Supreme Soviet of the USSR:
Vyacheslav Mikhaylovich Molotov, Chairman of the Council of People's Commissars of the USSR and People's Commissar for Foreign Affairs
Andrey Aleksandrovich Zhdanov, member of the Presidium of the Supreme Soviet of the USSR
Aleksandr Mikhaylovich Vasilevsky, brigade commander

For the President of the Republic of Finland:
Risto Ryti, Chairman of the Council of Ministers of the Republic of Finland
Juho Kusti Paasikivi, Minister
Karl Rudolf Walden, General
Väinö Voionmaa, Professor

The aforesaid representatives, after exchange of credentials which were found to be in due form and good order, have agreed as follows:

Article I
Hostilities between the USSR and Finland are to cease immediately, in accordance with the protocol appended to this treaty.

Article II
The state boundary between the USSR and the Republic of Finland is to be redrawn along a new line, which assigns to the territory of the USSR the entire Karelian Isthmus with the city of Vyborg (Viipuri), the Gulf of Vyborg and its islands, the western and northern shores of Lake Ladoga along with the towns of Keksholm, Sortavala, Suojärvi, a number of islands in the Gulf of Finland, the area to the east of Märkäjärvi, including the town of Kuolajärvi, and part of the Rybachiy and Sredniy Peninsulas—in accordance with the map appended to this treaty.
 A more detailed delineation of the border will be established by a joint commission of both Contracting Parties. This commission is to be appointed within ten days of signing this treaty.

Article III
Both Contracting Parties undertake each to refrain from any attack on one another,

and to make no alliances and participate in no coalition directed against one of the Contracting Parties.

Article IV
The Republic of Finland agrees to lease to the Soviet Union for a period of thirty years against an annual rent of eight million Finnish marks to be paid by the Soviet Union the Hanko Peninsula and its coastal waters to a radius of five miles to the south and east and three miles to the west and north, and a number of nearby islands, in accordance with the appended map, for the establishment there of a naval base capable of defending the entrance to the Gulf of Finland from attack. Moreover, in order to protect this naval base, the Soviet Union is granted the right to station the necessary number of ground and air forces there at its own expense.

Within ten days of this treaty coming into force, the government of Finland is to withdraw all its troops from the Hanko Peninsula, and the Hanko Peninsula and its adjoining islands will come under the jurisdiction of the USSR, in accordance with this Article of the treaty.

Article V
The USSR undertakes to withdraw its troops from the Petsamo region, which the Soviet state had voluntarily conceded to Finland in accordance with the Peace Treaty of 1920.

Finland undertakes, as envisaged in the Peace Treaty of 1920, not to station warships and other armoured vessels in its coastal waters in the Arctic Ocean, with the exception of armoured vessels with a displacement of less than 400 tonnes.

Finland undertakes, as envisaged in the same treaty, not to station submarines or armed aircraft in the same waters.

Likewise, Finland undertakes, as envisaged in the same treaty, not to establish military ports, naval bases or naval repair yards of greater capacity than required for the above-mentioned vessels and their armaments.

Article VI
As envisaged by the Peace Treaty of 1920, the Soviet Union and its citizens are granted the right of free transit to Norway and back through the Petsamo region. Moreover, the Soviet Union shall have the right to establish a consulate in the Petsamo region.

Goods imported into the USSR from Norway through that region shall be exempt from customs inspection and control, with the exception of such controls as are required for regulating transit links. They shall also be exempt from customs, transit and other duties.

The above-mentioned control of goods in transit is permissible only in the form customarily observed in such cases according to the established norms of international communication.

Citizens of the USSR travelling through Petsamo to Norway and back from

Norway to the USSR have the right of free passage on the basis of passports issued by the appropriate Soviet institutions.

Unarmed Soviet aircraft have the right to maintain air services to and from Norway overflying Petsamo, observing the current general air-traffic regulations.

Article VII

The government of Finland shall grant the Soviet Union the right of transit for goods between the USSR and Sweden. With a view to developing this transit by the shortest railway route, the USSR and Finland consider it essential to construct, each side on its own territory, a rail link between the towns of Kandalaksha and Kemijärvi, if possible in the course of 1940.

Article VIII

Upon this treaty coming into force, trade relations will resume between the Contracting Parties, and to this end the Contracting Parties will enter into negotiations to conclude a trade agreement.

Article IX

The Peace Treaty comes into force immediately upon signing and is subject to subsequent ratification. The exchange of ratification documents will take place in Moscow within ten days.

This treaty has been drawn up in two original copies, each in Russian, Finnish and Swedish, in Moscow, 12 March 1940.

V. Molotov
A. Zhdanov
A. Vasilevsky
Risto Ryti
J. Paasikivi
R. Walden
Väinö Voionmaa

[Source: *Vneshnyaya politika SSSR. Sbornik dokumentov*, Vol. 4 (Moscow 1946), pp. 494–96.]

3

Military Reform and Buffer-Building against Germany

The setbacks and humiliation suffered in Finland, coming on top of the heavy weather made of partial mobilization and then occupation of eastern Poland, led to bitter recriminations. While publicly Stalin boasted of the Red Army's prowess, official analyses of what had gone wrong highlighted a vast catalogue of weaknesses.[10] The report made by Voroshilov when he was 'promoted' to make way for Timoshenko as Defence Commissar spread the blame far and wide, from outdated military regulations and instructions, through inadequate operational plans and defunct mobilization plans, to shortages of officers and of the most basic military training.

Document 20 | **'The People's Commissariat for Defence does not have a new mobilization plan'—report at the handover of the USSR People's Commissariat for Defence from K.E. Voroshilov to S.K. Timoshenko**

May 1940

Top secret

Organization and structure of the central apparatus
... 2. The army has up to 1,080 service regulations, instructions and principles in force. The basic regulations—on service in the field, discipline, and certain operational statutes—are out of date and require a fundamental overhaul. We lack instructions for directing large-scale troop formations, instructions for the attack and defence of fortified areas, and instructions for troop movements in mountainous regions.

---

10 For the verbatim account of the frank post-mortem carried out by Stalin and the leadership in April 1940, see E.N. Kulkov and O.A. Rzheshevsky (eds), *Stalin and the Soviet–Finnish War, 1939–1940* (London 2001).

3. Most troop units are organized on a provisional basis which has not been confirmed by the People's Commissar. The maintenance of staff lists and rotas has been neglected. Around 1,400 staff lists and rotas, in accordance with which troops are living and being supplied, have not been confirmed by anybody and have been issued to the leadership as provisional.

Operational preparedness

1. At the moment of handover, the People's Commissariat of Defence has no operational war plan. Neither general nor specific operational plans have been worked out, nor do they exist.

The General Staff has no data on the state of border defences. The decisions of the military councils of districts, armies and the front on this question are unknown to the General Staff. . .

3. The preparation of the theatre of military operations for war is extremely weak in every respect. As a result:

. . . d. As far as airfields are concerned, the territories of western Belorussia, western Ukraine, and the Odessa and Transcaucasus military districts are very ill-prepared.

e. There is no clear and precise plan for preparing the theatre of war for the engineering tasks which will flow from the operational plan. Neither the basic parameters nor the overall system of engineering preparations has been determined.

Troop levels and deployment

1. At the moment of handover, the People's Commissariat does not have a precise figure for the size of the Red Army. Personnel assessments are in an exceptionally neglected state. This is the fault of the Chief Administration of the Red Army. . .

4. On the deployment of troops—there are no statutes on the administration of individual units (regiments), or combinations of units (divisions and brigades). The statutes on provisioning are out of date and need reworking. The statute on field command has not been worked out.

Preparation for mobilization

1. Owing to the war and a significant redeployment of troops, the mobilization plan has broken down. The People's Commissariat for Defence does not have a new mobilization plan. Measures for efficient total mobilization have not yet been fully worked out.

2. The People's Commissariat for Defence has not yet ironed out the following deficiencies in the mobilization plan revealed in the partial mobilization of September 1939:

a. Serious neglect in assessing the men liable for military service, as there has been no review since 1927.

b. The absence of any overall assessment of those liable for military service, yet the existence of individual assessments of railwaymen, water transport and the NKVD.

c. Weakness and incompetence in the work of the military commissariats.

d. The lack of any systematic order in total mobilization, leading to the overload of the first days of mobilization.

e. Impractical plans for troop dispositions during total mobilization.

f. The plan for issuing uniforms during mobilization has not been worked out.

g. A patchy response in the mobilization of men liable for call-up, of horses and of road-transport.

h. The absence of firmly set out procedures for reserved occupations during wartime.

i. The unrealistic and unsatisfactory state of the inventory of horses, conveyances, gear and road transport.

3. Among those liable for call-up are 3,155,000 untrained men. The People's Commissariat for Defence has no training plan for them.

Condition of staff

At the moment of handover of the Commissariat of Defence, the army has a significant shortfall in its officer corps, especially in the infantry, where the shortfall was up to 21% on 1 May 1940.

It was established that the annual output from military schools has not been sufficient to provide enough men to increase the size of the army and create the necessary reserves.

Military training

The most important defects in the training of troops are:

1. Poor training of middle command at platoon and company level, and exceptionally poor training at junior officer level.

2. Poor tactical training for all forms of battle and reconnaissance, especially of subunits.

3. Unsatisfactory practical training of troops in the field and their consequent inability to carry out what is required in a combat situation.

4. Extremely weak training of troop units in how to co-operate on the battlefield: infantry troops do not know how to flatten themselves against a barrage or rise from one; artillery troops do not know how to support tanks; aircraft do not know how to support ground troops.

5. Troops are not taught to ski.

6. The use of camouflage has been poorly worked out.

7. Weapons training among troops has not been worked out.

8. Troops have not been taught how to attack fortified positions, construct and overcome obstacles and ford rivers.

The reasons for this are:

1. Incorrect education and training of troops. In battle training for the troops many

old practices are retained, and troops do not undergo real battle simulations which correspond to the demands of the theatre of war. . .

K. Voroshilov handed over his duties.
S. Timoshenko assumed his duties.
Also present at the handover: Zhdanov, Malenkov, Voznesensky.

[Source: *Izvestiya TsK KPSS*, No. 1, 1990, pp. 193–208.]

Dismay at the malfunctioning of the army led to a series of reforms.[11] There was a major shake-up of the high command with almost a thousand senior promotions, and as many as 4,000 of the officers disgraced or arrested during the Great Terror were rehabilitated. Political commissars were somewhat more firmly subordinated to commanders and, to bolster officer morale and authority vis-à-vis the rank and file, many of the titles and trappings of seniority abolished with the revolution were reintroduced, including saluting superiors. Yet the call by Timoshenko and others to raise the level of initiative throughout the army was in tension with simultaneous emphasis on stricter discipline and obedience among officers and men.

During spring and early summer 1940, while initial changes were set in train and plans drawn up for the demobilization of some 700,000 reservists, alarming news came of Hitler's advances westward. In April, Denmark and Norway were both rapidly brought under German control, and on 10 May the Germans invaded Holland, Belgium and Luxembourg and swung southward, encircling the Anglo-French forces in northern France. To the astonishment of the Soviet leadership, French resistance collapsed and British forces fled the continent. On 10 June Italy joined the war against Britain and France and on 14 June the Germans entered Paris. The USSR faced a sea change in the balance of power, a terrifying demonstration of the effectiveness of the German army, and the realization that Germany now had at its disposal vast new resources. The assumption that as a result of the Nazi–Soviet Pact the Soviet Union would have a substantial breathing space while Germany and the western powers wore each other down was shattered.

---

11 For two fine accounts, see J. Erickson, *The Road to Stalingrad* (London 1975), pp. 13–49, and, more recently, D.M. Glantz, *Stumbling Colossus: The Red Army on the Eve of World War* (Lawrence, KS, 1998).

Annexation of the Baltic states, Bessarabia and Bukovina

The result was the injection of an atmosphere of near panic into Soviet planning. From late May Stalin and Molotov moved hurriedly to tighten their hold on the Baltic buffer between Germany and the Soviet heartland. On the pretext that the governments of Estonia, Latvia and Lithuania were colluding against the Soviet Union and contravening the agreements signed the previous year, an ultimatum was issued to each of them on 14 June insisting on the formation of governments sympathetic to the USSR. In the eyes of the authoritarian regimes in power in each of the three, this was straightforward crushing of national independence and they derided the new governments as puppets of the USSR. They protested internationally and in the Lithuanian case the idea appears to have been floated, without official authorization, of appealing for help to Germany—where President Smetona fled on 15 June. This was the account given to Ribbentrop a month later by the Lithuanian ambassador to Germany.

Document 21 | **Note from the Lithuanian ambassador to Ribbentrop**

21 July 1940

. . . on 14 June 1940 the Union of Soviet Socialist Republics on some unfounded and unjustified pretext delivered an ultimatum to Lithuania in which it demanded:
1. that the constitutional government of Lithuania resign.
2. that the Minister of Internal Affairs and the head of the political police be committed for trial, without any charges with any legal basis having been made against them.
3. that Soviet military units be allowed free and unrestricted access into Lithuania.

The next day the Russian Red Army, after attacking Lithuanian border guards, crossed the Lithuanian frontier and occupied the whole of Lithuania. In addition a puppet government was formed, foisted on us by high-ranking Soviet officials sent from Moscow, and the entire administration was placed under the control of the government of the Union of Soviet Socialist Republics.

In order finally to include Lithuania into the Union of Soviet Socialist Republics, we were ordered to conduct elections to the Sejm on 14 July, as a result of which the grossest falsification of the will of the Lithuanian people took place.

[Source: SSSR—Germaniya. Dokumenty i materialy o sovetsko-germanskikh otnosheniyakh s aprelya po oktyabr´ 1939 g. [sic] Vol. II (Vilnius 1989).]

Opposition opinion in the Baltic states, on the other hand, was initially elated at 'liberation' from regimes which had flouted the parliamentary democracy established in the 1920s and had failed to entrench their popular legitimacy. At first, their overthrow triggered enthusiastic demonstrations and applause from left-wing and liberal commentators and, in Lithuania, even from the substantial Catholic press. Moreover, the formation of temporary new governments headed by leading left-wing democrats was accompanied by the announcement of a range of social and economic changes with wide appeal. Excitement was greatest in Lithuania, which was the least advanced in socioeconomic terms and whose nationalist regime under Smetona had been the most oppressive of the three.[12] Here there had been the strongest pressure for land reform, the lifting of restrictions on trade unions, the imposition of progressive taxation and improvement in social security. The effect of voluble expressions of popular enthusiasm was not only to ease the subordination of the three states to the status of protectorates but also to encourage Moscow to go much further.

As reported to the Kremlin, quite wrongly, the popular upsurge amounted to support both for social revolution and for fusion with the USSR. Whereas initially the local communist leaders involved in the new provisional governments appear to have expected to retain at least the trappings of independence, by the end of the month Molotov was informing them that the three republics were to be incorporated into the Soviet Union. This was not made public in the run-up to the fresh national elections organized in each of them. Where the rumour did spread, there was sufficient enthusiasm in some quarters, orchestrated by local communists backed by the NKVD, to create a façade of popular support for merger. As Anna Louise Strong recalls in the following memoir for a western audience, promoted as 'the only eye-witness account of the coming to power of the People's Government of Lithuania', there were voices hailing the idea of the country joining the USSR as 'the thirteenth Soviet Republic'.

Document 22 | **An extract from Anna Louise Strong's *Lithuania's New Way* (1941)**

The big 'Get Together' of workers and peasants on July 10 in Kaunas climaxed the election campaign. All day the peasants poured into the city: groups of girls in youthful national costumes, clusters of youths on bicycles from distant farms. Trains, trucks and carts poured their human freight into the boulevards, and the newcomers formed in line to march. Hour after hour the streets were filled with singing: old Lithuanian folk-songs sad with the darkness of peasant life mingling with the new

---

12 For a close analysis, see L. Sabaliunas, *Lithuania in Crisis: Nationalism to Communism, 1939–1940* (Bloomington, IN, 1972).

triumphant songs of the Red Army, sung by Kaunas workers.

I stopped by some big auto-trucks of the Pieno-Centras, the dairy co-operative. 'Where are you from?' I asked. They named a village a hundred kilometres from Kaunas. 'We started at two o'clock,' they said.

'What do they say there about the elections? Are they for Soviet Lithuania?' I inquired.

'Thirteenth Soviet Republic,' shouted several of the girls.

'All of them?' I asked, and they shook their heads. 'No, not the old ones. They don't know what they want. . . but *we* know.'

In the late afternoon they gather on the great grass field above Kaunas. Here is a long row of peasant carts, smelling of manure and horse-flesh; here are auto-trucks festooned with flowers. Nearby a heap of bicycles surrounded by a dozen youths. Here are bearded men, kerchiefed women, high-booted soldiers, peasants with brown bare feet thrust into rough wooden-soled shoes. Children are playing in the dusty sand or trailing, tired, behind their parents.

Cutting across the vast field come the marchers from the city. Organized! Not long since organized, only since last Sunday, a matter of three or four days. They have not yet learned to march; their banners are crude and the spacing of their ranks is haphazard. The new People's Militia clears a way for them among the crowd and they move steadily towards the tribune, bearing portraits of Stalin, Voroshilov, President Paletskis.

[Source: Anna Louise Strong, *Lithuania's New Way* (London 1941), pp. 39–40.]

In practice, the electorate in each of the three states was presented with a single slate of left-wing candidates vetted by the Communist party; opposition voices and press were silenced; and heavy pressure was brought to bear against abstention. Once the elected assemblies convened they were rapidly marshalled behind formal requests for admission to the USSR as three new Union Republics. Socioeconomic and cultural revolution was imposed, banking and business nationalized, drastic land reform implemented, and education and the media Sovietized. There was a bloody purge of thousands of assumed opponents of the new order: in one night almost 130,000 were arrested and deported to Siberia. Much of the propertied and educated elite of the three small Baltic states was eliminated.[13]

While the Baltic takeover was still in progress, the Soviet regime moved in the south-west to wrest Bessarabia and Bukovina from Romania. The former had been part of the Russian Empire before 1914, and as we have

---

13 See the account by V. Vardys, 'The Baltic States under Stalin: The First Experiences, 1939–1941', in K. Sword (ed.), *The Soviet Takeover of the Polish Eastern Provinces 1939–1941* (London 1991), pp. 268–87.

seen (Document 2), Germany had acknowledged that it would fall into the Soviet sphere of influence in the secret protocol of the Nazi–Soviet Pact. However, Bukovina had not been mentioned. The German government tried to dissuade Stalin and Molotov from acting hastily and threatening force, but was able to do no more than pare back Soviet demands in Bukovina to the northern part. When Moscow proved adamant, Berlin reluctantly signalled to the Romanian authorities that they must give way. Here, too, Soviet occupation was followed by the decimation of the propertied elite and forced incorporation into the USSR, the bulk entering a newly created Moldovan Union Republic.

By the end of July 1940, the Soviet Union had annexed a broad swathe of territory running from the Baltic to the Black Sea. On the face of it, Soviet military security had been much enhanced. The danger of a hostile bridgehead being created in the north and threatening Leningrad had been pre-empted; likewise, Bessarabia and Bukovina cut across the route to the Ukraine; while effective control of the mouth of the Danube enhanced Soviet power in the Black Sea and deepened Odessa's defences. A substantial buffer zone had been created, seemingly capable of absorbing the initial shock of any attack while the Soviet heartland mobilized.

In practice, however, to exploit the potential of the newly acquired territory involved pouring men and resources into constructing and manning new defence lines—and maintaining existing ones until they were ready. Defence expenditure, which had already climbed steeply under the Third Five-Year Plan (1938–42), now soared.[14] The strain on the economy, which the discipline drive of the Great Terror (1937–38) had exacerbated rather than addressed, became acute. Summer 1940 saw the issue of a series of draconian decrees extending the working day and threatening dire criminal punishment for workers or managers responsible for poor performance (see Volume I, pp. 326–29).

Moreover, just as the USSR was annexing this additional territory, relations with Germany sharply deteriorated. Contrary to the secret protocol of the Nazi–Soviet Pact, Germany began to supply arms to Finland and secured Finnish permission for German troops to be sent via their territory to Norway. Soviet unease was increased when Berlin moved to bind Romania tightly to Germany. On the German side, Hitler objected to Moscow's strong-arm tactics over Bukovina and over control of the mouth of the Danube. He objected even more strongly when Stalin and Molotov demanded that Bulgaria be firmly acknowledged to belong to the Soviet

---

14 R.W. Davies, 'Industry', in R.W. Davies, M. Harrison and S.G. Wheatcroft (eds), *The Economic Transformation of the Soviet Union, 1913–1945* (Cambridge 1994), pp. 143–46.

sphere of interest. Moscow's concern, in direct line with Imperial Russian tradition, was to have a foot in the Balkans and to ensure that no hostile power, be it Germany or Britain, should gain control of the Straits.

What made both sides prepared to raise the stakes was Germany's war with Britain in the west. Stalin, though badly shaken by the speed with which France had collapsed, retained an exaggerated notion of Britain's strength, reinforced by the Royal Air Force's victory in the Battle of Britain that summer—Germany's first defeat. Despite being well aware that Germany was building up its troops in the east, therefore, he doubted any imminent threat. Hitler, for his part, was convinced that after the fall of France all that prevented British resolve from cracking was the hope that eventually the USSR would go to war with Germany. Between July and November, he reined in his frustration with Moscow and allowed the approach favoured by Ribbentrop and Schulenburg, the German Ambassador in Moscow, to be tested. Their hope was that by dangling before Moscow's eyes a possible carve-up of the British Empire, the Soviets could be persuaded to align themselves with a broad, anti-British front, thereby bringing home to the British that no help would come from the east.

It was when this approach foundered, Stalin and Molotov remaining firmly focused on Europe and intransigent both over Bulgaria and over the mouth of the Danube, that Hitler ordered preparations for the alternative: Operation Barbarossa, a full-scale invasion of the Soviet Union.

Document 23 | An extract from the Barbarossa plan of 18 December 1940

The German *Wehrmacht* must be prepared *to crush Soviet Russia in a quick campaign* (Operation Barbarossa) even before the conclusion of the war against England.

For this purpose the *Army* will have to employ all available units, with the reservation that the occupied territories must be secured against surprises.

For the *Luftwaffe* it will be a matter of releasing such strong forces for the Eastern campaign that a quick completion of the ground operations can be counted on and that damage to eastern German territory by enemy air attacks will be as slight as possible. This concentration of the main effort in the east is limited by the requirement that the entire combat and armament area dominated by us must remain adequately protected against enemy air attacks and that the offensive operations against England, particularly against her supply lines, must not be permitted to break down.

The main effort of the *Navy* will remain unequivocally directed against England, even during an Eastern campaign.

I shall order the *concentration* against Soviet Russia possibly eight weeks before the intended beginning of operations.

Preparations requiring more time to get under way are to be started now, if this has not yet been done, and are to be completed by 15 May 1941.

It is of decisive importance, however, that the intention to attack does not become apparent.

The preparations of the High Commands are to be made on the following basis:

1. *General Purpose*

The mass of the Russian *Army* in western Russia is to be destroyed in daring operations, by driving forward deep armoured wedges; and the retreat of units capable of combat into the vastness of Russian territory is to be prevented.

In quick pursuit a line is then to be reached from which the Russian Air Force will no longer be able to attack the territory of the German Reich. The ultimate objective of the operation is to establish a cover against Asiatic Russia from the general line Volga–Archangel. Then, in the case of necessity, the last industrial area left to Russia in the Urals can be eliminated by the *Luftwaffe*.

In the course of these operations the Russian *Baltic Sea Fleet* will quickly lose its bases and thus will no longer be able to fight.

Effective intervention by the Russian *Air Force* is to be prevented by powerful blows at the very beginning of the operation.

Hitler

[Source: J. Noakes and G. Pridham, *Nazism 1919–1945, Vol. III: Foreign Policy, War and Racial Extermination* (Exeter 2001), pp. 201–02.]

4

Stalin's Disastrous Miscalculation

Just eleven days later, Soviet military intelligence informed Stalin of the essence of Hitler's instruction, indicating that war would be declared in March 1941. Yet throughout late 1940 and the first half of 1941, Stalin remained unconvinced that Hitler was bent upon early conflict with the USSR. The price the Soviet Union paid for his misreading of the situation was, as we shall see, catastrophic. When Hitler launched Barbarossa on 22 June 1941, the Soviet army and air force were caught off guard and as a result suffered massive losses. Post-Soviet study of the diplomacy of 1940–41 has done much to illuminate what, given that Germany mounted the largest and most laborious military build-up the world had ever seen, had long seemed astonishing gullibility on Stalin's part.[15]

Stalin's suspicion of Britain

One factor behind Stalin's misreading of the situation was his exaggeration of British power and his concern over British intentions. He found it difficult to imagine Hitler going to war with the USSR while still being locked in the struggle against Britain. He feared lest London would suddenly come to terms with Germany. And he was convinced that British intelligence was bending every sinew to manoeuvre him into war against Germany. Even when in March Germany sealed its grip on Bulgaria, and in April both drove the British out of Greece and invaded Yugoslavia in response to the overthrow of the pro-German government there, Stalin's attention focused on how London would react.

---

15 The finest analysis is G. Gorodetsky, *Grand Delusion: Stalin and the German Invasion of Russia* (New Haven and London 1999).

Acute suspicion of Britain dovetailed with and reinforced what was the critical aspect of Stalin's mind-set: the belief that there was a rift in the German leadership. The notion was that whereas the German military were impatient to launch an attack on the USSR, the civilians were not because they were confident that sabre-rattling would be sufficient to secure a thoroughly satisfactory diplomatic and economic deal from Stalin. Hitler himself, so the theory went, was uncertain which side to favour. It was this hypothesis that moulded Stalin's actions in the weeks leading up to Barbarossa.

From the Kremlin, it seemed compatible with all the available evidence. Stalin knew full well of German troop movements, airspace infringements, and the arms build-up along the Soviet border: Churchill's well-known warning, which reached Stalin on 21 April, was late in the day and much less convincing than most. But Stalin took reports of military manoeuvres as confirmation that Germany intended to blackmail and bargain with the USSR, rather than invade, and that Hitler was open to persuasion by the 'civilian' camp. The Soviet leader believed that provided the USSR acceded to German demands, above all for exports, they could come to terms. By the same token, if he acted on the assumption of war, halted exports to Germany, abandoned his diplomatic efforts, and mobilized the Soviet army, he would play straight into the hands of the 'war party' in Berlin—and the efforts of the British to lure him into conflict. The fact that Schulenburg was a genuine opponent of Barbarossa, apparently living proof of a 'peace party', provided what seemed indisputable confirmation of Stalin's reading of the situation. When, in early May, Schulenburg urged that Stalin should appeal directly to Hitler, it seemed the most convincing evidence possible that there was a peace to play for and that it was vital to avoid any move which could be portrayed by German warmongers as a provocation.

Stalin and military intelligence

This was a mind-set which Soviet intelligence information could not shake. The intelligence Stalin received included reports which contained seemingly point-blank announcements of military build-up and, eventually, imminent invasion. But it also contained caveats and let-out clauses which, given Stalin's presupposition, could be read in an entirely different way. This reflected in part the disinformation fed by double agents and foreign powers. But it reflected, too, the tendency, by no means unique to Stalin's regime but epitomized by it, especially after the ravages of the Terror, for the spy service itself to select and highlight material that corresponded to the suppositions of their political masters. When Stalin asked 'What are the terms Hitler seeks?', nervous agents were much more inclined to try to provide plausible answers than to contradict the premise of the question. For the senior figures summarizing and editing intelligence material for the leadership, there was a powerful incentive to avoid being identified in Stalin's eyes with unwelcome claims. The commentary which General Golikov, chief of Red Army intelligence, appended to detailed reports tended to echo Stalin's own belief that Hitler would not attack while still at war with Britain. Officials lower down the hierarchy suspected him of crudely manipulating the raw intelligence material. The following extract, from the memoirs of V.A. Novobranets, a mid-ranking intelligence officer, conveys the frustration and dilemmas they faced.

Document 24 | 'The time to produce a report on Germany was approaching'— from the memoirs of V.A. Novobranets

. . . In his memoirs Marshal Zhukov says that by 4 April 1941, according to the General Staff's data, 72–73 German divisions were lined up against the USSR. . . Back in December 1940 Soviet military intelligence had reported that 110 divisions, including 11 tank ones, were lined up against the USSR. How come there were 38 fewer divisions by April 1941? This was the work of General Golikov, the Head of Military Intelligence. He simply 'removed' 38 divisions from the list and slipped the General Staff some disinformation. . .

The time to produce a report on Germany was approaching, but we were still having long and tortuous discussions about how many German divisions were really on our borders and where Hitler would strike his blow—Britain or the USSR?

On one occasion Colonel Gusev, red with fury, burst into my office after his regular report to Golikov and said, 'He's cut some again!'

'How many?'

'15 divisions!'

I realized that we could neither delay nor put up with this any longer. It was vital to make some kind of firm decision. But which one? To give the information the bosses wanted? That would mean betraying the Motherland! But to give reliable data would mean to conflict sharply with the leadership and official line, that is, in the final analysis, to go against the opinion of Stalin, and to risk 'disappearing in mysterious circumstances'.

. . . The next day I compiled a report. It was report No. 8 for December 1940. . . Basically, it said this: Massive transfers of German troops to our borders have been noticed recently. . . This enormous concentration of troops is not to improve their accommodation conditions, as Hitler claimed, but for war against the USSR. . .

[Source: *Znamya*, No. 6, 1990, pp. 177–80.]

Where troop estimates are concerned, the charge against Golikov may be misplaced. In purely military terms, the news reaching Stalin was anything but reassuring. Indeed, it was quite sufficient to make him, with good reason, alarmed at the prospect of early war with Hitler. But the effect was to give him a powerful additional incentive to cling to the belief that a clash could be postponed. His self-deception, though no doubt rooted in overweening confidence in his own judgement and irremovable suspicion of Britain and the capitalist world, fed too on wishful thinking. Early in 1941 he was made aware of how shockingly ill prepared the USSR was for a German assault. Two elaborate war games in January 1941 demonstrated beyond doubt that in the face of an early German attack, the Red Army would be in grave trouble. It was vital therefore to play for more time while military reorganization, defence construction and the switch of capacity from civilian to arms production proceeded. Far from being complacent, Stalin's actions were guided by the desperate wish to delay war until the USSR could face Germany effectively. As a result, convinced that Hitler's mind was not made up and that the one thing certain to precipitate war was for the Red Army to give provocation, thereby strengthening the position of the hawks in the German camp, Stalin repeatedly resisted pressure from his commanders to put the army on full alert.

When a report from Golikov on 5 May indicated that in just two months the number of German divisions facing Soviet borders had soared from 70 to 107, Stalin did reluctantly agree to authorize the deployment of some 800,000 men from the rear to bolster the most vulnerable points of the front. But he insisted it be done as discreetly as possible and would go no further. Over the following weeks, he time and again rejected his generals' urgent request to intensify preparations. One such proposal, drafted by Zhukov just three days after the partial deployment and endorsed by Timoshenko, urged a pre-emptive strike to disorganize Germany's preparations.

Document 25 | **Considerations on the plan for the strategic deployment of the armed forces in the event of war with Germany and its allies— from the USSR People's Commissar for Defence to I.V. Stalin.**

May 1941

For your eyes only
No copies

Herewith for your perusal considerations on the plan for the strategic deployment of the Soviet Union's armed forces in the event of war with Germany and its allies.

I. According to Red Army Intelligence, Germany at present has deployed some 230 infantry, 22 tank, 20 motorized, 8 air and 4 cavalry divisions, about 284 divisions in all. Of these, as of 15 April 1941, 86 infantry, 13 tank, 12 motorized and 1 cavalry divisions, up to 120 [*sic*] in all, are concentrated on the borders of the Soviet Union.

In current political conditions it is assumed that in the event of an attack against the USSR, Germany will be able to deploy against us up to 137 infantry, 19 tank, 15 motorized, 4 cavalry and 5 parachute divisions, up to 180 in all. . .

Germany's likely allies could deploy against the USSR: Finland—up to 20 infantry divisions, Hungary up to 15, Romania up to 25.

In all, Germany and her allies could deploy some 240 divisions against the USSR.

Since Germany at present maintains its army and rear services fully mobilized, it could *anticipate* us in deployment and strike a sudden blow.

To prevent this, I consider it absolutely vital not to give the German Command the initiative, *forestall* the enemy and attack the German army while it is being deployed, before it has managed to organize the front and the interaction of troop units.

II. The Red Army's first strategic goal should be to destroy the main part of the German army, which is deployed south of a line from Brest to Dęblin and a month later form a front along a line from Ostrolęnka, the river Narev, Łowicz, Łódź, Kluczbork and Opole to Olomouc. The next strategic goal should be to attack from the region of Katowice in a northerly or north-westerly direction in order to destroy the large concentrations in the central and northern wings of the German army, thereby taking control of the territory of former Poland and East Prussia.

The immediate task is to destroy the German army east of the Wisła and in the direction of Kraków, emerge along the Narev and Wisła and take control of the Katowice region. To do this, we must:

a) use the forces of our south-western front to strike the main blow in the direction of Kraków and Katowice, thereby cutting Germany off from its southern allies;

b) use the left wing of our western front to strike an auxiliary blow in the direction of Siedlce and Dęblin with the aim of pinning down the Warsaw group and taking Warsaw, thereby also helping the south-western front to destroy the enemy's Lublin group;

c) wage an active defence against Finland, East Prussia, Hungary and Romania and be ready—if circumstances are favourable—to inflict a blow on Romania. Thus, the Red Army would commence offensive action from the Czyżewo–Lutowiska front with 152 divisions against 100 German ones. Active defence would be envisaged along the rest of our state frontier.

III. On the basis of this conception of strategic deployment, the following grouping of the USSR's armed forces is envisaged:

1. The land forces of the Red Army: 198 infantry divisions, 61 tank divisions, 31 motorized divisions and 13 cavalry divisions, totalling 303 land divisions, with 74

artillery regiments from the GHQ reserves, should be deployed as follows:

a. The main forces of 258 divisions and 53 artillery regiments should be retained in the west as part of the GHQ reserves for the south-western and western fronts;

b. The remaining forces of 45 divisions and 21 artillery regiments in GHQ reserves should be used to defend the far eastern, southern and northern borders of the USSR.

2. The airborne forces of the Red Army, consisting of the 218 currently available and battle-ready air squadrons should be distributed as follows:

a. The main forces of 165 air squadrons to be deployed in the west;

b. The remaining forces of 53 air squadrons should be retained for the defence of the far eastern, southern and northern borders and Moscow's anti-aircraft installations.

Apart from the air forces indicated above, another 115 squadrons are in the process of formation but are not yet ready for action. They should be fully prepared by 1 January 1942. . .

VI. Covering concentrations and deployments

To protect ourselves against a possible sudden enemy attack, and to cover troop deployments, we must:

1. Organize a firm defence and cover of the state border, using all the troops of the border districts and almost all the aircraft earmarked for deployment in the west;

2. Work out a detailed plan for defence against air attack and have all anti-aircraft installations on full alert.

I have already issued orders on these matters, and the drafting of the plans for the defence of the state borders and for anti-aircraft defence will be fully complete by 1 June 1941.

At the same time we must speed up the construction and arming of fortified areas, begin construction in the rear of the fortified areas of Ostashkov and Pochep. We must envisage similar ones in 1942 on the Hungarian border and continue constructing fortified areas along the old frontier. . .

IX. I accordingly request:

1. That the plan for the strategic deployment of the USSR's armed forces and the plan setting out military actions in the case of war with Germany be confirmed;

2. Timely approval for the thorough implementation of secret total mobilization and secret concentration in particular of all the land and air forces in the GHQ reserves;

3. That the People's Commissariat for Transport be required to carry out the 1941 railway construction plan, especially in the direction of L'vov, fully and in good time;

4. That industry be obliged to fulfil its plan for the production of tanks and aircraft,

and for the production and delivery of ammunition and fuel strictly on schedule;
5. That the proposal for constructing new fortified districts be confirmed.

Marshal of the Soviet Union S. Timoshenko, USSR People's Commissar for Defence
General G. Zhukov, Chief of the General Staff of the Red Army

[Source: *Novaya i noveyshaya istoriya*, No. 3, 1993, pp. 40–44.]

The discovery of the above draft was among the fragments used to give plausibility to the now thoroughly discredited notion, briefly in vogue in the early 1990s, that Stalin was planning a war of aggression against Germany. An offensive military strategy was fully compatible with Moscow's defensive military–diplomatic stance. Timoshenko's recommendation of an offensive was foursquare in line with established Soviet military thinking: faced by an invading army, the Red Army must immediately go onto the attack.[16]

During early June, intelligence reports on the massing of German troops and their full battle-readiness became ever more alarming. On 6 June, Stalin, who now replaced Molotov as Chairman of Sovnarkom, did issue a decree ordering preparation for a massive switch to arms production from 1 July, should it prove necessary. But he remained adamant that no military moves which could be interpreted as provocation be undertaken. The following statement issued on 14 June by the Soviet news agency derided all talk of imminent war as British propaganda.

Document 26 | **'Rumours of Germany's intention to annul the pact and prepare an attack on the USSR are groundless'—TASS announcement**

14 June 1941

Even before the arrival of Mr Cripps, the British ambassador to the USSR, in London, and especially after his arrival, the British and foreign press as a whole began whipping up stories about 'the imminence of war between the USSR and Germany'. According to these rumours:
1. Germany has supposedly made territorial and economic claims against the USSR and at this very moment talks are taking place between Germany and the USSR about the conclusion of a new and closer agreement between them;
2. The USSR has supposedly rejected these claims, as a result of which Germany is massing its troops on the border with the USSR ready for an attack upon the USSR;

---

16 In addition to the analysis in Glantz, *Stumbling Colossus*, see the crisp resumé in E. Mawdsley, *The Stalin Years: The Soviet Union, 1929–1953* (Manchester 1998), pp. 85–87;

3. The Soviet Union, in its turn, is supposedly preparing more intensively for war with Germany and massing its troops on the border with Germany.

Despite the obvious senselessness of these rumours, responsible circles in Moscow still consider it necessary, in view of the relentless exaggeration of these rumours, to authorize TASS to declare that these rumours are the crudely cooked-up propaganda of forces hostile to the USSR and Germany, with an interest in extending and unleashing war.

TASS declares that:

1. Germany has made no claims of any kind against the USSR and is not proposing any kind of new and closer agreement, thus talks on such matters simply could not have taken place.

2. According to our own information, Germany is observing the conditions of the non-aggression pact just as strictly as the Soviet Union; thus, in the opinion of Soviet circles, rumours of Germany's intention to annul the pact and prepare an attack on the USSR are groundless, and the recent redeployment of German troops, released from operations in the Balkans, to the eastern and north-eastern regions of Germany is presumably for other reasons not connected with Soviet–German relations.

3. In accordance with its policy of peace, the USSR has observed and intends to observe the conditions of the Soviet–German non-aggression pact, in view of which rumours about the USSR preparing for a war with Germany are false and provocative;

4. The current summer mustering of reserve units of the Red Army and the forthcoming manoeuvres are intended for nothing more than the training of reserves and the testing of the railway system which, as everyone knows, take place every year. Thus, to present these Red Army measures as hostile to Germany is, to say the least, absurd.

[Source: *Pravda*, 14 June 1941.]

The more ominous the military information coming in, the more tense Stalin became, and the greater the courage and independence of mind required to confront him with the monumental misjudgement he was making. The mood in the Kremlin is captured in the following message to Stalin from Beria, head of the NKVD, written the day before disaster struck. What Beria himself believed by this stage is impossible to say: he was among the most obsequious as well as the most unsavoury of Stalin's lieutenants. In the same breath as he drew attention to warnings from the Soviet Embassy in Berlin— naming the ambassador, Dekanozov, Novobranets and the military attaché, Tupikov—he heaped scorn on them, totally disassociated himself from them, and identified himself wholeheartedly with Stalin's 'wise plan' [*mudroye prednachertanie*].

Document 27 │ '... Hitler will not attack us in 1941...'—
from L.P. Beria's note to I.V. Stalin

21 June 1941

... I again insist on the recall and punishment of Dekanozov, our ambassador in Berlin, who is still bombarding me with disinformation about Hitler preparing to attack the USSR. He tells me that this 'attack' will begin tomorrow.

Major-General V.I. Tupikov, our military attaché in Berlin, has radioed me the same. This stupid general reckons that three *Wehrmacht* armies will attack Moscow, Leningrad and Kiev, which he got from his agents in Berlin. He has the cheek to demand that we supply these liars with radio sets.

Lieutenant-General F.I. Golikov, the Head of the Intelligence Administration, where Berzin's gang were active until recently, has been complaining about Dekanozov and about his Lieutenant-Colonel Novobranets, who is also spreading lies to the effect that Hitler has massed 170 divisions against us on our western border...

But, Iosif Vissarionovich, I and my people still keep your wise plan firmly in mind: Hitler will not attack us in 1941!

[Source: *Argumenty i fakty*, No. 4, 1989.]

PART TWO

INVASION AND THE GREAT PATRIOTIC WAR (1941–1945)

Initial Soviet losses were catastrophic and by October 1941 German forces were in sight of Moscow. The regime resorted to ruthless coercion to halt desertion and retreat. But the scale of the disaster also compelled the leadership to cast its net as wide as possible for support, couching its popular appeal in terms that went beyond narrow party language: the struggle was almost immediately labelled the 'Great Patriotic War'. What guaranteed popular determination to repel the invasion was the brutality of German occupying forces. On the home front, the regime's desperate drive to shift the entire economy onto a war footing worked with the grain of popular resolve. The civilian economy was squeezed dangerously close to collapse. But the upshot was a phenomenal increase in munitions production which saw the USSR rapidly recover to outperform the Nazi empire. The military turning point came at Stalingrad in the latter part of 1942 and by the end of 1944 the Red Army was driving the Nazis back across eastern Europe. By the time victory was declared in May 1945, the USSR had suffered human and economic destruction on a scale unprecedented in history. The wartime experience, disruption making party control of necessity much less rigid in many areas of life, raised popular expectations that the return of peace would see a milder form of Soviet rule. But, although victory conferred on the regime a legitimacy it had never enjoyed in the 1930s, these expectations were confounded. A number of minority nationalities were forcibly uprooted from their homelands for supposed collaboration; on the same grounds, returning POWs were despatched en masse to the swelling labour camps in the east; reconstruction was to be accompanied by the violent reassertion of party control.

5

Barbarossa

Hitler launched Operation Barbarossa at dawn on Sunday 22 June.[17] At first Stalin refused to believe it. Even when Molotov was formally informed by Schulenburg—at 5.30 a.m., some two hours after the attack began—that Germany had in effect declared war, Stalin hoped for possible mediators. The initial military orders he approved, at 7.15 a.m., forbad crossing the border lest that close off any chance that a way out might yet be found. But though communication with the different fronts was severely disrupted, each piece of news that came through could hardly have been worse. By the time that instructions were at last given for full-scale war, after 9 p.m., the Soviet army and air force had already suffered devastating initial losses. The terrible situation was compounded by the order now to go directly onto the offensive, encircle and smash invading forces, and move straight into enemy territory. It had long been the premise of Soviet military planning that Soviet forces would immediately go onto the offensive in the case of war. But the quixotic attempt to do so with an army that was reeling and an air force that had been decimated on the ground plunged the front into chaos.

Stalin remained so shocked by the collapse of his entire political–diplomatic strategy that, although he was chairman of Sovnarkom as well as head of the party, he declined to announce the dreadful news himself. That was left to Molotov. His radio speech was made at noon. Speaking without the slightest pretension to charisma, and opening and closing with deferential reference to Stalin, he repudiated the German charge that the Soviet side had provoked the war and denounced the Germans for launching an attack without an ultimatum or warning of any kind. The number he cited killed

---

17 Erickson's *Road to Stalingrad* remains the classic account, while two excellent single-volume syntheses are D.M. Glantz, *When Titans Clashed: How the Red Army Stopped Hitler* (Lawrence, KS, 1995), and R.J. Overy, *Russia's War* (London 1999).

and wounded, two hundred, bore no relation to the scale of initial losses, but he did indicate that attacks had been made from the Baltic to the Black Sea. And in summoning Soviet resistance, he dubbed the war a 'Patriotic War', drawing what was to become the standard analogy with Russia's defeat of Napoleon's ill-fated invasion in 1812.

Document 28 | 'The Red Army will once more wage a victorious Patriotic War...'—from V.M. Molotov's radio broadcast

22 June 1941

Citizens of the Soviet Union!

The Soviet government and its head, comrade Stalin, have authorized me to make the following announcement.

At four o'clock this morning, without making any claims against the Soviet Union and without a declaration of war, German troops attacked our country. They attacked our borders in several places and used their aircraft to bomb our cities— Zhitomir, Kiev, Sebastopol, Kaunas and several others, killing and wounding over 200 people in the process. Enemy air raids and artillery fire were also launched from Romanian and Finnish territory...

At half past five this morning, after the attack had already begun, Schulenburg, the German ambassador in Moscow, informed me, as People's Commissar for Foreign Affairs, on behalf of his government that the German Government had decided to launch a war against the USSR because of the massing of Red Army units on the eastern borders of Germany.

In the name of the Soviet Government I replied that up to the very last moment the German Government had made no claims whatsoever against the Soviet Union, that Germany had launched an attack on the USSR despite the Soviet Union's peace-loving stance, and that fascist Germany was therefore the aggressor.

On behalf of the Government of the Soviet Union, I must also state that neither our troops nor our air force have committed any border violations at any point whatsoever, and so this morning's statement on Romanian radio that Soviet aircraft had supposedly attacked a Romanian aerodrome is a downright, provocative lie. Hitler's whole announcement today, trying belatedly to concoct some accusation against the Soviet Union for not observing the Soviet–German Pact, is likewise a lie and provocation.

Now that the attack against the Soviet Union has taken place, our troops have been ordered to repel this villainous attack and drive the German troops from the territory of our Motherland...

This is not the first time our people has had to deal with an aggressive enemy. During Napoleon's campaign against Russia our people responded with the Patriotic War and Napoleon suffered defeat and ruin. The same will happen to this puffed-up Hitler, who has instigated a new campaign against our country. The Red Army and our entire people will once more wage a victorious Patriotic War for the Motherland, honour and freedom. . .

Citizens of the Soviet Union, the government calls upon you once again to close ranks around our glorious Bolshevik party, around our Soviet Government and around our great leader, comrade Stalin.

Our cause is just! The enemy will be defeated! The day will be ours!

[Source: *Izvestiya*, 24 June 1941.]

The bewildered leadership began to take a series of emergency steps. On 23 June a 'High Command Headquarters' (*stavka*) was set up, although as yet with no clear Commander-in-Chief, and military authority in front areas was extended over civilian administration. The same day, authorization was given for the arms production plan drawn up on 6 June to be implemented at full speed. On 26 June, a decree to maximize the labour effort was issued. Enterprise directors were empowered to impose compulsory (paid) over-time, extending the working day for many to eleven hours, and holidays were cancelled.

Document 29 | **On the working hours of manual and white-collar workers in wartime—decree of the Presidium of the Supreme Soviet of the USSR**

26 June 1941

To ensure the fulfilment of those production quotas related to wartime needs, the Presidium of the Supreme Soviet of the USSR decrees as follows:

1. Directors of industrial, transport, agricultural and trade enterprises are to be given the right—with the permission of the USSR Sovnarkom—to institute 1–3 hours' compulsory overtime per day for both their factories as a whole and for individual shops, sections and groups of manual and white-collar workers.

2. Persons under the age of 16 may be required to do up to two hours' overtime per day.

3. Overtime is not compulsory for women from the sixth month of pregnancy, nor for nursing mothers for six months.

4. Compulsory overtime for manual and white-collar workers is to be paid at time-and-a-half.

5. Usual and extra leave is to be cancelled and replaced with financial compensation for leave not taken in all state, co-operative and public enterprises and institutions. Leave is to be granted only in case of sickness. Maternity leave is to be granted in accordance with Article 14 of the Decree of the USSR Sovnarkom, the CPSU CC and the VTsSPS of 28 December 1938.

M. Kalinin, chairman of the Presidium of the Supreme Soviet of the USSR
A. Gorkin, secretary to the Presidium of the Supreme Soviet of the USSR
Moscow, Kremlin.

[Source: *Izvestiya*, 27 June 1941.]

Soviet evacuation

The following day, as desperate news continued to come in from the
Western Front, a secret decree on evacuation from the invaded areas was
issued. German forces were threatening the industrial heartland of Ukraine,
thereby placing at risk armaments production and thus the very mainsprings
of the country's ability to wage war. At the top of the agenda, which was
co-ordinated by the head of Gosplan, N.A. Voznesensky, was the immediate rescue and removal of industrial machinery that would be vital for the
supply of arms and munitions, and where possible raw materials and grain.
The managers, technicians and skilled manual-labour force necessary to re-
establish production were to be evacuated with the plant. Where evacuation
was impossible, a scorched-earth policy was ordered: anything that could be
of use to the invaders—food, fuel, property of any kind—was to be destroyed
rather than be allowed to fall into German hands.

Document 30 | **Instructions on the evacuation and relocation of people and valuable property—decree of the Central Committee of the CPSU and the USSR Sovnarkom**

27 June 1941

Top secret

The Central Committee of the CPSU and the Sovnarkom of the USSR decree as
follows:
1. The council for evacuation or the front-line military councils shall determine
which people and valuable items are to be evacuated and when. They shall have the
right independently to decide—according to circumstances—on the time and
manner of the evacuation.
2. Evacuation is to apply in the first instance to:
    a) the most vital industrial equipment (fittings and important machinery), valu-
able raw materials and provisions (non-ferrous metals, fuel and grain) and other items
of importance to the state;
    b) qualified workers, engineers, and white-collar workers along with those enter-
prises which can be evacuated from the front line, those members of the population,
especially the young, who are fit for military service, and crucial Soviet and Party
workers.

3. By order of the front-line military councils all valuable property, raw materials, food stocks and standing crops which cannot be removed and have to be left, but might be of use to the enemy, must, in order to prevent such use, be immediately rendered totally useless, i.e., destroyed and burnt.

4. Responsibility for removals, as instructed by evacuation or front-line military councils, is devolved upon local organs of Soviet power. The accommodation of evacuees and evacuated property is to be conducted by the Sovnarkoms of the Union Republics according to the instructions of the evacuation council.

5. Feeding of evacuees en route is the responsibility of the People's Commissariat for Domestic Trade and the Central Union of Consumers' Societies. At their resettlement points, it is the responsibility of the Union Republic Sovnarkoms and *oblast'* executive committees.

6. Reception, settlement and job allocation of the evacuees is the responsibility of the Sovnarkoms and regional executive committees of the Union Republics.

[Source: *Izvestiya TsK KPSS*, No. 6, 1990, p. 208.]

Two days later, when the orders for mass evacuation of people and industrial plant were made public, the phraseology was much more dramatic. The leadership's instinctive wish to seem in control of events was giving way to concern to overcome inertia and false rumours, and to bring home the magnitude of what was happening. The next day, 30 June, saw the formation of a new supreme body with absolute executive and legislative authority: the Council for State Defence (GKO). The initiative for its establishment came not from Stalin, whose nerve and confidence had been deeply shaken, but from Molotov and other members of the Politburo. According to Mikoyan's not entirely reliable memoirs, when a deputation of them went to see Stalin to ask him to head the new body, he seemed surprised and relieved that they should do so.[18] The GKO was given power over all existing party and state bodies, further diminishing the role of the Supreme Soviet TsIK, and overriding the Sovnarkom and the formal Politburo. Its members—initially Stalin, Molotov, Voroshilov, Malenkov and Beria—joined the military high command on the *stavka*, Stalin himself replacing Timoshenko as Defence Commissar before becoming Supreme Commander on 10 July and chairman of the *stavka* on 8 August. Operating through the state, soviet, party and police hierarchies as well as through special plenipotentiaries, the GKO's orders were to be binding on all institutions and all individuals.

---

18 For the key excerpt in English, see the account by Mikoyan's son, S.A. Mikoyan, 'Barbarossa and the Soviet leadership', in J. Erickson and D. Dilks (eds), *Barbarossa: The Axis and the Allies* (Edinburgh 1994), pp. 123–33. In his memoirs, Khrushchev cited Beria as his source on Stalin's loss of nerve, *Khrushchev Remembers* (Boston 1974), Vol. II, p. 7.

The establishment of the GKO epitomized a frantic drive towards hyper-centralization: strategy, plans and instructions were hurled down from above on the expectation of obedience and scrupulous execution of orders from below. However, at the very same time, the leadership recognized that it was necessary to give wider discretion and more scope for initiative to subordinate authorities. The massive disruption across an ever longer and deeper Western Front, combined with the virtual breakdown in communication, made delegation essential and unavoidable. Countless decisions about the evacuation of people and industrial plant, about civilian and military mobilization, and about priorities, timing and detailed implementation in unpredictable circumstances had to be left to local discretion. The following decree of 1 July was couched in terms of giving members of Sovnarkom additional powers, the better to implement the general economic mobilization plan which the government had approved the previous day. In practice, however, the scale of the invasion quickly rendered the plan a dead letter, and the additional powers were largely powers of delegation, authorizing local officials and enterprise directors to deviate from established rules and norms in a manner unthinkable hitherto.

Document 31 | **On extending the powers of USSR People's Commissars in wartime—from a USSR Sovnarkom decree**

1 July 1941

To ensure timely and rapid implementation of operational questions connected with the wartime responsibilities of USSR People's Commissars and, primarily, the fulfilment of construction and production plans, the Sovnarkom of the USSR decrees that USSR People's Commissars be granted the power:

1. To distribute and redistribute the commissariat's material resources, including surplus materials and equipment, among individual enterprises and construction projects in accordance with the progress of the plan and the receipt of equipment and materials allotted to the commissariat.

2. To permit directors of enterprises and heads of construction sites to issue necessary materials from their own resources to other enterprises so as to expedite the fulfilment of production plans and orders. . .

4. To allow projects running over estimated costs to deviate partially from fixed schemes and estimates while remaining within the overall cost of each site laid down in the general budget estimate.

5. To permit as yet unfinished factories or individual sections thereof to start operating, with the USSR Sovnarkom informed subsequently.

6. To hold up to 5% of the commissariat's total officially allotted wage fund in reserve to ensure the fulfilment of additional production tasks, without, however, the right to raise wages. . .

9. In cases where enterprises are removed to a new locality, to permit renting of accommodation from individual citizens to house the workers and staff of the relocated enterprise, as well as of new constructions. The payment is not to exceed the rents established by the local Soviets of Workers' Deputies by more than three times, so that workers and staff can pay normal rents. . .

[Source: *Resheniya partii i pravitel'stva po khozyaystvennym voprosam (1917–1968)*, Vol. III (Moscow 1968), pp. 40, 41.]

Stalin's public address

Only on 3 July did Stalin himself go public with a radio address at 6.30 a.m., published in *Pravda* the same morning. A direct radio address by this towering figure, whom the personality cult had lifted far above ordinary mortals, began to bring home the momentous nature of what was happening. Stalin did not gloss over the threat. By then the leadership was gaining some idea of the scale of early Soviet losses, and of the astonishing speed of German advances, first across the recently acquired buffer, and then into central Ukraine. Stalin confirmed what until then had only been rumoured: Soviet cities and whole regions had been taken and the onslaught was continuing. Part of the speech was devoted to exonerating the policies he had pursued, defending the Nazi–Soviet Pact as an essential manoeuvre to buy time to prepare for war, and explaining in terms of German deception and surprise attack the failure of the supposedly invincible Red Army to hurl back the enemy. But what came over most strongly was his admission of the disaster that had befallen the country, and instead of soothing reassurance about the regime having matters in hand, his desperate endorsement of every means to save the country—partisan resistance in occupied areas, scorched-earth destruction in new areas facing invasion, ruthless punishment for the slightest hint of cowardice or defeatism whether at the front or behind the lines. Scarcely less striking was the tone and manner in which he addressed the Soviet people. Instead of the language of Marxism–Leninism and revolutionary struggle against capitalism and imperialism, he evoked the image of military heroes of pre-revolutionary Russia and hailed the emergent alliance with Britain and support from the US. Instead of conventional emphasis on party and class, he spoke in the name of the various peoples of the USSR, citing the major nationalities by name, and appealed to his fellow citizens as 'my friends', my 'brothers and sisters'. The break with precedent, evidently reflecting intense anxiety to channel patriotic reactions into support of rather than fury against the regime, could hardly have been more marked.

Document 32 | 'It is I who am speaking to you, my friends!'— from Stalin's radio broadcast

3 July 1941

Comrades! Citizens!

Brothers and sisters!

Warriors of our army and navy!

It is I who am speaking to you, my friends!

Nazi Germany's treacherous military attack on our Motherland, begun on 22 June, is still going on. . .

How is it possible that our glorious Red Army has surrendered cities and regions to the fascist troops? Are the German fascist troops really invincible, as the boastful fascist propagandists never tire of declaring?

Of course not! History shows that there can be no invincible armies. . . We can say the same now about Hitler's German fascist army. This army has not yet met with serious resistance on the European continent. It is only on our territory that it has met with serious resistance. . .

As for the fact that some of our territory has nonetheless been seized by German fascist troops, that is largely explained by fascist Germany's war against the USSR having been started in circumstances favourable to German troops, and unfavourable to Soviet troops. The point is that the troops of Germany, a country already waging war, were fully mobilized. . . It is also very important here that it was fascist Germany which unexpectedly and treacherously violated the non-aggression pact, concluded in 1939 between the USSR and Germany. . . It might be asked, 'How come the Soviet Government concluded a non-aggression pact with such treacherous monsters as Hitler and Ribbentrop? Wasn't this a mistake on the part of the Soviet Government?' Of course not! A non-aggression pact is a peace treaty between two states. That is what Germany offered us in 1939. Could the Soviet Government have declined? I don't think any peace-loving state could turn down a peace agreement with a neighbouring power, even a state headed by such monsters and cannibals as Hitler and Ribbentrop. . .

What did we gain by concluding a non-aggression pact with Germany? We ensured peace in our country for a year and a half and a chance to prepare our forces to resist if, despite the pact, fascist Germany were to risk attacking our country. . .

The enemy is tireless and cruel. He aims to seize our lands, grain and oil. . . He aims to bring back the power of the landowners and restore Tsarism, destroy the national culture and statehood of Russians, Ukrainians, Belorussians, Lithuanians, Latvians, Estonians, Uzbeks, Tatars, Moldovans, Georgians, Armenians, Azerbaijanis and other free peoples of the Soviet Union, Germanize them and turn them into the slaves of German princes and barons. So, it is a matter of life and death for the Soviet state, life and death for the peoples of the USSR. Are the people of the Soviet Union to be free or fall into slavery? The Soviet people must understand this and cease to be carefree; they must mobilize themselves and restructure all their work on a new wartime basis, showing the enemy no mercy. . .

We must organize every kind of help for the Red Army, ensure its ranks are replenished more intensively, ensure it is supplied with everything it needs, organize the rapid movement of troop and materiel transports and fully assist the wounded. . .

We must organize a merciless struggle against all disorganizers on the home front, against deserters, scaremongers, rumour-mongers, spies and saboteurs. . . Anyone at all who gets in the way of our defence with their scaremongering and cowardice must immediately face a Military Tribunal.

In the event of the Red Army's forced withdrawal, rolling stock must be removed. . . not a kilo of bread or a litre of fuel must be left for the enemy. . . Anything valuable which cannot be moved out must definitely be destroyed.

Partisan units must be created in the areas occupied by the enemy. . . We must make conditions intolerable for the enemy and all his accomplices in all the areas that have been seized. . .

A war with fascist Germany is no ordinary war. It is not only a war between two armies. It is also a great war of the whole Soviet people against the German fascist troops.

The aim of this people's patriotic war against the fascist oppressors is not just to get rid of the immediate danger threatening our country but also to help all the peoples of Europe groaning beneath the yoke of German fascism. . . We shall not be alone in this war of liberation. In this great war we shall have true allies in the peoples of Europe and America, including the German people, enslaved by the Hitlerite bosses. Our war to free our Fatherland will merge with the struggle of the peoples of Europe and America for their independence and democratic freedoms. This will be a united front of peoples standing up against slavery and the threat of slavery by Hitler's fascist armies. In this respect, the historic speech of Mr Churchill about aid to the Soviet Union and the US government's declaration of readiness to help our country, which can evoke only a feeling of gratitude in the hearts of the peoples of the Soviet Union, are completely understandable and significant. . .

In order quickly to mobilize all the forces of the people of the USSR, to repel the enemy which has so treacherously attacked our country, a State Defence Committee has been formed, and the entire power of the state has been placed in its hands.

Put all the people's forces into routing the enemy!

Forward to our victory!

[Source: *Pravda*, 3 July 1941.]

Stalin's speech made a significant impact. Elements of the positive response it evoked are captured in the following extract from the wartime diary of Konstantin Simonov. Simonov, later to become a prominent writer, poet and literary editor, read the transcript while serving as a war correspondent near Mogilev, west of Moscow.

Document 33 | **'The words "my friends" touched my heart'—**
from Konstantin Simonov's war diaries

July 1941

In the forest near Mogilev I sat among the political officers and read a transcript of Stalin's speech. His call to set up a partisan movement in the occupied territories closed the enormous gulf which had existed up to then between the official newspaper reports and the real extent of the territory already occupied. It made sombre reading, but for us who knew the truth, it was a relief to know that it had been admitted. I had another feeling as well: it suddenly became clear that the lingering faint hopes that only our border units had been routed, that a mighty response was under way somewhere, that the Southern Front was advancing and had already taken Kraków—all these were fantasies engendered by the disparity between the beginning of the war as we had previously imagined it, and the way it turned out in reality. The truth, although bitter, was now clear: it was obvious that everywhere was the same as here near Mogilev—a bit better or a bit worse, but we had only our own strength to rely upon. And there was one more feeling: I liked the words 'my friends'. They touched my heart. We had not heard that sort of thing in speeches for a long time. For years we had not had enough of that.

[Source: *Novoe vremya*, 1965, No. 17, p. 23.]

Positive though the response to Stalin's speech was, this should not obscure the depth either of resentment against the regime by the early 1940s, or of the leadership's unease over popular attitudes.

6
Allies

The west

Scarcely less dramatic than the new tone of Stalin's speech was the transformation in the image of and language used about the western powers. The British government, so long depicted as the political centre of international imperialism hell-bent on the destruction of the USSR and willing to descend to the most cynical manoeuvres to achieve this, was recast as a comrade-in-arms. Moreover, aghast at the disastrous opening weeks of the war, the Soviet regime was at pains to paint in glowing terms the help that was at hand. Stalin publicly welcomed Churchill's famous speech on the day of the invasion in which he promised assistance, expressed solidarity and forswore negotiations of any kind with the Nazi regime.

Although Hitler's invasion forced the Soviet Union and Britain into an accommodation against their common enemy, relations were from the outset much less easy than appeared on the surface. Moscow remained intensely nervous that Britain might pursue a separate peace and urgently pressed for tangible military collaboration. In London, on the other hand, the dominant view was that although the invasion gave Britain a respite, it would not last long. The Soviet Union would suffer crushing defeat. There could therefore be no question of diverting any significant resources to help the Red Army. Churchill's emotional rhetoric failed to mask British reluctance to be drawn into any close co-operation. He made quite clear that his hostility to communism was as great as ever and at first carefully avoided use of the term 'alliance'. The formal agreement signed in the Kremlin three weeks after the invasion, and published in *Pravda*, was limited to a vague commitment to mutual assistance and a far from watertight reassurance against either side pursuing a separate peace with Germany.

Document 34 | From the Anglo-Soviet agreement of 12 July 1941

His Majesty's Government in the United Kingdom and the Government of the Union of Soviet Socialistic Republics have concluded the present Agreement and declare as follows:

1. The two Governments mutually undertake to render each other assistance and support of all kinds in the present war against Hitlerite Germany.

2. They further undertake that during this war they will neither negotiate nor conclude an armistice or treaty of peace except by mutual agreement.

[Sources: *Pravda*, 14 July 1941; [US] *Department of State Bulletin*, 27 September 1941.]

The following week saw an exchange of telegrams between Stalin and Churchill. The tone was cordial but mutual suspicion ran deep. On the British side, although the Foreign Secretary, Anthony Eden, and the Ambassador in Moscow, Stafford Cripps, had begun to take more seriously the Red Army's ability to offer sustained resistance to Germany and were pressing Churchill to make more than empty gestures to encourage the Soviets, the Chiefs of Staff remained deeply pessimistic about the Red Army's resilience. On the Soviet side, Stalin was quick to press for the opening of a new front either in western Europe or, through what he insisted was relatively easy use of British sea and air power, in northern Europe to draw off German forces.

Document 35 | 'We really have become allies...'—Stalin to Churchill

Stalin to Churchill

18 July 1941

Your messages have marked the beginning of an agreement between our governments. Now, as you say, we really have become full allies in the fight against Hitlerite Germany. I have no doubt that, despite the difficulties, our two states have the strength to defeat our common enemy...

I think that both the Soviet Union's and Britain's military situation would be significantly improved if fronts against Hitler were opened in the West (Northern France) and North (the Arctic)... It would be easiest to create such a front right now, when Hitler's forces have been diverted to the East and when Hitler has not had the chance to consolidate his Western positions...

However, the manifest coldness of the British side in military talks, and Churchill's emphasis on the difficulties, made plain to Stalin that the chances of any significant British action on the mainland were poor. He would continue to press as the most valuable move and the most convincing proof of solidarity what he began to call 'a Second Front'—not unfairly casting the Anglo-German war in North Africa as a mere sideshow compared to the German–Soviet war—but he appears to have done so more as a lever than out of expectation of success.[19] His attention became focused, instead, on demanding naval and air help in the North Sea to keep the passage open for the transport of supplies. Within a week of Hitler's invasion the Americans had signalled their willingness to provide military and other supplies and Moscow had drawn up an enormous list of requests. And on this issue Stalin succeeded in extracting increasingly ambitious undertakings from Churchill.

Stalin to Churchill

3 September 1941

I wish to thank you for promising to sell the Soviet Union another 200 fighter planes in addition to the 200 already promised. I am quite sure that our pilots will soon get the hang of them and go into action. However, I do have to say that these aircraft, which obviously cannot go into action straightaway, cannot make a major difference to the situation on the Eastern Front. In the last three weeks our situation has got dramatically worse in such important places as Ukraine and Leningrad. . .

The Germans believe the threat from the West to be a bluff, and are diverting all their forces from the West to the East with impunity. They are convinced that there is not and will not be a Second Front in the West. The Germans believe it is quite possible to pick us off one by one: first the Russians, then the English. . .

I think there is only one way out of this situation: open a Second Front somewhere in the Balkans or France this year, able to draw off thirty or forty German divisions from the Eastern Front, while supplying the Soviet Union with 30,000 tonnes of aluminium by the beginning of October, and at least 400 aircraft and 500 tanks *per month*. . .

[Source: *Perepiska Predsedatelya Soveta Ministrov SSSR c prezidentom SShA i prem'yer-ministr Velikobritanii vo vremya Velikoy Otechestvennoy voyny, 1941–1945 gg.*, Vol. 1 (Moscow 1976), pp. 18, 19, 28, 29.]

The scale and terms on which the American 'Lend–Lease' arrangement already agreed with Britain should be extended to the USSR was one of the issues covered in the talks between Roosevelt and Churchill in August which saw the drawing up of the Atlantic Charter. The Charter underlined the growing likelihood that America would presently enter the war. It set out the principles in terms of international relations to which Britain and the US

---

19 See the account by G. Gorodetsky, 'An Alliance of Sorts: Allied Strategy in the Wake of Barbarossa', in Erickson and Dilks, *Barbarossa*, pp. 101–22.

were committed. In large measure it endorsed the values proclaimed by the League of Nations—the core being the self-determination of peoples and the repudiation of forcible acquisition of territory—but it looked towards a stronger and 'permanent system of general security' in a manner which fore-shadowed the United Nations.[20] Although much about the Charter's language—notably the commitment to free trade—fitted uncomfortably with Marxist–Leninist discourse on international relations, it was endorsed by the Soviet delegation at a conference called the following month in London. While stressing that in applying its principles full account must be taken of 'the circumstances, needs and historical character of each particular country', the USSR welcomed the opportunity for a public show of solidarity with the Anglo-Saxon powers.

Document 36 | **From the Soviet statement at the London Conference on the Atlantic Charter**

24 September 1941

This Conference has come together in London at a time when Hitlerite Germany, after enslaving and laying waste a number of European countries, is waging its piratical war against the Soviet Union with great force and unprecedented cruelty. . .

In its foreign policy the Soviet Union has applied and does apply the high principles of respect for the sovereign rights of peoples. In its foreign policy the Soviet Union has been and is guided by the principle of the self-determination of nations. In its whole national policy, the basis of the Soviet state structure, the Soviet Union operates on the principle of the recognition of the sovereignty and equality of nations. Starting from that principle, the Soviet Union defends every nation's right to independence, territorial integrity and right to establish a social structure and choose the kind of government it feels fit and necessary to ensure the country's economic and cultural well-being. . .

The Soviet Government expresses its agreement with the fundamental principles of the declaration by Mr Roosevelt, the President of the United States of America, and Mr Churchill, the Prime Minister of Great Britain, principles which are so important in the contemporary international situation.

The Soviet Government, aware that the practical application of the above principles must inevitably accord with the circumstances, needs and historical character of each particular country, feels it must declare that the consistent application of these principles will enjoy the most energetic support of the Soviet Government and the peoples of the Soviet Union.

At the same time the Soviet Government considers it necessary to stress most emphatically that the main task facing all peoples who recognize the need to destroy

---

20 http://www.yale.edu/lawweb/avalon/wwii/atlantic.htm

Hitlerite aggression and remove the Nazi yoke is to concentrate all the economic and military resources of freedom-loving peoples on the complete and rapid liberation of those groaning beneath the oppression of the Hitlerite hordes. . .

[Source: *Pravda*, 26 September 1941.]

The Church

The momentous realignment provoked by Hitler's attack on the USSR extended beyond diplomacy and inter-state relations. At home it saw a shift in relations between the regime and the Russian Orthodox Church as the hierarchy called for full support for the war effort.[21] On the day the invasion was launched, Metropolitan Sergiy issued a pastoral letter (which, against the law, he circulated) in which he evoked the centuries-long tradition of Russian resistance to invasion, appealing to the memory of Orthodox heroes great and humble. Although he made no mention of the Soviet regime, the common enemy drew something of a veil over the irreconcilable clash between the regime and the Church. He explicitly repudiated 'cunning ideas about possible benefits on the other side of the border' and any thought of Nazi barbarism as a route to the Church's liberation.

Document 37 | **'Let us remember those sacred leaders of the Russian people like Aleksandr Nevsky and Dmitriy Donskoy'—address *To the Pastors and Flock of the Orthodox Christian Church***

22 June 1941

In recent years we, the inhabitants of Russia, have been consoling ourselves with the hope that the fires of war engulfing virtually the whole globe would not touch our country, but fascism, which recognizes only brute force and mocks the lofty claims of honour and morality, has on this occasion too proved true to itself. Fascist brigands have attacked our Motherland. Trampling on all treaties and promises, they have suddenly fallen upon us and so the blood of peaceful citizens is already watering our native land. The times of Batu, the Teutonic Knights, Charles XII of Sweden and Napoleon are repeating themselves. The wretched heirs of the enemies of Orthodox Christianity yet again want to force our people to their knees in the face of falsehood and by naked aggression force them to sacrifice the good and safety of our Motherland and their deeply cherished love of our Fatherland.

But it is not the first time that the Russian people has had to endure such ordeals. With God's help this time too it will turn the hostile fascist force into dust. Even in

---

21 See D. Pospielovsky, *The Russian Church under the Soviet Regime* (New York 1984), Vol. I, pp. 193–219.

the direst situation our forefathers did not lose heart because they thought not of their own safety and advantage, but of their sacred duty to their Motherland and faith, and they emerged victorious. Let us too, their Orthodox kin in flesh and faith, not sully their glorious name. The Fatherland is defended by arms, the people's common heroic efforts and its common readiness to serve in every way it can in these testing times. This is the cause of the workers, the peasants, the intelligentsia, men and women, young and old. Everyone can and must contribute their share of work, care and skill to the common effort.

Let us remember those sacred leaders of the Russian people like Aleksandr Nevsky and Dmitriy Donskoy, who laid down their lives for their people and Motherland. And it was not only the leaders who did this. Let us remember the countless thousands of simple anonymous Orthodox warriors, whose names the Russian people has immortalized in the legends of the heroes Il'ya Muromets, Dobrynya Nikitich and Alyosha Popovich, who routed Solovey-Razboynik. Our Orthodox Church has always shared the fate of the people. Along with the people the Church has endured ordeals and taken comfort in its successes. Nor will it abandon its people now. It calls for heaven's blessing for the forthcoming heroic efforts of the whole people.

We, of all people, should remember Christ's precept, 'Greater love hath no man than this, that a man lay down his life for his friends.' Not only he who dies on the field for the good of his people lays down his life, but anyone who sacrifices self, health and welfare for the sake of the Motherland. At a time when the Fatherland calls all of us to heroism it will be unworthy of us pastors of the Church merely to look on in silence at everything going on around us, not to encourage the faint-hearted, not to comfort the distressed and not to remind the wavering of their duty and of God's will. And if, moreover, a pastor remained silent and unconcerned about the tribulations of his flock as a result of cunning calculations about possible benefits on the other side of the border, that would be a direct betrayal of the Motherland and of his pastoral duty. The Church needs a pastor who truly does his duty 'for Jesus and not for a crust of bread', as the prelate Dimitriy Rostovsky put it. Let us lay down our lives together with our flocks. The path of selflessness has been trodden by countless thousands of our Orthodox warriors, who laid down their lives for the Motherland and faith whenever the Motherland was attacked. They died without thinking of glory; they thought only that the Motherland needed their sacrifice, and they humbly sacrificed everything, even their very lives.

The Church of Christ blesses all the Orthodox in the defence of the sacred borders of our Motherland.

May the Lord grant you victory.

Sergiy, Metropolitan of Moscow and Kolomna, and humble locum tenens of the Patriarchate.

[Source: *Zhurnal Moskovskoy patriarkhii*, No. 1, 1943, pp. 3–5.]

The regime allowed Sergiy to circulate this and a stream of subsequent patriotic addresses to every parish, and public attacks on religion ceased.[22] Solidarity with the Red Army and the Soviet plight came, too, from sectarian émigrés for whom the Soviet regime was anathema. Here an intelligence report to Malenkov describes the unloading of gifts for the Red Army sent by members of the Molokane sect in the US—and the blessing of the Soviet flag by a priest.

Document 38 | **'... he made the sign of the Cross over the Soviet flag fluttering at the stern'—communiqué from the Political Division of the USSR People's Commissariat for the Navy to the CPSU CC**

5 October 1941

To: comrade G.M. Malenkov, Secretary of the CC of the CPSU

The *Minsk* brought into Vladivostok ten tons (eighteen containers) of presents for the Red Army, sent by Russian émigrés, primarily from the Molokane sect in San Francisco. The presents included men's and women's clothing, shoes, medicines and surgical instruments.

The captain and deputy political officer told me the following: as they were loading the presents, a car drew up out of which stepped a Russian priest in full clerical garb. He made the sign of the Cross over the Soviet flag fluttering at the stern. Then they got the presents out of the car and took them on board.

The captain and deputy political officer say that among the Molokane a movement for solidarity with the Soviet Union has become very active. This expresses itself in particular in organized fund-raising for presents for the Red Army, and is being energetically led by the leaders of the religious communities themselves.

At the same time we have been informed that presents for the Red Army have also been sent on other ships coming from foreign ports.

Belakhov, Head of the Political Division of the USSR People's Commissariat for the Navy

[Source: *Sovetskiy soyuz v gody Velikoy Otechestvennoy voyny 1941–1945 gg. Tyl. Okkupatsiya. Soprotivlenie* (Moscow 1993), p. 17.]

---

22 For a close study of the regime's shifting approach to the Church, see S.M. Miner, *Stalin's Holy War: Religion, Nationalism and Alliance Politics, 1941–1945* (Chapel Hill, NC, 2003).

The Fourth International

Abroad, at the same time as the Anglo-American governments signalled the support of the capitalist powers, support came too from the opposite end of the political spectrum, from the Trotskyist Fourth International—a year after Stalin had succeeded in having Trotsky himself assassinated.[23] The detailed declaration issued in August roundly condemned Stalin's regime but held back from calling for its immediate overthrow and, instead, predicted his fall as well as the onset of Europe-wide revolution once victory was won.

Document 39 | The Fourth International's response to the attack on the USSR, August 1941

Manifesto of the Fourth International

The following manifesto, issued by the Executive Committee of the Fourth International, is reprinted from the International Bulletin Press Service.

The Soviet Union is at war! The Soviet Union is in mortal danger! In his desperate struggle to open the world to German imperialism, Hitler has turned to the east, hoping by a quick victory to strengthen his military and economic positions. At this hour of supreme danger the Fourth International proclaims what it has constantly said to the workers: Defend the USSR! The defence of the Soviet Union is the elementary duty of all workers true to their class.

We know very well—better than anyone—that the present government of the USSR is very different than the Soviet power of the first years of the revolution, but we have something to defend and we defend it against the class enemy independently of all the misdeeds of its present leaders. The Soviet workers accomplished a tremendous revolution which changed the face of a vast country. They stood alone, they lacked the forces to realize all their hopes, and they had to tolerate on their necks vile usurpers. But now Hitler comes to annihilate everything. That, neither the peoples of the USSR nor the world working class can permit.

How to defend the USSR? To answer this question we must before all know why the first workers' state, the first experiment in proletarian power, stands at the edge of the abyss. If a catastrophe is possible at this date, after almost a quarter century of survival, the cause lies above all in the internal degeneration of the workers' state, now ruled over by a parasitic bureaucracy. . . .

The country where 'socialism has finally triumphed' is at war, but the very word 'socialism' has disappeared from the vocabulary of spokesmen of the bureaucracy. The Kremlin, with its mercenary writers, revives all the patriotic memories of Tsarist

---

23 On Trotsky's understanding of the Second World War and its likely impact on the USSR, see S. Kudryashov, 'L.D. Trotsky and the Second World War', in T. Brotherstone and P. Dukes (eds), *The Trotsky Reappraisal* (Edinburgh 1992), pp. 84–97.

Russia. It does not even dare recall to the Soviet masses the great events of the civil war. There are two reasons for this: first, not to disturb Churchill with burning memories and new fears, and second, because it is itself in mortal fear of the revolutionary traditions of the masses. The Communist International plays dead. In the countries of the 'democratic' camp, the Stalinist parties made an instantaneous about-face. Their already long experience in this sort of drill step made it possible to carry it out without the slightest incident. . . .

The balance sheet of Stalinist policy shows an enormous deficit. The present catastrophe is only the bankruptcy of this whole policy. But if at the decisive hour the leaders in the Kremlin could only reveal their confusion, the Soviet masses on the other hand were able to demonstrate their courage and daring. The first weeks of war have shown the devotion and spirit of sacrifice of the Soviet troops. That is the fundamental fact of the campaign up to this time. . . .

The Fourth International has unceasingly proclaimed what the Soviet worker has grasped by his class instinct: *unconditional defence of the Soviet Union!* We defend the Soviet Union regardless of the betrayals by the bureaucracy and despite these betrayals. We do not demand this or that concession by the Stalinist bureaucracy as a condition for our support. . . .

Even in case of victory, the days of the Stalinist clique are numbered. A victory, even in the form of prolonged resistance, would awaken all the hopes of the Soviet masses, and would destroy the accumulated apathy engendered by the years of defeats. The workers and collective farmers would increasingly oppose the arbitrary actions of bureaucrats. Besides, the failure of the German armies would inevitably produce what Stalin dreads the most—workers' insurrections throughout all Europe. On the burning terrain of the revolution, Stalin would lose his footing and follow Hitler straight into the abyss. . . .

Defend the Soviet Union and you thereby defend yourselves, you will hasten the hour of your liberation!

For defence of the Soviet Union!

Long live the World Socialist Revolution!

Executive Committee of the Fourth International
August 1941

[Source: *Fourth International*, October 1941, pp. 229–31.]

7

Stiffening Soviet Resistance

Soviet losses during the first months of war were enormous. The battle-hardened German army smashed through Red Army lines, cut their communications, and swept into the interior. Much of the Soviet air force was destroyed on the ground. Within days the buffer zone annexed since 1939 had been forfeited. Minsk fell on 28 June, Smolensk on 16 August, and Kiev on 19 September after the army had paid an astronomical price, losing over a million soldiers, for Stalin's refusal to sanction retreat. By November, a broad swathe of the most heavily populated and industrially advanced Soviet territory, embracing Belorussia, the whole of Ukraine and part of the Crimean peninsula in the south, was under German occupation. The loss of industrial capacity, raw materials and manpower was awesome.[24] Almost two-thirds of coal and steel production were lost, together with some 40 per cent of the land under grain crops and the same proportion of the Soviet rail network. The area occupied had contained almost 80 million people, no less than 40 per cent of the population. Rushed evacuation of plant and people, combined with desperate scorched-earth measures—including the dyna-miting of the Dnieper hydroelectric dam, pride of the First Five-Year Plan—deprived the Germans of some of the resources forfeited. But the blows were devastating, casualties already ran into the millions, and up to three million soldiers had been taken prisoner.

Frantically the regime sought to stiffen resistance. Where military defeats were concerned, Stalin characteristically saw the critical issue not in terms of the strategic advantage Germany gained from its mass offensive at the

---

24 The set of tables provided by J. Barber and M. Harrison, *The Soviet Home Front 1941–1945* (London 1991), pp. 213–17, brings home the magnitude of the losses by contrasting 1942 with 1940 in terms of the size of the workforce and consumer products per head.

outset, nor Soviet lack of preparation for defensive fighting, nor yet the inferiority of Soviet arms and equipment. Instead he placed the blame squarely on feeble military leadership and cowardice among officers and men alike. He instigated ruthless and immediate punishment for failed commanders, however impossible their task had been. As early as 22 July, D.G. Pavlov, Commander-in-Chief of the Western Front, along with three other senior generals, was tried and shot to make plain to all commanders the fate that would befall 'defeatists'. Stalin's scepticism about the reliability of the officer corps was underlined by the reversal of some of the reforms introduced in spring 1940: in particular, dual command was reintroduced. Political propaganda and oversight was placed in the hands of a Main Political Administration of the Red Army, under L.Z. Mekhlis, who had played a prominent role during the Great Terror, and commanders were once again shadowed by military commissars charged with stamping out the slightest wavering in the ranks.

Order No. 270

The danger of morale cracking grew as the Red Army was forced into deeper and deeper retreat, time and again without sanction from the Supreme Command. Signs of dismay and disillusionment spread far beyond the divisions shot to pieces by the German army. The number of men detained by the NKVD for desertion or being AWOL soared at an alarming rate during the first weeks of the war, and would reach as many as 657,000 by October.[25] In mid-August, on the same day that Smolensk fell, Stalin dictated and had read to the entire military Order No. 270, imposing drastic punishments on officers who surrendered.[26] Most notorious was the command that the families of those taken prisoner—officers and men alike—were to be punished and deprived of all state benefits.

Document 40 | 'Their families are to be arrested...'—
from Order No. 270 of the GHQ of the Red Army

16 August 1941

To all members and candidate members of the CPSU CC. To secretaries of *oblast'* and *kray* committees, CCs of Union Republic Communist Parties, to chairmen of *oblast'* and *kray* executive committees, Union Republic Sovnarkoms, to all secre-

---

25 J. Barber, 'The Moscow Crisis of October 1941', in J. Cooper et al. (eds), *Soviet History, 1917–1953* (Basingstoke 1995), p. 206.
26 Though read publicly, the Order was not published.

taries of district and city committees and chairmen of district and city executive committees.

Not for publication.

. . . There have recently been a number of shameful acts of surrender into enemy captivity. Certain generals have given bad examples to our troops. . .

My orders are as follows:

1. Commanders and political workers who rip off their badges of rank in battle and desert to the rear or surrender to the enemy are to be considered malicious deserters. Their families are to be arrested as the families of deserters who have violated their oath and betrayed their Motherland. Commanders and commissars are obliged to shoot such deserting officers on the spot.

2. Units and subunits who are surrounded are to fight selflessly as long as possible, guard materiel as the apple of their eye, fight their way back through enemy lines, inflicting defeat on the fascist dogs.

If his unit is surrounded, every serviceman, regardless of rank, shall be obliged to demand that his superior officer fight as long as possible to break through and, if such a superior officer or Red Army unit prefers to be taken prisoner rather than organize resistance, they are to be annihilated by all means available by land or air, and the families of Red Army men who are captured are to be deprived of all state benefits and assistance.

3. Commanders and commissars of divisions are instantly to remove from their post any battalion or regimental commanders who hide in trenches in battle and are frightened of commanding on the battle field. They are to be reduced to the ranks for being impostors and, if necessary, shot on the spot, and replaced by brave and courageous junior officers or outstanding Red Army men from the ranks.

This order is to be read out to all companies, squadrons, batteries, air squadrons, detachments and headquarters.

Red Army GHQ:
I. Stalin, chairman of the State Defence Committee
V. Molotov, deputy chairman of the SDC
S. Budenny, Marshal of the Soviet Union
K. Voroshilov, Marshal of the Soviet Union
S. Timoshenko, Marshal of the Soviet Union
B. Shaposhnikov, Marshal of the Soviet Union
Army General G. Zhukov

[Source: *Sovetskiy soyuz v gody Velikoy Otechestvennoy voyny 1941–1945 gg. Tyl. Okkupatsiya. Soprotivlenie* (Moscow 1993), p. 63.]

The following month, at the climax of the catastrophe in Kiev, Stalin instigated another ferocious order to stem retreat. He dictated it to Shaposhnikov, who had replaced Zhukov as chief of staff when the latter recommended withdrawal during the defence of Kiev in early August. Commanders were instructed to establish elite 'blocking detachments' empowered to execute deserters on the spot.

Document 41 | **'Every rifle division is to have a blocking detachment...'— from Stalin's directive to front-line commanders**

12 September 1941

The experience of the fight against German fascism has shown that there are quite a few panicky or directly hostile elements in our rifle divisions, who at the first pressure from the enemy throw down their weapons, start shouting, 'We're surrounded!' and take the rest of the troops along with them. As a result of such activities by these elements the whole division takes flight, throws away weapons and ammunition, and later emerges one by one from the forest. Such things have been happening on all fronts... The trouble is that we do not have so very many tough and steady commanders and commissars...

1. Every rifle division is to have a blocking detachment of reliable troops, no larger than a battalion.

2. The tasks of the blocking detachment will be to give direct assistance to the commanders in maintaining firm discipline within the division, and preventing servicemen seized by panic from running away, by force of arms, if necessary...

4. The creation of such detachments is to be completed within five days of receipt of this order.

Dictated personally by comrade Stalin.
B. Shaposhnikov

[Source: TsAMO, fond 3, opis' 11556, delo 2, pp. 175–76.]

Raising military morale

Alongside the ruthless decrees Stalin hurled down during 1941, the leadership took a variety of more positive steps to raise morale and strengthen combat motivation. The conditions for securing membership of the party were sharply relaxed. Despite widespread hostility towards the regime and cynicism about party propaganda and corruption, admission to the party conferred, even for humble members, an undeniable rise in status and the promise of privileged treatment. The policy of widening access was followed aggressively, particularly among soldiers: by 1945, as many as one-quarter of those serving in the armed forces belonged to the party.[27] In the latter stages of the war, admission increasingly became a reward at the disposal of commanders but initially the procedure retained the aura of careful selection and personal as well as political affirmation. The following letter from Yu. Krymov, a writer and war correspondent accompanying troops on the front line during the disaster at Kiev, conveys the honour that many felt at being nominated, their candidature and worthiness discussed, and formal admission. Krymov's letter was found in the pocket of his field shirt, pierced by a bayonet and covered in blood.

Document 42 | 'How did we get surrounded?'—from Yu. Krymov's letter home

10 p.m., 19 September 1941

. . . How did we get surrounded? I could go on about it for ages, but don't really feel like it, because it's still not that clear. One thing's clear: wherever you look there are German tanks, machine gunners or weapon emplacements. For four days already our formation has been conducting an all-round defence within this ring of fire. At night the ring around us is marked by the glow of fires. They flicker here and there on the horizon, making the sky look a strange pink colour. Magnificent golden branches reach out into the darkness, dimming the stars. The glow creeps along the steppe, goes out and then reappears somewhere else.

We leave the village at dawn. The collective farmers have worried, stern faces. The women are talking quietly. Our commanders are shouting curtly and angrily. You can hear the roar of engines and the neighing of horses. 'Don't be sad, comrades, we'll be back, we'll soon be back.' 'Please do!' 'Who's gonna finish off Jerry?' 'Well, not us, but others will. Farewell, dear friends.' 'Let me straighten the reins and put a bit of straw on the seat. Some cold water in your flask.' 'Thanks. We'll soon be back. If not us, then others like us and no worse. The German parasite will just disappear like some bad dream. Farewell, comrades! No, not 'farewell', but 'see you again'!'

The road's dusty. Lines of lorries and carts. The rear guard assembles near the centre of the ring. The line units retreat to regroup for a decisive break-out. The Germans are closing in. There's nowhere left to go. We can expect a decisive battle any time now. There's no doubt that our formation will break out, but how and at what cost? That's what's going through the mind of every commander. . .

The Party bureau's having a meeting. On their agenda is me joining the Party. And here I am, filthy and unshaven, sitting amid the maize. Around me the comrades: Party bureau members and activists, every one of them with a rifle or submachine gun. Not far off you can hear the boom of artillery. There are scouts

---

27 T.H. Rigby, *Communist Party Membership in the USSR, 1917–1967* (Princeton 1968), p. 241.

wandering about in the maize. This is how I get accepted:

Aleksey Tsaruk, the Party bureau secretary and political director, is reading out my application and the references from my comrades, commanders and some communists. They've known me only since the beginning of the war. With our formation commander's approval I'm accepted into the Party as a Red Army soldier who has distinguished himself in battle, i.e., according to a new CPSU CC directive. The references are being read out—and they're remarkable—they have full descriptions of battles I've taken part in. The description, of the one near Bobritsa last month is particularly interesting. I stare at the ground because my eyes are filling up. You know, I've always felt that I'd join the Party in some battle situation, but the reality has exceeded all my expectations. I've joined the Party exactly when our entire formation is surrounded, i.e., just before a deadly and decisive battle for my comrades and me.

[Source: Yu.S. Krymov, *Tanker 'Derbent'* (Leningrad 1983), p. 341.]

A week later Stalin signed a decree to ensure a stiff daily vodka ration reached every man at the front. The Tsar had introduced outright prohibition at the outbreak of the First World War and alcohol had been forbidden to Red Army troops during the 1920s and 1930s. But the precedent had been set during the bitter winter of 1940, when troops engaged in the war in Finland received a daily ration of 100 grams (the brand distributed courtesy of the People's Commissar—*Narodnyy komissar*—being labelled 'Narkomskiy'). It was now reintroduced and remained the ration throughout the war, for a period being extended to soldiers in the rear as well.

Document 43 | **On the introduction of vodka rations for the Red Army in the field—decision of the State Committee for Defence**

22 August 1941

It is confirmed that from 1 September 1941, 40% vodka is to be issued to the rank-and-file soldiers and officers of the Red Army on the front line at the rate of 100 grams per person per day.

Chairman of the State Committee for Defence, I. Stalin.

[Source: *Voenno-istoricheskiy zhurnal*, No. 4–5, 1992, p. 22.]

The party at all levels was ordered to organize medical care for wounded soldiers. Stalin's generation knew how much political capital the tsarist regime had forfeited during the First World War for its incompetence in providing such care, and how much political momentum opposition groups had gathered in filling the vacuum. As the following decree issued in October shows, the leadership were determined that the party would be intimately associated with helping the hospitals and health service cope with the casualties.

Document 44 | **On the organization of the All-Union Committee to help sick and wounded Red Army men and officers— from a CPSU CC resolution**

6 October 1941

. . . Set up the All-Union Committee to help sick and wounded Red Army men and officers.

. . . Oblige *oblast'* and *kray* Party committees and the Party CCs of the Union Republics by 15 October 1941 to confirm the membership of *oblast'*, *kray*, and republican committees to help sick and wounded Red Army men and officers. These should be composed of representatives of Party, Soviet, Komsomol, trade-union and public organizations and consist of nine to eleven people under the chairmanship of one of the secretaries of the Party *oblast'* committee, *kray* committee, or Union Republic Party CC.

. . . The committees to help sick and wounded Red Army men and officers will have the responsibility to:

a. Organize broad public assistance to the health services in treating sick and wounded Red Army men and officers and supervise the day-to-day work of the hospital;

b. Organize patronage over hospitals by enterprises and institutions; assist the hospitals with equipment repair and the installation of radios in wards, canteens and political study corners; receive and distribute presents for the men and officers;

c. Assist the public health services at stations, jetties and airports where sick and wounded Red Army men and officers are being brought to hospitals in the rear;

d. Help organize cultural and political work among the wounded, e.g., lectures, reports, concerts, films and amateur performances.

[Source: *KPSS. O vooruzhennykh silakh Sovetskogo Soyuza. Dokumenty. 1917–1981* (Moscow 1981), p. 313.]

The GKO placed heavy emphasis on 'cultural and political work' among the wounded men, as it did among soldiers in general. At the same time, however, the tone set by Stalin's July speech, with its new willingness to appeal to traditional and patriotic currents unconnected with the party, was reflected in substantial adjustments to party propaganda. Hallowed Marxist slogans were not merely reinterpreted but abruptly dropped. Even the internationalist cry that had adorned the founding text, Marx's *Communist Manifesto* of 1848—'Workers of the world, unite!'—was removed from military newspapers lest it antagonize Soviet soldiers. As Mekhlis explained in the following order, with unconscious gallows humour, it was to be retained only for material addressed to enemy soldiers.

Document 45 | **'The slogan "Workers of the world, unite!" is to be removed from the mastheads…'—from an order of the head of the Main Political Administration (GPU) of the Red Army**

10 December 1941

The slogan 'Workers of the world, unite!' may send the wrong signals to certain strata of the armed forces. The slogan 'Workers of the world, unite!' is to be removed from the mastheads of all military newspapers and replaced with 'Death to the German occupiers!' The slogan 'Workers of the world, unite!' is to be used only in literature published for enemy troops.

Mekhlis

[Source: *Rodina*, No. 6–7 (1991), p. 73.]

Public criticism and repression

As portrayed in Soviet historiography, even if there were faulty elements in the army, the Soviet regime and people were united from the moment Barbarossa was launched. The evidence is overwhelming, however, that the criticism of and cynicism about the regime bred in the years immediately before the war continued after the invasion. Secret police monitoring of the popular mood in the early months provided the leadership with graphic confirmation that the bewilderment, demoralization and hostility towards the authorities that affected part of the army was fully replicated among civilians. Alongside the kind of respect and eagerness to join the party conveyed by Krymov, there was widespread antipathy. The following extract from a report of November 1941 on morale covered various different regions— Arkhangel'sk in the far north, Ivanovo north-east of Moscow, and Kaluga, which fell during the October march on the capital, to the south-west. It pieced together hostile comment condemning the prolonged shipment of Soviet goods to Germany under the terms of the Nazi–Soviet Pact, the leadership's inability to inspire loyalty and commitment, the emptiness of promises that in any conflict the Red Army would immediately carry the struggle into enemy territory, and the rumours that party and police officials were spiriting their own families away to safety while abandoning ordinary workers to their fate.

Document 46 | **'... he'd go and defend the Soviet land, but not that lot sitting in the Kremlin'—on morale among the population in the first months of the war in individual *oblasti*, from secret NKVD reports**

1941

This is the mood in the Arkhangel'sk region: 'Everybody was saying that we'd be fighting the enemy on his territory, but just the opposite. . . . Our government's been feeding the Germans for two years when they should've saved the food for our army and people, and now we'll be going hungry.' Such sentiments are not confined to ordinary workers and peasants. Ya.S. Romanov, a Party member and former Civil War partisan declared, 'The Germans are really giving us what for, but our people don't have the enthusiasm that was there in the Civil War, especially amongst us partisans. We went out and inspired them ourselves. The present leaders aren't able to organize the masses and raise their spirits.'

P.V. Lobanov, Party secretary of the Arkhangel'sk transport administration, declared, 'Our government made loads of boastful speeches, saying we had massive stocks of everything, about how we'd be fighting the enemy on his territory, but in fact it's turned out quite the opposite.'

In July 1941, Balakin, a miner from No. 16 pit in the Kaluga region, declared in everybody's hearing that he'd go and defend the Soviet land, but not that lot sitting in the Kremlin.

There was a demonstration by about 200–300 workers in October 1941 in Privolzhsk in the Ivanovo *oblast'*. The workers were expressing their dissatisfaction at the way mobilization and the construction of fortifications were being carried out, and at the state of food provision. At the same time, 15–20 October, there were disturbances in Ivanovo itself. People were shouting, 'The commissars, the NKVD and the *oblast'* Party committee have got their families out and left ours behind. . . We won't let them dismantle and take away our equipment. . . Without asking us they started dismantling our machines on our day off. . . We won't let 'em do it.' When the district committee members and Party activists tried to scotch these rumours, spread by provocateurs, people started shouting back, 'Don't listen to 'em, they don't know nothing, they've been pulling the wool over our eyes for twenty-three years now!'

[Source: *Istoriya Otechestva* (Moscow 1991), p. 259.]

In the pandemonium of the early months of the war, reports of this kind fed the dread among Stalin and the leadership that deliberate treachery could undermine war effort and regime alike. Their pre-war fear, which had been one motive behind the mass repression of 1937–38, that in the event of war hostile elements would form a 'fifth column' actively or tacitly supporting the enemy, was powerfully reignited.[28] And at the same time as extending emollient, inclusive appeals for patriotic solidarity, the regime also struck out ruthlessly at what it saw as potential sources of opposition and disloyalty, at the 'disorganizers, deserters, scaremongers, rumour-mongers, spies and saboteurs' about whom Stalin warned in his speech. Far from being slimmed down as men and resources were poured into the military, the NKVD expanded after war broke out and was free to dispense with formal and judicial proceedings when dealing with 'security risks' and act on the spot.[29] As Soviet forces retreated, the treatment of civilians regarded as recalcitrant or suspect became harsher: in many cases those in prison were executed rather than being evacuated from territories about to fall into German hands.

The largest-scale repressive measure of the first months of the war was the wholesale internal exile of the Volga Germans, settled for centuries and, though still ethnically recognizable, thoroughly Russified in their allegiance. The NKVD had charged no more than a handful of specific individuals among the Volga Germans with spying, terrorism or sabotage. Yet the whole people was summarily convicted of harbouring traitors.[30]

Document 47 | **'... there are thousands and tens of thousands of saboteurs and spies...'—decree of the Presidium of the Supreme Soviet of the USSR** *On the Resettlement of the Germans Inhabiting the Volga Districts*

28 August 1941

According to reliable information received by the military authorities, there are thousands and tens of thousands of saboteurs and spies among the ethnic Germans living along the Volga. At a signal from Germany they are to set off explosions in the districts inhabited by Volga Germans. No one had informed the Soviet authorities of the presence of so many saboteurs and spies among the Germans living in the Volga districts. This means that the German population of the Volga districts has been hiding enemies of the Soviet people and Soviet power in their midst.

Should acts of sabotage be carried out at the instigation of Germany by German saboteurs and spies in the Volga German Republic and adjacent areas, resulting in

---

28 See Volume I, Chapter 15.

29 A. Knight, *Beria: Stalin's First Lieutenant* (Princeton 1993), provides an overview of the NKVD during the war, pp. 113–29.

30 See the account by V. Tolz, 'New Information about the Deportation of Ethnic Groups in the USSR during World War 2', in J. Garrard and C. Garrard (eds), *World War 2 and the Soviet People* (London 1993), pp. 161–79.

bloodshed, the Soviet government will, in accordance with wartime legislation, be obliged to take reprisals against the entire German population along the Volga. To avoid such undesirable actions and to prevent serious bloodshed, the Presidium of the Supreme Soviet of the USSR deems it necessary to resettle all the German population living along the Volga in other regions where they will be allotted land and granted state aid to settle in their new areas. The abundant arable land in parts of the Novosibirsk and Omsk *oblasti*, the Altay *kray*, Kazakhstan and other adjacent areas has been allocated for their resettlement. Consequently, the State Defence Committee is instructed urgently to carry out the resettlement of all Germans living along the Volga, and to allot land and forests in the new regions to the resettled Volga Germans.

[Source: *Sovetskiy soyuz v gody Velikoy Otechestvennoy voyny 1941–1945 gg. Tyl. Okkupatsiya. Soprotivlenie* (Moscow 1993), p. 43.]

The Volga German Autonomous Republic was abolished and some 600,000 people were uprooted and deported wholesale to special settlements in Kazakhstan and Siberia under the authority of the GULAG. The detailed instructions on the mass deportation extended the net to concentrations of ethnic Germans beyond the borders of the Autonomous Republic and placed all ethnic Germans in peril. Neither the families of Germans serving in the Red Army nor German members of the party and Komsomol were to be exempt.

Document 48 | 'All ethnic Germans... are to be resettled'— instructions on resettlement

August 1941

All ethnic Germans living in towns and villages in the Volga German ASSR and the Saratov and Stalingrad *oblasti* are to be resettled.

Members of the CPSU and Komsomol are to be resettled along with the others.

Germans living in the above-mentioned regions are to be moved to the territory of the Kazakh SSR, Krasnoyarsk and Altay *kraya*, and Omsk and Novosibirsk *oblasti*.

Family members of those serving in the Red Army and its officer corps are also to be resettled on the same basis. They should be given priority in the places of settlement, especially with acquiring land and housing. . .

Operational procedure:

1. Those being resettled are to be allowed to take personal property, small agricultural implements and unlimited money and valuables with them. The total weight of all personal effects, clothes and tools may not exceed one tonne per family. Bulky items may not be taken.

2. Those being resettled are to be given a fixed time to collect and pack their property.

Town dwellers may sell by proxy any property left behind which belongs to them personally. The property is to be sold and the proceeds are to be remitted to the owner's new place of residence within ten days. . .

5. Those being resettled should be advised that they should bring food supplies along with them to last for at least one month.

[Source: *Voenno-istoricheskiy zhurnal*, No. 4–5 (1992), pp. 34, 35.]

Analogies have been drawn with the internment of German nationals by other belligerent powers, but the brutal treatment of Soviet citizens was directly in line with the mass ethnic deportations of minorities living on the borderlands before the war. It reflected the regime's bludgeoning reflex reaction to perceived sources of potential danger and, while it was superficially plausible that Soviet Germans should sympathize with the Nazi campaign, the action demonstrated a less realistic risk assessment than the leadership's more general anxiety regarding the level of discontent and disaffection.

This fear was fed by alarming reports on the level of anti-Soviet feeling that was revealed where the Germans eliminated party authority. In the western areas recently annexed by the USSR, the Baltic, western Belorussia and western Ukraine, many initially welcomed Germany's intervention as holding out the prospect of a form of liberation. Moreover, to Moscow's horror, where the Soviet system was more deeply entrenched, in eastern Ukraine and Belorussia, in occupied areas of western Russia, and later in the Crimea and the Caucasus, the Germans succeeded in securing a measure of co-operation from the local population. Assessing the scale of active collaboration as opposed to sheer subordination to the brute force of the occupying forces is fraught with difficulty.[31] As we shall see, German treatment of the peoples they had conquered, and their refusal to give any quarter to nationalist leaders, rapidly alienated the great mass of their new subjects. But that was by no means clear to Stalin and his lieutenants. Like later Soviet historiography and, from a very different angle, western cold-war treatments, they tended to exclude the space between heroic resistance on the one hand and anti-Soviet motivation on the other.[32] From the first days, the leadership suspected the worst and, in the same breath as Stalin wooed popular opinion with fraternal and patriotic appeals, he threatened the most drastic punish-

---

31 For the best-known treatment, see A. Dallin, *German Rule in Russia, 1941–1945: A Study of Occupation Policies* (London 1981, 2nd edn).
32 This is a major theme in the work of the leading Russian specialist S. Kudryashov. For an English-language sample of his work, see his grim case-study of active collaboration, 'Ordinary Collaborators: The Case of the Travniki Guards', in L. Erickson and M. Erickson (eds), *Russia: War, Peace and Diplomacy* (London 2004), pp. 226–39.

ment for any form of co-operation whatever the circumstances.

The regime's initiatives played some part in stiffening the resolve of the home front, of the vast flow of reservists called up to replenish the army, and of the men on the front line itself. German attackers, having initially exulted in the apparent collapse of Soviet resistance, began to express dismay at the willingness of Soviet detachments to fight on despite manifestly inferior arms, wretched rations and broken lines of communication and to absorb casualties at a rate that no German army would contemplate. But the key factor in gradually shifting the dominant mood in the USSR from shock, anger and confusion to resolute defiance was popular experience of foreign invasion and the sheer brutality of German forces.

8
German Onslaught

The combination of catastrophe and resilience displayed on countless battle-fields and in Soviet villages, towns and cities across a vast front was epitomized in three epic struggles. The first was the Siege of Leningrad from autumn 1941. In August Hitler shifted the focus of attack in two directions, south-wards towards Kiev, seeking to take the Donets basin and the Crimean peninsula, and northwards with a smaller thrust towards Leningrad.

The Siege of Leningrad

Here the German aim was not immediately to storm the city, but to bombard it, cut it off from outside supplies, and induce its collapse through destruc-tion and starvation. When the threat from the *Wehrmacht* became plain, the former capital mobilized frantically. As the German attack reached its climax, the party enrolled civilians—workers, teachers, students—in a People's Militia to support the front-line army. All able-bodied men up to the age of 50 and women up to the age of 45 were ordered to make themselves avail-able to help build the city's defences. And between July and December, prodigious efforts were made to shore up the city.[33] With arms and explo-sives being rushed to the front, effort was poured into throwing up crude defences, barricades, anti-tank ditches and other obstacles, as well as trenches and concrete artillery positions. At the height of the air and artillery bombardment in September, over a quarter of a million civilian men and women served in a citywide organization charged with backing up air defences, blackouts, fire fighting and air-raid shelters. Party officials, assisted

---

33 See D.M. Glantz, *The Battle for Leningrad, 1941–1944* (Lawrence, KS, 2002) for a recent account.

by those of Komsomol and the trade unions, scrambled to implement the orders pouring from the leadership. But the scale of the mobilization rapidly overstretched anything the authorities could closely monitor. This was true in terms of industrial production as well as civil defence: factories were desperately switched from civilian to military needs but with the regular planning and industrial and technical hierarchy thrown into confusion, much depended on the initiative shown in individual plants.

Document 49 | 'You'll have to work it all out for yourselves...'—from the memoirs of G.A. Kulagin, chief mechanic of a Leningrad metal factory

In peacetime our factory used to make power station turbines, but in August '41 they built an armoured train in just a fortnight. This is what they wrote in the factory newspaper, 'In peacetime... the factory used to have special talks with a lot of organizations. Then the designers would get down to it: general appearance... detailed design... working blueprints, standards, ordering of materials, etc., etc. But now, when assigning the work, A.I. Zakhar'in, the chief engineer, in reply to questions from his subordinates about jobs and blueprints, said, "There aren't and won't be any. We don't need any blueprints or agreements. Everything's in house. If we follow the rules, then nothing'll get done. You'll have to work it all out for yourselves..."'

[Cited in O.R. Latsis, *Vyyti iz kvadrata* (Moscow 1989), p. 36.]

On the front itself, the second half of August and September saw the German assault push Soviet defences further and further back towards the suburbs. The rate of attrition suffered by Soviet forces was horrendous, often running to one-third of the men engaged, and the People's Militia paid a heavy price for inadequate training, leadership and arms. With Finnish troops facing the city to the north, and the *Wehrmacht* moving in from the west and south, the situation became critical and preparations were made to gut military installations rather than allow the Germans to take them over. On 10 September, in desperation, Stalin replaced Voroshilov with Zhukov in charge of the Leningrad front.[34] Zhukov halted scorched-earth plans, endorsed orders from the city's military council that anyone retreating would be shot, and launched a series of counter-attacks on the approaching Germans. Stalin backed his ruthless resolution to the hilt. When rumours reached Moscow that the *Wehrmacht* were driving refugees from outside

---

34 For a vivid and highly readable new biography of Zhukov, see A. Axell, *Marshal Zhukov, The Man Who Beat Hitler* (London 2002).

Leningrad forward to implore the authorities to surrender, and that the city's leadership was divided over how to treat such pathetic victims of the invasion, he ordered that they be shot without hesitation.

Document 50 | '... they must be destroyed first of all, because they are more dangerous than the German fascists'—directive to the command of the Leningrad front

21 September 1941

Secret

It is said that those German bastards, as they approach Leningrad, are sending ahead of their own troops representatives—old men, old women, women and children—from the areas they have captured to ask the Bolsheviks to surrender Leningrad and bring peace.

It is said that there are those among the Leningrad Bolsheviks who do not think it possible to use weapons against this sort of representative. I think that, if there are indeed such people among the Bolsheviks, they must be destroyed first of all, because they are more dangerous than the German fascists.

This is my reply: stop being soft, and smack the enemy and his accomplices, willing or unwilling, in the teeth. War is implacable and brings defeat first of all to those who show weakness or allow wavering. If anybody in our ranks allows wavering, he will be the main culprit regarding the fall of Leningrad.

Really let the Germans and their representatives have it, whoever they are, harry any enemy, no matter whether they are willing or unwilling enemies. Show no mercy to those German bastards or their representatives, whoever they may be.

This is to be brought to the attention of commanders and commissars of divisions and regiments, and also of the Baltic Fleet Military Council, and the captains and commissars of its ships.

I. Stalin

[Source: *Sovetskiy soyuz v gody Velikoy Otechestvennoy voyny 1941–1945 gg. Tyl. Okkupatsiya. Soprotivlenie* (Moscow 1993), p. 35.]

At the end of September, the German advance ground to a halt, key troops being reassigned for the attack on Moscow. But by then Leningrad had been surrounded and almost completely cut off from the outside world: a terrible siege that was to last 900 days had begun.[35] Supplies of raw materials, fuel

---

35 See J. Barber and A. Dzeniskevich (eds), *Life and Death in Besieged Leningrad, 1941–1944* (Basingstoke 2005), for the best and most detailed study of the ordeal and, for a brief insight, C. Merridale, *Night of Stone: Death and Memory in Russia* (London 2000), pp. 299–306.

and above all food dwindled away. Rationing, introduced in July both in Leningrad and Moscow and subsequently extended across the country, became a matter of life and death. Bread was apportioned according to a steep hierarchy of priorities, from soldiers at the front to soldiers at the rear, priority manual workers, key white-collar workers and technicians, lower-level manual and non-manual labourers, dependants and children. By the beginning of November, the daily allowance had been cut five times, bread was being heavily adulterated, and many were now far below the level of subsistence. Even with rations savagely reduced, there were sufficient reserves for no more than seven more days. Desperately a lifeline was sought across the one gap in the encirclement, the twenty-mile route north-east-ward to Lake Ladoga. Small boats transported modest quantities of food and fuel but early in November the lake began to freeze over. Orders were then given for the construction of a supply route across the ice, opening what became known as the 'Road of Life'. During December the road was substantially strengthened as the ice grew thicker, and there was a rapid increase in incoming supplies. The recapture of the key railway linking the lake to the interior significantly accelerated provisions. As the convoys grew in size and number and the transport links on the other side of the lake became secure, it also became possible to pack the outgoing trucks both with refugees from the starving city and with vital industrial plant left idle once fuel and raw materials had dried up. The issue of whether to prioritize emaci-ated citizens over machinery (or museum and other cultural valuables) became charged with emotion which lingered long after the war, when party leaders were keen to gloss over less heroic features of the siege. Part of the controversy is captured in the following interview by D. Granin, a Soviet writer who had been a young Leningrader during the blockade, with A.N. Kosygin, the plenipotentiary Stalin sent to Leningrad to accelerate evacua-tion (and Soviet premier at the time of the interview, in the late 1970s).

Document 51 | **'We took both people and equipment out...'—the writer D. Granin recalls his conversation with A.N. Kosygin at the end of the 1970s**

A.N. Kosygin was speaking: 'At the end of August 1941 a commission was sent from Moscow to Leningrad; on it were the chairman, V.M. Molotov, G.M. Malenkov, L.P. Beria, A.N. Kosygin, N.G. Kuznetsov (People's Commissar for the Armed Forces), P.F. Zhigarev (commander of the Air Force), N.N. Voronov (head of artillery)... We arrived at the Smol'ny and the whole command were brought together.

'Voroshilov, commander for the North-west, gave a report on the situation at the front. They had not been able to halt the German advance... The situation was confused, because the chain of command had broken down. . . It was obvious even then that the city authorities, not realizing the danger threatening Leningrad, had not bothered to ensure the evacuation of people and industry. . .

'On 31 December 1941 Stalin said, "Kosygin, I think it'd be a good idea if you went up to Leningrad to sort out the evacuation, because you know all about the place." Once I got to Leningrad, all efforts were concentrated on the Road of Life—the one little vein through which the blood was just about flowing to keep the dying city alive. Some sort of daily rhythm was set up, and all the hold-ups and chaos on both banks of the Ladoga were sorted out. We had to get rid of all the unnecessary orders. . . and sort out the conflicts between civilian and military authorities, sailors and infantry, the sick and the healthy. . . A pipeline was put across the lake to supply the city and the front with fuel. Coal deliveries to the city power stations were organized. Communists were mobilized to establish order at the warehouses on the eastern shore of the Ladoga, because all sorts of things were going on there. . . I was going here and there along that road. Once I came under direct fire from the enemy shore. . . It was troublesome work, always on my feet, without any office or paper. It was urgent work, and it had definite results: every day some thousands of people were saved. . .'

D. Granin writes, 'One thing needed clearing up: the choice between the population and equipment, between those dying of starvation and the machinery needed for the war effort. . . There was no transport to spare, there was not enough, so you had to choose what to take out first—people or metal—and whom to save or help—those at the front, with tanks and planes, or the people of Leningrad themselves.'

Kosygin's reply was, 'We took both people and equipment out at the same time. What other choice was there?'

Granin writes, 'I knew exactly what the trouble was—that he hadn't been able to choose. They were demanding that he clear out and secure the factories as quickly as possible, and they were devoting everything to that. . . If only he'd dropped a hint about it. A little hint about the bitterness, about the times, however rare, when he'd felt bad. Just to know that he did help somebody, took pity and broke the rules—or, on the contrary, didn't. But no, I just couldn't get it out of him.'

[Source: D. Granin, 'Zapretnaya glava', *Znamya*, No. 2 (1988), pp. 119–28.]

Leningrad's ordeal became the supreme symbol of civilian resilience. The worst period was that first winter. The city was engulfed by hunger, cold, lice, disease and death. Electricity supplies ceased, water and sanitation broke down, medical facilities dried up, people collapsed in the street. The winter was unusually severe and for those who survived on meagre rations the struggle to keep warm became ever harder. 'We feed on wild herbs and grass,' wrote Ol'ga Freidenberg, a university professor, to her cousin Boris

Pasternak in Moscow. 'We make our own fires and warm ourselves by burning memoirs and floorboards. Prose, it turns out, provides more heat than poetry. History boils our tea kettle for us.'[36] In the grimmest weeks, the number of civilian deaths approached a thousand a day, bodies were piled up unburied, instances of cannibalism were reported. The following diary extract by Yura Ryabinkin, a teenage boy, records with painful honesty his sense of self-disgust at being unable to resist stealing food from his own mother and sister. He did not survive the dreadful winter.

Document 52 | **'Farewell, childhood dreams, never more to return!'—
from the diary of Yura Ryabinkin**

1941

9 and 10 November. . . . I sit and cry. . . after all, I'm only 16! They're bastards who brought this war down on us. . .

Farewell, childhood dreams, never more to return! I'm going to keep away from you like the plague. Everything's gone to hell and I don't even know what bread or sausage are any more! As long as I don't start dreaming about my happy past! Happy!! That's how my former life really was. . . Calm about the future! What a feeling! Never again to experience it. . .

15 December. Well, that's it. . . I've lost my integrity and belief in it and got my just deserts. A couple of days ago I was sent for some sweets. Never mind the fact that I bought sweet cocoa instead (reckoning that Ira wouldn't eat it and so I'd get more), I kept half of it for myself (about 600 grams, which was 10 days' worth), made up some story about 3 packets being snatched out of my hands, feigned tears back home and told Mum on my pioneer's honour that I hadn't kept any for myself. . . Then, despite Mum's tears and sadness that she'd have nothing sweet, I hard-heartedly ate the cocoa on the sly. Today, on my way back from the baker's, I took 50 grams of Mum's and Ira's bread and ate that in secret. Just now in the canteen I ate crab soup, rissoles with trimmings and one and a half portions of kissel, taking only one and a half portions home to Mum and Ira and then still eating a third of that.

I've slid into an abyss of dissipation, where there's no conscience, just dishonour and shame. I'm an unworthy son to my mother and an unworthy brother to my sister. I'm a self-centred person who forgets about his nearest and dearest when the going gets tough. And I'm doing all this at a time when Mum's almost exhausted. With swollen legs, a bad heart and in summer shoes despite the cold, she spends all day without a bite to eat going from office to office in her pathetic attempts to get

---

36 E. Mossman (ed.), *The Correspondence of Boris Pasternak and Olga Freidenberg 1910–1954* (London 1982), p. 223.

us out of here. I've lost hope in any evacuation. For me it's disappeared. For me the whole world has become just one thing—food. My whole purpose is to get food. . .

I'm lost. My life's over. What lies ahead isn't life, so now I want just two things: to die right now and let Mum read this diary. May she curse and denounce me as an unfeeling, hypocritical worm of a thing. I've fallen too far, too far. . .

24 December. Something's happened to me. Something good seems to have appeared in my character. It seems to have happened when I lost Ira's sugar-ration booklet. Oh how vilely I behaved towards Mum and Ira! I stood gawking in the shop and lost 200 grams of sugar, 100 grams of chocolate and 150 grams of sweets for Mum and Ira. I want to change and be different, but I can't make it without Mum's and Ira's support. They can straighten me out a bit, I can't put it any other way. Today—for the first time in ages—I brought home everything I'd bought at the canteen and shared the bread with Mum and Ira, although sometimes I still might just take the odd tiny little bit. But today Mum and Ira were so nice to me when they shared bits of their sweets with me: Mum gave me a quarter (which she took back later) and Ira a half for going to get little cakes, sweets and oilcake cookies. I almost burst into tears again. These are the very same people I had been cheating and who now know about it! That's what happens when you treat people nicely! But then. . . that same Mum took a little cake from me, promising me an extra sweet (and got an extra one for herself), and that same Ira cried, saying that Mum should give me and her the same amount. Then I gave Ira more of my sweet, so that she could eat a bit more. True, it was my fault today, because I hid a little cake from Mum and Ira. That was bad. . .

28 December. . . Mum's health is getting worse and worse. The swelling's reached her hip. I've finally got lice. . . Ira's and my faces have gone a bit puffy. The sweets ran out today. Tomorrow it'll be the end of the semolina and the day after tomorrow the meat and butter. And then. . .

Note: That new year was Yura Ryabinkin's last.

[Source: A. Adamovich, D. Granin, *Blokadnaya kniga* (Leningrad 1984), pp. 391, 392, 455–57.]

The wider horror of those months is conveyed here through the eyes of a 20-year-old student, M.D. Arbatskaya. Her diary captures her amazement at successive Soviet defeats, the nightmare that descended on Leningrad, her part in building the defence lines on different sides of the city, the icy temperatures, desperate appeals to the city soviet for help, the starvation rations, her own body turning skeletal, and the way delicate sensibilities survived even as deprivation and death became routine.

Document 53 | **'Damn the one who thought up this war!'—from the 1941–1942 diary of Mariya Dmitrievna Yarushok (née Arbatskaya), student at the Leningrad Mining Institute**

Second year over, on 15 June 1941 I went off to a practical course in Krivoy Rog. . .

Early in the morning of 22 June the alarm signal was sounded on the radio. We were utterly astonished and wondered whether this was part of the training. No, it's war! Who with? With Germany! So much for the Non-aggression Pact!

On 22 and 23 June we made dugouts (slit trenches). Early in the morning of 24 June I abandoned the mine. Our course leader was in a great hurry, because they wanted us to stop work. Experienced workers were being called up and so there was nobody left to get the ore out.

We got to Khar'kov in a roundabout way. As we approached stations, even before we saw them, we could hear the wailing of women seeing off their men. Even now it's awful to recall. . .

On 27 June I got back to my home town, my beloved city of Lenin. . .

All my plans were in ruins. Damn the one who thought up this war!

9 August. I haven't written anything for over a month—I just haven't had time. We've been going off to the suburbs to dig anti-tank pits, starting with Cholovo, and now around Gatchina. . .

We've all started smoking—me, too. If only Mum could see me!

17 August. We're billeted near Gatchina and are digging pits and slit trenches near pillboxes. We're billeted in a church and expect it to be blown to pieces any minute. There are constant air-raid warnings. The nice, dark-eyed machine gunner who was up in the bell tower has been killed.

Yesterday our retreating troops came up to our church. The Germans are about 20km away. All day today troops have been on their way to the front, dusty, wet and tired. . .

We give them the milk that has been brought for breakfast. That's the only way we can show our sympathy and compassion. Why are our lads retreating? According to official information, the best German units have been smashed and their army is falling apart; their losses are greater than ours and they're starving, but they keep on advancing, just as if they're going home, and they're not far from Leningrad now.

They've got better machinery, but our planes are supposed to be better than theirs. . . but where are they? And all our lads are supposed to be heroes, so what's wrong?

I'm acting a bit crazy. Every defeat almost finishes me off. All I think about is getting to the Front, but who'd have me with sight like mine?

3 September. We left the trenches 10 days ago. As soon as we'd dug them, we had to abandon them to the Germans. We left bombed and fired on, leaving behind us burning villages and towns. . . In our slit trenches at Duderhof we watched German planes destroying our fortifications on Voron'ya hill.

On 8 September they started bombing Leningrad, and on the very first day the Badaev food-stores went up in flames. Then I became a blood donor—I've got to help somehow, although with my diet it's suicidal. . .

7 October

> When, my Country, I feel glum,
> Off and away my thoughts go.
> Though much worse is to come,
> You shall not perish, I know!

Today we're off to work. The Institute's been converted into a grenade-packing workshop. We'll have clocking-in cards and a wage of sorts, but there's not a word from home. . .

19 October. I haven't been to any lessons since I started working here—a couple of hours there is pointless. It's horrible getting up in the morning, because the room's bitterly cold.

Filling grenades is very boring and monotonous, and my hands hurt much worse than in the trenches. We'll get paid every other month and I'll give blood every other month. Not a word from home. I don't know what I'll live on.

The Germans are now going for Vasil'evsky Island. They've burned down the funfair. Two bombs landed on our Institute. Without exploding, one of them went straight through the gallery and landed with such a thump in one of the courtyards that it completely smashed up the storehouse and shattered all the windows in the building. Now the wind and snow are blowing straight in, and the snow's started early this year—on 14 October. . .

19 November. We're cold and hungry, and they're shooting at and bombing us. . . There's a lot less food. Manual workers are getting 300 grams of bread. They're serving cabbage-leaf soup in the canteen and you can smell it two blocks away. In coupons it costs the same as 25 grams of buckwheat. There's also horsemeat cutlets without the trimmings (1 coupon gets you 50 grams' worth). I can hardly drag myself along.

On 6 November we had a party at the Institute, but we had to have the formal part in an air-raid shelter, because they'd started firing at us again. On the tram lines near the Institute 8 people were killed and a lot injured. In the shelter we listened to Stalin speaking on Radio Moscow.

Afterwards we had refreshments in the canteen: potato pie, a glass of fruit compote, 100 grams of bread with a microscopic bit of cheese and 2 real *Aida* sweets, instead of some saccharine and oil-cake things. It all cost 3 rubles and a 100-gram bread coupon each.

20 November. Happy birthday to me! I'm 20 and now in my third decade, but look like an old woman. . .

My first present was an announcement on the radio that they're reducing the bread ration. Manual workers will now get 250 grams of conglomerate, and non-manual—125 grams. I was in tears because I thought everybody at home had forgotten me, when in burst Klava Dyagtereva and Katya Erina with presents. But it wasn't the presents (some shiny brooches) that delighted me, but the fact that they hadn't forgotten me and had somehow found the strength to come and see me.

It's already midnight and it'll soon be lights-out, but I'm not at all sleepy. I recall days gone by, family, friends. . . If only I could go back then! Although it's not really, it seems so long ago!

25 December. They've increased the bread ration a bit—350 grams for manual workers, 200 for non-manual. As before there's no other food. In the canteen they're serving a vile yeast soup and some sort of water-based flour paste without any fat. . .

On top of all this I went and scalded my hand in the pitch-black corridor (there's no light, just crude oil-lamps in our rooms, if we have anything to put in them).

4 January 1942. My stomach started hurting really badly, so I dragged myself to the clinic. The doctor, an old man, examined me and suddenly started shouting, as if it were my fault, that it was food I needed, not medicine. I got very frightened. Then the doctor sat down, put his head in his hands and began to cry. It was terrible to see. I realized I wasn't the only one in that state, that he was crying because of helplessness and that even men have their limits. I quietly left his office.

The day before yesterday I felt a bit better and dragged myself from my cell at No. 40 Maly Street to the Institute: a bit closer to work and the canteen, because I just didn't have the strength to walk so far to eat and recently hadn't even been having the slops they were serving. I'm terribly weak—third-degree dystrophy. My hair's falling out, just as if I'd got typhoid; my skin's covered in a peeling red rash, I've got no breasts or muscles—I'm just a skeleton covered in skin.

I spent yesterday and last night at the Institute, sitting at a table. There's only one warm room at the Institute—where there's a stove—the rest have been wrecked by shelling. In that room, the former accounts office, there are students standing or sitting and keeping themselves warm. We sleep here as well: on the floor, on tables and chairs, under tables and even on cupboards. Students recalled from the Front are writing their theses here (there's not enough engineers in the mines), but they're dying like everybody else. It happens so easily: they stop eating their meagre ration and peacefully fall asleep.

At the hostel at No. 40 Maly Street there hasn't been any light for a month now, the pipes have burst, it's cold, and the corridors have been turned into toilets, because the toilets are flooded and frozen, so the doors won't open. There are corpses in the lobby, where they've been for several days now. . .

As I write this, a student delegation are writing a letter to the Smol'ny, which everybody signs. Perhaps the Smol'ny will somehow help to rehouse us students, because the administration and the Party committee don't seem to be doing anything.

Well, 'bye then! Perhaps this is my last entry and I won't wake up tomorrow. . . I'll add Mum's address just in case. . .

15 January. They've moved us to the Military Academy building. It is an old building, with stoves for heating. . .

We go down to the Neva with buckets to get water. There's a ship moored by our Institute, they're breaking the ice round it, and getting water from the holes in the ice. We need a lot of water. Just about everybody in our room is a blood donor and we have to be careful, because they reject not only those bloated with drinking too much hot water, but also those with any signs of scratching (they're worried about lice, which mean epidemics).

When somebody has a wash, everybody looks away because they look so awful.

We keep the stove going with anything: chairs, PE equipment, etc. Both gyms have been pillaged, but we've spared the grand piano—we just couldn't. It's horrible wandering about there looking for fuel: there are corpses piled up like logs; many of them are friends and acquaintances; the lads have grown long beards (I never used to believe that hair kept growing once you were dead).

We always buy bread for several people, because queuing has already become difficult. We carefully wrap each separate ration, and nobody touches anybody else's. For some reason the men have turned out to be worse than the women, whingeing and crying, demeaning themselves in the canteen, stealing off each other. . .

8 February. No sooner had I lavished praise on the women than there was a case of theft amongst us as well. Three days before the end of January, Vera Yaroshevskaya's ration book disappeared, so we shared ours with her. . .

23 February. On 14 February I went with some poor girl from our room to give blood. . . We went all that way not only out of patriotism. We really wanted to see an electric light (in the blood-transfusion institute dim bulbs ran off a little generator), eat some real bread and drink real tea with sugar in it. . . Donors get a worker's ration book (they never used to), but I'm not bothered, because I had one anyway; they give you a one-off ration, but it doesn't make up for the loss of blood. They also pay you 60 rubles, but that makes no odds: there's no food to buy anyway and it won't even get you tobacco at the market. Being a donor is very good discipline, because it makes you look after yourself and keep clean.

I had to go back on my own. On Vasil'evsky Island I suddenly fell into some snow piled up on both sides of the road as high as the first floor. It felt so cosy in the snow that I began to doze off, when I suddenly heard a muffled voice shout, 'A woman's fallen down!' Two women with scarves over their faces picked me up and I staggered on like some robot. I didn't even say thank you, although they'd saved my life. And it couldn't have been easy picking somebody up when you're starving yourself.

28 February. We were given a bit of mutton, some onion and dried potato on our ration cards. I made a whole pot of soup! Never have I eaten such wonderful soup before and I'm not likely to do so again! You could smell it all over Vasil'evsky Island! Even now I can still taste it.

6 March. They're giving us 600 grams of bread and they've started feeding us

better in the canteen, but the strange thing is that we're hungrier now than when we had only 250. All we talk about is bread and dream of eating a whole loaf in one go. We wander all over the island in search of a bakery which will give out bread for several days ahead, and have already collected almost a fortnight's worth.

There are rumours they might be evacuating the Institute. . .

People in Leningrad have been getting diarrhoea, either from the extra bread or something else. Some get caught short out in the street, but nobody's surprised and people just look away in sympathy.

15 April. On 14 March I left Leningrad. . .

[Source: *Na porokhovoy bochke. Sbornik vospominaniy studentov i sotrudnikov LGI, rabotavshikh v 1941–42 gg. na spetsproizvodstve* (Leningrad 1991), pp. 14–22.]

Mariya Arbatskaya was evacuated in mid-March, presumably along the Road of Life, and after the war returned to Leningrad to complete her studies.

By summer 1942 the very worst was over. Supplies across the Road of Life grew significantly and when the ice thawed, substantial ships maintained a flow strong enough to restore basic necessities to a much shrunken population. Industrial production, heavily concentrated on munitions, slowly restarted; parks and vacant areas were turned over to private vegetable plots, eventually as many as 200,000 being planted; and rations and conditions slowly improved. However, a population severely weakened by the famine months still faced a mammoth ordeal before the siege was eventually broken. Among the most haunting of many memorials to the epic was Shostakovich's 7th Symphony, which he began composing as the siege was laid. In October, to ensure he could complete the score, he was evacuated to Kuybyshev, where the symphony was first performed in March 1942. In Leningrad itself, the philharmonic orchestra suffered terrible attrition and the hall itself fell silent. But during the summer, despite everything, rehearsals proceeded. The following memoir by Ol'ga Berggol'ts, a Leningrad poet who lived in the city during the 900-day siege and whose work became well known through her radio broadcasts, recalls the impact the symphony had when it was eventually performed in August 1942.[37]

Document 54 | **Ol'ga Berggol'ts recalls the first performance of Shostakovich's 7th Symphony during the siege of Leningrad**

On 9 August 1942, after being empty for a long time, the white-columned Philharmonic Hall was brightly lit as though for a celebration, and so packed with

---

37 On Berggol'ts's wartime poetry, see K. Hodgson, 'Soviet Women's Poetry of World War 2', in Garrard and Garrard, *World War 2 and the Soviet People*, pp. 85–91.

Leningraders that some had to be turned away. The musicians came on stage. . .
They had hardly played at all in the winter: they did not have enough strength, especially the wind players. The orchestra was melting away. Some had joined the Army,
others had starved to death. It is hard to forget those grey winter dawns when Yasha
Babushkin, all grey and puffy, would dictate the latest report on the state of the
orchestra to his typist, 'The first violin is dying, percussion died on the way to work,
the French horn is close to death. . .'

But still, those who were left selflessly kept on rehearsing. . . The orchestra's
desire to perform the Seventh, the 'Leningrad symphony', was an almost impossible
wish—to perform it here in their own country, in their besieged, half-dead but
undaunted city. . . The brilliant powerful score needed a double orchestra, nearly
100 people, and there were 15 left alive, but still. . .

At the conductor's stand stood Karl Il'ich Eliasberg, in his fine tail-coat, as befits
a conductor, but he had lost so much weight in the winter that he looked like a
coat-hanger in it. . . After a moment of total silence the music began, and from the
very first bars we recognized ourselves and our way forward: the merciless force
bearing down upon us, our defiant resistance to it, our grief, our dreams of a brighter
world, and our undoubted eventual victory. And we who had not wept over those
dear to us who had died in the winter now could not and did not want to hold back
our joyful, silent, burning tears, and were not ashamed of them. . .

And all through this amazing music we could hear the quiet, calm and wise voice
of its creator, Dmitriy Shostakovich, saying, back in September 1941, when the
enemy was tearing at Lenin's city, 'I assure you, comrades, in the name of all the
people of Leningrad, that we will never give in and will always stand our ground. . .'

[Source: O. Berggol'ts, *Sobrannye sochineniya v 3–kh tomakh*, Vol. 2 (Leningrad 1973),
pp. 149–52.]

The Germans outside Moscow

Leningrad survived the onslaught of September 1941 in part because Hitler
decided to concentrate on a full-scale assault on Moscow. Initial German
optimism that the USSR was imploding under the onslaught of the
Wehrmacht had begun to fade, and with German concern over supply and
raw materials increasing, the goal was to deliver a knockout blow by seizing
the capital itself. Operation Typhoon was launched on 2 October, delivering heavy blows by air as well as on land. The evacuation of personnel
from most government offices and foreign embassies (and that of
Metropolitan Sergiy). The city chosen as the reserve capital was Kuybyshev
(as the city of Samara was then known), on the Volga 500 miles east of
Moscow, while some offices were sent even further afield. Lenin's embalmed

body was sent to safety. On 5 October, with the Red Army reeling, Stalin sent for Zhukov and once he had been assured Leningrad would hold on, he placed him in command of Moscow's defence. By then the Western Front had been pushed back to a line from Kaluga to Mozhaysk only sixty miles from the Kremlin. On the night of 14–15 October the *Wehrmacht* broke through that defence line and the Soviet predicament appeared so desperate that GKO issued a secret crisis decree. It ordered provisional plans for scorched-earth measures in the capital itself, the immediate evacuation of Sovnarkom and members of the General Staff, and declared Stalin, whose papers were sent on ahead, on stand-by to leave the following day.

Document 55 | '... **Stalin will be evacuated tomorrow or later, depending on the situation'—State Defence Committee decree** *On the Evacuation of the Capital of the USSR, Moscow*

15 October 1941

Top secret
Special attention

In view of the unfavourable situation at the Mozhaysk defence line the State Defence Committee has decreed as follows:

1. Comrade Molotov is instructed to inform foreign missions that they are to be evacuated today to Kuybyshev (People's Commissar for Transport comrade Kaganovich is to ensure that rolling stock for the missions is available on time, and People's Commissar for Internal Security comrade Beria is to organize their protection).

2. The Presidium of the Supreme Soviet and the Government, headed by the Deputy Chairman of Sovnarkom comrade Molotov, is to be evacuated today. (Comrade Stalin will be evacuated tomorrow or later, depending on the situation.)

3. The People's Commissariats for Defence and the Navy are to be evacuated without delay to Kuybyshev, and the chief personnel of General Staff to Arzamas.

4. Should enemy troops appear at the gates of Moscow, the NKVD, under the command of comrades Beria and Shcherbakov, are to blow up factories, warehouses and institutions that cannot be evacuated, along with all the electrical equipment in the metro (excluding water mains and sewer system).

I. Stalin, Chairman of the State Defence Committee

[Source: *Izvestiya TsK KPSS*, No. 12, 1990, p. 217.]

The decree was top secret, but a Soviet news agency report that night, broadcast and published in the newspapers the next morning, admitted to a German breakthrough. Combined with the visible emptying of official offices, this triggered a whirlwind of rumour—that collapse was imminent, that communist party leaders were deserting and packing their families off in terror, and that Stalin himself had fled. For almost four days there was panic as, amid food riots and looting, hundreds of thousands of Muscovites tried desperately to escape what was believed to be a doomed city.[38]

However, chaos was narrowly averted. Most of the population kept their nerve, as did the great majority of officials and party and Komsomol members. On 17 October, Radio Moscow announced that Stalin would not be leaving the city. On 19 October, the GKO decided to pledge itself to holding the capital, a state of siege was declared, and instant execution was decreed for any breaches of law and order. Ruthless NVKD measures to restore calm helped to halt the panic and brace popular determination to resist the German onslaught. Moreover, just at that point, from 20 October, the attack began to lose momentum. The launching of Typhoon had placed the German army at full stretch. Its advance in the first months of the invasion had been so rapid that supply lines to the rear were perilously thin. The onset of winter slush made the roads increasingly difficult. And the initial success of the advance on Moscow saw Hitler once again display fatal overconfidence, diverting significant forces from the main attack. Moreover, for all the territory lost, the Red Army had inflicted heavy losses on the Germans in terms of both men and materiel. Supported by a gigantic civilian effort analogous to popular mobilization in Leningrad, Soviet forces dug themselves in before Moscow and mounted repeated movements to disrupt and throw back the approaching army. News of the successes contributed to the change of mood in Moscow—the following war correspondent's report of heroic resistance in late October, one of many, was published in *Pravda*.

Document 56 | **V.P. Stavsky: '... the guards have been wearing down and striking the enemy'**

18 November 1941

. . . It is the middle of October 1941. The German fascist hordes are rushing onward. The enemy has obvious numerical superiority, especially in tanks. Sector 316 is exceptionally important. One of the motorways is here. There are a railway line and major road junction here as well. The Germans are well aware of this. They have thrown three infantry divisions, one motorized division and one tank division and a lot of aircraft at it. . .

First lieutenant Maslov's company were the first to clash with the enemy. A defence outpost had repelled German reconnaissance. Then the enemy brought up 20 tanks and more infantry companies. A defensive clash ensued. Next day the

---

38 On the panic, see Barber, 'The Moscow Crisis of October 1941'.

Germans went onto the offensive with up to 100 tanks and 80 lorry-loads of infantry.

First lieutenant Maslov skilfully organized the defence by making brilliant use of a heavy machine-gun platoon, two cannons and two anti-tank weapons commanded by lieutenant Ivanov.

Today the tanks came straight at our battalion. Our gunners fired at them point blank. Several tanks burst into flames. A group of the steel monsters veered left, heading for our trenches, crushing our brave lads, who were attacking them with hand grenades and incendiary grenades, under their caterpillar tracks.

Seventeen tanks were destroyed that day, the rest retreating in disarray, but the next day the Germans went on the offensive again.

Maslov's company were surrounded... They held out for three days until all their ammunition and food had run out. They had only five cartridges each and four grenades. Maslov kept the grenades back so that those who remained alive could blow themselves up, if they did not manage to break out of the enemy encirclement.

On the fifth day Maslov and a group of Red Army men did manage to break out...

All this time—yesterday, the day before that and today—the guards have been wearing down and striking the enemy, first retreating some hundreds of metres then going onto a swift counter-attack.

[Source: *Pravda*, 19 November 1941.]

Memories of heroism and resistance as Moscow stood in peril featured prominently among voluminous postwar reminiscences. The following extract is from the memoirs of a well-known war correspondent, P.I. Troyanovsky, who was sent to interview one of the key generals working alongside Zhukov, K.K. Rokossovsky. Rokossovsky was among the Red Army officers arrested in 1937 during the Great Terror and charged with treason. Unlike much of the senior command, however, he survived and was released from prison in March 1940 and the following year was entrusted with a leading role on the Western Front. By the end of 1941 he had been promoted to the rank of Marshal and was subsequently twice awarded the highest military honour.

Document 57 | K. Rokossovsky: 'Fighting near Moscow, you have to think *Berlin*'—from the memoirs of P.I. Troyanovsky

In October 1941, as the *Wehrmacht* was approaching Moscow, the editor of *Krasnaya zvezda* sent me to interview K.K. Rokossovsky, the commander of the 16th Army. In the course of the conversation we needed a map and I proffered mine to the general. It was a map of the Moscow area.

'Don't you have another one?', the general asked, 'For example, a strategic one of Europe?'

I replied that I did not. Konstantin Konstantinovich took me over to a wall, where he pulled up a white roller blind. A map of Europe was hanging on the wall.

'You can't fight without a long-term vision. Here, right now, near Moscow, I have to think *Berlin*. I'm absolutely sure that we will be in Berlin!'

Then the general called in his aide and asked him to bring a map of Europe from the operations room. We carried on talking while the aide went to fetch the map.

'Here's a map for you', said Rokossovsky.

I asked him to write what he had said to me on a corner of the map. Rokossovsky wrote, 'To the *Krasnaya zvezda* correspondent, political instructor P.I. Troyanovsky. Fighting near Moscow, you have to think *Berlin*. Soviet troops will definitely be in Berlin! Greater Moscow, 29 October 1941. K. Rokossovsky.'

[Source: *Novoe vremya*, No. 18, 1965, p. 3.]

By 1 November the attack had been halted. On the twenty-fourth anniversary of the October revolution, Stalin was able to make a defiant speech at the military parade staged on Red Square. In the same spirit as his speech of 3 July, he evoked the tradition of Russian military heroes from the medieval and tsarist periods. Rather than abandoning revolutionary rhetoric and the name of Lenin, as is sometimes implied, he blended the two, but for his listeners it was the ancient patriotic appeal that was most novel and striking. Moreover, with Ukraine and Belorussia, as well as the Baltic area, under occupation, and the front line now on Russian soil and the ethnically Russian composition of the Red Army now overwhelming, strains in that appeal that were specifically Russian became more pronounced.

Document 58 | **'In this war may you be inspired by the courageous example of our great forebears—Aleksandr Nevsky, Dmitriy Donskoy...'— from I.V. Stalin's speech to a Red Army parade on Red Square**

7 November 1941

Comrade soldiers, sailors, commanders, political officers and partisans! The whole world is looking to you as the force which can destroy the predatory hordes of German aggressors. The enslaved peoples of Europe who have fallen under the German yoke are looking to you as their liberators. A great mission of liberation has fallen to your lot. Be worthy of that mission! The war which you are waging is a war of liberation, a just war. In this war may you be inspired by the courageous example of our great forebears—Aleksandr Nevsky, Dmitriy Donskoy, Kuz'ma Minin, Dmitriy Pozharsky, Aleksandr Suvorov and Mikhail Kutuzov!

May the victorious banner of the great Lenin shield you. . .

[Source: *Pravda*, 8 November 1941.]

Local commanders were triumphant at their success in frustrating Hitler's attack. The achievement boosted their confidence vis-à-vis political Commissars. In the following extract, one of Stalin's commanders appealed to him directly, albeit as yet with little success, to halt the hounding that officers like him had received from party watchdogs under Mekhlis.

Document 59 | **'The Army has stopped retreating and has been pummelling the enemy for about 20 days now...'—from a report to I.V. Stalin by K.D. Golubev, commander of the 43rd Army**

8 November 1941

Comrade Stalin,

... 2. The Army has stopped retreating and has been pummelling the enemy for about 20 days now. They have not let him into Podol'sk, nor will they. In the heat of battle we had to shoot some 30 men, others needed the gentle touch, while up to 60 were recommended for decorations.

... 5. A request:

a) Stop using the policy of the whip against me as the commander, as happened for the first 5 days. The day after I had arrived, they promised to have me shot, on the third day to have me court-martialled and on the fourth day they threatened to shoot me in front of the men.

Comrade Stalin, the situation, my job and responsibilities are all perfectly clear to me; the Party and Motherland are no less dear to me than to the senior commanders. I will go flat out to get the job done, I am not scared of anything and several of us have been setting an example in battle. But crude abuse, threats of shooting and unnecessary pestering over trivia will serve only to pull the rug from under my feet. They are creating a situation where I am ashamed to look in the eye those under my command who read these documents, and they are creating unnecessary nervousness...

K.D. Golubev

[Source: *Izvestiya TsK KPSS*, No. 3, 1991, pp. 220–21.]

On 15 November the *Wehrmacht* tried to renew the offensive against Moscow. For a few days the capital's survival again seemed in the balance. In desperation, Stalin issued fresh and quixotically precise orders for blanket scorched-earth treatment of territory lost or about to be lost to the German army.

Document 60 | 'Our conceited and arrogant adversary was planning to spend the winter in the heated buildings of Moscow and Leningrad...'—from Supreme GHQ's Order No. 0428

17 November 1941

The experience of the last month of war has shown that the German army is ill-equipped for war in winter conditions, lacks warm clothing and, suffering greatly from the hard frosts, is huddled in populated areas near the front. Our conceited and arrogant adversary was planning to spend the winter in the heated buildings of Moscow and Leningrad, but the actions of our troops have prevented this. Over huge areas of the front, German troops, having met with stubborn resistance, have had to go on the defensive and are stationed in populated areas along roads for 20–30km each way.

To deprive the German army of the chance to settle in villages and towns, to drive the German aggressors out of all populated areas into the cold open country, to smoke them out of all buildings and warm sanctuaries and make them freeze under the open sky—these are the urgent tasks. The speed of the enemy's defeat and the disintegration of his army depend to a great extent on their implementation.

Accordingly, GHQ of the Commander-in-Chief commands:

1. All settlements behind the German front line to a depth of 40–60km and 20–30km either side of roads are to destroyed and burned to the ground.

To destroy the settlements over the designated area aircraft must be despatched immediately, artillery and mortar are to be widely used, along with reconnaissance teams, troops on skis and partisan diversionary groups armed with incendiary bombs, grenades and explosives.

2. Every regiment must form 20–30-strong teams of hunters, whose job is to blow up and burn down settlements where enemy troops are holed up. The bravest, politically and morally strongest troops, commanders and political instructors are to be chosen for these teams of hunters. The purpose of this measure in defeating the German army should be explained thoroughly. The most audacious of them should be recommended for decoration for bravery in destroying settlements where German troops are stationed.

3. In the event of a forced retreat on the part of our troops in one or another sector, the local Soviet population is to be evacuated with them, and all settlements without exception are to be destroyed, so that the enemy can make no use of them. The teams of hunters created within the regiments are to be used first and foremost for this work.

4. The military councils of the fronts and the individual armies are to check systematically how the orders to destroy settlements are being carried out over the designated area. Special reports are to be submitted to GHQ every three days on

how many and which settlements have been destroyed over the preceding days and what means were used to attain these results.

I. Stalin

[Source: *Sovetskiy soyuz v gody Velikoy Otechestvennoy voyny 1941–1945 gg. Tyl. Okkupatsiya. Soprotivlenie* (Moscow 1993), p. 69.]

In the event, the Red Army's defences as well as civilian morale stood much firmer than had seemed possible during the panic a month earlier. The *Werhmacht* approached to within ten miles of the city centre and German officers claimed that through their binoculars they were able to see the glint of Moscow's spires. But they came no closer: Moscow survived. By 5 December the Red Army was in a position to counter-attack, forcing Hitler's troops into a brief retreat.

However, although the Blitzkrieg and the attempt to deliver a swift, crushing blow on the USSR had failed, a war of terrible attrition lay ahead. Successive counter-offensives launched in January, February and March 1942 came to grief, and in spring and early summer the Red Army suffered further massive losses. May saw the collapse of a calamitous attempt to recapture Khar'kov, and thereafter the *Werhmacht* regained the initiative. In July the German grip on the Crimea was consolidated with the fall of Sebastopol. The low point was reached when on 23 July, after resistance that was a mere shadow of the epic efforts made to save Leningrad and Moscow, Rostov-on-Don fell. With the economy under desperate strain, Soviet morale was put to the gravest test.

German occupation

That the Soviet Union survived the Nazi onslaught can be explained in part by the foolhardiness of Hitler's adventure in the east. He set out to conquer a country which, although rocked by initial disaster, had longer-term military potential greater than Germany's. Despite Russia's legendary capacity to absorb initial defeat and retreat into the vast hinterland, he placed his faith in a swift knockout rather than planning for a sustained struggle. His racist contempt for Slavs led him to make catastrophic military misjudgements, committing German forces on too many fronts simultaneously and refusing to sanction tactical retreats.

Above all, the attempt to impose German rule provoked mass determination to resist. It was this determination which was critical: without it, the Soviet regime's capacity to galvanize and mobilize would have come to nought. The German invasion created fear, panic and despair. But it created, too, a blend of outrage, patriotism and social solidarity. And in the course of the war it was the latter, and the steely resolution it bred, that prevailed in the army and on the home front alike. A major part in shaping the popular mood was played by rumours and news reports about the horror and destruction that lay in store for those subjected to Nazi domination. Something of the grim tale is conveyed by the following three extracts. The first, by a 14-year-old girl, is drawn from a collection of accounts by children who witnessed a brief but terrifying visit from German troops arriving in Moscow province during the assault on the capital.

Document 61 | 'The Germans were with us for only four days...'—from a transcript of schoolchildren in 1941 talking about the war

The Germans entered our village of Lobachikha, part of the Shchekin village soviet, in the Klin district of Moscow *oblast'* on the night of 25 November 1941. There were about 400 of them, all on bikes and motorbikes. When they entered the village, it was deserted because everybody was in the shelters. Half an hour later they set fire to our hay barn. I got scared, thinking our house would catch fire as well, so I ran out of the dugout towards our house. I got as far as the yard when I suddenly heard somebody shout, 'Hey, Roosky, surrender!' I stopped and a German officer came up to me and asked, 'Where's your house?' I showed him and then he put me with the other captured Russians. When the officer went into our house, I ran back to the shelter. There were 350 captured Russians in our yard. Next morning we went home and saw them leading the prisoners away. They'd taken hats and felt boots from some of them and were wearing them themselves, while driving them away bare-headed and barefoot through the snow. Our wounded troops, left behind by our units, were lying in three of the houses. They were in agony, with lacerations, lying around by the windows. Near our gate was a soldier who'd been shot dead. Nearby was his Komsomol card. He was a second lieutenant. When all the prisoners had been led away, a couple of Germans had tortured and eventually shot him.

The Germans were with us for only four days during the retreat and just one night during the attack. The damned barbarians took our cow and looted beehives from four families.

A. Gracheva (14 years old)

[Source: *Neizvestnaya Rossiya. XX vek*, Vol. 4 (Moscow 1994), p. 374.]

The scale of German atrocities began to be revealed in full in areas where the Red Army's counter-attacks that winter recaptured territory temporarily occupied. Here a priest describes the bloody scene he found in the cathedral at Vereya, near Moscow, after its liberation from the Germans early in 1942.

Document 62 | **'... I just could not comprehend how in our day and age such bestial murders of totally innocent Christians could be committed in a holy cathedral...'—
from a report to the Patriarchate of Moscow**

17 April 1942

Vereya cathedral, where services were being held, was used as a house of arrest by the Germans. They put all suspect persons there. The upper floor was set aside for the wounded and prisoners of war. All the protests of believers were to no avail. . .

I entered my cathedral after the Germans had fled the town, hoping to find some Orthodox believers there who had been held under guard there by the Germans. I had hoped to hear them speak, share their joy at being freed and pray with them. To my horror instead of living people I found the corpses of people who had been shot. The corpses lay in the porch, in the cathedral itself and even by the altar. There were more than thirty corpses all told. On the floor and walls of the cathedral you could see fresh blood stains. On many of the corpses the fingers were in position for making the sign of the Cross. From the tortured expressions of many of them I could tell they had been begging for mercy. But neither the Holy Cross nor the entreaties of the innocent victims had stopped these fascist barbarians from committing an act of unprecedented evil. I was in shock for ages and could not come round. I cannot remember how I got home. I just could not comprehend how in our day and age such bestial murders of totally innocent Christians could be committed in a holy cathedral. The terror and shock turned me grey. . .

Next day I learned that in the very same Vereya cathedral, on the upper floor, the Germans had burned alive about 200 captured and wounded fighters of the Russian army, having first poured petrol over them. . .

During the occupation we believers did not lose our link with the Mother Church. In our services we prayed for the blessed Metropolitan Sergiy, the head of the Russian Orthodox Church. In secret we asked God to bring victory to Russian arms. . .

Aleksey Sobolev, priest of Vereya

[Source: *Pravda o religii v Rossii. Moskovskaya patriarkhiya* (Moscow 1942), pp. 353–56.]

No less harrowing was the treatment to which civilian and military prisoners of war were subjected. The following account was by a girl captured in the Belorussian town of Liozno. It is part of a letter to her father, Petr Susanin, written the day she turned 15, and discovered after the area was liberated. She tells how her mother had been shot in the mouth for defiance. She describes how she herself was subjected to abject humiliation, treated as subhuman and brutalized in the true sense of the word, being forced to eat from the same trough as her German boss's two pigs, in the spirit of Field Marshal Reichenau's notorious order of October 1941: 'To supply local inhabitants and prisoners of war with food is an act of unnecessary humanity.'[39] After recalling with nostalgia her thirteenth birthday—celebrated to the strains of her favourite among the songs written for the party's teenage organization, the Pioneers—she bids her father farewell, preferring to die than be dragged off to Germany. After her father's name, the only address the letter bore was 'Army in the field. Field post', and across it she had written 'Whoever finds this letter I've hidden from the Germans, please, please post it straightaway. By then my corpse will already be swinging from the gallows.'

Document 63 | **'Yes, Dad, I'm the slave of a German baron, too...'— from a letter by a victim of the German occupation**

12 March 1943, Liozno

Dear, kind Daddy,

I'm writing to you as a prisoner of the Germans. When you read this, I'll no longer be alive, but, father, I beg you: punish the German blood-suckers. This is the testament of your dying daughter.

When you get back, don't look for Mum. She was shot by the Germans. When they were interrogating her, the officer hit her across the face with his whip. This was too much for her and she defiantly said, 'You don't scare me with your beating. I'm sure my husband will come back and chuck you lousy invaders out.' The officer shot her in the mouth. . .

It's my 15th birthday today, but if you met me now, you wouldn't recognize your own daughter. I'm skinny, sunken-eyed, shaven-headed and with hands like wizened claws. I cough up blood because my lungs have packed up.

Dad, do you remember two years ago, on my 13th birthday? What a lovely party I had! You said to me then, 'May you grow up to be very happy, love!' The gramophone was playing, friends wished me a happy birthday and we sang our favourite Pioneer song. . . And now, when I look at myself in the mirror—my ragged dress,

---

39 W. Moskoff, *The Bread of Affliction: The Food Supply in the Soviet Union during World War II* (Cambridge 1990), p. 44.

a number round my neck like some criminal, a bag of bones—I weep bitter tears. What does it matter that I'm 15? Like a lot of people here, I don't matter. The starving walk the streets to be rounded up by dogs. Every day they're taken away and killed.

Yes, Dad, I'm the slave of a German baron, too. I do the laundry for Scharlen and wash the floors. I work for hours and eat twice a day from the trough with Rosa and Klara, his two pigs. That's his orders. 'Rooskies have always been pigs and always will be,' he said. I'm really scared of Klara, who's a big, greedy sow. She almost bit my finger off when I was getting a potato from the trough.

I live in a wooden barn. I'm not allowed into any of the rooms. Once the Polish maid Józefa gave me a bit of bread, but the mistress saw her and gave her a severe whipping on the head and back.

I've run away twice, but their yard-keeper found me. Then the baron tore off my dress and started kicking me until I lost consciousness. Then they threw a bucket of water on me and chucked me down the cellar.

I heard some news today: Józefa says that the masters are off to Germany with a lot of prisoners from the Vitebsk area, and will be taking me with them. No, I will not go to their damned Germany! I'd rather die here on my own soil than be trampled into the ground there. Only death can save me from a terrible beating. Farewell, dear Daddy, I'm off to die.

Your daughter.
I just know in my heart this'll get to you.

[The letter was discovered when some brickwork from a shattered house was being dismantled shortly after the liberation in 1944.]

[Source: *Molodoy kommunist*, No. 5, 1990, pp. 13–14.]

The ordeal described by Petr Susanin's daughter epitomized the racist nature of German policy in the east. During the first eight months of the invasion almost four million prisoners of war had been taken and upwards of two million had been killed or died of starvation and disease. The rate of attrition was vastly higher than for prisoners taken in the west. Eventually the Third Reich's increasingly desperate labour shortage persuaded parts of the German regime that the policy of virtual extermination was madness. Whereas in 1941 and 1942 French and Polish workers predominated among foreigners forced to work in the Reich, thereafter the Soviet proportion soared. By August 1943 Soviet citizens—POWs as well as civilians, the great majority being Ukrainian—provided a quarter of the foreign workers labouring for the Reich and over half the foreign women workers. The treatment of Soviet soldiers and civilians carried off was barbaric. Nothing could have been more certain to fire Soviet resistance than the knowledge of how their fellow citizens were being treated—and of the price that would be paid by anyone falling into Nazi hands.

Document 64 | The use of foreigners and POWs as forced labour by Nazi Germany 1941–1944

Year (end of May)	Total (millions)	Agriculture	Industry	Crafts	Transport	Others
1941	3.0	1.5	1.0	0.3	0.1	0.1
1942	4.2	2.0	1.4	0.3	0.2	0.3
1943	6.3	2.3	2.8	0.4	0.3	0.5
1944	7.1	2.6	3.2	0.5	0.4	0.4

[Source: V.I. Dashichev, *Bankrotstvo strategii germanskogo fashizma*, Vol. 2 (Moscow 1973), p. 643.]

As the Red Army began to get the upper hand and the *Wehrmacht* was pushed steadily backward, accounts of German atrocities uncovered at the front were spread across the country. The following report was made by I.I. Shapiro, a 22-year-old student at Urals University, Sverdlovsk, who from 1943 served as a divisional correspondent and later went on to be a radio journalist.

Document 65 | 'This is what we're avenging, fighting and dying for!'— from a letter by I.I. Shapiro, correspondent of a divisional newspaper, to her fellow students

February 1944

. . . Right now we're driving through a village only yesterday occupied by the Germans. I say 'village', but that's a misnomer. It's just ash, ruins and wasteland. Those German bastards blow up and burn down everything, and take the villagers off with them. People run away to hide in the rye, but come back to the ruins of their own homes. Yesterday I saw a skinny little girl sitting on the pile of stones and blackened timbers that used to be her house. That's all that was left. Head bowed, she sat gazing at a teapot with a broken spout which reminded her of her mother. The Germans had taken her mother away, but had killed her father and brothers. While they were taking the villagers away, the little girl had gone and hidden in the hemp. She watched the village burning, while shells exploded just above her head. She sat and waited for our troops. She told me all this calmly and dry-eyed, but it was awful to look in her eyes—those of an old woman.

We found a burnt Red Army soldier in the rye. Next to him was a petrol can.

He lay there, arms outstretched, fists clenched from the unbearable pain.
This is what we're avenging, fighting and dying for!

[Source: *Stalinets*, 23 February 1944.]

Equally grim was this account of Red Army troops south-east of Minsk liberating a camp infested with typhoid. It comes from the diary of E.A. Dolmatovsky, a Russian poet and writer serving as military correspondent at the front. Dolmatovsky's charge that the Germans had planned the scene in order to spread typhoid among Soviet troops fitted all too easily with the carnage left in the wake of the retreating *Wehrmacht*.

Document 66 | '... Perhaps laying these 'typhoid mines' would work!'— from E.A. Dolmatovsky's notebook

Parichi, 26 June 1944

A camp for local people struck down with typhoid. It turns out that it was not just a camp, but a weapon aimed directly at our advancing troops' chests. The typhoid cases had been rounded up from the area. Even the healthy had been stuck in as well, so as to get infected. A captured guard explained the rationale: Parichi would be liberated, but the Soviet troops would not catch on straightaway that they were liberating typhoid cases. There would be embraces and the children would be carried about. That way typhoid would be caught and spread all around. Perhaps laying these 'typhoid mines' would work!

It seems they thought they had worked out what makes us tick.

The camp inmates showed tremendous willpower. I saw it for myself, although it was so terrible that I am not even going to tell the press about it. As we raced across a swamp towards the camp, which had been left intact without a shot fired, and flattened the barbed wire, the typhoid cases started shouting, wheezing and wailing, 'Keep away, lads, we're infectious! Dear comrades, keep away!'

[Source: E.A. Dolmatovsky, *Bylo. Zapiski poeta* (Moscow 1983), p. 132.]

9

The Home Front, Legitimacy and the Economic War Effort

Knowledge of the horrific attrition on the battlefield, and of German brutality towards Soviet POWs, civilians, women and children confronted regime and population with an overriding common priority. It lent frantic communist decrees and orders, threats and punishments popular legitimacy of a kind those of the 1930s had never enjoyed even among workers, let alone peasants. It provided the tragic context in which, for all its dysfunctions, the Stalinist leadership was able to devote a much higher proportion of national income to the war effort than was any other country, and to outperform in terms of capacity for organization and co-ordination governmental systems far superior in terms of education, communications and infrastructure.[40] The impact was as powerful on the home front as it was on combat motivation, driving a civilian war effort that was to become no less prodigious than that of the Red Army.[41]

Economic mobilization

To arm and supply the forces, the whole balance of the economy was drastically recast. Energies were poured into munitions production while civilian output and agriculture were starved of labour and resources, and living standards collapsed. The early stages of the economic drama, and the synergy

---

40 Mark Harrison's treatment of the Soviet case, in M. Harrison, *The Economics of World War II: Six Great Powers in International Comparison* (Cambridge 1998), pp. 268–301, provides a wealth of material set in comparative context.

41 The finest two accounts are Barber and Harrison, *Soviet Home Front, 1941–1945*, and the multi-authored study edited by R.W. Thurston and B. Bonwetsch, *The People's War: Responses to World War II in the Soviet Union* (Urbana, IL, 2000).

between popular willpower and the often haphazard, improvised initiatives of highly centralized political authority, were epitomized by the evacuation from western regions of over 1,500 major enterprises vulnerable to capture during the initial German onslaught.[42] Along with key skilled labourers and millions of civilian refugees, the enterprises were transported to the east. Frantically reassembled beyond the Urals and converted to war production, they began to operate before the machinery, let alone the labourers, was securely housed. The following extract from the memoirs of A.S. Yakovlev, a dynamic aviation designer honoured as a Hero of Socialist Labour the previous year, recalls the frenetic activity in subzero temperatures and desperate living conditions.

Document 67 | **'Aircraft are starting to be produced when we still don't have windows or roofs'—from the memoirs of the designer A.S. Yakovlev**

Work was going on under the open sky on several levels. Down below they were setting up the machines, laying cable and putting the armature in the walls. Up above they were building the roof. Massive new blocks, constructed in 30–40 degrees of frost, were being brought into operation in sections. They would put a roof on something, build a wall round some area and put machinery in. They would move on, and the machines would start up.

20 December. They are setting up the machinery in the shops at the same time as building the walls.

Aircraft are starting to be produced when we still don't have windows or roofs. It's snowing on us and the machines, but the work goes on. Nobody's leaving the shops. They just live right here. There's still no canteens. There's a distribution centre somewhere, where they dish out something looking like soup.

[Source: *Sovetskiy soyuz v gody Velikoy Otechestvennoy voyny 1941–1945 gg. Tyl. Okkupatsiya. Soprotivlenie* (Moscow 1993), p. 13.]

The Red Army's direct dependence on the home front was constantly underlined in the reports and newspapers addressed to workers and soldiers alike. Typical was the publication, during the Soviet counter-attack of January 1942 launched after the German assault on Moscow, of the following correspondence between R. Usmanov, a much decorated Uzbek machine

---

42 See S.R. Lieberman, 'Crisis Management in the USSR: The Wartime System of Administration and Control', in S.J. Linz (ed.), *The Impact of World War II on the Soviet Union* (Totowa, NJ, 1985), pp. 59–67.

gunner on the Western Front, and N. Bazetov, a Tatar steel worker in Sverdlovsk. The exchange appeared in *Ural'skiy rabochiy* and *Krasnaya armiya*, and orchestration by the editors was reflected in the stylized tone of two men being held up as role models, the homage to Stalin, and the laboured emphasis on fraternal solidarity among the USSR's different ethnic groups. But there was nothing artificial about the patriotic fervour the men exuded.

Document 68 | **'... together let's defeat the enemy'—
machine gunner R. Usmanov to steel worker N. Bazetov**

January 1942

Dear comrade Bazetov,

I read in the paper that in competition with Aleksey Sorokovoy, comrade Bazetov, a steel worker at the Verkh–Isetsk works, achieved an output of more than 10 tons of steel per square metre from the sole of an open-hearth furnace, and that from the beginning of next year you'll be doing only high-speed smelting.

That's all I know about you. . . You won't have heard anything about me. No problem. If you like, we can write regularly and get to know each other better. As for me, I can tell you that, like you, I try to do everything using high-speed methods. You smelt steel, I kill fascists. . .

I've been at the Front since the first days of the war. Over that time quite a few fascists have fallen by my hands. I've been mowing them down all the way—from Peremyshl' to Kiev, and from Kiev to the point where we stopped retreating and are now heading back west. I've mown down more than I can remember. Now we're attacking, I'm going to start counting. So far this year I've sent 63 occupiers to the next world. The tally's growing every day and the number's growing. It's a tally of revenge, hatred and retribution.

You're a Tatar and I'm an Uzbek. Your mate in the competition, Aleksey Sorokovoy, is a Ukrainian. You and Sorokovoy at the furnace and me at my machine gun—together let's defeat the enemy who's burst into our beloved Motherland.

If you've got time, write me a couple of lines about yourself and what you're going to do for the Red Army's anniversary. If you write to the editors of our newspaper *The Red Army* on the South-western Front, addressing it to me, I'll be glad to answer.

'Bye for now. I shake your hand. Regards to Aleksey Sorokovoy.

Ruzimat Usmanov, Red Army soldier

[Source: *Ural'skiy rabochiy*, 22 January 1942.]

Document 69 | 'I promise to make steel only by high-speed methods'— steel worker Bazetov to machine gunner Usmanov

Sverdlovsk, January 1942

Dear comrade Usmanov,

Thank you very much for your warm and friendly letter. Although you and I have never met and are not personally acquainted, you're now closer and dearer to me than the best of friends. Just the other day, while listening to Radio Moscow, I heard that you'd been highly decorated and the workers of Uzbekistan had sent you congratulatory telegrams. Truly, sincerely, I too would like to shake your hand firmly and wish you new successes in battle.

You asked me to tell you a bit about myself. It'd be a pleasure. I'm 33 and have been working in industry for fifteen years now. I've been smelting steel for four years already. That's not long, of course, but I do try to produce as much good-quality metal as I can. I had fulfilled my 1941 plan-quota by 19 October, and I produced several thousand tonnes of steel over and above the annual plan. All the smelting has been done precisely as requested. Not only that, last year I saved a whole trainload of fuel.

At our works there are Russians, Ukrainians, Belorussians and Jews, and all these workers of different nationalities are trying their best to help the Front.

Just before the new year our collective, along with all the workers of the Sverdlovsk *oblast'*, solemnly promised comrade Stalin to double and triple our output for the Front...

I'm proud to say that our works is honourably fulfilling its promise to comrade Stalin. My main wish now is to do something worthy of the 24th Anniversary of the Red Army. Henceforth, I promise to make steel only by high-speed methods. I intend to learn to make some new grades of steel for defence as well. I hope our Urals metal will soon be giving that fascist scum something to chew on.

Dear comrade Usmanov, like you I'm convinced that, by honourably carrying out Stalin's instructions, the common efforts of fighters at the Front and on the Home Front will wipe out that brown plague and not let a single one of those Hitlerite bastards who burst into our Motherland slip away.

Once again, my family and I shake your hand: my wife Fagilya, my sons Shavkar, Rashid and Farid, and my daughter Svetlana.

We look forward to hearing from you.

Nurulla Bazetov, steel worker

[Source: *Ural'skiy rabochiy*, 22 January 1942.]

Bazetov's reply was that of a worker at the forefront of the surge of Stakhanovite-type campaigns (see Volume I, p. 315) that spread from late 1941, such as that of the 'two-hundreders', who undertook to make up in full for the output of a comrade absent at the front. Bazetov himself was part of the movement of 'accelerators' delivering record-breaking high-speed smelting. His reference to honouring the twenty-fourth anniversary of the Red Army foreshadowed the birth of the 'thousander' movement when the legendary milling machine operator D.F. Bosyi overfulfilled his output norm by more than a thousand per cent. As with the Stakhanovite movement, these feats were made possible only with specially contrived support from managers and could not be generalized. But in direct contrast with the 1930s, rather than decrying such heroic efforts as bogus managerial devices to raise norms and increase work pressure, rank-and-file workers celebrated them.[43]

In this context of popular will to victory, even brutal measures by the regime made sense. For the great majority, such measures were experienced not as arbitrary and authoritarian but as essential: free riders, idlers, those tempted to take advantage of the ordeal must be brought into line. Miserable rations, stentorian demands for discipline, direct coercion—all seemed justified in a way they had not in the eyes of most during forced collectivization and the social upheaval of the industrialization drive of the first Five-Year Plans. At the same time, as before the war, sheer compulsion could make limited impact in raising motivation and productivity. What was different now was that pre-war cynicism about and hostility towards the regime were gradually being overlaid by common resolution. Draconian legislation complemented the will of the majority. It matched popular determination that the war must and could be won; it buttressed popular morale at the moments of gravest peril. Along the front line, with German troops approaching, mass mobilization of labour was often achieved on local initiative spurred by immediate danger. Further into the interior, it took longer to harness underutilized labour reserves, the primary sources of such labour being among collective farm peasants in the countryside and among urban women and youths. In February 1942 the following decree ordered the mobilization throughout the whole country of all men aged 16–55 and all women aged 16–45.

Document 70 | **On the mobilization of the able-bodied urban population for work in industry and construction in wartime— from the decree of the Supreme Soviet of the USSR**

13 February 1942

In order to guarantee the provision of a labour force for the most vital enterprises and construction sites in munitions and other branches of the economy working for

---

43 On the issue of output per worker during the war, see M. Harrison, *Accounting for War: Soviet Production and the Defence Burden, 1940–1945* (Cambridge 1996), pp. 82–87.

defence needs, the Presidium of the Supreme Soviet decrees:

1. The mobilization of the able-bodied urban population during the war for local production and construction work is deemed necessary, especially in the aviation, tank, munitions, metallurgical, chemical and fuel industries.

2. It is established that mobilization for factory and building work shall apply to the urban population not already working in state institutions and enterprises as follows: men of 16–55 and women of 16–45.

3. Mobilization does not apply to:

a. Males and females aged 16–18 who are due to enter industrial training, trades and railway colleges, as determined by the USSR Sovnarkom.

b. Nursing mothers and mothers with children under 8 where no other member of the family is able to take care of them.

c. Students in secondary and higher education. . .

5. It is established that any person evading mobilization for work in industry or construction will be liable to criminal proceedings and may be sentenced by a People's Court to forced labour in their locality for up to one year.

[Source: *Pravda*, 14 February 1942.]

Few questioned the necessity of such measures. To those already working a 50–55-hour week, their rationale was self-evident. Equally, while the overriding priority of sending men to the front and manufacturing munitions and supplies to keep the army in the field was obvious, it soon became grimly apparent that it was vital that the shift in labour be co-ordinated and regulated. One challenge was the need to plug the huge gaps opening up as army after army suffered devastating losses, while at the same time shoring up and then expanding defence output. The headlong rush to recruit men for the front in the early months saw an exodus of experienced workers, draining vital branches of industry of essential skills. The problem is reflected in the following letter sent from the front by S.K. Tarnov, a skilled worker, to the Moscow machine-tool factory he had abandoned for the army. Like many cadre workers, Tarnov did not return to the bench: he was killed that winter.

Document 71 | **To the worker at the third machine on the right in row two— from S.K. Tarnov's letter from the front line.**

Winter 1942

Dear Comrade,

My name's Sergey Kuz'mich Tarnov and I used to be a turner in the same works as you. Now I'm a rifleman in reconnaissance. I'm writing to you because I've got no family left. My wife and daughter, Valentina, perished in an air raid. I used to work right where you're standing. I don't know if you're young or not so young, male or female, but you're sort of like family to me. . .

Our machine's getting on a bit. It needs special care. Mind the friction clutch. As you know, it hasn't got much grip. So don't change gear too fast. . . I know things are tough for you back there right now. Try and manage without the tool-makers. Fix things yourself. You'll have to work for two now. . .

[Source: *Literaturnaya gazeta*, 6 November 1985.]

On a broader scale, without planning and co-ordination the entire economy was in danger of becoming fatally unbalanced. The shift of labour and resources to man and supply the front was so drastic that it put the very survival of the home front at risk. In 1940 the ratio of those serving in the army and defence-related branches of the economy was 1:6. In 1942, by when the occupation of the west of the country as well as appalling military losses had reduced the total working population from some 85 to 53 million, the ratio was near parity. By some calculations, the armed forces and defence sector that year absorbed the majority of workers, having doubled to 28 million, while the rest of the working population had fallen from 72 million to 28 million. The fall in civilian labour power providing food and goods for the civilian population was in fact even more catastrophic than these figures indicate. Even priority sections of industry saw the level of skill, experience and strength of the labour force fall precipitately: in Leningrad, women came to make up four-fifths of the industrial workforce. Non-defence sectors of the economy were virtually drained of able-bodied men and became overwhelmingly dependent on the labour of women, young people prematurely taken out of education and pensioners returning to work. Most dramatic was the impact on the rural economy. The best land had fallen under German occupation. Three-quarters of the able-bodied menfolk of 1940 were drafted into industry or the army. Draught power shrivelled as most of the horses were requisitioned. And, with civilian manufacture shrinking drastically, mechanization virtually collapsed, undoing what progress had been made, as farmwork reverted to backbreaking manual labour with primitive implements. Excess shift of resources from the countryside into industry and the army saw output plummet, placing everything else in jeopardy by undermining the food supply. The regime's extraordinary capacity to mobilize and target resources came perilously close to destroying it. Desperately the government tried to restore some balance, the following decree of April 1942 empowering local authorities temporarily to reverse the flow into industry to ensure the land was worked.

Document 72 | 'On procedures for mobilizing the able-bodied population of towns and villages for agricultural work on collective farms, state farms and machine tractor stations'—from the decree of the USSR Sovnarkom and the CPSU CC

13 April 1942

. . . at the busiest times in agricultural work in 1942, Union and Autonomous Republican Sovnarkoms and *kray* and *oblast'* executive committees are to be allowed to mobilize workforces for collective and state farms and machine-tractor stations as follows:

a. The able-bodied population of urban and rural localities not already working in industrial and transport enterprises;

b. Some white-collar workers in state, co-operative and public bodies. . . but not to the detriment of the work of those bodies;

c. 6th–10th-year pupils of village and city schools, and technical college and HE students, with the exception of those in their final year.

2. It is established that men of 14–55 and women of 14–50 from the able-bodied population and the white-collar workers shall be liable to mobilization for agricultural work.

Women with children under 8 with no other member of the family able to look after them are exempted from mobilization. . .

5. Those mobilized for agricultural work are to be sent to collective and state farms and MTS, and on arrival are at the disposal of the collective farm management, or the directors of state farms and MTS, who are obliged to provide accommodation for those who have arrived for agricultural work. . .

6. Those mobilized for agricultural work on state farms and MTS are to be paid at their standard rates, on an equal basis with the staff of the state farms and MTS.

Those mobilized for agricultural work on collective farms are to be paid according to current work-day rates in cash on the same basis as the collective farm members.

The final payment for days worked by those mobilized for agricultural workers is to be made at the end of the year. Pending the final payment, the collective farm management is to pay those who have worked there an advance of 50% of the value of the work-days envisaged in the collective farm's production plan.

[Source: *Pravda*, 17 April 1942.]

In the course of 1942, rations, which much of the time did not extend beyond bread, were cut and cut again; social security and health provision withered; civilian life became dire. The regime responded in frantic, ad hoc fashion to the mammoth shocks reverberating across the economy. It was symbolic of the conflicting pressures on the government that on the very same day as the decree mobilizing labour for agriculture was passed, the GKO approved a crash programme for the iron and steel industry.

Soaring munitions production

What made possible the Soviet military resurgence after the nadir of summer 1942, marked by the fall of Rostov, was an astonishing rise in munitions production. By the end of 1942, the shift of resources to defence industry had been on a scale so dramatic that, notwithstanding the loss of the western part of the country and the tumultuous disruption that ensued, output had soared. Between 1941 and 1942, the manufacture of aeroplanes more than doubled; that of rifles and carbines rose two and a half times; the output of machine guns three and a half times; the number of tanks five times; the number of mortars nearly six times. The following table, based on an assortment of late Soviet data, brings out the scale of what was achieved in 1942 by comparing it with German production.

In terms of quality and sophistication, it is true, German military hardware was superior in almost every category. But by focusing on a limited range of weapons, tanks and aeroplanes, and keeping a much tighter grip on speculative innovations, the Soviet system was able to maximize effort on producing in huge volume.[44] In industrial terms, as in the field, Hitler and the *Wehrmacht* grossly underrated Soviet capacity to compete. In 1943, at full stretch, the Third Reich would reduce the gap that had opened up. But by then the military advantage had been irrevocably wrested from German hands.

---

44 See the comparative analysis by M. Harrison, 'Wartime Mobilization: A German Comparison', in J. Barber and M. Harrison (eds), *The Soviet Defence-Industry Complex from Stalin to Khrushchev* (Basingstoke 2000), pp. 99–117.

Document 73 | Armaments production in Germany and the USSR, 1941–1945

Item	1941		1942		1943		1944		1945		Total for 1941–45	
	USSR	Germany	USSR	Germany	USSR	Germany	USSR	Germany	USSR	Germany	USSR	Germany
Rifles and carbines	1,600,000	1,358,000	4,049,000	1,370,200	3,436,200	2,275,300	2,450,000	2,855,700	574,000	667,000	12,109,200	8,526,200
Tommy guns	89,700	316,300	1,506,400	232,000	2,023,600	234,300	1,970,800	228,600	551,000	86,700	6,141,500	1,097,900
Machine guns	106,200	8,550	356,100	117,000	458,500	263,000	439,100	509,400	117,500	25,400 (to Feb)	1,477,400	932,350 [sic]
Mortars	42,300	4,230	230,900	9,800	69,400	23,000	7,100	33,200	2,600	2,770	351,400 [sic]	73,000
Ordnance	30,200	49,000	127,100	38,800	130,300	73,500	122,400	149,000	62,000	1,040 (to Feb)	472,000	311,340
76mm and above	9,900	7,092	49,100	14,300	48,400	35,800	56,100	61,100	28,600	no data	192,100	118,292
Tanks, SPAIs	4,800	3,806	24,446	6,200	24,100	10,700	28,982	18,300	15,419	4,394	97,747	43,400
Aircraft	11,500	12,401	25,436	15,409	34,900	24,807	40,241	40,593	10,102	7,540	122,179	100,750

[Sources: *Velikaya Otechestvennaya voyna. Slovar'-spravochnik* (Moscow 1988), pp. 389–91; *Grif sekretnosti snyat. Poteri Vooruzhennykh Sil SSSR v voynakh, boevykh deystviyakh i voennykh konfliktakh. Statisticheskoe issledovanie* (Moscow 1993), p. 349; V.I Dashichev, *Bankrotstvo strategii germanskogo fashizma*, Vol. II (Moscow 1973), p. 645; *Istoriya vtoroy mirovoy voyny. 1939–1945* (Moscow 1975–1979), Vol. IV, pp. 158, 419; Vol. VII, pp. 57, 84; Vol. IX, pp. 394, 449.]

There were two important subsidiary sources contributing to the efforts and achievements of the Soviet defence industry. The first was forced labour.[45] The number of forced labourers was much lower than has often been suggested—early postwar guesstimates reached 20 million—but was nevertheless significant. At the outbreak of war, they totalled some three million or about 3.5 per cent of the working population. The overall number dropped sharply at the start of the invasion, over 400,000 being released to join the army by late November, and three-quarters of a million being evacuated eastward in barbaric conditions. By 1944, the number had fallen to close to two million, as a result of a trickle of escapees, large numbers freed and transferred to the armed forces, and above all the soaring death rate: mortality moved broadly in line with the collapse in living standards across the country, prisoners' rations falling far below survival levels. The release of men and non-political prisoners for military service caused a substantial rise in the proportion of female and political prisoners among wartime inmates. Detailed analysis of Soviet archives has in general terms confirmed the figures in the following self-satisfied report drawn up for Beria in August 1944 by the Director of the GULAG, General V.G. Nasedkin. The inmate figures he provides cover only those who worked directly under the NKVD, whereas half as many again, or about a third of the total, were contracted out to work under other commissariats desperate for labour. The overall drop in numbers he reports draws a veil over the number who passed in and out during the war years, and his estimate of almost three million leaving appears a substantial exaggeration. Although there is no easy way to compute the overall economic contribution of forced labour—and their productivity was well below average—it was clearly significant in specific branches of mining and munitions.

Document 74 | '... at its enterprises the GULAG organized for the needs of the front'—from a report of the Head of the GULAG, USSR NKVD

August 1944

At the beginning of the war the total number of prisoners held in corrective labour camps and colonies amounted to 2,300,000. The number of prisoners had dropped to 1,200,000 by 1 July 1944.

During the three years of the war 2,900,000 people left the camps and colonies, but 1,800,000 new prisoners arrived.

There was at the same time a change in the make-up of the prisoners in terms of

---

45 For detailed analysis of the size of the GULAG during the war, see E. Bacon, *The Gulag at War: Stalin's Forced Labour System in the Light of the Archives* (Basingstoke 1994).

the crimes they had committed.

Whereas in 1941 those sentenced for counter-revolutionary and other especially dangerous crimes accounted for only 27% of the total number of prisoners held in camps and colonies, by July 1944 the number sentenced in this category had risen to 43%.

In addition, at present the corrective labour camps contain 5,200 prisoners sentenced to hard labour.

Among the prisoners the number of men serving sentences has declined, while the number of women has increased. In 1941 men made up 93% of the total prisoners. At present the proportions are men—74%, women—26%.

Early release of prisoners and their transfer to the Red Army
By special decree of the State Defence Committee, in the course of 1942–1943 157,000 people from among those sentenced for petty crimes were released early and transferred into the ranks of the Red Army. Moreover, in accordance with the procedures laid down by the GULAG, all prisoners released from camps and colonies who had completed their sentences and were fit for active service were also transferred into the Army. In all, over three years of the Patriotic War 975,000 people have been sent to replenish the ranks of the Red Army. . .

Many former prisoners serving at the Front in the Patriotic War have shown valour and heroism and have received decorations and medals of the Soviet Union. The former prisoners Matrosov, Breusov, Otstavnoy, Serzhantov and Efimov have been awarded the title Hero of the Soviet Union.

Matrosov's heroic action was noted in a special order of the Commander-in-Chief, Marshal of the Soviet Union comrade Stalin.

In 1941–1942, in accordance with the decree of the Presidium of the Supreme Soviet of the USSR and the resolution of the State Defence Committee, 43,000 Polish and up to 10,000 Czechoslovak citizens were released from corrective labour camps, and most of them were sent to form national units.

The productive and economic activities of the USSR NKVD GULAG
The Patriotic War has radically changed the nature and content of the economic activities of the GULAG.

Whereas in peacetime the main output of the GULAG's industrial colonies was items of mass consumption, from the very first days of the war the GULAG has organized its enterprises to fulfil orders for the needs of the Front. It switched production at all industrial colonies to ammunition, specialized packing, uniforms for the Red Army and other military output.

Ammunition production
In the three years of the war the total output of all types of ammunition in GULAG enterprises has been 70,700,000 units, or 104% of the plan.

In fixed prices the total output of ammunition amounts to 125,000,000 rubles.

The USSR NKVD takes second place in the Soviet Union for the production of 82mm and 120mm landmines. . .

At the beginning of 1942 the GULAG began to learn how to produce new kinds of ammunition. . .

The total output of ammunition in 1942 was 15,500,000 units, or twenty times more than in 1941. . .

The total output of ammunition in 1943 was 21,700,000 units, or 140% of the 1942 level. This figure includes 12,500,000 82mm and 120mm landmines.

In 1944 the total output of ammunition per quarter has been 10,000,000 units.

This consistent growth in output has been achieved by systematic work to organize production, rationalization and technological improvement. All our enterprises work according to production-line methods, while some (the industrial colonies at Penza, Izvestkovaya, Omsk, Khovrino, etc.) have organized conveyer-belt production.

The organization of production lines and the abolition of 'rushed jobs' have ensured lower costs and an increase in labour productivity. . .

Financial indices

The GULAG's economic subdivisions organize their productive activities and maintain their prisoners on a completely self-financing basis.

The volume of goods produced by the GULAG's industrial enterprises over the three years of the war, amounts, at selling prices, to 3.651 billion rubles, agricultural production—1.188 billion rubles, income from labour hired out to other People's Commissariats—2.57 billion rubles, income extracted from those sentenced to hard labour—0.97 billion rubles, and in total with other sundry income—10.668 billion rubles.

Annual contributions to state budget income have increased, and in 1943 reached 1.029 billion roubles, as compared with 0.446 in 1940, i.e., they have increased 2.2 times.

In total, for the years of the war, 2.65 billion rubles have been transferred into the state budget, including 300,000,000 rubles over the planned quota. . .

Head of the USSR NKVD GULAG V.G. Nasedkin

[Source: GARF, fond 9411S, opis' 1, delo 68, pp. 3–6, 8, 10, 23, 24, 42, 50, 57, 58.]

A second important subsidiary contribution to the Soviet economic war effort was Lend–Lease. The key goods delivered were food and high-quality trucks, jeeps and communication equipment. The level of aid reached some 5 per cent of GDP in 1942 and rose to 10 per cent thereafter.[46] Soviet histo-

---

46 Harrison, *Economics of World War II*, p. 287.

rians were keen to play down the importance of Lend–Lease to the Red Army's triumph but the materiel imported filled key strategic shortages. Moreover, close analysis has suggested that where it made a major, and possibly critical, difference was in easing from late 1942 the almost crushing burden on the civilian economy. GNP in 1942 was as much as one-third below the level of 1940, and the harvest of 1943 was even lower than that of 1942; without the relief afforded from abroad, the home front might have unravelled under the impact of the mammoth switch to munitions production that year. With its help, and the gradual recapture of invaded territory, total economic output started to climb from the disastrous levels of 1942.

Document 75 | **Performance indices of the Soviet economy during the war, in percent relative to 1940**

	1941	1942	1943	1944	1945
National income	92	66	74	88	83
Industrial output	98	77	90	103	91
Engineering output	111	119	142	158	129
Agricultural output	62	38	37	54	60
Productive resources available	72	68	76	84	88
Capital investment	84	52	57	79	92
Freight, all transport types	92	53	61	71	76
Retail trade volume	84	34	32	37	43
Average annual number of workers and employees	88	59	62	76	87

[Source: *Narodnoe khozyaystvo SSSR za 70 let* (Moscow 1987), p. 43.]

Nevertheless, though forced labour and Lend–Lease played important roles, central to the drama was the symbiosis between regime and people: a political–administrative system already attuned to economic mobilization for a limited set of priorities, now focused wholeheartedly on defence; within this framework, much wider scope for local initiative than had been permitted in the 1930s; and, above all, voluntary, unremitting endorsement by the vast bulk of the population of the priorities chosen—the ingredient whose absence had and would hobble the Soviet economy both before and after the war. It is this symbiosis which explains why millions gave more to the war effort than coercion could ever have extracted, and worked to breaking point in industry and agriculture. It explains why industrial productivity held up so well despite malnutrition, the haphazard flow of fuel and raw material, barely human living and working conditions, and an industrial workforce drastically recast by the influx of untrained ex-peasants, youths and women. It explains how the country was fed at all, despite German occupation of the best land, the loss to the army and industry of three-quarters of able-bodied collective farmers, requisitioning of most horses, and the virtual collapse of mechanization.[47] The government concentrated its energies on feeding the army, and strove to organize a bare minimum of bread rations for civilians—and even here both were in large measure dependent on foraging and the black market. For the rest, food provision was largely left to local initiative and organization, epitomized by the expansion of private plots on collective farms, significant cultivation organized by industrial enterprises, and a much larger number of private gardens worked by city dwellers.[48]

The following extract from a diary kept by T.V. Tokmacheva, a young student at Urals University, conveys without romanticization something of the popular stoicism that withstood even the grimmest conditions, and the social solidarity that defeated Hitler.

Document 76 | '... there's nobody else to do it, so I will'—from the 1942–1944 diary of Sverdlovsk student T.V. Minina (née Tokmacheva)

August 1942

Since 4 August the whole university has been mobilized to work on a collective-farm for eight to ten weeks. . . We've got to go and do some real work. . .

October 1942

The collective farm's become a real work front for us. We've been working from dawn till dusk and are totally exhausted. We've been binding after the mower, reaping with sickles, pulling flax as the team-leader's ordered, digging up turnips, etc.

December 1942

I seem to have a different attitude to Saturday voluntary work. I just didn't want to do it before, but now I see it's got to be done; there's nobody else to do it, so I will. . .

February 1943

You listen to the radio in the morning and really take heart. . . go on, give 'em what for! It might be all over by autumn!

March 1943

They say the Germans are gathering their forces. The bastards sense that if they get defeated, then they're finished. But the end is far off, so far off. . . It reminds me of

---

47 Moskoff, *Bread of Affliction*, pp. 70–93.
48 Ibid., pp. 94–112.

Churchill's speech where he said that the war had not yet reached its climax and 'may God help Russia in the fight'. But will we have enough strength? Hitler's sent in another 25 divisions. What about us? It's unacceptable and unforgivable that in the cinema we show the Jerries as horrible and stupid. . . Easy to trick them, they're so stupid. . .

March 1943
Our hostel warden came this morning with orders from the Rector to go out and clean the cesspit and the toilets. It was utterly disgusting. We went to the bathhouse in the evening, but the water was stone-cold. . .

January 1944
Things are getting hard now. There's no water, the toilets don't work and we have to get our own firewood. People have started stealing, and some have lost their ration books. The food in the canteen is awful. In Room No. 8, our 'commune', we do everything together and the friendly, family atmosphere makes things easier.

An awful lot of people envy us, because the Trade Union committee has issued us with coupons for additional food rations and higher additional food rations.

February 1944
I'm definitely getting weaker. . . I'm finding it hard to get upstairs, and really hard sawing wood. I feel half-starved most of the time. I paid 100 rubles for 600 grams of bread at the market, but am so upset at life these days, I couldn't eat it. I am crying and the other girls stand over me and cry too, because we're all so hungry. . .

October 1944
For the October celebrations they hung up a really interesting map in the square showing the borders in 1942 and now in 1944. Amazing!

[Source: Personal archive of T.V. Minina-Tokmacheva.]

10

The Turning of the Tide:
Stalingrad and Kursk

The momentum gathered by the Soviet war economy made possible the Red Army's recovery from the perilous position of summer 1942. As in the civilian war effort, sheer coercion played a part in stiffening the Red Army. It was in the aftermath of the collapse of Rostov in July, as German forces prepared for further thrusts east and south, that Stalin issued his most famous decree, Order No. 227, under the slogan 'Not one step back!'

Order No. 227

Two features of the decree, which was not published but read out by army commanders, became notorious. First, it ordered the formation of 'punishment' battalions and companies, into which officers and men guilty of cowardice, wavering or panic were to be drafted and sent on missions that spelt almost certain death. Second, it ordered the formation of 'blocking' detachments to fire upon any soldiers who gave ground without authorization. Such orders seem to belie claims made for the heroism of the Red Army. They conjure up a picture of the most reluctant warriors forced at gunpoint to give battle. And indeed the number of executions for supposed cowardice ran into the hundreds of thousands. At the same time, however, the impact of 'Not one step back!' has with reason been compared to that of Churchill's May 1940 speech amidst the chaotic retreat of British forces from mainland Europe, and his promise of nothing but 'blood, toil, tears and sweat'.[49] The dire warnings were accompanied by a desperate appeal to patriotism. The lengths to which Stalin went to make the case that further retreat

---

49 G. Jukes, *Hitler's Stalingrad Decisions* (Berkeley 1985), p. 233.

was not an option and his insistence that to yield more ground to the *Wehrmacht* would only tip the scales further against the USSR struck home. So, too, did his plea to the Red Army to realize that popular confidence in it had been shaken.

The emphasis on shoring up the determination of the vast majority was underpinned among the upper ranks when Order No. 227 was followed by a sequence of measures, both symbolic and operational, to boost officers' morale and confidence. A number of new decorations named after Russian military heroes and reserved for officers alone were introduced; a few weeks later the much-resented political commissars were abruptly subordinated to military commanders; and shortly afterwards 'commanders' were renamed 'officers', replete with pre-revolutionary golden shoulder-pieces and stripes. Equally, among most rank-and-file soldiers, as in the wider population, the effect of the ruthless measures instituted against waverers was to stiffen resolve and encourage heroism rather than intimidate. Stalin's message matched the hatred, the defiance and the resolution the Nazi assault had inspired: this was the period of the most powerful and blood-curdling patriotic poetry and popular rhetoric.

Document 77 | 'Not one single step back!'—Order No. 227 of the USSR People's Commissar for Defence

28 July 1942

Not for publication

The enemy continues to throw more and more new forces at the front, and, despite suffering heavy losses, he is making his way deeper and deeper into the Soviet Union, seizing new districts, ravaging and destroying our towns and villages, and is raping, plundering and murdering the Soviet people. Battles are raging around Voronezh, along the Don, in the south and at the gates of the northern Caucasus. The German invaders are heading for Stalingrad and the Volga and are determined at any price to take the Kuban' and northern Caucasus with their oil and grain riches. The enemy has already taken Voroshilovgrad, Starobel'sk, Rossosh', Kupyansk, Valuyki, Novocherkassk, Rostov-on-Don and half of Voronezh. Some of the troops on the Southern Front have followed the panic-mongers, abandoning Rostov and Novocherkassk without serious resistance and without orders from Moscow to do so, thereby covering their banner with shame.

The people of our country, who love and respect the Red Army, are beginning to get disillusioned and lose their faith in the Red Army, and many of them are cursing the Red Army for fleeing east, leaving our people under the yoke of the German oppressors.

Some ignorant people at the Front are consoling themselves with talk that we can retreat even further east, as we have a lot of land, a large population and that there will always be plenty of bread. In this way they are trying to justify their shameful behaviour at the Front. But such talk is thoroughly false and mendacious and helps only the enemy.

Every commander, Red Army soldier and political officer must realize that our resources are not limitless. The territory of the Soviet Union is not an empty desert, and its people are workers, peasants, intellectuals, our fathers, mothers, wives, brothers and children. The territory of the USSR, which the enemy has been seizing and is still trying to seize, means bread and other foodstuffs for the army and the home front, metal and fuel for industry, mills and factories providing weapons and ammunition for the army, and railways. Following the loss of Ukraine, Belorussia, the Baltic states, the Donbass and other regions we now have much less territory, and consequently many fewer people, less bread, metal, factories and mills. In one year we have already lost more than 70 million people, over 13 million tons of grain and 10 million tons of metal. We no longer have the advantage over the Germans either in reserves of people or stocks of grain. To retreat any further would mean to destroy ourselves and our Motherland. Every new bit of land we surrender will greatly strengthen the enemy and greatly weaken our defence and our Motherland.

So we must root out this talk that we have the option of retreating endlessly, that we have plenty of land, that our country is vast and rich, has a large population and that there will always be plenty of bread. Such talk is false and harmful, weakening us and strengthening the enemy, for if we do not stop retreating, we shall end up without grain, without fuel, without metal, without raw materials, without mills and factories, and without railways.

It follows from this that it is time to stop retreating.

Not one single step back! That must now be our main slogan. We must stubbornly and to the last drop of blood defend every position, every metre of Soviet territory, cling on to every bit of Soviet ground and defend it as long as possible.

Our Motherland is going through difficult times. We must stop, throw back and rout the enemy at all costs. The Germans are not as strong as the scaremongers claim. They are straining every nerve. If we withstand their blows now and in the next few months, this will mean our victory is assured. Can we withstand their blows and then throw the enemy back westwards again? Yes, we can, for our mills and factories are now working very well and the Front is getting more and more planes, tanks, guns and mortars.

What then do we lack?

We lack order and discipline in companies, battalions, regiments, divisions, tank units and air squadrons. That is now our main weakness. We must now establish strict order and iron discipline in our army, if we want to save the situation and defend the Motherland.

We can no longer tolerate commanders, commissars, political officers, units and formations who abandon their positions without permission. We can no longer tolerate commanders, commissars and political officers who allow a few scaremongers to decide the situation in battle, cause other soldiers to retreat and leave the Front open to the enemy.

Scaremongers and cowards must be shot on the spot.

Henceforth the iron law of discipline for every commander, soldier and political officer must be this demand: not a single step back without orders from Supreme Command.

Commanders, commissars and political officers of companies, battalions, regiments and divisions who abandon their positions without permission are traitors to the Motherland. Such commanders and political officers must be treated as befits traitors to the Motherland.

That is the appeal of our Motherland.

Responding to that appeal means defending our land, saving the Motherland, destroying and defeating the hated enemy.

After their winter retreat under Red Army pressure, when discipline among the German troops was shaken, to restore discipline the Germans took certain severe measures and did so with considerable success. They formed more than 100 punishment companies from those troops guilty of breaking discipline either through cowardice or instability, stationed them at dangerous parts of the Front and made them atone for their sins with their own blood. They then went on to form ten or so punishment battalions from commanders guilty of breaking discipline either through cowardice or instability, stripped them of their decorations and stationed them at even more dangerous parts of the Front and made them atone for their sins. Finally, they formed special blocking detachments, put them behind the unstable divisions and ordered them to shoot on the spot any scaremongers who tried to leave their post without permission or get captured. As we know, these measures were effective and now the German troops are fighting better than they did in winter. And so it turns out that the German troops have good discipline, even though they do not have the lofty aim of defending their Motherland, but only the base aim of plundering someone else's country, while our troops, who do have the lofty aim of defending their desecrated Motherland, do not have such discipline and so are suffering defeat.

Should we not learn something from our enemies, as in the past our ancestors learnt from their enemies, whom they then defeated? I think we should.

The Red Army Supreme Command orders:

1. Military councils at the Front and especially front-line commanders

a) Without fail to eliminate among the troops all notions of retreat and with an iron fist put a stop to all propaganda about being able and having to retreat further east, because to do so would supposedly be harmless;

b) Without fail to dismiss and send to headquarters for court-martial any commanders who allow troops to leave their positions without orders from the Front command;

c) To form near the Front 1–3 punishment battalions (depending on circumstances) of about 800 men each, into which are to be sent middle-ranking and senior commanders or political officers of all kinds of troops guilty of breaking discipline through cowardice or instability, and station them at the more difficult parts of the Front, so that they may atone for their crimes against the Motherland with their own blood.

2. Military councils at the Front and especially front-line commanders

a) Without fail to dismiss any divisional and corps commanders and commissars who allow troops to leave their positions of their own accord, without any order of the army command, and send them to the Military Council at the Front for court-martial;

b) To form within the army 3–5 well-armed blocking detachments of up to 200 men each, station them just behind unstable divisions and, in the event of panic or disorderly retreat of part of the division, make them shoot scaremongers and cowards on the spot, thereby helping the honest fighters in the division to carry out their duty to their Motherland;

c) To form within the army 5–10 punishment companies (depending on circumstances) of 150–200 men each, into which are to be sent soldiers from the ranks and junior officers guilty of breaking discipline through cowardice or instability, and station them by the more difficult parts of the army, so that they may atone for their crimes against the Motherland with their own blood.

3. Corps and divisional commanders and commissars

a) Without fail to dismiss company and battalion commanders and commissars who allow troops to leave their positions of their own accord without orders from the corps or division commander, strip them of their decorations and send them to the Military Councils of the Front for court-martial;

b) To give all necessary help and support to the blocking detachments in their task of maintaining order and discipline within army units.

This order is to be read out to all companies, troops, batteries, air squadrons, ship's companies and headquarters.

I. Stalin, People's Commissar for Defence

[Source: A.M. Samsonov, *Znat' i pomnit'. Dialog istorika s chitatelyami* (Moscow 1988), pp. 343–44.]

The Battle of Stalingrad

How the Red Army would respond to the dire message spelled out in Order No. 227 was promptly put to the test in the monstrous battle for Stalingrad, which began the following month.[50] Hitler's overconfidence had been reinflated by the crushing defeat inflicted on the Red Army at Khar'kov and the sweeping victories that placed Rostov at his feet. His forces were ordered simultaneously to head south to capture the Caucasus and, to protect that thrust from counter-attack, eastward to take the straggling city of Stalingrad on the Volga (renamed in Stalin's honour in 1925). The strategic aim was to paralyse the Soviet ability to resist by severing the link between the vast oilfields of the Caucasus and the rest of the country.

On 19 August Germany's VIth Army under General Paulus advanced on the city, and this was quickly followed by mass bombing and the imposition of a siege. By mid-September, the Germans had reached the city centre, the *Wehrmacht* launching furious attacks on Soviet positions and squeezing the defending forces ever more tightly. But Soviet forces, precariously supplied from across the Volga, mounted a defence which proved among the most heroic and the most bloody in history. For two desperate months they held out. Every street, every square, every house became a battleground; the railway station changed hands more than a dozen times; the pitiless struggle epitomized the ferocity of the Soviet–German conflict. Despite the fog of wartime reporting and misinformation, it became ever plainer across the country just how high the stakes were. Stalingrad became the supreme test not only of the army but of the Soviet war effort as a whole. Early in November Hitler proclaimed that the city had fallen. If morale was ever going to crack it was now. Yet, to the astonishment of the German high command and the delight of the Allies and Soviet sympathizers across the world, it held. The following extract by F. Dan, one of the defeated Menshevik leaders in exile since his deportation in 1922, paid homage to Soviet resilience, attributing it to a fusion of patriotism and idealism.

Document 78 | F. Dan, 'The revolution… has given… hopes'—from an article in the October 1942 issue of the émigré journal *Novyy put'*

Nothing can be understood about this miracle if you close your eyes to the fact that, for all its degradations, failures, mistakes and even crimes, the revolution that began a quarter of a century ago has become ingrained in the flesh and blood of the people. For all its adversity, deprivations and sufferings. . . it has given them certain achievements and, perhaps, more importantly, certain hopes to which the masses cling with every fibre of their beings, hopes which in their eyes outweigh all its dark and difficult aspects; hopes for which they are prepared to accept inhuman suffering, to fight and to die.

---

50 For an excellent recent analysis, see G. Roberts, *Victory at Stalingrad: The Battle that Changed History* (London 2002), and for the most evocative account, A. Beevor, *Stalingrad* (London 1999).

The revolution has given the patriotism of the peoples of the Soviet Union the great new idea of social liberation.

[Source: *Pravda*, 13 October 1989.]

The fervour evoked by the battle is captured in the following breathless letter from a 14-year-old to his local Komsomol committee in Sverdlovsk *oblast'*.

Document 79 | '… send me to defend our native city of Stalin…'— request to be conscripted from a 14-year-old schoolboy

10 November 1942

To: Berezovsky Komsomol district committee

From: Gennadiy Vasilich Mezhevalov, class 6A, Berezovsky Secondary School

Application

I'm 14, but I beg you to send me to defend our native city of Stalin. And put me in intelligence. I promise to fight the enemy to the last drop of blood.
10 November 1942

P.S. My mother says it's OK.

[Source: *Sovetskiy soyuz v gody Velikoy Otechestvennoy voyny 1941–1945 gg. Tyl. Okkupatsiya. Soprotivlenie* (Moscow 1993), p. 73.]

While the battle raged in the city, the Soviet high command was methodically assembling a huge force for a counter-offensive. It was launched on 19 November. Red Army units converged on the city, pinning Paulus's 330,000-strong army up against the banks of the Volga. Hitler refused to permit an attempt at break-out, counting on airlifting adequate supplies while bringing to bear fresh divisions to force their way through from outside the encirclement. Neither proved possible. The *Luftwaffe* was unable to deliver anywhere near sufficient food or fuel and Paulus's army was sapped by malnutrition, freezing cold and disease. The attempted German break-through in mid-December petered out within a fortnight. By the New Year the die was cast. Hope of relief had faded away and Paulus was in no condition to break out. Yet on strict orders from Hitler, he refused one ultimatum after another and Soviet forces smashed into the centre. By 31 January, when Paulus was captured, the VIth Army had been destroyed, 150,000 German troops lay dead, and a bedraggled remnant of 90,000, including twenty-four German generals, were taken prisoner.

Stalingrad marked the turning point. It had not broken the *Wehrmacht*, it is true, and an even larger winter counter-attack planned west of Moscow had failed to deliver the knock-out blow. But the strategic advantage had swung dramatically and permanently against Hitler, and, notwithstanding attempts to reverse the tide in 1943, his forces began a long, slow but unremitting retreat.

Soviet victory at Stalingrad had a major impact on Soviet partisan activity behind German lines. The clear signs that the balance of power was swinging away from the Germans encouraged a surge in active support for the already swelling bands of partisans. From May 1942, the GKO had set up a Central Headquarters to try to co-ordinate partisan efforts and align them with Red Army strategy. A network of party committees was re-established to supervise the disparate groups of partisans, and in September Stalin called a conference to draw together advice on partisan tactics and co-ordinate partisan activity with Red Army strategy. Soviet partisans, the vast majority of whom were Ukrainian and Belorussian, grew from a minor nuisance to a major menace, disrupting German supplies, sabotaging German installations, undermining German confidence, and, by some estimates, from as early as summer 1942 tying up the energies of more *Wehrmacht* divisions than the total number committed at the time by the Germans and Italians to war in North Africa.[51]

The Battle of Kursk

Summer 1943 saw the advantage move steadily against Germany. The clash that demonstrated Soviet superiority most decisively took place in July and August. Soviet intelligence, better informed than in the previous two years, reported German preparations to attack the large concentration of Soviet forces west of Kursk, liberated earlier in the year. The *Wehrmacht*'s plan was to attack simultaneously from the south above Khar'kov, and from the north below Orel. The following intelligence report came from behind German lines.

Document 80 | 'The *Wehrmacht* General Staff is intending to break through near Orel...'—from the People's Commissariat of State Security to the State Defence Committee

23 May 1943

P.G. Lopatin's operational group, operating in the Borisov district of Minsk *oblast'*, has informed us as follows, 'The *Wehrmacht* General Staff is intending to break

---

51 L.D. Grenkevich, *The Soviet Partisan Movement, 1941–1944: A Critical Historiographical Analysis* (London 1999), pp. 323–24.

through near Orel this summer. . .To this end the enemy has been bringing troops, tanks, artillery, aircraft, and other materiel up to the Orel area since 5 April. . . The Germans have concentrated 1,000 aircraft at the central sector of the Front. The *Luftwaffe* Central Front HQ is quartered in the city of Orel. . .'

[Source: *Voenno-istoricheskiy zhurnal*, No. 5–6, 1993, p. 50.]

Unlike a year earlier, Stalin deferred to the caution of his generals. Rather than launching a pre-emptive assault, Zhukov and his colleagues recommended absorbing the planned German attack and then mounting a massive counter-attack. What followed was the greatest tank battle ever fought, the Red Army fielding almost three and a half thousand tanks against the *Wehrmacht*'s 2,700. On 5 July, the 9th Panzer Army struck from the north but, to the horror of the German high command, met deep resistance of a kind German tanks had never encountered. The advance ground to a halt after just four days and on 12 July a devastating counter-attack drove the Germans back in pandemonium, ripping out the heart of the 9th Army. To the south, where German forces were even stronger, the initial advance was more rapid but the Soviets raced reserves to the defence. Here, 12 July saw a mammoth tank battle, no fewer than 700 tanks being destroyed in the space of eight hours. The Panzer Army lost half its men. The effect of the Battle of Kursk was to destroy Hitler's hopes of victory over the USSR. The Germans were forced backwards across a vast front. On 5 August Stalin ordered a triumphant salute in Moscow.

Document 81 | **'Moscow will salute our valiant troops. . .'—**
Order of the Commander-in-Chief

5 August 1943

To:

Colonel-General Popov
Colonel-General Sokolovsky
General Rokossovsky
General Vatutin
Colonel-General Konev

Today, on 5 August, the troops of the Bryansk front, assisted by flanks of troops of the Western and Central fronts, took the city of Orel as a result of ferocious fighting.

Also today, troops of the Steppe and Voronezh fronts broke the enemy's resistance and took the city of Belgorod.

A month ago, on 5 July, the Germans began their summer offensive from the areas around Orel and Belgorod, hoping to surround and destroy our troops in the Kursk salient and take Kursk.

After repelling all enemy attempts to break through to Kursk from Orel and Belgorod, our troops themselves went on the offensive on 5 August, exactly one month after the beginning of the German July offensive, and retook Orel and Belgorod. This has debunked the German myth that Soviet troops were incapable of conducting a successful summer offensive.

To commemorate their victory the 5th, 129th and 380th rifle divisions, who entered and liberated Orel, are to be given the designation *Orel*. . .

The 89th guards and 305th rifle divisions, who were first to enter the city of Belgorod and liberate it, are to be given the designation *Belgorod*.

Today, 5 August, at 24:00 hours, the capital of our Motherland, Moscow, will salute our valiant troops who liberated Orel and Belgorod with a 12-salvo 120-gun salute.

For their excellent offensive actions I express my gratitude to all the troops under your command who took part in the operations to liberate Orel and Belgorod.

Eternal glory to the heroes who have fallen in the struggle for the freedom of our Motherland!

Death to the German invaders!

Commander-in-Chief, Marshal of the Soviet Union I. Stalin.

[Source: *Velikaya Otechestvennaya* (Moscow 1984), p. 218.]

Although it was able to push the Germans further and further backwards, the Red Army continued to suffer losses on an awesome scale. The *Wehrmacht* mounted one rearguard action after another, and as it retreated left a blanket of scorched-earth destruction in its wake. Just how brutal and dehumanizing the war was, even as victory began to come into view, is reflected in the following letter of disgust at the Red Army's failure to give fallen soldiers a decent burial.

Document 82 | **'. . . it is terrible to come across a corpse, just dumped by the roadside, like something forgotten and unwanted. . .'— from a letter by N.M. Petrenko, former deputy chairman of the L'vov *oblast'* executive committee, to the Chief political administration of the Red Army**

October 1943

I consider the question of the proper burial of fallen Soviet troops and commanders to be an important one, which influences the fighting morale of the army.

The Germans have a good grasp of the psychological effect on living soldiers of observing the rituals of burial, and see it as showing concern for someone, even after their death. We, on the other hand, are just the opposite, showing complete unconcern for the corpses of the fallen. On the way from Kamensk in Rostov *oblast'* to Khar'kov I came across many dead Red Army soldiers, whose corpses had been left lying for up to a fortnight by the roadside in mud, ditches and fields. Military units pass along these roads and see this unacceptable picture of our negligence. Although no Red Army man has any fear of death, I think it is terrible to come across a corpse, just dumped by the roadside, like something forgotten and unwanted.

Very occasionally I came across a properly done grave for senior commanders with a marker and an inscription from their comrades. As for the ordinary Red Army men, in the best cases the deaths might be recorded, but there are never any markers on the grave. I consider that the question of obligatory and timely burial of the fallen soldiers of the Patriotic War is an important one politically, which itself reflects on the psychology of the Red Army men. Both the procedure for burial and the erection of memorials on graves need to be laid down in law.

[Source: *Rodina*, No. 6–7, 1991, p. 152.]

By late September the Germans had been forced back across most of the length of the Dnieper.[52] Kiev was recaptured in early November and the enemy driven from their last holding on the river in January 1944. The following month the Siege of Leningrad, which had been breached early in 1943, was finally lifted. By mid-May 1944, almost all Soviet territory within the 1939 borders, the Crimea, eastern Ukraine, and a slice of Belorussia, had been liberated from occupation. That summer saw a huge assault on the final significant Soviet area still under German control, western Belorussia. The campaign was launched on 22 June, a fortnight after the Normandy landings of the western powers had at last opened the long-awaited Second Front. The Soviet assault inflicted irreparable damage on the German army, opening the way to the liberation of the Belorussian capital, Minsk, on 3 July. The following letter from the front conveys the combination of triumphalism, newfound disdain for the *Wehrmacht* and the *Luftwaffe*, and sheer exhaustion at the end of the summer drive.

Document 83 | **'It is, of course, the experience of Stalingrad, Minsk, the Dnieper and Nikolaev'—from a letter by guards' captain B. Markus**

September 1944

Dear Nina Dmitrievna,

I haven't been in touch for ages and have only occasionally sent you short little post-

---

52 On the Soviet Union's mounting ascendancy after Stalingrad, see the second part of J. Erickson's two-volume history of the war, *The Road to Berlin: Stalin's War with Germany* (London 1983).

cards, which isn't surprising as the last few weeks have been really eventful. . . On the surface, the official reports have been uninformative: 'No major changes have taken place at the Front.' But judging by the colossal number of destroyed tanks and aircraft you can well imagine what lies underneath the surface calm. Great artillery duels have intensified and become commonplace. Until recently the Germans have just been sniping at us and trying to avoid the danger of capture or encirclement. Things have changed now. They're trying to consolidate, as they once did on the Dnieper. The difference is that then they built a fortification—the Nikopol' bridge-head—on the left bank and tried to get through to Melitopol' to save the 'Crimean death-row', who had fallen into a trap. But now it's we who're holding the bridge-head on the right bank, and they're trying their best to push us into the water. Now that we've crossed the old state border, albeit by only a couple of hundred metres, there's no way we're going back. So, despite the shells raining down on us, we've got part of the right bank. . . There's a daily artillery duel, sometimes spiced up by air raids on each other. This is a novelty for us now, as we've got unused to seeing German aircraft. . . I recall 1941 and our terror at the word 'air raid'. It's almost laughable now. You look round during an air raid now and feel quite cheerful—nobody's bothered by it. It's even rare for people to stop what they're doing and dive into a ditch when they are in immediate personal danger. It is, of course, the experience of Stalingrad, Minsk, the Dnieper and Nikolaev.

[Source: *Molodoy kommunist*, No. 5, 1990, pp. 14–15.]

Soviet advance, German retreat and the Warsaw Uprising

In the autumn the Germans were driven from the Baltic states and by the end of 1944 all territory under Soviet rule at the time of the invasion had been freed. By then the Red Army had begun to force the *Wehrmacht* back across eastern Europe. Soviet forces entered Romanian territory in April, Polish territory in July, Bulgarian and then Yugoslav territory in September, the territory of Czechoslovakia in October, and Hungarian territory at the end of the year. The regimes that had allied with Hitler collapsed: in Romania, Hungary and Bulgaria new governments switched sides and declared war on Germany.

Military priorities remained paramount but they began to become inter-twined with questions about the postwar order in eastern Europe. Even in the darkest days of 1941, with the Germans closing in on Moscow, Stalin had made it crystal clear to his British allies that the USSR would insist both on retaining all the territorial gains made between the Nazi–Soviet Pact and the Nazi invasion, and that Moscow would never again tolerate a hostile government in Poland lest the country become the route for yet another assault on the USSR. During 1944, most famously in the so-called 'percentages agreement' struck between Stalin and Churchill, it became plain, too, that the USSR expected to exert influence right across the countries of eastern Europe.

The strongest indication of how that influence might be secured, regardless of public opinion in those countries, came as the Red Army moved into Polish territory.[53] On 26 July, eight days after it crossed the Soviet border of 1941, the USSR recognized the Polish communist leadership as the new Polish authority, installing it in the liberated city of Lublin. For the Polish government-in-exile based in London, as for the non-communist underground in Poland itself, fear that Moscow was bent on imposing a puppet government turned to certainty. The very next week, on 1 August, the underground Home Army in Poland launched a quixotic uprising against Nazi rule which the Germans were to crush with vicious brutality. Desperately the western Allies appealed to Stalin to help. His response was icy. In the following telegram he assured Churchill that he had ordered the dropping of supplies to the stranded Poles—and a single parachutist to liaise with them—but made plain his determination to wash his hands of the disaster unfolding.

Document 84 | From Stalin's message to Churchill

16 August 1944

Secret

Personal

After talking to Mr Mikołaczyk I have ordered the Red Army High Command to bombard the Warsaw region heavily. A liaison-parachutist has also been dropped, but did not make it according to High Command, as he was killed by the Germans.

Having found out more about what is happening in Warsaw, I am convinced that it is a reckless and terrible escapade which is costing many lives. This would not have happened if Soviet High Command had been informed before it started and the Poles had kept in touch with us.

Soviet High Command has therefore come to the conclusion that it must dissociate itself from the Warsaw escapade, as it cannot bear any direct or indirect responsibility for it.

[Source: *Velikaya Otechestvennaya*, Vol. III (1) (Moscow 1994), p.232.]

---

53 On the imposition of Soviet suzerainty over Polish territory, see K. Kersten, *The Establishment of Communist Rule in Poland, 1943–1948* (Berkeley 1991).

A week later, following further pressure from the west, he emphasized the military obstacles facing the Red Army, notwithstanding the massive overall advantage it was now establishing, and placed the blame squarely on the 'bunch of criminals' who had triggered the uprising.

Document 85 | Stalin's message to Churchill and Roosevelt

22 August 1944

Secret
Personal

I have received your and Mr Roosevelt's message about Warsaw and would like to express my opinion.

Sooner or later the truth about the bunch of criminals who started all this off just to seize power will come to light. These people have abused the trust of the people of Warsaw and sent virtually unarmed people against German guns, tanks and planes. We now have a situation where every passing day is not being used by the Poles to liberate Warsaw, but by the Nazis ruthlessly to annihilate the people of Warsaw.

In military terms the current situation is drawing in German firepower and is unfavourable both to the Red Army and the Poles. Meanwhile, Soviet troops, who have been subjected to a significant counter-attack by the Germans, are doing their best to halt it and go onto the offensive again near Warsaw. You can rest assured that the Red Army will spare no efforts to beat the Germans near Warsaw and liberate it for the Poles. This will be the best and most effective help for the Polish anti-Nazis.

[Source: *Velikaya Otechestvennaya*, Vol. III (1) (Moscow 1994), p. 238.]

As the following report from a Soviet agent in Warsaw demonstrates, the London Poles and Polish public opinion at home were of one mind: the purpose of the uprising was to keep the Soviets out—somehow to emulate the 'miracle' victory over the Red Army as it had approached Warsaw in the Russo-Polish war of 1920. In their eyes, Soviet failure to give any effective help against the Nazis was deliberate: Stalin was choosing to leave them to their fate. It was all of a piece with Moscow's complicity in destroying Poland in the Nazi–Soviet Pact of 1939; with the Katyn' massacre of 1940; with the mass deportations of 1940–41 from the territory annexed in 1939; with Stalin's insistence on re-annexing it as the Germans were driven out; and with his determination to subordinate the whole of Poland after the war. Such Soviet supplies as were dropped were scorned.

Document 86 | **From the report of agent 'Oleg' in central Warsaw to the Belorussian Front**

Early hours of 2 October 1944

Attitudes to the Red Army and the Soviet Union

In accordance with instructions from the London government-in-exile the Home Army leadership has been conducting anti-Soviet propaganda among the people and the insurgents. Their slogan is 'Another miracle on the Wisła', i.e., 'Don't let the Russians into Warsaw'. Home Army propaganda has been claiming that the Red Army will conduct mass deportations of Poles to Siberia and bring in Russians to replace them. Katyn' has been mentioned several times.

The Soviet Union and the Red Army were criticized again and again at the beginning of the uprising because they did not help the insurgents, unlike Britain and America. After Soviet planes started dropping supplies on Warsaw the Home Army leadership still insisted that they were from Britain via Moscow.

Reactionary political organizations have people going round among the soldiers and populace turning them against the Red Army.

It is well known that Soviet aircraft dropped supplies from low altitude without parachutes, causing damage to their contents. The propagandists have been claiming that the damaged supplies were Soviet and the rest British—because they were packed better.

[Source: *Velikaya Otechestvennaya*, Vol. III (1) (Moscow 1994), p. 283.]

Western disgust at Stalin's reluctance to make more effort to help to drop supplies for the rebels may have underestimated his insistence that to do so was futile since most would fall into German hands. In retrospect, too, it appears that the Red Army was not in fact in a position to break through to Warsaw in time to save the uprising.[54] But it was plain that the annihilation of the Home Army was by no means unwelcome to Stalin.

In Moscow's eyes, of course, the Red Army's progress westward constituted the liberation of Europe. Every step closer to Germany and Berlin, 'the lair of the fascist beast', was hailed as a step towards rescuing peoples enslaved to the Third Reich. Much of the time the language in which it was celebrated eschewed emphasis on Marxism–Leninism and class analysis. Instead, it expressed solidarity with the western Allies abroad and, as in the following appeal, published in *Pravda* in February 1945, even tried to draw on Panslav sympathies and the supposed solidarity between Slavs within the USSR—Russians, Belorussians and Ukrainians—and those in neighbouring Poland, Czechoslovakia, Yugoslavia and Bulgaria.

---

54 Overy, *Russia's War*, pp. 248–49.

Document 87 | **From the CPSU CC slogans for the 27th Anniversary of the Red Army**

21 February 1945

Long live the mighty Soviet Union, which has saved European civilization from the fascist murderers!

Let us punish the German fascist monsters for plundering and destroying our towns and villages, for their violence against our women and children, and for murdering Soviet people and driving them into German slavery! Vengeance and death to the fascist villains!

Long live the victory of the Anglo-Soviet–American fighting alliance over the German fascist aggressors!

Brother Slavs! All your strength for the final rout of the German aggressors, the mortal enemies of the Slavs! Long live the fighting union of Slav peoples, struggling for the destruction of the German fascist plunderers!

[Source: *Pravda*, 21 February 1945.]

Revenge on Germany

Though the Red Army's progress across eastern Europe was marked by widespread mistreatment of civilians in general and barbaric abuse of women in particular, the rage directed at them was as nothing compared to that felt towards the Germans. When Soviet troops reached the Third Reich itself, the urge to avenge the destruction, slaughter and humiliation meted out to their own people burst all bounds. Germans who fell into Soviet hands were bludgeoned; refugees crushed to death; women and girls raped and slaughtered. Something of the emotion at work, albeit in a distinctly sanitized form, is conveyed in the following account from Dolmatovsky's diary.

Document 88 | **From E.A. Dolmatovsky's notebook**

February 1945

Boris Gorbatov and I got there an hour after it had been liberated. . . No, that's wrong, not 'liberated', but 'taken'. There'd be no more liberating, just taking. I could hardly believe we were in Germany. We decided to stay the night. We had some correspondence to deal with. We found an abandoned German house. . . We were writing by candle-light. . . Suddenly the house shook and there was a kind of crash, not from above, but below, so it couldn't have been a shell. Boris and I slipped our greatcoats on, rushed outside and saw a strange sight—a T-34 was bashing the wall of our abode. The hatch was open and in the turret stood one of the crew. Boris ran up to it, managed to jump on and started swearing at the man, who then turned the tank into the middle of the street, got out and came over to us. His eyes blazed in a blackened face, like some Negro. Almost in tears, he said, 'The bastards burned down my house and killed my father, mother, wife and kids. I swore that when I got to Germany, I'd smash up their home, the first I saw.'

Boris began to calm him down and talk seriously to him, inviting the whole crew into the house. We drank stolen brandy by candle-light in the sitting-room. . . And that's how we spent our first night in Germany. . .

[Source: E.A. Dolmatovsky, *Bylo. Zapiski poeta* (Moscow 1983), pp. 137–38.]

The instinct for vengeance reached all the way to the top. As the forces of the Grand Alliance closed in on Germany from east and west, Stalin was determined that the capital should fall to the Red Army rather than the Americans. Eisenhower, Supreme Commander of Western Allied Forces, assured Moscow that he was not competing to reach Berlin but there were constant rumours of and speculation about a race for the ultimate prize. When Zhukov reported in April information that Hitler was bent upon desperate defiance, this was Stalin's response:

Document 89 │ A coded telegram from Stalin to General Zhukov, Commander of the 1st Belorussian Front

April 1945

I received your cipher communication with the account of the German prisoner's testimony about not surrendering to us and fighting to the last, even if the Americans are approaching. Ignore it. Hitler is weaving a tissue of lies around Berlin to try to sow discord between the Russians and the Allies. This we must stop by taking Berlin. We can and must do so. Butcher the Germans mercilessly.

[Source: *Rossiyskie vesti*, 12 January 1995.]

By the end of the month, Soviet troops had linked up with western forces on the River Elbe. Although the line of demarcation had already been agreed between the two high commands, the following instruction reflects Stalin's wariness in handling this new proximity.

Document 90 │ From Stalin to the commanders of the 1st and 2nd Belorussian and 1st Ukrainian fronts on meeting Allied troops, April 1945

The senior commander in whose section the meeting took place is first of all to contact the senior commander of the American or British troops and establish a demarcation line, as ordered by Headquarters. No information about our plans is to be passed on. Await orders concerning fraternization.

Stalin

Antonov

[Source: *Rossiyskie vesti*, 12 January 1995.]

Meanwhile, the assault on Berlin had been launched on 16 April.[55] Although the outcome was not in doubt, the defenders fought with the savage desperation that had characterized much of the German retreat from the east. The following anecdote, published in 1965, is from a junior officer's memoirs of the battle for Berlin. It describes an instance of humanity amidst the brutality, carnage and destruction of the city, and exemplifies postwar portrayal of the Red Army heroically upholding humane ideals against Nazi barbarism.

Document 91 | From the memoirs of platoon commander L. Kolobov on the taking of Berlin, April 1945

This happened at the end of April 1945. Battle was raging right in the centre of Berlin. Our battery was firing straight at some barricades and buildings where the Nazis were holed up. Along with the infantry two detachments of my platoon had occupied a building at a crossroads. Behind a small garden opposite there rose a great big gloomy-looking building. In it were the Nazis. The battle became very fierce. Shells were exploding, throwing up clouds of smoke and dust. Machine guns and tommy guns were chattering. During a brief lull a woman with a child in her arms suddenly rushed out. She had scarcely gone ten yards before someone opened fire. Some Nazi was shooting at her. The woman fell right in the middle of the crossroads.

We froze. The woman was motionless, but the little boy of 2 or 3 at her breast began to cry loudly. The Germans did not shoot, as if waiting for something. Sasha Merzoev, commander of the gun closest to where the dead woman lay, crawled up to me. 'Comrade commander, permission to go for the kid?' What could I say? The crossroads were dead ahead and full of cross-fire. Sasha knew this but still wanted permission to rescue the child. I agreed.

As soon as Sasha leapt out, the Nazis opened fire. Merzoev fell. His comrades got him and dragged him back, whereupon an infantryman came up to me with the same request.

The Nazis intensified their fire. I ordered rapid fire from all weapons at the building they were hiding in. The infantryman, tucking up his greatcoat, waited a few seconds while he eyed up the situation. Then he leapt out from behind a gun

---

55 See the graphic account by A. Beevor, *Berlin: The Downfall, 1945* (London 2002).

and rushed forwards. Stooping down and weaving about, he ran forwards. Reaching the dead woman, he grabbed the child and rushed back.

It was utterly unbelievable! The Nazis let rip at him with everything. Sparks were thrown up from the bullets hitting the cobbles, but not one touched the hero, as if he were invulnerable.

Gasping, the soldier rushed into the doorway of our building. I asked orderly Akbarov to look after the little boy. He was taken down into the cellar. I went down a few hours later, when the battle was nearly over.

The child, still trembling and sniffling, was greedily eating kasha from a mess-tin with a soldier's spoon.

'Where's the soldier who saved the child?', I asked Akbarov. He just shrugged his shoulders.

The infantrymen were on the upper floors of the building. I ran up there to try and find the hero. Nowhere to be seen. Nobody could help me—the subunits were changing: some had just arrived and others had gone back behind the lines. The little German boy, saved by an unknown soldier, stayed with us until 2 May. When we finally took Berlin, we handed him over to a German woman, explaining as well as we could what had happened.

[Source: *Pravda*, 5 May 1965.]

Two weeks after the assault began, while insisting despite the hopeless situation on defiance to the last drop of blood, Hitler committed suicide. His chief of staff, General Krebs, then tried to open negotiations but he and Goebbels rejected unconditional surrender, both subsequently committing suicide. On the evening of 1 May, Soviet forces pulverized remaining pockets of German resistance and by the early hours of 2 May Berlin had capitulated. Dolmatovsky describes the surrender of the Reich's bedraggled regulars and ageing volunteers (*Volkssturmer*), the joy of emaciated POWs and forced labourers from the USSR, German being spoken on the streets of the capital only in a whisper and the flags of Germany's victims springing up from nowhere.

Document 92 | From E.A. Dolmatovsky's notebook

May 1945

The first of May is drawing to a close. I hear from the division that the commander of the 56th tank corps, who is in charge of the defence of Berlin, General Weidling, is ready to surrender. General Weidling is brought in. His throat is caught in a spasm with his Adam's apple bobbing up and down. The General himself writes the order for the Berlin garrison to surrender:

'On 30 April 1945 the Führer committed suicide, leaving us who had sworn our loyalty to him on our own. The Führer had ordered you, German soldiers, to fight for Berlin despite being out of ammunition and a situation which makes further resistance pointless. You are ordered to cease resistance immediately.'

It was already morning—damp, rainy and unseasonably cold. I left the room where our officers were getting copies of Weidling's order. They were to take the order to various parts of the city and read it out in the streets through a megaphone, calling upon soldiers to surrender.

There was no longer any sound of firing. Marshal Zhukov had given the order to cease fire. I saw the artillery men covering their guns as the streets filled with people. Prisoners were no longer passing in single file, but in rows. Guns were being thrown with a clatter onto a growing heap.

Crowds of worn-out people carrying little national flags were going past. I saw the national flags of France, Italy, Czechoslovakia, Holland and Norway. They stopped by Soviet tanks, laughing and shouting out things. Two Negroes in ragged American uniforms cycled past, obviously ex-prisoners.

Young women with *Ost* sewn onto their sleeves went past. All around I could hear Russian, Belorussian and Ukrainian. Today German was spoken in a whisper. More and more white flags were appearing at the windows. . .

[Source: E.A. Dolmatovsky, *Bylo. Zapiski poeta* (Moscow 1983), pp. 202–04.]

As the *Wehrmacht* imploded, Stalin urged the advantages of treating the defeated Germans more humanely.

Document 93 │ Stalin's call for more humane treatment of Germans

May 1945

The men are to change their attitude both to German prisoners and non-combatants and treat them better. Harsh treatment is frightening them and making them stubbornly resist rather than surrender. Fearing revenge, civilians are forming gangs. This does not help us at all. A more humane attitude will make military operations easier in their country and undoubtedly decrease their resistance.

I. Stalin

[Source: *Rossiyskie vesti*, 12 January 1995.]

Victory

The short-lived government of Hitler's successor, Admiral Doenitz, accepted unconditional surrender on 8 May. The following day was named Victory Day. In towns and cities across the USSR, crowds converged to delight in the victory and the peace. The celebrations constituted by far the largest spontaneous demonstrations since the revolution. In Moscow, the numbers involved ran into millions. The mood of relief and pride was testimony to the profound emotional impact of the Great Patriotic War. The monstrous scale of the bloodshed and destruction wrought, the vicious, bestial Nazi treatment of Soviet civilians and POWs, and the insufferable racial insult constituted a common trauma surpassed only by that of the Holocaust. The following table sets out recent estimates of the human losses. The population of 196.7 million living within pre-war borders in 1941 had fallen to 170.5 in late 1945. Alongside 8.7 million military personnel, over 30 per cent of those called up, there were as many as 18 million civilian deaths overwhelmingly caused by sheer economic deprivation.

Document 94 | Soviet armed forces and losses during the war

Total serving as of May 1941	4,826,900
Attached to Defence Commissariat	74,900
Called up 1941–1945	29,574,900
Grand total serving	34,476,700
Serving (total) as of June 1945	12,839,800
Leaving 1941–1945	21,636,900
inc. demobilized through wounding or illness	3,798,200
disabled	2,576,000
transferred to war work	3,614,600
transferred to NKVD etc.	1,425,000
punishment battalions	422,700
imprisoned	436,600
dismissed	206,000
deserters	212,400
Total losses	11,444,100
viz., killed, mortally wounded or sick	6,885,100
missing or captured	4,559,000
Less: returned POWs	1,836,000
remobilized et al.	939,700
Actual losses	8,668,400
Total civilian and service losses	c.27,000,000

[Sources: *Krasnaya zvezda*, 22 June 1993; *Novaya i noveyshaya istoriya*, 1992, No. 3, p. 221.]

The calamity marked every ethnic group, every religious group, every social group and generated a sense of social solidarity within the USSR that had not existed even in the cities before the war and had been entirely absent in the countryside. As we shall see, bitterness, discontent and division resurfaced soon enough, but they now co-existed with the emotional bonds of triumph, victimhood, moral outrage and indignation. The war bred a new sense of allegiance and conferred on communist rule and the Soviet system an entirely new legitimacy in the eyes of the generation who had endured the ordeal. It transformed Stalin into a popular hero. The following epistle issued by the new Patriarch elected in 1945 (see below, pp. 162–63) was among innumerable formal and impromptu celebrations of triumph. No longer making any effort to distance the Church and hierarchy from the regime and Stalin, Aleksiy heaped praise on 'our victorious army and its Supreme Leader'.

Document 95 | **'Blessed art Thou, O God, who hast tamed the Beast and quenched the fire...'—to Right Reverend arch-priests, priests and all true children of the Russian Orthodox Church**

9 May 1945

Christ is risen!
'O come, let us sing unto the LORD: let us make a joyful noise to the rock of our salvation!'
(Psalms 95:1)

... With the glory of victories and the joy of peace I greet firstly our victorious army and its great Supreme Leader, and then all the true sons of our Motherland, united with their Leader and his victorious army, who have now been vouchsafed the happiness of seeing victory over the dark forces of the enemy which have tormented Europe for so long with their mad dreams of conquering the world and hoisting over it the bloody banner of fascism. But God has put to shame the impertinent dreams of robbers and scoundrels, and now we see them suffering a terrible retribution for their evil deeds.

We have confidently and patiently awaited this joyful day of the Lord, the day when the Lord has uttered his righteous judgement upon the bitterest enemies of mankind—and Orthodox Russia, after unprecedented martial feats and the incredible exertions of the entire strength of her people, who came as one to the defence of the Motherland, sacrificing their very lives for her, now offers up prayers to the Lord, gratefully calling upon the very source of victory and peace for His heavenly help in this time of battle, for the joy of victory and for the gift of peace to the whole world.

But does victory bear only consciousness of joy? It bears also consciousness of obligation, of duty, of responsibility for the present and future, of the need to work harder to consolidate the victory, to make it fruitful and to heal the wounds of war. . .

Difficult times lie ahead, but we can now breathe freely and with joy set about our hard but creative labours. . .

I call upon our Holy Church through its arch-priests, priests and true children to pray as zealously and fervently for the peacetime prosperity of our land as they prayed in the time of trials for victory over our enemies. May these prayers be acceptable in the sight of God. . .

'Blessed art Thou, O God, who hast tamed the Beast and quenched the fire. . .' (Canon in Praise of the Mother of God). Amen.

Aleksiy, Patriarch of Moscow and All Russia

[Source: *Zhurnal Moskovskoy Patriarkhii*, No. 5, 1945, pp. 10, 11.]

On its side, the regime took every opportunity to ram home the message that victory had been achieved through popular support for and unity behind the leadership of Stalin and the party. This was the insistent theme of official rhetoric and memorializing of every military feat, economic achievement, personal sacrifice. At local level, in the smaller Union Republics, Autonomous Republics, cities and towns across the country, the public narrative celebrated in memorials and embellished by the leadership, the press and teachers wove ethnic pride together with Soviet pride, all suffused with obeisance to Stalin and the party. In the master narrative forged at the centre, in Moscow, celebration of the great Soviet people was combined with emphasis on the dominant contribution to victory made by the Russian people: the appeals to Russian national pride made since the first days of the war reached their apogee, overlaying the internationalism of Marxism–Leninism as the party colonized Russian patriotism and made it its own.[56] The following extract from a speech Stalin gave at a victory reception at the Kremlin a fortnight after VE day set the tone. He expressed his gratitude to the Russian people for their support of his regime. He openly acknowledged the possibility that in 1941 and 1942, so dire were the straits in which the country stood, the government might have been rejected in favour of one willing to sue for peace—and acclaimed the unique steadfastness of the Russians. In his unmistakable Georgian accent he reeled off the lands of lesser peoples that had been surrendered—Ukrainian and Belorussian, Baltic and Moldovan—while heaping praise on the leading role of the Russians in their recapture. It was their loyalty even in the darkest

---

56 The process is finely traced in J. Brooks, *Thank You, Comrade Stalin! Soviet Public Culture from Revolution to Cold War* (Princeton 2000), pp. 159–232.

period of the Nazi invasion, their intelligence, their patience that had saved the USSR.

Document 96 | I.V. Stalin: 'I propose a toast to the health of the Russian people'—speech at a reception in the Kremlin

24 May 1945

Comrades, allow me to propose one more, final, toast.

I would like to propose a toast to the health of our Soviet people, and, above all, the Russian people. (Prolonged, thunderous applause, shouts of 'Hooray!')

I drink principally to the health of the Russian people because it is the most outstanding of all the nations making up the Soviet Union.

I propose a toast to the health of the Russian people because in this war it, among all the peoples of our country, has earned recognition as the guiding force of the Soviet Union.

I propose a toast to the health of the Russian people not only because it is the leading people, but also for its intelligence, steadfastness and patience.

Our government made quite a few mistakes: there were moments in 1941–1942 when we were in a desperate situation, when our army was in retreat, abandoning the villages and towns of Ukraine, Belorussia, Moldova, Leningrad *oblast'*, the Baltic states, and the Karelian–Finnish Republic. It retreated because there was no other way out. Any other people might have said to their government, 'You have failed us, so go! We'll bring in another government, which will make peace with Germany and give us some rest.' But the Russian people did not do this, because it believed in the correctness of its government's policy and sacrificed itself to ensure the defeat of Germany. And it was the Russian people's trust in the Soviet government which proved to be the decisive factor ensuring a historic victory over fascism, the enemy of mankind.

Thank you, Russian people, for that trust!

To the health of the Russian people! (Thunderous, prolonged applause.)

[Source: *Pravda*, 25 May 1945.]

11

Postwar Expectations

Popular relief at victory was intermingled with anticipation and myriad hopes that the terrible ordeal had bred about postwar life.[57] The war was invasive and pervasive, rupturing life at every level and in every part of the country. Of a population of about 200 million at the time of Barbarossa, some 80 million were subjected to German occupation, 25 million were evacuated from their homes to the east, and 29 million served in the armed forces. Even those who were not physically uprooted saw their education, their careers, their hopes and plans, their loved ones engulfed. The effect on public assumptions and expectations was profound. Families endured such disruption, suffering and loss that peace in itself came to seem an almost unimaginable blessing: simply to be secure, to be alive and well and provided for, and to know that relations and friends were safe too. Pleasures once taken entirely for granted seemed infinitely alluring. The heightened appreciation of life as such is captured in the following plaintive extract from a letter written to his wife by V.L. Zanadvorov, a geologist and writer who served and died at Stalingrad.

Document 97 | '... I often wonder how people will live after the war'—
from a letter by V.L. Zanadvorov to his wife.

Army in the field, 19 October 1942

You know, love, I often wonder how people will live after the war. I reckon that people will have learned to value life, even in its most commonplace manifestations.

---

57 New ground on public opinion at the end of the war is broken by E.Iu. Zubkova, *Russia after the War: Hopes, Illusions, and Disappointments, 1945–1957* (London 1998).

Every minute will be a pleasure and every movement special. Or maybe that's just how it seems. . .

[Source: V.L. Zanadvorov, *Veter muzhestva* (Molotov 1954), p. 293.]

Visions of a postwar era infused by a new, tolerant and harmonious ethos were replicated not only among millions of soldiers, but a thousand miles from the front line: this was total war which involved civilians in a manner that Anglo-Saxons of the 1940s—even Britons, never mind Australians and Americans—did not experience. The following document conveys some of the elements that contributed to the spread of expectations that the common ordeal would leave relations between regime and society transformed. It expresses thanks from troops at the front for the patriotic entertainment provided by artistes sent from distant Sverdlovsk in the summer of 1943, and underlines the interweaving of battle front and home front.

Document 98 | '... I offer them all my gratitude...'—from an order
for the political division of the Central Front

No. 15. Army in the field, 8 August 1943

A brigade of artistes from Sverdlovsk, consisting of Sarra Sven, laureate of the International Dance Competition; Aleksandra Sedlyarovaya, laureate of the All-Union Competition for Masters of Variety; Vera Kupresovaya; Boris Mikhaylovich Kazaris; Samuil Genrikhovich Kogan; Sergey Ignat'evich Prishchepa; Irina Modestovna Davidovich; and Lidiya Bravich; directed by Aleksey Petrovich Mesnyaev, Honoured Artist of the RSFSR, put on 76 concerts in units and formations on the Front between 22 June and 8 August this year. They have done a great deal to build up Red Army amateur theatricals and music.

By mixing day to day with officers and men in front-line positions, these comrades gave a fresh spurt to the decisive battles against the deadly enemy of our beautiful Motherland.

These masters of performance, with remarkable patriotic songs, live readings, and classical dance, provided excellent relaxation for everyone, and were justifiably popular with the infantrymen and mortar men, gunners and tank crews in all the units and formations they visited.

For their conscientious attitude to their work and their remarkable performances of their repertoire for all the men of the brigade I offer them all my gratitude. . .

Colonel Budkin,
pp. Deputy director of the political administration of the Front

[Source: *Ural*, No. 9, 1975, p. 121.]

Reconstruction in liberated territory

The following decree, issued two weeks later, seemed to confirm in the most heart-lifting fashion the significance of the summer triumph at Kursk. With the Germans being pushed further and further back across the territory they had invaded, Sovnarkom and the party listed measures to revive economic activity in liberated areas. Reconstruction was to begin. Houses, railways, schools and farms were to be restored and rebuilt. Life was to start again.

Document 99 | **'On urgent measures to restore the economy in areas liberated from German occupation'—from a decree of the USSR Sovnarkom and the CPSU CC**

21 August 1943

. . . I/6   The USSR People's Commissariat for Agriculture is to take charge of bringing back to those areas liberated from German occupation the livestock evacuated to eastern areas. It is also to be responsible for returning the livestock in good time, and for looking after it en route. . .

I/20   *Oblast'* and *kray* CPSU committees and executive committees are to ensure by 15 September that in every area liberated from German occupation stock-raising farms are fully manned, and are to take the necessary measures to hire managers, milkmaids, calf-herds, pig-men, stable-lads, and other staff. . .

II/4   In 1943–1944 the USSR People's Commissariat for Agriculture is to organize the purchase for the state in eastern and central *oblasti* of all kinds of stock for the areas, liberated from German occupation. . .

IV/1   District executive committees and district CPSU committees are to exempt—fully or partially—collective farm households, individual farms, and workers' and craftsmen's holdings that suffered under German occupation, from the obligation to deliver all their agricultural produce to the state in 1943. . .

With the permission of the *oblast'*, *kray* or republic representative of the People's Commissariat for Procurement, district executive committees and CPSU committees may permit some collective farms to increase or decrease their local delivery quotas of grain, sunflower seeds, potatoes, vegetables and hay to the state within a 50% range, provided, however, that deliveries for the district as a whole remain strictly in accordance with the quotas laid down for that district. . .

V/1   To ensure fulfilment of the plan for winter sowings for the 1944 harvest, 50,000 tons of winter seed are to be released from state reserves for loans to collective farms. . .

VI/42   By 5 September 1943 the RSFSR People's Commissariats for Ferrous Metals, Non-ferrous Metals, Machine-Building, Rubber Production, Textile Production, Small Machine-Building, Mining Equipment and Local Industry are to despatch, on instructions from the USSR People's Commissariat for Agriculture, materials and spare parts for agricultural machinery to the Smolensk, Kalinin, Orel, Voronezh and Stalingrad *oblasti*, the Krasnodar and Stavropol *kraya* and the Ukrainian SSR. . . .

VI/46   Republican economic councils, *kray* and *oblast'* executive committees, CCs of Republican CPs, and *kray* and *oblast'* CPSU committees are to return senior agricultural workers and specialists who had been evacuated from the Voronezh, Kursk, Stalingrad, Rostov, Kalinin, Orel and Smolensk *oblasti*, the Krasnodar and Stavropol *kraya* and the Ukrainian SSR to their former places of work no later than 15 October 1943. . . .

VII/1   Party and Soviet organizations in the Kursk, Orel, Voronezh, Kalinin, Stalingrad and Rostov *oblasti*, and the Krasnodar and Stavropol *kraya* are to treat as a matter of urgency the restoration and construction of dwellings, using local materials, in villages, towns and workers' settlements liberated from German occupation, to ensure that collective farmers, and manual and white-collar workers at present living in dugouts and ruins are rehoused in accommodation fit for habitation. . .

VIII/1   The People's Commissariat for Transport and local Party and Soviet organizations are to regard the restoration and construction of track, stations, signal boxes and dwellings on the railways liberated from the enemy as a matter of urgency. . .

IX   On the allocation of garden plots for railway track workers and their exemption from obligatory deliveries of agricultural produce. . .

IX/2   *Oblast'* and *kray* executive committees and Republican Sovnarkoms are permitted to grant those railway track workers concerned with getting trains running parcels of trackside land belonging to the railway and spare land from the state fund of up to 0.5 hectares of arable land and a 1-hectare hayfield each.

X/1   For the settlement, upbringing and education of the children of Red Army soldiers, Patriotic War partisans, as well as the children of those Soviet and Party workers, manual and collective farm workers killed at the hands of the German occupiers, the following are to be organized in the Krasnodar and Stavropol *kraya* and the Rostov, Stalingrad, Voroshilovgrad, Voronezh, Khar'kov, Kursk, Orel, Smolensk and Kalinin *oblasti*:

a. Nine Suvorov military schools, like the old cadet corps, with 500 students in each. . .

b. Twenty-three special trade schools with 400 students in each. . .

c. Special orphanages for 16,300 children and nurseries for 1,750 babies.

d. Twenty-nine reception centres for 2,000 children. . .

[Source: *Pravda*, 22 August 1943.]

Conditions in liberated territory, much of which had been subject to scorched-earth treatment as the Red Army had retreated, denuded during the occupation, and then put to the torch again by the Germans as they in turn withdrew, were desperate. People returned to ghost cities, flattened villages, the most primitive conditions and backbreaking labour. Yet the relatively permissive tone of the reconstruction decree, from the assignment of private plots to the lightening of tax burdens on collective farms, seemed to match other evidence of the regime adopting a lighter hand as victory began to become imaginable. Popular delight was palpable. The following exultant letter home was sent four days later by a young sergeant, a Sverdlovsk graduate, E.N. Davydov, serving on the Leningrad front. He was killed in 1944.

Document 100 | '... **everybody understood it'—from a letter by sergeant E.N. Davydov to his mother**

Leningrad front, 25 August 1943

With me reading it out to the whole company, we studied the Sovnarkom and CPSU joint decree 'On measures to restore agriculture in liberated areas'. If only you could have seen how happy and heartened our lads were! Half of the men don't know Russian properly, but everybody understood it...

[Source: *Ural'skiy universitet*, 1 April 1965.]

Accommodation with the Church

One of the most striking symptoms of the regime's less dogmatic and more inclusive line was its treatment of religion.[58] The League of the Godless was disbanded and atheist propaganda halted. Greater toleration was shown most denominations, from the Armenian and Georgian Churches to Catholic and Protestant congregations, but the greatest beneficiary was the Orthodox Church. In addition to welcoming the Church's patriotic appeals and contribution to raising morale, Stalin and the leadership were aware of the vigorous religious revival in German-occupied territories, notably Ukraine, and the use that could be made of a loyal hierarchy in reintegrating liberated territory and subordinating it to Moscow. In January 1943 Stalin sanctioned and formally acknowledged the hierarchy's efforts to collect contributions to help with the war effort—in sharp contrast with Lenin's scathing reaction two decades earlier to clerical collections to help with the famine of 1921. In September, he summoned Sergiy to the Kremlin and authorized the convocation of a Council (Sobor) of the hierarchy empowered to elect a Patriarch, forbidden since the death of Tikhon in 1925. Although some

---

58 See Miner, *Stalin's Holy War.*

bishops, especially among those imprisoned, rejected the accommodation with the regime, as did clergy operating in German-occupied territory, Sergiy had no hesitation. Stalin urged Sergiy to act with 'Bolshevik tempo' and the Council met within a week. In stark contrast to the 564-strong Sobor of 1917, half of whose delegates had been lay (and where ironically Sergiy had been among those opposing the restoration of the Patriarchate), it was made up of just 19 bishops. Before his unanimous election, Sergiy gave the following fiercely patriotic report of the Church's wartime activities, with strong emphasis on the Church's role in fateful conflicts of the past, notably the struggle to throw off the Tatar yoke six hundred years earlier.

Document 101 | **'I shall report on what we have been doing during the war'— from Metropolitan Sergiy's report to the Council of Bishops**

September 1943.

Right Reverend archbishops and all gathered here! I shall report on what we have been doing during the war and on the circumstances which have permitted us to gather for this Synod.

We need not dwell on what stance our Church must adopt during the war, because before we had even had time to work out any kind of position, it was decided for us: the fascists attacked our country, laid it waste, captured our countrymen, tortured, pillaged, etc. Thus, simple decency would not allow us to adopt any stance other than the one we have adopted, which is one of unconditional hostility to everything bearing the stamp of fascism, the stamp of hostility to our country.

The archbishops considered it their duty not only to adopt this stance themselves but also to call upon their flocks to do so. For example, I have despatched twenty-three different epistles on various occasions, but their theme has, of course, been the same, namely, trust that, as before, God will not abandon us and will ultimately grant us victory. As has happened so many times before in our history, the Russian people with a smaller army and even less technical skill have conquered the most powerful foes. Thus was thrown off the Tatar yoke at Kulikovo and so on.

Our people willingly responded to our call. We called upon them to make sacrifices for the war effort. This they have been doing and a very significant sum has been collected. Moreover, as has been noted several times before, these sacrifices did not come from wealthy people, giving a small proportion of their riches to the war effort. These were the sacrifices of the simple devout who contributed their usual mite, but for a special purpose. It is from these individual sacrifices that millions have been collected; our believers were filled with the desire to help our warriors, laying down their lives for the Fatherland.

I myself proposed to our Church society a collection for a tank division named after Dmitriy Donskoy. I was guided by the desire to repeat the example of Saint

Sergiy, who despatched two of his monks to the battlefield. In physical terms they were, of course, of little use as soldiers, but they did bear with them the blessing of Saint Sergiy and the Troitskaya monastery. Thus, their appearance among the Russian ranks undoubtedly raised the spirits of the men and contributed to the defeat of Mamai.

Likewise our tanks, I thought. God alone knows what help they might have rendered to our troops, but it was with our blessing and was a sign that the Church does not abandon troops on the battlefield, that it blesses them and is prepared to be there with them in battle until Holy Russia is liberated from foreign invaders. . .

[Source: *Zhurnal Moskovskoy patriarkhii*, No. 1, 1943, pp. 7–8.]

The assembled bishops went on to sign collectively a denunciation of those priests and lay people who had sided with the Germans. Although Sergiy had condemned such traitors soon after the German invasion began, his language had at first been more moderate. The most prominent bishop to collaborate actively with the German authorities, the Bishop of the Baltic area, was a personal friend of his and, more important, the chaos of the early months made it difficult to know what options were open to the hierarchy in areas taken by the Germans. Here, however, the full weight of excommunication and defrocking was brought to bear.

Document 102 | Condemnation of traitors to Faith and Fatherland

8 September 1943

Alongside the heartening manifestations of patriotic activity among both the Orthodox laity and clergy, it is all the more sad to observe phenomena of a contrary nature. There are those among the laity and clergy who, no longer fearing God, dare to profit from our common misfortune. They greet the Germans as welcome guests, find employment in their service and even sink to outright betrayal by giving away their brothers, such as partisans and others, who are sacrificing themselves for their Motherland. An obliging conscience is, of course, always prepared to provide justification for even this kind of behaviour. But the treachery of a Judas will always be the treachery of a Judas. Just as Judas destroyed his soul, and his body suffered severe punishment here on Earth, so these traitors, preparing eternal damnation for themselves, likewise cannot avoid the fate of Cain on Earth. The fascists will receive a just punishment for their pillage, murders and other evil deeds. Similarly, the minions of the fascists cannot expect mercy, if they think they can profit behind the backs and at the expense of their brothers.

The Holy Orthodox Church, both Russian and Eastern, has already condemned the traitors to the cause of Christianity and the betrayers of the Church. We, gathered here today in the name of the Father, Son and Holy Ghost, also confirm this condemnation and decree: Anyone who is guilty of betraying the cause of the whole Church and has gone over to the side of fascism, is excommunicated or, in the case of bishops and clerics, defrocked as an enemy of the Cross of the Lord. Amen.

Sergiy, Metropolitan of Moscow and Kolomna; Aleksiy, Metropolitan of Leningrad; Nikolay, Metropolitan of Kiev and Galicia; Luka, Archbishop of Krasnoyarsk; Ioann, Archbishop of Sarapul; Andrey, Archbishop of Kazan'; Aleksiy, Archbishop of Kuybyshev; Stefan, Archbishop of Ufa; Sergiy, Archbishop of Gorky and Arzamas; Ioann, Archbishop of Yaroslavl' and Rostov; Aleksiy, Archbishop of Ryazan'; Vasiliy, Archbishop of Kalinin and Smolensk; Varfolomey, Archbishop of Novosibirsk and Barnaul; Grigoriy, Archbishop of Saratov and Stalingrad; Aleksandr, Bishop of Molotov; Pitirim, Bishop of Kursk; Veniamin, Bishop of Kirov, Dimitriy, Bishop of Ul'yanovsk; Elevferiy, Bishop of Rostov.

Moscow

[Source: *Russkaya pravoslavnaya tserkov' i Velikaya Otechestvennaya voyna* (Moscow 1943), p. 13.]

The Sobor and the rehabilitation of the Patriarchy signalled formal recognition by the regime and was followed by the establishment of a department of state, the Council of the Affairs of the Russian Orthodox Church, headed by a former NKVD officer, to oversee church matters. Permission was given to reopen a significant number of churches as well as several seminaries, the first being re-established in June 1944. The Church gradually extended the range of its activities, acquiring printing presses, opening bank accounts, organizing workshops producing candles, icons and other holy articles, and re-establishing the monthly *Journal of the Moscow Patriarchate* and thus a means of countrywide communication. The Patriarch's pastoral letters were now printed in *Izvestiya*. Sergiy's death in May 1944 was followed, in late January 1945, by a further Sobor, this time attended by forty-one Russian bishops, eighty-seven priests and thirty-seven laymen, to elect a new Patriarch, Metropolitan Aleksiy, and endorse a new Statute on the Church's internal structure.[59] The obsequious tone of some Orthodox sermons and prayers, as well as the vehement support which the hierarchy gave to Soviet foreign policy, notably Metropolitan Nikolay, who became a familiar spokesman, continued to alienate dissident members of the clergy and discouraged the many underground sects that had developed during the heavy repression of the 1930s from rejoining the Church. So, too, did the fact that the Church was firmly restricted to purely spiritual activity and denied any wider social

---

59 Pospielovsky, *The Russian Church under the Soviet Regime*, Vol. I, p. 212.

role or function. And even as its status improved and thousands of churches were reopened, the legal position remained unstable, the regime tolerating activities without formally repealing pre-war anti-religious decrees by which they were forbidden.

Nevertheless, the Church's partial rehabilitation and greatly enhanced visibility raised expectations that extended far beyond the concessions the regime had made by 1945. The following report in March 1945 from the party in Penza gives a flavour of the ideas in circulation about the Church's possible future role. It is a compilation of the kind of questions raised by local people in discussions triggered by an address which had been issued by the Church Council. They ranged from speculation about the reintroduction of holy days and religious instruction in schools, the suggestion that the leeway granted to the Orthodox Church be extended to other denominations, and the prospect of Komsomol members being married in Church, to the prediction that having made this concession to peasant faith and mores the regime would be dissolving the collective farms next.

Document 103 | **A list of questions asked at reports, lectures and in conversations about the Russian Orthodox Church Council's *Address to Christians throughout the World*—from a letter to the CPSU CC from the Penza CPSU *oblast'* committee**

5 March 1945

Top secret

1. What gave rise to this Council and the election of a Patriarch of All-Russia?
2. Will the clergy be disenfranchised?
3. Will the state allot funds for building churches and seminaries?
4. Will Scripture be taught in school?
5. What part will the clergy play in the work of the Soviets?
6. How are we to understand the recognition of religion by the government: as permanent or a temporary concession in the interests of finishing the war quickly?
7. Will churches be opened now?
8. Will religious holidays be observed?
9. Will Komsomol members get married in church?
10. How do you explain increased clerical activity?
11. Will the seminaries be opened?
12. How are we to understand the separation of Church and state at the present time?
13. Can Komsomol members enter a seminary and who in general can be admitted?
14. What is the Soviet government's attitude to the Church?
15. Why were churches being closed before, but are now being opened?

16. Why are they talking only about the Orthodox Church?
17. What influence did the Church and clergy have and how did they help in waging the Patriotic War?
18. Are Soviet organs monitoring the services being held in the Penza *oblast'*?
19. Won't the opening of churches and the revival of the clergy affect young people?
20. Will bell-ringing be allowed?
21. Why was religion considered the opium of the people before the war, but is now being advertised in the papers?
22. Is the Party going to conduct propaganda against religion now?
23. Why has Soviet power changed its attitude to the Church?
24. Who gives permission for a church to be opened?
25. Will seminarists continue to be exiled to Siberia?
26. Isn't the recognition of the Church Council and the presence in the Sovnarkom of a representative for the affairs of the Russian Church an infringement of the Stalin Constitution, where it says that the state and Church are separate?

In connection with the publication of the Address of the Church Council local people voiced the following opinions:

Erokhin, a worker at factory No. 50, said, 'The election of the Patriarch and opening of churches are being allowed for the moment, while the war's on, to keep our Allies happy, but as soon as the war ends, all these bishops and synods will disappear. We know the Communists don't need the Church.'

Proskurin, shop manager at factory No. 744, said this: 'The Church is an additional and extremely powerful means of agitation among many strata of the population. Hence we may conclude that the organization of the Church as a force supporting state measures is particularly important in the countryside.'

Belyakov, a fitter at Central Design No. 22, said, 'They pulled down all the churches and turned them into warehouses, and now they're wasting money on restoring them. They've just had to make concessions to the masses, because they still believe in God. They'll be dissolving the collectives before too long.'

Ponimatkin, a worker at factory No. 50, said, 'During the Patriotic War the government needed to do this, so let them pray, but after the war we'll see how they deal with the Church. . .'

[Source: RGASPI, fond 17, opis' 88, delo 429, pp. 3–4 ob.]

The mood generated among optimists may be detected from the tone of the following extract from the observations of Metropolitan Veniamin, the Church's representative in North America, on a visit to Moscow in 1945.

Document 104 | Metropolitan Veniamin, 'A happy... new young breed is growing up'—from his 1945 article *Russian Impressions*

Children, dear children. There are so many everywhere. A youthful new Russia is clearly already growing up. What happy little faces, intelligent little eyes, lively movements and often lovely faces. Everywhere they are warmly dressed. This future generation is growing up happy, not downcast. Their fathers and mothers suffered so that they can live in peace and radiant joy.

A happy and cheerful new young breed is growing up. . .

Veniamin, Metropolitan of the Aleutians and North America

[Source: *Zhurnal Moskovskoy patriarkhii*, No. 3, 1945, p. 24.]

The dissolution of Comintern

Another shift in the regime's stance and rhetoric that fostered speculation about thoroughgoing change was the way in which it projected relations with foreign powers. On 22 May 1943, Comintern was formally abolished: much of the apparatus, as well as émigré European communists, remained in Moscow, it is true, but the symbolism of rapprochement with western governments hitherto targeted for revolutionary overthrow was striking. And although the move was designed to impress foreign rather than domestic opinion, as the following statement by Stalin makes clear, in the USSR, too, it seemed to mark a permanent break with the invective and tension of pre-war years.

Document 105 | '... it simplifies the organization of a common onslaught by all freedom-loving nations...'—Stalin's reply to Reuter's Moscow correspondent

28 May 1943

Dear Mr King,
I have received from you a request to reply to a question about the dissolution of the Communist International. I am sending you my answer:

Your question was: British comment on the decision to dissolve the Comintern has been very favourable. What is the Soviet point of view on this question and its effect on the future of international relations?

My reply is: The dissolution of the Communist International is correct and timely, because it simplifies the organization of a common onslaught by all freedom-loving nations against the common enemy—Hitlerism.

The dissolution of the Communist International is correct, because:
a) It exposes the lie of the Hitlerites that Moscow supposedly intends to interfere

in the affairs of other states and 'bolshevize' them. We have now put an end to that lie.

b) It exposes the slander of the enemies of communism in the workers' movement that the communist parties in different countries are supposedly operating not in the interests of their own people but on orders from outside. We have now put an end to that slander.

c) It simplifies the work of patriots in freedom-loving countries in uniting the progressive forces of their own country, regardless of party or religious affiliation, into a single camp of national liberation—to broaden the struggle against fascism.

d) It simplifies the work of patriots in all countries in uniting all freedom-loving peoples into a single international camp to struggle against the threat of Hitlerite world domination and thereby clearing the way for the organization in future of a community of peoples on the basis of equality.

I think that all these circumstances, taken together, will lead to a further strengthening of the united front of the Allies and other united nations in their struggle for victory over Hitlerite tyranny.

I consider that the dissolution of the Communist International is entirely timely because it is precisely now, when the fascist beast is making its final supreme effort, that we must organize a common onslaught of freedom-loving countries to finish this beast off and save the peoples from the fascist yoke.

With respect
I. Stalin

[Source: I.V. Stalin, *O Velikoy Otechestvennoy voyne* (Moscow 1947), pp. 107–08.]

Relations with the west

The replacement, the following month, of the Internationale as the state anthem by a new fiercely patriotic one seemed to confirm a downgrading of the militancy and dogmatism of the party. More generally, while the authorities remained acutely suspicious of informal contacts with foreigners, this suspicion was expressed in terms of the danger of pro-Nazi spies, and was counter-balanced by the thaw in relations with the western powers. A meeting of allied foreign ministers in Moscow in October 1943, followed in November by the meeting Stalin held with Churchill and Roosevelt at Teheran in Iran, pointed in the same direction. The very fact of a face-to-face conference with western leaders suggested an end to the international isolation of the pre-war years. So, too, did the tone of the Teheran Declaration published in *Izvestiya* in December.

Document 106 | The Tri-partite Declaration, Teheran, 1 December 1943

We—the President of the United States, the Prime Minister of Great Britain, and the Premier of the Soviet Union—have met these four days past, in this, the capital of our ally, Iran, and have shaped and confirmed our common policy.

We express the determination that our nations shall work together in war and in the peace that will follow.

As to war, our military staffs have joined in our round-table discussions, and we have reached complete agreement as to the scope and timing of the operations to be undertaken from the east, west and south.

The common understanding which we have here reached guarantees that victory will be ours.

And as to peace, we are sure that our concord will win an enduring peace. We recognize fully the supreme responsibility resting upon us and all the united nations to make a peace which will command the good will of the overwhelming mass of the peoples of the world and banish the scourge and terror of war for many generations.

With our diplomatic advisors we have surveyed the problems of the future. We shall seek the co-operation and active participation of all nations, large and small, whose people in heart and mind are dedicated, as are our own peoples, to the elimination of tyranny and slavery, oppression and intolerance. We will welcome them, as they may choose to come, into a world of democratic nations.

No power on earth can prevent our destroying the German armies by land, their U-boats by sea, and their war plants from the air.

Our attack will be relentless and increasing.

Emerging from these cordial conferences, we look with confidence to the day when all the peoples of the world may live free lives, untouched by tyranny, and according to their varying desires and their own consciences.

We came here with hope and determination. We leave here friends in fact, spirit and purpose.

[Source: http://www.ibiblio.org/pha/policy/1943/431201c.html]

As Soviet and western forces closed in on Germany from 1944, the sense of the USSR more and more closely interacting and co-operating with its allies increased. News of the long-awaited Second Front in June was greeted with delight. The following month, Soviet representatives attended the Bretton Woods conference, at which the World Bank and the International Monetary Fund were established. With America proffering a large loan to assist postwar reconstruction, Moscow gave general endorsement to agreements on exchange rates and international trade.[60] In October, Churchill

---

60 On the regime's policy at Bretton Woods and the economic dimension to Soviet–western relations at the end of the war, see A.R. Pollard, *Economic Security and the Origins of the Cold War, 1945–1949* (New York 1985).

visited Moscow and diplomatic exchanges became fast and frequent. In February 1945 both he and Roosevelt travelled all the way to the Soviet Crimea to meet Stalin at Yalta. In April 1945 the Soviet Union, the US and Britain took the leading role at the founding conference of the United Nations in San Francisco. A tussle over how many seats the USSR should take in the planned General Assembly—Moscow initially proposed that in addition to a seat for the Union as a whole, each of the fifteen Union Republics should be represented, but eventually pressed only the case of Ukraine and Belorussia—conveyed to the Soviet public real engagement with the new organization, while the key role of the Security Council and the USSR's permanent membership and veto power within it prevented the issue's souring the atmosphere.[61] Tensions between the Allies seemed altogether secondary alongside the profound satisfaction of Germany's surrender and occupation. The Soviet press naturally celebrated victory as essentially that of the Red Army, and in its treatment of international relations emphasized above all the spectacular rise in the Soviet Union's international status. But the portrayal of relations with the western powers was sufficiently benign to feed expectations of relative postwar harmony.

Popular attitudes

The following party report of questions being raised in the Penza region in May 1945 conveys the way in which the fluid international situation was interwoven with uncertainty, impatience and excitement about demobilization, the possible repeal of rigid labour legislation forbidding unauthorized changing of jobs, the abolition of rationing and the restoration of the eight-hour day.

Document 107 | **Questions asked at meetings of collective farmers, manual workers and white-collar workers, and at lectures and conversations in the Penza *oblast'* after 9 May 1945— note from the Penza CPSU *oblast'* committee to the CPSU CC**

19 May 1945

Top secret

1. If the war is over, why do reports of battles keep coming from the Soviet Information Office?
2. When will front-line soldiers be sent home?
3. What sort of government will be set up in Germany?

---

61 R. Crockatt, *The Fifty Years War: The United States and the Soviet Union in World Politics, 1941–1991* (London 1995), places the negotiations in context, pp. 39–63.

4. Where is Hitler now and are the reports of his death true?
5. What are our present relations with Japan and might we find ourselves at war against her?
6. We don't need to wage war against Japan, but we should make Japan cede Port Arthur and the Chinese railway to us.
7. Why has the Soviet government insisted that just two Union republics—Belorussia and Ukraine—participate in the San Francisco conference?
8. Will Germany be divided up into a number of smaller states?
9. After the war will we be prosecuted for leaving an enterprise without authorization?
10. If the war is over, why are we still being called up for the army and mobilized for factory work?
11. When will we be allowed free access to the liberated areas?
12. Will those imprisoned for desertion from their enterprises be freed, and will there be an amnesty?
13. Will captured machinery be given to the collective farms to use?
14. Will agricultural specialists soon be demobilized?
15. When will shops selling manufactured goods at commercial prices be opened in our area?
16. Will women with children be allowed a shorter working day?
17. Will wounded soldiers of the Patriotic War be offered resort holidays on a mass scale?
18. Will some war-work factories soon be returned to civilian production?
19. When will the rationing system be abolished?
20. When will the war tax be abolished?
21. When will an eight-hour working day be introduced?
22. Will we get holidays and when will we get compensation for unused holidays?
23. Why have comrades Molotov and Kuznetsov left the San Francisco conference to come back to Moscow?
24. When will workers mobilized for transport work be demobilized?
25. Will students at technical colleges and higher education institutions be demobilized?
26. Will mothers of children under 4 be allowed not to work?
27. Will servicemen be given leave?
28. Where are they sending German prisoners and will they be sent back to Germany?
29. Why wasn't Poland invited to the San Francisco conference?
30. How are things proceeding at the San Francisco conference?

[Source: RGASPI, fond 17, opis' 88, delo 429, pp. 12–13.]

Expectations of a less repressive and more open order as victory and peace became foreseeable were most pronounced and most openly articulated among members of the intelligentsia. The war raised both the prestige and the confidence of scientists and technical specialists. Self-evidently of critical importance, and overwhelmingly committed, to the war effort, they enjoyed new respect from the regime and workers alike. They gained greater scope for taking initiatives, formulating proposals, solving problems and collaborating with each other with only light party supervision. The war's effect on the role of the cultural intelligentsia was analogous.[62] With war news tightly censored and official sources of information and commentary as closely controlled as ever, they played a central role in articulating the horror, hatred, hopes, patriotism and courage the war evoked. Patriotic creative artists, journalists and academics gained relatively free rein, and a new dispensation seemed to be heralded by the popular response to films and plays, symphonies and works of history, and novels and poems which conveyed the common ordeal without much reference to Marxism–Leninism.

Some saw the impact of the war in terms of a regime that had learned that it must and could trust the population; others in terms of a population that had earned a reward; yet others, in terms of a new bond, a common ordeal, and a yearning, shared by officials and party activists as well as workers and peasants, for less coercion and violence. Regular reports by the NKVD on public attitudes captured the different elements that fed a widespread expectation that there would be no reversion to the harshest features of the pre-war years. The following is a police account of the mood among the cultural intelligentsia—teachers, academics, writers—in Khar'kov in the months after its final liberation in August 1943. It records both the new patriotism and greater legitimization of the Soviet system born out of the war, and the expectation of greater democratization, openness and tolerance.

Document 108 | '... the government must change its policies'—
from a report on the mood among the intelligentsia of
Khar'kov in 1944

... Some of the old intelligentsia were happy to see the Germans at first, but the shooting of Jews, forcing young people to work in Germany, restrictions of all kinds, evictions from flats, requisitioning of furniture and property, public executions... meant that that section of the intelligentsia began to react differently to the Germans—with suspicion and hostility.

... There was a quip going round town, 'What comrade Stalin couldn't do in 24 years the Germans have done in one.' Fedorovsky, a lecturer, said, 'I was never

---

62 Barber and Harrison, *Soviet Home Front*, pp. 104–12.

a great patriot, but unless you've lived through the occupation, you can't really appreciate Soviet power. . . for a while all we got from the Germans were a kilo each of damp rye and a few beetroot and salted cucumbers a month. And now bread, just imagine, real bread, and so soon! Will we really be riding in trams again and have water and light? Will our shoulders and hands really be relieved of the burden and can we start looking human again?'

However, the absence of information about the life and struggles of the Soviet people as well as fascist lies and demagoguery have produced politically unhealthy attitudes among certain groups of intellectuals. . .

Here, for example, is the reasoning of Seligeev, a lecturer at Khar'kov university (a former member of the CPSU who left 'because of disagreements with Party policy'): 'We are at the beginning of a major political and ideological shift. . . The best thoughts and ideas of Western culture not only in the scientific and technological sphere, but also in the moral and political, are bound to percolate through to us and imprint themselves on our lives.

'The cornerstone of this. . . restructuring will be the rejection of implementing any social ideas by force of arms, a general penetration of real democracy with its complete tolerance of all varieties and currents of ideology and world view, and the triumph of freedom and humanity in the best western European sense of the words.'

Professor Tereshchenko thinks: 'After all we've been through, the government must change its policies. Serious changes must take place—and are already doing so—in the political life of the country, such as agreements with capitalist Britain and the USA, the dissolution of Comintern, the separation of educational institutions into male and female, the creation of a Church committee, private trade, etc. These changes must go further, especially towards a greater democratization of the life of the country. . .'

[Source: RGASPI, fond 17, opis' 125, delo 181, pp. 51, 52.]

During 1944, clashes over issues of censorship and the control of cultural and artistic expression began to increase. The regime became uneasy at the new assertiveness among the cultural intelligentsia. A number of prominent writers were publicly criticized and found their work rejected for publication. However, as is indicated by the following anxious NVKD report, sent by Beria's second-in-command at the NKVD, Merkulov, to Zhdanov, responsible for cultural matters, the experience of the war encouraged greater willingness to resist. There was a measure of confidence among intellectuals and students that the efforts of the new chief censor, Polikarpov, to re-establish tight Central Committee control over public discourse would fail and that, as the war drew to a close, the tide was with those seeking greater freedom of expression.

Document 109 | **Letter from Merkulov to A.A. Zhdanov, CPSU CC Secretary, on the political attitudes and utterances of Soviet writers**

Top secret   31 October 1944

... According to information coming to the USSR People's Commissariat of State Security from our agents... criticism of the politically harmful works of Sel'vinsky, Aseev, Zoshchenko, Dovzhenko, Chukovsky and Fedin has provoked... mainly hostile reactions and responses from the above persons with a wide resonance in the literary world in general.

The poet N.N. Aseev... has declared, 'My last booklet has not been published. I was summoned to the CC for it and told off for not using it to foment hatred of the enemy... I did, of course, agree with them, but I personally think they're wrong. I didn't see any point in arguing with them. We must learn to shut up for five years or so and teach ourselves not to get exasperated. Still, the young are with us... With the demobilization people will be coming back who've seen everything. These people will bring with them a new measure of things...' Chukovsky defines the situation in Soviet literature from a hostile viewpoint, '... The CC openly admits that the situation in all areas of life except literature is clear to them. They want to make us writers, like everybody else, perform a service. A stupid and limited person, Sergeant-Major Polikarpov, has been appointed to make us do it... Not a single manuscript can be accepted without permission. Everything has to be ratified by the CC, so editorial boards have just turned into government registries. I really long for the destruction of Hitler and the collapse of his crazy ideas. After the collapse of Nazi despotism the democratic world will come face to face with Soviet despotism. Let's wait and see...'

The writer V. Shklovsky says, 'They're recruiting people for the literary world who are willing to write to order. Fresh thinking is in a sorry state... We're so sick of getting slated, intimidated and banned that we're not scared any more, and there's an unspoken agreement that we take no notice, don't react, and play no part in this farce...'

The writer L.A. Kassil' says, 'Literature's degenerated completely. The Union of Writers should be closed down immediately and writers given the opportunity to gather at each other's flats and discuss what they have written in accordance with their creative sympathies and views...'

The works of Sel'vinsky, Aseev, Zoshchenko, Chukovsky, Fedin and Dovzhenko, which are alien to Soviet ideology, have met with a favourable response among students of the Union of Writers' Institute, who are rejecting the principles of Socialist Realism and trying to work out 'new theories' of the development of literature and art.

Merkulov, USSR People's Commissar for State Security

[Source: *Rodina*, No. 1, 1992, p. 96.]

The assertive tone among writers, and the anticipation of new openness and scope for constructive criticism, was by no means restricted to non-party members. Many of those within the party expected communists to take the lead in articulating popular needs and legitimate concerns, and within closed party meetings frankly denounced evidence of military arrogance, party corruption and indifference to abject poverty. The following report from the local party secretary of the Krasnaya Presnya district party committee, in Moscow, describes the outspoken criticisms of M.S. Shaginyan, and the general endorsement of her dismay at the presence of callous attitudes within the party. As the evident nervousness of the party secretary in making his report to his boss suggests, however, by summer 1945 among party officials higher up the ladder patience with dissent was wearing thin.

Document 110 | '… this is what we writers should be writing about'—
from a note on a speech by M.S. Shaginyan, sent to G.M.
Popov, secretary of the Moscow city and Moscow *oblast'*
committees of the CPSU

23 August 1945

… During the discussion at a Party meeting, M.S. Shaginyan, CPSU member since 1942, came out with the following, 'Can I have your attention, please!? I want to tell you some terrible things! I've been in the Urals, where 1,500 workers rioted because of bad conditions. The CPSU district and *oblast'* committees found out about this only when they turned up in the middle of the riot. The factory manager had not turned up at the factory for two months. After the riot he allotted 2 million rubles for improvements. Invalids of the Great Patriotic War are being fed swill. They are starving. There are a lot of kids working in the factories, where they're exploited and worked to exhaustion… I've been in the Altay and it's just awful there! *Oblast'* and district committees are getting fat, feeding their faces with workers' rations while the workers go hungry, walking about like fatigued, exhausted shadows. Where are Lenin's teachings, where's the Stalin Constitution? I was on my way to Kuybyshev. I'll show you the appalling things the generals are getting up to. Some general and another officer came into a second-class carriage. While they were checking people's papers, they saw a young woman and asked her to give up her seat for the general. I ask you, is this right? There was a wounded lieutenant-colonel next to her, who gave up his seat for the general. While such things are going on, we are writing masses of paeans. This is what we should be looking at, this is what we writers should be writing about.'

Shaginyan's outrageous anti-Party speech met with approval rather than condemnation among a certain (albeit small) number of communists, who applauded her.

Lev Nikulin spoke after Shaginyan, but made no comment on Shaginyan's speech.

Comrade Zorich responded sympathetically to Shaginyan's speech. . .

In all, eight people spoke at the meeting. Most of them spoke in general rather than concrete terms, without touching on the life of the local Party organization. All this I bring to your attention, Georgiy Mikhaylovich.

N.B. The speeches have not been reproduced in full. They were not taken down in shorthand. With your permission, I shall tell you in detail about the Party organization in person.

Likovenkov, Secretary of the Krasnaya Presnya district CPSU committee

[Source: RGASPI, fond 17, opis´ 125, delo 310, pp. 28–30.]

12

Repression

These expectations were to be dashed. Though the cultural, social, economic and administrative rupture caused by the war called into question much about the pre-war order, there was much about that order that it reinforced. It seemed, in the eyes of the Stalinist leadership, to confirm key features of the view of the world they had developed during the 1930s, and to validate the repressive political instincts and political methods they had forged before the war. Barbarossa had apparently demonstrated how right they had been to view foreign powers with deepest suspicion, to be ever alert to domestic sedition and 'fifth-column' activity, and to maximize official secrecy. It had placed a premium on swift, pre-emptive steps to forestall any potential opposition and on maintaining close surveillance of the population.

The role of the NKVD and NKGB

As before the war, the leadership continued to treat the NKVD as the key agency on which political control depended. In April 1943 it was split into two parts, the NKVD and the NKGB (People's Commissariat of State Security). This reflected the increased importance of its military role and its rapid expansion during the war. It continued to have responsibility for the GULAG, including the influx of Axis POWs, and the semi-autonomous economic base which this forced labour provided gave it powerful leverage vis-à-vis the commissariats and regional authorities. It was charged with counter-espionage abroad at a time when the stakes could not have been higher.[63] It was responsible for counteracting panic, and monitoring party

---

63 Under the reorganization of 1943, military counter-intelligence was for a period subordinated to the Red Army.

and Komsomol efforts to maintain morale—seeking to ensure demoralization or disaffection did not spread from wounded and retreating soldiers. It
oversaw punishment battalions in the army and ruthlessly repressed civilians
charged with subverting the war effort. It played a role establishing contact
with and co-ordinating partisans beyond the front lines. And within the
NKVD, despite rising expectations elsewhere, the definition of suspect and
anti-party activity changed relatively little. Autonomous initiatives, protests,
criticisms and expressions of discontent which became commonplace and
were widely accepted even among party members were here viewed much
more severely. And though its grip had been shaken by the initial disruption
of the war, after the supreme crisis of Stalingrad the NKVD gradually sought
to tighten its control.

In NKVD eyes, the developments that enthused reform-minded intelligentsia, workers and peasants were ominous: the partial rehabilitation of
religion; the erosion of the authority of collective farm managers; the heightened level of consciousness of and contact with the outside world, be it in
terms of military news, POWs, Lend–Lease or the popularity of those
western films whose distribution was permitted. The dangers were made
even greater by the variety of ways in which party discipline had slackened,
undermined by the rapid admission of new members with minimal screening
or political instruction, and by the disruption of party organization and lines
of communication amidst massive population shifts. The fact that Moscow
now depended so much on local initiative for growing and distributing food,
securing fuel and maximizing munitions production greatly increased the
discretion in the hands of local officials, military as well as civilian. This, too,
from the viewpoint of the secret police, made it much more difficult to
prevent the erosion and circumvention of official policy and to maintain
tight boundaries around public debate and discussion.

The following excerpt from an NKGB report of May 1943 illustrates the
conflicting attitudes among the authorities. In Kaluga, near the front, the
army's political directorate had agreed to allow the local church to sponsor
a military hospital. The clergy, according to the report, had seized the opportunity, vigorously raising money (which Stalin had sanctioned earlier in the
year), organizing entertainment for the wounded men, and throwing their
energies into this new role. The fact that the posters purchased to adorn the
walls of the hospital were of party leaders suggests that, far from providing
surrogate opposition, the local religious leaders were closely associating their
efforts with the authorities. But the implications—the failure of the regime
and the widening scope for public activity by the Church—seemed intolerable to the secret police, as the curt conclusion to the report indicates.

Document 111 | **From the USSR Deputy People's Commissar for State Security to the Secretary of the CPSU CC, A.S. Shcherbakov**

2 May 1943

I have been informed by the NKVD directorate of the Tula district that in the city of Kaluga, Pitirim, Bishop of the Orthodox Church, suggested the Church adopt military hospital No. 2751/FEP No. 1 as sponsors. Having agreed this with Major Medved'ev, head of the hospital's political section, and the political directorate of the Western Front, the management of the hospital accepted the Bishop's offer.

Thereafter, in its capacity as sponsor, the Church council collected 50,000 rubles, with which it bought 500 presents for the wounded. With this money they also acquired posters, slogans and portraits of Party and Government leaders for the hospital, and hired accordionists and barbers. The church choir organized two concerts of Russian folk songs and songs by Soviet composers in the hospital.

On being informed of this, the NKGB of the USSR has taken measures not to permit any further attempts by churchmen to enter into direct relations with the managements of hospitals and the wounded under the pretext of sponsorship.

Kobulov

[Source: RGASPI, fond 17, opis' 125, delo 188, p. 13.]

Potentially much more explosive were instances of local officials failing to implement directives on collective farm work norms and in some cases failing to prevent open protest against the very continuation of collective farms. As we have seen, the imposition of forced collectivization at the end of the 1920s, virtually eliminating independent household farming by the end of the 1930s, had involved coercion and upheaval on a mass scale, ensuring that morale and motivation on collective farms was desperately low and that the peasants' energy was poured into the small household plots the state had reluctantly permitted them to work.[64] Conditions and the recompense for *kolkhoz* work, pitiful enough in the late 1930s, had deteriorated even further during the war.[65] With food the supreme concern, and a vigorous black market evident, the urge to devote effort instead to tending the household plot became overwhelming, and in many parts of the country, peasants were given much greater latitude to expand their household plots, albeit while being subjected to steep increases in agricultural taxation and to compulsory

---

64 See Volume I, Chapter 12.
65 See A. Nove, 'Soviet Peasantry in World War II', in Linz, *Impact of World War 2*, pp. 77–90, for a lucid account.

deliveries from their own produce. The upshot was to give currency to the idea that collective farming was ceasing to be sacrosanct and to feed the expectation that, by way of acknowledging the peasantry's wartime efforts, the collective and state farms would be disbanded once war was over. The following report conveys the NKGB's alarm at peasants' demonstrating against collective farming in a village in Penza *oblast'*. It emphasizes their prayers and use of icons, and seeks to portray the protest as religious in inspiration.

Document 112 | **'... thirty active believers organized a procession round the village with icons'—special communiqué from the Penza *oblast'* NKGB administration**

5 June 1943

Top secret

On 30 May in the village of Nikolo–Azyasi (Mokshin district of Penza *oblast'*) a group of about thirty active believers organized a procession round the village with icons and hymn-singing, accompanied by shouts of anti-Soviet slogans, 'Down with collective and state farms! Let everyone have his own farm and we'll be better off!'

After they had passed through the village and gathered a crowd of over 1,000 people, they organized a prayer meeting for absolution.

While this was going on, some of them shouted at passing collective farmers, 'If there were no collectives, you wouldn't be suffering so much!'

Preliminary investigations have established that the organizers of the above-mentioned mob were T.E. Kolchina, O.A. Potapova and M.F. Firsova-Ageeva.

The above persons have been arrested and an investigation is under way, the results of which will be conveyed to you later.

Acting deputy director of the NKGB administration for Penza *oblast'* Major of state security Davydov
Director of the 2nd division of the NKGB administration for Penza *oblast'* Lt.-Col. of state security Klimashev

[Source: RGASPI, fond 17, opis' 125, delo 181, p. 13.]

Secret police anxiety about the erosion of political control over the population was compounded by fears, shared by Stalin and the leadership, about the level of hostility to communist rule revealed in parts of the USSR temporarily subject to German occupation. The abundant if unquantified evidence that in some areas the German invaders had initially been positively welcomed by Soviet citizens planted seeds of suspicion deep in the leadership's psyche. In the course of the war that mistrust was nurtured by everything that went wrong: by the failure of soldiers and civilians to halt further German advances, by army units failing to fight to the last man, by conquered civilians seeming so slow to mount partisan resistance. Moreover, when local underground party committees at least nominally in charge of partisan activity were unable to satisfy the demands emanating from Moscow, they all too readily resorted to crass, sweeping accusations about supposed connivance and collaboration among those they were meant to be galvanizing for resistance. The groups most vulnerable to these charges were small non-Russian minorities. From Moscow's vantage point, accusations against such minorities were credible: Stalin's leadership had demonstrated in the 1930s its inclination to view minorities ethnically linked to groups outside Soviet borders as prime suspects of disloyalty. Nazi propaganda about the supposed support they enjoyed from some minorities seemed to corroborate the accusations levelled by local party committees. So, too, did German efforts to exploit the hopes of émigré minority-nationalist leaders, holding out the promise of concessions, religious toleration and autonomy in exchange for support against Soviet partisans and troops.

Mass deportation in the Crimea

The two areas under German occupation where wholesale denunciation of national minorities led ultimately to drastic action by the NKVD were the Crimea and the Caucasus. In both cases, underground party officials, playing upon the fears and prejudices of the leadership, triggered the accusation eventually taken up by Moscow. The following denunciation of the Crimean Tatars, sent to the central headquarters of the partisan movement, contains many of the key ingredients: plausible detail in terms of named villages and the armed strength of specific hostile units; undifferentiated condemnation along racial grounds; emphasis on the supposed role of deserters from the Red Army, ex-kulaks returning from their period of exile following collectivization, and committed nationalists.

Document 113 | '... the attitude of a certain section of the Tatar population to the partisan movement...'—from a report
from the Crimean regional committee of the CPSU
to the central headquarters of the partisan movement

7 July 1942

The Russian and Greek population express sympathy for the partisans and assist them; the Bulgarian population also has a loyal attitude to the partisans.

One particularly negative influence deserves special mention—the attitude of a certain section of the Tatar population to the partisan movement. . .

In all the Tatar mountain villages the German commands have formed volunteer anti-partisan detachments from among the Tatars, headed by German or Romanian instructors. All those joining these detachments are fitted out with Romanian or German uniforms and armed with weapons seized after the retreat of the Red Army, as well as machine guns and mortars. . . These volunteer detachments do patrol duty, and immediately raise the alarm as soon as any partisans appear. The villagers of Yeni–Sala, Ülü-Üzen, Üsküt, Baksan, Küçük–Üzen, Şelen, Voron, Kouş, Beşüi, Arpat, Ortalan, and others have shown themselves to be particularly hostile.

In the village of Kouş there is a 345-man volunteer detachment of Tatar deserters and local inhabitants. Kouş is the place where counter-revolutionary Tatar detachments are being raised. From the very start of partisan activity in the Crimea this village has been a supplier of guides, traitors and agents provocateurs to the Germans and Romanians.

Under German orders, Osman Hasanov, the headman of Kouş, has been robbing those loyal to Soviet power. . . On 24 March the Kouş punitive detachment completely burned down the village of Lakı for involvement in helping the partisans. Savage reprisals against the village inhabitants were taken, in which many women and children were shot. . .

Provisionally, we can say the following concerning what we know about the behaviour of a certain part of the Tatar population.

Fascist demagoguery, deceit and bribery have played a large part. The Germans are promising them 'autonomy' and 'Crimea for the Tatars'.

1. When our troops started retreating (November 1941), the Germans started arming the Tatar population from the mountain villages, stirring them up to form self-defence groups, supposedly to defend the villages from banditry and looting, because 'Soviet power has gone and we don't have time to bother with internal matters'. These 'self-defence' groups were then put into barracks and obliged to carry out the orders of German commanders.

It should be noted that, when our troops retreated (November 1941), there were many deserters from the Red Army among the Tatars, and it was these the Germans used in the first instance.

2. At the same time kulaks and nationalist elements, who had been repressed by the organs of Soviet power, were returning to the Crimea, to their former places of residence, on the expiry of their sentences, especially during the period from the end of 1940 to the beginning of 1941. . . As we are now establishing through the partisans, they were the material used by the Germans as their representatives [as headmen, police chiefs etc.—[original] ed.]. For example, in the villages of Baksan, Kouş and Yeni–Sala, these enemies evicted anybody sympathetic to the partisans and forced many to work for the enemy out of fear.

3. Inflaming national discord. When allocating gardens, vineyards, tobacco plantations, livestock, and other property to the fighters in these anti-partisan militias,

the Germans confiscate them from the population of non-Tatar nationality and allot them to Tatars. . .

[Source: *Krym v period Velikoy Otechestvennoy voyny. 1941–1945. Sbornik dokumentov i materialov* (Simferopol' 1973), pp. 227–30.]

The accusations levelled by local underground committees by no means went unchallenged. In the following memorandum of a year later, for example, P.R. Yarmol'sky, head of the underground in the Crimean *oblast'*, gives a much more differentiated picture, emphasizing the presence of pro-Soviet activists among the Tatars. He specifically named two of the villages condemned in the report of 1942, Baksan and Küçük–Üzen, where, he said, although all the villagers knew about the partisans, not one gave in to German pressure to break their trust.

Document 114 | **'We did have representatives from the Tatar villages as well. . .'—from a report by P.R. Yarmol'sky, Head of the *oblast'* underground party centre, to V.S. Bulatov, CPSU *oblast'* secretary**

3 November 1943

On 29 October the Germans issued an order for the 'voluntary' evacuation of the population from the Crimea. We sent our representatives out to the villages. . . to get the people to go off into the forests with the partisans. . . A whole string of villages did so, and everybody, young and old alike, went off with their livestock and chattels into the forest. . . We did have representatives from the Tatar villages as well, even from Baksan. [Baksan was a village which the Crimean *oblast'* committee of the CPSU considered to be particularly hostile to the partisans in 1942—[original] ed.] But, so far, few of the Tatar population have come to us. Everything is still undecided. . .

[Source: *Krym v period Velikoy Otechestvennoy voyny. 1941–1945. Sbornik dokumentov i materialov* (Simferopol' 1973), pp. 295–96.]

Document 115 | **'. . . nobody betrayed them. . .'—from a report by P.R. Yarmol'sky, Head of the *oblast'* underground party centre, to V.S. Bulatov, CPSU *oblast'* secretary**

17 November 1943

The fascists have worked out a system for struggling against us. . .
3. They organize meetings of peasants in the villages to get them to betray the partisans. At one such meeting in the village of Küçük–Üzen [Küçük–Üzen was a village

which the Crimean *oblast'* committee of the CPSU considered to be particularly hostile to the partisans in 1942—[original] ed.], run by a Romanian captain, there were two of our partisans there, and one of them was even acting as the captain's interpreter at the meeting. All the villagers knew about the presence of our partisans, but nobody betrayed them. . . In the same village the headman sent a note to the shepherds, telling them to let him have one of the sheep. The shepherds refused, saying, 'Kurt-Umerov, the senior political officer, has told us not to do anything without informing him, so we can't let you have a sheep without his say-so.' (As you know, Kurt-Umerov's our representative in the Alushta district.)

[Source: *Krym v period Velikoy Otechestvennoy voyny. 1941–1945. Sbornik dokumentov i materialov* (Simferopol' 1973), p. 306.]

As Soviet forces drove the Germans from the Crimea, however, and the party's authority was reasserted, it was the blanket denunciation of the Tatars that prevailed. One element at work was Moscow's concern lest Turkey play upon the supposed Turkic sympathies of Muslim tribesmen. The fact that, during the early stages of occupation, Germany had sought to use the notion as a bridge to draw Turkey in on the Third Reich's side gave it added credence in Soviet eyes. In this sense, what followed was a direct echo of the pre-war, 'prophylactic' ethnic cleansing of the borderlands.[66] In summer 1944, Beria oversaw preparations for the wholesale deportation of the entire Tatar population. In the telegram he sent Stalin seeking approval, he set out the timetable, estimated the numbers involved (recent calculations suggest the number uprooted exceeded 190,000[67]), and reported the agreement of the Uzbekistan party secretary that they be resettled there.

Document 116 | 'Considering the treacherous actions of the Crimean Tatars...'—from a telegram from L. Beria to Stalin

10 May 1944

. . . Considering the treacherous actions of the Crimean Tatars against the Soviet people and in view of the undesirability of the Crimean Tatars' continuing to inhabit a border region of the Soviet Union, the NKVD submits for your consideration a draft resolution of the State Committee for Defence on the evacuation of all Tatars from the territory of the Crimea.

We consider it expedient to resettle the Crimean Tatars as special deportees in districts of the Uzbek SSR, to be used for work in agriculture—on collective and

---

66 See Volume I, Chapter 15.
67 Tolz, 'New Information', p. 168.

state farms, as well as in industry and transport. The question of resettling the Tatars in the Uzbek SSR has been agreed with comrade Yusupov, Secretary of the Uzbekistan CPSU.

According to preliminary data, the current population in the Crimea is 140–160,000. The evacuation operation will begin on 20–21 May and finish on 1 July. I enclose the text of the draft resolution and await your decision.

L. Beria, USSR People's Commissar for Internal Affairs

[Source: GARF, fond 9401 S, opis' 2, delo 65, p. 132.]

Mass deportation in the Caucasus

The condemnation of minority nationalities in the Caucasus followed a very similar trajectory.[68] Again, distrust was nurtured in Moscow by German attempts to mobilize support, manipulating nationalist leaders and pursuing a relatively lenient occupation policy: unlike elsewhere, forced labour was not introduced and freedom was given for the disbandment of collective farms. A case in point is the fate of the Balkars. German policy during their brief and violent occupation of the North Caucasian Autonomous Republic of Kabardino–Balkar was to give prominent roles to émigré nationalists and propose a Turkish protectorate uniting the Balkars with their fellow Muslims in the neighbouring Karachay Autonomous Republic. Against that background, Moscow listened with a sympathetic ear when some local party activists chose to make scapegoats of Balkars or at the very least laboured the ethnic identity of the minority who actively collaborated with the Germans: all too easily their accusations mutated into charges against the 39,000-strong Muslim people as a whole. The following report was written by a senior political commissar in the Red Army soon after the German capture of the Autonomous Republic and its capital Nal'chik, which fell late in October 1942. It claimed that locals had joined bands of 'brigands' and in some cases worked hand-in-glove with the Germans; that it was not only deserters, ex-kulaks and criminals who had done so, but workers and local party activists and officials; and that one such gang had captured a Soviet anti-aircraft gun and sought to turn the gunners against the Red Army.

---

68 For the now classic path-breaking account, see the work of the émigré Soviet historian A.M. Nekrich, *The Punished Peoples: The Deportation and Fate of Soviet Minorities at the End of the Second World War* (New York 1978), pp. 36–65.

Document 117 | '... the brigands even went so far as to capture a 772 anti-aircraft gun...'—a report from Colonel Osadchiy, head of the political section of the 37th Army

No earlier than 16 November 1942

With the enemy's advance and the capture of districts of the Kabardino–Balkar ASSR and the town of Nal'chik, various gangs have become active. There is considerable evidence that some of the partisan detachments organized earlier and some of the Soviet and Party activists joined forces with the brigands once they had been given weapons.

Owing to the sclerosis of the Soviet and Party apparatus in a number of districts and individual *oblasti*, former key workers have gone off to join the gangs. I also gather that the Germans have appointed the former Deputy Procurator of the republic, who went off to join a gang back in August, as Minister of Kabardino–Balkaria. The chairman of Nal'chik town soviet left the town when it was taken, but later returned to Nal'chik and, apparently, is now burgermeister of the town.

Gang activity is most marked in the villages of central Balkaria. As soon as army staff left the village of Mukol on 16 November, the brigands came out into the open, captured a number of mountain settlements, fired upon some of our units and terrorized the pro-Soviet section of the population. Their emergence has been heralded by the burning and destruction of state and public buildings erected in the years of Soviet power, they have stolen state property, and have also seized part of the property, foodstuffs and vehicles belonging to units of the 11th section of the NKVD. Fully aware of their superiority, the brigands even went so far as to capture a 772 anti-aircraft gun with the intention of forcing the gunners at gunpoint to turn their fire against our units. This failed because our soldiers refused to obey the brigands' orders. Two Red Army men managed to escape the brigands' retribution. I gather that their armed offensive has been accompanied by the coming together of all sorts of diverse elements: criminals, kulaks and Red Army deserters, Kabardins and Balkars. According to preliminary estimates, the brigand group in the Balkaria district totals more than 200 people. Moreover, part of the population, while not active in organized gangs, has been providing the brigands with all kinds of assistance.

The re-emergence of banditry in a series of districts of Kabardino–Balkaria is the result of the poor situation in Party and political work among the local population in the pre-war period and even more so during the war. Hostile elements, agitating against Soviet power, have won over part of the local population which was loyal to Soviet power, but which has followed the hostile elements owing to the lack of political work among them.

The sclerosis of Party and Soviet organs in a series of districts, and even in individual *oblasti*, has led to a position where those who had got themselves into leading posts have carried out anti-state activity and then gone off to join the brigands.

Throughout the Patriotic War, the organs of the NKVD have not done enough to combat the emergence of brigandage. They failed to wage a decisive struggle against open brigandage as the enemy was approaching districts of Kabardino–Balkaria, and in particular against counter-revolutionary and brigand armed actions as the enemy was entering the territory of Kabardino–Balkaria.

[Source: *Voenno-istoricheskiy zhurnal*, No. 8, 1991, p. 41.]

In February 1944, a year after the liberation of the Autonomous Republic, Beria, evidently on his own initiative rather than on that of Stalin, drew up an indictment against the whole Balkar people. He repackaged the charges associated with the period of occupation: the supposed mass collaboration, the role of the émigré leaders, the proposed fusion with the Karachay Autonomous Region (the Karachay had been deported wholesale three months earlier), and the episode of the gun. He urged Stalin's approval, recommending that the deportation be tacked onto the agenda of the troops already preparing the larger operation of expelling two other Caucasian peoples, the Chechens and the Ingush, from the neighbouring Autonomous Republic.

Document 118 | **'I could… make all the necessary arrangements on the spot for the removal of the Balkars'—from a telegram from L. Beria to Stalin**

22 February 1944

Top secret

I have familiarized myself with the materials on the behaviour of the Balkars both during the advance of the German fascist troops on the Caucasus and after they had been driven out. When the Germans were breaking through the front lines near Rostov in 1942, anti-Soviet elements in Balkaria intensified their hostile work behind the Red Army lines and created gangs and insurgent groups. The situation was particularly difficult as units of the 37th Army were retreating through the passes in the Caucasus mountain range, through Balkaria. In the Cherek region the Balkars disarmed an army subunit. . . They killed the officers and stole an artillery piece. One gang was headed by the former chairman of the executive committee of the district Soviet. . . At the bidding of the Germans and the émigrés they had brought with them, Shokmanov and Kemmetov, the Balkars made a deal with the Karachaevtsy to unite Balkaria and Karachay.

In 1942–1943 alone 1,227 people were arrested for anti-Soviet activity and banditism, among them 186 communists and Komsomol members. 362 people fled Balkaria with the Germans.

In connection with the forthcoming final expulsion of the Chechens and Ingush, I think it essential that we use some of our spare troops and Chekists to remove the

Balkars from the northern Caucasus so as to get it finished by 15–20 March before the forests get foliage cover. There are 40,900 Balkars, the overwhelming majority of whom live in four administrative districts, situated in the gorges of the main Caucasus range, with a total area of 503,000 hectares, of which about 300,000 are hayfields, pasture and forest.

If you are in agreement, I could, before my return to Moscow, make all the necessary arrangements on the spot for the removal of the Balkars.

I await your orders.

L. Beria

[Source: GARF, fond 9401s, opis' 2, delo 64, pp. 163, 163 ob.]

The same day, Beria reported to Stalin on the expulsion of the Chechens and the Ingush. This was the largest of the 'operations' in the Caucasus, the total number uprooted approaching half a million. The Chechens in particular were viewed in Moscow as inveterately hostile to Soviet rule. In the atmosphere of 1944, the fact that the capital of the Chechen–Ingush Autonomous Republic, Grozny, had been furiously and successfully defended against German invasion weighed as nothing against the belief that the level of resistance to Soviet rule in 1942–43 was higher than it was anywhere else. People were violently herded into cattle trucks and, after travelling in inhuman conditions and suffering a terribly high mortality rate, forced to live in 'special settlements' marked out in Kazakhstan, Central Asia and Siberia. As in the case of all four of the 'punished peoples' of the northern Caucasus, the Kalmyks further north, as well as the Tatars, Bulgarians, Greeks and Armenians uprooted from the Crimea, and the Turks, Kurds, Khemshils and Azerbaijanis from Georgia, party and state officials of the selected nationalities were deported along with the rest, albeit in marginally less bestial conditions. The very names of damned republics as well as of the villages of the condemned peoples were erased from the map. The blanket categorization in ethnic terms, in complete defiance of Marxist theory and class analysis, could hardly have been more brazen.

Document 119 | **'The expulsion begins at dawn...'—
from a telegram from Beria to Stalin**

Special file, 22 February 1944

Top secret

In order to carry out the operation to expel the Chechens and Ingush successfully, in line with your instructions, the following has been carried out in addition to the Cheka and military measures:

1. Molaev, the chairman of the Sovnarkom of the Chechen–Ingush ASSR, was

informed of the government decision to expel the Chechens and Ingush and of the reasons underlying that decision.

After receiving this information from me, Molaev burst into tears, but then pulled himself together and promised to carry out all the tasks which will be required of him in connection with the expulsion. Subsequently, in Grozny he and nine leading cadres from among the Chechens and Ingush were selected and summoned. They were informed of the expulsion of the Chechens and Ingush and of the reasons for it.

. . . We assigned forty Chechen and Ingush Party and Soviet personnel from the Republic to the twenty-four regions with the task of choosing two or three people for agitation work in each settlement from among the local activists.

We held talks with B. Arsanov, A.G. Yandarov and A. Gaysumov, the most influential spiritual figures in Checheno–Ingushetia. They were called upon to provide assistance through the mullahs and other local authorities.

The expulsion begins at dawn. On 23 February districts will be sealed off to prevent the population's leaving the territory of their settlements. The population will be called to a meeting, one part will be sent to collect their things, while the remainder will be disarmed and sent to despatch points. I think that the operation to expel the Chechens and Ingush will be carried out successfully.

L. Beria

[Source: GARF, fond 9401s, opis' 2, delo 64, pp. 161–62.]

Five days later Beria proudly reported his mission virtually accomplished and the process of handing over the vacated territory to new settlers well in hand. He pronounced that 'the operation [had] proceeded in an organized manner without incident or resistance'. Beria's ice-cold indifference to the violence, bewilderment and suffering involved was matched only by his blindness to the determination of the victims and their descendants one day to return home, and the capacity of the Chechens, in particular, to defy the will of Moscow.

Document 120 | **'I am reporting on the results of the operation to expel the Chechens and Ingush...'—
from a telegram from Beria to Stalin**

Special file, 29 February 1944

Top secret

I am reporting on the results of the operation to expel the Chechens and Ingush. The expulsion was begun on 23 February in most districts, with the exception of settlements high in the mountains.

By 29 February 478,479 people, including 91,250 Ingush, had been evicted and loaded onto special trains. 177 trains have been loaded up, and 159 of them have already set off to the new places of settlement.

Trains were despatched today containing the former leading cadres and religious authorities of Checheno–Ingushetia who were used in carrying out the operation.

Heavy snowfall and impassable roads have meant that 6,000 Chechens from various points in the Galanchozh district have still not been expelled. The process of removing them and loading them up will be completed in two days. The operation proceeded in an organized manner, without serious cases of resistance or other incidents.

The forested areas are still being combed, where as much as a garrison of NKVD troops and an operational group of Chekists have been temporarily retained. During the preparation and implementation of the operation 2,016 persons from the anti-Soviet element among the Chechens and Ingush were arrested. 20,072 firearms were confiscated, including 4,868 rifles and 479 machine guns.

. . . The leaders of Party and Soviet bodies in Northern Ossetia, Dagestan and Georgia have already set to work taking charge of the new districts assigned to these republics.

. . . To ensure the preparation and successful execution of the operation to expel the Balkars all the necessary measures have been taken. The preparatory work will be completed by 10 March, and on 15 March the expulsion of the Balkars will take place. We are finishing our work here today, are going to Kabardino–Balkaria for one day, and from there on to Moscow.

L. Beria

[Source: GARF, fond 9401s, opis' 2, delo 64, pp. 161–62.]

Repression in Ukraine and Belorussia

These monstrous steps seemed, in NKVD eyes, to deal satisfactorily with the 'betrayal' of and 'threat' to the USSR in the Crimea and Caucasus. But analogous challenges that had emerged in other areas during German occupation could not be so summarily addressed even though in some ways they seemed more ominous still. There was clear evidence of overt and sustained anti-Soviet activity (albeit of a small minority) in western occupied areas, in the Baltic territories, Belorussia and Ukraine. Initially, here too, nationalist committees prepared to co-operate with the Germans were set up and émigré leaders hailed the new possibilities for national liberation and the dismantling of the communist order, while members of the clergy seized on the greater religious freedom permitted.[69] The hopes raised were quickly

---

69 On the interaction between religious allegiance and minority nationalism during the occupation, see W.C. Fletcher, 'The Soviet Bible Belt: World War II's Effects on Religion', in Linz, *The Impact of World War 2*, pp. 91–106.

destroyed by the racist nature of Nazi rule and the vicious contempt with which Slavs were treated. Only in 1944, once German occupation was close to collapse, did the *Wehrmacht* in desperation try to mobilize local support by giving Ukrainian and Belorussian nationalists greater scope—including belatedly sanctioning the dismantling of collective farms. But by then the advancing Red Army precluded an effective challenge to the re-establishment of Soviet power. Throughout the period of German rule there were minority currents of active hostility to the USSR among those subject to occupation. Many of these were not ideologically motivated: hostility to Soviet partisans often reflected conflict over food and scarce resources as well as terror at the reprisals threatened by the Germans. But there were prominent instances of organized anti-Soviet military activity. Best known and numerically most significant were the Ukrainian nationalist bands brought together in the course of 1942 and 1943 under the umbrella of the 'Ukrainian Insurgent Army'. Its heartland was in western Ukraine, annexed by the USSR in 1939, and at its height the UIA numbered, according to some estimates, as many as 200,000.[70] Its nationalist programme placed it formally as much at loggerheads with the Third Reich as with the USSR, but in practice most of its energy was directed against Soviet partisans and from Moscow's vantage point its activity was treason.

Document 121 | *What is the Ukrainian Insurgent Army Fighting For?—* **leaflet issued by the UIA**

August 1943

The Ukrainian Insurgent Army fights for a Ukrainian Independent Conciliar State, and for every nation to live freely in its own independent state.

The UIA fights against all imperialists and empires, because they involve one ruling nation enslaving other peoples culturally and politically and punishing them economically. For this reason the UIA fights against both the USSR and the German 'New Europe'.

We stand for:
- the destruction of the Bolshevik system of feudal exploitation in the organization of agriculture;
- large-scale industry to be national state property, small-scale industry to be co-operative and social;
- a general eight-hour working day;
- free labour and free choice of profession;
- full equality of women and men in all social rights and obligations;

---

70 Grenkevich, *Soviet Partisan Movement*, p. 134.

- compulsory secondary education;
- the all-round harmonious development of the younger generation: moral, intellectual and physical;
- free access to all humanity's scientific and cultural achievements;
- honour for the work of intellectuals;
- full security for all working people in their old age and in case of illness or disability;
- freedom of the press, of thought, persuasions, religious beliefs and world view; We are against the imposition of ideological doctrines and dogmas on society;
- full rights for national minorities to nurture and maintain their forms of national culture.

Ukrainian Insurgent Army

[Source: www.history.univ.kiev.ua/ukrbooks/doc1921_85.html]

Repression of former prisoners of war

Even more diabolical in Moscow's eyes were the national battalions—Baltic as well as Ukrainian, Belorussian and, the largest and most effective among them, Cossack—organized under German command and used against Soviet partisans. Nor was treason of this kind restricted to the national minorities. The German authorities succeeded, too, in drafting Russian POWs into supporting their occupation. The following furious appeal called down every curse upon them for their cowardice and treachery, threatening that the only way they could ever earn forgiveness was to switch their loyalty to the partisans. The fact that the appeal was signed not by a Russian but by a Belorussian party leader—the republic's party secretary, Ponomarenko, who became head of the Central Partisan Headquarters on its formation in May 1942— added to the contempt poured upon them for besmirching the heroic tradition of Russian warriors.

Document 122 | '… you and your families may be granted forgiveness by Soviet power…'—addressed to prisoners of war serving in German punishment brigades

When things got difficult, you, to save your own miserable, cowardly, selfish skins, laid down your arms and allowed yourself to be captured.

You did not fight the enemy to the last drop of blood, as required by the Oath and your duty as a warrior in the Red Army.

You violated the age-old tradition of the Russian warrior: to die yourself to save your comrade.

You besmirched the name of 'warrior', the name of a Russian man, your families, your nearest and dearest, and your friends.

You committed the gravest crime against your people.

You will bear forever the shameful mark of Judas the traitor. . .

The German occupiers are using you to kill Soviet people—your wives, children and parents.

With your help the German slave-traders are driving your brothers and parents off to Germany for slave labour.

The Germans are raping your sisters and wives before your very eyes.

Your cowardice has made you traitors twice over.

However, you and your families may be granted forgiveness by Soviet power if you start honestly serving the Soviet people.

What must you now do?

Do harm to the Germans in every way possible. Hide your food and livestock from them. Trick them. Give them false information. Hide those being sought by the Germans.

Help the partisans. Tell them and the Red Army about all the enemy's intentions. Disrupt enemy communications by cutting telegraph and telephone lines.

On your own or in groups, wreck railway lines. Destroy wagons and render engines useless. Destroy their war materiel. Set fire to German warehouses.

If you see that you are in danger from the Germans, hide in other villages with other families.

Get weapons from the enemy, organize partisan groups and cause havoc behind enemy lines. Destroy the German brigands.

If you do this, your Motherland and Soviet power will forgive you and not a single hair on your head will be harmed.

P. Ponomarenko, secretary of the CC of the Communist Party of Belorussia
I. Bylinsky, chairman of the Sovnarkom of the Belorussian SSR

[From the collection of the Museum of the Revolution, Moscow.]

The Russian POWs who gained greatest notoriety were those who joined the so-called 'Russian Liberation Army' headed by the former Red Army General, Vlasov. The following oath of allegiance, adaptable for those joining the less well-known 'Liberation Armies' of Ukraine and the Caucasus, brings home how explicitly its adherents were called upon to endorse Hitler and the Third Reich.

Document 123 | '... I do solemnly promise Adolf Hitler... to be loyal and utterly obedient'—text of the oath for volunteers serving in units of the German army

29 April 1943

I, a loyal son of my Motherland, enter the ranks of the Russian (Ukrainian or Caucasus) Liberation Army of my own free will and do solemnly swear that I will honestly fight against Bolshevism for the well-being of my people.

In this struggle, fought alongside Germany and her Allies against the common enemy, I do solemnly promise Adolf Hitler, the Führer and Commander of the Liberation Armies, to be loyal and utterly obedient.

I am prepared at any time to sacrifice my life for this oath.

[Source: *Voenno-istoricheskiy zhurnal*, No. 4, 1991, p. 22.]

An estimated 800,000 POWs consented to serve under Vlasov alongside the *Wehrmacht*. Their military impact was limited: Hitler himself was acutely suspicious of the notion of a Russian Liberation Army and when he redirected them to face the Allies in southern and western Europe their combat motivation, always low, dwindled away. The 'Vlasovites' have been a touchstone of conflicting attitudes to the Great Patriotic War. For some, the horrors of the Stalinist system made Vlasov the figurehead of a movement that, as its leaders claimed, stood for Russia's liberation.[71] For others, Vlasov's subservience to the Nazis makes that claim a travesty. Soviet historiography regarded him and his movement as semi-fascist in complexion as well as treacherous. As the following reflection from a veteran writing in 1987, during the Gorbachev period, suggests, in Stalin's eyes the Vlasovites were traitors pure and simple. But as the war recedes in time, there has been greater readiness to acknowledge that many of them signed up only because they were demoralized beyond endurance by their treatment at the hands of German captors and had no other hope of survival.

Document 124 | '... Stalin reduced it all to a simple equation: *prisoner = enemy*'—from a letter by N.I. Vasil'ev

Do you know how many innocent, honest people who had been captured naively ended up with Vlasov? The Germans had a carefully worked-out way of recruiting for Vlasov, based on the fact that Soviet prisoners of war had been ditched by the USSR government. They were kept on the very edge of physical and moral annihilation. In the morning the dead were removed from their two- or three-tier bunks,

---

71 On the ideas propounded by Vlasov and in his name, see C. Andreyev, *Vlasov and the Russian Liberation Movement: Soviet Reality and Émigré Theories* (Cambridge 1987).

and many of them had already had their ears, noses and fingers gnawed off by rats. The prisoners of war, just like ants, carried off their dead, loaded them onto carts and buried them—everybody who saw this knew it could be them the next day. . . Who helped them? Nobody gave them even a crust of bread, a potato, a mitten or a short line from home. . .

That was the fate of nameless millions. The courage and endurance of some, the despair and collapse of others—Stalin reduced it all to a simple equation: *prisoner = enemy*.

[Source: A.M. Samsonov, *Znat' i pomnit': dialog istorika s chitatelyami* (Moscow 1988), pp. 195–96.]

On their liberation and return to Soviet territory, ex-POWs were notionally 'screened' by the NKVD to separate out those who had betrayed the USSR. In practice, the vast majority were automatically arrested and sentenced to the GULAG.

Thus at the very same time that hopes of far-reaching moves in the direction of greater democratization, freedom of speech and openness were gathering pace, the regime was resorting to mass repression of entire categories of its citizens. The paradox reflected in part the way in which disinformation and attempts at secrecy limited public knowledge about these measures. It reflected, too, the fact that for many, official rhetoric about collaboration in western Ukraine and among some POWs, and such allusions as there were to the 'treachery' of non-Slav 'tribes' in the Caucasus and the Crimea, rang true. Moreover, these groups could all be regarded as set apart, their treatment a series of special cases rather than a foretaste of the general way in which the postwar order was likely to evolve. Yet this treatment proved all too indicative of what was to come.

The war had elevated Stalin's own prestige and domination over government and party to a new pinnacle, thus ensuring that the suspicious view that he and Beria took of these huge categories of Soviet citizens who had suffered from the war, and the supremely authoritarian manner in which they chose to respond, bled across to many other areas of immediate postwar policy. Their pursuit of blanket repression both extended the power of the secret police and gave a further lease of life to the violent, ruthless culture bred within it during the 1930s. Moreover, whereas in theory the USSR's wartime relationship with the western powers might have yielded international conditions favourable to liberalizing trends—massive loans for reconstruction together with a diplomatic environment conducive to arms reduction—in practice it did no such thing. Instead, the rapid deterioration in that relationship itself intensified the trend towards re-establishing much of the pre-war Stalinist order. It all but guaranteed that once again, as in the 1930s, a desperately poor country would be called upon to make massive investment in developing heavy industry, thereby maintaining a pressure on living standards that was scarcely compatible with democratic consent. Following the dictator's death in 1953, it is true, the most vicious and oppressive features of his rule would be reined in and policy would be reoriented in directions which at least to some extent echoed, albeit in diluted form, the hopes and expectations of 1945. But as we shall see, victory in the Great Patriotic War entrenched the authority of a generation of party leaders, a set of ideas, and an economic, social and political order which would frame the USSR long after the dictator himself was dead.

PART THREE

STABILIZATION AND STAGNATION (1945–1985)

The impact of the Great Patriotic War on the USSR proved definitive. Internationally, it conferred superpower status on the country and dominance over eastern Europe. At home it gave the regime an entirely new legitimacy and entrenched a political system, an economic model, and an ideological orthodoxy that proved highly resistant to change. Stalin's last years (1945–53) were markedly more brutal than those of his successors, and Soviet international relations more fraught. But, notwithstanding far-reaching economic and social development, the essentials of his postwar legacy remained unaltered through the more stable period presided over by the next four General Secretaries, Khrushchev (1953–64), Brezhnev (1964–82), Andropov (1982–84) and Chernenko (1984–85). The Cold War persisted despite periods of détente; bouts of unrest in eastern Europe kept the communist regimes of that region dependent on the threat of Soviet force and, in 1956 and 1968, its use; repeated attempts at economic reform made modest impact on malfunctions of the command economy; one-party rule backed by the secret police remained firmly in place; a courageous but limited current of overt dissent challenged the regime, notably over minority nationalist issues, but education, the media and public debate remained bound by the constraints of Marxism–Leninism. By the mid-1980s, economic growth had slowed dramatically; armed intervention in Afghanistan instigated in 1979 had highlighted the country's military overstretch; and a vastly better-educated and more urban society was giving rise to increasingly sophisticated reformist currents operating within legal limits. But through four decades of rapid international, economic, social and cultural change, the recipe for rule shaped by the Great Patriotic War shored up the power of the CPSU and its ageing elite.

13

The Cold War

Postwar Soviet history between 1945 and 1985 has long been subdivided at the point of Stalin's death on 1 March 1953.[72] Those last years of Stalin's, the short decade from 1945 to 1953, have been treated as a postscript to the drama of the 1930s and the Great Patriotic War, linked to it by mass poverty, overt repression, political violence at the summit, and above all the absolute domination of the *vozhd'* (leader) himself. No death, according to conventional wisdom, so profoundly altered a country's whole landscape as did that of Stalin. And indeed, so great was the dictator's authority that it remains difficult to escape the sense that his removal from the scene constituted an epoch-making break.

Stalin's heirs moved swiftly to reduce political violence and arbitrary arrest. In the immediate succession struggle, the only combatant arrested and executed was Beria, whose record and continuing control of the secret police alarmed his colleagues. But neither the immediate struggle for power which saw Khrushchev establish primacy (1955–64), nor the attempt by Malenkov, Molotov and a Presidium majority to eject Khrushchev in 1957, nor yet the successful drive to eject him seven years later, involved political violence. The new party leader, L.I. Brezhnev, who by 1968 had established primacy over the Prime Minister, A.N. Kosygin, remained in office for almost two decades, until his death in 1982; the very few Politburo members he demoted faced no disgrace; and his successors, Yu.V. Andropov (1982–84) and K.U. Chernenko (1984–85), died in office. Moreover, this change in the political culture at the summit was mirrored in a radical curtailment of political violence more generally. The secret police were firmly subordinated to the party again, lost control over the GULAG economy, and from the mid-

---

72 Among numerous examples, see R.G. Suny's fine overview, *The Soviet Experiment: Russia, the USSR and the Successor States* (Oxford 1998).

1950s the camps themselves were rapidly run down and dismantled, millions being restored to civilian life. The number of arrests for political activity fell precipitately. Though punishment for officials and managers held responsible for economic failure continued to be harsh, it ceased to be the norm that they were denounced for subversion and they were no longer subject to arrest. More broadly, these decades saw a sustained improvement in real wage and consumption levels, welfare provision, access to education, cultural life and public amenities. This enhancement in living standards underpinned a major shift in the balance between coercion and consent as the leadership sought to embed the legitimacy of communist rule.

Stalin's death, then, released forces for change which significantly altered the quality of life and which appeared to have the capacity to reconfigure the USSR along lines quite different from those laid down under the old dictator. And as long as the Soviet story remained open-ended, a periodization taking the year 1953 as a caesura seemed compelling. Now that the story is over, however, the case looks less sound and the countervailing arguments in favour of making 1945 rather than 1953 the benchmark year have taken on additional weight. For, as it turned out, the Soviet Union was not to be successfully refashioned. Far-reaching though the changes during the post-Stalin generation were, what stands out in retrospect is that they were limited by and achieved within the diplomatic, military, economic, political, ideological and cultural structures entrenched in Stalin's last years.

In this sense, the Great Patriotic War cast its shadow right across the period to the mid-1980s. The country attained superpower status and became the sole rival to the US, one of two fixed points in a bipolar world, and the USSR remained locked in an open-ended arms race against the US-led western alliance. Throughout these decades, the territory claimed as Soviet at the end of the war was neither extended nor retracted; within it, the key administrative division remained that between fifteen ethnically based Union Republics; and in the eastern European People's Republics established along the Soviet border the authority of communist-led regimes lacking domestic legitimacy was upheld by Moscow. Central features of the socioeconomic system remained firmly in place, from state ownership of industry, collective and state farming, to a state monopoly on (strictly limited) foreign trade, and the mechanisms of the command economy. The party's monopoly on power was set in stone, along with its control over public debate and cultural life, backed by the successors to the NKVD, the MVD and later the KGB, and a formidable array of sanctions and rewards. And Stalin's last years saw, too, the central pillars of Marxist–Leninist ideology consolidated with the victory over Nazi Germany: the world-power status of the USSR and its domination of eastern Europe were portrayed as the supreme vindication of the party's leading role and proof of its claim to be pioneering the route which post-capitalist humanity was destined to follow. The change that took place after Stalin's death was extensive, but it was contained within this framework right across the period from the mid-1940s to the mid-1980s.

Conflict over eastern Europe

The fundamental issue over which the wartime alliance with Britain and the United States broke down was the manner in which Moscow secured influence over the Soviet Union's eastern European neighbours.[73] By late 1944, as we have seen, Soviet insistence on friendly governments presiding over Poland, Romania and Bulgaria had been made plain. What was much less clear was how this was to be secured. Everywhere, it is true, the political tide flowed strongly leftward.[74] Parties left of centre, and especially those actively engaged in underground resistance, gathered momentum, while parties of the right and those implicated in collaboration with the Nazi overlord were thrown onto the defensive and then totally discredited. Yet the only parties that Moscow felt confident would give unswerving fealty were communist parties. And while all communist parties in eastern Europe had recovered from the bloody purges of the late 1930s and gained some prestige from their role in the resistance, only in south-east Europe, in Yugoslavia and Albania, did they command sufficient popular base and military muscle to secure power essentially through their own efforts: no effective opposition was mounted when Tito's Yugoslav People's Front organized elections in November 1945, or when Hoxha's Democratic Front followed suit the following month. Nowhere else did the communist parties have either partisan militia of equivalent weight or any chance of unfettered popular endorsement—not least because of their allegiance to the awesome giant in the east. Though communist demands for a massive shift in power and property everywhere resonated among peasants and workers, the national party's appeal was severely limited not least by being identified with a power that was foreign, intensely anti-religious, charged with extracting maximum reparations for the USSR, and personified in the often brutal form of the liberating Red Army. Moscow gained massive leverage, of course, from the

---

73 For considered reflection on recent work on the Cold War, see J.L. Gaddis, *We Now Know: Rethinking Cold War History* (Oxford 1997), and his new synthesis, *The Cold War* (London 2005).

74 Two good surveys are J. Rothschild, *Return to Diversity: A Political History of East Central Europe since World War II* (Oxford 1994, 2nd edn), and D.S. Mason, *Revolution in East-Central Europe: The Rise and Fall of Communism and the Cold War* (Boulder, CO, 1992).

arrival of Soviet forces. With the economy of each country thrown into disarray, and basic food supplies in chaos, the Red Army's patronage became critical. It became the decisive arbiter/guarantor of the territorial ambitions of the re-emerging states of eastern Europe, securing for Poland a broad swathe of ex-German territory in compensation for the lands now incorporated in the USSR; buttressing Czechoslovak confidence that there would be no revenge for the mass flight of Germans; and adjudicating between the conflicting claims of Hungary and Romania, Bulgaria and Yugoslavia. By the time the war ended, this leverage had enabled national communist parties to take the leading role in provisional coalition governments in Poland, Romania and Bulgaria, and to establish footholds within the provisional coalition governments of Hungary and Czechoslovakia.

Yet there were good grounds for Stalin exercising this leverage with some caution. The death and destruction the country had just endured made the prospect of head-on confrontation with American might all but unthinkable. With a gargantuan task of reconstruction lying ahead, the tantalizing prospect of large-scale loans from Washington exercised a strong attraction. Accordingly, Stalin's approach appears to have been pragmatic. He hoped somehow to consolidate Soviet influence in eastern Europe in a manner which made it possible to keep relations with the west on an even keel. Yet, his American and British allies placed stronger and stronger pressure on him to abide by Allied commitment to the installation of free multi-party democratic systems across liberated Europe. To do so while entrenching governments unswervingly loyal to Moscow would be to square the circle. Only in Czechoslovakia did it, for a period, seem possible. President Edvard Beneš commanded respect in the west and was determined on friendly relations with Moscow; the Social–Democratic prime minister, Fierlinger, worked closely with the communists; the communists themselves had a substantial electoral base and were well aware of the advantages of securing power democratically. In Hungary, the communists' attempt to do so in the relatively free elections of November 1945 saw them humiliated with a mere 17 per cent of the vote. When in the same month the communist-dominated Fatherland Front in Bulgaria secured electoral victory by blatant manipulation, in the west it was rejected as fraudulent. Elections in the largest two countries in eastern Europe, Romania and Poland, were repeatedly postponed.

Western suspicions grew, and anxiety was heightened by the momentum which communist parties in France, Italy, Belgium and Greece had gained through their role in the resistance. The fact that Europe's overseas colonies, especially in Asia, had become severely destabilized by the end of the war, and the continuing advances made by the Chinese communists in the civil war with the nationalists further intensified western concerns. The scope for Soviet/communist expansionism—and in western eyes the two amounted to the same thing—seemed almost limitless. In the US, Truman, who had succeeded Roosevelt in April 1945, took a markedly firmer line, and stiff resistance to the supposed Red threat became an increasing electoral asset. In February 1946, George Kennan's famous Long Telegram from Moscow laid out cogently the case for regarding Soviet ambitions as open-ended and for making it crystal clear that the US would resist, by force if necessary, further expansion. The following month, Winston Churchill, out of office since summer 1945 but commanding enormous prestige, delivered in Fulton, Missouri, what was quickly recognized as a landmark speech.[75]

In it he drew together many of the elements fuelling demands for more robust handling of the USSR. While reaffirming general goodwill to what he quaintly called 'the peoples of all the Russias', he painted an alarming portrait: the countries of east-central Europe were being brought under rigid Soviet control exercised through illegitimate and highly unpopular communist governments. Along with Poland, Romania, Czechoslovakia, Bulgaria and Yugoslavia, he included Vienna and Berlin, warning that Moscow was nurturing communist support within the zones of occupation it controlled, thereby, he claimed, opening the way for German manoeuvre between the members of the Grand Alliance. He warned that the threat extended even further: during the summer of 1945 Soviet pressure on Turkey for concessions over control of the Straits, together with apparent Soviet foot-dragging over the agreement that all foreign troops would be withdrawn from Iran (Persia), appeared deeply ominous in the west. And he urged that the way to halt any further Soviet 'adventure' was for Britain and the US to present Moscow with resolute and armed resistance.

Document 125 | **Excerpts from Churchill's Fulton speech, 5 March 1946**

I have a strong admiration and regard for the valiant Russian people and for my wartime comrade, Marshal Stalin. There is deep sympathy and goodwill in Britain— and I doubt not here also—towards the peoples of all the Russias and a resolve to persevere through many differences and rebuffs in establishing lasting friendships. We understand the Russian need to be secure on her western borders by the removal of all possibility of German aggression. We welcome Russia to her rightful place among the leading nations of the world. We welcome her flag upon the seas. Above all, we welcome constant, frequent and growing contacts between the Russian people and our own people on both sides of the Atlantic. It is my duty, however,

---

75 For an illuminating treatment, see F. Harbutt, *The Iron Curtain: Churchill, America and the Origins of the Cold War* (Oxford 1986).

for I am sure you would wish me to state the facts as I see them to you, to place before you certain facts about the present position in Europe.

From Stettin in the Baltic to Trieste in the Adriatic, an iron curtain has descended across the Continent. Behind that line lie all the capitals of the ancient states of Central and Eastern Europe, Warsaw, Berlin, Prague, Vienna, Budapest, Belgrade, Bucharest and Sofia, all these famous cities and the populations around them lie in what I must call the Soviet sphere, and all are subject in one form or another, not only to Soviet influence but to a very high and, in many cases, increasing measure of control from Moscow. Athens alone—Greece with its immortal glories—is free to decide its future at an election under British, American and French observation. The Russian-dominated Polish government has been encouraged to make enormous and wrongful inroads upon Germany, and mass expulsions of millions of Germans on a scale grievous and undreamed of are now taking place. The communist parties, which were very small in all these eastern states of Europe, have been raised to pre-eminence and power far beyond their numbers and are seeking everywhere to obtain totalitarian control. Police governments are prevailing in nearly every case, and so far, except in Czechoslovakia, there is no true democracy.

Turkey and Persia are profoundly alarmed and disturbed at the claims which are being made upon them and at the pressure being exerted by the Moscow government. An attempt is being made by the Russians in Berlin to build up a quasi-communist party in their zone of occupied Germany by showing special favours to groups of left-wing German leaders. At the end of the fighting last June, the American and British armies withdrew westwards, in accordance with an earlier agreement, to a depth of some 150 miles upon a front of nearly 400 miles, in order to allow our Russian allies to occupy this vast expanse of territory which the Western democracies had conquered.

If now the Soviet government tries, by separate action, to build up a pro-Communist Germany in their areas, this will cause new serious difficulties in the British and American zones, and will give the defeated Germans the power of putting themselves up to auction between the Soviets and the Western democracies. Whatever conclusions may be drawn from these facts—and facts they are—this is certainly not the liberated Europe we fought to build up. Nor is it one which contains the essentials of permanent peace. . .

From what I have seen of our Russian friends and Allies during the war, I am convinced that there is nothing they admire so much as strength, and there is nothing for which they have less respect than weakness, especially military weakness. For that reason the old doctrine of a balance of power is unsound. We cannot afford, if we can help it, to work on narrow margins, offering temptations to a trial of strength. . . .

If the population of the English-speaking Commonwealths be added to that of the United States with all that such co-operation implies in the air, on the sea, all over the globe and in science and in industry, and in moral force, there will be no quivering, precarious balance of power to offer its temptation to ambition or adventure. . .

[Source: http://www.cnn.com/SPECIALS/cold.war/episodes/02/documents/churchill]

Stalin responded with an interview published in *Pravda* a week later. It addressed the domestic Soviet audience as well as the western powers.[76] No doubt with an eye to continental European opinion, Stalin charged Churchill with Anglo-Saxon arrogance and drew attention to his characteristic hyperbole about the vast economic, military and moral weight of an alliance between the British Commonwealth and the US. He waved away Churchill's concern about Soviet political activity in the Soviet zones of occupation in Berlin and Vienna by dwelling on the fact that, formally speaking, the occupation of the two capitals was under the joint control of the four occupying powers. On the issue of the political regimes taking shape in eastern Europe, he gave no ground at all. Far from it. And the key points that he made were points which not only informed his own attitude but were widely shared in the USSR and would remain fundamental to the Soviet approach to eastern Europe for decades ahead.

The Soviet Union had shed untold blood. The figure of 7 million losses he gave was, as we have seen (Part I, document 94), but a fraction of the reality, probably reflecting inhibitions both about informing the Soviet public just how grievously the country had paid for what was now being glorified as a brilliant triumph, and about informing foreign powers just how gravely the country had been weakened. But it was sufficient for him to drive home the point, which *Pravda*'s readers would heartily endorse, that the relative insignificance of western sufferings deprived Churchill of any right to pontificate on postwar eastern Europe. Equally, he made quite plain that in Soviet eyes there was no cause whatsoever to be apologetic about insisting that the governments of eastern Europe must have 'a loyal attitude to the Soviet Union'. In any conflict between the needs of Soviet security and the wishes of the electorate in the countries in question, there could be no question about which should take priority. At the same time, Stalin characteristically used Churchill's warning about the rise of communist influence to celebrate the popularity which the fraternal parties supposedly enjoyed, portraying the prominent role they were acquiring in postwar governments not as the product of the Red Army but as the fruit of their own role in the resistance. Finally, neatly underlining the urgency of Soviet security

---

76 For Stalin's approach in the immediate aftermath of the war, see H. Thomas, *Armed Truce: The Beginnings of the Cold War, 1945–46* (London 1986).

concerns, he accused Churchill of warmongering. He implied that the threatening tone of the Fulton speech lent direct confirmation of the warning he had given the previous month (see below, document 151) of capitalism's inherent instability and hostility towards the communist world. And he drove the point home by alluding to Churchill's long record of militant anti-Bolshevism, his support for the Whites during the Russian civil war of 1918–20, and the resounding defeat inflicted on them and their 'imperialist sponsors'.

Document 126 | **From an interview given by Stalin to *Pravda* on Churchill's Fulton speech**

March, 1946

Interviewer: How do you rate Mr Churchill's most recent speech, which he made in the USA?

Stalin: I consider it a dangerous act, aimed at sowing the seeds of discord between allied states and making co-operation difficult.

Interviewer: Is it fair to say that Mr Churchill's speech is damaging the cause of peace and security?

Stalin: Absolutely. In essence, Mr Churchill has now adopted the position of the incendiaries of war. . . In effect, Mr Churchill and his friends in the USA and Britain have issued something like an ultimatum to non-anglophone countries: accept our supremacy voluntarily and everything will be fine—if not, war is inevitable. . .

Interviewer: How do you rate that part of Churchill's speech where he attacks the democratic systems of the European states neighbouring us and criticizes the good-neighbourly relations established between those states and the Soviet Union?

Stalin: That part of Churchill's speech is a mishmash of slander, rudeness and tactlessness. . . It is utterly absurd to talk about the USSR's exclusive control in Vienna and Berlin, where there are Allied Control Councils with representatives of four states and where the USSR has only one-quarter of the vote. Some people cannot resist slandering others, but they ought to know where to stop. . .

As a result of the German invasion, the Soviet Union lost about 7 million people irrevocably, in battles with the Germans, and thanks to the German occupation which drove Soviet people off into German slavery. . .

Maybe in certain places they are inclined to bury these colossal sacrifices in oblivion, sacrifices which ensured the liberation of Europe from Hitler's yoke. The question arises—is it really surprising that in wishing to safeguard itself in the future the Soviet Union is trying to ensure that there are governments in these countries with a loyal attitude to the Soviet Union?. . .

Mr Churchill gets nearer the truth when he talks about the rising influence of communist parties in Europe. . . Such a rise is not accidental, but an entirely natural phenomenon. Communist influence has grown because during the dark days of fascist domination in Europe the communists were trustworthy and bold fighters against the fascist regime, for the freedom of the peoples. . .

I don't know whether after the Second World War Mr Churchill and his friends will succeed in organizing a new crusade against 'Eastern Europe'. But if they do succeed—which is unlikely, because millions of ordinary people will stand up for peace—then we can confidently say that they will be beaten, just as happened in the past, twenty-six years ago.

[Source: *Pravda*, 14 March 1946.]

For a further year, Stalin's approach in eastern Europe continued to be some-what more pragmatic than Churchill's portrait allowed.[77] Relatively free elections in Czechoslovakia in May 1946 saw the communists fall far short of an overall majority—38 per cent of the vote—and they continued to operate within a genuine coalition, albeit now headed by their leader, Gottwald: their most high-handed reaction to the inconclusive outcome was sharply to curtail the constitutional autonomy of Slovakia where they had been heavily outvoted by the Social Democrats. In Hungary, the coalition government continued to be headed by a non-communist, the Smallholder Party leader Ferenc Nagy, although as everywhere the interior ministry and police were brought under firm communist control. In Romania, by contrast, a National Democratic Front, analogous to the Polish Democratic Bloc, gradually splintered, subordinated and suppressed independent parties and secured a massive majority in elections in November 1946. And in Poland, the monopoly power of the communist party (renamed the Polish Workers' Party) headed by Gomułka was eventually endorsed by a carefully orchestrated election in January 1947, their 'Democratic Bloc' inflicting crushing defeat on the main opposition, the Peasant Party, and subsequently compelling their Social Democratic partners to fuse within a new Polish United Workers' Party.

Each step was met by mounting western protest, culminating in March 1947 in Truman's commitment to containment. American financial and if necessary military power would be deployed to halt the further spread of communist influence, starting in Turkey, Iran and civil-war-torn Greece, where Soviet pressure seemed most intense. Two months later, as tension between east and west rapidly mounted, the French and Italian communists were driven from their respective places in coalition governments. The decisive break was triggered when the American Secretary of State, George

---

77 For a rich collection of essays, see N. Naimark and L. Gibianskii (eds), *The Establishment of the Communist Regimes in Eastern Europe, 1944–1949* (Oxford 1997).

Marshall, announced the European Recovery Program, channelling large-scale loans to rebuild the continental economy. Having momentarily responded positively to the invitation to take part, Stalin quickly changed course, and denounced the scheme as a plot to reduce participating countries to dependence on the US.[78] The eastern European delegations to the Paris Conference of June–July organized to discuss the programme were ordered to withdraw. Two months later (22–27 September), the founding congress of the Communist Information Bureau (Cominform) signalled the tightening bonds between the Soviet communist party, those of Poland, Romania, Hungary, Czechoslovakia, Bulgaria and Yugoslavia, and the fraternal parties of France and Italy. In language that mirrored Churchill's, Zhdanov's opening speech warned of American aggression on the fascist model and the division of the world into two hostile camps.[79]

Thereafter, Soviet policy was much less inhibited by concern to minimize western protest. In Czechoslovakia, the communist party became increasingly assertive and when most of its coalition partners resigned in January 1948, the party quickly moved to establish an effective monopoly of power, driving through industrial, agricultural and censorship policies in line with the rest of the emergent Soviet bloc. Likewise in Hungary, from the latter part of 1947 the communist party extended its authority to that of monopoly, dissolving the opposition parties, subordinating the media, and enforcing a Stalinist Five-Year Plan. By May 1949 it was in a position to orchestrate a 95.6 per cent vote for a single government list.

The clash with Tito and Yugoslavia

The sharp deterioration in relations with the west from summer 1947 coincided with a crisis which enormously increased Stalin's impatience to cement his control over the governments of the 'People's Democracies'. At issue were the recurrent demonstrations of independence by one of their number: Yugoslavia.[80] Given that Tito had adopted the most militant communist line since the war, and pushed ahead with imposing Soviet-style central planning

---

78 See the account by G. Roberts, 'Moscow and the Marshall Plan: Politics, Ideology and the Onset of the Cold War, 1947', *Europe–Asia Studies* 46 (1994), pp. 1371–86.

79 On the foundation of Cominform, see G.R. Swain, 'The Cominform: Tito's International?', *Historical Journal* 35 (1992).

80 On the crisis, see R. Pearson, *The Rise and Fall of the Soviet Empire* (Basingstoke 1998), pp. 23–44. For a useful comparative analysis bringing out the features distinguishing Moscow's relationship with communist Yugoslavia, see J. Tomaszewski, *The Socialist Regimes of East Central Europe: Their Establishment and Consolidation, 1944–1967* (London 1989).

much faster than his neighbours had, this fissure gave the lie to the idea that Moscow's control was smooth and absolute. On numerous issues, the stance adopted by Tito, his Vice-President, Kardelj, and the Yugoslav government provoked Stalin: clandestine support for the Greek communists regardless of the effects on wider Soviet–Anglo-American relations; an apparent assumption that the Yugoslavs had the right to dominate Albania; a hectic pace of industrialization which assumed economic support and terms of trade with the Soviet Union that Moscow had no intention of providing; the vision of a Balkan federation large enough to develop considerable independence vis-à-vis the USSR. Unlike the other government leaders in Cominform, palpably dependent on Moscow for coming to and retaining power, Tito was set apart by his leadership of the partisans during the war, by the modest debt owed the Red Army for the country's liberation, and by his secure grip on a loyal, self-confident, united and relatively popular party. As is shown by the following report from the Soviet Ambassador in Belgrade, written on the closing day of the Cominform's founding congress, the thread running through each disputed question was the issue of Yugoslavia's deference to the USSR.

Document 127 | **The Soviet–Yugoslav conflict—extracts from declassified documents, 1947–1948**

i. A.I. Lavrent'ev, the Soviet ambassador to Yugoslavia, on Josip Broz Tito's speech at the 2nd Congress of the Yugoslav National Front on 27 September 1947

. . . Tito did not mention once Soviet aid to Yugoslavia in this struggle or Soviet influence on the whole course of the liberation struggle, although it is patently obvious that Yugoslavia was liberated by the Red Army and that the Soviet Union played a decisive foreign-policy role in the making of Yugoslavia. . . The reason for all these omissions is that Tito sees the process of the liberation of Yugoslavia and of the socio-economic formation of the country only from local national positions, thereby lapsing into national narrowness. . .

The following excerpts track the rapid decline in relations. In December, Stalin himself reproached Tito over Yugoslavia's high-handed intervention in Albania.

ii. A personal message from Stalin to Tito on 23 December 1947

. . . as you suggested, Zhdanov, a member of the Politburo, has had two conversations with comrade Popović (the Yugoslav ambassador in Moscow) on the question of Albania. As new questions came to light in the course of the conversations, we would like you to send a senior comrade to Moscow, Djilas, perhaps, or someone else well up on the position in Albania. I am prepared to do as you wish, but I do need to know what these wishes are.

With comradely greetings,

I. Stalin

By the beginning of February, infuriated at Tito's continuing unsanctioned initiatives on sending troops via Albania to support the Greek communists, Moscow had the ambassador, Lavrent'ev, deliver an icy reproach.

iii. To comrade Tito

1 February 1948

It is clear from your conversation with comrade Lavrent'ev that you consider a situation normal where Yugoslavia, which has a mutual aid treaty with the USSR, considers it acceptable not only not to consult the USSR about sending troops into Albania, but also not to inform the USSR about this thereafter. For your information, the Soviet Government found out entirely by chance from our representatives' private conversations with Albanian officials about the Yugoslav Government's decision on sending your troops into Albania. The USSR considers such a situation abnormal. But if you consider it normal, then I must inform you on behalf of the Soviet Government that it cannot agree with being presented with a *fait accompli*. It is also, of course, understandable that the USSR, as an ally of Yugoslavia, cannot accept responsibility for the consequences of actions taken by the Yugoslav Government without consulting or informing the Soviet Government. Comrade Lavrent'ev has informed us that you have delayed sending your troops to Albania, of which we take cognizance. It is, however, clear that there are serious disagreements between our governments about the nature of relations between our two allied countries. To avoid misunderstandings these disagreements should be settled in one way or another. . .

According to Lavrent'ev, Tito was badly shaken.

iv. The Soviet ambassador on the mission given him by the Soviet government on 1 February 1948

I gave Tito your telegram today. After reading it twice, Tito became extremely agitated and said that he never expected the Soviet Government to ascribe the matter such significance. He admits he made a mistake, should first have consulted the Soviet Government and that henceforth there will be such consultation on foreign policy matters. He realizes that reactionary circles would lay the blame on the Soviet Union for such incorrect steps in foreign policy. A Yugoslav division will not be sent into Albania. . .

Seeking to bring Tito to heel while he was unnerved, the following day Molotov issued a curt demand that he send a delegation to Moscow for talks.

v. An extract from Molotov's urgent telegram to Tito on 2 February 1948

We think that on foreign-policy matters there are serious differences between us. In view of the tense international situation we think it necessary to iron out these differences by having an unofficial meeting in Moscow for an exchange of views. To this end, please send a couple of senior Yugoslav representatives to Moscow no later than 8–10 February. Representatives of the Bulgarian government have also been invited.
Your response please.

Molotov

When the talks took place in the Kremlin on 10 February, Stalin made his anger quite plain. As Tito feared, the purpose of inviting Bulgarian representatives at the same time was to instruct both parties that the two countries were to form a federation. This was anathema to Tito: not only was it designed to short-circuit his exploration of a much wider Balkan federation, but amalgamation of the subservient Bulgarian party with his party would give Moscow the foothold within the latter that it lacked. The standoff became interwoven with conflicting economic expectations, and on 18 March, Soviet military and civilian experts and advisers were withdrawn.

vi. Molotov's instructions to the Soviet ambassador in Belgrade on 18 March 1948 concerning his message to Tito or Kardelj on their refusal to give information on economic matters to Soviet government bodies

We were astonished by this news, because there is an agreement between us that the organs of the Soviet Government should receive such information without hindrance. We were even more astonished by the fact that Yugoslav Government organs are carrying out this measure unilaterally, without any warning or explanation of the reasons. The Soviet Government regards such actions on the part of the Yugoslav Government as showing lack of trust towards Soviet personnel in Yugoslavia and as an expression of hostility towards the USSR.

Clearly, given this mistrust towards Soviet staff in Yugoslavia, the latter cannot consider themselves safeguarded against similar unfriendly actions by the Yugoslav Government.

Consequently, the Soviet Government has issued instructions to the ministries of ferrous metals, non-ferrous metals, the chemical industry, power stations, transport and health immediately to recall all their specialists and personnel to the USSR.

The list of Soviet accusations grew rapidly: ideological heresy, slandering the CPSU, nationalist deviations, analogies with Trotskyism, Menshevism, undemocratic party processes. The Yugoslavs stoutly rejected each charge and defended their right to pursue a path towards socialism marginally different from that of the USSR. The Soviet side responded on 4 May with furious denunciation of this arrogance from a party which, it claimed, owed everything to Soviet power, and demanded that the issues be placed before Cominform for resolution. Tito and Kardelj replied on 17 May.

vii. An extract from Tito and Kardelj's reply to the Soviet government on 17 May 1948

Dear comrades Stalin and Molotov
We have received your letter of 4 May 1948. We hardly need to describe the sad impression it made on us. It convinced us of the futility of all our efforts to show that the accusations made against us are the result of mistaken reporting.

We do not reject criticism on matters of principle, but in all this matter we feel ourselves at such a disadvantage that we cannot now agree to this matter being settled by the Cominform. . .

We wish to clear up this matter in such a way as will in fact show that the accusations against us are unjust, in that we shall tirelessly build socialism and remain loyal to the Soviet Union and to the teachings of Marx, Engels, Lenin and Stalin. . .

[Source: *Pravda*, 6 March 1990.]

The following month the Yugoslav party was expelled from Cominform and denounced for flouting every precept of Marxism–Leninism. 'Titoism' became a cursed heresy, the eastern European party leaders hurrying to add their own castigation. The challenge to Stalin's authority which Tito had thrown down triggered a drastic tightening of Moscow's control over the other European communist parties. Between 1948 and 1950 there were repeated and bloody party purges and show trials of 'exposed' former leaders charged with various permutations of Titoism and Trotskyism as well as responsibility for economic failures.[81] The main victims were party members who had been active in the resistance and showed signs of independence of mind, while the main beneficiaries were those who had spent the war in exile in Moscow and were most ready to do Stalin's bidding. Everywhere the leaders brought to the fore were, and were seen to be, even more directly dependent on Moscow's support than their predecessors had been. In Poland, Gomułka, who had headed the Polish communist resistance since

---

81 On the purges, see G.H. Hodos, *Show Trials: Stalinist Purges in Eastern Europe, 1948–1954* (New York 1987).

1943, was removed as General Secretary and subsequently arrested; in Bulgaria, Kostov, whose wartime role was analogous, was ousted and hanged; in Czechoslovakia, Gottwald moved with the tide which swept away many relatively moderate voices of the immediate postwar years as well as party advocates of greater autonomy for Slovakia. The following subsequent reflections by M. Djilas, at the time a leading figure in Tito's party, endorse the view that though Yugoslavia's assertiveness stood out, the communist leaders of the other People's Democracies had analogous if milder aspirations to a measure of autonomy.

Document 128 | From a *Discussion on the Events of 1948 and Their Consequences* conducted by *Literaturnaya gazeta* and *Nedeljne Informativne Novine*

March 1990

M. Djilas: In Stalin and Molotov's letters to the Yugoslav leadership it said that the Yugoslavs were too full of themselves. We did overestimate our strength and capabilities back then. . . Stalin suspected that Yugoslavia wanted to take a leading position in the international communist movement. . .

I think Stalin was pursuing two aims. The first was to subordinate Yugoslavia and through her all of Eastern Europe. There was also another reading of this. If things didn't work out with Yugoslavia, then subordinate Eastern Europe without her. The second one succeeded.

The problems were fairly complex. Nobody said so in writing, but I can remember from confidential chats that there was a tendency to independent development in the countries of Eastern Europe—Poland, Romania and Hungary.

I'll give you an example. In 1946 I was at the Congress of the Czechoslovak Party in Prague. Gottwald said that the cultural levels of Czechoslovakia and the Soviet Union were different. He emphasized that Czechoslovakia was an industrially advanced country and in it socialism would develop differently, in more civilized forms and without the turmoil the Soviet Union had had, where industrialization had been traumatic. Gottwald spoke out against collectivization in Czechoslovakia. In essence his views were not that different from ours.

Gottwald was not a strong enough character to stand up to Stalin. But Tito was a strong man. . . Gomulka was not able to defend his position. At one session of the Cominform, Gomulka had spoken about a Polish way to socialism. Dimitrov was also thinking about independent development. . .

[Source: *Literaturnaya gazeta*, 21 March 1990.]

Mounting friction with the West

Growing tension between the USSR and the west, fuelled by the increasingly brutal and blatant enforcement of communist puppet governments
ruling in the image of their Soviet master, conditioned and was itself exacerbated by the breakdown in the joint occupation of Germany.[82] The issue of
reparations did much in itself to sour relations. In Soviet eyes, the west
seemed to be deliberately obstructing the agreed payments in kind to be
made to the USSR; from the western viewpoint, the prospect of endlessly
subsidizing Germany only to see the resources bleed away to the east became
increasingly hard to tolerate. By the beginning of 1947, Britain and the US
began to favour restoring the German economy as part of what became the
Marshall Plan, and proceeded to merge their zones, the French one joining
in 1948. The same year the western zones introduced a new currency and
began to construct German institutions at the national level. At this point,
in June, though similar steps were being taken in the eastern zone, Moscow
tried to halt the slide towards a division which would see the bulk of German
territory fall to the capitalist 'bloc': Stalin's method was to exploit Berlin's
position deep in the Soviet zone, blockading the western sectors of the city.
An Anglo-American airlift defeated the manoeuvre and, far from bringing
the west to the negotiating table, it hastened the process it had been designed
to halt. Coming hard upon the communist consummation of power in
Czechoslovakia, the blockade was seen in the west as an attempt to drive
Allied troops out and extend Soviet/communist power. In March, Britain,
France and the Benelux countries had established a military alliance (sometimes known as the Western European Union), and talks followed swiftly
about building an alliance between North America and western Europe. The
upshot was the announcement in January 1949 which heralded what was to
become the North Atlantic Treaty Organization (NATO). In vain the Soviet
government protested that the new organization could not genuinely be
defensive since there was no threat, and that it was in fact a device to install
Anglo-American domination and threaten the USSR and the People's
Democracies.

Document 129 | **Declaration of the Soviet Foreign Ministry on a North Atlantic
Pact, January 1949**

On 14 January 1949 the US State Department published a lengthy declaration with
the brash title *Building Peace: Collective Security in the North Atlantic*.

---

82 On the division of Germany and the emergence of the GDR, see N. Naimark, *The Russians
in Germany: A History of the Soviet Zone of Occupation, 1945–1949* (Cambridge, MA, 1995).

This official document sets out the USA's position on the question of this so-called 'North Atlantic Pact', talks about which the governments of the USA and Canada have been holding since last summer with the governments of Great Britain, France, Belgium, Holland and Luxembourg.

If last year under the pretext of collective self-defence the ruling circles of the above European states, with US patronage, created a military and political union, this year a far-reaching Anglo-American plan to create a North Atlantic union of the same countries and Canada, directly headed by the USA, is being implemented.

In his 20 January speech Truman declared that a draft North Atlantic Pact will soon be put before the Senate, the official aims of which are stated to be a desire to strengthen security in the North Atlantic... Just as the implementation of the Marshall Plan is directed not at the genuine economic regeneration of European states, but is a means of adapting the politics and economics of the 'Marshallized' countries to the selfish military and strategic plans of Anglo-American domination in Europe, in the same way the formation of a new grouping is not at all for the mutual assistance and collective security of the Western Union, in so far as by the Yalta and Potsdam Agreements these countries are not threatened with any aggression. Its aim is to strengthen and considerably extend the dominant influence of Anglo-American ruling circles in Europe, and to subordinate all the domestic and foreign policies of the corresponding European states to their own narrow interests.

As with the creation of the Western Union, the instigators of the North Atlantic Pact have from the outset precluded any possibility of participation by the People's Democracies and the Soviet Union in that pact, making it clear that not only could these states not be participants, but that the North Atlantic Pact is directed precisely against the USSR and the new democracies...

[Source: *Izvestiya*, 29 January 1949.]

For the Soviet alliance, as for the emerging western one, military and economic considerations were tightly entwined. The following week the creation of COMECON, the Council for Mutual Economic Assistance, was announced. It aimed to foster the growing economic links between the five People's Republics and the USSR.[83] The language of mutual assistance concealed a very unequal relationship: the USSR laid down the terms of trade and in large measure shaped the development plans of the People's Democracies to complement the needs of the Soviet economy. This did not prevent the Soviet declaration proclaiming, in order to point up the contrast with the western military pact, that membership of the Council was open to other European countries.

---

83 See J.M. van Brabant, *Socialist Economic Integration* (Cambridge 1980), pp. 31–34.

Document 130 | **The creation of the Council for Mutual Economic Assistance, January 1949**

An economic conference of representatives from Bulgaria, Hungary, Poland, Romania and Czechoslovakia took place in Moscow in January this year.

The conference noted significant successes in the development of economic relations between the above countries, witnessed primarily by a big growth in trade. Owing to the establishment of these economic relations and the implementation of a policy of economic co-operation the People's Democracies and the USSR have been able to speed up the restoration and development of their economies.

Moreover, the conference established that the governments of the USA, Britain and certain Western European countries are in effect boycotting trade relations with the People's Democracies and the USSR, because these countries find it impossible to submit to the dictates of the Marshall Plan, as this plan infringes the sovereignty of these countries and the interests of their economies.

In view of these circumstances, the conference discussed the possibilities of organizing broader economic co-operation between the People's Democracies and the USSR. In order to make economic co-operation between the People's Democracies and the USSR a reality, the conference deemed it necessary to create a Council for Mutual Economic Assistance of representatives of the countries attending the conference on the basis of equal representation with the aim of the exchange of expertise, mutual technical assistance, mutual assistance in raw materials, food, machinery, equipment, etc.

The conference stated that the Council for Mutual Economic Assistance is an open organization which other European countries can join, if they share the Council's principles and wish to participate in broad economic collaboration with the above-mentioned countries.

[Source: *Izvestiya*, 25 January 1949.]

NATO came into existence in April, and in May the establishment of the Federal Republic of Germany was proclaimed, its first Chancellor being the fiercely anti-Soviet Christian Democrat Konrad Adenauer. In Soviet eyes, western de-Nazification measures had been entirely inadequate and such rapid rehabilitation of the recent enemy was regarded as palpable hostility. From the western viewpoint, on the other hand, the proclamation in October of the People's Republic of China, following Mao's victory in the protracted civil war, suggested Soviet/communist expansionism was rampant. By then both sides in what was now 'cold war' were significantly expanding their military capability—the USSR reversing postwar demobilization from 1948 to bring the army to a level above 4 million, developing a substantial navy and submarine fleet, and, in 1949, successfully exploding its first atomic bomb. Each side regarded itself as under threat. This was the portrait of the American military build-up given in November by the Soviet ambassador to the UN, A.Ya. Vyshinsky, chief prosecutor in the show trials of the 1930s.

Document 131 | From A.Ya. Vyshinsky's speech at a meeting of the UN General Assembly's political committee, 16 November 1949

. . . In September 1945, the Assistant Secretary of the Navy, Mr Hensel, outlining the view of his Department at a public press conference, said that the United States 'must secure for itself a gigantic postwar ring of naval bases encompassing the Pacific Ocean and including bases which formerly belonged to Britain'. And indeed, according to authoritative data which no one has as yet disputed, the USA, in the course of the war, built 256 bases of all dimensions and all types in the Pacific theatre of war and 228 military, naval and air bases in the Atlantic theatre of war, that is 484 bases in all. Since then the number of these bases has increased.

In October 1948, a communiqué was issued in London that there are permanent bases for American Super Fortresses in Britain and that stationed at these bases were 90 American B-29 Super Fortresses, subdivided into three groups of the strategic bomber air force. . .

[Source: A.Ya. Vyshinsky, *On Condemning the Preparations for a New War and for the Conclusion of a Five-Power Pact to Strengthen Peace* (London 1949), pp. 5–6.]

In June the following year, the army of communist North Korea invaded South Korea with Stalin's sanction. The US secured UN approval—the USSR was boycotting the Security Council at the time in protest against communist China being excluded from the organization—for it to send forces to halt the invasion, and the Chinese poured 'volunteers' in to assist the North. After a year's fighting, a stalemate was reached but by then the war had dramatically intensified the arms race. Washington extended its defensive umbrella to anti-Soviet regimes across Asia, notably in Indo-China, where the US gradually took over from France the armed resistance to the Vietnamese nationalist movement led by Ho Chi Minh. By the time Stalin died in March 1953, the USSR had firmly established its domination of eastern Europe, and its status as one of only two superpowers to which nationalist as well as communist protest movements looked for succour. But in doing so it had bound its prestige to regimes which lacked legitimacy and had committed itself to an arms race against an alliance whose wealth vastly outstripped its own.

Khrushchev and partial thaw

How far this postwar geopolitical position depended on the looming presence of Stalin himself was quickly put to the test after his death. Summer 1953 saw unrest in Bulgaria and Czechoslovakia and a series of mass protests and strikes in East Germany, fuelled by grinding poverty and triggered by expectation that the removal of the Soviet dictator heralded major change. They were swiftly and ruthlessly repressed. There would be no sea change. However, the arrest and execution of Beria, coming on top of Stalin's death, made a strong impression not only in the USSR, as we shall see (document 182), but also abroad, and was particularly unsettling for the secret police leadership in the People's Democracies. Moreover, Stalin's heirs did begin to shift the terms in which east–west confrontation was discussed. Malenkov, briefly Prime Minister, asserted that notwithstanding either the tendency for capitalism to generate war or the imperialist powers' inveterate hostility to the socialist world, nuclear weaponry had in effect made the USSR invulnerable. In the course of 1954, Moscow helped smooth the way to a treaty to end the Korean War, withdrew from the zone it had occupied in postwar Austria, and gave up its military bases in Finland.[84] As Khrushchev began to assert his pre-eminence among the 'collective leadership', he energetically pursued a rapprochement with Tito. To win Yugoslavia back into the fold would raise Khrushchev's prestige at home and abroad, and would position him to out-manoeuvre those among Stalin's lieutenants still within the Politburo, headed by Molotov, most closely associated with the rift and purges of the late 1940s. Tito was not easily won round and insisted that Yugoslavia would accept no part of the blame for the rupture. But Khrushchev was persistent, laying the blame at the door of Beria and secret police chief V.S. Abakumov and, on a goodwill visit to Belgrade in May 1955, fulsomely apologizing for the rupture.

Document 132 | **From N.S. Khrushchev's 1955 declaration at Belgrade airport**

May 1955

. . . We sincerely apologize about what happened and are decisively sweeping away all the accumulated dirt of that period.

For our part, we consider the provocative role played in relations between the USSR and Yugoslavia by those now unmasked enemies of the people—Beria, Abakumov, and others—to be part of that dirt. We have made a thorough study of the materials on which the serious charges and slanders made against the Yugoslav

---

84 For a lucid treatment of the post-Stalin years, see J.P.D. Dunbabin, *The Cold War: The Great Powers and their Allies* (London 1994).

leadership at that time were based. The facts show that these materials were fabricated by enemies of the people, despicable imperialist agents who had wormed their way into the ranks of our Party.

We are deeply convinced that the period of bad relations is now behind us. For our part, we are ready to do whatever is required to remove all of the obstacles hindering the full normalization of relations between our states and the strengthening of friendly relations between our peoples.

[Source: *Pravda*, 27 May 1955.]

The formal statement drawn up at the end of Khrushchev's visit was signed by Malenkov's successor as Soviet Premier, Bulganin, rather than Khrushchev, the party leader, reflecting a failure to iron out ideological differences. And it underscored what was for Tito the key point: Yugoslavia's right to pursue its own path to socialism.

Document 133 | **From the 1955 declaration of the Soviet and Yugoslav governments**

June 1955

... Both governments proceed from the following principles:... mutual respect and non-interference in domestic affairs for any reason, be it economic, political or ideological, since questions of internal organization, differences in social systems and differences in the concrete forms in which socialism develops are the exclusive affair of the peoples of the individual countries.

... The cessation of any form of propaganda and disinformation, as well as other actions which sow distrust and in one way or another make it difficult to create an atmosphere for constructive international co-operation and peaceful coexistence among peoples.

N.A. Bulganin, Chairman of the Council of Ministers of the USSR, for the government of the USSR

J. Broz Tito, President of the FPRY, for the government of the FPRY

[Source: *Pravda*, 3 June 1955.]

Khrushchev's initiative did not imply any intention to weaken the bonds between the USSR and the satellite states of eastern Europe. There he envisaged the kind of piecemeal domestic reform he was himself moving towards, but there was to be no questioning either of the communist monopoly of power or of permanent inclusion in the Soviet-led 'socialist family of nations'. Indeed, in May 1955, a fortnight before his trip to Belgrade, the latter principle was emphatically underlined. In part in response to West Germany being incorporated into NATO, the military alliances between the People's Democracies of eastern Europe and the USSR were formally brought together under a unified (Soviet) command in the Warsaw Pact.

Document 134 | **From the 1955 Treaty on Friendship, Co-operation and Mutual Assistance, signed by Bulgaria, Hungary, the GDR, Poland, Romania, the USSR and Czechoslovakia**

May 1955

. . . Article 4

In the event of an armed attack in Europe on one or several of the states participating in the Treaty by any state or group of states, then the Treaty signatory, exercising the right to individual or collective self-defence in accordance with Article 51 of the United Nations Constitution, shall render to the state or states under attack immediate assistance, either individually or by agreement with other Treaty signatories, by all means deemed necessary, including the use of armed force. . .

Article 5

The Contracting Parties have agreed upon the creation of a unified command for their armed forces. The exercise of this command is to be apportioned by agreement between the parties on the basis of jointly established principles. They will also take other agreed measures necessary for the reinforcement of their defence capabilities in order to safeguard their peoples' peaceful labour, secure the inviolability of their borders and territory and guarantee defence against the possibility of aggression.

[Source: *Pravda*, 15 May 1955.]

Nevertheless, the Soviet rehabilitation of Tito played an important role in unsettling the leadership of the satellite states. Cominform repudiated the diatribes it had issued against 'Titoism', before being disbanded altogether in April 1956, and in doing so cast a dark shadow over the record of those leaders who had benefited from the purges and show trials of 1948–50. The trigger for political upheaval was the sensational 'Secret Speech' which Khrushchev delivered to the Twentieth Congress of the CPSU in February 1956, denouncing the 'cult of personality' and many of Stalin's crimes (see below, document 186). The combination of conciliation towards Tito and this attack on Stalin played an important role in the gradual souring of relations in the late 1950s both with Mao's China and with Hoxha's Albanian regime. Closer to home, the consequences were most dramatic in Poland and Hungary.[85]

---

85 There is a good account in G. Swain and N. Swain, *Eastern Europe since 1945* (Basingstoke 1993), pp. 77–200.

Crisis in Poland and Hungary, 1956

In Poland, public debate burst open and police powers were curbed, the privileges of the *nomenklatura* attacked, and political prisoners released. Attempts to stem the tide by a range of minor economic and religious concessions were swept away in June (the month in which Khrushchev's Secret Speech was made known universally when it appeared in the *New York Times*) by mass workers' riots and their bloody repression. Public demand grew for the current leadership to be replaced by Gomułka, who had been quietly released from prison eighteen months earlier. But Gomułka was willing to take office only on his own terms, which included an explicit loosening of Moscow's control, including the freedom to dismantle the collective farms. The Soviet leadership looked askance at developments and Khrushchev himself flew to Poland to try to browbeat Gomułka. The attempt at intimidation failed, yet a head-on collision between Moscow and Warsaw was averted. Khrushchev drew back from attempting military coercion, reassured by Gomułka's insistence that neither the communist political monopoly nor membership of the Warsaw Pact was in doubt. And radical voices in Poland raised against both promises subsided in part because of the much grimmer events unfolding in Hungary.

Here the apparent analogue of Gomułka was Imre Nagy, a moderate communist leader who, following Stalin's death, was appointed premier to work alongside the hard-line party leader Rákosi. He had been empowered to implement a relatively radical version of the 'New Course' favoured by Malenkov, which envisaged shifting the economic priorities sharply from the classic Stalinist emphasis on heavy industry to consumer industry. By 1955, inadequately supported by the USSR and actively undermined by Rákosi, Nagy's reforms seemed to have foundered and he was removed. In the eyes of reformists, however, he was regarded like Gomułka as a relatively liberal communist leader and one willing to assert Hungarian interest vis-à-vis Moscow. After Nagy's fall, Rákosi tried to restore the rigid discipline of the late Stalin years but was unable to intimidate and silence critics against the background of Khrushchev's rapprochement with Tito and denunciation of Stalinist methods. In July 1956, Rákosi was replaced by Gerő, who found it impossible to calm the gathering storm, energized as it was by the unrest in Poland.

On 23 October mass demonstrations in favour of a raft of reforms and calling for the return of Nagy triggered upheaval. The security police fired on the crowds, and the following day parts of the Soviet garrison stationed in Hungary briefly went on the offensive. By then, however, with Soviet consent, Nagy was reinstalled as premier, while on 25 October, Janos Kádár, another reformist party leader repressed under Rákosi, took over as First

Secretary. In Moscow, the best possible gloss was put on events, the following account published on 25 October claiming both that Nagy had requested action by the Special Corps and that their intervention had resolved matters.

Document 135 | TASS communiqué on Hungary

25 October 1956

Late last night underground reactionary organizations in Budapest made an attempt to stage a counter-revolutionary putsch against the people's government. . . . Rebel detachments which had managed to seize weapons caused bloodshed in a number of places. The forces of revolutionary order began to repulse the rebels. On the orders of Imre Nagy, the reappointed chairman of the Council of Ministers, the city was declared to be in a state of siege. The government of the HPR appealed to the government of the USSR for help. In fulfilment of this request, Soviet military units stationed in Hungary in accordance with the Warsaw Pact rendered assistance to the troops of the Hungarian Republic in restoring order in Budapest. . . . By the end of today the hostile escapade had been suppressed. Order has been restored in Budapest.

[Source: *Izvestiya*, 25 October 1956.]

In reality, it was the discredited government of Gerő, against whom the demonstrators were protesting, which appealed for help via the Soviet ambassador, the future CPSU party leader, Yu. Andropov. By contrast, Nagy, once in office, pressed for the Special Corps to be recalled to barracks even though mass demonstrations continued. Moreover, he went much further. Breaking with Kádár, who was less willing to defy the USSR, he decided to endorse popular demands both that Soviet troops be withdrawn from Hungary altogether and that free competitive elections be held, with the Social Democrats and possibly other parties being permitted to organize and stand against communist candidates. On 1–2 November, he announced Hungary's withdrawal from the Warsaw Pact, proclaimed the country's neutrality, and appealed to the UN for support. In doing so he broke the two taboos respected by Gomułka. In Budapest it seemed possible that a peaceful compromise might yet be found not least because, as is brought out in the following memoir by V. Fomin, propaganda officer with the Soviet garrison in Hungary, many Hungarian officers both trusted their Soviet opposite numbers and had no illusions about the futility of pressing matters to a trial of strength. Yet by 1 November the die had been cast. Soviet troops began to cross into Hungary, and mass unrest was ruthlessly and bloodily crushed.[86]

---

86 For the sequence of events in Budapest, see B. Lomax, *Hungary 1956* (London 1976).

Document 136 | **A memoir of the Hungarian uprising of 1956 by the military historian V. Fomin**

A Special Corps was formed from among our troops in Hungary in March 1956. I had the job of special propaganda officer in its political division. . .

The Corps was directly answerable to the Ministry of Defence in Moscow; that's why it was called 'Special'. It was comprised of two mechanized and two air divisions. The task of the Corps was to help the Hungarian army in case of a NATO attack. No other tasks had been assigned to the troops. . .

In October 1956 the Hungarian public, and especially young people, were worked up about events in Poland, where strikes were still going on after people had been shot in a demonstration that summer in Gdańsk. On 23 October Hungarian students were going to organize a demonstration of solidarity with the young people of Poland. The demonstrators also had a 14-point list of demands. The young people did not aim at overthrowing the socialist system. It was about improving it and getting real national independence, which they reckoned had been prevented by Soviet troops being stationed in Hungary for eleven years.

In other words, it was about continuing the reforms which had started with the government programme as far back as 1953. A group of demonstrators moved towards the radio building, which was protected by state security forces. They began to storm the building, and in the course of this the first shots rang out. Finally, the building was seized. . . There were casualties on both sides. Another, even bigger crowd, set out to destroy the statue of Stalin, which they cut through with blow-torches and knocked off its pedestal. All that was left of the 'Peoples' Leader' were his boots.

Round about this time they started seizing weapons and ammunition from police stations and from an ordnance factory. After 8 p.m. Yu.V. Andropov, the Soviet ambassador to Hungary, passed on to the military the Hungarian government's request to bring in the Special Corps to 'maintain order'. And the Special Corps moved into Budapest. . .

After 28 October, when Imre Nagy's government declared the events a 'popular movement', the presence of our troops in Budapest became unnecessary. At the same time the Hungarian government raised the question of the complete withdrawal of Soviet troops from Hungary. Our government agreed to talks about this. The 'popular movement' decision proved really tragic for the Hungarian defenders of the existing order, who had been honestly doing their duty. On 30 October extremists destroyed the Budapest Party building and shot its defenders without investigation or trial, just when our troops were moving out of Budapest. As for the talks about Soviet withdrawal from Hungary, at which I was present as an interpreter, they, as it transpired, had another purpose. On 3 November 1956 our military delegation, headed by General M.S. Malinin, Deputy Chief of General Staff, arrived in Budapest. The talks took place in the Parliament building. When they finished, it was agreed that a final decision would be taken that evening at a meeting at the quarters of our troops. . . . After everything had been decided, the Hungarian delegation was waiting for cars to take them to Budapest, and we even offered them a glass of wine each. Into the room came a group of KGB men, headed by General I.A. Serov, the KGB chairman. The members of the Hungarian delegation were arrested.

I was shocked by the arrest, not only because it was so unexpected (not one of us had been warned about it) but also by its crudity. To this day I still cannot understand why it was necessary. I am fully convinced that we could have reached an agreement with the delegation. The three military men had a friendly attitude towards the Soviet Union and two others had taken part in our partisan movement during the war. They did not need to be told what armed resistance to overwhelming Soviet forces might mean for Budapest. In any case, the Hungarian officer who was director of 'Maleter', a mobile radio station, and on duty in his vehicle outside the building, understood straightaway and agreed to give an order 'in the Minister's name' not to fire on the Soviet troops who were supposedly beginning to be restationed. The main purpose of this military trick was to neutralize the anti-aircraft batteries which we believed formed the outer ring of Budapest's defence. . . . The guns remained silent as our tanks rolled into the city, except for one gun positioned near the village of Soroksár which destroyed a tank and the ATC in which, by a twist of fate, Serov's men were riding. . .

On 2 November 1956, the Commander-in-Chief of the Unified Forces of the Warsaw Treaty, Marshal of the Soviet Union I.S. Konev. . . gave the order to 'put down the counter-revolutionary revolt in Budapest'. The Corps was accordingly reinforced with tanks, artillery and paratroopers. The military operation was carried out on the orders of our senior Party and government leadership headed by N.S. Khrushchev. They took the decision. . . at the request of Hungarian communists, the Chinese and Yugoslav leaderships and the member-states of the Warsaw Treaty.

[Source: *Komsomol'skaya pravda*, 5 December 1990.]

Khrushchev and 'the correlation of forces'

The repression of the Hungarian revolution made plain the severe limits on the extent to which Khrushchev and his successors, even when they were distancing themselves from some of Stalin's methods and image, would countenance altering the framework he had bequeathed. Domination of eastern Europe had become integral to that framework. Just how deeply they were committed to retaining suzerainty over it was demonstrated by the fact that, in contrast to Stalin's exploitative approach, they now allowed the terms of trade to swing in favour of the satellite People's Democracies, and particularly in favour of Poland and Hungary. Soviet overlordship was non–negotiable but they would seek to underpin it by giving the client regimes more leeway in domestic affairs and some chance, through economic and social development, to build legitimacy. In part this absolute commitment remained a matter of military security. Even though the strategic significance of eastern Europe would slowly decline with the development of nuclear weapons with ever longer range, for the generation of Soviet leaders who had endured the horrors of Barbarossa the need to maintain buffer states and a major military presence along NATO's front line seemed axiomatic. What drove this commitment, over and beyond military concerns, was the critical role that the 'socialist commonwealth' had come to play in terms of Soviet ideology, Soviet status and the authority of the Soviet regime at home and abroad. Thus threats to hegemony in eastern Europe were experienced as mortal threats to the entire Soviet order. That hegemony had become embedded in the manner in which the regime staked its ideological claims and sought to reinforce its international prestige. It had become integral to the Marxist–Leninist narrative in which 'progressive' forces, aligned with the USSR against the forces of reaction spearheaded by 'warmongers' in the US, were steadily advancing.

The key to the regime's optimistic reading of the Cold War—a trial of strength in which by the laws of history the Soviet side, the 'peace camp', was destined to prevail—was the manner in which the relative weight and trajectory of the two alliances were analysed. This was in terms of what was labelled 'the correlation of forces' between them, an amalgam of the economic power, military strength, support from other states (notably those in the Third World), and the extent to which governments aligned with each side were stable or faced social unrest. And on each score Soviet prospects were portrayed in glowing terms: a rate of economic growth that put western economic expansion in the shade; a rate of military–scientific progress that would soon enable the USSR to match American nuclear capability; and wave upon wave of anti-colonial, socialist and radical nationalist rebellion—in South-east Asia, in Latin America, in the Middle East, and in Africa—which, even when not explicitly pro-Soviet, was decidedly anti-western. During the late 1950s and early 1960s, there were sufficient grounds for this assessment to seem plausible not only within the USSR but abroad. And Khrushchev saw enormous potential gain in terms of extending Soviet influence and entrenching his own position by inflating Soviet claims on each front.

He maximized the capital to be made from the successful launch of Sputnik into orbit in October 1957. The impression it made both at home and internationally gave credence to speculation that the Soviet Union was rapidly narrowing American technical, military and economic superiority. The USSR, so Khrushchev boasted, was now in a position to target rockets on any region on earth, and there was real alarm in the west that the Soviet Union had established a 'missile gap' between its capabilities and those of the US. Waxing equally eloquent on Soviet economic progress shortly before the launch of Sputnik, Khrushchev had coined the phrase 'we will bury you'. Questioned about the remark in an interview two years later, he rehearsed the orthodox Marxism–Leninism assumptions to explain his prediction.

Document 137 | **'We have to co-exist'—Khrushchev's conversation with American journalists**

September 1959

Khrushchev was asked, 'People keep referring to you supposedly saying at some diplomatic reception that you'd bury us. If you didn't, then perhaps you'll deny it, but if you did, could you explain what you meant?'

Khrushchev replied, 'In this hall there is only a tiny part of the American population. But my life wouldn't be long enough even to bury each one of you. I did say such a thing, but what I actually said was deliberately twisted. It wasn't a matter of actually burying somebody sometime, but about changing a social system during the historical development of society. Anybody who can read knows that at present there is more than one social system in the world. As a society develops, its social system changes. There was feudalism, which was replaced by capitalism. Capitalism was more progressive than feudalism. Compared with feudalism, capitalism created better conditions for the development of productive forces, but capitalism produced irreconcilable contradictions. As each system outlives itself, it gives birth to its heirs. As Marx, Engels and Lenin showed, Communism will replace capitalism. This is what we believe. Many of you don't believe this. But even in your country there are people who believe it. . .

You may disagree with me. I disagree with you. What are we to do? We have to co-exist.'

[Source: *Litsom k litsu s Amerikoy* (Moscow 1959), pp. 111–12.]

On each front, however, Khrushchev overplayed his hand. In terms of economic growth, although the Soviet economy did indeed grow rapidly in the post-Stalin period, the American lead in terms of GNP remained huge. Moreover, for all his bluster about long-term trends, the immediate implications of the imbalance proved difficult to escape. In Europe, the contrast in terms of consumer goods and living standards between east and west was marked and at the most sensitive point, Berlin, politically explosive. Whereas free passage westward had been blocked off elsewhere across the 'iron curtain', here there was a relentless flow of Germans opting to leave the Soviet zone and migrate to the west. The effect was to bleed the nascent state of key educated cadres, and intensify the anxiety of Ulbricht and the GDR leadership to see the USSR engineer a peace treaty ending four-power occupation and securing international recognition for the GDR. In 1958 Khrushchev tried to lever the western powers out of the capital, threatening unilaterally to hand over control of the Soviet zone of the city to the GDR. He succeeded only in increasing American commitment to its defence. In summer 1961, under heavy pressure from an East German leadership desperate to halt the stream of migrants, he ordered the construction of the Berlin Wall.[87]

The Cuban Missile Crisis, 1962

In military terms, too, Khrushchev himself admitted by 1960 that American investment in intercontinental ballistic missiles had eliminated any gap there had been, and the scale of military expenditure under President Kennedy plainly swung the balance the other way. Khrushchev's eagerness to bring military and diplomatic reality more closely into line with Soviet pretensions played a major part in the Cuban Missile Crisis of 1962, the most dangerous Cold War clash.[88] It arose in part because, a year after coming to power without any help whatsoever from Moscow, Castro's revolutionary government began to look to the USSR for protection, trade and arms. This seemed to the Soviet leadership a glorious demonstration that the 'correlation of forces' was shifting inexorably in their favour, made all the more delicious by Washington's alarm, threats and disastrous attempt to overthrow Castro in April 1961. Khrushchev took it as a golden opportunity to drive home the shift: by installing nuclear missiles just ninety miles from the American mainland he saw the possibility of reducing the US's nuclear superiority at a stroke and at remarkably modest cost.[89] The precedent and a factor in his reasoning was the US's installation of nuclear missiles on the Soviet doorstep,

---

87 Friction over Berlin is placed in the wider context of the Cold War by M. Beschloss, *Kennedy v Khrushchev: The Crisis Years, 1960–63* (London 1991).

88 For the most detailed account of Soviet decision-making, see A. Fursenko and T. Naftali, *'One Hell of a Gamble': Khrushchev, Castro and Kennedy and the Cuban Missile Crisis 1958–1964* (London 1997). See Gaddis, *We Now Know*, pp. 260–80, for a succinct synthesis of recent work on the Cuban crisis.

89 On the interaction between Khrushchev's domestic and foreign agendas in his policy in Cuba, see the essays by W. Taubman, A. Yanov, and G.F. Minde II and M. Hennessey, in R.O. Crummey (ed.), *Reform in Russia and the USSR* (Chicago 1989).

in Turkey, the previous year. The upshot, however, was President Kennedy's threat on 27 October to go to war unless the missiles were withdrawn. The following memoir by G.N. Bol'shakov, a KGB agent at the Soviet Embassy at the time who was used by both sides as a channel for secret exchanges, recreates the fraught atmosphere of that October. He emphasizes the key role played by the clandestine negotiations which Robert Kennedy carried out on behalf of his brother with the Soviet ambassador, A.F. Dobrynin. It was in the course of these that President Kennedy, unknown to most of his own advisers, made a key concession to Khrushchev: though Washington could not publicly concede Khrushchev's demand that the US withdraw its bases in Turkey, Kennedy promised to do so within a few months of resolving the Cuban crisis.

Document 138 | **From the memoirs of G.N. Bol'shakov, an adviser in the Soviet Embassy in Havana, on the Cuba Crisis**

The events of October 1962 were the first and, fortunately, only thermonuclear crisis in our history. . . 'a moment of fear and illumination', when N.S. Khrushchev, John Kennedy, Fidel Castro and the whole of mankind felt that for the first time they were 'in the same boat' at the epicentre of a nuclear abyss. . . Some thought that the causes of the crisis were military: by deploying missiles in Cuba the USSR was, they reckon, trying to correct the 'imbalance' in the number of nuclear warheads with the USA, which, so they claimed, was something like 15:1 or 17:1 in the latter's favour at that time. Others put forward political reasons: the USA's intention to destroy the Republic of Cuba, and the USSR's desire to consolidate the position of the socialist camp on the American continent. I myself think that the Cuban crisis was primarily a failure of trust—between states and people. . .

This was the first time the Americans felt the breath of war on their own doorstep. Those thirteen days in October made the USA, and the whole world, really think about the unity of human security. . . The most dangerous moment was the night of 27–28 October. The trouble was that on the morning of 27 October a Soviet surface-to-air missile had shot down a U2 high-altitude spy-plane, piloted by Major R. Andersen. He was the first and last human victim of the blockade. USAF command proposed an immediate air strike on Cuba. The situation became extremely tense. The President was having difficulty restraining the military. Robert Kennedy called in ambassador A.F. Dobrynin to warn him that war might break out. We had to make an urgent decision about the proposal, discussed the previous day, to withdraw the missiles from Cuba in exchange for a guarantee from the USA that it would not interfere in Cuba's internal affairs and would respect its sovereignty. A few minutes after the conversation with Dobrynin, Robert Kennedy phoned me and suggested we meet in his car near my house. He said exactly the same as he had just said to the ambassador. He emphasized that the President, by beginning the blockade of Cuba, had now become 'a prisoner of his own actions' and could 'restrain the military only for a few more days, unless a positive answer came from Moscow'.

Early on the morning of 28 October. . . Moscow Radio broadcast the Soviet government's message to President Kennedy, agreeing to withdraw the missiles and bombers from Cuba in exchange for the above-mentioned guarantees from the USA to Cuba. . .

[Source: *Komsomol'skaya pravda*, 4 February 1989.]

Days later Mikoyan, the Soviet Deputy Prime Minister, flew to Havana to pick up the diplomatic pieces. He had been the first senior Soviet official to visit Cuba two-and-a-half years earlier and his enthusiasm for the authentic revolutionary spirit on the island had made him a highly popular figure. His task was to reassure Castro's government, bewildered as it was by discovering that either Soviet military power or the anti-imperialist resolution of its leadership or both fell far short of expectations. His approach was in step with the approach adopted by Khrushchev in rationalizing the dénouement. To meet the deep unease of his own colleagues and parry the scorn of the Chinese government that this was a humiliating climb-down in the face of imperialist aggression, he insisted that the critical issue had been warding off American determination to overthrow Castro and restore capitalism. By raising the stakes dramatically, Moscow had successfully forced the US publicly to abandon its planned military intervention: thus, despite appearances, the Soviet Union had emerged the victor. Mikoyan's purpose now was to ensure that, despite the ceiling that had been placed on the Soviet military presence, the Cubans would remain firmly embedded in the Soviet alliance. As the notes of his meeting with Castro underline, he did so by emphasizing continuing Soviet commitment to Cuban security and proffering not only heavily subsidized trade but straight-forward aid.

Document 139 | From notes of the talks between A.I. Mikoyan and Fidel Castro on 3 November 1962

After greetings A.I. Mikoyan conveyed regards from the CC of the CPSU and N.S. Khrushchev to Fidel Castro, remarking that the CC of the CPSU had a high opinion of the courage of comrade F. Castro and the Cuban people in their stalwart defence of the freedom and independence of their country. A.I. Mikoyan said that he person-ally was glad to carry out the CC of the CPSU's wishes, since he knew Cuba and the leaders of the Cuban revolution. . .

F. Castro replied that the Cuban leaders were glad to see A.I. Mikoyan again in

Cuba and talk with him about matters of mutual importance. 'We know,' joked F. Castro, 'that N.S. Khrushchev once said that "there's a Cuban on the CC of the CPSU, and that Cuban is A.I. Mikoyan".'

. . . 'The Soviet Union's concessions [to the USA] had had a depressing effect. Psychologically our people were not ready for it. There was a feeling of deep disappointment, bitterness and pain. It was as if we had been deprived not only of missiles but of the very symbol of solidarity. Our people thought that the report that the missile installations were being dismantled and returned to the Soviet Union was a barefaced lie. The Cuban people did not know about the agreement, they did not know that the missiles still belonged to the Soviet side. The Cuban people had no idea of the weapons' legal status. They had got used to the Soviet Union giving us weapons which then became our property. . .

'Why was the decision taken unilaterally? Why are they taking the missiles away? Are they going to take all weapons back? These are the questions which have been bothering our people. Over the last couple of days these feelings of bitterness and pain have spread right across the country. It has been one thing after another. On 27 October came the proposal to remove the missiles from Cuba on condition that the Turkish bases were shut down. On 28 October came the order for dismantling and agreement to inspection. Nobody could believe it and thought it was all a pack of lies.'

Mikoyan replied, 'We considered and consider it our international duty as communists to do everything we can to defend the Cuban revolution and scupper the imperialists' plans.

'A short while ago our comrades told us that the economic situation in this country was getting worse, caused by American pressure and high defence expenditure. We were afraid that the deteriorating situation might be the result of a plan to stifle Cuba economically. The CC of the CPSU discussed the Cuban situation and, unsolicited (you are a modest people who don't like to pester us with requests), decided to take a number of measures to increase aid to Cuba. Whereas once you used to get part of your weapons from us on credit and only part of them free of charge, in the new conditions we have decided to supply weapons and some uniforms (100,000 sets over 2 years) and equipment free of charge. We could see that the Cuban trade negotiators taking part in the negotiations were having some difficulties. To balance the books they needed more than $100 million. That's why we took up all their suggestions, in order to scupper Kennedy's plan, which counted on Cuba imploding.

'The same can be said about foodstuffs and industrial products. To make Cuba's economic position easier, we delivered essential industrial goods and foodstuffs to the tune of 198 million rubles. To be frank, we gave you everything without counting the cost.

'The way I see it is we're now entering a new phase in our relations, which have a different character. In the first phase there was some sort of appearance of mutually beneficial trade. But now these deliveries have the character of purely fraternal assistance.'

[Source: *Mezhdunarodnaya zhizn'*, No. 4, 1992, pp. 130, 131, 135.]

The Cuban crisis, bringing the world to the brink of catastrophe, had a sobering effect on both sides in the Cold War. To reduce the danger of nuclear war being triggered by misunderstanding or accident, a 'hot line' was installed between the Kremlin and the White House. And in summer 1963 negotiations on limiting the testing of nuclear weapons, initiated as far back as 1957, at last yielded a treaty. Concern both about the broader issue of the cataclysmic capacity of nuclear weapons and about the narrower one of radiation fallout from tests had generated worldwide popular demand for action since the late 1950s. In the aftermath of the Cuban crisis, both the USSR and the US proved readier to compromise. From the Soviet point of view it was a matter of satisfaction that the final breakthrough was achieved in direct negotiations in Moscow, tangible recognition of the USSR's super-power status.

Document 140 | **Treaty Banning Nuclear Weapon Tests in the Atmosphere, in Outer Space and under Water**

5 August 1963

The Governments of the United States of America, the United Kingdom of Great Britain and Northern Ireland, and the Union of Soviet Socialist Republics, here-inafter referred to as the 'Original Parties',

Proclaiming as their principal aim the speediest possible achievement of an agreement on general and complete disarmament under strict international control in accordance with the objectives of the United Nations which would put an end to the armaments race and eliminate the incentive to the production and testing of all kinds of weapons, including nuclear weapons,

Seeking to achieve the discontinuance of all test explosions of nuclear weapons for all time, determined to continue negotiations to this end, and desiring to put an end to the contamination of man's environment by radioactive substances,

Have agreed as follows:

Article I
1. Each of the Parties to this Treaty undertakes to prohibit, to prevent, and not to carry out any nuclear weapon test explosion, or any other nuclear explosion, at any place under its jurisdiction or control:
(a) in the atmosphere; beyond its limits, including outer space; or under water, including territorial waters or high seas; or

(b) in any other environment if such explosion causes radioactive debris to be present outside the territorial limits of the State under whose jurisdiction or control such explosion is conducted. It is understood in this connection that the provisions of this subparagraph are without prejudice to the conclusion of a treaty resulting in the permanent banning of all nuclear test explosions, including all such explosions underground, the conclusion of which, as the Parties have stated in the Preamble to this Treaty, they seek to achieve.

2. Each of the Parties to this Treaty undertakes furthermore to refrain from causing, encouraging, or in any way participating in, the carrying out of any nuclear weapon test explosion, or any other nuclear explosion, anywhere which would take place in any of the environments described, or have the effect referred to, in paragraph 1 of this Article. . .

Article III

1. This Treaty shall be open to all States for signature. Any State which does not sign this Treaty before its entry into force in accordance with paragraph 3 of this Article may accede to it at any time. . .

6. This Treaty shall be registered by the Depositary Governments pursuant to Article 102 of the Charter of the United Nations.

Article IV

This Treaty shall be of unlimited duration.

Each Party shall in exercising its national sovereignty have the right to withdraw from the Treaty if it decides that extraordinary events, related to the subject matter of this Treaty, have jeopardized the supreme interests of its country. It shall give notice of such withdrawal to all other Parties to the Treaty three months in advance.

[Source: http://www.nuclearfiles.org/menu/library/treaties/partial-test-ban/trty_partial-test-ban_1963-10-10.htm]

However, the Treaty's scope was narrow. Not only did France and China decline to sign, but the ban did not extend to underground testing. Moreover, although it demonstrated a minimum level of trust between the two sides, it did nothing in itself to limit the arms race. And following Khrushchev's fall in October 1964, his successors, led by Kosygin and Brezhnev, committed the USSR to a sustained and major programme of military investment, both nuclear and conventional and including massive expansion of the navy. By the late 1960s, Soviet nuclear capability had begun to match that of the US and in the early 1970s, with American resources stretched by the Vietnam War, the USSR achieved broad nuclear parity.

Crisis in Czechoslovakia, 1968

The mounting cost of the arms race was among the factors placing a new strain on relations between the Soviet Union and the eastern-European satellites. Relatively lavish subsidy of the economies of its COMECON partners weighed increasingly heavily on the Soviet budget but Moscow's preparations to cut it back provoked strong opposition from allied capitals. Moreover, a series of economic reforms, vigorously taken up by Kosygin as we shall see, fostered pressure for wider social and cultural change. The impact was most unsettling in Czechoslovakia, where the post-1956 regime headed by Novotný had been particularly centralized, rigid and repressive.[90] When sharp decline in Czechoslovakia's economic growth forced him grudgingly to accept the need to follow the Soviet example of economic reform, momentum began to gather for more far-reaching change, much of the pressure coming from Slovak demands for greater autonomy. Novotný's attempt to halt the momentum by force was vetoed by Moscow and in January 1968 he was replaced by the Slovak party leader, Alexander Dubček.[91] Dubček reassured Moscow that he was firmly committed both to the party's leading role and to the Warsaw Pact, but within that framework he sanctioned a battery of measures to implement 'socialism with a human face', including an end to censorship and competitive elections for party posts. Although at first the Soviet leadership was relaxed, when domestic radicals and ebullient student demonstrators publicly pressed Dubček to resist external diktats, Moscow began to send out ever sharper warning signals. Moreover, the neighbouring satellite governments, notably those of the GDR and Poland, became increasingly alarmed lest the 'Prague Spring' prove infectious. On 15 July, a collective letter was sent by the five 'fraternal parties' of the Warsaw Organization (the Romanian leadership declined to sign) calling on Dubček and his colleagues to reimpose effective control. When the Prague leadership resolutely rejected the demands, Moscow invited them to talks which were held in Čierna nad Tisou and Bratislava.

On the eve of the talks, the hardening line in Moscow helped to trigger an appeal to Brezhnev, written from Čierna, by more cautious Czech and Slovak leaders who feared the party was losing its grip. That they wrote in Russian underlined their loyalty to Moscow and signalled the risk they were running that, prior to Soviet action, they might in the eyes of Czechoslovak public opinion be exposed as traitors to their own country.

---

90 H. Renner, *A History of Czechoslovakia since 1945* (London 1989), pp. 49–58, provides a sound narrative.
91 On Moscow's handling of the crisis, see J. Valenta, *Soviet Intervention in Czechoslovakia, 1968: Anatomy of a Decision* (revised edn, Baltimore 1991).

Document 141 | **Request for Soviet intervention in Czechoslovakia—the appeal from A. Indra, Secretary of the CPCz CC, D. Kolder and A. Kapek, members of the CPCz CC Presidium, O. Švestka, editor-in-chief of *Rudé právo*, and V. Bilák, First Secretary of the CC of the CP of Slovakia, to the leadership of the CPSU and the USSR**

29/30 July 1968

Dear Leonid Il'ich, aware of our full responsibility for what we are doing, we are addressing the following appeal to you.

Our essentially healthy post-January democratic process, the correction of the mistakes and failings of the past and overall political leadership are slipping from the grasp of the Party's Central Committee.

The press, radio and television, which are effectively in the hands of right-wing forces, have had so much influence on public opinion that elements hostile to the Party are now beginning to participate in the political life of the country without public resistance. They are fostering a wave of nationalism and chauvinism and fomenting an anti-Communist and anti-Soviet psychosis.

... The very existence of socialism in our country is under threat... Right-wing forces have created conditions favourable to a counter-revolutionary coup.

It is in such difficult circumstances that we are appealing to you, Soviet communists and leading representatives of the CPSU and USSR, with a request to give us active support and help with all the means available to you. Only with your help can we rescue the CzSSR from the imminent danger of counter-revolution... In view of the complex and dangerous developments in our country we ask you to keep our statement top-secret and for this reason we are writing it directly to you, personally, in Russian.

[Source: *Izvestiya*, 18 July 1992.]

During the talks, which spanned the four days from 29 July to 1 August, Dubček tried to persuade the Soviet leaders that there was no question of his government leaving the Warsaw Pact and that the party was not losing control of the situation. The communiqué issued at the end of the talks implied a meeting of minds, but in reality he had failed to convince Brezhnev and Kosygin. The following report on the talks, written a week later, was designed for CPSU activists. Despite the veneer of agreement, what it ominously underlined were the differences between the two sides and the failure of members of the Prague leadership to take action to uphold socialism, Marxism–Leninism and 'proletarian internationalism' against the threat of counter-revolution.

Document 142 | **Information from the CPSU CC for Party activists on the situation in Czechoslovakia**

8 August 1968

On the initiative of our Party, discussions were held between the Politburo of the CC of the CPSU and the Presidium of the CC of the CPCz in Čierna nad Tisou, followed by a meeting of fraternal Parties of the socialist countries in Bratislava. The situation in which the meeting between the CPSU CC Politburo and the CPCz CC Presidium took place was extremely complex.

On the one hand, the Warsaw letter from the five fraternal Parties was favourably received by many communists and workers in the CzSSR and promoted the process of consolidating all those who take the position of Marxist–Leninism and proletarian internationalism. On the other hand, however, the same letter was used by right-wing forces to fan the flames of nationalist and above all anti-Soviet feeling in the country. The leadership of the CPCz has not rebuffed such sentiments. On the contrary, as the document 'The point of view of the CC of the CPCz', published in connection with the letter of the five Parties showed, it was effectively encouraging them, counting on using the wave of nationalist sentiment to support and consolidate its own position. The real threat of a sharp shift to the right in the political life of Czechoslovakia was beginning to become apparent. That is why the Politburo of the CC of the CPSU decided to force the question of talks with our Czechoslovak comrades.

In entering into talks with the Presidium of the CC of the CPCz, the Politburo of the CC of the CPSU had set itself the following aims:
– yet again to direct the attention of the leadership of the CPCz to the extreme seriousness of the situation in the CzSSR and the necessity for urgent, effective measures to be taken against counter-revolutionary elements;
– to exert influence in the necessary direction on those members of the leadership of the CPCz who are adopting a conciliatory line towards right-wing, anti-socialist forces;
– yet again to use the influence of the CPSU to prevent the CPCz and its leadership from abandoning the internationalist positions of the fraternal Parties of the socialist states and to strengthen the CzSSR's traditional friendly ties with the Soviet Union and the other socialist countries.

The Politburo of the CC of the CPSU felt that, given the circumstances, it was appropriate to put the question as bluntly and frankly as possible. This was the only way to ensure a clearer exposure of the positions within the Presidium of the CC of the CPCz and provide support to those comrades standing on consistent Marxist–Leninist positions.

Such a line was consistently taken by other members of the Politburo of the CC of the CPSU both in their speeches and in their conversations with individual members of the Presidium of the CC of the CPCz, which took place throughout the talks.

The speeches of comrades Dubček, Černík and Smrkovský did recognize in general the negative phenomena in the Party and country and spoke of the need to combat right-wing forces, while emphasizing the wish of the leadership of the CPCz to maintain and develop fraternal relations with the Soviet Union and the CPSU. However, as before they denied any immediate danger of counter-revolution and showed an uncritical attitude to their own actions in trying to depict a position in which the situation in the country was becoming increasingly normal. They regarded the collective letter from the five fraternal Parties as a factor which complicated their work, and expressed disagreement with its evaluation of the political situation in the CzSSR. . .

The Politburo of the CC of the CPSU notes that this bilateral meeting was timely and has great significance for the further development and strengthening of relations between the two Parties and countries.

A joint declaration based on a draft prepared by the CPSU delegation was produced by the Bratislava conference. It set out a united position on current important questions in the development of socialism and the international situation. . .

At the same time, in the present complex international situation, when imperialism is increasing its efforts aimed at undermining the socialist system, the declaration of the Bratislava conference is a blow against imperialist reaction and its plans.

The CC of the CPSU is sure that the results of the Bratislava conference are in keeping with the interests of the whole world socialist system and the entire international communist movement and will play an effective part in rallying anti-imperialist forces in the struggle for their great common aims.

In summing up the results of this work, it should be said that a serious new success for the CPSU's principled Marxist–Leninist policy has been achieved and an important step has been taken which will help the leadership of the CPCz and healthy forces in the Party and country to go onto the attack against right-wing, revisionist, counter-revolutionary elements, become more active and get the country out of the difficult situation it currently finds itself in.

The Politburo of the CC will continue to watch developments in Czechoslovakia attentively, and in accordance with the decisions of the July plenary session of the CC of the CPSU, take all necessary measures to help the working class and communists of the CzSSR to defend their country's socialist achievements.

[Source: *Otechestvennye arkhivy*, No. 3, 1993.]

Two weeks later, hopeful that a significant portion of the Czechoslovak party leadership would accept the verdict, Soviet-led forces of the Warsaw Pact invaded. The announcement by the Soviet news agency claimed that the troops would stay no longer than the Czechoslovak leadership required. But the final sentence baldly spelled out the lesson to be learned both by would-be eastern-European reformers and by the west, the kernel of what was to become known as the 'Brezhnev Doctrine': 'No one will ever be allowed to remove a single link from the commonwealth of socialist states.'[92]

Document 143 | **The TASS declaration on intervention in Czechoslovakia**

21 August 1968

During the night of 20–21 August 1968 troops from five countries of the Warsaw Pact—the USSR, the PRB, the GDR, the HPR and the PPR—crossed the Czechoslovak border, which is why TASS has made the following declaration.

TASS is authorized to declare that Party figures and statesmen in the Czechoslovak Socialist Republic have appealed to the Soviet Union and other allied states with a request that immediate assistance, including the assistance of their armed forces, be rendered to the fraternal Czechoslovak people. This appeal was prompted by a threat which had arisen to the existing socialist system in Czechoslovakia, and its constitutionally established statehood, from counter-revolutionary forces, in league with foreign forces hostile to socialism. . .

Any further aggravation of the situation in Czechoslovakia affects the vital interests of the Soviet Union and the other socialist countries and the security interests of the states of the socialist commonwealth. Moreover, a threat to the socialist system of Czechoslovakia is also a threat to the foundations of European peace.

The Soviet government and those of the allied countries—the People's Republic of Bulgaria, the Hungarian People's Republic, the German Democratic Republic and the Polish People's Republic—proceeding from the principles of indissoluble friendship and co-operation and in accordance with existing treaty obligations, have decided to comply with the above appeal to render the necessary assistance to the fraternal Czechoslovak people. . .

On 21 August Soviet military subunits, along with military subunits of the above-mentioned allied countries entered the territory of Czechoslovakia. They will be immediately withdrawn from the CzSSR as soon as the threat which has arisen to the achievements of socialism in Czechoslovakia and the security of the socialist countries is removed and the lawful authorities consider that these military subunits need no longer remain.

The actions being taken are not directed against any state and in no way encroach upon the interests of any state. They are serving the goals of peace and are dictated by a concern for reinforcing it.

---

92 For an analysis setting the 'doctrine' in wider context, see R.A. Jones, *The Soviet Concept of Limited Sovereignty from Lenin to Gorbachev: The Brezhnev Doctrine* (London 1990).

The fraternal countries will firmly and decisively oppose any threat with their indissoluble solidarity. No one will ever be allowed to remove a single link from the commonwealth of socialist states.

[Source: *Pravda*, 21 August 1968.]

Though there were mass demonstrations of popular opposition to Soviet action, there was no attempt at a military response and the effective authority of the invasion forces was swiftly established. Dubček was retained in post for several months in an attempt to minimize the affront to reformist Czechoslovak opinion. At the same time preparations were made to grant Slovakia substantial autonomy under a new federal constitution, the Soviet hope being that this would provide a platform from which to reconstruct Slovak allegiance.

In terms of the Soviet image internationally, the intervention in Czechoslovakia was deeply corrosive. Though the leadership continued to use the language of the 'correlation of forces', the premise that popular protest and the non-communist Left could be counted as broadly sympathetic to the USSR ceased to be plausible. Even fraternal communist parties in western Europe condemned the action outright, sharply accelerating the detachment of 'Eurocommunism' from Moscow. In the eyes of the Soviet leadership, however, the decision was vindicated by the efficiency with which intervention had been carried out and by the speed with which the west, despite initial expressions of disgust, came to terms with the Brezhnev Doctrine.

Détente

Securing formal western acceptance of the postwar settlement and of Soviet domination in eastern Europe was a paramount goal for Brezhnev, as it had been for Khrushchev. The dramatic demonstration that despite limited rein granted the satellite People's Republics the fundamentals were impermeable, combined with the achievement of virtual nuclear parity, gave Moscow a significantly stronger bargaining position than it had enjoyed under Khrushchev. At the same time, by the late 1960s the prospect of a substantial reduction in tension with the west had become highly attractive. Steep deterioration in relations with China, reaching the point in 1969 of serious border clashes, and a Chinese boycott of the last international communist congress organized by Moscow, counselled détente elsewhere. Now that a broad balance of nuclear potential had been reached, it was highly desirable that the heavy cost of the arms race should be eased. And in the search for ways of accelerating Soviet economic growth, a level of understanding that opened the way to an expansion of foreign trade and in particular imports of western technology was most appealing. In 1969 when the West German Chancellor Willy Brandt began to pursue his *Ostpolitik*, edging towards recognizing the GDR, and the US backed him, the Soviet response was positive. In parallel with inter-German talks, the superpowers opened negotiations to agree limitations on their respective nuclear arsenals.[93]

Taking stock of developments of the previous five years and of the Soviet Union's geopolitical position at the Twenty-fourth Congress of the CPSU in 1971, Brezhnev exuded confidence. His language no longer had the militancy and urgency of Khrushchev's. In proclaiming Soviet commitment to bringing an end to war in Southeast Asia, and in solving the Arab–Israeli conflict in the Middle East, he spoke not of the onward march of the forces of progress but of the need for international security. The enthusiasm of the early Khrushchev years for any and every sign of unrest in the Third World had tapered away, Brezhnev allotting a single sentence to support for 'the peoples' struggle for democracy, national liberation and socialism'. All too often the radical new governments patronized by the USSR had gradually become more and more conservative and unpopular and were themselves threatened by popular unrest. In numerous cases, too, they had proven fickle, even those adamantly hostile to the US being as willing to seek succour from China, Europe or the non-aligned states as from the USSR. Although a handful of states moved into the Soviet orbit in the course of the 1970s— South Yemen and Syria in the Middle East, Vietnam, admitted to COMECON in 1978, and Afghanistan, with whose military regime a Treaty of Friendship was signed the same year—by the end of the decade the number of Soviet-oriented governments outside eastern Europe had declined steeply since the peak of the Khrushchev era.[94] And Brezhnev's conclusion celebrated not the historically guaranteed spread of socialism but quite simply the prestige and security of the USSR. In many respects, the Soviet Union had mutated from a revolutionary and revisionist to a status quo power, ready to take advantage of instability but primarily concerned to buttress its existing status and areas of hegemony.

---

93 For two accounts of détente, see Crockatt, *Fifty Years War*, pp. 203–98, and S.J. Ball, *The Cold War: An International History, 1947–1991* (London 1998), pp. 115–70.

94 See R.F. Laird, 'Soviet Geopolitical Momentum: Myth or Menace?', in R.F. Laird and E.P. Hoffmann (eds), *Soviet Foreign Policy in a Changing World* (Hawthorne, NY, 1986), pp. 701–12.

Document 144 | From L.I. Brezhnev's speech on international relations to the 24th CPSU Congress

30 March 1971

The Soviet Union has countered the aggressive policy of imperialism with its policy of active defence of peace and strengthening of international security. The main lines of this policy are well known. Our Party, our Soviet state, in co-operation with the fraternal socialist countries and other peace-loving states, and with the whole-hearted support of many millions of people throughout the world, have now for many years been waging a struggle on these lines, taking a stand for the cause of peace and friendship among nations. The CPSU regards the following as the basic concrete tasks of this struggle in the present situation.

First:

To eliminate the hotbeds of war in Southeast Asia and in the Middle East and to promote a political settlement in these areas on the basis of respect for the legitimate rights of states and peoples subjected to aggression.

To give an immediate and firm rebuff to any acts of aggression and international arbitrariness. For this, full use must also be made of the possibilities of the United Nations.

Repudiation of the threat or use of force in settling outstanding issues must become a law of international life. For its part, the Soviet Union invites the countries which accept this approach to conclude appropriate bilateral or regional treaties.

Second:

To proceed from the final recognition of the territorial changes that took place in Europe as a result of the Second World War. To bring about a radical turn towards a détente and peace on this continent. To ensure the convocation and success of an all-European conference.

To do everything to ensure collective security in Europe. We reaffirm the readiness expressed jointly by the participants in the defensive Warsaw Treaty to have a simultaneous annulment of this treaty and of the North Atlantic alliance, or—as a first step—dismantling of their military organizations.

Third:

To conclude treaties putting a ban on nuclear, chemical, and bacteriological weapons.

To work for an end to the testing of nuclear weapons, including underground tests, by everyone everywhere.

To promote the establishment of nuclear-free zones in various parts of the world.

We stand for the nuclear disarmament of all states in possession of nuclear weapons, and for the convocation for these purposes of a conference of the five nuclear powers—the USSR, the USA, the PRC, France and Britain.

Fourth:

To invigorate the struggle to halt the race in all types of weapons. We favour the convocation of a world conference to consider disarmament questions to their full extent.

We stand for the dismantling of foreign military bases. We stand for a reduction of armed forces and armaments in areas where the military confrontation is especially dangerous, above all in central Europe.

We consider it advisable to work out measures reducing the probability of accidental outbreak or deliberate fabrication of armed incidents and their development into international crises, into war.

The Soviet Union is prepared to negotiate agreements on reducing military expenditure, above all by the major powers.

Fifth:

The UN decisions on the abolition of the remaining colonial regimes must be fully carried out. Manifestations of racism and apartheid must be universally condemned and boycotted.

Sixth:

The Soviet Union is prepared to deepen relations of mutually advantageous co-operation in every sphere with states which for their part seek to do so. Our country is prepared to participate together with the other states concerned in settling problems like the conservation of the environment, development of power and other natural resources, development of transport and communications, prevention and eradication of the most dangerous and widespread diseases, and the exploration and development of outer space and the world ocean.

Such are the main features of the programme for the struggle for peace and international co-operation, for the freedom and independence of nations, which our Party has put forward.

And we declare that, while consistently pursuing its policy of peace and friendship among nations, the Soviet Union will continue to conduct a resolute struggle against imperialism, and firmly to rebuff the evil designs and subversions of aggressors. As in the past, we shall give undeviating support to the peoples' struggle for democracy, national liberation and socialism.

Comrades, it is clear from what has been said that the past five years have been a period of vigorous and intense activity by our Party and state in the sphere of international policy.

Of course, in international affairs not everything depends on us or our friends alone. We have not advanced in every sphere as fast as we should like towards the goals we set ourselves. A number of important acts have yet to be brought to completion, and their importance will become fully evident later. But the overall balance is obvious: great results have been achieved in these five years. Our country's international position has become even stronger, its prestige has been enhanced, and the Soviet people's peaceful endeavour has reliable protection.

[Source: Leonid Brezhnev, *Report of the CPSU Central Committee to the 24th Congress of the Communist Party of the Soviet Union* (Moscow 1971), pp. 35–38.]

The following year, the first Strategic Arms Limitation Talks agreement (SALT I) was signed, and the diplomatic blockage opened by West Germany's recognition of the GDR and of the Polish borders established in 1945 paved the way for a wide-ranging agreement on European affairs. The seal was set on a series of treaties by the European Conference on Security and Co-operation held in Helsinki in 1975. Although the Conference's Final Act included articles on human rights which provided unwelcome leverage for foreign and domestic critics of the regime, the USSR at last secured formal western recognition of the postwar political and territorial settlement.

Document 145 | **An extract from the Final Act of the European Conference on Security and Co-operation, Helsinki, 1 August 1975**

The High Representatives of the participating States solemnly. . . declare their determination to respect and put into practice, each of them in its relation with all the other participating States, irrespective of their political, economic or social systems as well as of their size, geographical location or level of economic development, the following principles, which all are of prime significance, guiding their mutual relations:

I.   Sovereign equality, respect for the rights inherent in sovereignty.
II.   Refraining from the threat or use of force.
III.   Inviolability of frontiers.
IV.   Territorial integrity of states.
V.   Peaceful settlement of disputes.
VI.   Non-intervention in internal affairs.
VII.   Respect for human rights and fundamental freedoms, including the freedom of thought, conscience, religion or belief.
VIII. Equal rights and self-determination of peoples.
IX.   Co-operation among States. . .

Co-operation in humanitarian and other fields

1. Human contacts.
The participating States, considering the development of contacts to be an important element in the strengthening of friendly relations and trust among peoples. . . make it their aim to facilitate freer movement and contacts, individually and collec-

tively, whether privately or officially, among persons, institutions and organizations of the participating States, and to contribute to the solution of the humanitarian problems that arise in that connection. . .

a. Contacts and regular meetings on the basis of family ties.

In order to promote further development of contacts on the basis of family ties the participating States will favourably consider applications for travel with the purpose of allowing persons to enter or leave their territory temporarily, and on a regular basis if desired, in order to visit members of their families.

. . .

5. Re-unification of families.

The participating States will deal in a positive and humanitarian spirit with the applications of persons who wish to be reunited with members of their families. . . The receiving participating State will take appropriate care with regard to employment for persons from other participating States who take up permanent residence. . .

[Source: http://www.osce.org/documents/html/pdftohtml/4044_en.pdf.html]

The 'Second Cold War'

However, even as the Helsinki Accords were being signed, the thaw in Soviet relations with the US was coming to an end.[95] American opinion had become increasingly suspicious that the USSR might be establishing superiority in terms of nuclear weapons. The speed with which nuclear technology developed created deep uncertainty about the strategic balance, notably in terms of short-range weapons, which had not been covered by SALT I. Although SALT II negotiations edged slowly forward from 1976, there were loud voices in Washington warning that the US must substantially increase its weapons investment. Relations were further soured when from 1977 President Carter's administration proposed making progress on arms talks dependent on Soviet respect for human rights as laid down in the Helsinki Accords, provoking Moscow to furious rejection of any such linkage. Moreover, Washington's view of developments in the Third World was very different from Moscow's. The notion of the USSR as the centre of a world revolutionary movement had taken such deep root in the US that virtually every threat to the international status quo was regarded as favourable to and probably sponsored by the CPSU. And between 1974 and 1980, as many as fourteen Third World states in the Middle East, Asia and Latin America saw radical new regimes come to power. The causes of these

---

95 For a lively analysis that has aged well, see F. Halliday, *The Making of the Second Cold War* (London 1983).

upheavals varied widely, from the overthrow of the Portuguese empire in Africa to the change of regime in Cambodia, Laos and South Vietnam, as did the political affiliation of the newly established governments. And in most cases the Soviet role was secondary at best. But there were high-profile instances of what seemed clear Soviet intervention by proxy, notably the arrival of Cuban troops in Ethiopia and Angola, and in the aftermath of defeat in Vietnam, Washington was disposed to see the hand of Moscow everywhere. The USSR found itself confronted by a steep increase in American military expenditure, the establishment of full diplomatic relations between Washington and Beijing, and, no less ominous, a considerable rapprochement between China and Japan.

Military intervention in Afghanistan

It was in this context that Brezhnev's government took steps that proved fatal to its attempts to prolong détente.[96] In the course of 1979, the radical government of Afghanistan headed by Nur Muhammed Taraki, installed following a left-wing military coup in April 1978 and quick to sign a Treaty of Friendship with Moscow, encountered mounting opposition. The land reforms and vigorous assaults on Islamic religious practices championed by Taraki's prime minister, Hafizullah Amin, provoked ill-assorted but widespread resistance. It ranged from displaced elites looking to the west for support, to Islamic fundamentalists inspired by Ayatollah Khomeini's revolution in neighbouring Iran. By March 1979 the Soviet Embassy in Kabul was sufficiently anxious to recommend that the modest Soviet military presence be surreptitiously strengthened, notably at the main airports, thereby keeping open the option of either significantly increasing intervention or evacuating Soviet personnel.

Document 146 | Afghanistan, March–December 1979—suggestions from Soviet representatives in Kabul on sending Soviet subunits to Afghanistan

In the event of a further deterioration of the situation it will evidently be expedient under some appropriate pretext to review the question of some kind of participation by our troops in the guarding of those buildings and important installations created with Soviet assistance. In particular, the question could be considered of sending subunits of Soviet troops:

---

96 Soviet intervention in Afghanistan is skilfully set in context in O.A. Westad (ed.), *The Fall of Détente: Soviet–American Relations during the Carter Years* (London 1997).

a. to Bagram military airport under the guise of technical advisers by using as cover the intended rebuilding of a maintenance shop;

b. to Kabul airport under the guise of overseeing its reconstruction, especially because this is stipulated by a recent inter-governmental agreement, reported in the press;

In the event of a further deterioration of the situation the presence of such strong points would allow us a specific choice of options and also, if necessary, to guarantee the safe evacuation of Soviet citizens.

Ivanov, Gorelov, 19 March 1979

In the course of the summer, the Embassy reported more and more urgent requests from Taraki that Moscow take this further and quietly introduce small concentrations of troops at key points within the capital.

11 July. . . Taraki has also expressed the idea that it would be good if the Soviet side decided secretly to station several Soviet special force groups of up to one battalion each in Kabul, in the event of a sudden deterioration of the situation in the capital.

The KGB representative, 11 July 1979

. . . the leadership of the DRA is making serious preparations for new clashes with counter-revolutionaries, but is to a considerable extent counting on direct Soviet assistance should a crisis situation arise.

Puzanov, Ivanov, Gorelov, 12 July 1979

The Kremlin responded by sending a delegation headed by Politburo member B.N. Ponomarev for talks. Taraki and Amin now urged that Moscow hold in readiness a force as large as two divisions should the government's position trigger a request. No exception could be taken internationally to such action, they insisted, since it would be in response to a request for help from the legitimate government. As Ponomarev reported, the Kremlin firmly refused to do so.

Both Taraki and Amin have returned several times to the question of increasing the Soviet military presence in the country. They put the question of sending approximately two divisions to the DRA in case of emergency 'at the request of the lawful government of Afghanistan'.

In reply they were informed that the Soviet Union was not prepared to do so.

Ponomarev, 19 July 1979

No sooner had Ponomarev returned to the USSR than Amin called in Puzanov, the Soviet Ambassador, and asked for immediate help in the form of Soviet helicopters replete with trained crews. Again the Afghan leadership were rebuffed and firmly told that Soviet forces would not take part in military action.

On 21 July H. Amin invited the Soviet Ambassador in and, referring to Taraki's commission, asked him to send the following appeal to the Soviet leadership.
    . . . the Afghan armed forces urgently require 8–10 Soviet helicopters and crews with which to make sorties.
    I have said to H. Amin that, as Soviet leaders have indicated more than once and B.N. Ponomarev emphasized during his last talks in Kabul, the Soviet side is not prepared to let Soviet military personnel take part in military action.
Puzanov, 21 July 1979

Whether because the government's position looked so fragile, or because Soviet refusals failed to carry conviction, Taraki and Amin kept up the pressure.

Amin has again brought up the question of stationing three Soviet army subunits in Kabul, should an emergency situation arise. In his opinion, they could be secretly stationed in the military club, the Soviet embassy and Tane–Tajbek, to where the head of state's residence will be moved at the end of the year and where there are some barracks. Amin said that comrade Taraki expects the imminent arrival of a Soviet battalion at the military club.
The KGB representative, 24 July 1979

A week later, the Soviet Ambassador began to support the Afghan requests, recommending that limited forces be despatched to Kabul.

. . . In view of the possibility of intensification of the rebel insurgency in August and September we must give a positive reply to our Afghan friends' request to send a special force brigade to Kabul in the next few days.
Puzanov, Ivanov, Gorelov, 1 August 1979

. . . It would be expedient to send a special force battalion. . . and transport helicopters with Soviet crews to Kabul soon. . . We also request that sending another two special force battalions be considered—one to reinforce the guards at the Bagram air base, the other to be stationed at the Bala-Khazar fortress just outside Kabul.
Puzanov, Ivanov, Gorelov, 12 August 1979

The following month, however, the situation was gravely complicated as simmering friction between the two Afghan leaders reached crisis point. When Taraki tried to sack Amin, he was himself deposed and executed. The following instructions from Gromyko, the Soviet Foreign Minister, to the Embassy in Kabul aimed to restrain Amin's repressive drive against Taraki's allies. Soviet personnel were to continue to work with Afghan forces against 'counter-revolutionaries', but they should not take sides in the new internecine conflict, and a careful assessment was to be made of how far Amin could be regarded as a reliable ally of the Soviet Union.

A coded telegram to the Soviet representatives in Kabul.

1. It is considered expedient, in view of the real position that is developing in Afghanistan, not to refuse to deal with Amin and his government. At the same time it is essential to restrain Amin by all means possible from taking repressive measures against Taraki's supporters and other persons out of favour with him who are not enemies of the revolution. Moreover, it is vital to use contacts with Amin to ascertain further his political colours and intentions.
2. It is also considered expedient for our military advisers in the Afghan forces and for our advisers on state security and internal affairs to stay put. They should fulfil their direct functions connected with the preparation and conducting of military action against rebel formations and other counter-revolutionary forces. They must, of course, not take any part in repressive measures against persons out of favour with Amin, if units and subunits containing our advisers are drawn into such actions.

Gromyko, 15 September 1979

Having disposed of Taraki, Amin resumed pressure on Moscow for troops to be sent to Kabul, emphasizing the threats to his own personal security and giving the Soviets carte blanche over the form it should take.

Nevertheless, in the course of a conversation H. Amin repeated his request for a battalion of Soviet servicemen to be sent to Kabul for his personal protection in the new residence, to which he intends to move after 25 October this year.

The KGB representative, 2 October 1979

On 12 and 17 December the KGB representative met H. Amin. From Amin's remarks the following deserve consideration.

He kept bringing up the question of direct Soviet participation in restraining the bandit insurgency in the north of the DRA. His thinking comes down to this: the present Afghan leadership will welcome the presence of Soviet armed forces in a variety of strategically important spots in the northern provinces of the DRA. . .

Amin said that the forms and methods of military assistance must be decided by the Soviet side:

The USSR can have military garrisons wherever it likes;

The USSR can defend all joint Afghan–Soviet installations;

Soviet troops could guard the DRA's communications network.

The KGB representative, 17 December 1979

[Source: *Komsomol'skaya pravda*, 27 December 1990.]

Although Moscow's confidence in Amin steadily declined, viewed from the Kremlin the case for military intervention seemed increasingly powerful. The triumph that November of Ayatollah Khomeini and the movement for radical Islamic revolution in Iran crystallized long-standing anxieties about the danger of fundamentalism spreading via Afghanistan to the USSR's Central Asian republics. The fact that détente already seemed stalled weakened the counsels of caution in the Kremlin. In their extended debates over whether or not to intervene, the ageing members of the Politburo thought in traditional Marxist–Leninist terms. The perils of becoming drawn into a highly complex civil war in which political, social and economic conflicts were inextricably intertwined with religious, ethnic and regional issues were obscured by the language of 'revolution' and 'socialism', and by the assumption that Soviet forces would work in harmony with a substantial and growing Afghani constituency. Amin would be replaced and a less radical Marxist government installed. From mid-December, preparations were made for a substantial invasion from Tajikistan, and on 24 December the invasion began.

Document 147 | **A list of commands given by the General Staff based on orders from the Soviet Ministry of Defence in December 1979**

14 December. Re-station a bomber squadron from the Transcaucasus Military District to Mary and place it under the command of the Turkmen Military District [TMD].

16 December. Have field control of the 40th Army ready for action. Have motorized infantry and tank regiments from another TMD division ready for action.

19 December. Re-station those motorized infantry and tank regiments made ready for action on 16 December in the Takhta–Bazar district towards Kushkinsk by 21 December. Have communications units of the 40th Army ready for action.

23 December. Have the Central Asian Military District (CAMD) motorized infantry division ready for action.

24 December. The USSR Minister of Defence announced at a meeting of

Ministry of Defence chiefs that the decision had been taken to send troops into Afghanistan. Present at the meeting were the Deputy Ministers of Defence and heads of the Chief and Central Directorates. Lieutenant-General Yu.V. Tukharinov, commander of the 40th Army, was ordered to meet Lieutenant-General Babajan, head of operations in the DRA General Staff, to discuss stationing Soviet troops in Afghanistan.

The Minister of Defence signed the order for sending Soviet troops into Afghanistan, and sent them in encrypted form to the army. The time for crossing the state border was set at 15.00 on 25 December.

25 December. Have artillery and anti-aircraft units of the 40th Army ready for action. Have all TMD aircraft ready for action. Have another CAMD motorized infantry division ready for action.

26 December. Put the CAMD motorized infantry division made ready for action on 25 December at the disposal of the TMD. Send to the Takhta–Bazar district all the units of the TMD motorized infantry division made ready on 23 December.

27 December. Have the TMD pontoon-bridge regiment ready for action.

[Source: *Komsomol'skaya pravda*, 27 December 1990.]

The international uproar that followed was much fiercer than the Kremlin had expected. For those who had seen Moscow's hand behind the international instability of the 1970s, the spectacle of the Soviet Army now for the first time since the Great Patriotic War taking military action outside eastern Europe was deeply alarming. There was all but universal condemnation— from western Europe, from China and across the Middle East itself. Carter warned that world peace was in danger, froze moves to ratify SALT II, imposed a grain embargo, and instituted a damaging boycott of the Olympic Games, Moscow's prestige project of 1980. And far from a brisk re-establishment of authority, Afghanistan proved impossible to pacify.[97]

Crisis in Poland, 1980–1981

Though not in itself sufficient to undermine the Soviet Union's international position, the debacle in Afghanistan made certain that the regime would react with caution in the face of the parallel threat that unfolded during 1980–81. This came from the heartland of the 'socialist commonwealth': Poland. Since the mid-1970s, Poland's communist government had seen its

---

97 For a crisp and penetrating account, see M. Galeotti, *Afghanistan: The Soviet Union's Last War* (London 1995).

fragile legitimacy steadily eroded.[98] During the first part of the decade, in order to buttress the regime's position, Moscow had sanctioned a sharp rise in Polish living standards funded primarily through loans both from the USSR and from the west. By 1976, however, the burden of debt led the government abruptly to raise prices, triggering widespread unrest and a quick retreat. Opposition currents were fed by the election of Cardinal Wojtyła as Pope in 1978, and even more by his tumultuous visit to Poland in June 1979. The economic and financial crisis continued to mount. By 1980, as the following table on Soviet aid and debt-deferment shows, the country was unable to meet its obligations either to the west or to the USSR and its economic dependence on the latter was rapidly deepening.

Document 148 | A report on Soviet aid to Poland in 1980–1981

	1. Credits granted	*Date*	*Million US$*
1	To purchase sugar. USSR Council of Ministers order.	1 Aug. 1980	30
2	To regularize accounts with capitalist countries. USSR Council of Ministers order.	23 June 1980	250
3	To create banking consortia to help the PPR. CPSU CC resolution.	6 June 1980	70
4	To regularize accounts with capitalist countries. USSR Council of Ministers order.	11 Nov. 1980	150
5	To purchase grain and foodstuffs. USSR Council of Ministers order.	11 Nov. 1980	190
			Total: 690
	2. Repayments deferred		
1	Deferment of repayments to Soviet banks. CPSU CC resolution.	6 June 1980	219
2	Deferment of repayments to Soviet banks. USSR Council of Ministers order.	11 Sept. 1980	280
3	Deferment of repayments to Soviet banks. USSR Council of Ministers order.	11 Nov. 1980	280
4	Deferment of repayments of debt on all previously granted credits. USSR Council of Ministers order.	16 Aug. 1981	up to 1,000
			Total: 1,779

[Source: *Novaya i noveyshaya istoriya*, No. 1, 1994.]

---

98 On the Polish crisis, see the vivid contemporary account by T. Garton Ash, *The Polish Revolution: Solidarity 1980–82* (London 1983), and the analysis by G. Kolankiewicz and P.G. Lewis, *Poland: Politics, Economics and Society* (New York 1988).

When Gierek's demoralized government made a further abortive attempt to control expenditure by abruptly raising prices in July 1980, the response was disastrous. Wave upon wave of workers' strikes were actively supported by opposition intellectuals, students and the Catholic hierarchy and a broad-based opposition movement, 'Solidarity', was formed. Unable to conceal just how narrow its constituency had become, the regime bowed to pressure and on 31 August made a series of far-reaching concessions to Solidarity, including wage increases, the right to form independent trade unions and to strike, and a drastic reduction in censorship. Gierek's successor, Kania, appointed a week later, struggled to find a way to shore up the regime without resort to force but by February was reduced to handing over to his defence minister, General Jaruzelski. Jaruzelski tried to use his greater personal prestige as well as the unmistakable threat of the use of force to reach an understanding with Solidarity. Despite the willingness of the Solidarity leader Lech Wałęsa to co-operate, the unresolved economic problems and mounting consumer shortages encouraged more radical voices to denounce the government outright.

The following Politburo memorandum signed by Brezhnev's senior lieutenants outlines Moscow's reactions. The language of Marxism–Leninism, drained of virtually all class content, was stretched to the very limit to fit events to the orthodox pattern. Despite the manifest support of the vast majority of workers, Solidarity was labelled 'counter-revolutionary'; Polish communists most ready to countenance reform were condemned in time-honoured fashion as 'revisionists'. At the same time, hard-headed realism was woven into the text: it was fear of Soviet troops that restrained the opposition; support for the sound left wing of the Polish United Workers' Party (PUWP) came largely from the generation (most of them past pensionable age) who had lived through the war and re-establishment of the Polish state; unsatisfactory though Kania and Jaruzelski were, the loyal Left could muster no credible alternative leadership; the best chance of taming the tide was to bring home to the Poles that the USSR was their only hope of economic relief.

Document 149 | **From minutes of the CPSU CC Politburo meeting of 23 April 1981 on the development of the situation in Poland and steps taken**

23 April 1981

The internal political crisis in Poland has acquired a chronic character. To a significant extent the PUWP has lost control of the processes taking place in society. At the same time *Solidarność* has turned into an organized political force capable of paralysing the activity of Party and state bodies and effectively of taking power into its own hands. If the opposition has not yet gone that far, it is primarily out of fear that Soviet troops would be brought in, and hopes of achieving its aims without bloodshed, through counter-revolution by stealth.

In the recent period a new tactical approach has been emerging more clearly, around which this motley opposition is effectively uniting. Well aware that Poland's geopolitical situation deprives them of the possibility of encroaching upon the country's participation in the Warsaw Treaty Organization and the principle of the leading role of the Communist Party, these forces have decided to demoralize the PUWP from within, take the process as far as its degeneration, and thus take power 'on a legal basis'.

It is in such a situation that we must yet again evaluate our attitude to the policies of the Polish leadership and more clearly ascertain what forces we can ultimately rely on to defend the achievements of socialism in Poland.

On the right of the CC of the PUWP are people of a revisionist bent. Ideologically they are close to some of the leaders of *Solidarność* and are for recasting the socio-economic structure of Poland along Yugoslav lines. In politics they talk about a 'partnership' of various political forces, concurring with the 'eurocommunist' and Social-Democratic ideas of pluralism.

The speeches from comrades on the left wing are ideologically closest to our positions. They express the views of that section of the Party which consistently comes out for socialism, for friendship with the Soviet Union, against revisionist distortions, and is demanding decisive action against *Solidarność*. Behind them stand, mainly, old Party members who went through the school of the war and the class struggle in the first stages of the emergence of People's Poland. Unfortunately, representatives of this tendency in no way constitute a majority.

Comrades Kania and Jaruzelski in essence take a centrist position. In the complex situation after August last year they spoke for the dominant mood of the Party which wanted to solve the acute problems which had arisen through dialogue and agreement with *Solidarność*. Time has shown that, while Kania and Jaruzelski talk about the necessity of defending the achievements of socialism in Poland, they are pursuing this course passively, wavering and making frequent concessions to *Solidarność*. Hence the unjustified compliance with *Solidarność*'s demands, the panic when confronted by it and the fear of bringing in Soviet troops.

At the same time Kania and Jaruzelski stand on a position of friendship with the Soviet Union and loyalty to Poland's obligations under the Warsaw Treaty. Both of them, especially Jaruzelski, have standing in the country. In effect, there are at present no other figures capable of handling leadership of Party and state.

In view of all the above, for the immediate future the following course is expedient:

We continue providing political support to comrades Kania and Jaruzelski, who, despite a certain amount of wavering, come out in defence of socialism. At the same time we continuously try to get more consistent and decisive action from them in order to overcome the crisis on the basis of maintaining Poland as a socialist country, friendly to the Soviet Union.

In view of the exceptionally difficult economic situation in Poland, we continue to render whatever help we can, while intensifying our propaganda to the maximum extent, so that every Pole knows how dependent the country is on Soviet aid and support.

K. Chernenko

Yu. Andropov

A. Gromyko

D. Ustinov

K. Rusakov

I. Arkhipov

L. Zamyatin

[Source: *Novaya i noveyshaya istoriya*, No. 1, 1994.]

As turmoil continued Jaruzelski edged Kania out of the party leadership, taking it over himself while at the same time implicitly subordinating the party. He now attempted to project himself as a national figure above political and social divisions, a patriotic leader in the tradition of the interwar Polish hero Marshal Piłsudski. He manoeuvred to parry the conflicting pressures upon him by playing Solidarity's leaders off against the Kremlin. On the one hand, he would use the danger that social unrest and anti-Soviet passion might reach the point where Poland would slip from the 'socialist commonwealth' to persuade Moscow to increase the already formidable economic aid it was providing the indebted and beleaguered Polish economy. On the other, he would use the possibility that the patience of Moscow and the other Warsaw Pact governments might run out and military intervention follow to dissuade opposition leaders from escalating protest. And meanwhile, both to put an end to social unrest, strikes and political free-for-all, and to reassure Moscow that the country would remain firmly within the Warsaw Pact, he prepared to impose martial law.

In fact, exasperated and deeply insulted by open expressions of anti-Soviet feeling in Poland though the Politburo was, the Soviet leadership had resolved that this time to invade was out of the question.[99] The mood is shown in the minutes of a Politburo meeting of 10 December, called to consider the situation and in particular a report from Baybakov, a senior economic official on the CPSU's Central Committee, on Jaruzelski's

---

99 See M.J. Ouimet, *The Rise and Fall of the Brezhnev Doctrine in Soviet Foreign Policy* (Chapel Hill, NC, 2003), for a detailed account of the Soviet decision.

economic demands. Brezhnev and his colleagues had little faith in Jaruzelski. They regarded his economic demands as excessive and possibly deliberately so, especially given what was by then, as we shall see, a serious deterioration in the Soviet Union's economic position. Yet Jaruzelski had made his economic terms the condition of implementing martial law, as called for by his own Polish Central Committee. Senior members of the Politburo— including Andropov, poised to succeed Brezhnev—were uncertain whether Jaruzelski would indeed act, and disliked his downgrading of the Polish party. Yet they were resigned to hoping for the best. They suspected that Jaruzelski was playing up the possibility of Soviet military intervention for domestic purposes (hence his misinterpretation of a speech by Kulikov, Deputy Defence Minister), and they were of one mind in being unwilling to countenance it. The risks—of Polish resistance, of triggering wider eastern European protest, of international outcry and unpredictable American reaction—were too great, especially given the heavy price still being paid for the invasion of Afghanistan, where the army was being drawn deeper and deeper into a military quagmire against guerrilla forces supplied from abroad. Even when Andropov conjured up the nightmare scenario that Solidarity would prevail in Poland, and that the west would use Soviet discomfiture here and in Afghanistan to attack, he and the party's long-standing chief ideologue, Suslov, ruled out military intervention as inviting catastrophe.

Document 150 | From the minutes of the CPSU CC Politburo meeting of 10 December 1981 on the situation in Poland

10 December 1981

Chair: comrade L.I. Brezhnev
Present: comrades Yu.V. Andropov, V.V. Grishin, A.A. Gromyko, A.P. Kirilenko, A.Ya. Pel'she, M.A. Suslov, D.F. Ustinov, K.U. Chernenko, P.N. Demichev, B.N. Ponomarev, M.S. Solomentsev, I.V. Kapitonov, V.I. Dolgikh, K.V. Rusakov

Brezhnev: In the first quarter of next year the Polish comrades are hoping to receive from the USSR and the other socialist countries an extra $1.5 billion worth of raw materials and products. This includes iron ore, non-ferrous metals, fertilizers, oil, tyres, grain, etc.

Moreover, as you can see, the Polish comrades are assuming that deliveries of goods from the USSR in 1982 will remain at 1981 levels. Comrade Baybakov has told them that their requests will be conveyed to Moscow.

Baybakov: As instructed by the Politburo, I've been to Warsaw. There I met all the comrades with whom I needed to discuss the questions entrusted to me.

I have to say that the list of goods deemed as aid comprises 350 items totalling 1.4 billion rubles. It includes such things as 2 million tonnes of grain, 25,000 tonnes of meat, 625,000 tonnes of iron ore and many other goods. Bearing in mind what we intended to give Poland in 1982, the aid total comes to about 4.4 billion rubles, if we include these requests from the Polish comrades.

The time is coming for Poland to pay off its debts to western European countries. To do so Poland needs at least 2.8 million rubles in hard currency. I heard the Polish comrades talk of balanced economic relations with us. I did notice that Polish industry is not fulfilling its plan to a significant extent. The coal industry, the main source of hard currency, is essentially disorganized and is doing nothing to remedy this as the strikes continue. Although there are no strikes at present, coal output is at a very low level.

Or, for instance, the peasants have produce, there is grain, meat, vegetables, etc., but they are giving nothing to the state, they are waiting and seeing. The private markets are fairly busy, but at very inflated prices.

I told the Polish comrades straight that they must take more decisive measures, given the situation which has developed. Perhaps they should introduce something like requisitioning.

If we consider grain reserves, Poland took in more than 2 million tonnes this year. The people aren't going hungry. The townspeople go to the rural markets and buy all the foodstuffs they need. The food is there.

As you know, we're helping them by supplying 30,000 tonnes of meat, as requested by the Polish comrades and agreed upon by the Politburo. Of this, 16,000 tonnes have already been exported. I have to say that food, in this case meat, is being delivered in filthy, uncleaned iron-ore wagons and in a very unsightly form. Serious sabotage takes place when the stuff's unloaded at Polish stations. The Poles say very rude things about the Soviet Union and its people, refuse to clean the wagons, etc. The insults being hurled at us are just innumerable.

Rusakov: Comrade Baybakov's given an accurate picture of the state of the Polish economy. What should we do now? I think we have to supply the goods mentioned in the economic agreement, but we should not supply more goods than in the first quarter of last year.

Brezhnev: Are we able to do so now?

Baybakov: Only from our state reserves or by reducing the quantities supplied at home, Leonid Il'ich.

Rusakov: Their provincial committee secretaries had a meeting yesterday. According to comrade Arestov, the provincial committee secretaries do not understand comrade Jaruzelski's speech at all, which did not give any clear, definite line. Nobody knows what's going to happen in the next few days, but there was talk of some Operation 'X'.

Jaruzelski himself says that he intends to make an address to the Polish people. But in this address he is not going to mention the Party, but will appeal to the people by playing on their patriotic feelings. Jaruzelski's talking about the need to declare martial law, as Piłsudski did, pointing out that the Polish people will understand that better than anything else. . .

At the same time Jaruzelski intends to link up on this matter with the allies. He says that if the Polish forces can't cope with resistance from *Solidarność* on their own, the Polish comrades are hoping for help from other countries—even going as far as sending armed forces into Poland. Moreover, Jaruzelski has referred to the speech of comrade Kulikov, who is supposed to have said that the USSR and the allied states would give Poland military assistance. However, as far as I know, comrade Kulikov didn't exactly say that, but was simply repeating what L.I. Brezhnev had previously said, that we will not abandon Poland.

As for what is happening in the provinces, we should say straight that the Party organizations have no force there. Essentially all the power is in the hands of *Solidarność*. As for what Jaruzelski is saying, he seems to be leading us up the garden path, because his analysis is wrong. If they don't get organized quickly, don't gather their forces and come out against the onslaught from *Solidarność*, they won't succeed at all in improving the situation in Poland.

Andropov: It's clear from talking to Jaruzelski that they haven't yet made a firm decision to introduce martial law, and, despite the Politburo of the PUWP CC's unanimous resolution on introducing it, we still cannot see any concrete measures from the leadership. The *Solidarność* extremists have got the Polish leadership by the throat. In the last few days the Church made its position clear. In effect is has taken the side of *Solidarność*. . .

I'd like to point out that Jaruzelski has been putting forward economic demands to us fairly insistently, and has been making the implementation of Operation 'X' conditional on our economic help. Moreover, I would say he has been posing the question, although not directly, of military assistance.

If we look at the list of goods our Polish comrades are asking for, I have to say that serious doubts arise about the necessity of supplying these products. For example, what has the delivery of fertilizers and suchlike got to do with the success of Operation 'X'?

As for economic aid, it will of course be difficult for us to supply it on the scale they have requested. It's obvious we have to do something. But I want to say yet again that the way the question of delivering goods as economic aid has been put is impudent. It is all being done so that if we fail to deliver something, the blame can be placed on us. If comrade Kulikov really did talk about sending troops, then he made a mistake. We're not going to risk it. We don't intend to send troops to Poland. That's the correct line and we must stick to it to the end. I don't know how things'll turn out in Poland, but even if *Solidarność* ends up running Poland, so be it. If the capitalist countries attack the Soviet Union, and they already have the necessary agreements concerning economic and political sanctions, it'll be very hard for us. We've got to look after our own country and strengthen the Soviet Union. That's our principal line. . .

Suslov: We've been doing a great deal of work on peace and must not change our position now. World public opinion won't understand us. We've done a great deal to strengthen peace through the UN. Witness the effect of L.I. Brezhnev's visit to the FRG and of other similar actions for peace. This has enabled all peace-loving countries to understand that the Soviet Union is firmly and consistently championing a policy of peace. That's why we mustn't change the position with regard to Poland which we took from the very outset of the Polish events. Let the Polish comrades themselves decide what measures to take. It's not for us to push them to more decisive action. But we shall, as before, tell the Poles that we understand what they're doing.

It seems to me that Jaruzelski is showing a certain cunning. He wants to cover himself with all these requests to the Soviet Union. Of course, we cannot physically comply with them, and Jaruzelski'll then say 'I did ask the Soviet Union for help but didn't get any.'

At the same time the Poles are saying directly that they're against sending in troops. If troops are sent in, it'll be a catastrophe. I think we're all unanimously agreed that sending in troops is quite out of the question.

[Source: *Novaya i noveyshaya istoriya*, No. 1, 1994.]

Three days later Jaruzelski implemented 'Operation X', proclaimed martial law and proceeded to suppress Solidarity. In the short term he succeeded in restoring order, but his regime never established popular legitimacy. Moreover, although the repression was the work of the Polish rather than the Soviet army, in western eyes it was the handiwork of Moscow, of what the new American president, Reagan, dubbed 'the evil empire'. SALT II remained frozen. American military expenditure soared, rising by as much as 50 per cent between 1980 and 1985. And in 1983 the US introduced its Strategic Defence Initiative (SDI), purporting to herald a space-based shield which would make American territory invulnerable to Soviet missiles.

By the mid-1980s, for all the changes through which Soviet international relations had passed, the country remained encased within the framework bequeathed by Stalin: the weaker of two superpowers; locked in an exorbitant arms race against a much wealthier rival; and committed to a 'socialist commonwealth' whose ruling regimes, lacking domestic legitimacy, relied on the threat of Soviet intervention for their stability. Nor was this the only part of Stalin's legacy that proved highly resistant to fundamental change right through to the mid-1980s.

14

The Command Economy

Where the economic structure was concerned, the imprint left by the war was no less profound.[100] Features of the pre-war economy that were regarded as having worked successfully during the war and those that were introduced to mobilize the war effort became firmly entrenched. The state's economic monopoly was reaffirmed. Policy was projected in terms of successive Five-Year Plans—Khrushchev's experiment with a seven-year variant did not take root—each supposedly based on a comprehensive blueprint for all parts of the economy. The central planning agencies continued to identify for the different branches of the economy output targets and resources, which were then allocated via the ministries region by region and enterprise by enterprise. The terms in which targets and output were measured were first and foremost quantitative: despite constant exhortation for managers and workers to raise quality, sanctions and incentives operated overwhelmingly to focus effort on volume measures. Although financial controls supplemented the critical physical allocation made by the ministries, most prices, retail as well as wholesale, were fixed and bore distant relationship to costs. Beneath the formal centralized system were myriad 'horizontal' links, deals, barter and exchange. These served to correct the rigid and impractical allocations of resources—fuel, machinery and raw materials—contained in official plans. Likewise, as before the war, informal rule-bending and trade-offs between management and labour did something to deflect the pressure on workers to maximize output.[101] The factory model that had proven so

---

100 For an excellent exposition, see A. Nove, *The Soviet Economic System* (London 1977). On the postwar decades, see P. Hanson, *The Rise and Fall of the Soviet Economy: An Economic History of the USSR from 1945* (London 2003).

101 See D. Filtzer, *Soviet Workers and Late Stalinism: Labour and the Restoration of the Stalinist System after World War II* (Cambridge 2002).

successful in out-producing the Third Reich between 1941 and 1945 became dominant for industry at large: huge enterprises employing mass production lines to turn out vast quantities of a very limited range of standardized products.

Within this overall structure, the highest priority was given to the defence sector, which had first call on investment, material, manpower, research and innovation. This dominance was assured by the prestige that the armed forces, the defence industries and the leadership of both had acquired in victory; by the regime's determination never again to be caught unready for war, as in 1941; and by the fierce military competition of the Cold War. The privileged position of the defence sector coloured the entire economy. The proportion of GNP devoted to defence remained steadily far above the equivalent peacetime ratios elsewhere, and the channelling of resources both into current military strength and future development placed a permanent constraint on personal consumption. Defence expenditure also underpinned and itself constituted the core element in the tendency to privilege investment over consumption, and heavy industry over light industry and agriculture. In terms of the latter, collectivization was reaffirmed and both state and collective farms were subject to quotas set in the light of the requirements of the state and urban sectors.

As we shall see, in the first three decades after 1945 the Soviet economy grew rapidly within this framework. The war damage inflicted on both agriculture and industry—flooded mines, factories reduced to rubble, railways networks fractured—was restored and great tracts of agricultural land were brought back into production during the reconstruction of the late 1940s. Five massive new hydroelectric power stations initiated under Stalin were among the factors providing a major boost in the later 1950s, along with a rapid expansion in the acreage of land sown. Despite the vagaries of the weather and recurrent harvest setbacks in one area of the country or another, agricultural output more than doubled by 1985. Industrial growth was much greater, and by the mid-1970s is estimated to have quadrupled. On the other hand, even when growth was at its most impressive, the economy was marked by severe dysfunctions and by the late 1970s, the rate of growth itself had slowed dramatically. The limitations of the Stalinist economic framework were becoming increasingly plain.

Postwar reconstruction

The skewed balance between defence and heavy industry on the one hand, and consumer and light industry on the other, was at its most extreme during

Stalin's last years.[102] As he had done ever since the drafting of the First Five-Year Plan in 1927–28, he made rhetorical commitment to devoting 'special attention' to improving living standards and the output of consumer goods. The reality, however, was massive investment in heavy industry alongside desperate poverty. The postwar tone is captured in the following excerpt from his speech before the Soviet elections of 1946, in which he heralded the Fourth Five-Year Plan (1946–50), exulting over visions of gigantic outputs of steel, coal, oil and pig iron, surely rendering the USSR invulnerable.

Document 151 | **From Stalin's speech at a constituents' meeting in the Stalin electoral district of Moscow**

9 February 1946

The main tasks of the new five-year plan are to rehabilitate the devastated regions of our country, to restore industry and agriculture to the pre-war level, and then to exceed that level to a more or less considerable extent. Apart from the fact that the rationing system is to be abolished in the very near future (*loud and prolonged applause*), special attention will be devoted to the expansion of the production of consumers' goods, to raising the standard of living of the working people by steadily reducing the prices of all commodities (*loud and prolonged applause*), and to the extensive organization of scientific research institutes of every kind (*applause*) capable of giving the fullest scope to our scientific forces. (*Loud applause.*)

I have no doubt that if we give our scientists proper assistance they will be able in the very near future not only to overtake but even to outstrip the achievements of science beyond the borders of our country. (*Prolonged applause.*)

As regards long-term plans, our Party intends to organize another powerful upswing of our national economy that will enable us to raise our industry to a level, say, three times as high as that of pre-war industry. We must see to it that our industry shall be able to produce annually up to 50,000,000 tons of pig iron (*prolonged applause*), up to 60,000,000 tons of steel (*prolonged applause*), up to 500,000,000 tons of coal (*prolonged applause*) and up to 60,000,000 tons of oil (*prolonged applause*). Only when we succeed in doing that can we be sure that our Motherland will be insured against all contingencies. (*Loud applause.*) This will need, perhaps, another three five-year plans, if not more. But it can be done, and we must do it. (*Loud applause.*)

[Source: J. Stalin, *Speeches Delivered at Meetings of Voters of the Stalin Electoral District, Moscow* (Moscow 1950), pp. 40–41.]

---

102 See T. Dunmore, *The Stalinist Command Economy: The Soviet State Apparatus and Economic Policy, 1945–1953* (London 1980).

The Fourth Five-Year Plan did indeed achieve huge growth in the indices of heavy industry and rapid reconstruction of much of the urban and industrial economy. As before and during the war, however, the investment resources were accumulated by restraining consumption, allowing for only very slow recovery from the grinding poverty of the war years. In the course of 1946, far from being cut, prices were permitted to soar, the average cost of non-food products peaking early in 1947 at more than double the pre-war level, and that for food rising to more than triple. The heaviest burden of the squeeze on consumption was borne by those employed in the consumer industry par excellence: agriculture.[103] The key mechanism by which the state had secured its hold on grain, collectivization, was both extended to the western areas newly incorporated into the USSR and bolstered across the country. Far from the looser wartime management of the farms leading to their disbanding, as peasants had hoped, the regime announced in September 1946 a major drive to tighten discipline. The decree attacked abuses by local officials exploiting peasant labour and making unauthorized demands on the collective farms, and made much of calls for democratic procedures to be respected. The centrepiece, however, was a campaign, to be overseen by a new 'Special Council on Collective-Farm Affairs', to reverse the wartime trend for peasant households to expand the private plots of land which they farmed, consuming the produce or selling it at collective farm markets.

Document 152 | **From the joint decree of the Council of Ministers of the USSR and the CC of the CPSU on measures to prevent violations of the Agricultural *Artel'* Code on collective farms**

19 September 1946

On the basis of information received and checks made in a number of areas the Council of Ministers of the USSR and the CC of the CPSU have detected the existence of serious violations of the Agricultural *Artel'* Code on collective farms.

These violations involve the incorrect expenditure of work days, misappropriation of the common land on collective farms, pilfering of collective property, abuses by regional and other Party and Soviet workers and violation of the democratic basis of the administration of an agricultural *artel'*—elections for the management and chairmen of collective farms, and their accountability to meetings of collective farmers. . .

The Council of Ministers of the USSR and the CC of the CPSU resolve:

---

103 A succinct portrait is drawn by S. Fitzpatrick, 'Postwar Soviet Society: The "Return to Normalcy", 1945–1953', in Linz (ed.), *Impact of World War II on the Soviet Union*, pp. 129–56.

1. To condemn the distortions of Party and government collective farm policy and the violations of the Agricultural *Artel'* Code indicated in this decree as anti-collective-farm and anti–State, and institute court proceedings against the guilty parties as criminals.

2. To oblige the leaders of Union Republic, *oblast'* and *kray* Party and Soviet organizations to put a stop to these violations of the Agricultural *Artel'* Code immediately, fully restore the operation of the Agricultural *Artel'* Code and protect the collective farms from encroachments on collective farm property.

3. To do away with the practice of misappropriation of work days on collective farms and the incorrect distribution of collective farm income.

To inspect all farms within two months, reduce the excessive number of administrative and service personnel and the use of work days to pay them and bring administrative costs into line with the Agricultural *Artel'* Code.

To remove from the work-day payroll those having no connection with collective farms, and forbid district Soviet and Party bodies to demand work-day payments for work unrelated to the collective farms. . .

6. To forbid under threat of prosecution district and other organizations and staff to demand bread, food and money from collectives for the needs of various organizations, for holding congresses, meetings and celebrations, and for financing district building projects. . .

8. To re-establish basic democratic procedures, violated in many collective farms, for calling general meetings of collective farmers to discuss and sort out farm problems, for electing the management and chairmen of collective farms by general meetings, for accountability of management and chairmen to the collective farmers and audit commissions.

To strictly forbid Party district committees, district Soviets and land bodies from appointing or dismissing collective farm chairmen without a general meeting of collective farmers. . .

10. To set up a government Council on Collective Farm Affairs in order to establish strict observation of the Agricultural *Artel'* Code, protect collective farms from attempts at violating the Code and deal with questions of collective farm construction.

[Source: *Pravda*, 20 September 1946.]

The drive against expanded private plots was one facet of an approach to collective farms that perpetuated hostility among rank-and-file peasants and indeed among some farm chairmen. Terrible drought hit much of European Russia and Ukraine in 1946–47, reducing villages in some areas to starvation. Peasant discontent was intense. The sources and depth of this discontent are brought out in the following report to the party on a (relatively rare) instance of violent protest on a collective in Chelyabinsk *oblast'*. In line with the pre-war language in which those who opposed collectivization were denounced as 'kulaks' or 'kulak hirelings', regardless of their economic position within the village, the report labels the protesters 'people from former kulak families'. It sets out at length a critique of collectivization supposedly made by the farm chairman, Lapov, in the immediate aftermath of the war at a time of widespread speculation that the government might disband the collective farms. The explanation the report gave for matters running so far out of control seemed to confirm just the kind of breakdown in formal lines of authority that the party leadership was seeking to reverse. During the war, the rural party here as elsewhere had been drained of young and better-educated activists, few of whom had returned to their villages when peace came. As a result, the district party officials and police, the local 'eyes and ears' of Moscow, were politically inadequate and failed to inter-vene: indeed, they had apparently allowed themselves to become dependent on the goodwill of, rather than exercising control over, the collective farm chairman.

Document 153 | **Report on peasant unrest from the minutes of a meeting of the CPSU Chelyabinsk *oblast'* committee**

13 November 1946

On 12 October this year a band of people from former kulak families committed a counter-revolutionary terrorist attack against senior staff and students from Trade School No. 3, who had arrived at the 'Forward!' collective farm to help with the harvest and grain collection...

The investigation at the scene of the crime established that Limonov, Karpov and other active participants in this band of about 15–20, armed with shovels, stakes and knives, made a pre-planned terrorist attack on representatives of the working class mobilized for grain collection, as a result of which comrades Il'inykh, a master at Trade School No. 3 and a decorated communist, and Kryuchkov, a candidate-member of the CPSU, were killed, while comrades Sharkov and Zhavoronkov were badly wounded... The essence of the political platform of the kulak management of the collective farm was most clearly expressed by Lapov, the head of the 'Forward!' *artel'*, who had declared in August 1945 to his close colleagues, 'Now under Soviet power the people and peasants feel oppressed. They work from one whistle blow to the next. The peasants have nothing and are restricted in everything; the common lands are covered in weeds and cultivation's poor quality, worse than in the old days. The farm tools and machinery aren't looked after and get broken, because the collec-tive farmers don't think of them as their own, but as somebody else's, the farm's. A lot of collective farm land lies fallow, whereas, before, the individual farmer used to work every inch. The peasants are not their own masters, but are forced to work whether they like it or not. If our agriculture had kept developing as it did under NEP, by now every peasant-farmer would have a tractor, a car and other equipment on his own farm. The peasants would've had plenty of produce and want for nothing.' . . .

The reason for the blunted political vigilance on the part of the leading personnel of the CPSU district committee, the district executive committee and the district departments of the Ministries of State Security and Internal Affairs is their low ideological and political level, and also the fact that most of the leading personnel in the district were directly materially dependent upon the chairman of the administration, Lapov, from whose farm they got their bread, eggs, chickens, meat, dairy and other farm produce.

[Source: *Slovo*, No. 6, 1991.]

During 1947, pressure on the peasantry remained fierce. Delivery targets were raised to a new height, as were taxes on income arising from private plots, while retail outlets in the countryside remained few and far between. That year, in part to cut peasant demand for consumer goods in short supply, a currency reform was carried through, carefully designed to devalue drastically the savings that more entrepreneurial peasants had accumulated during the war. The price the state paid for grain remained abysmally low, and the rate of pay to collective farmers for work days served was derisory, as this letter from the management of a collective farm in western Siberia to Andreev, the Politburo member responsible for agriculture, lamented.

Document 154 | **Extract from a letter sent by the management of the Altay 'Kyzyl Beacon' collective farm to A.A. Andreev**

13 September 1948

We'd like you to explain to us why year in year out we have to hand over our whole harvest and don't get a single gram back for our work days, which is undermining the economy of collective farms and the farmers' wish to work. We realize that during the war more grain was needed to supply the army, and we gladly and uncomplainingly gave up everything to defeat the enemy. As there were poor harvests in 1945, '46 and '47, we also handed over everything to rebuild the economy as quickly as possible. For 1948 we hoped that once we had achieved our state grain delivery quota, we could distribute about a kilo each per work day. Now we have fulfilled the state plan by 200%; we have delivered double the plan quota. But, despite this, the CPSU *oblast'* and district committees have given us and other collective farms firm instructions to deliver above the quota, exceeding the state plans by several times, so there's nothing left to give out for work days and there's not even enough seed to sow densely enough in 1949.

The collective farmers in our *aymak* live in extremely difficult conditions and nobody's interested that we work day in day out all year round, but don't get a thing for work days. We don't see a crumb of bread and live on potatoes. When the potatoes run out in the spring, we go on to grass. . .

[Source: *Slovo*, No. 6, 1991.]

The following letter, this time addressed to the Collective Farm Council by a peasant woman in the Urals, makes an equally desperate plea itemizing the starvation diet to which peasants were driven. She lays part of the blame on 'speculators'.

Document 155 | **From a letter by Nikiforova, a peasant woman, to the Collective Farm Council of the USSR**

December 1948

Many collective farms in the Chernushinsky district of the Molotov *oblast'* are in a bad way. After they've delivered their quotas and paid the MTS, many of the villages are left with almost no bread grain. All they've got to eat is potatoes, sometimes with some milk. This is how they bake their bread in the village of Kopytovo: they grate a bucket of potatoes and add a handful of flour to bind it. Bread like this has almost no protein, which is what the body needs. As for milk, a lot of the cows have gone to the slaughterhouse to make up the meat quota; they send calvers in the last stages of pregnancy. I've heard of a calf falling out of a slaughtered cow and standing up. And there's lots of cases when the unborn calves were moving.

Cattle are going under the knife to pay debts, but slaughtering cows is disastrous, because milk is used to replace bread, because there is protein in it.

Children have got to have milk to grow properly. If there's little bread grain (a handful of flour for a bucket of potatoes) and no milk, then the body gets starved and feeble.

It is absolutely vital to establish a minimum quantity of bread, which must remain untouchable, even if it is only 300 g. of flour per person per day. Potatoes are a deceptive food—they're more to do with taste than nourishment. These are some of the places that are short of bread grain: Kopytovo, Bol'shoy Esaul, Malyy Esaul, Kreshchenskoe, Grun, Bizyar, etc. It is not in the state's interest to reduce its population to exhaustion and dressing it in rags. If the cities don't take so much bread grain and meat, then the people who produce it won't be hungry and embittered.

Since there's a lot of villages without any bread grain in the Chernushinsky district, it is vital to stop the leakage of bread to the speculators. At every market, on Wednesdays, Saturdays and Sundays lots of speculators turn up to buy up the bread grain and take it home to Revda, Druzhinino, Sverdlovsk and Sergi, where they sell it at 2½ times the price. It's there where they get wheat flour for, say, about

6 rubles a kilo and then go and sell it for 13–15 rubles a kilo. Then when they've got the money, they rush back here and buy more bread grain again and again. Each speculator—and there's a lot of them—hauls off about 5–6 *pudy*. The buildings next to the station are crawling with them. There's a couple of dozen at every market. The police have often searched Pioneer St, where they hang about, but they're only interested if they've got textiles. They get about in heated goods vans. They pay the people in charge of the vans 20–25 rubles, sometimes they also bribe the guards.

Nikiforova

[Source: RGAE, fond 9476, opis' 1, delo 144, pp. 44, 45.]

These pleas made little impact. In terms of organization, from 1949 there were rapid moves to amalgamate smaller collective farms into larger units, the number being cut by almost two-thirds in two years. Collective owner-ship became even less meaningful and the management, into which ex-soldiers and party members were increasingly drafted, became even more remote from the villagers. Stalin's last years also saw the renunciation of the policy, championed for a time by Andreev, of permitting the formation of small teams of peasants—'links'—charged with responsibility for an area of the farm and given some autonomy and tangible incentive.

Peasant policy after Stalin

Stalin's successors remained wedded to the essentials of this structure, yet they sought to ease the pressure on the peasantry. Within days of Stalin's death, at the same time as they signalled their intention to reduce the levels of repression and political violence, both the Prime Minister, Malenkov and the party First Secretary, Khrushchev, as they manoeuvred for primacy, placed heavy emphasis on improving the quality of life. They were conscious of the need to foster the post-Stalin regime's legitimacy by demonstrating its ability to deliver material improvement. They tried to find ways simultane-ously to raise rural productivity and to improve living standards, welfare provision and amenities. They embarked on the first of a whole series of attempts, within the framework of the collective farm system, to link effi-ciency and incentives. Among the variables was the issue of how to treat the peasants' private plots. Even after the postwar drive to cut them back and reclaim collective land temporarily used privately, they remained a major supplementary source of overall output. Policy oscillated. In this excerpt from a speech by Malenkov, delivered during the summer following Stalin's death, at a time when he was championing a 'New Course' in economic policy making greater use of market incentives, he announced moves which, without allowing peasants to expand their plots, would positively encourage them to maximize the amount they produced and marketed from the land they were permitted to use.

Document 156 | From a speech by G.M. Malenkov to the Supreme Soviet

7 August 1953

. . . In order to ensure a steep rise in the production of items of mass consumption, our first concern must be the further growth and development of agriculture, which provides food for the people and raw materials for light industry. . .

. . . In connection with this, the government and Party Central Committee consider it necessary to go for a significant reduction in compulsory delivery quotas from the private plots of collective farmers, and have decided, as the Minister of Finance comrade Zverev has already reported, to change the system for levying the agricultural tax on collective farmers, to reduce the money tax on each collective farm household by approximately a half, and to cancel completely the remaining agricultural tax arrears from previous years.

[Source: *Pravda*, 8 August 1953.]

The following month, Khrushchev announced a sharp increase in the hitherto derisory procurement price paid to collective and state farms for their produce.[104] He underlined, at the same time, that there would be no equivalent increase in the retail price at which the state marketed food to consumers. On the contrary, the reduction in food retail prices that had begun during 1947, halving them by 1954, would continue. Thus to square the circle of improving incentives for peasants while avoiding passing the cost on to workers, the regime began to curtail the mechanism through which, under Stalin, resources from the countryside had been extracted for investment in industry. Yet striking though these initial increases in procurement prices sounded, they were far from sufficient to break collective farmers' apathy.

---

104 On Khrushchev's agricultural policies, see D. Filtzer, *The Khrushchev Era: De-Stalinization and the Limits of Reform in the USSR, 1953–1964* (Basingstoke 1993), pp. 38–57.

Document 157 | **From Khrushchev's report to a plenary meeting of the CPSU CC**

3 September 1953

It is very important to increase the material interest of collective and state farms in raising crop yields and developing socialized animal husbandry. With this aim in view the Council of Ministers of the USSR and the Presidium of the Party CC have recognized the necessity of raising the current fixed state procurement and purchase prices of animal products, potatoes and vegetables. Thus, fixed state procurement prices for compulsory cattle and poultry deliveries to the state will go up by more than 5.5 times, for milk and butter by more than 2 times, for potatoes by 2.5 times and for vegetables on average by 25–40%. As for purchase prices, they will go up by about 30% for meat and by 1.5 times for milk. At the same time it is important to point out that the retail prices of animal products, potatoes and vegetables will not go up, but, on the contrary, will fall year on year. The policy of reducing retail prices for consumer goods will be continued.

[Source: *Pravda*, 7 November 1953.]

The 'virgin lands' campaign

A dramatic effort to increase output, with which Khrushchev identified himself very closely, was the campaign to bring vast tracts of 'virgin land' under the plough.[105] Huge unused expanses in Kazakhstan, the Urals and Siberia were brought under cultivation. The campaign was conducted with a fanfare of publicity and an appeal to communist idealism reminiscent of the early days of the revolution and the First Five-Year Plan.

Document 158 | **From an address to Moscow Komsomol members and young people keen to go to develop virgin and fallow lands**

January 1955

Komsomol members and young people of the Soviet Union!
   . . . Dear friends!
   Let us prove worthy of the trust and care of our mother the Communist Party!
Let us gladden our Motherland with further success in reclaiming millions of hectares of virgin and fallow land! Let us give our unbreakable Komsomol word to the Party

---

105 See the account by M. McCauley, *Khrushchev and the Development of Soviet Agriculture: The Virgin Lands Programme* (London 1976).

Central Committee and the Soviet government that we shall toil honestly and in a spirit of self-sacrifice on the new lands.

Let us go, comrades, and develop the virgin lands!

[Source: *Pravda*, 8 January 1955.]

The 'virgin lands' campaign had some success in mobilizing popular and especially young people's enthusiasm, and the propaganda that accompanied it was highly effective. For a few years it did contribute to a very steep rise in output. Yet the policy was deeply flawed. Not only was most of the newly farmed land highly susceptible to drought and wind erosion, but inadequacies in terms of management, infrastructure, storage and transport led to colossal waste. The whole approach—the reckless commitment to a drastic solution dependent more on the willpower of the political leadership than economic calculation—was redolent of the authoritarian mindset and semi-military approach to economic priorities ingrained during the Great Patriotic War and bequeathed by Stalin. The following recollections and later reflections by Eduard Shevardnadze, the longtime First Secretary in Georgia who was to become Gorbachev's Foreign Minister, capture both the enthusiasm of the time and the later realization of how ill-conceived the campaign had been.

Document 159 | Eduard Shevardnadze: Memoir of the 'virgin lands' campaign

. . . The opening up of the virgin and fallow lands had begun. Special trains for young volunteers went to Kazakhstan and the Altay. I was given the job of being in charge of the Georgian Komsomol contingent. We lived for several months on the steppes of Kazakhstan, tilled the virgin land, built housing and farm buildings. . . I owe a lot to those times and still have fond memories of them. . .

The organizational deficiencies of the grandiose virgin lands epic, the foolishness of some decisions and the ill-considered strategies which later in many respects nullified what we did achieve are all so clear to me now. The machinery, brought there from all over the country, broke down before our very eyes. Thousands of people who couldn't harvest such vast areas just couldn't cope. Crops were left to rot and there was nowhere to store the grain. There was a colossal waste of billions of rubles, machinery and labour. The virgin lands cost the country dearly. I now believe that all that expenditure could have brought large returns, had a different approach to solving the grain problem been adopted. But in those days a different approach was not possible.

[Source: E. Shevardnadze, *Moy vybor: v zashchitu demokratii i svobody* (Moscow 1991), p. 57.]

In parallel with the 'virgin lands' campaign, Khrushchev embarked on what was to become by the early 1960s, following a visit to the US during which he had observed the vast fields of the corn belt, an almost equally ill-conceived drive to make maize the country's main fodder crop. The following extract from a 1955 report to the Central Committee shows him waxing eloquent about the potential benefits which maize, farmed with the most modern machinery, held out for the USSR.

Document 160 | **CPSU CC Plenum resolution on increasing agricultural productivity, adopted on the basis of a report by N.S. Khrushchev**

31 January 1955

. . . III. On increasing the output of meat, milk, eggs, wool and other products of animal husbandry.

. . . The USSR Ministry for the Meat and Dairy Products Industry is to expand the feeding and fattening up of cattle and pigs by 1960 by approximately 2.5 times compared with 1954. . .

IV. On increasing fodder production.

. . . The tried and tested square-cluster way of sowing maize and harvesting with combines opens up great possibilities for cultivating maize, completely mechanizing sowing and harvesting, greatly reducing the labour costs of producing this crop, raising the yield and making maize the leading crop in creating a firm basis for animal fodder.

[Source: *Pravda*, 2 February 1955.]

Directly in line with the ethos established in the First Five-Year Plan, and entrenched by the triumphant achievements of munitions production during the war, the faulty assumptions on which the leadership's agricultural policies were constructed became built into All-Union, Republican and regional targets. The wild optimism about agricultural growth extended to irrational projections and estimates, enthusiastically promoted by Khrushchev, of increased livestock and output of meat and milk. It was bombast of the kind that led local leaders who had publicly committed themselves to unattainable targets to resort to desperate and often counterproductive measures —such as slaughtering dairy cattle for beef—to disguise their inevitable failure. The most notorious instance was in Ryazan' *oblast'*, where the local party secretary, A.N. Larionov, undertook to treble the sale of meat within two years, was celebrated as a Soviet hero, and was then driven to suicide when the reality was exposed. The level of fantasy, analogous to that of the First Five-Year Plan, is illustrated in the following table, paraded in *Pravda*.

The local leadership of the Krasnodar region north of the Caucasus put their names to estimates of increased output that defied all reason (as well as the laws of mathematics, where the 'all types of farm' calculation is concerned).

Document 161 | The socialist production obligations of agricultural workers in the Krasnodar *kray* (1957)

Production of meat per 100 hectares of land (live weight in quintals)

Produced in 1956		Envisaged for 1957		Envisaged for 1960		Increase since 1956	
Coll.	State	Coll.	State	Coll.	State	Coll.	State
22	45	44	61	151	200	7 times	4.5 times

All types of farm

47	72	203	4.2 times

Milk production per 100 hectares of land (in quintals)

Produced in 1956		Envisaged for 1957		Envisaged for 1960		Increase since 1956	
Coll.	State	Coll.	State	Coll.	State	Coll.	State
105	131	145	149	375	375	3.7 times	2.9 times

All types of farm

197	268	529	2.6 times

D. Polyansky, secretary of the CPSU Krasnodar *kray* committee
B. Petukhov, chairman of the Krasnodar *kray* executive committee
V. Pribylov, head of the agricultural administration

[Source: *Pravda*, 8 June 1957.]

Meanwhile, the leadership wrestled with the continuing evidence that none of the measures taken had made a significant impression on the inefficient and listless work of the collective farms. It was not easy to deny an element of truth in the following gloomy criticism, an interesting example of the deeply embedded tradition of humble citizens sending pleas and petitions to the Kremlin in the hope that a frank exposition might get through to the very top.

Document 162 | From a letter by M. Nikolaeva to Khrushchev on the failure of collective farming

November 1956

Comrades, you think a lot about yourselves but little about ordinary people. The people aren't living well and their [negative] state of mind isn't in our interest. Food's tight all over the country. In effect you can eat properly only in Moscow. All you see in the shops in a lot of towns are crabs and peas. They hardly eat any sugar in the countryside. The main thing is that the food problem is not getting any better year on year.

We, in Russia, are importing meat from New Zealand. Just take a look at the state of the houses of individual collective farmers—they're just wrecks. The odd success doesn't alter the picture. Has it ever happened before that people ran away from the countryside?! But our countryside is emptying. . .

Comrade Khrushchev! You're a brave man, so be brave again and say outright that 26 years' experience has shown that the collective farms haven't worked. We need another way of organizing agriculture.

[Source: *Izvestiya TsK KPSS*, No. 6, 1989, pp. 148–49.]

From the late 1950s, Khrushchev was persuaded to sanction a number of local experiments with the 'link system' which Andreev had sponsored after the war.[106] The idea was to tie incentives to effort by entrusting a team of some nine to eleven peasants with the responsibility of planting, tending and harvesting a designated piece of land, and to be directly rewarded according to the surplus they succeeded in producing. The evidence is that, in many cases, the experiments were highly promising, the combination of the incentive, the esprit de corps, the autonomy and the direct involvement in micro management enabling them to outperform the apathetic brigade system. However, there was powerful resistance from ideologues hostile to what was easily portrayed as a halfway house to private enterprise; from collective farm managers and local party officials, whose efforts were put in the shade and whose role might ultimately be threatened; and from the majority of peasants who resented the success of the links and the way their performance showed up the slackness and inefficiency of regular collective farm work practices. The collective farm bequeathed by Stalin remained impervious to fundamental change. The hostility provoked by Khrushchev's efforts here fed into a growing current of criticism within the party of his repeated reform initiatives. The most dramatic, instituted in 1962, saw the party abruptly divided between parallel hierarchies responsible for agriculture and industry, and the number of times leading officials could be elected to the same office limited to three. Both of these reforms contributed directly to the resentment that led to his dethronement in 1964.

As we have seen, at the same time as Khrushchev and his colleagues set

---

106 Though it may overstate Khrushchev's reformist instincts, A. Yanov, *The Drama of the 1960s: A Lost Reform* (Berkeley 1984), provides a lively and coherent treatment of his agricultural aims.

about trying to ease the conditions of the peasantry and raise agricultural output, they sought also to improve urban living standards. In the course of the 1950s they pursued a range of policies to tackle the deprivation of the postwar years. First and foremost was the drive to increase the provision of and access to food. The following announcement of sharp price reductions, made within a month of Stalin's death, added dramatically to the gradual reduction in train since 1947.

Document 163 | **From a decree of the USSR Council of Ministers and the CPSU CC on further reductions in state retail prices for foodstuffs and industrial goods**

1 April 1953

. . . The Council of Ministers of the USSR and the CC of the CPSU have resolved:
1. From 1 April 1953 to reduce state retail prices for foodstuffs and industrial goods as follows:

- wheat and rye bread, white loaves, rolls and bakery products by 10%;
- beef, mutton, pork, poultry, salami, sausages. . . by 15%;
- chilled, frozen, salted and smoked fish by 10%;
- animal fat, lard, margarine and vegetable oil. . . by 10%;
- potatoes by 50%;
- fresh cabbage and other vegetables by 50%;
- granulated and lump sugar by 50%;
- vodka by 11%;
- beer by 15%;
- chintz, satin, calico and other cotton products by 15%;
- dresses, blouses, underwear and other ready-mades by 14%;
- medicines and other sanitary and hygiene products by 15%;
- petrol and grease by 25%.

. . .

[Source: *Pravda*, 1 April 1953.]

The continuing reduction in food prices succeeded in edging downwards the very high proportion of their budgets that families spent on food in the postwar years, and gradually heavy state subsidies underwriting cheap food became embedded in popular expectations. Although Khrushchev initially confronted Malenkov for taking too far the shift of emphasis towards consumer industries in his 'New Course', and defeated him in the competition for primacy in part by winning the support of officials in the military and heavy industry, once firmly in power, he too took a variety of steps to improve workers' quality of life. He sponsored a high-profile programme to tackle the desperate housing shortage and to increase urban living space. In 1956 the minimum wage was sharply raised and pension provision for the aged, disabled and sick was greatly expanded. So too, incrementally, was the scope of the free health service.[107] Khrushchev made particular play of his measures to expand educational provision at all levels, the numbers enrolled in higher education almost trebling between the early 1950s and the mid-1960s. And throughout he placed emphasis on making upward social mobility through education more easily available to the children of workers and peasants. In 1958, reverting to the principle enunciated in the Stalin Constitution of 1936 but quickly flouted, he abolished fees both for senior classes of secondary and for tertiary education.

Document 164 | **The law amending Article 121 of the USSR Constitution and abolishing fees for education**

14 July 1956

In view of the introduction of general seven-year schooling in all urban and rural localities of the USSR and the abolition of fees for education in the senior classes of secondary schools, secondary special schools and higher education institutions, the corresponding amendments to Article 121 of the Constitution (Fundamental Law) of the USSR are to be made as follows, 'Article 121. Citizens have the right to education. This right is guaranteed by compulsory general seven-year schooling, the broad development of secondary education, no fees for any types of education, secondary or higher, and a system of state grants for outstanding students in higher education.'

[Source: *Vedomosti Verkhovnogo Soveta SSSR*, No. 15, 1958, p. 404.]

Khrushchev's optimism: New Party Programme, 1961

Each improvement was accompanied by loud trumpeting and greatly inflated claims about his economic, social and welfare initiatives. Alongside Khrushchev's bravado about the speed with which the Soviet system would outperform its capitalist rivals, momentum gathered for the most grandiose speculation on and then commitment to the swift transformation of Soviet society. The epitome was the flamboyant ambition he wrote into the text of the new Party Programme introduced in 1961 to replace that of 1919.[108]

---

107 On the rise in living standards between the 1950s and the 1970s, see V. George and N. Manning, *Social Welfare and the Soviet Union* (London 1980).

108 See the discussion in M. Sandle, *A Short History of Soviet Socialism* (London 1999), pp. 318–25.

The transition from socialism to communism, from a society in which goods were distributed according to work done to one in which, because they were produced in such abundance, they could be distributed according to need, would be made within a period of two decades.

Document 165 | From the Programme of the CPSU, 1961, on building a communist society

The material and technical basis of communism will be built up by the *end of the second decade* (1971–80) ensuring an abundance of material and cultural values for the whole population; Soviet society will come close to a stage where it can introduce the principle of distribution according to needs, and there will be a gradual transition to one form of ownership—public ownership. Thus, *a communist society will in the main be built in the USSR . . .*

With these aims in view, the CPSU plans the following increases in *total industrial output*:

within the current 10 years, by approximately 150 per cent, exceeding the level of US industrial output;

within 20 years, by not less than 500 per cent, leaving the present overall volume of US industrial output far behind.

To achieve this, it is necessary to raise *productivity of labour* in industry by more than 100 per cent within 10 years, and by 300–350 per cent within 20 years. In 20 years' time labour productivity in Soviet industry will exceed the present level of labour productivity in the USA by roughly 100 per cent, and considerably more in terms of per-hour output, due to the reduction of the working day in the USSR.

. . .

THE PARTY SOLEMNLY PROCLAIMS: THE PRESENT GENERATION OF SOVIET PEOPLE SHALL LIVE UNDER COMMUNISM!

[Source: *The Programme of the Communist Party of the Soviet Union, adopted at the 22nd Congress of the CPSU, 31 October 1961* (London 1961), pp. 46, 48.]

Given that Soviet productivity per worker still trailed far behind that of the US, and in the case of rural workers did not belong in the same league at all, and given what was by western standards the modest provision and quality of everything from household goods to clothes in the USSR at the time, the optimism that underlay these projections was breathtaking. Defending the notion of approaching material abundance at a time of serious shortages involved Soviet commentators in some highly contorted reasoning. It was only against the background of wartime destitution, and a highly restrictive notion of relevant material goods, that the programme made sense at all.

The Novocherkassk protests, 1962

The fact that the following year saw severe economic difficulties seemed to make a virtual mockery of the new programme. There were acute shortages not only of luxuries, but of essentials, including food itself. The government responded by raising procurement prices paid to collective and state farms, continuing the effort to bring them to levels which might serve as a real incentive for greater efficiency and output. In parallel, in order to pass on the increased cost of produce to consumers, rather than commit the state to a sizeable price subsidy, as well as to reduce queuing, a sharp increase in the retail price for food was announced, on 31 May 1962. There was outcry the very next day. Fixed, cheap food prices had come to be taken for granted and built into the assumptions of every worker and family. There were signs of unrest in several cities across the Union and in the town of Novocherkassk, in Rostov *oblast'* in southern Russia, a major disturbance broke out. It was the most serious urban protest since the war and left a permanent mark.[109]

What exacerbated feeling here was that at just that moment, the management of the large local electrical works, the Budenny plant, announced a cut in wages. The following report, sent to Khrushchev by N. Trubin, the Chief Prosecutor, after the ensuing trial, conviction and subsequent review of most of the cases, put the best possible face on the sequence of events. The disturbances were labelled 'pogroms', drunks and 'loutish elements' were prominent among the demonstrators, those shot dead had supposedly forced the troops involved to fire out of sheer self-defence despite the absence of an order to do so, and the number killed had been limited to twenty-four.[110] Yet even this sanitized account could not disguise the crass style of Kurochkin, the works' manager; popular disdain for the regional party secretary; the way in which efforts to stamp out the protest by arresting ringleaders led to its escalation; the speed with which men, women and children from nearby converged on the headquarters of the local soviet, the party and the police; the haste with which Kozlov, Khrushchev's deputy, Mikoyan and other top Kremlin figures rushed to the town; or the panic-stricken resort to both KGB and army troops.

---

109 The extent to which the events in Novocherkassk stood out from numerous lesser disorders in the Khrushchev years is made clear by V.A. Kozlov, *Mass Uprisings in the USSR: Protest and Rebellion in the Post-Stalin Years* (New York 2002).
110 The most comprehensive subsequent study is by S.H. Baron, *Bloody Saturday in the Soviet Union: Novocherkassk, 1962* (Stanford 2001). Baron numbers those killed at twenty-one.

Document 166 | **From the report of I. Trubin, USSR Chief Public Prosecutor, on Novocherkassk, 1962**

On the eve of the events there was an announcement on the radio and in the press about countrywide retail-price rises for meat and dairy products with effect from 1 June 1962. This coincided with measures by the management at the 'Budenny' electric locomotive works in Novocherkassk to reduce workers' wage rates. All this combined to cause a spontaneous strike of the workers there on 1 June 1962, which turned into a meeting attended by thousands. The strikers demanded the withdrawal of the wage reductions and representations to the government to halt the price rises for meat and butter, but Kurochkin, the works' director, rejected their demands rudely. His remarks aggravated the situation and further inflamed the anger of those at the meeting, amongst whom people had appeared who were inebriated and were demanding reprisals against the works' management. . . Comrade Basov, First Secretary of the Rostov *oblast'* Party committee, who had arrived on the factory premises that very day, went out on the balcony of the administration building to try to pacify the meeting, but was met with a hail of bottles, stones, sticks and other objects. Some people tried to switch off the public address system. At the same time a significant number of the participants in these disorders went to Lokomotivstroy station, which is near the works and on the main railway artery in the south of the country. They blocked the tracks and brought all trains to a standstill. Loutish elements started smashing carriage windows. . .

On the morning of 2 June a crowd of many thousands, including women and children, made for Novocherkassk to voice their demands and obtain the release of those people held at the city militia department who had been arrested the previous day near the works. To stop the march going any further, on the morning of 2 June on the orders of Pliev, the commander of the tank division of the Novocherkassk garrison Colonel Mikheev had stationed his men with 9–10 tanks and ATCs on the bridge across the Tuzlov. Arriving at the bridge, people ignored the orders of the unit commander to stop and carried on into town. . .

Comrades Kirilenko, Kozlov, Mikoyan, Il'ichev, Polyansky and Shelepin, all senior government figures, had arrived at the city's Party headquarters on the morning of 2 June. . . F.R. Kozlov reported back to N.S. Khrushchev in Moscow about the situation and asked permission from the Minister of Defence to order commander I.A. Pliev to use troops to stop any possible pogroms in the city. On 2 June weapons and ammunition were brought up from Rostov-on-Don and handed out to all the Interior Ministry troops, and by 10.00 all the subunits of these troops were ready for action. . . The crowd of thousands of people had reached a position 60–100 metres from the City Executive Committee building. . .

Comrades Zamula, the City Executive Committee chairman, and Stepakov, head of the local CPSU CC section, went out on the balcony with microphones and tried to persuade the throng to disperse and go back to work. Zamula, Stepakov and others on the balcony were met by a hail of sticks, stones and angry threats. The most aggressive group burst into the building and started a pogrom. Windows were smashed, doors broken down, furniture damaged, phone lines ripped out, and chandeliers and portraits torn down.

Major-General Oleshko, commander of the Novocherkassk garrison, arrived with fifty Interior Ministry servicemen armed with submachine guns, who pushed people back from the building and formed two lines in front of it... From the balcony Oleshko ordered people to stop the rioting and go home... The crowd did not respond, there were shouts, threats of retribution, and the square became a sea of noise. The servicemen fired a warning shot into the air from their submachine guns, which made the people who had been pressing against the soldiers move back. Shouts were heard from the crowd, 'Don't be frightened, they're just blanks!', after which the crowd again rushed at the City Executive Committee building and the troops spread out along it. There was another volley of shots into the air and immediately some individual shots into the crowd, leaving ten to fifteen people lying on the square. Following these shots panic broke out, people started running in all directions and a crush began... The subsequent investigation ascertained that Major-General Oleshko had not given any order to fire. The soldiers fired after violent elements from the crowd had rushed them and tried to snatch their weapons. Defending themselves and protecting their submachine guns, the soldiers had fired straight at them.

At the same time... an angry crowd had also gathered at the city militia and KGB buildings. They... made an active attempt to get into militia headquarters through smashed windows and doors to release those held there. There were calls from the crowd to seize weapons... One of the rioters managed to seize a submachine gun from private Repkin, and tried to open fire on the servicemen from this weapon. Forestalling him, private Azizov fired several shots and killed him. Another four people from among the rioters were killed and others were injured at the same time. More than thirty rioters who had burst into the corridors and yard of the city militia department were detained and locked up. Troops and officers of the Interior Ministry drove rioters out of the building of the State Bank, into which they had managed to penetrate for a short time...

As a result of the use of firearms in self-defence by Interior Ministry servicemen on 2 June on the square and at the city militia headquarters, twenty-two participants in the disorders were killed and thirty-nine injured. A further two people were killed in the evening of 2 June in unexplained circumstances. KGB and USSR Interior Ministry bodies opened and investigated fifty-seven criminal cases, for which 114 people were sentenced, including seven for banditry and organizing mass disorders, eighty-two for participating in mass disorders and twenty-five for malicious damage. All these criminal cases have now been reviewed. Owing to juridical mistakes, on the objection of the public procurator forty-six of those sentenced have been fully rehabilitated. In the cases of a further forty-five persons, sentences have been changed as charges were not made correctly and the punishments were excessively harsh. . .

[Source: *Pravda*, 3 June 1991.]

The following contemporary reports and later recollections largely tally with Trubin's account. The estimate of the numbers killed given to Khrushchev by the head of the KGB, V.E. Semichastny, within a fortnight of the disaster was very much the same and remained the official headcount. That was the number internalized by the leadership, although accounts reaching the west suggested a number three times as high.

Document 167 | **Report by V.E. Semichastny, Chairman of the KGB, on Novocherkassk**

14 June 1962

Top secret

To comrade N.S. Khrushchev
Herewith data on the persons killed during the mass disorder in Novocherkassk. A total of 23 persons were killed, of whom 18 have been identified, while the identities of 5 persons remain unknown.

[Source: *Istoricheskiy arkhiv*, No. 1, 1993, p. 131.]

This excerpt from an account by a N. Artemov, a team leader at the Budenny plant, underlined the price paid for Kurochkin's response to the initial protest among workers.

Document 168 | **Recollections of Novocherkassk, 1962**

These are the recollections of team leader N. Artemov from the Novocherkassk works:
On 1 June 1962 I was about five minutes late, so I went straight to the steel mill, changed into my overalls, switched on my machine and started putting a mould box together. Some of the lads came up to me and said, 'What are you working for?'
'That's what I'm here for!', I replied.
'Didn't you know there's a strike on? Come on, they're talking to the boss.' They'd gathered at the summerhouse next to our section. Men were asking Kurochkin, the director, how on earth they were supposed to make ends meet now.
He answered, 'You'll have to get by on offal pies then, won't you?' He said it rudely, which was really offensive to the workers. People from all the sections started heading for the factory admin building. By the time I got there, they were already holding a meeting.

If the boss had found the right words at that summerhouse meeting, perhaps there wouldn't have been any 'Novocherkassk events', but he didn't.

Did you really need to have some special kind of skill just to listen to people, talk to them as human beings and try to understand what they want? The bosses then didn't know how to, that was the trouble—and I don't mean just the director, Kurochkin.

An account by the chief engineer at the works, S. Elkin, who despite being part of the management structure appears to have sympathized with the protesters, pours scorn on how badly Basov, the First Secretary, misjudged the mood. He emphasizes the peaceful spirit of the protest and suggests the probability that local 'bosses' actively incited violence so that they could send for armed help in silencing the protests. And, underlining his portrait of the workers as thoroughly law-abiding and politically loyal, he describes them going to protest to the local Soviet Executive Committee bearing red flags and portraits of Lenin.

Somebody switched on the works' siren. People packed in work and made for the admin building. The situation began to heat up. In the course of the meeting, Basov, First Secretary of the Rostov *oblast'* committee, turned up. But I don't think he handled it properly. He started off by saying, 'Me, I was an orphan. . .' and began to moan about his hard life. But he still looked well-padded and well-dressed. Some louts started chucking bottles at him. We decided Basov should go, helped him get out through a window and into his car—and off he went.

Having given up hope of getting anybody at the works to understand, the workers weren't asking for very much—just to tell the government what they thought. Tell them they were dissatisfied and were stopping work in protest. Such a demand seemed unthinkable!

It would've been a sight easier and less painful for the local bosses to portray it all as some loutish escapade and egg people on to break the law. That is what they tried. It's difficult now, but you could still probably find out who was urging the workers on to disorder and riot, where the empty bottles were thrown from and who was shouting 'Beat up all those in suits!' The pushing, shoving and hitting had already started.

All the same, the workers were soon able to snuff this provocation out: they all agreed to go to the City Committee with red flags and portraits of Lenin and put their demands. They sent delegations to other factories with a call to support them.

This account by the deputy commander of the North Caucasus military district, Lieutenant-General M.K. Shaposhnikov, a war veteran, reflects the dismay among some officers that troops should be sent against peaceful civilian demonstrators.

I was put in charge of the units sent to the Novocherkassk electric locomotive works. General Pliev, commander of North Caucasus military district, assumed direct command of the units in Novocherkassk itself. Right from the start I was against sending our troops, especially with weapons and ammunition, against a crowd of factory workers and citizens, but my warnings were ignored.

I decided to order my units to unload their submachine guns and rifles and hand their ammunition in to their company commanders, who would not issue any ammunition without my orders.

General Pliev told us over the radio that thousands of workers with red banners were heading for the town centre.

'Stop them, don't let them through!', he shouted down the phone.

'The front of the procession's already crossed the Tuzlov and I just don't have the forces to stop so many people,' I said.

'I'll put tanks at your disposal.'

'What I don't see here is an enemy that should be attacked with tanks,' I replied firmly.

At this point the line went dead.

My assistant and I raced downtown in a jeep, but hadn't gone more than 100 metres before we heard automatics firing. . . The result was twenty-two or twenty-four dead, including a child of school age, and thirty wounded. Next morning I heard that the dead had been buried secretly.

Here the bloodshed and the hasty attempts to erase the evidence left behind on 2 June are recalled by A. Simonov, a correspondence course teacher in Novocherkassk:

A huge crowd had gathered at the city internal affairs building. They were demanding the release of people arrested that morning. The doors burst open under the sheer weight and people flooded in. Shots rang out and people rushed back out.

The uproar moved to the square in front of the Party headquarters. I got there just as the soldiers opened fire from their submachine guns. Panic ensued. The older ones, probably war veterans, fell to the ground and crawled across the square.

I can't remember very well what happened next. They spent a long time trying to wash the blood off the square. They tried a fire engine first and then something with brushes, but in the end brought in a roller and resurfaced the whole square with a thick layer of asphalt.

[Source: *Komsomol'skaya pravda*, 2 June 1989.]

The embarrassment and alarm the outbreak caused the Kremlin was palpable. As soon as the disorder had been crushed, Kozlov and his colleagues moved to ensure there were no copycat incidents elsewhere. On the one hand, Novocherkassk and the surrounding district were semi-quarantined; on the other, the area was abruptly given the highest priority for food supplies, the sentences meted out to those convicted were rapidly reduced and in many cases quashed, and the local party was placed under strict orders to ensure there were no further incidents requiring overt military force. Moreover, unlike in the 1930s, the leadership did not take refuge in the notion that this flare-up was the product of espionage and counter-revolutionary agitation, and did not follow up the restoration of order with heightened repression. Instead, on the scattered occasions during the following years on which local strikes and protests broke out, the response tended to be rapid concessions. The disaster, in short, left the regime highly circumspect about measures that might serve to trigger popular and especially working-class protest. In terms of national economic policy, the repercussions of Novocherkassk reverberated across the next quarter of a century. Food prices were set in stone. It became axiomatic that, however strong the economic case for bringing them more closely into line with the costs of food production, food prices remained sacrosanct. And from the mid-1960s the gap between costs and prices yawned ever wider, embedding at the very core of the command economy a disjunction that was to frustrate numerous attempts at economic reform.

The Kosygin reforms

Following Khrushchev's fall in 1964, Kosygin presided over a determined effort at such reform. He abandoned some of Khrushchev's wilder experiments or 'hare-brained schemes' as they were promptly dubbed. In agriculture, the Central Committee drove procurement prices upwards, convinced like Malenkov and Khrushchev before them that the poor performance of collective and state farms reflected first and foremost inadequate material incentives. The following Central Committee resolution, adopted in March 1965, set out the premises of the Kosygin reforms in agriculture: while reiterating the traditional emphasis on the quality of leadership and key role of scientific and technological progress, at the heart of the analysis was the need to raise the price paid for rural produce so as to provide incentives to the peasantry.

Document 169 | **From the resolution of the CPSU CC plenary session of 24–26 March 1965 *On Urgent Measures for the Further Development of the Agriculture of the USSR***

Agricultural growth has slowed down in recent years. Development plans have not been fulfilled. Crop yields have been rising very slowly. Growth in the production of meat, milk and certain other foodstuffs has also been insignificant. All of this has been creating certain difficulties for the country's economic development.

The basic reasons for the backwardness of agriculture have been violations of the laws of economic development of socialist production, of the principle that collective and state farmers should have a material interest in increasing social production, and of the proper balance of public and private interests. Subjective attitudes in management have had a significant effect, leading to mistakes in planning, financing, and providing credit to agriculture, and in price policy. Too little has been set aside for investment in building for both productive and welfare purposes, and the material and technical basis of agriculture has developed feebly. Great harm to both collective and state farm production has been done by pointless reorganization of its leading bodies, resulting in a situation of irresponsibility and insecurity in their work.

There have been serious defects in the organization of procurement and purchase of agricultural produce. The present system of procurement and purchase of crops and animal products does not create the necessary conditions for the development of collective and state farm production. . . .

The Plenary meeting accordingly decrees:

. . . 2. The successful implementation of the measures set out by the Party for further strengthening the collective- and state-farm economy and raising farm workers' material interest in the outcome of their work demands radical improvement in the work of all Party, Soviet, economic, Komsomol and trade-union organizations. The most important and decisive factors in their activities are the day-to-day concern for people, for the development of the collective- and state-farm economy, for increasing agricultural production, lowering costs and ensuring the profitability of all branches of production.

We must decisively reject the practices of managerial high-handedness, of giving orders, of displacing the managers and specialists of the collective and state farms themselves, and must root out manifestations of ostentation and show.

It is vital to win the active participation of the broad mass of the people in carrying out these economic and political tasks, and to ensure the correct recruitment, placing and education of personnel, and systematic verification of the carrying out of Party decisions. Discipline must be tightened up at all levels of Party and state apparatus and in all areas of social production, and every worker must take more responsibility for the tasks entrusted to them.

Particular attention must be paid to strengthening and raising the role of the primary Party organizations on collective and state farms. District committees must rely on them on a daily basis and help them in the smooth running of organizational and political-educational work among the masses.

3. This Plenary meeting of the CPSU CC considers the development of scientific agriculture particularly important. The scientists' duty is to expand their theoretical research, raise its level and get more results, and provide all-round help to collective and state farms to apply scientific achievements and advanced practices on a wide scale in the interests of further developing all branches of collective and state farm production.

4. Party, Soviet and agricultural bodies must decisively strengthen the democratic bases of the collective farm system, strictly observe *artel'* management principles, and ensure the wide involvement of collective farmers in dealing with the basic questions of collective farm production. Measures are to be taken to strengthen further and protect public socialist property, bring order into land use and put a stop to instances of selling off land. Work on the new-model rule-book for the agricultural *artel'* and preparations for the 3rd All-Union Collective Farmers' Congress must begin.

[Source: *KPSS v rezolyutsiyakh i resheniyakh s˝ezdov, konferentsiy i plenumov TsK*, Vol. 10 (Moscow 1986), pp. 426–29.]

Over the next two decades, procurement prices were raised and raised again, to the point where by the early 1970s rural wages were at last approaching those of unskilled urban workers. At the same time, a higher and higher proportion of annual investment was poured into mechanization, irrigation, fertilizer and storage. Total output rose significantly: indeed UN figures indicate that in the quarter of a century from 1950, the USSR was the fastest-growing agricultural region of the world.[111] Yet even in years of clement weather, the harvest recurrently fell short of targets. The managerial problems on Soviet collective and state farms proved highly resistant to solution. Rural work was associated with relatively low status and the calibre of most managers was modest. Nor were the difficulties of raising the quality of work overcome: peasants evaded efforts at close supervision, while the nature of most tasks made it impossible to develop an individual piece-rate system. Time and again, the bureaucratic structure responsible for agriculture was reconfigured, the last and most ambitious reform being the introduction of a super-ministry in 1982 to oversee the industrial sectors serving the farms as well as agriculture itself. By then the issue of disaggregating teams of labour to form 'links' entrusted with a given piece of land was also back on the

---

111 For an early collection of articles exploring the achievements and problems of the period that retains its value, see H.G. Shaffer (ed.), *Soviet Agriculture: An Assessment of its Contribution to Economic Development* (New York 1977).

agenda, promoted by M.S. Gorbachev, the Politburo member responsible for agriculture in the early 1980s. But one initiative after another ran into the sands.

In industry, too, the Kosygin reforms attempted to make much greater use of market mechanisms while remaining within the confines of the command economy and state ownership.[112] In September 1965, steps were announced designed at one and the same time to give enterprise managers more control over the product mix of their enterprises, and managers and workers alike stronger incentives to take what steps were necessary—cutting costs, reducing waste, shedding labour and introducing new machinery and techniques—to raise productivity and improve quality. In theory, as the key Central Committee resolution of 1965 emphasized, managers and workers were to be given much greater leeway by the reduction in the range of targets laid down.

Document 170 | **From the CPSU CC plenary meeting resolution *On Improving Industrial Management, Perfecting Planning and Strengthening Economic Stimuli for Industrial Production***

27–29 September 1965

A serious deficiency in the management of industry is that administrative methods have predominated, to the detriment of economic methods. Self-financing in many enterprises is a mere formality and the economic rights of enterprises have been constrained.

The work of enterprises is regulated by a large number of planning indices, which limits the independence and initiative of enterprise collectives, and reduces their responsibility for improving the organization of production. The system for material incentives for industrial workers does little to interest them in improving the overall results of the enterprise's work, in raising the profitability of production, and in improving the quality of industrial output.

The administration of industry on a territorial basis, whilst it did broaden the opportunities for inter-sector specialization and co-operation in industrial production within economic regions, at the same time hindered the development of sector specialization and rational production relations between enterprises in different economic regions, separated science from production, and led to multilayered managerial fragmentation and a loss of effectiveness in work.

In order to develop industry further and increase the efficiency of social production. . . . we need to improve planning methods, strengthen economic stimuli in industrial production and increase the material interest of workers in improving the results of their enterprise's operation.

---

112 See the analysis in Hanson, *Rise and Fall*, pp. 98–127.

This CC plenary meeting deems it necessary to reorganize industrial administration on a branch basis and form republican and all-Union ministries for each branch of industry.

It is deemed expedient to abolish the excessive regulation of industrial activity, reduce the number of planning indices being sent to enterprises from above, and provide them with the necessary means to develop and improve production and make better use of such vital economic levers as profit, price, bonus and credit.

The whole system of planning, industrial management and material incentive must be directed at ensuring high rates of development in social production and at raising its efficiency. The most important condition for attaining these goals is to ensure that enterprise collectives have a material interest in developing higher planning tasks, in improving use of production funds, the labour force and material and financial resources, in improving technology and the organization of labour, and in raising the profitability of production.

[Source: *KPSS v rezolyutsiyakh i resheniyakh s˝ezdov, konferentsiy i plenumov TsK*, Vol. 10 (Moscow 1986), pp. 440–45.]

In practice, however, here too the command economy proved resistant to thoroughgoing change. For all the fanfare of the Kosygin reforms, the primary call on the time and effort of managers and workers alike remained ministerial orders for the fulfilment of targets; and the primary measure for such fulfilment continued to be not a matter of cost or quality but of sheer volume. Thus, however rational the case at the macro-economic level for the introduction of new machinery and learning of new methods, at the micro-economic level, from the perspective of the individual enterprise, the short-term penalty of failing to achieve targets was simply too high. The command economy was adept at 'extensive growth', at increasing output by building new factories, opening new mines, laying new railways on patterns closely modelled on what already existed. What it proved very poor at doing was embedding a process of renewal and innovation, whether technological or managerial. Despite the prestige of and investment in scientific and technological research, the productivity gap between the USSR and the industrialized west widened. Repeated, milder efforts at industrial reform in the 1970s, undertaken without the panache or confidence of those of Kosygin, lost momentum even more quickly. There were local successes, but the obstacles to generalizing them across the system as a whole proved intractable. From the early 1970s industrial expansion began to slow down markedly.

The decline in economic growth

By the early 1980s, as the following table shows, two of the key ingredients which had underpinned the swift growth of the first two postwar decades were fast dwindling. The first was population growth: family sizes outside Central Asia rapidly shrank, as did reserves of female labour to be drawn into the labour market. The second was the availability of readily recovered or generated fuel and energy.

Document 171 | **Average annual percentage growth rates of productive resources over Five-Year Plan periods, 1961–1984**

Resource	1961–70	1971–75	1976–80	1981–84
Number of workers, employees and collective farmers engaged in material production	1.9	1.4	1.0	0.5
Production of fuel and energy resources	5.9	5.1	3.9	2.4

[Source: *Politicheskoe samoobrazovanie*, No. 10, 1986, p. 81.]

The next two tables, published during the years of reform under Gorbachev, attest to the declining rate of growth across the post-Stalin period. Though the exact scale of the change has remained a matter of keen dispute since the collapse of the USSR, its direction has not.[113] On every score—the rate of return on investment, average annual growth of national income, the rate at which industrial production expanded, the rate at which agricultural output increased, productivity per worker, and the increase in real per capita income—the trend was downwards.

Document 172 | **Basic indices of social and economic development in the USSR—average annual percentage rates of growth over Five-Year Plan periods, 1966–1985**

Index	1966–70	1971–75	1976–80	1981–85
National income	7.2	5.1	3.8	3.1
Industrial production	8.5	7.4	4.4	3.7
Average annual agricultural production	3.9	2.5	1.7	1.1
Social sector labour productivity	6.8	4.5	3.3	3.1
Changes in investment returns	–0.4	–2.7	–2.7	–3.0
Real per capita income	5.9	4.4	3.4	2.1

113 For an authoritative treatment, see W. Easterly and S. Fischer, 'The Soviet Economic Decline', *The World Bank Economic Review*, (1995), Vol. 9, no 3, pp. 341–71.

[Sources: L.I. Abalkin, *Kursom uskoreniya* (Moscow 1986), pp. 26–27; *Narodnoe khozyaystvo SSSR v 1985 godu* (Moscow 1986), p. 38; G. Khanin, 'Ekonomicheskiy rost: al'ternativnaya otsenka', *Kommunist*, No. 17, 1988, p. 85.]

By the same token, the shortfall between planned and actual increases both in national income generally and in agriculture in particular widened.

Document 173 | Soviet economic growth as a percentage of economic growth targets in the 9th, 10th and 11th Five-Year Plans, 1971–1985

Index	1971–75	1976–80	1981–85
Gross industrial production	91	67	77
Gross agricultural production (average annual figure)	68	56	42

[Source: B.P. Orlov, 'Tseli srednesrochnykh planov i ikh osushchestvlenie', *EKO*, No. 11, 1987, p. 50.]

The Novosibirsk Report

Try as they might, Stalin's heirs had found that within the structures sanctified by the Great Patriotic War, there were severe limits on their ability to shift the pattern of economic development from extensive to intensive growth; to embed technological refinement and innovation; to tie incentives to improvement in quality as well as quantity, productivity as well as gross output.[114] By the early 1980s the most daring social scientists were beginning to diagnose a malaise deep within the command economy. The following extracts are from what became known in the west as the 'Novosibirsk Report', a devastating critique penned in 1983 by Tatiana Zaslavskaya, a leading sociologist at the Novosibirsk Institute of Economics, and read by Andropov's leadership. Aspects of the analysis echoed that of the Kosygin reforms two decades earlier, criticizing excessive reliance on 'administrative' rather than 'economic' methods of management. It asserted explicitly that the economy had become too complex for centralized micromanagement and that there was a need to increase the use of market mechanisms.

---

114 For a lively critique, see M.I. Goldman, *USSR in Crisis: The Failure of an Economic System* (New York 1983).

Document 174 | From the Novosibirsk Report, 1983

. . . The branch, departmental and territorial structure of the national economy has become much more complex, the number of its links has grown colossally and even more its technological, economic and social ties. The structure of the national economy long ago crossed the threshold of complexity when it was still possible to regulate it effectively from one single centre. Regional, branch and economic disproportions in the national economy of the USSR, which emerged and can be observed in the past five-year plans, are growing relentlessly; and, more than anything else, indicate the exhaustion of possibilities for centrally-administered economic management; the necessity for more active use of 'automatic' regulators in balancing production, linked to the development of market relations. . .

. . . The centralized system of rules and norms of economic activity, which was created over the course of decades, has now become tangled to an unbelievable degree and many of its elements have become outdated.

More striking were two arguments Zaslavskaya advanced to explain malfunctions in the economy. On the one hand, she warned that the Soviet system was stultifying and distorting the individual morality and powerful work ethic to which socialism aspired. Potentially, Soviet workers were vastly more sophisticated and creative than they had been in the 1930s. But by denying scope to these more educated and reflective workers, the system was stunting their development, warping their attitude to work, and fostering a culture of what she called 'shady deals'.[115]

. . . Important changes have also taken place in the social type of worker in the socialist economy. The level of his education, culture, general information, and awareness of his social position and rights, has grown incomparably. The main body of skilled workers, on whom above all the effectiveness of the production process depends, nowadays has a rather wide political and economic horizon, is able to evaluate critically the leaders' economic and political activities, accurately recognizes its own interests and can defend them if necessary. The spectrum of needs and interests of workers is today more abundant and broader than that of workers in the 1930s; moreover, in addition to economic, it includes social and spiritual needs. It testifies to the substantial increase in the level of the workers' personal development, but at the same time it is an indication that they have become a much more complex object of management than previously. . .

Thus, it is in the interests of socialist society, while regulating the key aspects of

---

115 On the scale of corruption, see K.M. Simis, *USSR: Secrets of a Corrupt Society* (London 1982).

the socio-economic activity of the workers, to leave them a sufficiently wide margin of freedom of individual behaviour. Hence the necessity for directing behaviour itself, i.e. the subjective relationship of the workers to their socio-economic activity. Administrative methods of management are powerless here. The management of behaviour can only be accomplished in an oblique fashion, with the help of incentives which would take into account the economic and social demands of the workers and would channel their interests in a direction which would be of benefit to our society.

. . . In the light of what has been said, we must admit that the social mechanism of economic development as it functions at present in the USSR does not ensure satisfactory results. The social type of worker formed by it fails to correspond not only to the strategic aims of a developed socialist society, but also to technological requirements of contemporary production. The widespread characteristics of many workers, whose personal formation occurred during past five-year plans, are low labour- and production-discipline, an indifferent attitude to the work performed and its low quality, social passivity, a low value attached to labour as a means of self-realization, an intense consumer orientation, and a rather low level of moral discipline. It is enough to mention the various 'shady' deals made at public expense, the development of illegal output, of irregular registrations, of procuring wages which are not dependent on the results of labour.

It is our conviction that both the expansion of these negative phenomena and the lowering of the rate of growth of production come about as a result of the degeneration of the social mechanism of economic development. At present, this mechanism is 'tuned' not to stimulate, but to thwart the population's useful economic activity. Similarly, it 'punishes' or simply cuts short initiatives by the chiefs of enterprises, in the sphere of production organization, aiming at the improvement of economic links. Nowadays, higher public value is placed not on the activities of the more talented, brave and energetic leaders, but on the performances of the more 'obedient' chiefs, even if they cannot boast production successes.

Equally striking was Zaslavskaya's explicit challenge to the orthodox insistence that common ownership had eliminated conflicts of interest between different social groups. In her view, this was a dangerous myth which obscured the key source of opposition to effective reform. Such reform need pose no threat to elite officials responsible for the broad planning parameters within which market mechanisms would be allowed to take root. It would positively empower enterprise managers who had the talent and dynamism to match the new opportunities that a more market-oriented system would afford them. It would radically broaden the scope for initiative and higher earnings among rank-and-file technical and manual workers.[116] Each of these groups would include those who feared change and additional responsibility. But there was no inherent threat to any of them. The group which had every reason to fear reform, and which would inevitably see its role, rights and responsibilities drastically reduced, were the myriad and ever-increasing middle-ranking officials.

. . . The realization of these tasks presupposes a serious reorganization of the system of state management of the economy and especially the rejection of administrative methods of management with a high degree of centralization of economic decision-making, and the subsequent complex transition to economic methods of regulating production.

Any serious reorganization of economic management must be accompanied by a certain redistribution of rights and responsibilities among various groups of workers. Thereby, the expansion of every group's rights is, as a rule, combined with an increase of responsibilities; and a decrease of responsibilities goes hand in hand with a reduction of rights. Because of this, the attitude of the majority of groups to possible transformations in production relations, and to the economic mechanism which is their reflection, is not unambiguous.

. . . Logically speaking, the group which must be most interested in the transition to economic methods of management is the managerial 'staff' of the enterprises (associations), whose rights it has been proposed to widen sharply, and . . . the ordinary workers and ITR (Engineering and Technical Workers), who could use their individual capabilities more fully, work more effectively and receive a higher salary.

Thus, a good number of workers in the central organs of management, whose prospective role ought to be increased, are afraid that its responsibilities will become substantially more complicated, as economic methods of management demand much more of highly qualified cadres than do administrative methods. The guarded response of this group of workers to the idea of a transition to and a consistent implementation of economic methods of management often manifests itself in unfounded assertions, as though such transition was going to undermine the centralized motive power in the development of the socialist economy, or to reduce the real importance of the plan.

The reorganization of production relations promises a substantial narrowing and simplification in responsibilities for workers in departmental ministries and their organs. However, it is pregnant with just as significant a reduction in their rights, in their economic influence and also in the number of their apparatuses: the liquidation of many departments, administrations, trusts, branches etc. that have grown

---

116 The constraints which doomed the efforts by Stalin's heirs to remotivate Soviet workers are brought home in D. Filtzer, *Soviet Workers and De-Stalinization: The Consolidation of the Modern System of Production Relations, 1953–1964* (Cambridge 2002).

like mushrooms in recent decades. Naturally, such a prospect does not suit the workers, who at present occupy numerous 'cosy niches' with ill-defined responsibilities, but thoroughly agreeable salaries.

[Source: *Survey*, 28, No 1, Spring 1984, pp. 88–108.]

15

The One-Party State

Much of the political structure developed during the 1930s and hallowed by victory over Hitler endured across the postwar generation. The Stalin Constitution of 1936 was in force until 1977, and the 'Brezhnev' Constitution which replaced it left the essential framework in place. That framework was built around the political power of the CPSU, backed by the secret police and a network of informers. The party formed a unitary hierarchy which extended across the whole country, was embedded within every town, city, region and autonomous republic, and bound together the fifteen Union Republics.[117] In theory, it was composed of a politically conscious and high-minded elite, entry requiring nomination by current members and endorsement by the local committee. In form, it was democratic, the key personnel at each level—the party secretaries, the delegates to periodic Congresses, and the Central Committee and Presidium/ Politburo which emerged from the Congress—all being notionally subject to election. In practice, however, it was highly centralized; elections were not competitive; and appointments were dependent on selection from above. This process of selection and the vast patronage that went with it were concentrated in the hands of the Central Committee Secretariat. To head the Secretariat, as Stalin, Khrushchev, Brezhnev, Andropov and Chernenko all did, was to occupy the pivotal post in terms of policy as well as personnel: chairman of the Politburo/Presidium. Moreover, the policies adopted by the narrow elite right at the top of the party dictated all aspects of public policy: no rival parties were allowed to exist and the CPSU dominated every public institution. It controlled government and the media, all arms of the military and civil apparatus, the hierarchies responsible for cultural, leisure, welfare

---

117 See R.J. Hill and P. Frank, *The Soviet Communist Party* (3rd edn, London 1986), for a crisp account of the party's structure and development in the post-Stalin era.

and educational provision, every branch of the economy and every significant economic enterprise, as well as the formal legislative pyramid of soviets as elected at local, regional, republican and All-Union level. This framework proved sufficiently malleable to encompass the far-reaching economic and social development we have traced. Between Stalin's last years and the early 1980s, as we shall see, there were extensive changes in the political culture of the leadership, in the level of coercion, in the function of party membership, and in the measure of the regime's legitimacy. Yet the basic architecture remained.[118]

Stalin's last years

During the war, as we have seen, much of the party's formal mechanism had been disrupted, the GKO (the Council of State Defence set up in response to the Nazi invasion) had displaced the Politburo, local officials had gained considerable autonomy from the centre, and access to party membership had been freely conferred, especially in the Red Army. In Stalin's last years, many of the formalities began to be restored, albeit slowly and imperfectly. The Politburo regained authority over policy-making from the GKO, although critical decisions continued to be made by ad hoc groups under Stalin's purview and his word was decisive on any issue over which he cared to intervene. The Central Committee, too, regained its formal position, despite the fact that it failed to meet between 1947 and 1952, and eventually, in 1952, Stalin reactivated the formal link between rank-and-file members and the elite by summoning for the first time in thirteen years a Party Congress, the Nineteenth. The relationship between the Kremlin and party and state officials also began to mutate. Although there were violent echoes of the drastic purges carried out in the 1930s, the trend for them to establish greater autonomy and immunity from intervention by Moscow began to set in. Likewise, although immediately after the war there was a fierce drive, particularly associated with Zhdanov, to 'cleanse' the party, to raise the level of political consciousness and commitment among its members, and to tighten entry criteria, the attempt to return to the Leninist ideal of a membership restricted to an ideologically enthused elite soon lost steam. Steady, less discriminating growth resumed, with CPSU membership approaching 7 million by the time of Stalin's death. The incentives for joining were strong enough to make it unlikely that only the

---

118 For two systematic overviews of late Soviet society and the party's role within it, see D. Lane, *Soviet Economy and Society* (Oxford 1985), and B. Kerblay, *Modern Soviet Society* (London 1983).

politically zealous would do so, for there was a growing association between party membership and upward social mobility. To join was a fruitful career move, and by 1953 over three-quarters of party members occupied white-collar posts.[119] These included a wide range of humble clerical office jobs, but membership opened the way to promotion. The most successful minority could rise to the ranks of the *nomenklatura*, the elite deemed appointable to key posts in every hierarchy, who enjoyed not only power and access to restricted information but an expanding range of material privileges including special access to food, consumer goods and housing.

Among many pressures militating against the restriction of the party to the small vanguard it purported to be was the leadership's concern to deepen the party's roots and entrench popular acceptance of its dominant political role. Here, too, trends began under Stalin that would develop much further after his death. In 1946 he reintroduced the Soviet elections sanctioned by the Constitution of 1936. They were non-competitive, voting was compulsory, and there was no kind of independent verification of the results. From the vantage point of a multiparty parliamentary system, therefore, they seemed an empty charade. Yet the regime set considerable store by them. On the one hand, they served as a vehicle for parading public endorsement of the party and its policies. On the other, they were used to convey current policy initiatives and, to some extent, to take stock of public opinion. Even in Stalin's last years, meetings between candidates and constituents, though heavily formalized and imbued with Marxist–Leninist rhetoric and celebration of the great leader, provided a forum in which, within careful limits, popular concerns could be expressed. And the secret police compiled detailed memoranda on the mood revealed in informal discussions during the elections. The following report, from the town of Borovichi in Novgorod *oblast'*, halfway between Leningrad and Moscow, in the run-up to the Supreme Soviet elections of February 1946, is typical in spelling out detailed instances of cynicism and discontent.

Document 175 | **From a report on political attitudes among the population of the Novgorod region before the elections**

February 1946

. . . There are some individuals among the populace with a hostile attitude to Soviet power who are trying to discredit the forthcoming elections to the USSR Supreme Soviet. A significant number of instances point to this, as when they criticize the

---

119 For a recent study of the consolidation of the position of the technical intelligentsia in the postwar years, see J.E. Duskin, *Stalinist Reconstruction and the Confirmation of a New Elite, 1945–1953* (London 2001).

Soviet electoral system or use food, housing and other difficulties in order to blame the Soviet government.

Here are a number of examples from the town of Borovichi:

'First give us more bread, then explain what you want.' 'Why is it always take, take, take and never give?' 'Is it worth voting when the communists will be elected anyway?' Malyshev, head clerk at Borovichi state farm declared, 'Our elections aren't democratic, they only choose the one appointed by the Party. They're not elections, but just a joke.' P.A. Lebedev, a teacher in the Lyubytino village school, said, 'I've read the Law on Elections. I thought I'd find some changes towards democracy, as in Britain or America. I didn't. As before they'll be just for show and the ones the Party wants will go to the Supreme Soviet.' F.I. Ivanov, a teacher from another school in the Lyubytino district, said the same sort of things. A.I. Bochkov, an electrician at the Red Ceramics factory, said, 'Right now all the papers are full of stuff about the elections to the Supreme Soviet, but it's just a farce. We don't have any democracy here. You read about what happens abroad, where they elect people from different parties and even religious groups. Like it or not, here they're all from just one party, so we have to elect it. Where's the freedom there, then? I'll just cross all the candidates out.'

Balygeev, a collective farmer at the '12th Anniversary of October' agricultural *artel'* in the Utorgosh district, declared at a study group to learn about the Law on Elections, 'They've never told us the truth and won't tell us now about which candidate got more votes and which got less. You can count me out. What's the point in me voting? It won't change my position.'

At a meeting of members of the Sunrise collective farm in the Khvoynaya district, after a talk on 'The Stalin Constitution—The Constitution of Victorious Socialism', E.I. Dorozhkina, a Leningrad evacuee, spoke. She dedicated her speech to the advantages which the state supposedly confers only on workers. 'What does the state give the collective farmer? There's no paraffin, no matches, no soap, and as for consumer goods—forget it! That's how much the state cares about collective farmers. True, the state doesn't forget collective farmers, it's always turning to us and demanding everything: give it to the state and you can go hungry. Although I don't belong to a collective farm, I mix with collective farmers all the time and can see that our state has reduced them to complete wretchedness. If you gave collective farmers a medical examination, to a man they would be declared unfit for physical labour. I blame our state, which just doesn't care about having able-bodied people on the collective farms. The collective farmers work day and night, but still can't keep up with the work.'

N.G. Lerman, who lives in Velikoe Selo village, Zaluch'e district, declared, 'Speeches are fine when you've got enough to eat. They come round, checking for lice. If they gave us enough bread, we wouldn't have lice. Under the Germans we had enough to eat and we didn't have lice. I wrote to my son, telling him to get out of the Red Army. He'd be better off in prison than in the army. I'm not going out to vote, because I'm going hungry. . .'

Kir'yanov, Head of organization of the CPSU *oblast'* committee training division

[Source: GARF, fond 17, opis' 88, delo 469, pp. 104–06.]

Secret police and party officials presented disaffection of this kind as restricted to a small minority, and it remains difficult to gauge how widespread it was. There is also evidence of spontaneous expressions of loyalty and warmth on the reverse side of some ballot slips, and in many cities the mood during the elections seems to have been festive rather than restive. It appears to have been quite possible for individual voters to scorn the process, be it the All-Union elections of 1946, those for the Union Republics of 1947, or the parallel local elections, and to be acutely hostile towards local party bosses and officials, while at the same time remaining broadly supportive of the Soviet regime and order as a whole. Critical here was the emotional and psychological impact of the war. It conferred on communist rule and the Soviet system a measure of legitimacy of a qualitatively different kind from any it had been able to establish before the war. The shared ordeal, the combination of outrage and of moral superiority born of the suffering endured, the absolute priority given defence against any sequel to Barbarossa—all this bound regime and people together in an entirely new manner. Both celebration of the victory and indignation at the racial insult and devastation visited on the country endowed the regime's rhetoric and narrative with themes which resonated across every social group. It provided the richest material for fostering positive identification with the USSR, and a common, multinational allegiance embracing the country's myriad different national groups. In his speech before the February 1946 elections, Stalin pronounced the definitive triumph of the Soviet solution to the national tensions which had torn apart the Austro-Hungarian Empire and, by 1946, left the USSR and Yugoslavia as the only European states which did not base their claim to legitimacy on the notion of representing a single nation.

Document 176 | **The USSR as a 'model multinational state'—from Stalin's speech at the pre-election meeting in the Stalin electoral district of Moscow**

9 February 1946

. . . Secondly, our victory signifies that our Soviet *state* system was victorious, that our multinational Soviet state passed all the tests of the war and proved its viability. As we know, prominent foreign journalists have more than once expressed themselves to the effect that the Soviet multinational state is an 'artificial and short-lived structure', that in the event of any complications arising the collapse of the Soviet Union would be inevitable, that the Soviet Union would share the fate of Austria–Hungary.

Now we can say that the war refuted these statements of the foreign press and proved them to have been devoid of all foundation. The war proved that the Soviet multinational state system successfully passed the test, grew stronger than ever during the war, and turned out to be quite a viable state system. These gentlemen failed to realize that the analogy of Austria–Hungary was unsound, because our multinational state grew up not on the bourgeois basis, which stimulates sentiments of national distrust and national enmity, but on the Soviet basis, which, on the contrary, cultivates sentiments of friendship and fraternal cooperation among the peoples of our state.

Incidentally, after the lessons of the war, these gentlemen no longer dare to come out and deny the viability of the Soviet state system. The issue now is no longer the viability of the Soviet state system, because there can be no doubt about its viability. Now the issue is that the Soviet state system has proved to be a model multinational state, that the Soviet state system is a system of state organization in which the national problem and the problem of the collaboration of nations have found a better solution than in any other multinational state.

[Source: J. Stalin, *Speeches Delivered at Meetings of Voters of the Stalin Electoral District, Moscow* (Moscow 1950), pp. 27–29.]

Right to the end of Stalin's rule, Moscow's confidence that the danger posed by minority nationalism and separatism had been laid to rest was in fact much more fragile than his words suggest. In both the Baltic Republics and western Ukraine there was active resistance by armed bands to the imposition of Soviet authority after the war, to which the regime's response was drastic. The purges carried out in the newly incorporated Baltic Republics, western Ukraine and Moldova were directly analogous to the wholesale exile of the 'punished peoples' of the Caucasus and Crimea (see documents 116–120) in 1944, albeit focused on the political, economic, social and cultural elite rather than on the whole people. The following grim report of 1992, drawing on archival research published in 1988 and 1989, attempts to compute the numbers, running together three very different categories of victim: purged local party leaders, Soviet personnel killed by nationalist bands, and the tens of thousands decimated and uprooted by the regime.

Document 177 | A chronicle of resettlements, repressions and deportations

On 26 November 1948, a Decree of the Presidium of the Supreme Soviet was adopted, announcing that Germans, Kalmyks, Ingush, Chechens, Balkars, Crimean Tatars and other groups had been resettled in remote locations for ever, and that for leaving their place of settlement without permission they would be sentenced to up to twenty years' hard labour.

In 1948, in connection with the 'Leningrad affair' [see document 180], virtually the whole Party leadership of the Estonian SSR was subject to repression.

In 1949, immediately before collectivization, more than 20,000 people were deported from Estonia.

On 22–23 May 1948, as decreed by the USSR Council of Ministers on 21 February 1948, 11,345 families of active members of the armed nationalist underground and of kulaks were deported from Lithuania: a total of 39,766 people (12,370 men, 16,499 women and 10,897 children under 15).

Between 25 and 28 March 1949, as decreed by the Council of Ministers on 29 January 1949, 6,845 families of kulaks and 1,972 families of nationalists were deported from Lithuania: a total of 29,180 people (9,199 men, 11,736 women and 8,245 children under 15).

Between 1944 and 1956, 25,108 people were killed and 2,965 wounded by Lithuanian nationalist terrorists. These included: adult Lithuanians—21,259 killed and 1,889 wounded; children under 16—993 killed and 103 wounded; infants under 2—52 killed and 15 wounded.

In Latvia between 1944 and 1952, 702 nationalist groups with a total of 11,042 members were broken up: of these people 2,408 were killed, 4,341 arrested and 4,293 gave themselves up to the authorities.

During the same period in Latvia 1,562 Party, Komsomol and state representatives, 50 Soviet Army servicemen, 64 from the MVD/KGB, 386 from special forces and many members of their families were killed.

When the Riga Forest Brotherhood was broken up in July 1946, a blacklist of 168 Latvian cultural and scientific figures was discovered.

14,000 people, including children and the elderly, were deported from Latvia on 25 March 1949.

[Source: A.P. Nenarokov, compiler, *Nesostoyavshiysya yubiley. Pochemu SSSR ne otprazdnoval svoego 70-letiya* (Moscow 1992).]

Stalin's suspicions extended well beyond these newly incorporated areas. Leaders of the established Union Republics who pressed the claims of their constituents too strongly were acutely vulnerable to denunciation for 'nationalist deviations'. The treatment of the Russian people as the senior partners in the USSR, begun in the 1930s, reached its apogee after the war, interwoven within the celebration of Soviet superiority over the west.[120] And Stalin's appointment policy, making Russians Party Secretary in almost all the Union Republics, demonstrated his distrust of the minorities. Yet he did not reverse the national–territorial structure of the USSR or the policy of *korenizatsiya* (nativization), whereby the party sought to ensure native participation and leadership in non-Russian areas. This, too, was part of the postwar framework that would endure to the 1980s.

His distrust and readiness to detect sedition epitomized and itself intensified the regime's low level of tolerance for disaffection not only among national minorities but of any kind in the immediate aftermath of the war. The leadership feared that the grim quality of life, acute shortages and frustrations, and desperate competition over resources might precipitate political opposition. The number arrested for civil crimes soared, too, in these repressive years. The following table, compiled in the Gorbachev period from GULAG archives, suggests that the proportion of political convicts was somewhat more than one-fifth of the total. The great majority of this category were in camps, those run by the central GULAG in which the discipline regime appears to have been made harsher than in the so-called 'colonies' which were in the hands of local MVD branches. The table, it should be noted, does not include the population of the GULAG labour settlements, although conditions there were often at least as harsh as in the camps: in 1949 their numbers were almost as great as the combined total for camps and colonies.

Document 178 | **The make-up of the GULAG in 1951**

	In corrective labour camps	In corrective labour colonies	Total
Total imprisoned as of 1 January 1952	1,713,905	789,170	2,503,075
Of which for counter-revolutionary crimes	492,188	90,344	582,522 [*sic*]
Of these:			
For betraying the Motherland	236,839	44,107	280,946
For spying	19,321	296	19,117 [*sic*]
For terrorism	8,564	329	8,899 [*sic*]
For sabotage	3,725	55	3,780
For nationalist activities	95,377	1,134	96,511
For misc. counter-revolutionary crimes	128,362	43,913	172,275

120 For the best account, see D. Brandenberger, *National Bolshevism: Stalinist Mass Culture and the Formation of Modern Russian National Identity* (Cambridge, MA, 2002).

Prisoners not sentenced for			
counter-revolutionary crimes	1,221,717	698,836	1,920,553
for 3 years	75,012	146,587	221,599
for 10 years	1,164,743	486,423	1,651,166
for 20 years	136,191	20,612	156,803
Number of prisoners released during 1951	248,838	351,892	600,730

[Source: *Voenno-istoricheskiy zhurnal*, No. 7, 1991, p. 69.]

In a sense it was paradoxical that Stalin's own mindset contributed so much to the repression of the postwar years, for a major factor strengthening the legitimacy of the regime was the enormous prestige that he himself now enjoyed. The personality cult so assiduously manufactured during the 1930s had, as a result of military victory, put down popular roots. Yet rather than bask in his popularity or take it for granted, he was tireless and ruthless in fostering the cult, ensuring that the glory of victory reflected on the party and above all its beloved leader. Very shortly after peace had been restored, he took steps, eagerly supported by members of the Politburo, to remove the military commanders from the limelight. Even Zhukov, now a household name and the military figure for whom Stalin appears to have had the most personal liking, was hurried off the stage. The following excerpt from Zhukov's recollections recounts his clash in 1946 with Bulganin, then Defence Minister; his removal from the Central Committee; the purge organized by Beria and V. Abakumov, the head of the MGB (formerly part of the NKVD), of senior military figures some of whom had supposedly conspired with him; and his own (temporary) demotion and exile to Odessa.

Document 179 | G.K. Zhukov on the postwar purge of officers

. . . At the beginning of March 1946 Stalin rang me in Berlin and said, 'Bulganin's given me a draft plan for the postwar reorganization of our armed forces high command. You're not on the list of the main senior commanders. I think this is wrong. What position would you like? Vasil'evsky has expressed a desire to be head of General Staff. Wouldn't you like to be Commander-in-Chief of ground forces, as they are our largest forces?'

I replied that I hadn't thought about it, but was prepared to take on any task entrusted to me by the CC. . .

After going through the draft statute on the People's Commissariat of Defence, Deputy Defence Commissar Bulganin and I had serious differences about the legal status of the heads of the various armed forces.

Bulganin reported all this in a distorted form to Stalin, adding, 'Zhukov's a Marshal of the Soviet Union, so he doesn't want anything to do with me, a mere general.' This was Bulganin's scheme for getting Stalin to appoint him, too, a Marshal of the Soviet Union.

And, in fact, a day later a decree was published granting Bulganin the title of Marshal of the Soviet Union, but Stalin said to me that more work was needed on the draft statute on the Commissariat. . .

Thanks to Bulganin's hints, Stalin saw separatism in my actions. There was a long and unpleasant talk about the contents of my draft decree, especially in the section about involving land forces and units of GHQ reserves in joint exercises and training. . .

I began to feel that something ominous was going on around me. And finally something really unpleasant happened to me.

Stalin brought together the Chief Military Council, to which were invited all the members of the Politburo, marshals, generals. . . Into the meeting room walked Stalin. He had a face like thunder. Without saying a word he took a piece of paper out of his pocket, threw it at General S.M. Shtemenko, the Council secretary, and said, 'Read it!' It was an accusation against Marshal Zhukov from former aide-de-camp Lieutenant-Colonel Semochkin and airforce Marshal A.A. Novikov, now both in prison. . . What it said in essence was that Marshal Zhukov was disloyal to Stalin, thought that he, Zhukov, and not Stalin, had been mainly in charge in the last war, and that Zhukov had allegedly often said things against Stalin. During the war I had supposedly gathered round me a group of dissatisfied generals and officers. . .

It ended with me being dismissed from the post of Commander-in-Chief of land forces and sent off to command the troops in the Odessa military district. At the plenary session of the CPSU CC then taking place I was removed from the CC without any explanation. A.A. Zhdanov said, 'Zhukov's still young, and is not mature enough for the CC.'

In 1947 a large group of generals and officers were arrested, particularly those who had once worked with me. . . They were physically compelled to admit to preparing some 'military conspiracy' against Stalin's leadership, organized by Marshal Zhukov.

This 'case' had been cooked up by Abakumov and Beria. . . Stalin would not let them arrest me. And when Abakumov himself was arrested, it transpired that he had made the whole thing up, just as he had made things up back in the dark days of 1937–1939.

Abakumov was shot, and at the 19th Party Congress Stalin personally recommended that I be brought onto the CPSU CC.

[Source: G.K. Zhukov, 'Korotko o Staline', *Pravda*, 20 January 1989.]

Stalin was equally ruthless in ensuring that none of his acolytes developed an independent political base within the party.[121] The most notorious instance of political persecution of senior party figures in these years was the so-called 'Leningrad affair'. During and after the war, the two chief rivals among Stalin's lieutenants were Malenkov and Zhdanov, party secretary in Leningrad since 1934. One of the factors casting a shadow over the Leningraders was that Zhdanov and his allies had developed close ties with Tito, providing ammunition for their rivals following the estrangement between Yugoslavia and the USSR. Though Zhdanov himself died suddenly in 1948, Malenkov and Beria appear to have pursued a campaign to cast suspicion on his former associates, and in 1949 there was a major purge, several leading figures being shot or confined to the GULAG. The following account comes from an investigation and rehabilitation carried out forty years later, during the Gorbachev years.

Document 180 | **Report from the CPSU CC Committee for Party Control and the Institute of Marxism–Leninism on the 'Leningrad affair'**

1989

One act of mass repression after the Great Patriotic War was the so-called 'Leningrad affair', the victims of which were hundreds of Party and Soviet workers, including members of the Politburo, Orgburo and Secretariat of the CPSU CC.

On 1 October 1950 the Military Board of the USSR Supreme Court sentenced the following to the highest measure of punishment—shooting: N.A. Voznesensky, CPSU CC Politburo member and deputy-chairman of the Council of Ministers of the USSR; A.A. Kuznetsov, Orgburo member and CPSU CC secretary; M.I. Rodionov, CPSU CC Orgburo member and chairman of the Council of Ministers of the RSFSR; P.S. Popkov, CPSU CC candidate member and first secretary of the Leningrad city and *oblast'* Party committees; Ya.F. Kapustin, second secretary of the Leningrad city Party committee, and P.G. Lazutin, chairman of the Leningrad city executive committee. I.M. Turko, secretary of the Yaroslavl' *oblast'* Party committee, and F.E. Mikheev, administrator of the Leningrad *oblast'* and city Party committees, were both sentenced to long periods of imprisonment.

All those sentenced had been charged with creating an anti-Party group, engaging in subversive wrecking activities directed at breaking the Leningrad Party organiza-

---

121 Two useful analyses of postwar factional struggle among Stalin's lieutenants are W.G. Hahn, *Post-War Soviet Politics: The Fall of Zhdanov and the Defeat of Moderation, 1946–1953* (New York 1982), and T. Dunmore, *Soviet Politics 1945–1953* (London 1984). The best account of Stalin's *modus operandi* in his last years, as his energy and appetite for detailed direction declined without slackening his grip on power, is Y. Gorlizki and O. Khlevniuk, *Cold Peace: Stalin and the Soviet Ruling Circle, 1945–1953* (Oxford 2004).

tion away from and setting it against the CPSU CC, and turning it into a bastion for struggle against the Party and the CPSU CC. The victims of the repression in connection with the so called 'Leningrad affair' were all the leaders of the Leningrad city and *oblast'* Party organizations, the leaders of the district Party organizations of Leningrad city and *oblast'*, and almost all those Soviet and state leaders who had been moved out of Leningrad after the Great Patriotic War to leading positions in the central Party and Soviet apparatus and other *oblast'* Party organizations. In the Leningrad *oblast'* alone more than 2,000 communists were relieved of their Party or Soviet jobs, and many of them were subjected to persecution and victimization over a long period. Members of the families of the sentenced leaders of the Leningrad organization were also subjected to repression.

The so-called 'Leningrad affair' was provoked and organized by Stalin, who tried to maintain among the top leadership an atmosphere of suspicion, envy and mistrust in order to bolster his own personal power. The so-called 'Leningrad affair' is connected with a number of people who were close to Stalin and formed his entourage: G.M. Malenkov, L.P. Beria, M.F. Shkiryatov, V.S. Abakumov and others. They were the ones who actually carried out these illegal acts of making false accusations and organizing reprisals against hundreds of innocent people.

[Source: *Izvestiya TsK KPSS*, No. 2, 1989, p. 126.]

Stalin's heirs

In Stalin's last months, some of his long-serving lieutenants, including Beria, Molotov and Mikoyan, appeared to be in danger of getting caught up in the aftermath of the so-called 'Doctors' Plot' in which Stalin had several (predominantly Jewish) Kremlin doctors arrested for supposedly conspiring to assassinate party leaders.[122] Certainly following Stalin's death there was swift relaxation, and the leading contenders for primacy—Malenkov, Khrushchev and Beria—each identified themselves with one or another aspect of reform. At the same time, his senior lieutenants were quick to narrow the circle of those at the summit of power, reversing the steps Stalin had taken to promote younger leaders when at the Nineteenth Congress he replaced the Politburo with a much larger Presidium. In the realignment of the top party and government posts announced in the week after Stalin's death, its full membership was cut right back to ten, among whom Malenkov emerged as *primo inter pares*. He was appointed chairman of the Council of Ministers while at the same time remaining, with Khrushchev, Central

---

122 For a detailed account, see L. Rapoport, *The Doctors' Plot: Stalin's Last Crime* (London 1991).

Committee Secretary. The line of continuity running across the post-Stalin era is underlined by the mention, albeit in a secondary post, of the man who would still be in post as General Secretary almost three decades later: Leonid Brezhnev.

Document 181 | **From the resolution of the joint plenary session of the CC of the CPSU, the USSR Council of Ministers and the Presidium of the USSR Supreme Soviet on continuity in leadership after Stalin's death**

March 1953

. . . In order to prevent any interruptions in the direction of the activities of state and Party bodies, the Central Committee of the Communist Party of the Soviet Union, the USSR Council of Ministers and the Presidium of the USSR Supreme Soviet deem it necessary to bring in a number of measures concerning the organization of Party and state leadership:

I. On the chairman and the first deputy chairmen of the Council of Ministers

1. Comrade Georgiy Maksimilianovich Malenkov is appointed chairman of the USSR Council of Ministers.

2. Comrades Lavrentiy Pavlovich Beria, Vyacheslav Mikhaylovich Molotov, Nikolay Aleksandrovich Bulganin, Lazar' Moyseevich Kaganovich are appointed first deputy chairmen of the USSR Council of Ministers. . .

II. On the Presidium of the CPSU CC and the CPSU secretaries

1. It is considered essential to have, instead of two CC bodies in the CPSU Central Committee (the Presidium and the Presidium Bureau), one single body, the Presidium of the Central Committee of the CPSU, as laid down in the Party Constitution.

2. To make the leadership more effective the membership of the Presidium is to be set at ten full and four candidate members.

3. The following composition of the Presidium of the Central Committee of the CPSU is confirmed:

Full members of the CC Presidium: comrades G.M. Malenkov, L.P. Beria, V.M. Molotov, K.E. Voroshilov, N.S. Khrushchev, N.A. Bulganin, L.M. Kaganovich, A.I. Mikoyan, M.Z. Saburov and M.G. Pervukhin.

Candidate members of the CC Presidium: comrades N.M. Shvernik, P.K. Ponomarenko, L.G. Mel'nikov and M.D. Bagirov.

4. Comrades S.D. Ignat'ev, P.N. Pospelov and N.N. Shatalin are elected as CC secretaries.

5. It is considered necessary that comrade N.S. Khrushchev concentrate on work in the Central Committee of the CPSU and is consequently relieved of his duties as first secretary of the Moscow committee of the CPSU.

6. CPSU CC secretary N.A. Mikhaylov is confirmed as first secretary of the

Moscow committee of the CPSU.

    7. Comrades P.K. Ponomarenko and N.G. Ignatov are relieved of their duties as CPSU CC secretaries to lead work in the USSR Council of Ministers, along with comrade L.I. Brezhnev, in connection with his transfer to the post of head of the political division of the Naval Ministry.

Central Committee of the Communist Party of the Soviet Union
USSR Council of Ministers
Presidium of the USSR Supreme Soviet

[Source: *Pravda*, 7 March 1953.]

Just a week later Malenkov's primacy was called into question when he was prevailed upon to stand down as party secretary. This reflected the consensus on the Presidium that collective leadership should replace the concentration of power in the Stalin mould. Stalin's successors were also quick to agree on condemning his use of secret-police methods in resolving political disputes, the violence and mutual suspicion that characterized Stalin's court, and the bogus charges so readily trumped up against those who fell from favour. However, there was to be one last exception. During the spring and early summer, several members of the leadership became increasingly nervous of Beria.[123] Despite the fact that he had been vehement in denouncing Stalin's ruthless arrest of innocent men, Beria's colleagues feared his ambition, and that his control of the MVD gave him the potential to establish his own authority. On 26 June, Khrushchev orchestrated Beria's arrest and two weeks later, his disgrace endorsed by the Central Committee, the following denunciation appeared in *Pravda*.

Document 182 | Denunciation of Beria in *Pravda*, July 1953

Now unmasked as an enemy of the people, Beria wormed his way into the leadership's trust by a variety of careerist machinations. Whereas previously his criminal anti-Party and anti-state activities were well-hidden and masked, more recently Beria, emboldened and unrestrained, began to show his true face—the face of a malicious enemy of the Party and people. This increased criminal activity on Beria's part can be explained by a general intensification of the subversive anti-Soviet activity of international reactionary forces hostile to our state. As international imperialism becomes more active, so do its agents.

    Beria began his base machinations, aimed at seizing power, by trying to set the Ministry of Internal Affairs above the Party and the government. He used the Ministry's organs both centrally and locally against the Party leadership, against the

---

123 On Beria's fall, see Knight, *Beria: Stalin's First Lieutenant*, pp. 176–229.

government of the USSR, and promoted staff within the Ministry of Internal Affairs on the basis of personal devotion to himself.

As has now been established, Beria employed a variety of false pretexts to hinder solutions to the most important and urgent questions in agriculture. This was done so as to undermine the collective farms and cause problems in the supply of food within the country.

Obliged to carry out the direct orders of the Party CC and the Soviet government to improve the Soviet economy and get rid of certain instances of illegality and maladministration, Beria deliberately slowed down the implementation of these orders, and in several cases attempted to distort them. Incontrovertible facts show that Beria had lost the mentality of a communist, had turned into a bourgeois degenerate, and had in fact become an agent of international imperialism. This adventurist hireling was hatching out plans to seize the leadership of the country in order in effect to destroy our Communist Party, and replace policies worked out by the Party over many years with policies of capitulation, which would eventually have led to the restoration of capitalism. . .

Political lessons and the necessary conclusions must be drawn from the Beria affair. The strength of our leadership lies in its being collective, united and monolithic. Collectivity in leadership is the most important principle of leadership in our Party. This principle is in complete accord with Marx's well-known theses on the danger and unacceptability of a personality cult.

[Source: *Pravda*, 10 July 1953.]

The language in which the denunciation of Beria was couched, including the charge that he was an enemy agent, gave little indication that Stalin's heirs would consistently distance themselves from the political culture that prevailed while he ruled. Beria was kept in custody and six months later executed. Yet his fall was followed by an immediate resolution that the secret police be firmly subordinated to the party and that, as in the days before Stalin's ascendancy, it should be deprived of the right to arrest party members without explicit sanction by the relevant party committee. Moreover, the Presidium reiterated both its commitment to collective leadership and its condemnation of the 'cult of personality', a guarded but unmistakable public criticism of Stalin himself.

Document 183 | From *50 years of the CPSU (1903–1953)*—theses of the CPSU CC Propaganda and Agitation Department and its Marx–Engels–Lenin–Stalin Institute, 1953

We must root out of the Party's propaganda work the incorrect and un-Marxist approach to the question of the role of the individual in history, which has expressed itself in the ideological theory of the personality cult, so alien to the spirit of Marxism–Leninism. The personality cult contradicts the principle of collective leadership, leads to a reduction in creative activity by the Party masses and Soviet people and has nothing at all in common with a Marxist–Leninist conception of the great significance of the directing activity of leading bodies and leaders. . .

[Source: *Pravda*, 26 July 1953.]

A more general reduction in the use of overt coercion began.[124] The powers of the secret police (reorganized in 1954 as the KGB) were not only reined in, but its numbers and the extent of the informer network were cut back. There was an immediate amnesty for over a million convicts, cautious first steps towards shrinking the size of the GULAG, and repeated public calls for the restoration of 'socialist legality'. In 1954 the leadership set up an inquiry into the manner in which party officials had been arrested and tried under Stalin. The signals that the leadership was seeking to earn public approval ranged far and wide. One symptom of moves to shift the balance of public rhetoric about the superiority of all things Great Russian and cultivate approval among the national minorities was the announcement in 1954 that the Crimea was being transferred from the RSFSR to the Ukrainian Union Republic.

Document 184 | **The law on the transfer of the Crimean *oblast'* from the RSFSR to the Ukrainian SSR, 1954**

The Supreme Soviet of the Union of Soviet Socialist Republics resolves:

1. to ratify the decree of the Presidium of the USSR Supreme Soviet of 19 February 1954 on the transfer of the Crimean *oblast'* from the RSFSR to the Ukrainian SSR;

2. to make the corresponding changes to Articles 22 and 23 of the constitution of the USSR.

The Kremlin, Moscow, 26 April 1954
Chairman of the Presidium of the Supreme Soviet of the USSR K. Voroshilov
Secretary of the Presidium of the Supreme Soviet of the USSR N. Pegov

[Source: *Vedomosti Verkhovnogo soveta SSSR*, No 10, 12 May 1954, p. 343.]

---

124 For a succinct account, see Filtzer, *The Khrushchev Era*.

There was a palpable relaxation of tension, nurtured by both the foreign policy and the economic initiatives taken by Khrushchev and Malenkov, as the leadership actively sought to broaden public support. Tentatively, public discussion began to become somewhat more open. By the time of the Soviet elections of March 1955, KGB and party reports on the voters' mood echoed many of the complaints and charges of official corruption and incompetence of the immediate postwar years. But with living standards beginning to rise above the extreme hardship of the late 1940s and early 1950s, the demands made were less desperate. And despite the reduction in overt coercion, expressions of radical opposition to the Soviet system appear to have receded rather than grown. The following report from Sverdlovsk provides a sample of negative comments by voters.

Document 185 | **Voters' proposals and mandates—from a report to the RSFSR department of party bodies and the CPSU CC on local and Supreme Soviet elections**

2 March 1955

'The situation regarding living space is appalling.'

'Stiffer sentences for robbers and murderers.'

'Give us more foodstuffs.'

'We need more meat and fish, otherwise we've got nothing.'

'I vote for you, but why are we still queuing for bread?'

On ballot papers for comrade Zemlyanichenko (chairman of Sverdlovsk city executive committee and regional Soviet candidate) was written, 'He builds a chiming-clock, but can't see that us workers live in barracks.'

On certain ballot papers, hostile, anti-Soviet comments had been written, 'We've had no life for 37 years. Our whole life is work, higher prices and queues.'

'Our rights exist only on paper.'

'I vote for the truth, but there isn't any! There's no democracy anywhere.'

'They reduce our wages so that we have to spend them all on food. The bosses live better.'

'He's a toady. The whole thing's a joke. It's the same as the USA, Britain and Germany—violence, hunger, unemployment, drunkenness, murder and depravity.'

'There's nothing to eat. They've oppressed the people totally, so let's go on strike. We demand meat, butter and sugar.'

Sverdlovsk *oblast'* CPSU committee

[Source: TsDOO SO, fond 4, opis' 54, delo 100, pp. 81–84.]

'De-Stalinization' and its limits

In 1956, Khrushchev took the single most dramatic step in what became known as 'de-Stalinization'.[125] At a closed session of the Twentieth Party Congress, he delivered a long speech itemizing some of Stalin's crimes. The account he gave was carefully restricted so as to cast no shadow on the achievements of the revolution, collectivization, industrialization and the overall record of the party in power. Far from allowing the slightest hint that the revelations might cast doubt on the legitimacy of communist rule, he couched his whole speech in terms of Stalin's distortion of and offences against Marxism–Leninism and much was made of Lenin's distrust of him. It was not for the repression of 'kulaks' during collectivization, for the ethnic cleansing of the border regions, or for the notorious NKVD Order No. 00447 ordering mass executions of 'former kulaks and criminals' (see Volume I, document 194) that he was condemned. Rather it was first and foremost for his attacks on party figures, loyal communists, that Khrushchev denounced Stalin. And he projected an aura of heroism around them: ill-fated delegates to the Seventeenth Party Congress of 1934, made up overwhelmingly of hardened party officials, were in time-honoured fashion classified as 'workers' on the grounds of their employment at the time they joined the party. The details he provided, including the breathtaking figures given in the following extract on the portion of the party elite struck down in the 1930s, caused consternation.

Document 186 | From Khrushchev's 'Secret Speech', *On the cult of the personality and its consequences*, to the closed session of the 20th Congress of the CPSU

25 February 1956

. . . After Stalin's death the Central Committee adopted a strict and consistent line of explaining that it was alien and unacceptable to Marxist–Leninism to elevate a single individual and turn him into some kind of superman with godlike, supernatural qualities. This person supposedly knows everything, sees everything, thinks for everyone and can do anything; he is without fault in his actions.

Such a conception of an individual, specifically, Stalin, was fostered in our country for many years. . .

Since not everyone yet understands what the personality cult led to in practice and what immense damage was done by the violation of the principle of collective

---

125 For high politics in the Khrushchev era, see S. Bialer, *Stalin's Successors: Leadership, Stability and Change in the Soviet Union* (Cambridge 1980), and the major biography by W. Taubman, *Khrushchev: The Man and His Era* (London 2003).

leadership within the Party and the concentration of unlimited power in one person's hands, the Party Central Committee considers it necessary to report on the matter to the 20th Congress of the Communist Party of the Soviet Union. . .

It turns out that many of the people working in the Party, Soviet and economic apparatus who were declared to be 'enemies' in 1937–1938 were in fact never enemies, spies, wreckers, etc., that they had, in effect, always remained honest communists. They had been slandered and sometimes, unable to withstand bestial torture, accused themselves of all sorts of serious and improbable crimes, as dictated by interrogator–falsifiers. . . It has been established that of the 139 members and candidate-members of the Party CC elected at the 17th Congress, 98 were arrested and shot, mainly in 1937–1938. That is 70%. (*Consternation in the hall*.) . . . We know that 80% of the voting delegates to the 17th Congress had joined the Party in the days of the revolutionary underground or during the Civil War, that is, up to 1920. As for their social position, most of the delegates were workers (60% of the voting delegates).

It is thus utterly inconceivable that a Congress of such a composition would have elected a Central Committee in which the majority turned out to be enemies of the Party. It is only because honest communists were slandered and falsely accused, and monstrous violations of revolutionary legality were permitted, that 70% of the members and candidate-members of the CC elected by the 17th Congress were declared to be enemies of the Party and people.

This fate befell not only CC members but also the majority of the delegates to the 17th Congress of the Party. Of the 1,966 voting delegates to the Congress, 1,108, well over half, were arrested on charges of counter-revolutionary crimes. . . This happened because of Stalin's abuse of power, when he instituted a reign of terror against Party cadres. . . By this time Stalin had raised himself so far above the Party and people that he no longer took account of either the Central Committee or the Party. . .

Stalin's autocracy also had particularly serious consequences in the course of the Great Patriotic War. . .

Particularly serious consequences, especially during the early period of the war, followed from the fact that between 1937 and 1941, as a result of Stalin's suspiciousness, numerous army and political officers were falsely accused and exterminated. Thus, the grave danger which hung over our Motherland in the early period of the war was in many respects the result of defective ways of leading the Party and country on the part of Stalin himself. . .

We must decisively, once and for all, debunk the personality cult and draw the proper conclusions both in our ideological and theoretical work, and in our practical work. . .

Khrushchev went on to denounce the mass deportation of the 'punished peoples' as contrary not only to Marxism–Leninism but to common sense.

> . . . Comrades, let us look at some other facts! The Soviet Union is quite rightly considered to be a model multinational state, because the equality and friendship of all the peoples living in our great Motherland are safeguarded in reality.
>
> All the more scandalous therefore are the actions initiated by Stalin, which represent a crude flouting of the basic Leninist principles of the national policy of the Soviet state. We are talking about the mass evacuation from their places of residence of whole peoples, including communists and Komsomol members, without any exceptions whatsoever. Moreover, such evacuations were in no way dictated by wartime considerations. . . The Ukrainians escaped that fate because there were too many of them and there was nowhere to send them. (*Animated laughter in the auditorium.*)
>
> No Marxist–Leninist or any sensible person can imagine a position where responsibility for the hostile acts of individuals or groups can be laid upon whole peoples, including women, children, the elderly, communists and Komsomol members, who are then subjected to mass repression, deprivation and suffering.

[Source: *Izvestiya TsK KPSS*, No. 3, 1989, pp. 127–28.]

Over the next two years most of the victims of the national deportations of 1944 were officially pardoned and the restrictions on them were lifted, albeit without granting them either compensation or the right to return to the homes from which they had been uprooted.

Document 187 | USSR Supreme Soviet decree *On the Lifting of Resettlement Restrictions on Chechens, Ingush, Karachaevtsy and Members of Their Families Evacuated during the Great Patriotic War*

16 July 1956

Bearing in mind that the implementation of the restrictions on the legal status of. . . [those]. . . currently in special settlements, is no longer necessary, the Presidium of the USSR Supreme Soviet resolves:

1. To strike the special settlements off the register and to free the Chechens, Ingush, Karachaevtsy and their families, evacuated from the north Caucasus during the Great Patriotic War from the administrative supervision of the USSR Ministry of Internal Affairs.

2. To establish that the removal of the special settlement restrictions from those persons listed in Article One of the decree does not entail the restoration of any

property confiscated at the time of their evacuation, nor do they have the right to return to the places from which they were evacuated.

The Kremlin, Moscow, 16 July 1956
Chairman of the Presidium of the Supreme Soviet of the USSR K. Voroshilov
Secretary of the Presidium of the Supreme Soviet of the USSR N. Pegov

[Source: *Istoriya SSSR*, No. 1, 1991, p. 159.]

Once pardon had been granted, the issue of the right to return became potentially explosive. To deny the right provoked the 'punished peoples', but to acknowledge it ran the risk of inter-ethnic clashes between them and those who had settled in their former homeland. In explaining why the Azeris deported from Georgia were not to be permitted to return there, the Kremlin firmly laid the responsibility at the door of the Georgian government.

Document 188 | **USSR Supreme Soviet decree lifting restrictions on Azeris evacuated from Georgia in 1944**

31 October 1957

On the lifting of restrictions from USSR citizens of Azerbaijani nationality, evacuated in 1944 from the Adzhar ASSR and the Akhaltsikhe, Akhalkalaki, Aspindza and Bogdanovka districts of the Georgian SSR, upon whom restrictions on movement were subsequently placed.

The Presidium of the USSR Supreme Soviet decrees:

1. To lift all restrictions on citizens of Azerbaijani nationality evacuated in 1944 from the Adzhar ASSR and the Akhaltsikhe, Akhalkalaki, Aspindza and Bogdanovka districts of the Georgian SSR.

2. Bearing in mind that the districts of the Georgian SSR from which the Azerbaijani population was evacuated are at present settled and that there are no possibilities, according to the government of the Georgian SSR, of resettlement and employment in other districts of the republic, these citizens are to be granted the right to settle permanently in the Azerbaijani SSR, if they so wish.

The Kremlin, Moscow, 31 October 1957
Chairman of the Presidium of the Supreme Soviet of the USSR K. Voroshilov
Secretary of the Presidium of the Supreme Soviet of the USSR M. Georgadze

[Source: *Istoriya SSSR*, No. 1, 1991, p. 159.]

Khrushchev's 'secret speech', which quickly became widely known, suddenly and dramatically broadened the scope for public discussion of taboo subjects in the USSR, and as we have seen helped spark mass unrest in Poland and open rebellion in Hungary. The shock this gave the Kremlin led Khrushchev for a period to be more cautious in denouncing Stalin. But his critics in the Presidium, headed by his earlier rival, Malenkov, Stalin's long-time foreign commissar, Molotov, and his senior lieutenant, Kaganovich, decided to try to overthrow him.[126] In June 1957, citing his unpredictable and ill-considered initiatives across foreign and domestic policy but moved too by the scale of the liberalization he had sponsored, they secured a Politburo majority against him. However, Khrushchev insisted on putting his case to the Central Committee by which he had been elected. The consensus on resolving political conflict without violence was sufficiently established for his enemies to accept the move, probably optimistic that there too he would be rejected. But instead he won a resounding victory in the Central Committee, in part no doubt because of the significant number of members who owed their promotion to him. Khrushchev thereupon moved to have the leading trio, along with their younger ally D.T. Shepilov, removed from office. The Central Committee resolution expelling them denounced them for opposing party policy on a whole range of issues. The resolution echoed many of the fatal accusations Stalin had levelled against rivals and doomed officials, but in more restrained tones. They were given a catch-all label, the Anti-Party Group, which set them apart as untouchables, yet the resolution did not associate them with foreign espionage, treason or Trotskyism. They were 'unmasked' after having concealed their evil intentions, yet their machinations extended just three or four years back rather than stretching all the way to the moment they joined the party. They were condemned for 'factional methods' banned by Lenin in 1921, and for opposition to formally adopted party policy, yet the primary emphasis was on tangible issues such as administrative reorganization, economic management, the 'virgin lands' scheme, and foreign policy. Molotov was singled out for the harshest treatment, including reference to his long years as Stalin's foreign commissar/minister and his responsibility for the regrettable 1948 breach with Yugoslavia. The Central Committee vote was carefully recorded as unanimous in the Stalinist tradition—Molotov was the only one among those condemned who refused to endorse the resolution. It was also highly symbolic of the shift in political culture that instead of suffering arrest and/or execution they were punished by demotion to minor posts. Molotov went to the embassy in Mongolia, Malenkov was sent to a power station in Kazakhstan, and Kaganovich became director of a cement works in Sverdlovsk.

---

126 N. Barsukov, 'The Rise to Power', in W. Taubman, S. Khrushchev and A. Gleason (eds), *Nikita Khrushchev* (New Haven 2000), pp. 44–66, includes a good account.

Document 189 | **Resolution of the plenary meeting of the CC of the CPSU**
On the Anti-Party Group of G.M. Malenkov, L.M. Kaganovich
and V.M. Molotov

June 1957

At meetings between 22 and 29 June 1957 the CC of the CPSU in plenary session looked into the question of the Anti-Party Group of Malenkov, Kaganovich and Molotov, which had formed within the Presidium of the CPSU CC. . . Aiming to change the political line of the Party, this group used anti-Party and factional methods to try to change the make-up of the leading Party bodies elected at the plenary session of the CPSU CC. . . Over the last three to four years, when the Party had been taking a decisive course of action to correct the mistakes and failings caused by the personality cult, the participants of this Anti-Party group, now uncovered and completely unmasked, constantly tried to oppose, directly or indirectly, the course of action approved by the 20th Congress of the CPSU.

They were against extending the rights of the Union Republics in matters of economic and cultural construction, and in matters of legislation. They were also against widening the role of local soviets in solving these tasks. . . The Anti-Party Group not only did not understand but also resisted the Party's measures to fight bureaucratism and reduce the size of the state apparatus. . . This group doggedly resisted and tried to undermine such important measures as the reorganization of the administration of industry and the creation of Economic Councils in economic regions. . . As for agriculture, the participants in this group showed no understanding of the urgent new tasks.

They did not accept the need to strengthen the material interest of collective farmers in increasing agricultural output. They objected to replacing the old bureaucratic farm planning system with a new one which would unleash the initiative of collective farms in running themselves. . . They fought against the Party's calls to overtake the USA in per capita milk, butter and meat production in the next few years. . . Comrade Molotov, displaying conservatism and rigidity, not only did not understand the need to open up new virgin land but also resisted developing the 35 million hectares of new land which have come to play such an important part in the economy of our country.

Comrades Malenkov, Kaganovich and Molotov stubbornly resisted those measures introduced by the Central Committee and our whole Party to get rid of the consequences of the personality cult, do away with violations of revolutionary legality which had previously been permitted and create conditions which would preclude the possibility of their recurrence.

In the area of foreign policy this group, particularly comrade Molotov, showed inflexibility and tried in every way to block timely new measures designed to reduce international tensions and strengthen peace throughout the world. . . Over a long period comrade Molotov, as Minister for Foreign Affairs, not only did nothing through his Ministry to improve the USSR's relations with Yugoslavia but spoke out more than once against the measures the CC's Presidium was taking to improve relations with Yugoslavia. . . He dragged his feet on concluding a state treaty with Austria. . . was also against normalizing relations with Japan, whereas this normalization has since played a major part in reducing international tensions in the Far East. . . On many of these questions comrade Molotov was supported by comrades Kaganovich and, sometimes, Malenkov. . . Having agreed among themselves on an anti-Party basis, they set out to change Party policy and return the Party to those incorrect methods of leadership which had been condemned by the 20th Congress of the Party. . .

The CC Plenary meeting therefore resolves:
1. To condemn as incompatible with our Party's Leninist principles the factional activities of the anti-Party group of comrades Malenkov, Kaganovich and Molotov, and of Shepilov, who joined with them.
2. To remove comrades Malenkov, Kaganovich and Molotov from membership of the CC Presidium and the CC, and to remove comrade Shepilov from the post of CPSU CC secretary, and from membership of the CC and candidate membership of its Presidium. . .

(Adopted unanimously on 29 June 1957 by all the members of the Central Committee and candidate members of the Central Auditing Commission with one abstention—that of comrade Molotov.)

[Source: *KPSS v rezolyutsiyakh i resheniyakh*, Vol. 9 (Moscow 1986), pp. 184–89.]

Three months later, confident of his own position, Khrushchev dismissed Zhukov as Minister of Defence, in part over his resistance to the leader's efforts to reduce non-nuclear military expenditure. The grounds on which he denounced him were that he had fostered a personality cult which did no justice to the role in victory that had been played by the mass of the people, the army, the other commanders, and 'the guiding and inspiring role of the Communist Party of the Soviet Union'.

Document 190 | **From the minutes of the October 1957 plenary meeting of the CC of the CPSU, condemning G.K. Zhukov**

The plenary meeting of the CC has established that, with G.K. Zhukov's personal participation, a cult of his personality began to take root in the Soviet Army. With the complicity of obsequious toadies he began to be extolled in lectures, reports, articles, films and pamphlets which inordinately elevated his person and his role in the war. To please G.K. Zhukov this entailed a false history of the war, which distorted the facts and played down the stupendous efforts of the Soviet people, the heroism of all our Armed Forces, the role of commanders and political officers, the military skill of front-line, army and naval commanders, the guiding and inspiring role of the Communist Party of the Soviet Union. . .

Comrade G.K. Zhukov has not thereby merited the trust placed in him by the Party. He has proved to be politically bankrupt, and inclined to adventurism both in his understanding of the most important tasks of the Soviet Union's foreign policy, and in his leadership of the Ministry of Defence.

In view of this, the CPSU CC plenary meeting has resolved to remove comrade G.K. Zhukov from the CC Presidium and has requested the CPSU CC Secretariat to offer G.K. Zhukov alternative employment.

(Passed unanimously by all CC members and CC candidate-members, Central Audit Commission members and approved by all the military, Party and Soviet figures present at the CC Plenary meeting.)

[Source: *Pravda*, 10 November 1957.]

Despite the reverberations of the upheaval in Poland and Hungary, and the evidence of unease within the party, Khrushchev pressed ahead with steps towards 'de-Stalinization'. The GULAG was run down and Khrushchev proudly boasted that the USSR no longer held political prisoners. Along with millions of ordinary citizens who had sentences lifted or revoked, tens of thousands of party members who had been expelled and/or repressed were rehabilitated, many of them posthumously.[127]

Document 191 | **From the report of the CPSU CC Party Control Committee for the period 1956–1961—results of a review of applications for the reinstatement of persons expelled from the Party on the basis of false accusations**

As instructed by the CC of the CPSU, the Party Control Committee and local Party bodies have done a great deal of work towards reinstating in the Party communists who had previously been groundlessly brought before the courts on serious political charges and expelled from the Party. Over the period since the 20th CPSU Congress, 30,954 communists have been reinstated (many posthumously). Among them were 3,693 former leading Party and Komsomol workers, 4,148 leading workers in Soviet bodies, 6,165 leading workers in the economic apparatus and 4,394 commanders and political officers in the Soviet Army.

[Source: *Izvestiya TsK KPSS*, No. 11, 1989, p. 53.]

127 On the limitations of rehabilitation as well as the tangible relaxation of tension that came with it, see the account in R. Medvedev, *Khrushchev* (London 1982), pp. 83–103.

The Twenty-Second Party Congress, held in 1961, saw Stalin and his crimes denounced openly. The Central Committee resolved that his body was to be removed from its place alongside Lenin in the mausoleum on Red Square. The public and ritual repudiation of much of what Stalin had come to stand for was combined with resolute reaffirmation of the power of the party. The following lines from the new Party Programme adopted by the Congress convey just how malleable was the Marxist–Leninist justification for that power. What had once seemed integral could be freely jettisoned—its longtime leader exposed as a villain and its proletarian make-up replaced by an 'all-class' identity. The party's right to rule rested on the key role it had in enabling the Russian revolution to succeed where others had failed, and on its supposed monopoly of scientific understanding of the laws of history which made it the indispensable guide in the building of socialism.

Document 192 | From the Programme adopted at the 22nd CPSU Congress *On the Role of the Party*

31 October 1961

. . . As a result of the victory of socialism in the USSR and the consolidation of the unity of Soviet society, the Communist Party of the working class has become the vanguard of the Soviet people, a party of the entire people, and extended its guiding influence to all spheres of social life. The Party is the brain, the honour and the conscience of our epoch, of the Soviet people, the people effecting great revolutionary transformations. It looks keenly into the future and shows the people scientifically motivated roads along which to advance, arouses titanic energy in the masses and leads them to the accomplishment of great tasks.

The period of full-scale communist construction is characterized by a *further enhancement of the role and importance of the Communist Party* as the leading and guiding force of Soviet society. . .

[Source: *The Programme of the Communist Party of the Soviet Union, Adopted by the 22nd Congress of the CPSU* (London 1961), p. 89.]

One of the functions played by the party which Soviet rhetoric did not labour was that of the prime mechanism through which the incentives were provided for political conformism. Already visible under Stalin, this trend became deeply embedded under Khrushchev and his successors. As we have seen, the post-Stalin generation enjoyed a sustained rise in living standards which affected all social groups, from the most poorly remunerated collective farmers and unskilled workers to the *nomenklatura*. There was also rapid if gradually decelerating upward social mobility. Urbanization, mechanization and further industrialization, combined with an expansion of education at each level, saw the children of peasants leave the countryside and become urban workers; a significant minority of unskilled workers join a skilled elite; and millions of children of both workers and peasants secure higher education and enter the ranks of the intelligentsia. Each layer of society was subdivided by myriad smaller inequalities and hierarchies—in access to scarce goods and amenities and to more desirable posts, education and housing, including residence permits for the bigger cities. And the surest single step to improve one's prospects of benefiting from the unequal distribution of life's chances was to join the party. Party membership brought with it contacts with powerful people and links to the central pool of patronage. Moreover, there was an expanding pyramid of perquisites over which party influence was a significant factor, rising from informal advantages vis-à-vis non-party members, through the growing range of minor posts for which local party support was an asset, to entry into the elite ranks of the *nomenklatura*. To be invited to join the party was a major opportunity; to turn it down and jeopardize promotion a difficult choice to make. Party membership in the period soared, rising from under 6 million in the early 1950s to 18 million by the early 1980s. Indeed, by the late 1970s, more than one-fifth of men over the age of thirty were party members, and in the white-collar stratum with higher education the proportion who were party members exceeded 50 per cent. The party, in short, was no narrow elite of dedicated political animals. Nor was it restricted to the elite establishment: it was proportionately far broader than the public school network of contemporary Britain. It constituted a vast recruitment ground for the ambitious and dynamic in every walk of life and in every part of the Union. To join the party was markedly to increase the chances of conventional success, career advancement, promotion—the good life Soviet style. And to join the party involved making a public, explicit commitment to uphold the values and authority of the CPSU.

This function of the party as the central channel for preferential social advancement was critical in the recipe developed under Stalin's successors for stabilizing Communist rule.[128] Its impact was particularly striking among the national minorities. In Armenia and Moldova, Estonia and Ukraine, it served to bind the local intelligentsia—in the economy, in the police, in the legal system, in the administrative hierarchy, in formal culture and education—to the party and, through the party, to Moscow. It thereby counterbalanced the risk of minority nationalist pressure. On the face of it,

---

128 There is a striking analysis in V. Zaslavsky, *The Neo-Stalinist State: Class, Ethnicity and Consensus in Soviet Society* (New York 1982).

after all, that risk was acute. Each of the fifteen Union Republics had its own government, its own Supreme Soviet or parliament, and the trappings of statehood. Education in the vernacular was guaranteed both in the Union Republics and in the smaller national–territorial units, actively nurturing minority national consciousness. The structure of the Union provided ready-made ingredients for the government of each republic to be pressurized by its own national constituency and for it to mobilize that constituency vis-à-vis the Kremlin. Moreover, the reduction of overt coercion, the public repudiation of Stalinist crimes against specific national minorities, and the curbing of Russian nationalist rhetoric—all contributed to the potential for centripetal nationalist self-assertion.

The new Party Programme of 1961 celebrated the absence of significant friction of this kind as an achievement of socialism. But the socioeconomic explanations it advanced—the common ownership of the means of production; the achievement of (formal) political, cultural and economic equality, and advancement of the most backward republics; the mingling and inter-marriage of peoples as industrial and agricultural development led to migration—were partial at best. Common ownership did not prevent lobbying by different national republics, and indeed the Central Committee served increasingly as the forum for compromise between them as well as between the representatives of different regions of the RSFSR and different branches of the economic, civil and military apparatus. The formal equality of and active investment in the poorer republics by no means overcame the differentials in terms of per capita income and public amenities between the European republics and those of Central Asia or between the Baltic republics and most of the rest. Though intermarriage did become more common, the largest single element in the mingling of peoples was the migration of Russians to the minority republics. The steady erosion of the dominant position of the titular nationality by Russian immigration bred deep resentment, notably in the Baltic as well as in Kazakhstan, where by the late 1970s they would constitute the largest nationality. These official explanations drew a veil over the way in which the party as the conduit for upward social mobility underpinned the unity of the USSR.

Document 193 | **From the Programme adopted at the 22nd CPSU Congress**
On the National Question

31 October 1961

. . . The solution of the *national question* is one of the greatest achievements of socialism. This question is of special importance to a country like the Soviet Union, inhabited by more than a hundred nations and nationalities. Socialist society has not only guaranteed the political equality of nations and created Soviet national statehood, but has also abolished the economic and cultural inequality inherited from the old system. . .

. . . Under socialism the nations flourish and their sovereignty grows stronger. The development of nations does not proceed along lines of strengthening national strife, national narrow-mindedness and egoism, but along lines of their association, fraternal mutual assistance and friendship. The appearance of new industrial centres, the prospecting and development of mineral deposits, virgin land development and the growth of all modes of transport increase the mobility of the population and promote greater intercourse between the peoples of the Soviet Union. People of many nationalities live together and work in harmony in the Soviet republics. The boundaries between the Union Republics of the USSR are increasingly losing their former significance, since all the nations are equal, their life is based on a common socialist foundation, the material and spiritual needs of every people are satisfied to the same extent, and they are all united in a single family by common vital interests and are advancing together to the common goal—communism. . .

[Source: *The Programme of the Communist Party of the Soviet Union, Adopted by the 22nd Congress of the CPSU* (London 1961), pp. 14, 75.]

The fall of Khrushchev

In 1964, the different constituencies which Khrushchev had offended—his colleagues in the leadership, the military and civilian elite, middle-ranking officials in the party and the economic and cultural ministries, as well as much popular opinion—coalesced and he was peacefully removed from office. Unlike in 1957, he was unable to call upon the loyalty of senior officials, among whom there was bitter hostility towards the repeated administrative reorganizations he introduced in his efforts to energize the party and state apparatus. When those at the summit of the party moved against him, few voices were raised in his defence. The Presidium resolution condemning him was intensely personal in its criticisms, expressing his colleagues' exasperation with his impetuous method of rule. Its reference to his deteriorating health and advanced age (70) seems ironic in view of the fact that of his successors Brezhnev was to remain party leader until his death at 76, Chernenko was already 73 when he took up the post, and Andropov would be bed-ridden for much of his two-year period in power.

Document 194 | From the CPSU CC Presidium resolution condemning Khrushchev

13–14 October 1964

It is acknowledged that as a result of comrade Khrushchev's mistakes and incorrect actions, which violate Leninist principles of collective leadership, a completely abnormal situation has developed within the CC Presidium recently, making it difficult for CC Presidium members to carry out their responsible duties in leading the party and country.

As First Secretary of the CC of the CPSU and chairman of the Council of Ministers of the USSR, comrade Khrushchev has concentrated great power in his hands, and in several instances has slipped out of the control of the CPSU CC, and has ceased to take account of the opinions of members of the CC Presidium and CPSU CC, deciding the most important matters without due collective consultation.

In displaying impatience and rudeness to his Presidium and CC comrades and spurning their opinions, comrade Khrushchev has allowed a number of serious mistakes to be made in carrying out the line indicated in the decisions of the 20th, 21st and 22nd Congresses of the CPSU.

The CC Presidium believes that because of his unacceptable personal qualities as a colleague, his advanced age, and deteriorating health, comrade Khrushchev is incapable of correcting his mistakes and his non-Party style of work.

Taking into account comrade Khrushchev's own declaration as well, the Presidium of the CC of the CPSU resolves:

1. To comply with comrade Khrushchev's request to be relieved of his duties as First Secretary, member of the CC Presidium and Chairman of the USSR Council of Ministers owing to his advanced age and deteriorating health.

2. To recognize that it is inexpedient for the duties of CC First Secretary and Chairman of the USSR Council of Ministers to continue to be exercised by one person.

3. To consider it necessary to call another CPSU CC Plenary session on 14 October 1964.

[Source: *Istoricheskiy arkhiv*, No. 1, 1993, pp. 4–5.]

At the Central Committee meeting which followed and which unanimously confirmed Khrushchev's dismissal, the key speech was given by Suslov, who was emerging as the guardian of ideological orthodoxy. He reaffirmed the broad line of policy adopted at the three party congresses over which Khrushchev had presided, before going on to criticize him for being high-handed and arbitrary, for setting his comrades against each other, for failing

to consult the Central Committee properly, and for endorsing wild initiatives—his 'hare-brained schemes' as they were subsequently dubbed—
ranging from his obsession with maize to the preposterous meat-procurement promises that had led to the suicide of the Ryazan' party secretary,
Larionov, in 1959 (see above, p. 268). But the charges were now far removed
from those characteristic of the Stalin years, there was no equivalent of the
'Anti-Party Group' rhetoric Khrushchev himself had used in 1957, and he
was allowed comfortable if anonymous retirement.

Document 195 | From M.A. Suslov's speech on Khrushchev at the CPSU CC plenary meeting

14 October 1964

Comrades! Members and candidate members of the CC Presidium and CC secretaries have recently been greatly troubled by the abnormal situation obtaining
because of comrade Khrushchev's incorrect methods of Party and State leadership.
It was decided to discuss this question at a meeting of the CC Presidium and recall
comrade Khrushchev, who was then in the south. The Presidium discussed the question in minute detail over two days and comrade Khrushchev's incorrect methods
of work were subjected to severe criticism. All members of the Presidium, candidate members of the Presidium, and CC secretaries showed complete unanimity in
their contributions.

In our contribution we all started from the position that the Leninist general line
of the Party, as set out in the decisions of the 20th, 21st and 22nd Congresses and
the Party Programme, is correct and inviolable. For us this line is sacred and unshakeable in the areas of both domestic and foreign policy. (*Thunderous and prolonged
applause.*)

We know that our Party has achieved significant successes in economic and
cultural construction in recent years. The decisions of the 20th, 21st and 22nd
Congresses set out the correct Leninist line in the domestic and foreign policy areas.
Comrade Khrushchev did make a certain contribution in the elaboration of this
collectively developed line. His positive role should be acknowledged in unmasking
Stalin's personality cult, pursuing a Leninist policy of peaceful co-existence of states
with different social systems, and in the struggle for peace and friendship between
peoples.

However, our successes would have been much more significant had there been
a different situation in the CC Presidium. The abnormal situation created by
comrade Khrushchev in recent years has inflicted and is inflicting serious damage
on the practical work not only of the CC Presidium but also of the whole CC, and
even of the Party itself. In what way has it been abnormal? It has been abnormal
first and foremost in comrade Khrushchev's crude disregard for Leninist standards
of Party leadership.

Comrade Khrushchev, having concentrated the posts of First Secretary of the Party Central Committee and Chairman of the Council of Ministers in his own hands, has certainly not always used these rights and duties in the correct manner. By infringing the Leninist principles of collectivity in leadership, he began to try to solve very important questions of Party and State work on his own. In the recent period he has been deciding even the most major questions essentially autocratically, crudely foisting his subjective and often quite incorrect viewpoint on others. He imagined himself to be infallible and claimed a monopoly on truth. To all comrades who voiced their own opinions or made comments displeasing to him, comrade Khrushchev has arrogantly given all sorts of derogatory, offensive and demeaning nicknames.

Because of comrade Khrushchev's incorrect behaviour the CC Presidium became less and less a place for the collective and creative discussion and solution of problems. Collective leadership was becoming, in effect, impossible.

The normal work of the CC Presidium has also been hampered by the fact that comrade Khrushchev was systematically engaging in intrigue and tried in every way to set members of the Presidium against one another. (*Cries of 'Shame!'*)

Comrade Khrushchev's impermissible wilfulness has been evident in a number of cases of awarding Orders of the Soviet Union, where the CC Presidium had agreed one thing, but comrade Khrushchev foisted other decisions upon them, presenting the Presidium with a *fait accompli*.

Comrade Khrushchev's urge to break free of the control of the Presidium and the Central Committee is also attested to by the fact that in recent years we have, in effect, not had any real plenary sessions of the Central Committee, summoned to consider current problems in a businesslike way, but only to stage vacuous parades. In fact, there were no plenary meetings of the CC, but All-Union conferences of 5,000–6,000 people, where people sang the praises of comrade Khrushchev from the rostrum.

Without investigating the matter thoroughly and without any foundation whatever, comrade Khrushchev extolled such a shameless thing as the Ryazan' affair. You may recall how he advertised the experiment of that trickster and adventurist Larionov, who proposed to complete a three-year meat-procurement plan in one. This adventurist experiment did serious damage to animal husbandry on collective and state farms. . .

[Source: *Istoricheskiy arkhiv*, No. 1, 1993, pp. 5, 7, 8.]

The Brezhnev era

Khrushchev's successors, as we have seen, reversed many of his administrative changes, notably the subdivision of the party and the regional Economic

Councils, and the new prime minister, Kosygin, sponsored a series of economic reforms designed to make greater use of market mechanisms. In foreign affairs, while Brezhnev and his colleagues adopted a more cautious approach than had Khrushchev in terms of specific initiatives and crisis management, they greatly increased arms investment, making a determined drive to achieve nuclear parity with the USA. But the broad lines of policy, and the mechanisms which stabilized the USSR, underwent no dramatic change.[129] The social pyramid built around the structure of the party remained firmly in place, and for the elite in each republic the rewards of political conformity became even richer, from chauffeur-driven cars and household staff, through assured niches for their children, to graceful apartments and carefully guarded holiday dachas. Something of the flavour of *nomenklatura* privilege is conveyed by the following secret Central Committee resolution of 1971 on the construction of a sumptuous sanatorium for the Moscow elite.[130]

Document 196 | **Resolution of the CC of the CPSU on building a special *nomenklatura* sanatorium, 1971**

1. The proposal from the Committee for State Security of the USSR Council of Ministers to establish a special sanatorium at the Semenovskoe state dacha is to be accepted.
2. The Moscow City Executive Committee is to:
    a) compile the technical specifications as instructed by the Committee for State Security of the USSR Council of Ministers by 1 August 1971...
3. The USSR Ministry for Special Construction Work, the USSR Ministry for the Timber and Woodworking Industries, the Ministry for the Aviation Industry, the USSR Ministry for the Building Materials Industry and the USSR Ministry of Communications are to ensure the work is carried out.
4. The USSR Gosplan, the USSR Ministry of Finance and the USSR State Supply Commission are to allot and transfer to the Moscow City Executive Committee at its request the necessary capital resources, including foreign currency and material and technical resources for building the sanatorium at Semenovskoe...
11. The use in limited quantities of non-ferrous metals for non-standard fittings and also of hard woods, marble and granite for constructing the said sanatorium is to be allowed...
13. The USSR Ministry of Defence is to provide the Moscow City Executive

---

129 For a recent reappraisal of the Brezhnev period, see E. Bacon and M. Sandle (eds), *Brezhnev Reconsidered* (London 2003).
130 On *nomenklatura* privilege, see M. Voslensky, *Nomenklatura: Anatomy of the Soviet Ruling Class* (London 1984).

Committee with 150 soldiers to carry out this work from 1 May 1971 to 15 December 1972. . .

[Source: *Izvestiya*, 25 May 1992.]

When a new constitution was introduced in 1977, it confirmed in large measure the structures that had evolved under Khrushchev.[131] And enshrined in Article 6 and spelled out with greater clarity even than in the Stalin Constitution of 1936 was the central political role of the party.

Document 197 | Article 6 of the USSR Constitution

1977

Article 6. The leading and guiding force of Soviet society and the nucleus of its political system, of all state organizations and public organizations, is the Communist Party of the Soviet Union. The CPSU exists for the people and serves the people.

The Communist Party, armed with Marxism–Leninism, determines the general perspectives of the development of society and the course of the home and foreign policy of the USSR, directs the great constructive work of the Soviet people, and imparts a planned, systematic and theoretically substantiated character to their struggle for the victory of communism.

All party organizations shall function within the framework of the Constitution of the USSR.

[Source: *Constitution (Fundamental Law) of the Union of Soviet Socialist Republics* (Moscow 1977), p. 21.]

By the 1980s, therefore, the bombast of the Party Programme of 1961 had fallen away, and there were no hostages to fortune such as Khrushchev's commitment to advance beyond socialism to communism within two decades. But equally there was little of the dynamism of Khrushchev's leadership among what became known as Brezhnev's 'gerontocracy'—the average age of the Politburo exceeded 70 by 1980. The style and rhetoric of the regime, epitomized by Brezhnev himself, exuded complacency, drawing a veil over the implications of the new stage in the arms race, the guerrilla warfare in Afghanistan, the instability in Poland, and the declining rate of economic growth. The following extract from Brezhnev's address to the Twenty-Sixth Party Congress in 1981 is characteristic, glorying in the

---

131 For the text and detailed commentary, see A.L. Unger, *Constitutional Development in the USSR* (London 1981).

harmony and supposed equality among all the nationalities of the USSR and the 'disinterested' generosity of the Russian people.

Document 198 | From L.I. Brezhnev's speech to the 26th CPSU Congress *On the National Question*

23 February 1981

. . . Ever since Soviet power was established our economic and social policy has been framed in such a way as to bring the outlying regions of old Russia inhabited by national minorities up to the development level of the central regions as quickly as possible. This task has been successfully accomplished. Here a key role was played by close co-operation among all the nations of the country and, chiefly, by the disinterested assistance of the Russian people. Comrades, there are no backward ethnic outskirts today.

[Source: L.I. Brezhnev, *Our Course: Peace and Socialism* (Moscow 1982), p. 65.]

Brezhnev's successor, Andropov, was more alive to and open about the multifaceted problems facing the USSR. In the following extract on the nationality question from a speech to celebrate the sixtieth anniversary of the founding of the USSR, for example, he alluded to the tension arising in Central Asia generally and Kazakhstan in particular from the predominance among the urban working class of Russians rather than the titular nationality. But he did so in the most general terms and his primary message was the notion that the national question had been resolved 'finally and irrevocably'.

Document 199 | From a speech by Yu.V. Andropov on the 60th anniversary of the formation of the USSR *On the National Question*

December 1982

The real qualitative changes in national relations over the past 60 years show that the national question, as bequeathed to us by the old exploitative system, has been successfully resolved, resolved finally and irrevocably. . . For the first time in history the multinational composition of a country has turned from a source of weakness into a source of strength and prosperity. . . However, these successes in resolving the national question do not mean that all problems have disappeared.

Contemporary productive forces. . . require the close and skilful combination of the efforts of different regions. . . The most sensible use of natural and labour resources, the climatic peculiarities of each republic and the most rational inclusion of this potential into the All-Union whole—this is what will bring the most benefit to each region, each nation and national group, as well as to the state as a whole. . .

We need to improve further the allocation of productive forces, regional specialization and co-operation. . . It is a task we must deal with.

We should remember that in the spiritual legacy, traditions and way of life of every nation there is not only that which is good, but also that which is bad and has outlived its time. And this is another task—not to conserve what is bad, but to free ourselves from all that is out of date, that runs contrary to the standards of Soviet communal life, socialist morality and our communist ideals. . .

It is important that natural pride in one's achievements does not turn into national arrogance and conceit, does not engender a tendency to aloofness and disrespect towards other nations and national groups. But such negative phenomena can still be encountered. It would be wrong to explain them merely as vestiges from the past. They are sometimes encouraged by our own mistakes in our work. . . In this respect everything matters—attitudes to language and historical monuments, the interpretation of the past, and how we change villages and towns. . .

As a result of natural population shifts each republic, *oblast'* and city is becoming more and more multinational. . . Workers now make up the biggest social group in every republic. However, in some of them the titular nationality needs to be more fully represented within the working class. . . This is necessary for the development of the economy. It is also important politically.

We must work consistently to make sure that every national group in a given republic is duly represented at all levels of Party and Soviet bodies. . . Great tact in the recruitment and allocation of personnel is especially necessary where the union and autonomous republics are multinational in composition. . .

We speak boldly about the problems we have, and about unsolved tasks, because we know for sure that we are equal to these problems and tasks, and that we can and must solve them.

[Source: Yu.V. Andropov, *Izbrannye rechi i stat'i* (Moscow 1983), pp. 9–12.]

16

Marxism–Leninism and Dissent

If three of the pillars on which the postwar architecture of the USSR rested were superpower status together with chronic insecurity, the command economy, and the political and social domination of the CPSU, the fourth was Marxism–Leninism. Just as the Great Patriotic War helped to perpetuate the key features of the country's geopolitical, economic and sociopolitical structure, so too it set firm the core elements of the official ideology. The war lent new credence, certainly in the eyes of the leadership and party, to the selection of ideas drawn from Marx and Lenin which had been codified in the 1930s. And it provided a context far more conducive than that of the 1930s to propagating a virtual fusion between that official ideology and Soviet patriotism.

The Nazi assault on the Soviet Union offered confirmation that the forces of reaction were a permanent threat to humanity's first socialist society. The country's central role in the defeat of Nazism matched the claim that it constituted the vanguard of human progress and was working with the grain of the law-governed historical process uncovered by Marx. The Soviet economy's out-performance of the Third Reich could be read as proof of the innate superiority of common ownership and central planning. The party's leading role in organizing the great victory corroborated the assertion that it was precisely the presence of Lenin's 'party of a new kind' in 1917 which had enabled Russia's socialist revolution to succeed where others had failed, and that the party was the indispensable repository of scientific guidance in pioneering the building of socialism. Thus the Great Patriotic War gave a new lease of life to the Soviet regime's claims on the ideas of Marx and Engels, the most formidable intellectual product of the Enlightenment. It rooted those claims in an historical experience that for the generation which had endured Barbarossa was far more resonant than the fading memory of the revolution of 1917.

The result was to arm the regime with an ideology that enabled Stalin and his heirs to colonize the modern language of social protest, the conceptual tools of social analysis, and the entire record of human history; to project the CPSU as the authentic product of universal laws governing the historical process; and to give shape to the claim that the Communist-ruled USSR was the culmination of human progress, the fulfilment of mankind's aspiration for social justice, altruism, democracy, liberty, equality, international fraternity, solidarity and peace. It enabled the regime to exploit to the very full both the pool of emotional capital which the ordeal and victory of the war placed at its disposal, and the gradual improvement in living standards delivered by the command economy as reconstruction was achieved. And it bound the elite and party together behind a coherent discourse which was readily systematized, simplified, packaged and propagated through the mass media and at all levels of education. Moreover, while the ideology made much play of its own logical rigour and supposed scientific validation, it was in reality supremely flexible. For within the language and worldview of Marxism it had embedded the unquestionable premise that the CPSU was the ordained and infallible vanguard of human progress: whatever the party chose to do was *a priori* justified, and even its own past leaders could be blithely repudiated and its own policies drastically altered without calling its authority into question. It could work almost any development, at home or abroad, negative as well as positive, into its narrative of class struggle, the inevitable replacement of capitalism by socialism, and the pioneering role of the USSR.[132] It was, for its critics, maddeningly difficult to falsify. And at the same time, while it provided apparent justification for the most rigid form of censorship over all forms of public communication, from political analysis to music, it also gave successive leaders considerable freedom of manoeuvre in altering the line between what was and what was not permissible. Between the late 1940s and the 1980s, while Marx, Lenin and the leading role of the party remained sacrosanct, that boundary moved dramatically, thereby accommodating wide-ranging cultural, social and international change. Against the backdrop of the Great Patriotic War, Marxism–Leninism proved intellectually compelling to some and broadly plausible to many. It provided the ideal discourse in which to unite the elite and maximize the legitimacy of communist rule. And it played a key role in the regime's remarkable success, despite the rapid rise in the size and sophistication of the educated public, in limiting overt opposition.

---

132 See Sandle, *Short History of Soviet Socialism*, for a sophisticated analysis of both change and continuity in the ideology.

The *Zhdanovshchina*

In the immediate aftermath of the war, the regime took drastic measures to reverse the relative wartime loosening of its control over public discussion and education, confirming the undiluted ideological monopoly of Marxism–Leninism and the Central Committee's absolute authority over its interpretation. Stalin's partial rehabilitation of the Orthodox Church remained in place, but its ability to affect public discourse was kept to a minimum while other denominations were even more severely repressed. From 1946, censorship over literature, art, cinema and theatre were sharply tightened, and as the Cold War gathered momentum, evidence of contact with the west or susceptibility to its influence became highly dangerous. A new edition of the *History of the CPSU(b) Short Course*, enshrining orthodoxy, was published. The social sciences were paralysed by the secrecy enveloping key statistics, the rigidity of censorship, and the treatment of Stalin's every word as infallible guidance. Natural science was subject to devastating interference by the Central Committee apparatus, fruitful lines of research were denounced as manifestations of 'bourgeois science', and sometimes unproven and even absurd hypotheses were adopted as proletarian orthodoxy.

It was in the creative arts that the tensions between the regime and innovative intellectuals were keenest and were fought out most publicly.[133] The obligation for artists in every genre from music to literature to conform to 'socialist realism', the orthodoxy established in the 1930s, was reaffirmed and it was defined in the most rigid manner. As in the 1930s, to be charged with ideological neutrality was enough to forfeit the right to publication. The tone was set by the following Central Committee resolution, sponsored by Zhdanov, the Politburo member with chief responsibility for ideology, criticizing two relatively bold literary journals published in Leningrad.[134] The resolution condemned their willingness to publish the works of two authors in particular, those of the satirist M. Zoshchenko, citing as outrageous his tale (which might easily have been dismissed as innocuous) of an escaped monkey who after a day's exposure to Soviet life opted to return to the zoo, and those of the highly popular lyrical poetess Anna Akhmatova, notoriously denounced by Zhdanov as 'half-nun, half-harlot'.

---

133 R. Medvedev, *Let History Judge: The Origins and Consequences of Stalinism* (New York 1989, revised edn), ch. 14, provides a chilling account.
134 For a recent account, see K. Boterbloem, *The Life and Times of Andrei Zhdanov, 1896–1948* (Montreal 2003), the first full biography of Zhdanov.

Document 200 | **From the CPSU CC resolution *On the Journals* Zvezda *and* Leningrad, 14 August 1946**

The CC of the CPSU notes that the literary and artistic journals *Zvezda* and *Leningrad*, published in Leningrad, are not being run at all satisfactorily.

Along with some notable and successful works by Soviet writers a lot of unprincipled and ideologically harmful works have been appearing recently in *Zvezda*. It has made a great mistake in giving a platform to the writer Zoshchenko, whose works are alien to Soviet literature. The editors of *Zvezda* know that he has long specialized in writing empty, dull and vulgar things which propagate a putrid, banal and apolitical lack of principle and are designed to disorient our young people and poison their consciousness. His most recent short story, *The Adventures of a Monkey* (in *Zvezda* No. 5–6, 1946) is a vulgar lampoon against Soviet life and people. Zoshchenko portrays the Soviet order and people in grotesque caricature, slanderously depicting Soviet people as primitive, uncultured and stupid, with philistine tastes and ways. His maliciously destructive portrayal of our reality is accompanied by anti-Soviet attacks.

Giving space to such philistine literary scum as Zoshchenko is all the more unacceptable because *Zvezda*'s editors know all about his nature and unworthy behaviour in the war when, instead of helping the Soviet people in their struggle against the German invaders, he wrote something as disgusting as *Before Sunset*, an evaluation of which, along with all his literary 'work', was given in the journal *Bol'shevik*.

The journal *Zvezda* has also been very busy popularizing the work of the authoress Akhmatova, whose work and sociopolitical nature have long been known to the Soviet public. Akhmatova is a typical representative of the empty, unprincipled poetry alien to our people. Her poems, infused with the spirit of pessimism and decadence, expressing the tastes of the old salon poetry, are still stuck in the time of bourgeois–aristocratic aestheticism and decadence. Her 'art for art's sake' has no desire to keep pace with the Soviet people, is doing harm to our young people's education and cannot be tolerated in Soviet literature.

Allowing Zoshchenko and Akhmatova an active role in the journal has undoubtedly brought elements of ideological disorder and disorganization among Leningrad writers. Works have begun to appear which cultivate an un-Soviet spirit of servility to contemporary bourgeois Western culture.

The CC notes that the journal *Leningrad* is being particularly badly run. It has constantly been giving space to Zoshchenko's empty and slanderous efforts and Akhmatova's vacuous and apolitical poetry. Like the editorial board of *Zvezda*, the editorial board of *Leningrad* has made a grave mistake in publishing a number of works infused with the spirit of servility to all things foreign.

What is the essence of the mistakes of the editorial boards of *Zvezda* and *Leningrad*? The leading staff of these journals, particularly their editors-in-chief, comrades Sayanov and Likharev, have forgotten the Leninist tenet that our journals, be they scientific or artistic, cannot be apolitical. They have forgotten that our journals are a powerful means for the Soviet state to educate the Soviet people, especially the youth, and must therefore be guided by what is the lifeblood of the Soviet system— its politics. The Soviet system cannot allow the young to be educated in a spirit of indifference to Soviet politics, in a spirit of contempt and lack of principle.

The CC of the CPSU resolves:

1. The editors of *Zvezda*, the leadership of the Union of Soviet Writers and the Propaganda section of the CC of the CPSU must take steps to correct the mistakes indicated in this resolution and the failings in the journal, and correct its line by not publishing the works of Zoshchenko, Akhmatova and their ilk.

2. In view of the fact that the conditions in Leningrad at present are not right for publishing two literary and artistic journals, *Leningrad* is to cease publication, and its literary forces are to be concentrated around the journal *Zvezda*.

3. To introduce the necessary order into the work of the editorial board of *Zvezda* and seriously improve the journal's content there must be an editor-in-chief with an editorial board under him. The editor-in-chief of the journal will bear full responsibility for ideological and political direction and the quality of the pieces it publishes.

4. Its editor-in-chief is to be comrade A.M. Egolin, who is also to remain deputy director of the Propaganda Section of the CC of the CPSU.

[Source: *O partiynoy i sovetskoy pechati, radioveshchanii i televidenii: sbornik dokumentov i materialov* (Moscow 1972), pp. 258–62.]

The next month a parallel resolution was adopted sharply narrowing the scope granted to filmmakers, and Eisenstein was among those targeted. The trigger was the following attack on L.D. Lukov's new film *A Great Life II*. Here the charge was of denigrating the party, the state and the level of Soviet technology, as well as of wasting space on everyday trivialities rather than celebrating what the regime saw as the mighty achievements of postwar reconstruction.

Document 201 | From the CPSU CC resolution on the film *A Great Life II*

4 September 1946

The CC of the CPSU notes that the film *A Great Life II*, produced by the Ministry of Cinematography (director L. Lukov, script-writer P. Nilin), is ideologically and politically flawed and exceptionally weak artistically.

What are the flaws and faults of *A Great Life II*?

The film shows only one insignificant episode in the first phase of the rebuilding of the Donbass, which does not give a true picture of the real scale and significance of the rebuilding being undertaken by the Soviet state in the Donets basin.

Moreover, this rebuilding occupies an insignificant space in the film, the main attention being given over to a primitive depiction of all kinds of experiences and everyday scenes. The content of *A Great Life II* therefore comes over as a mockery of Soviet reality.

Two different eras in our industrial development have obviously been mixed up in the film. Judging by the technological level of industry depicted in the film, the post-Civil War rebuilding is portrayed rather than the current one with the advanced technology created over the period of Stalin's Five-Year Plans. The film's producers give the viewer the false impression that the restoration of the Donbass mines after their liberation from the German invaders and the coal mining there have been taking place not with advanced technology and the mechanization of labour processes, but by brute force, long-outdated machinery and conservative work methods. The film thereby distorts the image of our postwar industrial restoration, based as it is on advanced technology and a developed industrial culture.

The rebuilding of the Donbass is shown in the film *A Great Life II* as if the initiative of the workers in restoring the pits not only did not receive state support but was accomplished by the miners against the resistance of state organizations. Such a depiction of the relationship between state organizations and workers' collectives is utterly mistaken and wrong, because it is well known that any worker initiative or innovation in our country enjoys the full support of the state.

Party activists are falsely portrayed in the film. The Party secretary at the mine is shown in a deliberately absurd situation in so far as his support for the miners' rebuilding initiative puts him outside the Party. The film's producers depict the situation in such a way as to suggest the Party might expel anybody who shows any concern for economic restoration. . .

The CC of the CPSU resolves:

1. In view of the above *A Great Life II* is not to be released.

2. The USSR Ministry of Cinematography and its artistic council are to draw the necessary conclusions from this resolution of the CPSU CC on the film *A Great Life II* and organize future work on artistic cinematography in such a way that such films cannot be made again.

[Source: *O partiynoy i sovetskoy pechati: sbornik dokumentov* (Moscow 1994), pp. 573–74, 576.]

The roll-call of those who were reduced to the so-called 'genre of silence' included Shostakovich and Prokofiev among major Soviet musicians and Pasternak among major writers. The *Zhdanovshchina*, as the repressive campaign became known, wove together Marxist–Leninist orthodoxy and an insistence on active propagation of the party line with outlandish claims for Soviet and in particular Russian superiority over the rest of the world. It was fed by xenophobia and anti-Semitism in particular: Jewish organizations, journals and individual intellectuals were most at risk of repression. The following *Pravda* denunciation in January 1949 of a number of theatre critics typifies the language of the *Zhdanovshchina* (though Zhdanov himself had died suddenly the previous summer), its crude insistence on didactic art, and its ominous call that art be 'cleansed'. The charge of being 'rootless' or of 'bourgeois cosmopolitanism' implied obeisance to foreign criteria of artistic merit, disloyalty to the USSR, and, more often than not, Jewishness. To prioritize 'aestheticism' above ideological meaning was at best frivolous and at worst both reactionary and unpatriotic; so, too, was sneering at the lack of artistic sophistication of a sound Soviet author who provided 'truthful depiction of the heroic beauty of our life and the beauty of the spiritual world of Soviet Man'. There was especial venom against those 'unmasked' for daring to criticize Gorky, elevated ever higher in the Soviet artistic pantheon since his death in 1936, and for seeking to use Turgenev, accepted as one of the giants of the Russian tradition, to belittle Soviet art.

Document 202 | **From a *Pravda* editorial *On an Anti-Patriotic Group of Theatre Critics***

28 January 1949

. . . In the field of theatre criticism an Anti-Party Group of epigones of bourgeois aestheticism has formed. . . These critics have forgotten their responsibility to the people and are the bearers of bourgeois cosmopolitanism, something profoundly repulsive and hostile to the Soviet people; they are hindering the development of Soviet literature. . . A feeling of Soviet national pride is something alien to them. Critics like these are trying to discredit the most advanced features of our literature and art by furiously inveighing against patriotic and politically purposeful works under the guise of their supposed artistic inadequacy. . .

The figure of the worker–revolutionary Nil in Gorky's *Philistines* is of enormous ideological and artistic significance. But the critic Yu. Yuzovsky, in amongst his Jesuitical praise for the play, tries to persuade the reader that Nil is 'not one of Gorky's fully rounded characters' and that its author is acting 'at this point as a political commentator who does not always bother to consider whether this political commentary interferes with the artistic thread of the play'. The 'artistic thread', the logic of the plot, which Nil's actions supposedly infringe in Gorky's remarkable play—here is the mask of the bourgeois aesthete, behind which he conceals his true anti-revolutionary and anti-patriotic essence. . .

. . . His article is full of mockery in which he vents his sarcasm on 'the happy and jolly' type of hero in Soviet plays and on our playwrights who supposedly often start from the 'premise' of a 'self-satisfied' main character; on tendencies which are supposedly 'corroding our art'; on our playwrights who allegedly do not want to think and thereby 'stop their characters from thinking'. What are we to make of the following comment, 'Since the character is Soviet, he must necessarily. . . be victorious, but this sort of philosophy has nothing to do with the dialectics of life'?. . . The critic's deliberately nebulous phrase is all the more outrageous because it was written in 1943, after the Soviet Army's great victory at Stalingrad. . .

A. Gurvich makes a malicious attempt to contrast Soviet and classic Russian drama by using the authority of Turgenev. When speaking of Soviet plays, he pontificates thus, 'Only one character rouses us and makes us sense something familiar and significant, and that was Verochka from Turgenev's *A Month in the Country*. Deep within we felt that only this shy and passionate girl reaches out to shake hands with Zoya Kosmodem'yanskaya over the centuries and over the heads of many female characters in our plays.'

Let us dot the 'i's. 'We' means those lacking a feeling of Soviet patriotism, to whom neither the figure of Zoya Kosmodem'yanskaya nor the works of our literature are dear; a literature highly esteemed by the Soviet people for its truthful depiction of the heroic beauty of our life and the beauty of the spiritual world of Soviet Man. What sort of idea of Russian Soviet national character does A. Gurvich have, if he can write that 'in the good-natured humour and naively trusting optimism' of Pogodin's plays, in which 'the national character of the dramatist's worldview' is expressed, the audience saw its own reflection, because 'Russians are not lacking in good humour'? This is slander against Soviet Russian Man. . .

These are not one-off, individual mistakes, but a system of anti-patriotic views, which are damaging the development of our literature and art, a system which must be eliminated. . . We must decisively and once and for all put an end to liberal tolerance of these aesthetic nonentities who do not have a healthy love for their Motherland and people and have nothing in their spirits save malevolence and inflated conceit. The atmosphere of art must be cleansed of these anti-patriotic philistines. . .

[Source: *Pravda*, 28 January 1949.]

The fact that a note struck during the war, when censorship had been less tight, could now be dredged up as damning evidence, as was done here against the critic Yuzovsky, placed artists, intellectuals and academics in every field at risk of denunciation. The *Zhdanovshchina* bred mutual suspicion and inhibited innovation and experimentation. Even when the Central Committee appeared to encourage bolder artistic treatment, the insistence on 'socialist realism' and an idealized portrayal of Soviet life was unrelenting, as in this excerpt from Malenkov's speech to the Nineteenth Party Congress in 1952.

Document 203 | **From G.M. Malenkov's report on behalf of the CC to the 19th CPSU Congress**

October 1952

In their work our writers and artists must castigate the defects, failings and unhealthy phenomena widespread in society, and show in positive artistic images people of a new type in all the greatness of their human virtues. In this way they will help to inculcate, in the people of our society, characters, habits and customs free of the evils and vices caused by capitalism. Meanwhile, our Soviet fiction, drama and cinema still lack such artistic genres as satire. It would be quite wrong to think that our Soviet reality does not provide plenty of material for satire. We need Soviet Gogols and Shchedrins, who are able to use the flame of satire to excise from our lives all that is negative, rotten and dead, all that is holding us back.

We need to achieve a cultural growth in society that can ensure the all-round development of the physical and mental capabilities of all members of society, so that members of society have the opportunity to receive an education which will make them active participants in social development, so that they have the chance freely to choose a profession and not be shackled all their lives, because of the current division of labour, to just one profession. . .

[Source: *Pravda*, 6 October 1952.]

Partial thaw under Khrushchev

In the 'thaw' that followed Stalin's death—the label was taken from the innovative novella of that name published in 1954 by Il'ya Erenburg—the boundaries of what was permissible were gradually pushed back. The greatest single stimulant to intellectual debate was Khrushchev's 'secret speech' at the Twentieth Party Congress in February 1956. It gave immediate hope to those whom censorship had turned into 'internal émigrés'; it enthused a younger generation who would soon refer to themselves as 'children of the Twentieth Party Congress'; and it was a devastating shock to those who had identified themselves wholeheartedly with the late-Stalinist reading of 'socialist realism'. The following cri-de-coeur came from one of the latter, A.A. Fadeev, head of the Writers' Union during the *Zhdanovshchina* and an ardent supporter of Zhdanov himself. Fadeev's best-known book, *The Young Guard* (1951), had been slavishly rewritten to come fully into line with the postwar demands of 'socialist realism' and to celebrate and idealize the Komsomol's role in the partisan resistance. He had been responsible for or endorsed numerous denunciations that now appeared indefensible; this excerpt comes from a rambling suicide note he addressed to the Central

Committee three months after Khrushchev's speech, at one and the same time devastated by the revelations about the Stalin regime and scathing about those now directing literary policy.

Document 204 | From A.A. Fadeev's letter to the CC of the CPSU

13 May 1956

I cannot go on living, because the art to which I have given my whole life has been ruined by a self-assured but ignorant Party leadership and is now beyond repair. . .

. . . Literature—that holy of holies—has been thrown to the bureaucrats and the most backward types among the people, and from the 'highest' rostra—of such events as the Moscow conference or the 20th Party Congress—we hear a new slogan, 'After it!'

The self-satisfaction of these upstarts, nouveaux riches from Lenin's great teaching, has meant that even when they swear by this teaching, I completely distrust them, because we can expect even worse from them than from Stalin's satrap. He was at least educated, unlike this bunch of ignoramuses.

Fadeev

[Source: Izvestiya TsK KPSS, No. 10, 1990, p. 147.]

The authority of the *Short Course* began to be questioned; the social sciences were resuscitated with the publication of social and economic statistics that had long been suppressed; intellectuals gained at least limited access to western work; the number of journals multiplied rapidly. Yet the change in atmosphere did not involve the slightest official concession on the absolute validity of Marxism–Leninism or the continuing right of the Central Committee to define the limits of what could and what could not be published. In literature, for example, on the one hand, the most daring journal *Novyy mir* (*New World*), edited by A.T. Tvardovsky, serialized the path-breaking novel *Not by Bread Alone* by V. Dudintsev, in which the ranks of conventional party and state officials were subject to a withering critique. On the other, *Novyy mir* rejected Pasternak's much more radically independent novel of the revolution, *Doctor Zhivago*, and when its appearance in the west in 1957 won him the Nobel Prize he was forbidden to accept it and expelled from the Writers' Union. The poetry of Evgeny Evtushenko and Andrey Voznesensky spearheaded the ebullient and mischievous work of a younger generation unthinkable before 1953. But at the same time, there was a backlash among those who saw the thaw as a decline from a purer age. This was symbolized by the formation of a markedly more conservative Writers' Union of the RSFSR alongside that of the USSR, and by the journal

Oktyabr' (*October*), which established itself as the conservative alter ego of *Novyy mir*.[135]

The key role played by the party leadership in shaping the pace and extent of change across the whole cultural field was epitomized by the impact of Khrushchev's personal and unpredictable interventions.[136] On the one hand, he tended to condone work which discomfited die-hards sympathetic to the viewpoint of Molotov and the 'Anti-Party Group'; on the other, he could take a violent dislike to new work, notably modern art. After compelling his colleagues on the Presidium to read the manuscript of Aleksandr Solzhenitsyn's sensational portrayal of life in Stalin's GULAG, *A Day in the Life of Ivan Denisovich*, he authorized its appearance in *Novyy mir*, in November 1962. The manner in which the work broke this taboo was so stark, striking and authentic that it became an instant classic and made Solzhenitsyn a household name. More conservative figures in the leadership, including L. Il'ichev, who as head of the Central Committee's Ideological Commission oversaw the key editors and censorship generally, strove to rein in Khrushchev's openness to experiment. At the beginning of December 1962, apparently at Il'ichev's instigation, Khrushchev visited an exhibition of unofficial artists. To conservative delight, he was appalled at what he regarded as the decadence and irrelevance to popular needs of some of the modern art to which Il'ichev drew his attention. He had an open row with the sculptor Ernst Neizvestny, and was reported in *Pravda* condemning pictures 'that make you wonder whether they were painted by the hand of a man or daubed by the tail of a donkey'. At a meeting with artists and intellectuals two weeks later, on 14 December, Il'ichev and his allies tried to cajole more adventurous writers and painters into abandoning 'formalism', 'abstractionism' and 'lyrical twitterings' and to 'sing out for the victory of communism'. The artist B. Zhutovsky subsequently recalled some of the exchanges, including clashes over Evtushenko and Pasternak, and the spirited ripostes which he, Neizvestny and other creative artists gave.

Document 205 | **From B. Zhutovsky's recollections of meetings between Party leaders and artists**

. . . On 14 December 1962 I set off for the first of a series of planned meetings. This was to be a meeting between a group of young intellectuals and Leonid Fedorovich Il'ichev, the head of the CPSU CC's Ideological Commission.

Around the table were L. Il'ichev, Aleksey Adzhubey, the editor-in-chief of

---

135 The fluctuating picture is illuminated by E.R. Frankel, Novy Mir: *A Case Study in the Politics of Literature, 1952–58* (Cambridge 1981).

136 See the portrait in Taubman, *Khrushchev*.

Izvestiya, P. Satyukov, the editor-in-chief of *Pravda*, ten in all. . . I can remember the names of some of those who were there: B. Okudzhava, E. Belyutin, the head of our studio, B. Akhmadulina, I. Glazunov, N. Andronov, P. Nikonov, N. Vorob'ev, F. Zbarsky, R. Shchedrin, E. Isaev. . . The meeting proceeded as planned.

L. Il'ichev: Talk in the Ideological Commission is friendly, comradely and open. . . We decided to warn against getting carried away with formalism and abstractionism. This is not a game—it's about abandoning principles. . . There is formalism in literature, cinema, music, and theatre. . . Lyrical twitterings—do we really need such stuff?. . . We're not talking about whipping, humiliating or ridiculing anyone, we're just asking them to sing out for the victory of communism. . .

D. Starikov: Why is *Pravda* indulging Evtushenko? Why has Ruch'ev been forgotten? Kulemin, Fedorov, Anatoly Peredreev—why have they been forgotten?

B. Okudzhava: There's no left or right, but just those with more or less talent. They're all ours, all of them. . . Many young talented poets are doing readings abroad. Leningrad's closed to them. (Prokof'ev: As long as I live, I won't let them appear.)

B. Akhmadulina: Firsov likes Sofronov—and nobody can change his mind. I like Pushkin, Pasternak, Shchipachev, and I'm allowed to. We're serious and involved with the people.

B. Zhutovsky: There was a time when, after serious Party criticism of this or that mistake or error, those who had made these mistakes immediately admitted them—it was a question of survival. But it is hard to believe that it was really sincere. . . I think that eliminating mistakes isn't that easy. . . I would not be being sincere if I said, 'I understand now and will write in a different way.' What I do understand is something else, that the artistic search needs a lot of time and you have to do a lot of thinking before you tackle something that's not just an experiment in technique. Artists think with their brushes and I reckon that each of us can show by deeds and not just words that we're useful to the people.

E. Neizvestny: Time to get started, then.

[Source: *Literaturnaya gazeta*, 5 July 1989.]

Later that week, on 17 December, Khrushchev himself attended a larger meeting between government and party leaders and prominent members of the cultural intelligentsia. He greeted Solzhenitsyn warmly and he allowed Evtushenko among others to make the case openly for allowing different schools of art to compete. On the other hand, Zhutovsky recalls the abuse he heaped on those whose works he disliked.

17 December—the next meeting. N.S. Khrushchev spoke up after a break and what he said made quite an impression. . .

N.S. Khrushchev: The situation's fine with writers, but needs cleaning up a bit, that's your job!. . . Is this sculpture (pointing to Ernst [Neizvestny's] work)? I asked them whether you're a bunch of pederasts. You'd expect it from a 10-year-old, but how old are you lot?

(He obviously did not know the difference between a 'pederast' and 'masturbator'.)

N.S. Khrushchev: I'm a politician, not an artist. Just look at Zhutovsky's self-portrait. If you cut a hole in a piece of plywood and stuck it on these portraits, I reckon 95% of us here would know what part of the body it'd be. You had the divine spark in you, Zhutovsky, but you've buried it. That's formalism. . . Who gave you the right to mock the people?

Neizvestny looks down on us. He's a medium. He's created something, but we're thinking 'What is it?' Comrade Neizvestny, it makes me want to spit. I said to Shelepin, 'Where do they get the copper?'. . . Let's stand up for the old stuff and not give in to decadence. . . What're we going to do with Neizvestny and Zhutovsky? If they don't get the message, they can leave. We're not going to stand for this sort of stuff. . .

[Source: *Literaturnaya gazeta*, 5 July 1989.]

At a much more formal meeting nearly three months later, Khrushchev reaffirmed that though taboos might have been broken, the duty to endorse and propagate the party's leading role, patriotism and the inevitable triumph of Soviet socialism over capitalism remained the core duty of creative artists. He spoke approvingly of Solzhenitsyn, Tvardovsky and Evtushenko and yet, as Zhutovsky recalls, his tone towards Voznesensky, who boldly emphasized that he did not belong to the party, was crude and threatening.

There was a gap of ten weeks between the second and third (the last) meetings. The third meeting was set for 7 March 1963 in the Kremlin's Sverdlov Hall.

A. Voznesensky: Like my teacher Mayakovsky I'm not a Party member. . .

An increasingly irate Khrushchev immediately interrupted.

N.S. Khrushchev: Don't show off, traitor. You're a go-between for our enemies. You're no member of my Party, Mr Voznesensky! You don't have a Party stance. Your lot can all freeze. Just you wait, we'll show you what for. You're just another Pasternak! Get yourself a passport and go to the devil! Go to the devil!

A. Prokofev: I cannot understand Voznesensky and that's why I'm protesting. Our literature has not and will not tolerate such unprincipled stuff. . . I support Mayakovsky, but Rozhdestvensky and Voznesensky—no way!

The discussions drew to a close. Interrupting only himself, Khrushchev now summed up. . .

Many years later, N.S. Khrushchev explained to me the reasons for this vicious campaign: 'I didn't need to get involved. I was Head of State. It was nothing to do with me. But I do get a bit heated. . .'.

[Source: *Literaturnaya gazeta*, 5 July 1989.]

Dissent in the Brezhnev era

Khrushchev's occasional radicalism and apparent contradictions—at the same meeting of 7 March he spoke positively of Stalin and signalled a limit to the public criticism that he had himself started—were among the frustrations that led his colleagues to overthrow him in October 1964. Under Brezhnev and Kosygin, the regime attempted to clarify and strengthen the boundaries of the permissible. In addition to the mixed signals conveyed by Khrushchev himself, those boundaries were being blurred by increased contact with the west, by the opportunities for some writers to follow Pasternak's example and publish their works abroad, and by the small but ominous amount of unsanctioned literature now circulating in 'self-published', or *samizdat*, copies. In September 1965, two prominent satirical writers, Sinyavsky and Daniel', who had been close to Pasternak and had published abroad as well as being involved in *samizdat*, were arrested and the following February publicly tried for circulating short stories which were condemned as 'anti-Soviet propaganda'.

The case became a *cause célèbre*.[137] To maximize support for its view and make a public example of the two authors, the regime sought to rely not on the array of sanctions available to it to entice, intimidate, punish or forcibly silence its critics, but to use the law in open court. The prosecution alleged that the stories made a mockery of the USSR and as such broke the law and amounted to treason. The defendants insisted that the tales had to be read as literature, not political texts, that they did not necessarily endorse the comments made by the characters they had created, and that they had not broken the law.

Document 206 | From notes taken during the trial of A. Sinyavsky and Yu. Daniel'

February 1966

The morning session, 10 February 1966.

The resolution of 4 February on bringing Sinyavsky and Daniel' to trial under Article 70, Part 1, of the Criminal Code of the RSFSR is read out.

---

137 See M. Hayward (ed.), *On Trial: The Case of Sinyavsky and Daniel* (London 1967).

Judge: Accused Sinyavsky, do you admit to some or all of the charges laid against you?

Sinyavsky: No, I do not admit to them, neither to some, nor to all of them.

Judge: Accused Daniel', do you admit to some or all of the charges laid against you?

Daniel': No, I do not admit to them, neither to some, nor to all of them.

The evening cross-examination of Sinyavsky was adjourned until the next day. He tried to explain to the court that his article and three works did not contain his political views and convictions, but his position as a writer, and that fantastic realism with its hyperbole, irony and grotesqueness were close to him as a writer, but the Procurator demanded that he refrain from giving the court a literary lecture. This demand was upheld by the judge. . .

Procurator: Does your work express your political views and convictions?

Sinyavsky: I am not a political writer. A writer's works do not convey political views. . . You cannot ask either Pushkin or Gogol about their political views. (*Commotion in the courtroom.*) My work expresses how I see the world, but not my politics.

Procurator: I beg to differ. . .

The trial continued on 12 February.

Public Prosecutor O.P. Temushkin: I accuse Sinyavsky and Daniel' of anti-state activity. They have written and published under the guise of literature grubby lampoons calling for the overthrow of the system and disseminated slander, all disguised as literature. What they have done is not an unfortunate mistake, but an action tantamount to treason. . . In view of their lack of remorse and Sinyavsky's leading role I request Sinyavsky be given the maximum sentence—seven years' imprisonment, to be spent in a hard labour colony, and five years' exile (*applause in the courtroom*), and Daniel'—five years' imprisonment, to be spent in a hard labour colony, and three years' exile. . .

[Source: *Mif o zastoe* (Moscow 1991), pp. 70–71.]

The accused were duly convicted and punished as the prosecution demanded. Yet the outcome was far from definitive and the trial served to stir rather than dampen debate. A 'White Book' setting out the court proceedings and the difficulty the prosecution had had in winning the argument was circulated in *samizdat*. A collective letter of protest to the leadership was sent by a large number of members of the Writers' Union. Abroad, the repression, the manipulation of legal procedure and the regime's hypocrisy in affirming its commitment to 'socialist legality' were widely condemned. At the same time, within the USSR, viewed through the prism of Marxism–Leninism, the charge that Sinyavsky and Daniel' had shown themselves unpatriotic carried weight. To ridicule the claims of the socialist order was to denigrate the country, manifestly so when it was done in collusion with deeply hostile foreign powers. The emotions behind this response may be seen in the following extract from a speech made by the novelist M.A. Sholokhov to the Twenty-Third Party Congress a few weeks later. Sholokhov, whose *Quietly Flows the Don* (1928–40) had won him domestic and foreign acclaim as a young man, was scathing about those writers who defended Sinyavsky and Daniel′ or criticized the severity of the sentences.

Document 207 | From M.A. Sholokhov's speech to the 23rd CPSU Congress

1 April 1966

. . . We Soviet writers determine the place of the writer in public life as communists, as sons of our great Motherland, as citizens of a country building a communist society and as exponents of the revolutionary–humanist views of the Party, the people and Soviet Man. (*Thunderous applause.*)

We get quite a different picture when some storyteller comes to light who writes one thing here, but something totally different abroad. He uses the same Russian language, but does so on the one hand as a disguise and on the other in order to pollute this language with rabid hatred and malice for all things Soviet and for all that is dear and sacred to us.

. . . We call our Soviet land our mother. We are all members of a great family. How are we supposed to react to the behaviour of traitors who attack that which is dearest to us? The old saying is sadly true, 'There's a black sheep in every family.' But there are black sheep and black sheep. I think everybody understands that there is nothing more blasphemous and loathsome than to slander your own mother, hurl abuse at her and raise your hand against her! (*Thunderous, prolonged applause.*)

I feel ashamed of those who have slandered the Motherland and slung mud at what is so radiant for us. They are amoral. I feel ashamed of those who have tried and are trying to defend them, for whatever reason. (*Prolonged applause.*)

I feel doubly ashamed of those who offer their services and offer to stand bail for these criminal renegades. (*Thunderous applause.*)

We have paid too high a price for what we have achieved and Soviet power is too dear to us to let slander and denigration go unpunished. (*Thunderous applause.*)

Others, hiding behind phrases about humanism, moan about the severity of the sentences. I can see here delegates from the Soviet Army's Party organizations. What would they do if there were traitors in their midst?! They, our soldiers, know what humanism is—and it's not slobbering. (*Prolonged applause.*)

One more thing. If these black-hearted rogues had been around in the twenties when people were sentenced, not on the basis of the strictly defined articles of the Criminal Code, but on the basis of a 'revolutionary legal consciousness' (*applause*), these werewolves would have got a very different punishment! (*Applause.*) And there they are going on about the 'severity' of the sentence.

I'd like to say to the bourgeois defenders of these lampoonists: Don't worry about the fate of criticism here. We're supporting and developing criticism, it can be heard sharply at this very Congress. But slander is not criticism, and filth from a swamp is not paint on an artist's palette! (*Prolonged applause.*)

[Source: *XXIII s˜ezd Kommunisticheskoy partii Sovetskogo Soyuza. Stenograficheskiy otchet*, Vol. 1 (Moscow 1966), pp. 357–58.]

The dividing line between intellectuals who fell foul of the authorities and were becoming known as 'dissident', and those who, while sharing some of their views, continued to operate within the bounds of officially sanctioned publication, was still indistinct.[138] Within the 'legal' world, the primary target for those who shared Sholokhov's view was Tvardovsky's *Novyy mir*, still the flagship of bolder publications in literature. At the beginning of 1967, attacks on it intensified, including the following *Pravda* broadside, which took it to task for selecting for publication gloomy new depictions of Soviet life, for employing literary critics who revelled in the negative, and for sneering at its rivals.

Document 208 | *Pravda* editorial attacking *Novyy mir*

27 January 1967

Unfortunately, from our diverse reality *Novyy mir*'s attention has not been attracted by facts and phenomena which show that our Party and people have emerged even stronger and harder from all their experiences, with unshakeable revolutionary optimism, but mostly by phenomena of one type, connected with various seamy and abnormal aspects of 'rapid growth'. . . . The magazine is not interested in publishing the best broadly life-affirming works, representing that which is new, that which has been created and is being created on a daily basis by our people's labours and struggles. Instead, the journal has lapsed into depressing monotony, and distortion of the truth. Moreover, as *Novyy mir* travels over the roads of the past, it notices only the traces of mistakes and not the evidence of the people's unparalleled achievements. It can offer its readers nothing but mournful, and at times frightening, edification. . . . The editors of *Novyy mir* pass heroism and romance by. Furthermore, the journal never misses a chance to poke fun at and even mock works published in other organs of the press where an attempt, albeit sometimes unsuccessful, is being made to affirm a heroic theme and depict a heroic character. The literary critics working on *Novyy mir* quite often elevate works which one-sidedly depict difficult

---

138 D.R. Spechler, *Permitted Dissent in the USSR: Novy Mir and the Soviet Regime* (New York 1982), provides a close analysis.

situations in our past, the various 'tight corners' or our 'back yard'. Instead of revolutionaries and fighters these critics put at centre stage characters damaged by fate, people with disturbed psyches and morals, and socially passive, open 'anti-heroes'. The critic V. Lakshin has devoted many pages in the journal to defending such positions. . . . What is now most typical of the journal *Novyy mir* is an excessive emphasis on the negative, suspicion about depicting positive phenomena and a stubborn defence of mistaken positions.

[Source: *Pravda*, 27 January 1967.]

In his response, Tvardovsky insisted that he remained firmly loyal to Marxism–Leninism. In championing the finest work, he claimed, *Novyy mir* demonstrated its faith that Soviet society could afford to look the truth square in the face and was thus more faithful to the spirit of Lenin than were its attackers. And in bringing to light the greatest Soviet authors, it was bringing glory to the USSR. In the following speech at a meeting of the secretariat of the Soviet Writers' Union, he reminded his critics of the role the journal had played as far back as Stalin's last years in power, when it published the boldest sketches to appear in that era, V. Ovechkin's *Local Daily Life*. He tried to make them admit their admiration for Akhmatova, who had been given her due in Khrushchev's day through the efforts of the journal. And far from retreating, Tvardovsky pressed for the re-issue of long-suppressed works by Bulgakov, and for the publication of those of Pasternak that had never appeared in the USSR.

Document 209 | **A. Tvardovsky's speech defending *Novyy mir* at a meeting of the Union of Soviet Writers' Secretariat**

15 March 1967

In fact, what *is Novyy mir*? What sort of journal is it? On the one hand, it is obvious that at least two-thirds of those works which have recently attracted the greatest interest among readers, and comprise an inalienable part of what society is justifiably proud of in our literature, have appeared in the pages of *Novyy mir*. That seems like a good thing. A leading Soviet journal worthy of all kinds of approval.

On the other hand, this journal's activities are characterized as vicious and slanderous, both in the press and in public pronouncements (there are examples of this, and such speeches have been published).

You often hear the phrase '*Novyy mir*'s line', by which they mostly mean a line which is bad, vicious and contrary to our Party's line in literature. The general implication is that the very presence of a line is something sinful, contraindicated for a Soviet journal.

I think there is a conceptual confusion here. We have a single Party line in literature, obligatory for all journals and newspapers. But a journal's line is a particular, concrete expression of the Party line, it is the journal's identity, formed from the totality of its ideological and aesthetic predilections and principles. A journal without such a line is something characterless and indiscriminate in terms of the form and content of what it publishes, i.e., a grey journal, of which, unfortunately, we have enough.

Novyy mir openly expresses its ideological and aesthetic partiality and sees the strange reproach that it 'pushes its own line' as praise. To 'push one's own line' means having principles and sticking to convictions acquired from that teaching which is all-powerful because it is true.

It has always been obvious to me that in the realm of aesthetics, Marxism–Leninism has a penchant for realism, truthfulness to life, and for penetrating the complexity of reality as it actually is, not just as it might be represented, for one can influence reality by truly seeing reality itself, not a schema standing in for it. . .

Yes, we hold to the line of realism and the truthful reflection of reality, and are true to the great legacy of classic Russian literature, which presented the world with unsurpassed exemplars of realistic art.

. . . We know that it is precisely by being so exacting and so irreconcilable to vacuous hack-work that we win our readers' approval and sympathy. If we are talking about what *Novyy mir* sees as its starting point, then we can point to Ovechkin's *Local Daily Life*, published in 1952, which was the first in Soviet literature to touch on poor conditions in agriculture and the inadequacies of the collective-farm management of that time.

As we know, this material, the starting point for the 'line' of *Novyy mir*, engendered a new wave in our literature and a whole array of such talents as Dorosh, L. Ivanov, Mozhaev, Yu. Chernichenko and others.

I would like to share one more gloomy observation. If one opens *Novyy mir*, *Moskva*, *Literaturnaya Rossiya*, one comes across bits and pieces of Zoshchenko, Platonov, Bulgakov or Anna Akhmatova. Let's be honest, all of these are names we know. It is a good thing that in her final years Anna Akhmatova did hear herself well spoken of in her own country and died knowing that she was a Russian poetess, while the others we buried, but are now publishing selected bits and pieces by them. And just fifteen years have passed, not a hundred. The same is true concerning Pasternak and Bulgakov. Why should the fates of writers in our country follow this same dismal pattern, albeit different from the fates of those writers of 1937? Why do we have to bury them before we can publish bits of them?. . .

[Source: *Oktyabr'*, No. 8, 1990, pp. 180–82.]

Stalin's role and reputation continued to be central to the struggle over the boundaries of the permissible. Brezhnev and his colleagues upheld the call Khrushchev had made in his last years in power for a halt to further attacks on the dictator, and from the mid-1960s conservative voices adopted a markedly more positive tone about him. Much of the response from those appalled at any attempt to rehabilitate Stalin paralleled Tvardovsky's approach. To condone Stalin's monstrous crimes, they protested, was the surest way to blacken the reputation of the party and demoralize the USSR as it strove to build a true and just socialist order. The following striking letter of September 1967 was sent to the Central Committee by the children of famous victims of Stalin, including N.I. Bukharin, two other leading Bolsheviks of 1917, V.A. Antonov-Ovseenko and A.G. Shlyapnikov, and the prominent military commander executed along with Tukhachevsky in 1937, I. Yakir.

Document 210 | From a letter sent to the CPSU CC by surviving children of communists repressed under Stalin

24 September 1967

At the present time Stalin's 'services' are being trumpeted from rostra, in the press, and on the radio and television. This is in effect going back on the resolutions of the 20th and 22nd CPSU Congresses.

We are worried by this, and not just because our parents and we ourselves, like millions of others, were victims of the criminal machine created by Stalin. It is painful to realize that at one time masses of cruelly deceived people were induced to approve his arbitrary rule. This must not happen again. The revival of the past is striking a blow at the ideas of communism, discrediting our system and presenting the destruction of innocent millions as natural.

Any attempt to whitewash Stalin's black deeds bears within it the danger of repeating a terrible tragedy for our Party, people and the whole communist movement.

. . . We ask you to bear the above in mind and look upon our letter as a component part of the struggle for communism. We hope that this letter will contribute to averting a mistake which cannot be corrected.

P. Yakir
L. Petrovsky
A. Antonov-Ovseenko
Yu. Larin-Bukharin
Yu. Vavilov
A. Boky
I. Shlyapnikov and others (43 signatories in all)

[Source: *Istochnik*, No. 2, 1994.]

Likewise, in extending their appeals beyond the USSR, it was initially to foreign communists that the voices of protest turned, consistently underlining that they were true patriots and presenting their critique as coming from loyal adherents of the same ideological community. The following address sent to an international meeting of communist leaders in Budapest in spring 1968 listed the growing measures of repression against those who spoke out—public trials, police intimidation, imprisonment, internal exile, withdrawal of rights, and, most sinister, incarceration for psychiatric treatment.

Document 211 | **From a letter of protest to the Presidium of the Conference of Communist Parties in Budapest**

30 April 1968

A number of political trials have been held in our country in recent years. The essence of these trials is that, in contravention of basic civil rights, people have been tried for their beliefs. That is why these trials have involved crude violations of legality, most importantly, an absence of openness.

The public is no longer prepared to put up with such lawlessness, and this has led to indignation and protests, increasing with each trial. A large number of individual and group letters have been sent to various legal, government and Party bodies, up to and including the CC of the CPSU. These letters have remained unanswered. The answer to the most active protesters has been sacking, a summons to visit the KGB and the threat of arrest and, finally, the most disgraceful form of reprisal—forced incarceration in a psychiatric hospital. These illegal and inhuman actions cannot bring any positive results. On the contrary, they heighten tension and cause more indignation.

We consider it our duty to point out that there are several thousand political prisoners in camps and prisons nobody knows about. They are held in inhuman conditions of hard labour on semi-starvation rations and left to the whim of those running the camps and prisons.

Having served their time, they are subjected to extra-judicial and often illegal persecution such as restrictions on their choice of place of abode and police supervision, putting free people in the position of exiles.

We also wish to draw your attention to instances of discrimination against small nations and the political persecution of people struggling for national equality—a particularly glaring example being the Crimean Tatars.

We know that many Soviet and foreign communists have frequently expressed their disapproval of the political repression of recent years.

We ask the participants of this consultative meeting to weigh up the danger which the flouting of human rights is causing our country.

Signed by:
Aleksey Kosterin, writer
Larisa Bogoraz, linguist
Pavel Litvinov, physicist
Petr Yakir, historian
Viktor Krasin, economist
Il'ya Gabay, teacher

[Source: *Mif o zastoe* (Moscow and Leningrad 1991), p. 144.]

Spring 1968 also saw the appearance of the first number of what was to establish itself as the best-known regular *samizdat* publication, *Chronicle of Current Events*.[139] The *Chronicle* adopted the standard dissident platform: its purpose was not to undermine but to uphold the Soviet Constitution and Soviet law. It proclaimed itself legal: that it could only be circulated in secret was, it insisted, because the regime itself was breaking the law. And its method was simply to record, with as much precision and detail as possible, cases where the Soviet regime had flouted the constitutional and legal rights of its own citizens.

Protest against the invasion of Czechoslovakia, 1968

The event that drove a committed core of those operating on the borderline of the regime's rules into open dissent was the Soviet invasion of Czechoslovakia and repression of the Prague Spring in August 1968 (see documents 141–143). It triggered a flurry of protest and also rudimentary efforts to rouse wider popular support. Two of the signatories of the April 1968 letter to Budapest, L. Bogoraz and P. Litvinov (grandson of the Soviet foreign minister of the 1930s), were among a small group of men and women who boldly staged a demonstration at the Place of Execution on Red Square with banners denouncing Soviet intervention. The KGB's swift response is described in a letter which one of the demonstrators, Natal'ya Gorbanevskaya, sent to several foreign newspapers, including one in Czechoslovakia: the Soviet Embassy in Prague hastily sent the text to Moscow.

---

139 See M. Hopkins, *Russia's Underground Press: The Chronicle of Current Events* (New York 1983).

Document 212 | **Protest against the occupation of Czechoslovakia**

August 1968

. . . A whistle blew almost immediately and plain-clothes KGB men ran towards us from all corners of the square: a Czechoslovak delegation was expected in the Kremlin, which is why they were keeping watch there. They ran towards us shouting, 'They're all yids! Let's beat up these anti-Soviet elements!' We sat there calmly and offered no resistance. They tore the banners out of our hands. They smashed Viktor Faynberg's face in and knocked some of his teeth out. Pavel Litvinov was hit across the face with a stout stick. They tore the Czechoslovak flag out of my hands and smashed it. They shouted at us, 'Clear off, you scum!', but we just sat there. Very soon some cars raced up. They chucked everybody in, except me. I had a 3-month-old son, which is why they didn't take me straightaway. I sat by the Place of Execution for about another ten minutes.

I was beaten in the car. . . My friends and I were happy that we were able to take part in this demonstration, albeit briefly stem the flow of unfettered lies and cowardly silence, and show that not all the citizens of our state agreed with the violence perpetrated in the name of the Soviet people. We hope that the Czechoslovak people know or will know about this. And we believe that the Czechs and Slovaks won't think of the Soviet people only as invaders, but will think of us as well. Such a belief gives us courage and strength.

[Source: *Izvestiya*, 1 August 1992.]

Although hostility to intervention in Czechoslovakia was common among members of the cultural intelligentsia, there was no substantial, overt response from among them, and it is doubtful that anti-government sentiment extended much further. The following secret report was sent to the Central Committee on 21 August 1968, the day of the invasion, by V. Grishin, secretary of the Moscow party committee. It suggests that although there were some expressions of dissent among non-intellectuals, they were not widespread even in the capital, and there is no indication of working-class protest.

Document 213 | **Moscow City report on reactions to the invasion of Czechoslovakia**

August 1968

In order to acquaint the broad mass of workers with the TASS declaration more than 9,000 meetings were held in factories and institutes. They were attended by about 885,000 people, and some 30,000 workers, technical staff and other white-collar employees spoke at them. Those who spoke at them expressed their full support for the domestic and foreign policy and actions of the CC of the CPSU and Soviet government. . .

However, in some research institutes there were speeches made against the measures taken by the Soviet government and the governments of the fraternal countries. For example, in the automatic equipment research institute, the senior scientist and Candidate of Technical Sciences Andronov, non-Party, declared that he could not understand who in Czechoslovakia—and in whose name—was asking for help from the Soviet Union and other countries, and suggested that voting on the resolution of the general staff meeting be put off until the situation was clarified. His speech was condemned by the participants at the meeting.

Some people are expressing unhealthy and sometimes hostile attitudes in private conversations. For example, Torstensen, a producer at the Central Television Studio and not a Party-member, said, 'Our actions don't tie up with declarations about non-interference in Czechoslovakia's internal affairs.'. . .

Similar assertions were made in conversations by Petrov, an engineer at the state experimental agricultural institute, Sidorova, a surgeon at Hospital No. 16, Afanas'ev, a kiln operator at the vacuum glass institute (all non-Party). . .

[Source: *Izvestiya*, 1 August 1992.]

Five of the participants in the Red Square demonstration were tried and in October convicted both for slandering the USSR and, under new articles of the Criminal Code introduced to make it easier to ensure convictions against dissidents, for disturbing the peace.

Document 214 | From the notes of the lawyer D.I. Kaminskaya on the case against P. Litvinov and others

October 1968

. . . The formulation of the case brought against the accused: 'The investigation has ascertained that Pavel Litvinov, who does not agree with the policy of the CPSU and Soviet government on rendering fraternal assistance to the Czechoslovak people in defence of their socialist achievements, approved by all the workers of the Soviet Union, did enter into a criminal conspiracy with the other accused in this case (K. Babitsky, L. Bogoraz, V. Faynberg, V. Delone, V. Dremlyuga, N. Gorbanevskaya) to organize a group protest against the temporary entry of the troops of five socialist countries into the CzSSR.

'He prepared banners on which were written fabrications known to be false, slandering the Soviet state and social system, namely, 'Hands off the CzSSR! For your and our freedom! Down with the invaders! Free Dubček! Long live a free and independent Czechoslovakia!' (in Czech). At midday on 25 August of this year he went to the Place of Execution on Red Square, where, together with the above-named, he took part in a group action which crudely disturbed the peace and the normal flow of traffic: he unfurled the above banners and shouted out slogans of similar content, thus committing the crimes stipulated in Articles 190/1 and 190/3 of the Criminal Code of the RSFSR.'

Testimonies in court:
Konstantin Babitsky, 'Since I considered that the entry of Soviet troops into Czechoslovakia would above all be detrimental to the prestige of the Soviet Union, I thought it necessary to bring this conviction to the notice of the government and people. That is why I went to Red Square at midday on 25 August... I went there fully aware of what I was doing and of the likely consequences.'

Pavel Litvinov, 'On 21 August Soviet troops crossed the Czechoslovak border. I consider these acts of the Soviet government to be a gross violation of the norms of international law... the verdict which awaits me is obvious. I knew what this verdict would be in advance, when I went into Red Square. Nevertheless I went into the Square. For me there was no question of not going.'

[Source: *Znamya*, No. 8, 1990.]

In protest against the sentence, ninety-five people, the great majority of whom were intellectuals now crossing the line into the ranks of dissidents, addressed the following letter to the deputies of the Supreme Soviet of the USSR and that of the RSFSR, with copies to the editors of *Izvestiya* and *Sovetskaya Rossiya*, albeit without any hope of publication.

Document 215 | **Letter of protest against the sentence of P. Litvinov and others**

October 1968

On 11 October 1968 the Moscow city court sentenced Konstantin Babitsky, Larisa Bogoraz, Vadim Delone, Vladimir Dremlyuga and Pavel Litvinov.

These are the five who took part in a demonstration in Red Square on 25 August 1968 against the entry of troops into Czechoslovakia. Their participation in a peaceful demonstration and their attempt to express their protest in this constitutional manner were characterized as a 'crude disturbance of the peace'.

Their slogans 'Long live a free and independent Czechoslovakia! For your and our freedom! Hands off the CzSSR! Down with the invaders! Free Dubček!' were characterized as 'fabrications known to be false, slandering the Soviet state and social system'.

We believe that a sentence known to be unjust was passed on the demonstrators. This sentence is retribution for the open and public expression of their convictions. We believe that there were absolutely no legal bases for instituting a criminal case.

Citizen Deputies of the Supreme Soviet! We are not dealing [merely] with the scandalous procedural violations committed by the court and the investigation, but with something more important. There has been a violation of the civil rights guaranteed by the Soviet Constitution: freedom of speech and assembly. It is your duty to defend these freedoms. This is why we are asking you to intervene and insist on the quashing of the sentence and the discontinuance of proceedings in the absence of *corpus delicti*.

[Source: *Rodina*, No. 4, 1990, p. 19.]

On the anniversary of the invasion of Czechoslovakia, a group of dissidents, including Gorbanevskaya, who had not been imprisoned for the Red Square demonstration, P. Yakir, who was closely involved in the launch of the *Chronicle of Current Events*, and P. Grigorenko, a former major-general who was to become a prominent dissident figure, addressed the leadership with the following further letter of protest.[140]

Document 216 | **Letter of protest against the invasion of Czechoslovakia and the unjust verdict on P. Litvinov and others**

August 1969

A tragic event took place on 21 August last year: Warsaw Pact troops invaded friendly Czechoslovakia.

The purpose of this act was to block the democratic path of development this country had taken. The whole world was following the post-January development of Czechoslovakia with high hopes. It looked as if the socialist idea, discredited in the Stalinist period, would now be rehabilitated. The tanks of the Warsaw Treaty countries crushed these hopes. On this sad anniversary we declare that we still do not agree with this decision, which threatens the future of socialism.

We are in solidarity with the people of Czechoslovakia, who wanted to show that socialism with a human face is possible.

These lines are dictated by our feeling of pain for our country, which we wish to see truly great, free and happy.

We are absolutely convinced that a people cannot be free and happy if it oppresses other peoples.

P. Yakir, L. Petrovsky, G. Pod"yapol'sky, N. Gorbanevskaya, M. Dzhamilev, L. Ternovsky, P. Grigorenko, I. Gabay, V. Krasin, S. Kovalev, A. Levitin-Krasnov, T. Baeva, Yu. Vishnevskaya, N. Emel'kina, L. Plyushch, I. Yakir, A. Yakobson.

[Source: *Rodina*, No. 4, 1990, p. 19.]

---

140 P.G. Grigorenko, *Memoirs*, transl. T.P. Whitney (London 1983), provides an evocative first-hand account of the emergent dissident movement.

Thus the invasion of Czechoslovakia pushed a small but vocal number of intellectuals into illicit activity. Both among them and among the larger number who resisted stepping beyond the limits laid down by the regime, there was now much greater pessimism about achieving any significant reform within the existing order, and for them the language of Marxism–Leninism rang more and more hollow.

At the same time, those who longed to see firmer measures taken against work they regarded as corrosive of Soviet values took heart. Tvardovsky's critics kept up a steady barrage of attacks on *Novyy mir*. In 1968 they succeeded in heading off its attempt to publish Solzhenitsyn's *Cancer Ward* and in 1970 they finally succeeded in dislodging the editor himself. Yet the disillusionment of innovative intellectuals reflected their frustration at censorship and at the KGB preventing them extending further the boundaries of the permissible rather than the success of die-hards in their efforts to roll those boundaries firmly back. The obstacles to achieving the latter proved formidable. Because of the potential for leading writers to publish in the west or circulate their work through *samizdat*, blanket suppression was liable to be counterproductive. The rapidly expanding number and range of specialist journals, in pure and applied science as well as social sciences and the humanities, made it increasingly difficult for the Central Committee apparatus to deploy the necessary expertise to cut off lines of discussion and access to western work without stultifying valuable Soviet scholarship. And with the steady expansion in the size and sophistication of the educated public, there was a strong incentive for the regime to avoid any drastic action that might alienate a significant proportion.[141]

The Solzhenitsyn affair

That both sides could simultaneously feel themselves losing ground was shown, for example, in the furore over Solzhenitsyn's nomination for the Nobel Prize for literature in July 1970. The Cultural Section of the Central Committee assembled a raft of suggestions about how to prevent this potentially embarrassing celebration of a writer recently expelled from the Soviet Writers' Union and now regarded as viciously anti-Soviet. By the time these proposals reached the Central Committee Secretariat, however, Solzhenitsyn had been awarded the prize. The Secretariat did not react by preventing Solzhenitsyn from accepting the prize, as had happened to Pasternak in Khrushchev's early years, still less by arresting him as might have

---

141 On the gathering pace of intellectual exchange within legal bounds, see M. Lewin, *The Gorbachev Phenomenon: A Historical Interpretation* (London 1988).

happened a decade earlier than that. Instead it felt able to do no more than adapt the Cultural Section's spoiling action to launch a propaganda barrage, at home and abroad, in an attempt to discredit the award as inspired not by any literary merit of Solzhenitsyn's but by the malign machinations of anti-Soviet forces.

Document 217 | **Note from the CPSU CC Cultural Section to the CPSU CC Secretariat on measures to prevent A.I. Solzhenitsyn from being awarded a Nobel Prize**

9 October 1970

This July a number of French intellectuals from the *Art and Progress* association (the writer Armand Lanoux, the film director René Clair, the sociologist Raymond Aron et al., some fifty in all) put forward A. Solzhenitsyn's name for a Nobel Prize in 1970.

The organizers of this proposal have sent letters to many writers and artists all over the world, including the USSR, asking them to support the nomination of A. Solzhenitsyn.

Such a letter was received, for example, by comrade Mikhalkov, the Secretary of the USSR Writers' Union, who sent a reply to the *Art and Progress* association which stressed that he saw their action as 'another political provocation directed against Soviet literature which had nothing at all to do with a real concern for the development of literature'. . . .

Comrades Markov and Voronkov, Secretaries of the USSR Writers' Union, comrade Udal'tsov, chairman of the *Novosti* Press Agency, and representatives of certain other bodies have put forward a number of proposals which might prevent A. Solzhenitsyn from being awarded a Nobel Prize. The following measures are suggested:

a) A small amount of material could be placed in the Soviet press which would show the public that A. Solzhenitsyn's nomination has a political, rather than a literary, character, supported as it is by confused or openly anti-Soviet circles. Material published in No. 8, 1970, of the White [Guard] journal *Chasovoy* might be particularly useful for this purpose.

b) Have the *Novosti* Press Agency (comrade Udal'tsov) prepare, distribute abroad and broadcast on our overseas radio services a group interview with representatives of Soviet public opinion (writers, academics, teachers, workers, etc.) on this topic.

c) Use the trip of comrade B.L. Suchkov (Director of the Gorky Institute of World Literature) to France to make personal contact with prominent French writers and explain the position of the USSR Writers' Union on the works and public behaviour of A. Solzhenitsyn.

d) Perhaps the Soviet ambassador to Sweden should be instructed urgently to clarify and provide detailed information on the situation within the Nobel Committee in connection with the nomination of A. Solzhenitsyn, and make his own suggestions.

e) If necessary, the Soviet ambassador to Sweden could also be instructed to make a verbal unofficial representation to the Swedish government, explaining that Soviet public opinion regards the intention of the Committee to award the prize to A. Solzhenitsyn as an unfriendly act which could complicate the development of links between the writers of our countries.

f) Have the Soviet ambassador to France appeal to our friends there with a request to take any possible measures to neutralize the propagandist campaign in support of A. Solzhenitsyn among sections of the French intelligentsia.

[Source: *Istoricheskiy arkhiv*, No. 1, 1992.]

Document 218 | **The CPSU response to Solzhenitsyn's Nobel Prize—from Minute No. 112 of the Secretariat of the CC of the CPSU**

9 October 1970

Top Secret

Agree with proposals below in the note from the CPSU CC Department of Culture and Department of Propaganda.

M. Suslov, CPSU CC Secretary.

On measures in connection with the provocative act of awarding the 1970 Nobel Prize for literature to A. Solzhenitsyn.

9 October 1970

On 8 October this year the Nobel Committee (Stockholm, Sweden) awarded the 1970 Prize for literature to A. Solzhenitsyn with the words: 'For the ethical force with which he is developing the priceless traditions of Russian literature.' As we know, Solzhenitsyn has been nominated for that prize in previous years as well.

The works and behaviour of A. Solzhenitsyn have long been used by bourgeois propaganda for anti-Soviet purposes. Awarding him the Nobel Prize is intended to develop that campaign further.

The following would be expedient:

1. To publish in the Soviet press (*Izvestiya, Trud, Komsomol'skaya pravda, Literaturnaya gazeta*) a brief announcement from the USSR Writers' Union Secretariat explaining that the Nobel Committee's action has a political, rather than a literary. character. The USSR Writers' Union Secretariat announcement could take the form of an answer to a question from an *Izvestiya* correspondent.

2. To publish a long article in *Literaturnaya gazeta* exposing the nature of the political speculation around the name and work of Solzhenitsyn in the West.

3. To instruct the USSR Council of Ministers State Committee for Radio and Television (comrade Lapin), and *Novosti* Press Agency (comrade Udal'tsov) to

prepare and distribute to foreign countries by the appropriate channels the necessary propaganda materials concerning the decision of the Nobel Committee.
4. To inform the leaders of local Party committees verbally of the provocative nature of awarding a Nobel Prize to A. Solzhenitsyn.

CPSU CC Cultural Department
CPSU CC Propaganda Department

[Source: *Istoricheskiy arkhiv*, No. 1, 1992.]

Amongst Solzhenitsyn's admirers, on the other hand, there was furious indignation at the campaign against him. To them what was striking was not that the regime did not dare to prevent him accepting the prize, or that he remained at liberty to continue writing with every prospect of publishing in the west, but that his name was being blackened. In the following letter sent to the Soviet press but not published, his close friend Rostropovich, the world-famous cellist, likened Solzhenitsyn's critics to participants in the *Zhdanovshchina* in the late 1940s and to those who had persecuted Pasternak a decade later; he scorned those who had called for Solzhenitsyn's expulsion from the Writers' Union as 'cat's paws' of the regime; and he denounced the shadowy pressure repeatedly brought to bear against numerous creative artists (including his wife, the soprano Galina Vishnevskaya) of whom the authorities disapproved.

Document 219 | **From an open letter by Mstislav Rostropovich to the editors-in-chief of the national newspapers in defence of Solzhenitsyn**

31 October 1970

Dear Comrade Editor,

It is an open secret that A. Solzhenitsyn spends most of his time in my house near Moscow. I witnessed his expulsion from the Writers' Union just when he was working hard on his novel *1914*, and now he has been awarded the Nobel Prize and there is a newspaper campaign around this. It is the latter that has impelled me to write to you.

As I recall, this is the third time a Soviet writer has received the Nobel Prize. On two occasions out of the three, we regarded the award of the prize as a sordid political game, and on the other occasion (Sholokhov) as a just recognition of the leading world importance of our literature. If Sholokhov had refused to accept the prize from the same hands that had awarded it to Pasternak 'for Cold War reasons', I could understand that we continue to mistrust the honesty and objectivity of the Swedish academicians. It now turns out that we are selective about it: we either accept the Literature Prize gratefully or we heap abuse on it. And what if it is awarded to comrade Kochetov next time? We shall have to accept it, won't we? Why is it that only a day after the prize was awarded to Solzhenitsyn a strange article appeared in our papers about a conversation between an unnamed correspondent and a representative of the Writers' Union Secretariat, claiming that all public opinion (i.e., apparently all academics, all musicians, etc.) actively supported his expulsion from the Writers' Union? Why does *Literaturnaya gazeta* tendentiously select from a multitude of Western newspapers only the utterances of some American and Swedish communist ones, studiously avoiding such incomparably more popular and significant communist papers as *l'Humanité, Lettres Françaises, l'Unità*, not to mention the numerous non-communist ones? If we believe some critic called Bonosky, what about the opinions of such major writers as Bell, Aragon, François Mauriac?

I can remember, and would like to remind you of, our papers in 1948 and of all the rubbish that was written about people now recognized as giants of our music, such as S.S. Prokof'ev and D.D. Shostakovich, e.g., 'Comrade D. Shostakovich, your atonal music is organically alien to the people. . .' Has time really failed to teach you to be a bit more careful about crushing talented people? That you should not speak for the whole people? Not to force people to express an opinion on something they patently have not read or heard about? I proudly remember not attending a meeting of cultural figures at the Central Artists' Building where B. Pasternak was being reviled and my speech, wherein I was 'authorized' to criticize *Dr Zhivago*, was noted—even though I still had not read it out.

Back in 1948 there were lists of forbidden works. Verbal warnings are now preferred, saying that 'the opinion is' that publication is not recommended. Where this opinion is, and by whom it is held, we never find out. For example, why was G. Vishnevskaya forbidden to perform Boris Chaykovsky's brilliant song cycle based on I. Brodsky's poetry at her concert in Moscow? Why on several occasions have barriers been put in the way of performances of Shostakovich's cycle with words by Sasha Cherny, even though the texts were published in our country? Why have there been strange problems associated with the performance of Shostakovich's 13th and 14th symphonies? That 'opinion' again, it would seem. Who was of the 'opinion' that Solzhenitsyn should be expelled from the Writers' Union? I have not been able to find out, although I have been very interested in the matter. It is highly unlikely that five Musketeer-writers from Ryazan' would have done it off their own bat—without the mysterious 'opinion'. It looks like 'opinion' has prevented my compatriots seeing Tarkovsky's *Andrey Rublev*, which we have sold abroad and I had the good fortune to see among delighted Parisians. And again it is obvious that 'opinion' has blocked the publication of Solzhenitsyn's *Cancer Ward*, although it had already been typeset to appear in *Novyy mir*. If it had been published here, that is when it should have been openly and widely discussed for the benefit of readers and writers. . .

Everyone should have the right to think and speak independently and without fear about what they know, have personally thought through or experienced, and not just feebly regurgitate received 'opinion'. We must move towards free discussion without being prompted or silenced.

I know an 'opinion' about me is bound to follow this letter, but I am not afraid and will openly say what I think. Those talents, of which we should be proud, must not be subjected to a prior drubbing. I know a lot of Solzhenitsyn's works, like them and think he has earned the right to write the truth as he sees it, and see no reason to hide my attitude to him when there is a campaign going on against him.

Mstislav Rostropovich.

[Source: *Izvestiya*, 13 April 1992.]

Although the increasingly pronounced Russian Orthodox and nationalist motifs in Solzhenitsyn's work limited his appeal among dissidents, his fame and the power of his protest against Soviet repression drew foreign attention to the growing dissident current and increased the concern of the authorities. The following 'top secret' report was written at the end of 1970, by Andropov, head of the KGB since 1967. Andropov recognized that the self-styled 'democratic movement' had a core of activists in the major cities and that, though it had little formal organization, through *samizdat* it had the potential to grow. He outlined the police measures being taken to contain the problem and advocated careful thought on how to limit the spread of *samizdat*. He drew particular attention to the ideas and influence of A.D. Sakharov, a leading nuclear physicist and member of the Academy of Sciences renowned for his work on the Soviet atomic project. The previous month, Sakharov had founded a 'Human Rights Committee' and advocated legalizing opposition, thereby challenging the core principle of Marxism–Leninism: the monopoly role of the CPSU.

Document 220 | From a KGB report on dissidents

21 December 1970

Top secret

Documents propounding various theories of 'democratic socialism' are being distributed among the scientific, technical and part of the creative intelligentsia. According to the schema of one of these theories of 'democratic socialism', the author of which is academician Sakharov, the evolutionary path of the USSR's internal political development is bound to lead to the creation of a 'truly democratic system' in the country. To this end mathematicians and economists must draw up in good time a model which will be a synthesis of all the positive aspects of currently existing sociopolitical systems.

The 'limitation or abolition of the CPSU's monopoly of power and the creation of an opposition loyal to socialism' are envisaged in a number of schemes for the 'democratization' of the USSR. Their authors and disseminators, believing that the present level of development of socialist democracy permits the existence of opposition views, are demanding to be granted legal means to express their disagreement with the official line. They accordingly declare the criminal legislation which punishes people for anti-Soviet agitation and propaganda and for the dissemination of knowingly false fabrications which denigrate the Soviet state and social system to be unconstitutional.

The preparation and dissemination of *samizdat* is bringing together like-minded people, and attempts to create some sort of opposition are being carefully watched.

Round about the end of 1968 and beginning of 1969 a political core known as the 'democratic movement' was formed from opposition elements. They believe that their movement has three characteristics of an opposition: 'Although it does not adopt definite forms of organization, it has leaders and activists, relies on a significant number of sympathizers, sets itself specific aims and has chosen a specific tactic in striving to operate legally.'

The main tasks of this 'movement', as set out in No. 13 of the *Chronicle of Current Events*, put out by the Moscow group of the 'democratic movement' led by Yakir, include 'democratization of the country by inculcating democratic and scientific convictions in people, resistance to Stalinism, self-defence against repression, and struggle against any kind of extremism'.

The centres for disseminating uncensored materials remain, as before, Moscow, Leningrad, Kiev, Gorky, Novosibirsk and Khar'kov. We have uncovered in these and other cities about 300 people who style themselves 'anti-Stalinists', 'fighters for democratic rights' and 'participants in the democratic movement'. They put out both individual documents and collections.

The KGB is taking the necessary steps to stop the attempts of certain people to use *samizdat* to spread libel against the Soviet state and social system. They are being prosecuted under existing legislation, while preventative measures are being taken against those who have fallen under their influence.

At the same time. . . it would be expedient to have the ideological apparatus, after having studied the problem, come up with the necessary ideological and political measures to neutralize and unmask the antisocial tendencies represented in *samizdat*, as well as some suggestions for taking account, when devising policy, of the factors which facilitate the appearance and distribution of *samizdat* materials.

Andropov, Chairman of the KGB

[Source: *Istochnik*, No. 2, 1994, pp. 75–76.]

Andropov's figure of 300 was only a fraction of the number of activists at the time, and during the early 1970s networks of dissenters were growing fast, *samizdat* output expanding, and interaction with the west giving opposition circles hope.[142] In 1971, the major dissident historian Roy Medvedev succeeded in publishing abroad a devastating account of Stalin's rule, *Let History Judge*. Western criticism of the regime's repression of dissidents intensified, and demands grew for progress on détente to be dependent on improvements in the Soviet record. In 1974 the US Congress even made this a condition for the ratification of a major trade agreement. In 1975, stimulated by the Helsinki Accords (see document 145) and the Soviet Union's public commitment to the human rights affirmed there, 'Helsinki Watch Groups' were set up in several cities.

Yet, despite the moral grandeur of their protest, the dissidents were unable to shake the regime's stability and indeed in the later 1970s, especially within the RSFSR, their movement lost momentum. Notwithstanding contemporary expectations and the claims of some western historians,[143] they failed to make more than a very limited impact on public opinion in the USSR. This is not to deny the widespread fall in respect for the leadership in the 1970s and early 1980s; the popular lampooning of Brezhnev and his ageing colleagues; the growth in cynicism about the privileges of the *nomenklatura* and the level of corruption in every official hierarchy; the evidence of friction and frustration as slower economic growth restricted upward social mobility and intensified competition for resources; or the decline in the conviction carried by Marxism–Leninism. But the potential for opposition to gather momentum that these trends created makes the very modest impact of the dissidents all the more striking.

No doubt part of the explanation must be sought in the legacy of Stalinist repression and the recurrent assaults mounted against the dissidents by Andropov. Between 1972 and 1974, the KGB launched repeated drives to arrest key activists, broke up the lines of dissident communication, and disrupted the flow of *samizdat* material, for some eighteen months silencing altogether the flagship *Chronicle of Current Events*. At the same time, a significant toll on the vitality and optimism of the movement was taken by many leading figures being driven into exile abroad. The signal for this change in tactics was the announcement of Solzhenitsyn's deportation in 1974.

---

142 Optimism was echoed by western commentators: see, for example, P. Reddaway, *Uncensored Russia: The Human Rights Movement in the Soviet Union* (London 1972).

143 See, for example, G. Hosking, *The Awakening of the Soviet Union* (Cambridge, MA, 1990); R.V. Daniels, *The End of the Communist Revolution* (London 1993); R. Pipes, *Communism: The Vanished Spectre* (Oxford 1994).

Document 221 | **Decree of the Presidium of the USSR Supreme Soviet on the deprivation of citizenship and expulsion of A.I. Solzhenitsyn from the USSR**

12 February 1974

Solzhenitsyn has been systematically perpetrating acts incompatible with citizenship of the USSR and has been inflicting damage on the USSR by his hostile behaviour. The Presidium of the Supreme Soviet of the USSR accordingly resolves as follows: in conformity with Article 7 of the USSR Statute of 19 August 1938 *On Citizenship of the Union of Soviet Socialist Republics*, Aleksandr Isaevich Solzhenitsyn, born 1918 in Kislovodsk, shall be stripped of his citizenship and deported from the territory of the USSR for actions bringing the title 'citizen of the USSR' into disrepute.

[Source: *Svobodnaya mysl'*, No. 6, 1992.]

The action provoked scattered protest not only from prominent disaffected artists and intellectuals in Moscow and Leningrad but from humbler folk in the provinces. The first of the two letters below addressed to the Presidium of the Supreme Soviet came from a village in Voronezh *oblast'*, in southern Russia. Though unpolished, the author, P.P. Laptev, was evidently well-read, contrasting the regime's action unfavourably even with the manner in which in the mid-nineteenth century Nicholas I's notoriously repressive autocracy treated Nekrasov and Gogol for their unwelcome works. The second, by G.V. Dubchenko, advances a carefully reasoned argument for allowing Solzhenitsyn to make the case in public for his own defence.

Document 222 | **Letters of protest to the Presidium of the USSR Supreme Soviet**

1. *To the Presidium of the USSR Supreme Soviet*

17 February 1974

Dear Members of the Presidium,

This is about the repressions being inflicted on a former front-line soldier and artillery captain, the writer Solzhenitsyn.

Before trying to find out why he should deserve such harsh repression, we should remember a similar case, also concerning a writer, Pasternak. He got persecuted in the same way for the fact that his novel *Doctor Zhivago* got published abroad. . . And when the book came out and he got the Nobel Prize as well, then so much persecution was launched against him that it was suggested that he might leave the country. What for? Because he went and published abroad and bypassed the Writers' Union. But, in the end, what harm did his book really do to our state? What was all the fuss about? No harm was done at all, no state or military secret was leaked, there were no calls for war, etc. So I don't really know what he did wrong. The same sort of thing's happened with Solzhenitsyn. Because I've not been able to get my hands on anything else, I've read only his little story *One Day in the Life of Ivan Denisovich*. Well, what can you say about it? It's based on real material and was at that time put forward for a Lenin Prize because it's so true to life. But I gather that he's in trouble because he's supposed to have written that Prague was taken by Vlasov's lot, so he's now been lumped in with them. Come on, accusers, you shouldn't do things like that... He did use some kind of material and didn't just make it up... In short, Solzhenitsyn's not some 20-year-old kid who's taken liberties; he's based it all on some kind of material and sources, so it can be discounted only by facts and not just by labelling him a traitor—that's too harsh an accusation... He wrote about the camps because he saw what it was like himself, and he did it so it won't happen again. The radio commentator Zhukov attacks him for it, saying that the Party put things right ages ago, but he wrote what he did so that lawyers and the Party *would* do so, and Solzhenitsyn was one of the many who were rehabilitated. But now there are new attacks on him. If our publishers turned his manuscripts down, then, as I said before, he's got every right to publish wherever in the world he pleases... To resort to such extreme and harsh measures—that is the unconstitutional ruining of one of my countrymen... They didn't resort to such measures even in the time of the autocracy. Neither Nekrasov for *Who Can be Happy and Free in Russia?* nor Gogol for *The Government Inspector* got stripped of their Russian citizenship, did they? No, brothers, we can't live like that. It's bad enough that the Writers' Union's turned into some sort of extra-constitutional outfit that can give orders to writers outside that union, but you let it persecute them as well. And not just him, but his family as well. What for?... You are doing the wrong thing, citizens of the top Party bodies! Your actions are unacceptable! If you can't guarantee constitutional freedoms, and worse still you go around persecuting people, then stand aside for somebody who will guarantee them. Shame on you! Solzhenitsyn must be rehabilitated.

P.P. Laptev
17 February 1974
Arkhipovka village
Rossoshansk district
Voronezh *oblast'*

2. *To*: the Presidium of the Supreme Soviet of the USSR
   From: G.V. Dubchenko, citizen of the USSR

22 February 1974

I, G.V. Dubchenko, citizen of the USSR, worker and member of the CPSU, cannot support the decree of the Presidium of the USSR Supreme Soviet to strip A.I. Solzhenitsyn of his citizenship and deport him from our country. I think that a person who has citizenship of our country by birthright cannot be stripped of it just because he has his own views on certain processes in the life of our society and does not hide them from other people. And anyway, I do not think that it should be done on the whim of the government alone. I can neither condemn nor support Solzhenitsyn because I have had the opportunity to hear only the accusers' side and, like the overwhelming majority of Soviet people, have been deprived of the opportunity to hear what the accused has to say. If A. Solzhenitsyn has slandered the Soviet people, then the people should be given the chance to get to know the content of this slander, demand an answer from the writer, and pass sentence themselves. The government's present actions make you wonder what it is trying to hide from the people.

I think that in Solzhenitsyn's case, like in any court, the accused should be given the right to defend himself before any sentence is passed, and the whole Soviet people should be the ones to judge him.

In view of the above I propose that:

1. A.I. Solzhenitsyn should be given the chance to return to the Soviet Union.
2. Extracts from his work, with appropriate annotations, should be published.
3. He should be given the chance to set out his position on the television, radio, and in the press.
4. There should be broad consideration of the case of A.I. Solzhenitsyn, and, in the event of divergent opinions, discussion on the television, radio, and in the press.
5. A decision about the case of A.I. Solzhenitsyn should be made on the basis of the free expression of the people's will.

I think that the measures I have proposed will lead to a strengthening of the USSR's international prestige. . . and of its leading bodies among the Soviet people, resulting in an increase in the people's political activity.

[Source: *Svobodnaya mysl'*, No. 6, 1992, pp. 82, 83.]

The limits of dissent

Many other leading creative artists emigrated voluntarily, frustrated by Soviet restrictions and no longer hopeful of early reform. Though detrimental to its international image, the regime welcomed the dampening impact on dissident activity and morale at home, and did all it could to portray the émigrés as traitors to the Motherland colluding with 'White Guard' émigré circles and journals from an earlier age. In 1978, for example, Rostropovich and Galina Vishnevskaya, who had been living in the west, were deprived of their citizenship and right to return.

Document 223 | **The deprivation of citizenship of M.L. Rostropovich and G.P. Vishnevskaya**

March 1978

Having left the Soviet Union several years ago on a trip abroad, M.L. Rostropovich and G.P. Vishnevskaya have shown no intention of returning, have engaged in unpatriotic activities and have besmirched the Soviet social system and the title 'citizen of the USSR'. They have systematically rendered material assistance to subversive anti-Soviet centres and other organizations abroad hostile to the Soviet Union. For example, they gave several concerts in 1976–1977, the proceeds of which went to benefit White émigré organizations.

Although formally remaining citizens of the Soviet Union, Rostropovich and Vishnevskaya have essentially become ideological degenerates, engaging in activities directed against the Soviet Union and the Soviet people.

Taking into account the fact that Rostropovich and Vishnevskaya have been systematically engaging in activities detrimental to the prestige of the USSR and incompatible with holding Soviet citizenship, the Presidium of the Supreme Soviet of the USSR has decreed, on the basis of Article 7 of the USSR Statute of 19 August 1938 *On Citizenship of the USSR*, that M.L. Rostropovich and G.P. Vishnevskaya be stripped of USSR citizenship for actions besmirching the title 'citizen of the USSR'.

[Source: *Izvestiya*, 16 March 1978.]

The exiled couple's appeal to Brezhnev for an open trial of their supposed offences went unpublished and unanswered.

Document 224 | **From the appeal by G. Vishnevskaya and M. Rostropovich to L.I. Brezhnev**

1978

Dear Chairman of the Presidium of the USSR Supreme Soviet,

The Supreme Soviet of the USSR, of which you are the head, has deprived us of our Soviet citizenship. . . We are musicians. We live and breathe music. . . You know as well as anybody else that our only 'crime' was that we gave refuge in our house to the writer Aleksandr Solzhenitsyn. For this, with your sanction, we were subjected to all sorts of persecution, which we found impossible to tolerate—cancellation of concerts, a ban on foreign concert tours, a boycott on the radio, television and in the press, and an attempt to paralyse our musical activities.

On three occasions, while still in Russia, Rostropovich appealed to you for help: once by letter and twice by telegram, but neither you nor any of your subordinates even replied to our heart-felt cries.

In this way, you obliged us to apply for an extended trip abroad, and this was done in the form of an official trip on behalf of the USSR Ministry of Culture. But clearly our tears in our homeland were not enough for you. You got at us even here.

We are now being morally shot in the back on fabricated charges and deprived of our citizenship—all in your name as 'fighter for peace and human rights'.

. . . We demand to be tried at any time and anywhere in the USSR, but under one condition—that the trial be open.

We hope that you will reply to this, our fourth, appeal to you, but, if not, may you at least blush with shame.

M. Rostropovich, G. Vishnevskaya

[Source: *Mif o zastoe* (Leningrad 1991), pp. 394–95.]

From the following year, the pressure on dissidents within the USSR was again stepped up. In January 1980, action against Sakharov, long urged by the KGB, was taken and he was exiled to the backwater of the city of Gorky. The leadership had been reluctant to incur the international opprobrium bound to follow sanctions against the scientist, and the timing of the action, shortly after Soviet troops invaded Afghanistan and amidst the international uproar that followed, probably reflected the regime's view that relations with the west were now so badly soured that further friction mattered little. Internal exile did not prevent Sakharov from publishing abroad the following appeal to Brezhnev to halt Soviet military action. And at the end of the letter he appended the core dissident demand that the regime uphold the civil liberties denied ever since the Bolshevik revolution.

Document 225 | From A.D. Sakharov's open letter to L.I. Brezhnev on Afghanistan

1980

I am writing to you on a matter of extreme importance—Afghanistan. As a citizen of the USSR and because of my position in the world, I feel a responsibility for the tragic events which are taking place. I am fully aware that your point of view is based on information available to you (which must be immeasurably greater than mine) and in accordance with your position. Nevertheless, the question is of such import that I beg you take this letter and the opinion expressed in it seriously.

Military actions in Afghanistan have been going on for seven months now. Thousands of Soviet people and tens of thousands of Afghans have been maimed or killed; the latter are not only partisans but mainly civilians—old people, women, children, peasants and townspeople. More than a million Afghans have become refugees. Reports about the bombing of villages aiding and abetting the partisans and the mining of mountain roads, thereby threatening hunger to whole regions, are particularly ominous. . .

Nor is there any doubt that events in Afghanistan have changed the political world. They have struck a blow against détente and have created a direct threat to peace not only in this region but everywhere. They have hampered (and perhaps made completely impossible) ratification of SALT II, vitally important for the whole world, especially as a precondition for future phases of the disarmament process. Soviet actions have contributed to (and how could it be otherwise!) increased defence budgets and the adoption of new weapons programmes by all the major powers, which will have repercussions for years to come and increase the danger from the arms race. At the UN General Assembly, Soviet actions have been condemned by 104 states, including many which hitherto unequivocally supported any actions by the USSR.

Within the USSR itself the destructive hyper-militarization of the country is intensifying, which is particularly damaging in economically difficult conditions; vitally important reforms in the social and economic spheres are not being implemented; and there is a strengthening of the dangerous role of the organs of repression, which could get out of control.

I do not intend to analyse the reasons for sending Soviet troops to Afghanistan in this letter—was it brought about by real defence interests or was it part of some other plan? Was it an expression of unselfish help with land reform and other social changes or was it interference in the internal affairs of a sovereign country? Perhaps there is a grain of truth in all of these suggestions. . . I am convinced that a political settlement involving the following actions is necessary:

1. The USSR and the partisans cease military action and conclude an armistice.
2. The USSR declares that it is prepared to withdraw its troops completely and have them replaced by UN troops. This will be a very important action by the UN in accordance with the aims proclaimed at its founding and the resolution of 104 of its members.
3. The neutrality, peace and independence of Afghanistan are guaranteed by the Security Council through its permanent members and, perhaps, the countries neighbouring Afghanistan.
4. The member countries of the UN, including the USSR, should offer political asylum to any citizen of Afghanistan wishing to leave. One of the conditions of the settlement should be unfettered right of exit.
5. Afghanistan is to be given aid on an international basis to preclude its dependence on any one country; the USSR should assume some of this burden.
6. Prior to elections Babrak Karmal's government is to transfer its powers to a Provisional Council, created on a neutral basis with the participation of representatives of both the partisans and Karmal's government.
7. The elections are to have international monitors; members of Karmal's govern-

ment and the partisans are to participate on the same basis. . .

I think I should also bring to your attention another chronic problem. For nearly sixty-three years there has never been political amnesty in the USSR. Free prisoners of conscience, arrested and sentenced for their convictions and non-violent actions. . . Such a humane act on the part of the USSR government would greatly enhance the country's authority, improve the internal situation, assist international trust and bring back happiness to many deprived families. . .

A. Sakharov, Gorky.

[Source: A.D. Sakharov, *Trevoga i nadezhda* (Moscow 1990), pp. 199–201.]

The attrition suffered by the dissident movement continued. In 1982, Sakharov's wife, Elena Bonner, announced that the last of the Helsinki Watch Groups to hold out in the USSR, that in Moscow, was ceasing activity. *Samizdat* persisted and the *Chronicle of Current Events* continued to appear, if more irregularly. But by the mid-1980s the demoralization and loss of momentum seemed undeniable.[144]

If the failure of the dissident movement to make a greater impact reflected the sheer weight of repression against it, it reflected too the resilience of the recipe for rule developed by the regime after the Great Patriotic War. The opponents of the CPSU were able to mobilize only a tiny proportion of the Soviet Union's educated public. Out of some 18 million with higher education by 1985, the number of dissident sympathizers, even by the most generous count, did not exceed some 300,000, of whom perhaps a tenth may have been activists. Unlike almost every significant modern European protest movement, they failed to elicit any powerful echo among the country's large student body. Unlike their opposite numbers in communist Poland, Hungary and Czechoslovakia, they failed to establish contact with, let alone mobilize, substantial social or class constituencies. The contrast could not have been stronger between their isolation and the alliance that the opposition intelligentsia in Poland succeeded in forging with the working class there in the late 1970s and early 1980s. The dearth of economic and social content in the *Chronicle* reflected the wider failure to forge an alternative socioeconomic vision of the future with mass appeal: capitalism had virtually none. They were unable to develop and give popular currency to a discourse to rival that of Marxism–Leninism: the language, ideals and conceptual tools identified in the west with social democracy had in the

---

144 See C.I. Gerstenmaier, 'Dissidents', in H.J. Veen (ed.), *From Brezhnev to Gorbachev: Domestic Affairs and Soviet Foreign Policy* (Leamington Spa 1987), pp. 172–77.

USSR been colonized and virtually exhausted by the regime.[145]

The one dissident current that did gain ground was minority nationalism. While studiously vague about their socioeconomic vision, those who concentrated their protest here and pointed towards the demand for national rights or even nation-statehood did offer a clear political alternative to the status quo. Although independence was a scarcely imaginable goal outside the Baltic region, it was minority nationalists who had most success in engaging a somewhat larger constituency and articulating wider concern among their co-nationals about their culture, traditional religion and historical record and monuments; about competition between their own language and Russian with its status as the second official language; about the remorseless rise in the number of Russians settling in their territory and encroaching on jobs, housing and educational provision; about the damage inflicted on their urban and rural environment; about discrimination against those living outside their 'own' Autonomous or Union Republic. *Samizdat* posters, leaflets, articles and larger texts addressing these issues made headway, and at different moments instances of significant protest flared up.[146]

In 1978, for example, there was a demonstration of some 5,000 people in the Georgian capital, Tbilisi, which persuaded the regime to retreat from a proposal that Russian and other minority languages should be given equal status with Georgian itself. There was intense indignation among Armenians over the Autonomous Region of Nagorno-Karabakh, which, despite their predominance within it, was part of and subordinated to Azerbaijan. Popular resentment was palpable in Kazakhstan over the resources taken by Russians, whose numbers in the Republic almost equalled those of the Kazakhs by the late 1970s. There were repeated, if small-scale, ecological protests in Ukraine and the Baltic republics. In 1980, a petition organized by the Catholic Church in Lithuania for the reopening of a cathedral secured almost 150,000 signatures. The most vigorous of several campaigns over the rights of smaller national groups was the one mounted, with the support of a number of prominent Russian dissidents, by the Crimean Tatars, who had been among those uprooted and exiled in 1944 (see document 116), and, despite Khrushchev's condemnation of the action, not permitted to return to their homeland. In 1977, the following appeal was addressed to the Belgrade Conference on Security and Co-operation in Europe of that year, to the Politburo, to the Supreme Soviet and to the public at large.

---

145 For further discussion, see E. Acton, 'Revolutionaries and Dissidents: The Role of the Russian Intellectual in the Downfall of Tsarism and Communism', in J. Jennings and A. Kemp-Welch (eds), *Intellectuals and Politics: From the Dreyfus Affair to Salman Rushdie* (London 1997), pp. 149–68.

146 Hosking, *Awakening of the Soviet Union*, contains an excellent overview.

Document 226 | **Appeal on behalf of the Crimean Tatars: 'Return what was confiscated and restore what was trampled underfoot'**

1977

On the eve of the 60th anniversary of the October victory let us restore the gains of the October revolution in Crimea, trampled down by the enemies of Soviet power in 1944.

The Russian Empire seized Crimea in 1783, 193 years ago. Empress Catherine II thereby directly set about implementing the Russian Empire's great-power chauvinistic plan of annexation in the south and east of Europe and Asia.

. . . In the course of twenty-four years of Soviet power the number of Tatars in Crimea increased by 220,000, i.e., an average annual natural growth of 2.7%, and the proportion of Crimean Tatars in the total population exceeded 45%.

. . . Leninism and revolution, marking the beginning of a new era on earth, finally put paid to the Imperial plan of 'Crimea without Crimean Tatars' and affirmed a new plan of equality and friendship among peoples—the plan of socialism on earth.

. . . And then on 18 May 1944, 161 years after Crimea's seizure by Russia and twenty-seven years after the victory of the Revolution, her Majesty the Empress Catherine's plan of 'Crimea without Crimean Tatars' was carried out in one night. 422,000 people—children, wives, brothers, sisters, the fathers and mothers of soldiers who were fighting on the front line against fascism—were exiled under the false and insidious pretext of 'betraying the Motherland'.

. . . After eighteen months under the 'special regime', 46.2% of the total number of those exiled perished according to the census data (the documents are kept by the CC of the CPSU). That means around 200,000 lives, of whom over 100,000 were children.

. . . In the name of the unshakeable founding laws of the revolution and socialism, the 20th Party Congress, wishing to stop the violations, expressed the will of the Party, the interests of the peoples of the USSR and the fate of socialism, and demanded the return of the exiled peoples and the restoration of socialist principles in the national question.

. . . In 1967 the CC of the CPSU organized a reception for the plenipotentiary representatives of the Crimean Tatar people. At the reception comrade Andropov, speaking in the name of and on behalf of the Politburo, announced that an extraordinary meeting of the Politburo on the day before had unanimously agreed to the political rehabilitation of the Crimean Tatars. 'Comrades, we know that your people want to return to their homeland and maintain their national integrity, language, schools and culture. Under Soviet law you have every right to seek a complete and final solution to your national question', comrade Andropov said emphatically. Then in September 1967 the Decree and Edict of the Presidium of the USSR Supreme Soviet were issued. These documents admitted that the accusations against and the evacuation of the Crimean Tatars were groundless. The Crimean Tatars were given the right to live anywhere in the USSR on the same basis as anyone else.

Meanwhile in Crimea cemeteries were being smashed and destroyed with axes, pick-axes and crowbars. Detachments were set to work redeveloping the land. They were wiping the history of the Crimean Tatars from the face of the earth. Neo-chauvinism and Ukrainian nationalism are robbing the dead, enriching an annexationist 'archaeology', destroying ancient monuments and preparing the 'literary ground' for creating a 'renewed history' of Crimea. Museums have been pillaged and all the relics of the material culture, art and daily life of the original population looted and destroyed, e.g., the Gasprinsky museum and mausoleum. The same thugs have been through all the museums with the same purpose, but this time using pens, scissors and fire. They have fabricated exhibitions in accordance with the tastes and aims of the thugs of 1944.

From 1967 onwards, the scope and scale of the people's national movement, its legality, its indisputable objective basis as an initiative of the entire people, and the Decree of the Presidium, all changed the nature of the national question. They defined precisely the goal and the means of restoring the national existence of the Crimean Tatars in Crimea.

In accordance with the decree, our people immediately began to flood back to Crimea. In the space of a few months 10,000 people had arrived in their Motherland. This flood demonstrated beyond dispute the baselessness of the decree's assertion that our people had 'put down roots' in their places of exile. Interested parties raised the alarm and, it would seem, quickly received sanction for putting obstacles in our way.

. . . In the documents our people put to the 25th Congress, the fate of the Crimean Tatar people as a result of the events of the 1940s and their consequences were clearly set out. They also contained a detailed exposition of the historical, legal, ideological and economic bases of our national movement for a return to our homeland and set out precise demands:

1. an organized return to Crimea, to our national Motherland, without any restrictions;
2. the return of everything that was confiscated;
3. the restoration of everything that has been trampled underfoot.

. . . Since in this document our people fully reaffirm all the documents of the national movement, we seek, on the eve of the 60th anniversary of the victory of the October Revolution, a resolution to the national question, an organized return of the Crimean Tatars to their native land and the restoration of Crimea's revolutionary achievements, trampled underfoot in 1944 by the enemies of the revolution and socialism.

The appeal was signed by 2,500 people.

[Source: A.P. Nenarokov, compiler, *Nesostoyavshiysya yubiley* (Moscow 1992), pp. 324–27.]

The minority national cause to which dissidents managed to give greatest prominence internationally was that of the Jews. Although the vicious anti-Semitism sponsored by the regime in Stalin's last years was toned down thereafter, popular resentment and discrimination against them, especially in the RSFSR and the western republics, continued unabated. In the late 1960s a trickle of demands for the right to emigrate to Israel grew into a strong current, with numerous small-scale public demonstrations, and some 250,000 Jews secured visas between 1968 and 1980. However, the impact on popular opinion of this campaign was not unhelpful to the regime; it provided the specious grounds on which dissidents could be portrayed as predominantly Jewish; and it contributed to the regime's success in smearing not only would-be émigrés but the movement as a whole as unpatriotic, disloyal and even treasonable. Here as elsewhere, inter-ethnic tension did not necessarily pose a danger to the authorities: in some respects it strengthened Moscow's position as the arbiter between competing minorities and potential protector of smaller minorities outnumbered and discriminated against by the titular majority of each Union or Autonomous Republic. Moreover, signs of minority national assertiveness tended if anything to rally the Russian majority behind the regime, while the manifestly privileged position of Russians in the USSR as a whole minimized the potential for dissidents to play upon Russian nationalism. Thus, while the regime's complacent statements about the harmony between the different nationalities of the USSR concealed considerable friction, even this dissident current posed no visible threat to the power and stability of the CPSU. For most among the elite of each minority, the motivation to uphold the status quo and the party ladder up which they had climbed was too strong.

The regime's success in frustrating the dissident movement bore witness to the resilience and flexibility of the diplomatic, economic, sociopolitical and ideological framework entrenched in Stalin's last years. It had shored up the power of the CPSU and its ageing elite through a period of unprecedentedly rapid international, economic, social and cultural change. And it had done so even though the country's international status had become increasingly embattled; its rate of economic growth had slowed markedly and the technological lag behind the west had widened; and the world that had generated the ideas enshrined in Marxism–Leninism was receding into an ever more distant past.

PART FOUR

CRISIS AND COLLAPSE (1985–1991)

The dénouement of the Soviet story was triggered by the new General Secretary appointed in 1985, Mikhail Gorbachev. He repositioned the USSR internationally. He attempted to accelerate industrial growth and later began to dismantle many of the structures of the command economy. He radically loosened the rigour of censorship and the scope for questioning the verities of Marxism–Leninism. He instigated dramatic reform of the party and of the entire political system, introducing competitive elections both at All-Union level and within each Republic. His confidence that the upshot would be the revitalization of the USSR proved gravely misplaced. The attempt to reform society from above unleashed forces for change which the government proved wholly unable to control. It unhinged the economy, turning stagnation into steep decline. It ignited a cultural and ideological revolution that swiftly stripped the regime of its legitimacy and ruptured the Communist Party. It set off an explosion which ripped apart the Soviet system and fractured the country along the fault-lines of the fifteen constituent Union Republics. The Union of Soviet Socialist Republics, for so long a major fixture in international relations and in the mental furniture of mankind, disappeared into history.

17

The End of the Cold War and of the 'Socialist Commonwealth'

Within seven short years of the death of Chernenko (February 1985), the CPSU had been disbanded and the USSR had ceased to exist. How long the regime might have remained in place had the leadership continued to operate firmly within the framework which had served it so well for four decades after the Great Patriotic War, it is impossible to say.[147] For the initiative behind the dramatic sequence of events which led to its fall came not from below but from above, not from the critics and enemies of the regime but from the new General Secretary appointed in March 1985, Mikhail Gorbachev.[148]

At 54, Gorbachev was the youngest member of the Politburo at the time. Born in 1931, he belonged to the generation that had grown up after the war and been permanently marked by the Twentieth Party Congress in 1956 and the Khrushchev thaw. In terms of his style and education, familiarity with the west and the cosmopolitan outlook of his wife, Raisa, he was very different from his predecessors. Indeed, so sharply did his policies come to diverge from those pursued till then that, in retrospect, it came to seem almost miraculous that such a man could have emerged as leader of the CPSU. Yet

---

147 For agonizing among western scholars over the general failure to predict the imminent collapse of the USSR, see M. Cox, *Rethinking the Soviet Collapse* (London 1998).

148 For highly accessible and cogent thematic coverage of the Gorbachev years, see S. White, *After Gorbachev* (Cambridge 1993). For the most authoritative account of Gorbachev's role, emphasizing the critical difference made by the General Secretary himself, see A. Brown, *The Gorbachev Factor* (Oxford 1996). For a much less sympathetic critique of Gorbachev's approach, see J.F. Hough, *Democratization and Revolution in the USSR, 1985–1991* (Washington, DC, 1997). A readable, eclectic account endorsing the widespread view that any attempt to resist liberal capitalism was doomed is S. Kotkin, *Armageddon: The Soviet Collapse, 1970–2000* (Oxford 2001). The most arresting diary-memoir is that of Anatoly Chernyaev, Gorbachev's assistant from early 1986, *My Six Years with Gorbachev* (University Park, PA, 2000).

in 1985 the lines of continuity between him and his predecessors were strong. He was able to carve so successful a career for himself within the apparatus of the CPSU, being brought from Stavropol' (where he was regional party leader from 1970) to the Secretariat in Moscow in 1978, and promoted to the Politburo in 1979, because of the confidence he inspired in key members of the 'gerontocracy'. The patronage he received from Suslov, Gromyko and above all Andropov would have been unthinkable had there been any question mark over his loyalty to the monopoly power of the CPSU. Moreover, ironically, it was not because he had any intention of abandoning the USSR's superpower status, state ownership, central planning, communist rule or Marxist–Leninist ideology that he embarked on radical reform. Rather, it was precisely because of his conviction that the fundamentals of the Soviet system were robust that he had the confidence to tackle the problems confronting the leadership far more energetically than had his predecessors. He believed the USSR's international status could survive a drastic break with its former combative military posture; that the inherent superiority of its economic system made it possible to achieve much more rapid growth; that the authority and unity of the CPSU were so secure that its effectiveness would be positively enhanced by internal reform and competitive elections; and that the credibility of Marxism–Leninism was sufficient to withstand a sharp reduction in censorship. He was proved wrong on all counts.

Internationally, Gorbachev launched himself into breaking the impasse over arms control. He ordered a freeze on the further deployment of short-range nuclear missiles in Europe; he halted Soviet nuclear testing, without insisting that the US do likewise; he actively sought to reduce every regional tension and curtailed Soviet aid to radical Third World movements; by the end of 1988 he was announcing a major reduction in the size of the Soviet army and number of tanks, and their redeployment to defensive positions in both Europe and Asia. This breath-taking range of measures taken to build western confidence, as well as that of China and Japan, in the benign intentions of the USSR was fully matched by his rhetoric.[149]

The following passage is drawn from the book he published and had translated and disseminated across the world, *Perestroika: New Thinking for our Country and the World*, drawing together the main themes of countless speeches during his first eighteen months in office.[150] He did not repudiate

---

149 For a fine overview of the transformation in international relations, see R.L. Garthoff, *The Great Transition: American–Soviet Relations and the End of the Cold War* (Washington, DC, 1994).

150 For an excellent analysis of the roots of Gorbachev's 'new thinking' amongst reformist intellectuals within the party, see R. English, *Russia and the Idea of the West: Gorbachev, Intellectuals and the End of the Cold War* (New York 2000).

the Marxist–Leninist assumption that the USSR was engaged in long-term competition with the capitalist world, or doubt that it would prevail. But what he emphasized were issues confronting the whole of humanity which transcended that struggle—environment damage, depletion of natural resources, Third World poverty and, above all, the danger of nuclear annihilation.

Document 227 | **Extract on international relations from Gorbachev's *Perestroika: New Thinking for our Country and the World*, 1988**

On the whole, we have long lived in peace. But the current international situation can't be described as satisfactory. The arms race, especially the nuclear arms race, goes on. Regional conflicts are raging. The war danger grows. To make international relations more humane is the only way out—and that is a difficult thing to do. This is how we pose the question: it is essential to rise above ideological differences. Let everyone make his own choice, and let us all respect that choice. And for that a new mode of political thinking is necessary, one that proceeds from realization of the general interdependence and from the idea that civilization must survive. If we reach an understanding on the criteria of such new thinking, we shall arrive at valid decisions for global issues. If political leaders realize that point and implement it practically, it will be a major victory for reason.

When we speak about improving the global situation, we single out two criteria for a realistic foreign policy: consideration for one's own national interests and respect for other countries' interests. That stance is sound and reasonable; one to be defended persistently. We think so and act accordingly.

[Source: Mikhail Gorbachev, *Perestroika* (London 1988), p. 221.]

Two decisions Gorbachev took to win trust abroad were particularly spectacular. The first was to withdraw from Afghanistan, notwithstanding the manifest blow to Soviet prestige that this effective admission of defeat entailed. Soon after coming to office he signalled his eagerness to end the war, cutting the number of Soviet troops there in 1986. Early in 1988, energetically pushing forward international negotiations in Geneva, he set a date for complete withdrawal.

Document 228 | **Gorbachev's declaration on Afghanistan**

8 February 1988

In trying to assist the rapid and successful conclusion of the Afghan–Pakistani talks in Geneva, the governments of the USSR and the Republic of Afghanistan have agreed to set a definite date for the beginning of a withdrawal of troops over ten months. This date has been fixed on the assumption that the settlement agreements will be signed no later than 15 March 1988 and come into force two months later. Should the agreements be signed before 15 March, the withdrawal of troops will be correspondingly earlier.

[Source: *Pravda*, 9 February 1988.]

Gorbachev publicly regretted that the decision to invade had ever been taken and endorsed the vote of censure passed the following year by the newly created Soviet Congress of People's Deputies, elected, as we shall see, in March 1989 (see below, pp. 406–13).

Document 229 | **Resolution of the Congress of People's Deputies of the USSR on the decision to send Soviet troops into Afghanistan**

24 December 1989

1. The Congress of People's Deputies of the USSR supports the political evaluation given by the Foreign Affairs Committee of the Supreme Soviet of the USSR to the decision to send Soviet troops into Afghanistan in 1979 and considers that this decision deserves moral and political censure.

2. The Congress instructs the Constitutional Commission, in preparing a new draft Constitution of the USSR, to take into consideration the proposal on spelling out the basic principles for deciding on the use of contingents of the USSR Armed Forces, as provided for in points 13 and 14 of Article 113 and point 13 of Article 119 of the current USSR Constitution, in connection with drawing up a Statute on the Defence Council of the USSR.

3. The Supreme Soviet of the USSR is to examine the question of setting up a Commission for the affairs of former Soviet servicemen in Afghanistan.

4. The Council of Ministers of the USSR is to be asked to draw up a state programme, aimed at solving the questions connected with arrangements for former servicemen and others who made up the Soviet military contingent in Afghanistan, as well as for the families of those killed in action.

[Source: *Spravochnik partiynogo rabotnika, vyp. 30* (Moscow 1990), p. 409.]

Gorbachev's speech to the United Nations, 1988

Gorbachev's most dramatic decision was to permit the eastern European satellites to move out of the Soviet orbit should pressure for that become fierce. This was the apparent implication of his public stance from at least

1986, and of his private remarks even earlier.[151] It was spelled out in a land-mark speech at the United Nations in December 1988. The language in which he couched the decision represented a further departure from the tradition of Marxism–Leninism. The idiom he used was still reminiscent of Marxism, great emphasis being placed on the 'objective processes' at work. But he insisted that what these processes now demanded was that ideology should cease to determine relations between states, and he made clear that when arguing that each country should be genuinely free to pursue its chosen sociopolitical structure he included the states of eastern Europe. In that spirit, he reiterated his commitment to human rights and to the jurisdiction of the International Court at the Hague. He signalled an end to the Soviet practice of 'jamming' foreign radio stations reaching the USSR. He then spelled out a series of arms reductions which, he stressed, were not dependent on the international talks proceeding in Vienna, but would be implemented unilaterally. As part of an overall cut in manpower and arms, 5,000 tanks and a variety of assault forces were to be removed from the three European satellites in which Soviet forces were concentrated, and those that remained were to be rendered 'unambiguously defensive'. Thus Gorbachev solemnly gave notice that he was abandoning the so-called 'Brezhnev Doctrine' which had bound eastern Europe to the USSR for ever, and confirmed that the Soviet government would no longer interfere in these states' internal affairs.

Document 230 | **Extract from Gorbachev's speech to the United Nations, 7 December 1988**

Further world progress is now possible only through the search for a consensus of all mankind, in movement toward a new world order. . .

If we wish to take account of the lessons of the past and the realities of the present, if we must reckon with the objective logic of world development, it is necessary to seek—and to seek jointly—an approach toward improving the international situation and building a new world. If that is so, then it is also worth agreeing on the fundamental and truly universal prerequisites and principles for such activities. It is evident, for example, that force and the threat of force can no longer be, and should not be, instruments of foreign policy. . .

The compelling necessity of the principle of freedom of choice is also clear to us. The failure to recognize it is fraught with very dire consequences, consequences for world peace. Denying that right to the peoples, no matter what the pretext, no matter what words are used to conceal it, means infringing upon even the unstable balance that it has been possible to achieve.

---

151 For Gorbachev's own account of how his expectations regarding the satellites evolved, see *Memoirs*, pp. 464–535.

Freedom of choice is a universal principle to which there should be no exceptions. We have not come to the conclusion of the immutability of this principle simply through good motives. We have been led to it through impartial analysis of the objective processes of our time. The increasing varieties of social development in different countries are becoming an ever more perceptible feature of these processes. This relates to both the capitalist and socialist systems. . .

The de-ideologization of interstate relations has become a demand of the new stage. We are not giving up our convictions, philosophy, or traditions. Neither are we calling on anyone else to give up theirs. Yet we are not going to shut ourselves up within the range of our values. That would lead to spiritual impoverishment, for it would mean renouncing so powerful a source of development as sharing all the original things created independently by each nation. In the course of such sharing, each should prove the advantages of his own system, his own way of life and values, but not through words or propaganda alone, but through real deeds as well. That is, indeed, an honest struggle of ideology, but it must not be carried over into mutual relations between states. Otherwise we simply will not be able to solve a single world problem; arrange broad, mutually advantageous and equitable cooperation between peoples; manage rationally the achievements of the scientific and technical revolution; transform world economic relations; protect the environment; overcome underdevelopment; or put an end to hunger, disease, illiteracy, and other mass ills. Finally, in that case, we will not manage to eliminate the nuclear threat and militarism. . .

We intend to expand the Soviet Union's participation in the monitoring mechanism on human rights in the United Nations and within the framework of the pan-European process. We consider the jurisdiction of the International Court in The Hague with respect to interpreting and applying agreements in the field of human rights should be obligatory for all states.

Within the Helsinki process, we are also examining an end to jamming of all the foreign radio broadcasts to the Soviet Union. On the whole, our credo is as follows: Political problems should be solved only by political means, and human problems only in a humane way. . .

Now about the most important topic, without which no problem of the coming century can be resolved: disarmament. . .

Today I can inform you of the following: The Soviet Union has made a decision on reducing its armed forces. In the next two years, their numerical strength will be reduced by 500,000 persons, and the volume of conventional arms will also be cut considerably. These reductions will be made on a unilateral basis, unconnected with negotiations on the mandate for the Vienna meeting. By agreement with our allies in the Warsaw Pact, we have made the decision to withdraw six tank divisions from the GDR, Czechoslovakia, and Hungary, and to disband them in 1991. Assault landing formations and units, and a number of others, including assault river-crossing forces, with their armaments and combat equipment, will also be withdrawn from the groups of Soviet forces situated in those countries. The Soviet forces situated in those countries will be cut by 50,000 persons, and their arms by 5,000 tanks. All remaining Soviet divisions on the territory of our allies will be reorganized. They will be given a different structure from today's which will become unambiguously defensive, after the removal of a large number of their tanks. . .

[Source: www.cnn.com/SPECIALS/cold.war/episodes/23/documents/gorbachev/]

In the west it seemed hard to credit that the Kremlin would in reality peacefully accept the dissolution of the 'socialist commonwealth', so central was it to established Soviet policy and self-perception. Yet when successive eastern European communist governments were confronted by an upsurge of popular protest, precipitated in part by the momentous changes under way in the USSR, Gorbachev made no move to save them. In the course of 1989, the regimes of Poland, Hungary, Bulgaria, Czechoslovakia and, with more violence than the others, Romania were overthrown.[152] He did not even stand in the way of the GDR being absorbed by West Germany.[153] And in 1991 both the Warsaw Treaty Organization and Comecon were disbanded.

Deeply suspicious though western reactions were initially, and profound though scepticism was about the party's new commitment to abolishing nuclear weapons by 2000, Gorbachev's consistency gradually won western trust. He had four summit meetings with Reagan in rapid succession and established an equally strong rapport with President Bush when he came to office in 1989. Going far beyond the tortuous agreements of SALT I and SALT II, the two sides signed a Strategic Arms Reduction Treaty. And by 1989 arms production was on a downward trajectory.

Document 231 | **Output of the main types of military hardware in the USSR and the USA**

Type	1987		1988		1989	
	USSR	*USA*	*USSR*	*USA*	*USSR*	*USA*
Tanks	3,500	950	3,500	775	1,700	725
ATC	4,450	800	5,250	1,000	5,700	650
Field artillery	2,250	298	2,500	273	1,850	147

---

152 On the wider debacle, see J. Rothschild and G. Stokes, *The Walls Came Tumbling Down: The Collapse of Communism in Eastern Europe* (Oxford 1993).

153 On Soviet decision-making and the critical role played by Gorbachev and Shevardnadze, see A.E. Stent, *Russia and Germany Reborn: Unification, the Soviet Collapse, and the New Europe* (Princeton 1999); the full drama is powerfully conveyed in T. Garton Ash, *In Europe's Name: Germany and the Divided Continent* (London 1993).

(continued)	1987		1988		1989	
	USSR	*USA*	*USSR*	*USA*	*USSR*	*USA*
AAB	100	0	100	0	250	0
Bombers	45	52	45	22	40	0
Fighters/LFAA	700	550	700	550	625	470
Helicopters	450	360	400	340	400	280
ICBM	125	34	150	12	140	9
SLBM	100	0	100	0	100	21
SRM	750	0	650	0	200	0
Long-range cruise missiles	200	170	200	260	200	240
Short-range cruise missiles	110	570	110	380	110	180
Attack subs	7	2	7	3	7	5
Aircraft carriers	0	0	0	0	1	0
Other naval vessels	8	6	9	3	11	4

[Source: S.M. Rogov, 'Tsena pariteta (sopostavlenie oboronnykh raskhodov SShA i SSSR', *SShA: ekonomika, politika, ideologiya,* No. 5, 1991, p. 6.]

The change in the international atmosphere was epoch-making. In the west, Gorbachev was lionized: in 1987 he was named Man of the Year by *Time* magazine and in 1990 he was awarded the Nobel Peace Prize. He had transformed Soviet relations with the rest of the world. Yet in doing so he had dismantled one of the four pillars which, as we have seen, had provided the framework for the rule of the CPSU, for the effect of his initiatives was to destroy the bases on which Soviet foreign policy had rested and on which, since the Great Patriotic War, so much of the party's claim to legitimacy had come to depend. The USSR's superpower status melted away and its military prestige and diplomatic influence declined precipitately. With the disappearance of the 'socialist commonwealth', the claim that Moscow stood at the head of one of two alliances shaping the world ceased to be credible; so, too, did the notion that the forces of 'imperialism' and reaction posed a mortal threat which only the party that had saved the country in the Great Patriotic War could fend off. One of the main threads in the narrative of postwar Marxism–Leninism had run its course.

18

The End of the Command Economy

On the face of it, by initiating what promised to be a steep retrenchment in Soviet defence spending, Gorbachev had achieved one of his central purposes in breaking the impasse of the Cold War, namely to make it possible to liberate resources for the civilian economy. He had apparently freed the USSR from the incubus that had weighed on its economic development since the 1930s, the overriding priority given to and massive scale of military expenditure. Yet, considering how swiftly the rest of the CPSU's system of rule was to fall apart, the impact on the domestic economy was painfully slow. By 1989, when the first substantial reductions began to be made, his economic reforms had not only failed to deliver more rapid growth but had destabilized the second pillar on which the regime's power and authority had come to rest, the command economy.

Initially, Gorbachev's approach to the economy directly echoed that of Andropov.[154] He did not have a ready-made recipe for reform and in his first major speech he explicitly emphasized the lines of continuity running from his immediate predecessors.

Document 232 | **From M.S. Gorbachev's speech to a plenary meeting of the CPSU CC**

11 March 1985

The strategic line developed at the 26th Congress and subsequent plenary meetings of the CC with the energetic participation of Yu.V. Andropov and K.U. Chernenko was and is immutable. This is the line of accelerating the socioeconomic development of the country and improving all aspects of the life of society. It is a matter of

---

154 The most influential account, written as the failure of Gorbachev's economic reforms unfolded, is A. Aslund, *Gorbachev's Struggle for Economic Reform* (revised edn, London 1991).

transforming the material and technological basis of production. It is a matter of improving the system of social relations, especially the economic ones. It is a matter of developing Man himself and of the qualitative improvement of the material conditions of his life and work and of his spiritual cast of mind.

We must try to achieve a decisive shift in the economy onto a path of intensive development. We must, indeed are obliged, to move as quickly as possible to the most advanced scientific and technical positions and to the highest world-class level of labour productivity.

To do this more successfully and speedily, we must continue trying to improve economic mechanisms and the whole management system. In following this route and choosing the optimum solutions, we must creatively apply the fundamental principles of socialist economic management. This involves the unswerving application of the planned development of the economy, strengthening socialist property, broadening rights, increasing the independence and responsibility of enterprises and strengthening their interest in the final results of their work. In the final analysis this means subordinating all economic development to the interests of the Soviet people.

The Party will unswervingly apply the social policy it has developed. Everything in the name of Man and for the good of Man—this programme position must be made deeper and more concrete. We realize that improvements in people's living conditions must be based on their growing contribution to our common cause. If deviations from this principle are permitted, social justice, the most important unifying and stabilizing factor in socialist society, will inevitably be flouted.

[Source: *Kommunist*, No. 5, 1985, pp. 8–9.]

Very much in Andropov's spirit, Gorbachev quickly committed himself to a rapid acceleration (*uskorenie*) in the rate of growth, confident of the command economy's potential to deliver it. The following extract from his speech to a Central Committee plenum in April is characteristic of his style in his early years in office. Alongside conventional emphasis on continuity with his predecessors, he signalled themes on which he would play for years ahead—notably the need to mobilize the 'human factor', the commitment and creativity of individual Soviet men and women. He exuded vigour and dynamism and his tone was of a leader in possession of a clear, highly focused prescription for the economy, pinpointing precisely what must be placed 'at the centre of all our work'. Closer analysis would show—as his critics would complain ever more loudly as the years went by and the economic benefits remained elusive—that this supposed precision and rigour over the selection of priorities turned out to encompass everything, from technological innovation, better management, planning and investment, to 'fundamentally improving the way we do things'.

Document 233 | **From M.S. Gorbachev's report to a CPSU CC plenary meeting**

23 April 1985

Today we are again affirming the continuity of the strategic course worked out at the 26th Party Congress and subsequent plenary sessions of the CC. In its Leninist sense 'continuity' means moving constantly forward, the exposure and solution of new problems, and the removal of everything which hinders development. We must follow this Leninist tradition unswervingly, enriching and developing our Party policy and our general line for social improvement under advanced socialism.

The main question is how, and with what, the country can speed up its economic development. When looking into this problem in the Politburo, we unanimously came to the conclusion that real possibilities for this do exist. The task of speeding up growth rates substantially is definitely feasible, if at the centre of all our work we put economic intensification, the acceleration of scientific and technological progress, the restructuring of management, planning, and structural and investment policy, tightening up organization and discipline all round and fundamentally improving the way we do things.

I think those at this plenary session will support such a conclusion. We can get a comparatively rapid return if we bring our organizational, economic and social reserves into action, and, in the first place, activate the human factor by having everyone working conscientiously and efficiently.

The chief slogans of the moment, which ought to become the leitmotifs of our pre-Congress meetings and all preparations for the 27th Party Congress, are creative labour, unity of word and deed, initiative and responsibility, and being exacting towards oneself and one's comrades.

[Source: *Kommunist*, No. 7, 1985, pp. 5, 7, 13.]

The methods by which Gorbachev's government sought to achieve this accelerated growth were closely in line with those that had been advocated by Andropov. The vast resources tied up in unfinished construction projects would be cut by targeting a limited number for swift completion. A major boost to investment in the machine-building industry would inject technological innovation across the economy. A new quality-control inspectorate, carefully selected and paid so well that, unlike every other Soviet hierarchy, they would resist corruption and the embrace of local elites, would bring to light the disastrously high proportion of products that were defective. To reduce corruption and embezzlement, scandals uncovered would be exposed to massive publicity. To encourage diligence and the acquisition of skills, differentials would be stretched. And, most dramatically, to reduce the heavy toll on work practices and the health services of very high rates of alcoholism, a nationwide campaign was announced to restrict the sale of alcohol.[155]

Document 234 | **From the decree of the Presidium of the USSR Supreme Soviet on intensifying the struggle against drunkenness**

16 May 1985

. . . 2. The consumption of alcoholic beverages at work (in the workplace or on the premises of enterprises, institutions and organizations) or arriving at work in an intoxicated state will entail the imposition of penalties in the form of a fine of between 30 and 50 rubles.

Foremen, heads of sections, shifts and shops, and other managers, who participate in the consumption of alcoholic beverages with their subordinates at work, fail to take measures to remove those found intoxicated from the workplace or attempt to hide instances of subordinates consuming alcoholic beverages or arriving at work intoxicated will be liable to a fine of between 50 and 100 rubles.

Persons committing the offences set out in this article may, in addition to the fine, be subject to disciplinary action. . .

[Source: *Spravochnik partiynogo rabotnika, vypusk XXVI* (Moscow 1986), pp. 617–23.]

The results of these reforms were uniformly disappointing. Not only were the restrictions on alcohol intensely unpopular but after a brief period of adjustment they were in most areas circumvented by soaring rates of illicit distilling. The quality inspectors rejected such a high proportion of output that there was uproar from workers and managers alike, and the authorities retreated from imposing the economic penalties intended. The capacity of the Soviet system—party and state officials, economic managers, workers and citizens—to evade initiatives from the centre frustrated Gorbachev just as it had Stalin, Khrushchev and Kosygin.

Perestroika

From 1987, therefore, Gorbachev played down the goal of instant acceleration and began to attempt more far-reaching 'perestroika' (restructuring). He sought to decentralize economic decision-making and to loosen the control of the planning apparatus and ministries over enterprises. Under a

---

155 For an excellent study, see S. White, *Russia Goes Dry: Alcohol, State and Society* (Cambridge 1996).

Law of State Enterprises introduced with much fanfare on 1 January 1988, Gorbachev gave managers a significant measure of discretion over their own product mix and pricing, and greatly increased the rewards and penalties—including bankruptcy and closure—of exercising this autonomy. He sought to engage the 'human factor', too, by giving workers power to elect managers and a Council of the Labour Collective in each major enterprise which was to be deeply involved in developing and refining the plans proposed by management. During 1987 and 1988, the regime continued to portray economic perestroika as a coherent package that was tapping untold reservoirs of enthusiasm and efficiency. In the following account, Gorbachev proudly listed the measures he saw energizing the economy, characteristically labelling them in the same breath as 'unprecedented' and as 'natural' or 'normal'.

Document 235 | Extract from *Perestroika: New Thinking for our Country and the World*, 1988

I am pleased that there's a growing understanding, both within the Party and in society as a whole, that we have started an *unprecedented* political, economic, social and ideological endeavour. If we are to implement everything we have planned, we must also carry out *unprecedented* political, economic, social and ideological work in both the internal and external spheres. Above all, we bear an *unprecedented* responsibility. And we are aware of the need for large-scale and bold efforts, especially at the first stage.

Many things are unusual in our country now: election of managers at enterprises and offices; multiple candidates for elections to Soviets in some districts; joint ventures with foreign firms; self-financed factories and plants, state and collective farms; the lifting of restrictions on farms producing food products for enterprises and run by them; wider cooperative activities; encouragement of individual enterprise in small-scale production and trade; and closure of non-paying plants and factories operating at a loss; and of research institutes and higher educational establishments working inefficiently; a press that is more incisive, taking up 'taboos', printing a rich variety of public points of view, and conducting an open polemic on all vital issues concerning our progress and perestroika. All that is natural and necessary, although all these things do not come easily, nor are they understood readily both among the public at large and among Party members. . .

[Source: M. Gorbachev, *Perestroika: New Thinking for our Country and the World* (London 1988), p. 66.]

Commentators differ in their assessment of the potential effect of these measures and the extent to which their failure arose from inconsistencies and
errors of policy or insoluble malfunctions embedded in the Soviet system.[156]
What seems certain is that to have had any chance of accelerating the growth
of the Soviet economy, these measures would have needed an extended
period in which to become effective. To make a positive impact, they
required far-reaching cultural and technical change, significant adaptation by
officials and managers, and the emergence of new attitudes and expectations
among workers and consumers. The attempt to bring greater use of market
signals to bear, in particular, necessitated a major reform of prices in order
to bring them into line with costs.

Yet the reforms had scarcely been announced and a start made on
implementing them when the Soviet economy began to unravel. Within a
mere four years of the introduction of the Law of State Enterprises, the
system Gorbachev had inherited had ceased to exist. In part, clearly, the
whirlwind that destroyed the USSR in those years was the result of disruption brought on by the economic reforms themselves. The ministries
attempted to minimize the erosion of their authority and constrained the
options of enterprises. Managers used their limited autonomy to raise prices
rather than innovate or, still less, respond to consumer demand. Workers
voted for those who would protect the status quo and raise wages rather than
experiment or cut costs.[157] The economic tensions at work fed a swelling
budget deficit. Already aggravated by Gorbachev's initial increases in investment, in white-collar wages and in welfare provision and by the loss of excise
revenue through the cut in legal alcohol sales, the deficit was exacerbated
by the wage increases doled out by enterprises and, in 1989, by the government's costly settlement of a rash of miners' strikes. A significant part in
increasing the budget deficit—by 1990 it was ten times what it had been in
1985—was played by the costs that arose from the nuclear disaster at
Chernobyl in 1986, and from the earthquake in Armenia in 1988. With
prices of many basic goods, including food, still controlled, the inflationary
effect of the deficit was dramatic.[158] There was a huge growth in the black
market and alarming shortages developed in one retail sector after another.
Both inflation and the consumer shortages were made considerably worse

---

156 M.I. Goldman, *What Went Wrong with Perestroika* (New York 1991); Aslund, *Gorbachev's
Struggle*; Hanson, *Rise and Fall*.
157 On workers' reactions to the Gorbachev reforms, see D. Filtzer, *Soviet Workers and the
Collapse of Perestroika: The Soviet Labour Process and Gorbachev's Reforms* (Cambridge 1994),
and L.J. Cook, *The Soviet Social Contract and Why it Failed: Welfare Policy and Workers'
Politics from Brezhnev to Yeltsin* (Cambridge, MA, 1994).
158 See Hough, *Democratization and Revolution*, on the significance of the authorities'
profound reluctance to alter retail prices.

by a downturn in the international terms of trade. Oil revenues in particular fell fast in the mid-1980s, which ruled out large-scale imports to plug consumer shortages. Combined with the decentralization of economic decision-making, this in turn triggered a growing trend for individual republics, cities and even factories and collective farms to hoard goods, or insist on direct barter rather than sell for rubles whose value was in steep decline. Vital trading links and the supply of fuel, raw materials, key components and semi-finished goods from one part of the country to another were disrupted and output not only ceased to increase but began to shrink. The following table contrasts official figures with much more sombre independent estimates drawn up by G.I. Khanin.

Document 236 | **The economic development of the USSR: the official data and G.I. Khanin's assessment**

(average annual rates in %)

Average annual indices	Source	1971–75	1976–80	1981–85	1986	1987	1988	1989	1990
National income growth rates	State Statistical Committee	5.7	4.2	3.5	2.3	1.6	4.4	2.5	-4.0
	G.I. Khanin	3.2	1.0	0.6	1.3	0.7	0.3	-4.25	-9.0
Labour productivity growth rates	State Statistical Committee	4.6	3.4	3.0	2.1	1.6	4.8	2.2	-3.0
	G.I. Khanin	1.9	0.2	0.0	1.2	0.8	1.3	-3.95	-8.0

[Sources: *SSSR v tsifrakh v 1990 g.* (Moscow 1991), pp. 40–41; *Kommunist*, No. 17, 1988; *EKO*, No. 4, 1989, pp. 120, 124; *EKO*, No. 1, 1990, p. 79; *EKO*, No. 5, 1991, p. 33; G.I. Khanin, *Dinamika ekonomicheskogo razvitiya SSSR* (Novosibirsk 1991).]

The regime failed to halt this dizzying decline in economic output and financial control. Indeed, rather than make a sustained attempt to stabilize the economy within its traditional framework, the government began from 1989 to abandon that framework altogether. In part this reflected the widening abyss between the expectations Gorbachev had stoked up—and had sincerely shared—first about *uskorenie* (rapid acceleration) and then about perestroika, and the reality of mounting disruption. As the long period of economic stability and (albeit decelerating) growth came to an end, a yawning gulf began to open up between the rhetoric of perestroika and shortages on the shelves.[159] The government's faith in the essentials of the Soviet economy—

---

159 The dramatic decline in living standards for many is explored in W. Moskoff, *Hard Times: Impoverishment and Protest in the Perestroika Years: The Soviet Union, 1985–1991* (Armonk, NY, 1993).

state ownership and central allocation—collapsed. The crisis of confidence in the rationality of central planning, part of the wider loss of faith in Marxism–Leninism, created a virtual vacuum in official Soviet economic strategy and laid it open to the vagaries of western fashion. Whereas three decades earlier it might have been filled by vigorous pursuit of a mixed economy, the intellectual context of the late 1980s ensured that the panacea on which critics of perestroika seized was that of Chicago economics and faith in private enterprise, possessive individualism and the capitalist free market.[160] Rival groups of economists found the government listening to, if hesitant about implementing, proposals for what was labelled 'shock therapy', at the core of which lay removal of all price controls, drastic cuts in public expenditure and wholesale privatization.

---

160 For a revealing example of blithe western free-market fashion of the period, see the commentary by P.J. Boettke, *Why Perestroika Failed: The Politics and Economics of Socialist Transformation* (London 1993).

19

Glasnost

It was in the context of this rapid erosion of two of the pillars on which Marxism–Leninism rested that two more of Gorbachev's closely intertwined reforms unfolded: radical curtailment of censorship and revitalization of politics. His policy of *glasnost* (openness) was prompted by a combination of factors. In the first place, it was becoming ever harder to insulate the Soviet public from foreign sources of information. In any case, to attempt to do so ran counter to his effort to bridge the gap between the USSR and the west. Moreover, secrecy was seen as an obstacle to economic reform and incompatible with greater reliance on local initiative and market relations. Finally, he hoped that more open public discussion would mobilize enthusiasm for his innovations and popular support against what he saw as the self-interested resistance of conservative officials wedded to the unreformed command economy.

From the second half of 1986, Gorbachev actively signalled to editors and writers greater and greater willingness to see taboos of the past broken. A powerful symbol of his commitment to relax restrictions on freedom of speech was his recall of Sakharov from exile in December of that year. The government began to publish social and economic data that had previously been available only to a narrow circle, to open archives which had long been closed, and to permit public debates and opinion polls. Editors, journalists and intellectuals rushed to make the most of the new opportunities opening up, and as one barrier after another was broken and open controversy gathered pace about the past and the present, about the economy, corruption and social problems of every kind, public interest and demand for the most innovative journals and newspapers soared. Long-suppressed works were published, Pasternak's *Doctor Zhivago* and Solzhenitsyn's *Cancer Ward* and *The First Circle* foremost among them. Journalists, playwrights and ordinary citizens raced ahead of most professional historians in recovering the full horrors of collectivization and terror under Stalin.[161] The mass participation in openly articulating repressed memories, grievances and grief amounted to a form of cultural revolution.[162]

The assault on what till 1985 had been orthodoxy did not go unchallenged. Despite Gorbachev's energetic use of his powers of appointment, there was division among the leadership over the pace of reform and the increasingly uncontrollable range of attacks on what was for Marxism–Leninism very delicate ground. Early in 1988 it seemed possible that there would be a sharp application of the brakes. In March a tremendous stir was caused by the publication of and high profile given to an open letter fiercely critical of the direction in which events were moving. It was signed by a Leningrad party member, Nina Andreeva, and manifestly sponsored by senior figures in the party, suspicion fastening on E.K. Ligachev, who ranked second in the Politburo, and V.M. Chebrikov, the KGB chief.[163] The letter was couched in terms of loyalty to the General Secretary, typifying the bind in which Gorbachev's initiatives placed all conservative defenders of Party discipline. Yet in spirit it was deeply hostile. It gave a defiant defence of Stalin himself, and had sinister anti-Semitic overtones, even echoing the synonym for Jew favoured during the *Zhdanovshchina* in Stalin's last years, 'cosmopolitan'. And it explicitly warned that the authority of the CPSU was threatened by the tide of criticism, together with the rapid growth of 'informal organizations' permitted, as we shall see, since 1986. The fact that it was published not only in *Sovetskaya Rossiya* in the capital but in provincial outlets across the country made it plain that it was a shot across the bows of radical voices extending the scope of glasnost.

Document 237 | **Extract from N.A. Andreeva's letter: 'I cannot give up my principles'**

March 1988

I am probably not alone in being struck by the fact that calls from Party leaders for those who specialize in 'revelations' to direct their attention also to real achievements at various stages of socialist construction just bring forth ever more bursts of 'revelation', as if to order.

161 For the transformation among historians, see R.W. Davies, *Soviet History in the Gorbachev Revolution* (Basingstoke 1989).

162 The drama that unfolded is brilliantly evoked in A. Nove, Glasnost' *in Action: Cultural Renaissance in Russia* (London 1989).

163 For Ligachev's bitter rejection of the charge, see E.K. Ligachev, *Inside Gorbachev's Kremlin: The Memoirs of Yegor Ligachev* (New York 1993), pp. 298–311. At the time, however, he made quite plain his support for the sentiments of the letter.

Let us take the question of the place of I.V. Stalin in our country's history. It is with his name that this whole obsession with critical attacks is connected, which I think concerns not so much the historic individual himself as the whole, extremely complex transitional period. A period connected with the unparalleled achievements of a whole generation of Soviet people who are now gradually retiring from activity. Industrialization, collectivization and the cultural revolution, which put our country into the front ranks of the Great Powers, are being forcibly dragged into the concept of 'cult of the personality'. This is all very dubious. It has now gone so far, that 'Stalinists' (amongst whom you can include whoever you want) are constantly being required to 'repent'. . . .

I support the Party's call to defend the honour and dignity of socialism's pioneers. I think that it is from such a Party and class position that we must evaluate the historic role of all the leaders of the Party and country, including Stalin.

The supporters of 'left–liberal socialism' are developing a tendency to falsify the history of socialism. They are suggesting that the only real things about our country's past are the mistakes and crimes, while hushing up the huge achievements of the past and present. Claiming absolute historical truth, they are substituting scholastic ethical categories for the sociopolitical criterion of social development.

Another feature of the 'left–liberal' outlook is an overt or covert cosmopolitan tendency, a sort of non-national 'internationalism'.

The problems of educating the young are being further aggravated by the fact that informal organizations and associations are being created around the ideas of the 'neo-liberals' and 'neo-slavophiles'. It sometimes happens that extremist elements, capable of provocations, become their leaders. In the recent period we have seen the politicization of these independent organizations on the basis of a pluralism which is far from socialist. The leaders of these organizations often talk of 'sharing power' in a 'parliamentary system' with 'free trade-unions', 'independent publishers', etc. All of this, in my opinion, leads one to conclude that the main and cardinal question in all the current discussions in the country is—do we or do we not accept the leading role of the Party and working-class in socialist construction and, therefore, in perestroika? And, of course, with all that this would mean in theory and in practice for politics, economics and ideology.

As M.S. Gorbachev said at the February plenary meeting of the CPSU CC, 'We must act in the spiritual sphere, and possibly first and foremost there, according to our Marxist–Leninist principles. Principles, comrades, which cannot be given up under any circumstances.'

On this we stand and shall stand. These principles were not given to us but hard-won at the great turning-points of our Fatherland's history.

[Source: *Ural'skiy rabochiy*, 25 March 1988.]

The response, however, was swift. Despite the sympathy among several Politburo members for the letter, Gorbachev commissioned his closest ideological ally, A.N. Yakovlev, to draft a clear rebuttal. A fortnight later, this appeared as an authoritative article in *Pravda*, firmly endorsing the public outcry which demanded the condemnation of Stalin and the rehabilitation of his countless victims.

Document 238 | **From a *Pravda* editorial on 'The principles of perestroika: a revolution in thought and action'**

6 April 1988

The figure of Stalin is extremely contradictory. Hence the furious arguments.

If we keep to a position of historical truthfulness, we must see both Stalin's unquestionable contribution to the struggle for socialism and defence of its achievements, and his gross political mistakes and the arbitrary actions committed by him and his entourage, for which our people paid dearly and which had serious consequences for the life of our society. It is sometimes said that he did not know about the acts of lawlessness. He not only knew about them—he organized and directed them. This is now proven fact. The guilt of Stalin and his entourage before the Party and people for the mass repressions and illegal actions is huge and unforgivable.

Yes, every historical figure is formed by concrete socioeconomic and politico-ideological conditions. But the cult was not inevitable. It is alien to the nature of socialism and possible only because of deviations from its basic principles.

We shall firmly and unswervingly follow the revolutionary principles of perestroika: more glasnost, more democracy, more socialism.

The past is vitally necessary for today and for dealing with the tasks of perestroika. Life's objective demand for 'more socialism!' obliges us to look at what we did yesterday and how we did it. At what we must jettison and what we must retain. What principles and values are we to consider truly socialist? If today we are taking a hard look at our history, it is only because we want to map out our future path better and more fully.

Hushing up the painful parts of our history means neglecting truth and showing no respect for the memory of those who were the innocent victims of lawlessness and arbitrary actions. The truth is indivisible. We need complete clarity, precision, consistency and a moral reference point for the future.

[Source: *Pravda*, 6 April 1988.]

At the momentous 19th Party Conference which, as we shall see, Gorbachev assembled that summer to press ahead with political reform, the following formal resolution endorsing glasnost was adopted.

Document 239 | **From the resolution of the 19th All-Union Conference of the CPSU *On Glasnost***

1 July 1988

1. Guided by the interests of socialism and perestroika, the All-Union Conference of the CPSU considers one of its most important political tasks to be the further development of glasnost.

This Conference sees glasnost as a developing process and emphasizes that its consistent extension is a necessary condition for the expression of the democratic essence of the socialist system, its orientation to humanity, and the association of the individual with all the affairs of society, the state and collective as an effective guarantee against the deformation of socialism, on the basis of popular control over the activity of all social institutions, managerial and government bodies.

In glasnost the Conference sees the necessary condition for realizing the socialist self-government of the people and of citizens' constitutional rights, freedoms and duties.

Glasnost in all spheres of life is one of the main conditions for further deepening the processes of perestroika and making it irreversible.

2. This Conference moreover notes that glasnost, the weapon of perestroika, also needs to be deepened and supported. . .

4. We must remove unjustified restrictions on the use of statistical information concerning the socioeconomic and political development of society and the environment, create a system for collecting, processing and disseminating it based on modern information technology, ensure that all types of library are accessible, and create a legal framework for the use of archive material.

5. This Conference considers the suppression of critical articles in the press and the publication of non-objective information denigrating individuals to be unacceptable. Glasnost presupposes the social, legal and moral responsibility of the media.

6. Glasnost must not be used to damage the interests of the Soviet State, society, the rights of the individual, to propagate war, violence, racism, ethnic and religious intolerance, for propagating cruelty, spreading pornography, and to manipulate glasnost itself.

[Source: *Materialy XIX Vsesoyuznoy konferentsii KPSS* (Moscow 1988), pp. 140–45.]

The sixth paragraph of the party's resolution, forbidding the use of the new dispensation to 'damage the interests of the Soviet State' or to 'manipulate glasnost', underlined that this was still less than full freedom of speech. But, with the party leadership coming down firmly in favour of more openness, the momentum lay clearly with those who would push the boundaries ever further. To cajole reluctant members of the Politburo, Gorbachev more than once threatened to resign, and in September Ligachev was demoted and Chebrikov was replaced by V.A. Kryuchkov. Where the fault-line over Stalin was concerned, the weight of the party leadership was thrown on the side of a clear break with the past. During 1988 there had been continual and widespread friction between traditionalist party and KGB officials and local branches of Memorial, a vigorous unofficial organization dedicated to bearing witness to and establishing permanent monuments in honour of the victims of Stalinism.[164] The following resolution, acknowledging the rehabilitation of Stalin's victims as an essential step towards Gorbachev's avowed aim of replacing abuse of power and arbitrary rule with 'a law-governed state', was adopted by the Politburo in January 1989.

Document 240 | **Politburo resolution on undoing injustices to the victims of repressive measures under Stalin**

5 January 1989

Documentary evidence and the experience of rehabilitation acquired in the wake of the 20th and 22nd CPSU Congresses, and quite recently, indicates beyond any doubt that the practice of mass repressive measures and arbitrary actions was pursued in the 1930s–1940s and early 1950s. Criminal behaviour reached its culmination with the establishment of special extra-judicial bodies, the so-called 'Troikas' and 'Special Conferences', and with the drawing up of lists of persons to be subjected to repressive measures.

These practices had tragic consequences for hundreds of thousands of Soviet citizens and an extremely negative effect on the socioeconomic development of the nation. They ingrained in the public mind a disregard for legal standards and human life. Serious damage was done to the progress of Soviet society, the cause of socialism, and the standing of the party.

It is of vast importance now to re-establish historical and legal justice. Progress towards a socialist law-governed state and the development of public consciousness depend to a large extent on this. The relatives of the innocent victims of these repressive measures and the public at large are awaiting their rehabilitation and commemoration.

The CPSU Central Committee Resolves

1. To bring before the Presidium of the USSR Supreme Soviet a proposal that all extra-judicial decisions made in the 1930s–40s and early 1950s by 'Troikas' and 'Special Conferences' be legislatively declared null and void. All citizens victimized by decisions of those bodies shall be considered rehabilitated.

---

164 On Memorial, see J. Devlin, *The Rise of the Russian Democrats* (Aldershot 1995), pp. 118–26.

To acknowledge at the same time that this measure does not extend to those who betrayed their Motherland and served in punitive forces during World War II, to Nazi criminals, members of nationalist bands and those who collaborated with them, to officials who falsified criminal cases, or to persons guilty of premeditated murder or other penal crimes. The above categories of persons shall be subject to the procedures established by the law for appeals, reviews of sentences and the reconsideration of other decisions.

To consider it necessary to speed up the review, as prescribed by law, of criminal cases of persons convicted by judicial bodies during the years of the repressive measures.

To carry out the work of materially reimbursing the rehabilitated persons and notifying their next of kin of their rehabilitation in keeping with prescribed procedures.

To support the proposals of the Soviet public for the setting up, under territorial, regional and city Soviets of People's Deputies and the Supreme Soviet of the autonomous and union republics, of Commissions of People's Deputies and members of the public to assist government bodies in assuring the rights and interests of rehabilitated persons, erecting monuments to the victims of repressive measures, and seeing to the upkeep of cemeteries where they are buried.

To approve the decrees of the USSR Supreme Soviet on this matter.

2. To publish the main points of the present decision of the CC CPSU in the press and to publish it in full in *Izvestiya Tsk KPSS*.

3. To appoint the Government and Legal Department of the Ideological Department of the CC CPSU to monitor the implementation of the present decision.

[Source: *Izvestiya TsK KPSS*, No. 2, 1989.]

On this matter the leadership went much further than Khrushchev could have conceived of doing, and on a whole range of historical, economic and social issues they implicitly called into question more and more of the elements that composed Marxism–Leninism. In the process, they unintentionally not only pushed to the outer limits of what was compatible with the ideology but opened the way for the boundaries to be broken down altogether. In the major cities especially, public and press debate went beyond what even the more tolerant leaders, including Gorbachev himself, could condone. Whereas in 1986 and 1987 those most enthusiastic about Gorbachev's new broom had made maximum use of the flexibility of Marxism–Leninism, calling whenever possible on the authority of Lenin himself to urge expanding the scope of the permissible, by 1989 and 1990 the tide of glasnost had risen far beyond that point. By then more radical voices were not only dispensing with a ritual genuflection in the direction of Lenin and conventional argument over the future direction of the party, but were beginning to damn the CPSU outright and castigate the entire history of communist rule.

The unravelling of Marxism–Leninism

Marxism–Leninism did not evaporate at once. Its inbuilt flexibility enabled party leaders including Gorbachev himself to continue to operate within its discourse right into 1990.[165] Indeed, the legitimacy of the party's political monopoly could not be upheld without recourse to Marxism–Leninism. Yet this third pillar on which the rule of the CPSU had rested was acutely vulnerable to exposure to open intellectual competition, especially at the very moment that two core themes of its narrative had imploded: the military–diplomatic and the economic. By 1991, a vibrant independent press was reporting that the 'socialist commonwealth' of eastern Europe had disappeared. This destroyed the last shreds of credibility for the notion that since 1917 the party had been pioneering a social order destined by history to be imitated by all humanity. The press was also publishing international comparative economic statistics which made a mockery of the party's economic pretensions. The following table, for example, was published in 1991 by *Argumenty i fakty*, the most vigorous of glasnost papers. It suggested that the USSR was a grossly inefficient backwater and that, after seven decades of party rule and Marxist–Leninist-style 'scientific' management of the economy, it was able to provide its citizens with a standard of living which, measured in consumption per head, was barely one-fifth that of the US. Amidst the shortages and mounting financial chaos of that year, the verdict rang all too true.

---

165 See Sandle, *Short History of Soviet Socialism*, for a lucid account.

Document 241 | **Production, consumer goods and productivity in the USSR and the west in 1991**

By volume of production: USA = 100

Country	Gross volume			Per capita		
	GNP	Industry	Agriculture	GNP	Industry	Agriculture
USA	100	100	100	100	100	100
Japan	42	72	42	84	144	82
Germany (unified)	25	41	24	80	133	63
France	19	22	32	84	96	115
UK	16	19	13	68	81	45
Italy	14	15	15	59	67	78
Canada	10	9	12	98	81	100
USSR	38	48	64	30	42	38

Consumption of goods and services, and labour productivity: USA = 100

Country	Per capita consumption	Annual output per employee	
		Industry	Agriculture
USA	100	100	100
Japan	65	90	22
Germany (unified)	70	85	45
France	80	85	56
UK	70	60	56
Italy	60	60	42
Canada	95	90	85
USSR	20	25	9

[Source: *Argumenty i fakty*, No. 26, 1991, p. 4.]

20

Democratization

Gorbachev's moves towards democratization developed in tandem with his adoption of glasnost and for parallel motives: above all, to engage public enthusiasm in economic reconstruction and to counter and expose foot-dragging by party and state officials, whom he considered the supreme obstacle to successful reform. In 1986, he loosened controls over informal discussion groups and clubs, opening the way to a surge of autonomous activity no longer directly controlled by the party. Many 'informals', as these organizations became known, were formed around leisure, sporting and artistic activity, and those which took up causes with clear political implications—the upkeep of historic monuments, the protection of the environment, the status of women—were by no means all of one political coloration.[166] But because perestroika had made their emergence possible, their rhetoric was overwhelmingly supportive of Gorbachev and provided a useful backdrop as he moved to shake up the CPSU itself. At the Central Committee Plenum in January 1987 he launched a remarkable critique of the party's shortcomings and in June 1987 he announced that there would be a special party conference the following summer whose main agenda would be democratization.

Preparations for the conference generated an unprecedented level of political expectation and activity. Within the party, friction over the implications of democratization was acute and began to fracture the long-established Marxist–Leninist convention that, even in periods of intense in-fighting, the public face of unity be maintained. The fact that divisions reached right into the Politburo was made public by the outspoken criticisms of Boris Yeltsin,

---

166 On the informals, see J. Sedaitis and J. Butterfield (eds), *Perestroika from Below: Social Movements in the Soviet Union* (Boulder, CO, 1991).

a flamboyant reformer whom Gorbachev brought to Moscow from Sverd-lovsk soon after he came to power.[167]

As Moscow First Secretary, Yeltsin conducted a high-profile campaign against corruption and became increasingly vocal about the incompetence of party officials and the unjustified privileges enjoyed by the *nomenklatura*. He also began to criticize Gorbachev himself for what he regarded as the unacceptably slow pace of change. Matters came to a head in October at a dramatic meeting of the Central Committee. The meeting was scheduled to consider the content of the public report Gorbachev was due to deliver during the celebration of the seventieth anniversary of the Russian revolution on 7 November. After Gorbachev's long presentation, Ligachev (in the chair) invited questions and was poised to record unanimous, unqualified support when Yeltsin signalled he wished to speak. His speech was unlike any that had been heard from a Politburo member since the 1920s. He attacked Ligachev's manner of running the Secretariat; he bemoaned the unrealistic expectations raised about the pace of perestroika; he criticized what he regarded as an incipient trend towards mindless deference to Gorbachev himself; and he offered his resignation as an alternate Politburo member.

Document 242 | From the Central Committee plenary meeting of 21 October 1987 reprimanding Yeltsin

Yeltsin: The draft reports, both today's and the one for the 70th Anniversary, were discussed in the Politburo, and, considering that I made my suggestions and some of them were taken into account, I have no comments to make on the report today and I fully support it.

Still, I'd like to make a few points, which have arisen in my mind in the time I have been working in the Politburo.

I fully agree that there are very big difficulties in *perestroika* and that a great responsibility and a great duty rest upon every one of us.

I would consider that the prime need is to restructure the work of party committees and of the party as a whole, beginning with the Central Committee Secretariat, as was said at the plenary meeting of the Central Committee in June.

I must say that though five months have passed since then, nothing has changed from the standpoint of the style of work of the Central Committee Secretariat and of comrade Ligachev.

---

167 The best treatment of the political struggle that developed between the two men is G.W. Breslauer, *Gorbachev and Yeltsin as Leaders* (Cambridge 2002). Yeltsin's hastily written and apparently ghosted autobiography, *Against the Grain* (London 1990), conveys something of the deep mutual animosity that came to divide them.

What was said here today, what Mikhail Sergeyevich said about all manner of upbraiding and berating being inadmissible at all levels, which applies to economic bodies or any others, is, in fact, permitted at that very level, this at a time when the party must take a truly revolutionary road and act in a revolutionary way. . . How are we to correct and prevent what happened before? In those days Lenin's principles of our life were simply discredited, and later this resulted in Lenin's principles being largely eliminated from our party's rules of behaviour.

I think what was said at the congress about two or three years of *perestroika*—two years have passed or are coming to an end, and now again reference is made to another two or three years—this misleads people very much, misleads the party, misleads all people, since we, aware of the people's mood, can now feel the undulating attitude to *perestroika*. At first there was enormous enthusiasm, an upsurge, high and strong, including the plenary meeting of the party's Central Committee in January. Then, after the Central Committee's plenary meeting in June, people began to lose some faith, and this worries us very much indeed. The thing is, of course, that these two years have mostly gone into drafting all these documents, which have not reached down to the people, and of course people are worried that they've gained nothing in real terms over this time.

So it would seem to me that this time we need, perhaps, to be more cautious about announcing the time of *perestroika*'s practical results in the next two years. The going is very, very hard of course, and we realise it, and even if the party, precisely the party, and the party committees revolutionise their actions very strongly—and this is necessary—still it isn't going to be two years. And in two years' time we might face the people, I would say, with a reduced prestige of the party as a whole.

I think there is another problem. It's not an easy one, but this is a plenary meeting of the party's Central Committee, of the most trustworthy and frank people, whom one can and should tell everything he has in his soul, in his heart, as a communist.

I must say that the lessons we've learned over 70 years are hard lessons. There have been victories, of which Mikhail Sergeyevich spoke, but there have been lessons too. Lessons of heavy, heavy defeats. The defeats came about little by little because collegiality was missing, because there were groups, because party authority was given to one man, because that one man was fenced off from any criticism whatever.

What worries me, for one, a great deal is that we don't yet have such an atmosphere in the Politburo; recently there have been signs of a definite growth, I would say, of eulogising of the General Secretary by some members of the Politburo, some permanent members of the Politburo. . .

I realise that now this hasn't yet resulted in any definite, inadmissible deformations, so to speak, still there have been some minor signs of such an attitude, and it would seem to me that, of course, this should be prevented in the future.

And the last thing. (Pause.)

It appears I am not succeeding in the Politburo for various reasons. Obviously it is a matter of experience and something else, perhaps, and the lack of some support, especially from comrade Ligachev, and this, I would say, has led me to think that I must raise the matter before you of relieving me of my position and duties as an alternate member of the Politburo. I have handed in the appropriate request, and concerning my duties as first secretary of the city party committee, apparently a full-scale meeting of the city party committee will decide that.

Gorbachev: Perhaps, I had better chair the meeting now.

Ligachev: Yes, please, Mikhail Sergeyevich.

Although Yeltsin had earlier told him of his increasing dissatisfaction and wish to resign, Gorbachev understood Yeltsin to have agreed not to press the issue until after the 7 November celebrations. He was taken aback by Yeltsin's breach of time-honoured Central Committee practice and intensely irritated by the attack. He invited comment and one after another the leading members of the party denounced Yeltsin for the style and the content of his intervention, for his pride and his ignorance, for his disloyalty and his gross ambition. The mood, as well as the continuity in terms of the almost liturgical rhetoric of the working class's loyalty to the party, was brought out by the last of Yeltsin's attackers to speak, Zatvornitsky, a longstanding worker-member of the Central Committee.

Gorbachev: Very well. We'll stop there, comrades. Actually, everything is now clear. If anyone has an opinion differing from the prevailing assessments voiced here, please speak up. With your permission, I am giving the floor to comrade Vladimir Andreyevich Zatvornitsky, a team leader with the Mosstroi No. 1 Trust of the Moscow Construction Administration.

Zatvornitsky: I am no different, I am like you are. But I would like to continue a little. Here we sit, Muscovites. I am a member of the City Committee, I've been a Central Committee member for several five-year terms, and this is what I now recall... We respect you so much, Boris Nikolayevich! With Khrushchev, for instance, we dealt one and a half times more quickly. But here we have such democracy—we keep lecturing you on and on. (Laughter.) We might lecture so much that you will forget in general what all this talk is about, whether you are being criticised or praised. You headed for this rostrum but stumbled. Here is the Politburo. You are an alternate member of the Politburo yourself and you stumbled on purpose, in order to push your comrades. Apparently, you wanted to push through and become a Politburo member. That's my personal opinion.

I respected you very much, Boris Nikolayevich, and I still respect you, but I regret that you stumbled politically so badly today. The working class will never fail the Communist Party, the Central Committee, the Politburo, the Secretariat, and we will always be loyal and committed to you, dear comrades. Thank you.

(Applause.)

Invited by Gorbachev to respond to the avalanche of criticism, Yeltsin qualified his earlier remarks but did not withdraw them. When he reiterated that there was a trend towards eulogizing the General Secretary, albeit now claiming he was referring to 'perhaps two or three comrades', Gorbachev pounced. Making explicit Yeltsin's hint that there were the first signs of a new cult of personality, akin to the notorious adulation of Stalin and, albeit in milder form, of Khrushchev, he browbeat Yeltsin into admission of error.

Gorbachev: Boris Nikolayevich. . .

Yeltsin: Yes?

Gorbachev: It is well known what a personality cult is. It is a system of definite ideological views, a situation characterising a mode of exercising political authority, democracy, a state of legality, an attitude to personnel, to people. Are you so illiterate politically that we must organise elementary school studies for you here?

Yeltsin: No, not any more.

Gorbachev: The whole country is now being drawn into the mainstream of democratisation. And the main thing in the reform is democratisation, for such elements of it as the new economic mechanism, associated with the independence of enterprises and the promotion of initiative, are aimed at helping people come increasingly into their own. That is, in the final analysis, we are talking about the development of democratisation. As for accusing the Politburo of not learning from the lessons of the past. . . wasn't that dealt with in today's report?

Yeltsin: By the way, about the report, as I. . .

Gorbachev: Not by the way. We even had to put off consideration of the report because of the act you put on here.

Yeltsin: No, I spoke of the report first. . .

Voices: You were concerned with yourself. With your unfulfilled ambitions.

Gorbachev: I think so too. And the Central Committee members understood you so. It is not enough for you that Moscow alone revolves around your personality. You also want the Central Committee to concentrate on you? Humour you, right? Comrade Zatvornitsky made a correct comment. Personally, I am upset that he had to tell you that to your face. But I don't regret that the conversation you started has taken place at the plenary meeting. It is a good thing it took place.

Just imagine developing such excessive self-admiration and conceit as to place one's own ambitions before the party's interests and our cause! And this at a time when we are in such a crucial phase of *perestroika.* Just imagine imposing this discussion on the party's Central Committee! I consider this an irresponsible action. The comrades have correctly characterised your show.

Tell us in substance what is your attitude to the criticism voiced.

Yeltsin: I have said what I think of it politically.

Gorbachev: Tell us what you think of the remarks of your Central Committee comrades. They told you many things and must know what you think. After all, they will have to make a decision.

Yeltsin: Except for some expressions, I agree with their assessments on the whole. I let down the Central Committee and the Moscow city organisation by speaking today. It was a mistake.

Voices: He can't. He must not be left in such a job.

Gorbachev: Wait a minute, please. I am asking him. Let us go about this democratically. We all need to hear his answer before making a decision.

Yeltsin: I said I let down the party's Central Committee, the Politburo, and the Moscow party organisation. And, judging from the reaction, unanimous enough, of the members of the party's Central Committee and the Politburo, I repeat what I said: I ask to be relieved of my duties as an alternate member of the Politburo and, accordingly, of the leadership of the Moscow city party organisation.

[Source: *Political Archives of the Soviet Union*, Vol. I (1990), pp. 57–126.]

Yeltsin was removed from the Politburo, and three weeks later he was summoned from his sickbed to be ceremoniously denounced and humiliated before the Moscow city party committee and removed as Moscow First Secretary. The rupture between him and Gorbachev delighted Ligachev, Chebrikov and the more cautious members of the Politburo. But it was a measure of the way in which the undisputed authority of the leadership within the party was beginning to waver that Yeltsin's dismissal did not consign him to permanent obscurity. His outspokenness and challenge to the *nomenklatura*, and the colourful rumours that spread about the showdown in the Central Committee, made him a popular figure, and Gorbachev's moves towards democratization gave his popularity political purchase. Provision had been made for delegates to the conference to be chosen by competitive elections among party members, and politicized 'informals' seized the opportunity, actively campaigning and demonstrating against conservative candidates and working to see the election of bolder critics of the status quo. Although in many areas party officials managed to prevent such competition, there were high-profile cases where they failed to do so. Yeltsin was one of those elected in defiance of the party leadership. In some parts of the country, the local leadership decided to sway with the tide of criticism and permit political mobilization within the party of a kind and on a scale that was unforeseen. Most dramatic was the outcome in the three Baltic republics. There, key party officials quickly judged it wisest to be highly tolerant and in each case a number of different organizations coalesced to form a 'Popular Front' committed to pressing for maximum republican autonomy.[168]

The conference itself fed public ferment and widened divisions within the party. Parts of it were broadcast live, the greatest excitement being generated by a head-on clash between Ligachev and Yeltsin over the explosive issue of *nomenklatura* privileges. Discipline was still sufficiently firm for Gorbachev to dominate the agenda and to secure approval for a far-reaching reshaping of political life. The control exercised by the party apparatus over the legislature, the executive and the economy was to be sharply cut back. Provision was to be made across the country for future elections to local, regional and republican soviets to be competitive. And to oversee the Union as a whole there was to be created a Congress of People's Deputies, which would elect from its number a new Supreme Soviet which, unlike its ineffective predecessors, would actively engage in legislation.

The Congress of People's Deputies

The build-up to the elections to the Congress, held in March 1989, extended much further the political awakening of the previous year.[169] Though party officials in many areas, especially in the countryside, succeeded in preventing competitive elections and in ensuring the return of established local leaders, a significant minority of more radical candidates secured nomination and, in direct competition, defeated local party worthies. Yeltsin, to the exasperation of his critics, was returned in Moscow with close to 90 per cent of the vote. His manifesto, characteristically populist in its attack on officialdom and *nomenklatura* privilege and its demand for immediate improvements in wages, was still within the idiom of Soviet socialism. But it epitomized how deep divisions within the party were becoming.

Document 243 | **Yeltsin's manifesto for the elections to the Congress of People's Deputies, 21 March 1989**

The country's supreme legislative body must express the people's will in the resolution of all fundamental matters and must prevent the adoption of unnecessary and at times even harmful decisions and resolutions. All government, political and public organizations without exception, including the party, must be legislatively accountable to it.

It is necessary to introduce a practice whereby central bodies report to the

---

168 See G. Smith (ed.), *The Baltic States: The National Self-Determination of Estonia, Latvia and Lithuania* (London 1994).
169 See the account in Hough, *Democratization and Revolution*, pp. 140–74.

Congress of People's Deputies and the USSR Supreme Soviet.

The current law on elections is not genuinely democratic. Elections of deputies and chairmen of soviets at all levels must be universal, direct, equal, secret and always contested, including the election of the Chairman of the USSR Supreme Soviet.

It is necessary to create a state–legal mechanism ruling out relapses into authoritarian forms of rule, voluntarism and a personality cult.

It is necessary to struggle against the existing elitist bureaucratic stratum via the transfer of power to elected bodies and the decentralization of political, economic and cultural life.

Legislation must not be anonymous: every draft law and amendment must be attributed to its authors, and those authors must be responsible for it.

A people's deputy must have the right to demand referendums on the most important issues of state life (the building and use of the armed forces, priority avenues of economic and social policy, construction of nuclear power stations and so on).

Concern for man is the main objective of socialism. It is necessary to give even greater priority to a strong social policy and to concentrate all efforts along the three most important avenues: supply of foodstuffs and industrial goods; the services sphere; housing. Larger sums must be appropriated for the solution of these tasks, including by means of reduced appropriations for the defence and other sectors. The implementation of a series of space programmes ought to be postponed for five to seven years. This will make it possible to substantially enhance Soviet people's living standards within two to three years.

Priority in social policy must be given to the socially least protected members of society: low-income families, pensioners, women and the disabled.

Bearing in mind the unjustified stratification of the population according to property criteria, it is necessary to intensify the struggle for social and moral justice. It is necessary to aim for equal opportunities for all citizens—from the worker to the head of state—as regards the acquisition of foodstuffs, industrial goods and services and the receiving of education and medical services. The fourth directorate of the USSR Ministry of Health, which today serves the leaders, should be reorientated to meet the needs of society's socially least protected members. The sundry special rations and special distribution centres must be eliminated. The sole incentive for good work ought to be the ruble, with identical purchasing power for all strata of society.

Only an efficient economy can provide a lasting foundation for a strong social policy. There is a need for a clear-cut scientific programme to improve the economy's health as soon as possible.

Within the framework of this programme

– the slogan 'Land to the peasants!' must be implemented. Land must be transferred under long-term leases. People must choose for themselves the forms of economic management;

– there must be a sharp reduction in the number of ministries and departments and their apparatus must be gradually transferred to full economic accountability. Enterprises must be given an opportunity to withdraw freely from ministries and the right to engage in autonomous economic activity;

– there ought to be a 40% reduction in appropriations for industrial construction and they ought to be excluded from the budget as lacking commodity backing. This ought to result in a sharp reduction of the state's internal debt and stabilization of the ruble's exchange rate.

The solution of economic and social problems is possible only under further development of democracy. The mass media must be given greater independence and a law on the press ought to be adopted defining the duties of press, radio and television workers and protecting their rights. The mass media must depend not on groups of people but on society.

Serious attention must be given to relations between nationalities. All USSR peoples must have de facto economic, political and cultural autonomy.

I share people's anxiety over the acuteness of the ecological problem. It is necessary to adopt a law on ecological responsibility. An ecological map of the country must be drawn up, and an end must be put to industrial construction in regions under ecological pressure, including Moscow.

A number of legislative acts covering young people ought to be adopted. Agreement in principle must be given to the possibility of alternative young people's organizations being created.

Restructuring and democratization must bring revolutionary changes in our society and the struggle for them ought to be waged in revolutionary fashion.

[Source: BBC World Broadcasts, SU 0421 CI, 30 March 1989.]

In each of the Baltic republics, candidates who had the endorsement of the Popular Front inflicted crushing defeat on those without it. Elsewhere, a number of prominent radicals secured seats benefiting, paradoxically enough, from the device whereby one-third of the 2,500 seats were reserved for nominations by key organizations. The party itself was foremost among them, ensuring uncontested seats for Gorbachev and other members of the elite. But this mechanism was also responsible for the inclusion in the Congress of some of the fiercest critics of the leadership. Among them was Sakharov, who had been languishing in exile in Gorky until little over two years earlier, and was now chosen to represent the Academy of Sciences.

When the Congress opened in May 1989, it immediately became clear that Gorbachev's encouragement of political engagement and openness had succeeded beyond his expectations. To popular astonishment and fascination—the proceedings broadcast live on television attracted a massive audience—deputy after deputy spoke out openly. Debate ranged across the board, fierce criticism being hurled at the government on issues political, social, economic, ethnic, cultural, military and diplomatic. The full implications for the party of the process which Gorbachev had set in train now began to become apparent. Party unity, rooted in the ban on factions in force since the Tenth Party Congress (1921) and underpinned by the Secretariat's control over appointments to party posts, was breaking down. The fact that almost 90 per cent of the deputies elected to the Congress were party members no longer guaranteed unanimity or even consensus. During the first two-week-long session of the Congress, the Soviet public saw before their very eyes the monolithic political establishment that was the party openly fracture.[170]

A majority still dutifully and in time-honoured fashion endorsed the proposals made by the General Secretary, who was duly elected Chairman of the standing Supreme Soviet chosen by the Congress. But those who identified themselves as more radical reformers created an 'Inter-Regional Group' of deputies, which included Yeltsin and Sakharov and which pressed for much more drastic changes than Gorbachev envisaged.[171] Central to its campaign for the introduction of fully fledged parliamentary government was the demand, repeatedly made by Sakharov, to revoke the party's monopoly of political power enshrined in Article 6 of the 1977 constitution. In the following draft decree on power, he proposed a range of constitutional changes which would have made the Congress and Soviet effectively sovereign, with the executive headed by a directly elected president. Although the draft did not spell it out, the result would have been to make the party's influence dependent on its success or failure in winning popular endorsement in contested elections.

Document 244 | **From A.D. Sakharov's speech to the 1st Congress of People's Deputies of the USSR**

9 June 1989

Comrade deputies, now—right now—you have an immense historical responsibility. Political decisions are necessary, without which it will be impossible to strengthen the power of local soviets and to solve economic, social, ecological and ethnic problems. If the Congress of People's Deputies of the USSR does not take power into its own hands now, there is not the slightest hope that soviets in the republics, *oblasti*, districts and villages will be able to do so. Without strong soviets in the provinces, land reform and any sort of effective agrarian policy not involving

---

170 See White, *After Gorbachev*, pp. 52–55.
171 On the Inter-Regional Group and the strengths and weaknesses of the 'radical reformers' generally, see Devlin, *Rise of the Democrats*.

pointlessly throwing money at unprofitable collective farms will be impossible. Without a strong Congress and strong independent soviets, it will be impossible to overcome the diktat of government departments, to draw up and implement laws on enterprises and to struggle against ecological insanity. This Congress has been called to defend the democratic principles of people's power and thereby the irreversibility of perestroika and the country's harmonious development. Again I call upon the Congress to adopt this *Decree on Power.*

Decree on Power

Proceeding from the principles of people's power, the Congress of People's Deputies declares:

1. Article 6 of the Constitution of the USSR is abolished.

2. The adoption of laws of the USSR is the exclusive right of the Congress of People's Deputies. In the Union Republics, laws of the USSR acquire legal force only after ratification by that Republic's supreme legislative body.

3. The Supreme Soviet is the Congress's working body.

4. Commissions and committees for drawing up laws on the state budget and other laws, and for permanent supervision of the activities of state bodies and of the economic, social and ecological situation in the country, are to be set up by the Congress and the Supreme Soviet on principles of parity and are answerable to the Congress.

5. The appointment and recall of senior officials of the USSR, namely,

a) The Chairman of the Supreme Soviet of the USSR,

b) The Deputy Chairman of the Supreme Soviet of the USSR,

c) The Chairman of the Council of Ministers of the USSR,

d) The Chairman and members of the Constitutional Inspection Committee,

e) The Chairman of the Supreme Court of the USSR,

f) The Procurator-General of the USSR,

g) The Supreme Arbitrator of the USSR,

h) The Chairman of the Central Bank,

i) The Chairman of the KGB of the USSR,

j) The Chairman of the State Broadcasting Committee,

k) The chief editor of *Izvestiya,*

are the exclusive right of the Congress. The above-mentioned functionaries are answerable only to the Congress and are independent of CPSU decisions.

6. Candidates for the post of Deputy Chairman of the Supreme Soviet and the Chairman of the Council of Ministers of the USSR are to be proposed by the Chairman of the Supreme Soviet of the USSR and, alternatively, by People's Deputies. The right to propose candidates for the remaining posts belongs to People's Deputies.

7. The functions of the KGB are limited to defending the international security of the USSR.

Note: In the future it will be necessary to make provision for direct national elec-

tion of the Chairman and Deputy Chairman of the Supreme Soviet of the USSR
on an alternative vote basis.

9 June 1989

[Source: A.D. Sakharov, *Trevoga i nadezhda* (Moscow 1990), pp. 262–63.]

Six months later, just before the Congress's second session (12–24
December), the Inter-Regional Group not only reiterated its demand for
the repeal of Article 6 but now explicitly called for the formation of opposition parties. It urged the case for formally legalizing their creation, mocking
those who continued to oppose official recognition being given even to
Memorial, which by now seemed a relatively moderate pressure group. The
Group called for those sympathetic to its appeal—whom it characterized as
the 'democratic Left' in contrast to the conservative current within the party
which it dubbed the 'Right'—to coalesce to form a coherent electoral bloc.
And it bemoaned the absence in Russia of an organized political movement
comparable to the Baltic Patriotic Fronts, citing in particular *Sajūdis* in
Lithuania.

Document 245 | From a declaration of the Inter-regional Group of People's Deputies of the USSR on the future of the CPSU

1989

We, the undersigned People's Deputies of the USSR forming the Inter-regional
Group, consider it our duty to the country's electorate, on the eve of the 2nd [session
of the] Congress of People's Deputies of the USSR, to give a concise evaluation of
the current situation from a broad historical perspective, and to put forward a platform which might serve in the foreseeable future as a basis for practical agreed action
by all consistently democratic forces, while maintaining the differences between
them.

As a result of the CPSU leadership's rejection of a neo-totalitarian course, thanks
to the transition to a policy of reform without precedent since October 1917, a
fundamentally new social situation has arisen. It is rich in hopes and opportunities
for doing away with the lack of personal rights, the poverty and the flouting of ethnic
interests and traditions to which we are accustomed. Perestroika is the outstanding
historical contribution of M.S. Gorbachev and his closest supporters.

. . . The first phase of perestroika (from April 1985 until M.S. Gorbachev's speech
in January 1987 at the CPSU CC plenary session) was just a new thaw; the second
phase, in 1987, saw the beginning of glasnost and a rejection of the old politics; the
third phase, beginning in 1988 and ending politically in March–June 1989, was
primarily marked by the appearance of independent social movements, and consequently the emergence of civil society. This ensured the rise of national-liberation

movements, especially in the advanced Baltic States, and the start of the unstoppable collapse of the centralized bureaucratic state. Although this process should, overall, be regarded positively by democrats, it has, however, been unusually painful in Transcaucasia and Central Asia, accompanied in many cases by explosions of inter-communal strife, extreme violence and genocide, to which neither government nor society has been able to find a consistent and effective response.

... The two main crises—the ethnic and the economic—have been growing in geometric progression, frequently interacting with and aggravating each other.

... Straight after the 1st Congress most people are losing or have already lost their trust in perestroika, seeing it predominantly as superficial and as verbiage. Many have become disenchanted even with M.S. Gorbachev. This potentially dangerous crisis of confidence, together with overt dissatisfaction and irritation, has been growing day by day and are colouring the fourth phase of perestroika, which began in spring and summer and unfortunately continues to this day.

The essence of the current phase is, in short, the stagnation of perestroika, the unconditional exhaustion of the resources and forms it had until recently and its halting before genuine structural reform of property and power relations.

The process of perestroika has reached a watershed, the resistance of reactionary apparatus bosses has grown. The indecisiveness of the Gorbachev leadership is under-standable, but mistaken. The remarkable events in Eastern Europe are an example and sufficiently audible warning to those who want to maintain indefinitely the obligatory 'vanguard and leading role of the CPSU', economic ministries, directive planning and the monopoly of the collective and state farming system. Sooner or later we shall need to start dismantling all this.

... This primarily concerns the state and role of the CPSU. As an effective mass political organization the CPSU no longer exists at all. Everybody knows that this is a propaganda function. The only real thing left is its self-reproducing apparatus. One can encounter honest, hard-working and intelligent people within it, but they do not comprise the majority. The main thing is the apparatus, as a system of power over all other power, including state power. It is a structure which is totalitarian in origin and function, and is incompatible with genuine perestroika.

... Getting rid of the shameful Article 6 from the Constitution, and a refusal to accept that the rearguard of the vanguard CPSU should be the eternal official mentor and guardian of society, in no way constitute a demand to remove the Communist Party from the political life of the country.

A genuine multi-party situation is already appearing in the USSR and in this respect 1990 will probably be decisive. It would be wise to legalize this unavoid-able process democratically and in good time. Will those who have hitherto been resisting even the registration of Memorial go this far?

As for the CPSU, its present structures, procedures, composition and very name will not last much longer. In fact, the CPSU is already split. It contains people, on a purely formal basis, who belong to the most extreme opposite shades of the political spectrum and to social movements sharply hostile to one another. We think an open split to be ultimately inevitable, followed by the replacement of the nominal 'CPSU' by maybe two or three real mass political parties in Russia, not to mention the Republican parties which will break away.

As for radical democratic forces independent of the CPSU, the future of perestroika depends to an enormous extent on whether these forces, especially in Russia, can come together in an electoral bloc of several really large, politically distinct movements or parties comparable in their combined size and influence to *Sajūdis* in Lithuania. In Moscow, Leningrad, the Volga region, the Urals, Siberia and the Far East—everywhere there are a lot of democratic fronts, movements, electors' clubs and workers' unions. But on the All-Russia scale they are disunited and feeble; there is no mature, organized democratic Left, although the necessary elements are already basically there.

There can be no normal political life without an opposition. In the abstract this is generally accepted. However, many far from timid, active people are still afraid to count themselves among the opposition, in 'factions', etc. There are usually two reasons for this: not giving the Right a chance to consolidate itself and go on the offensive and not driving away centrist deputies or harming Gorbachev himself.

[Source: *Vek XX i mir*, No. 2, 1990, pp. 42–45.]

21

Nationalism

As it called for the emergence of opposition parties, the Inter-Regional Group recognized that the movements showing much the most dynamism were those based on the minority nationalities—'national-liberation movements', as the Group labelled them.[172] During 1988, it is true, it had seemed possible that an All-Union popular front might emerge. After all, many of the grievances that fuelled protest against communist rule were common to the whole country—from the monstrous crimes of Stalin's day, through *nomenklatura* privilege and environmental damage, to consumer shortages and economic failure. Moreover, Russian reformers were happy to make common cause with many aspects of the emergent minority nationalist movements in attacking authoritarian features of communist rule, past and present.

Baltic nationalism

The Inter-Regional Group included Baltic deputies endorsed by their respective Popular Fronts, and the Group vigorously supported their denunciation of the three republics' treatment. It backed—and Gorbachev approved—demands from the Baltic deputies for an official inquiry into the coercive manner in which independent Estonia, Latvia and Lithuania had been incorporated into the USSR under the terms of the Secret Protocol to the Nazi–Soviet Pact (see document 9). The Congress set up a commission to investigate, Gorbachev choosing Yakovlev to chair it. While the commission was working, nationalists in the three republics marked the fiftieth

---

172 For an introduction to the nationality issue, see B. Fowkes, *The Disintegration of the Soviet Union: A Study in the Rise and Triumph of Nationalism* (Basingstoke 1997).

anniversary of the Pact with an astonishing demonstration linking the three capitals by a human chain whose members symbolically turned their backs to the east and faced westward. The commission's report to the second session of the Congress, while condoning the Pact itself as a desperate attempt to avoid war in 1939, confirmed the contents of the Secret Protocol, whose very existence had long been denied by the USSR, and in the following resolution condemned it outright.

Document 246 | **From the report by Aleksandr Yakovlev, Chairman of the Commission on the Political and Legal Assessment of the Soviet–German Non-aggression Treaty of 1939**

23 December 1989

The Commission came to the following conclusions regarding the protocol:

First, a secret additional protocol of August 23, 1939 did exist, although its original has not been found in either Soviet or foreign archives. The copies now in the possession of the Soviet and West German governments may be considered to be authentic on the basis of modern expertise. And indeed, the subsequent events themselves developed exactly according to the protocol.

Secondly, the original protocol was drawn up in the German Foreign Ministry and approved by Stalin and Molotov, with slight amendments. The Soviet negotiators—not to their credit—forgot about their original wish to have a dual guarantee of the independence of the Baltic states. They did not insist that the protocol reflect Germany's readiness to make Japan see reason, and were satisfied with verbal promises from Ribbentrop on that score.

Thirdly, the political and government bodies of the Soviet Union were not informed about the preparation of the protocol. Molotov did not have the appropriate formal powers to sign it. The protocol was exempt from ratifications and was not approved by the country's legislative or executive bodies.

Fourthly, signed in circumvention of the country's laws and in violation of its commitments under treaties with third countries, the protocol was inherently an illegal document, a collusion, reflecting the intentions of the actual persons who signed it.

Fifthly, the methods used to elaborate the protocol and the categories and terms it includes, such as 'territorial–political restructuring', etc., were an obvious departure from the Leninist principles of Soviet foreign policy.

It is true that the peoples of Ukraine and Belorussia regained their territorial integrity. But, with the same universal criteria in mind, it was surely possible to understand the feelings of those who had found themselves a powerless toy in the hands of the strong and who saw all the subsequent developments in the context of the injustices committed by Stalin.

Determined to have his share of the prey, Stalin began to speak the language of ultimatums and threats with the neighbouring nations, particularly the small ones. He did not stop short of open warfare in the dispute with Finland. He made Bessarabia part of the Soviet Union once again in a high-handed imperious manner, and likewise re-established Soviet power in the Baltic states. Those actions distorted Soviet political and state ethics.

This is probably the first time that the events of the difficult pre-war period have been described in such strong and unambiguous terms. But the whole truth, however bitter, had to be revealed some time.

The secret protocol of 23 August, 1939 epitomized the very essence of Stalinism. This is one of the most dangerous bombs from the minefield which we have inherited and are trying to clear with great difficulty. But it has to be done. Social mines are not subject to corrosion. We are obliged to do it in the name of perestroika, in order to establish new political approaches and to restore the honour of socialism which has been marred by Stalinism.

The view of the Commission is that the work performed has clarified a number of issues which people have on their minds and given rise to the formulation of a legally and morally correct verdict with respect to the secret protocol, first and foremost. In expressing their conclusions, the members of the Commission weighed up every word in the light of their convictions.

If the Congress finds it possible to agree with the Commission's proposals, this will help to sweep away the relics of the past which are incompatible with socialism and justice.

[Source: *On the Political and Legal Assessment of the Soviet–German Non-aggression Treaty of 1939* (Moscow 1990), pp. 29–30.]

The nationalist movements in the Baltic were much the strongest in the country.[173] Given a free vote at any time since their reincorporation into the USSR when the *Wehrmacht* was driven out, it is unlikely that their electorate would have opted to stay within the Union. But in the early Gorbachev years the scale and vigour of support for outright independence there was not matched in the other twelve republics. And of these, it was most pronounced in the smallest—Georgia, Armenia and Moldova—and distinctly feebler in the other nine, which embraced 90 per cent of the country's population and even more of its territory.[174] Nationalist support for independence formed a visible but minority current in Ukraine and Azerbaijan, was minimal in Central Asia and Belorussia, and virtually non-

---

173 The factors that set them apart are analysed in depth by K. Gerner and S. Hedlund, *The Baltic States and the End of the Soviet Empire* (London 1993).
174 For a lucid comparative approach, see M.R. Beissinger, *Nationalist Mobilization and the Collapse of the Soviet State* (Cambridge 2002).

existent among Russians themselves. On the face of it, therefore, it might seem that there were real prospects of an All-Union opposition movement emerging. It might have built on the close economic and trading ties between the Union Republics and the Autonomous Republics within them; on their common transport system, legal system, education system, currency, media and communications network; and on the military and defence arrangements they shared. Russian, widely known as a second language where it was not the first, provided a lingua franca and there was a measure of inter-ethnic marriage. Yet what tentative steps towards an All-Union opposition movement were taken, including by the Inter-Regional Group itself, made no headway. It proved impossible to mobilize and unite a coherent socioeconomic, as opposed to national, constituency. The abolition of private ownership of the means of production virtually precluded clear-cut class divisions of the kind that had formed the primary base for European political parties for the previous two centuries.[175]

Despite intense discontent among workers, dramatized by major coal miners' strikes in 1989, the Soviet working class as a whole proved an unviable social base.[176] In part this reflected its steep stratification and in part its successful subordination to official trade unions, whose grip had been strengthened by control over social benefits. But it reflected, too, the way in which the party had appropriated and exhausted the rhetoric and resonance of class politics and undermined the credibility of alternative socialist visions of the future. Collective farmers, only 9 per cent of the employed population by the mid-1980s, were the stratum slowest to engage in the new political climate and most suspicious of far-reaching change. On the face of it, the most likely constituency for an All-Union opposition lay among non-manual workers, and especially the upper echelons, the huge pool of graduates and networks of professional, cultural, recreational and scholarly organizations—the Soviet intelligentsia broadly defined.[177] Yet this stratum was riven by divisions, not least between reformers anxious to forge an opposition and those serried ranks of officials whom they accused of studied resistance to change. Moreover, among the national minorities it was the intelligentsia—professionals, teachers, intellectuals, journalists as well as officials, specialists and managers—for whom the strident assertion of national needs against the Kremlin and the Russian majority held greatest promise.

---

175 See D. Lane, *Soviet Society under Perestroika* (London 1990), for useful discussion of the potential for and obstacles to mobilizing coherent social constituencies, pp. 335–48.
176 For two thoughtful discussions, see Filtzer, *Soviet Workers and the Collapse of Perestroika*, and Cook, *The Soviet Social Contract*.
177 Lewin, *The Gorbachev Phenomenon*, brings home the rate at which this latent constituency had developed since the 1960s.

The Soviet social structure, then, militated against the mobilization of a broad constituency defined in terms of class, occupation, level of education or income. The deadening legacy of Marxism–Leninism militated against the development of any clearly defined left-wing socioeconomic vision to replace the status quo, while capitalism still had minimal appeal. By contrast, the ethno-territorial structure of the USSR provided ideal political and cultural preconditions for nationalist mobilization of the titular majority of each republic. Nationalists within each republic had no need to identify or forge unity around any specific socioeconomic alternative to Soviet-style 'socialism'. They could leave open the core issues that an All-Union movement could not avoid addressing—the proposed structure of a non-communist economy and society. Instead, they could play upon cultural themes with real resonance among the titular nationality and upon the suspicion easily nurtured in every republic that they were somehow penalized by the economic terms of the Soviet federation. Above all, they could hold out the inviting prospect that, whatever the social and economic model adopted, given independence from the USSR the state machinery of the republic in question could be marshalled to favour unreservedly the interests and culture of their co-nationals over others within the republic.

The potential for the political mobilization of the titular nationality had been implicit, of course, since the crystallization of the Soviet Union around ethno-territorial units in the 1920s. What had prevented it was the certainty that Moscow would forcibly crush signs of overt nationalism, and the hegemony of a unitary and centralized party embracing the entire Union. Yet even before the Congress of People's Deputies had met, Gorbachev's initiatives had both called into question Moscow's willingness to use force and shaken the unitary structure and central control of the party. The upshot at the All-Union level, as we have seen, had been increasingly open conflict within the leadership, dramatized by the furore over Yeltsin. At the republican level, the result had been instances of party leaders more or less willingly condoning or even themselves voicing minority national demands that clashed with established party policy. While in Estonia, Latvia and Lithuania this took the form of questioning the source and legitimacy of Moscow's authority, in the ethnic mosaic of the Caucasus, the commonest trigger was increasingly open inter-ethnic conflict around the status of and distribution of power within disputed ethno-territorial subunits.[178]

---

178 R.G. Suny, *The Revenge of the Past: Nationalism, Revolution and the Collapse of the Soviet Union* (Stanford 1993), places events in the Caucasus in context.

Armenian–Azerbaijani conflict

The most violent explosion took place between Armenians and Azerbaijanis over the disputed 'Autonomous Area' of Nagorno-Karabakh in Azerbaijan. The overwhelmingly Armenian population of Nagorno-Karabakh had long complained of economic and cultural discrimination by the Azerbaijani authorities against them, but it was only now that their discontent was given formal expression. A flurry of demonstrations in the enclave led the local soviet, despite being party-dominated like all the others, to challenge official policy on the inviolability of internal borders and to vote in February 1988 to apply to Moscow for transfer from Azerbaijan to Armenia. In this, it reflected the blend of heightened expectations, reduced fear of repression, and weakened party discipline arising from Gorbachev's reforms. The move ignited huge demonstrations in the Armenian capital, Erevan, and here too the party leaders came out in support of the demand for the transfer of Nargorno-Karabakh. Azerbaijani public opinion, however, was enraged: there were large-scale counter-demonstrations, and in the Azerbaijani city of Sumgait crowds hunted down and attacked Armenians, massacring at least thirty-two. Clashes on both sides saw tens of thousands of refugees flee across the border, fuelling mutual hatred. Moscow tried to impose order by force and by arresting militant leaders, and eventually announced in January 1989 that the area would be run by a Direct Rule Committee. This entirely failed to satisfy Azeri opinion yet at the same time accelerated a dramatic shift in Armenian public opinion against Moscow and ultimately against continued membership of the USSR.

The continuing crisis was passionately debated at the Congress in late May 1989, the open division within the party and the flouting of Moscow's authority plain for all to see. The Azeri viewpoint was given by P. Azizbekova, director of the Azerbaijani History Museum in Baku.

Document 247 | **From the debate on Nagorno-Karabakh at the first session of the Congress of People's Deputies: the Azeri viewpoint**

June 1989

Piusta Azizbekova, director, Azerbaijani History Museum, Baku (national deputy, Azerbaijan): . . . Each of the union republics making up the USSR has its own peculiarities which are reflected in its economy, social conditions, and culture. Clearly, the republics must not copy each other in developing their political institutions or economic models. . . But we do need comprehensive legislation to co-ordinate the interests of the USSR and those of the union republics. . .

Frequent calls are heard now for what will essentially mean disintegration of the constitutional foundation of our multinational state. But all those who make such calls represent the interests of narrow groups, rather than those of the entire nation. Our descendants will not forgive us if we allow a deterioration of the links between the Union and the republics, and between the republics themselves, that will result in weakening of the Union and the republics, and national self-isolation. . .

Recently we have seen grievous events caused by nationalist outrages in various regions of our country, including Transcaucasia. . . Unjustified demands for the absorption of Karabakh by Armenia destabilized the region and produced ethnic conflicts. The traditional economic links and friendship ties have been broken. The tragic events will shape the destinies of an entire generation. . . About 300,000 in Azerbaijan and Armenia lost their homes. Now 50,000 Armenian refugees have returned to their homes in Azerbaijan and we are happy about that. We would like the 165,000 Azerbaijanian refugees from Armenia to return to their homes, too. Refugees present a terrible problem and it is not just our regional problem. The non-indigenous population of any republic where ethnic conflicts are brewing may become refugees. We urgently need special legislation for refugees, to restore justice and protect their human and property rights. . .

Despite all complications and obstacles, the Karabakh problem can be resolved. Direct rule in Karabakh is contributing to stabilization and helps to find compromises for overcoming the ethnic disagreements and tensions. The Direct Rule Committee has done much in that respect. Yet its activities are efficiently hindered by forces that openly oppose perestroika: they organize strikes and obstruct the implementation of the decisions taken by Moscow authorities. Though the country faces a critical economic and financial situation, 500 million rubles were allocated for the economic and social development of Karabakh. For unclear reasons, however, this aid has been, in effect, rejected. What is lacking is goodwill and a sincere desire to co-operate in normalization of the conditions in the region. . .

The nations of Transcaucasia in the past lived through tragic events provoked by obsessed nationalists. In such periods leaders emerged who succeeded in bringing peace to the nations that can live in friendship for ages. I am proud to say that one of them was my grandfather, Meshadi Azizbekov.[179] To continue this tradition, I call all those who have forgotten about the ancient brotherhood of our nations to make peace. It would be naive to think that the conflict will resolve itself. Careful hard work by the healthy patriotic forces of both nations, political guidance by the party organizations, and the combined efforts of people's deputies will be able to do that, despite the blackmail by the forces opposing perestroika. . .

[Source: O. Glebov and J. Crowfoot (eds), *The Soviet Empire: Its Nations Speak Out* (London 1989), pp. 86–89.]

---

179 A prominent Bolshevik, one of the twenty-five Baku commissars executed by the nationalist Socialist government in Baku in 1918.

The response by the party First Secretary in Armenia, S. Arutyunyan was forthright.

Document 248 | From the debate on Nagorno-Karabakh at the first session of the Congress of People's Deputies: the Armenian viewpoint

Suren Arutyunyan, 1st Secretary, Armenian Communist Party Central Committee, Erevan (territorial deputy, Armenia): . . . Any regional problems, if they are not resolved in time, inevitably expand their scope and affect the entire country. . . For the last year and a half the Karabakh problem has been producing convulsions throughout our republic and the entire Transcaucasia, and the tremors of it are felt throughout the USSR. It provides a tragic illustration of the acute ethnic issues. For decades we repeated Lenin's maxim that all nations in our country were equal. And for decades we steadily cut, to the officially approved size, the live tissue of ethnic relations.

Even now some try to avoid an honest analysis of the problem by replacing it with standard phrases about ancient friendship and brotherhood of nations, trying to reduce the ethnic problems to the conspiracy of extremists and organized crime. . .

Biased mass media reports aimed at manipulating public opinion, and calls for mutual understanding unsupported by real actions, only make the problem more acute. . . What we are dealing with are the consequences of the Stalinist anti-demo-cratic attitude to nations. If such consequences are regarded as being sacred, it means justifying the regime that brought severe distortions into socialism. If we rehabili-tate individuals who were illegally persecuted in the past why can't we do the same for entire nations? [Applause.]

. . . For decades the Azerbaijanian authorities insulted the national dignity, and ignored the social and cultural needs, of the Armenian population of Karabakh. . . It was an open injustice that led to the crisis in the region. . . Unfortunately, even now, when it is especially important to calm ethnic enmity and distrust, steps are often taken to set in opposition the interests of Armenians and Azerbaijanians in Karabakh. . . We strive for normalization, for dialogue, for constructive approaches but encounter various obstacles in establishing normal links between Armenia and Karabakh. Any economic, social or cultural issues are elevated to the rank of polit-ical problems. Armenian officials and intellectuals have difficulties in visiting Karabakh. . .

In Armenia the Karabakh problem is the concern of the entire nation. Even the recent catastrophic earthquake failed to uproot it from the hearts of the people. The Direct Rule Committee was a compromise prompted by the realities. Unfortunately, the Committee failed to develop an administrative system directly governed from Moscow. The loss of confidence in the Committee led to an increase in tension in Karabakh and, hence, in Armenia. The authority of the Committee must be enhanced, it must be given a real right to administer independently all the vital functions in Karabakh.

The Karabakh problem remains an unhealed wound. . . This Congress has the right to conduct referendums. I suggest that the Congress exercise this right for Karabakh. Let the population of this autonomous region decide its destiny by its own free will. . .

The Sumgait tragedy, which still awaits proper analysis, gave rise to the terrible plight of refugees. At the moment Armenia has accepted 200,000 refugees from Azerbaijan. Tens of thousands of Azerbaijanians fled from Armenia. If you recall that 530,000 people were left homeless after the recent earthquake you will realize the full extent of the problem. Almost a third of the population in Armenia are homeless and many of them have lost their jobs. . .

The delays in solving urgent problems disturb the people in the republic, and produce a feeling of social and national vulnerability and a crisis of confidence in the republican leadership. . .

The heavy confrontation between the Armenian and Azerbaijanian nations is a sad fact that cannot be ignored. Our nations will have to live side by side in the future. It is extremely important, therefore, to prevent the crisis from deepening. Both republics and, primarily, their communist parties must make use of all opportunities to overcome animosity and to restore the atmosphere of mutual understanding and trust. . .

Many difficulties in ethnic relations are due to the lack of relevant legislation and the inconsistencies in the USSR Constitution. . . The Congress must work out guidelines for modifying the Constitution in accordance with present-day realities, particularly in the field of ethnic relations. . . The fundamental principle in this sphere, that must protect us from wrong decisions and extremist measures, is the strengthening of the Soviet state as a federation of sovereign republics. . .

[Source: O. Glebov and J. Crowfoot (eds), *The Soviet Empire: Its Nations Speak Out* (London 1989), pp. 86–89.]

Violence in Georgia

In neighbouring Georgia, the remaining Caucasian republic, tension between the titular majority and ethnic minorities, in this case the Osetins and in particular the Abkhaz, triggered violence and gave powerful impetus to nationalist demands. Abkhaz nationalists appealed to Moscow against discrimination by the Georgian government and, evidently supported by the Abkhaz Party Secretary, pressed for their Autonomous Republic to become, as it had briefly been in the 1920s, a Union Republic independent of Georgia. The demand and the threat to Georgia's authority over the Autonomous Republic—a majority of whose population was by the 1980s Georgian—infuriated Georgian nationalists. In early April 1989, just after the Congress elections, there were repeated demonstrations in the capital, Tbilisi, directed at one and the same time against the Abkhaz, against the Georgian communist authorities, and against the USSR. Unlike in Armenia or Azerbaijan, here the party leadership under the First Secretary, D. Patiashvili, appealed to Moscow for the use of paratroopers and security troops in an attempt to disperse the demonstrations and intimidate the nationalist upsurge.

Gorbachev and Shevardnadze, whose long period in office as Georgian First Secretary and prestige as Soviet Foreign Minister gave him considerable leverage in Georgia, were abroad at the time, and the Politburo under Ligachev and Chebrikov sanctioned some form of action. Gorbachev and Shevardnadze returned to Moscow late on 7 April, but Gorbachev's proposal that Shevardnadze go to Tbilisi to calm matters was shelved when Patiashvili assured him on 8 April that the situation was under control.[180] Yet early the next morning there was bloodshed. Preparations to stamp out the demonstrations had been entrusted to General I. Rodionov, a renowned disciplinarian, and under his authority the following instructions (which grossly underestimated the size of the crowds involved) were issued by the officers on the ground.

Document 249 | **Military orders on special operations to liquidate the mass disturbances in the square outside Government House and on Rustaveli Avenue, Tbilisi—from the orders issued by the commander of the operative group of troop unit 3419 of the USSR MVD troops**

9 April 1989

1. Unsanctioned meetings have been taking place over the course of 6, 7 and 8 April in Tbilisi, organized by extremist groups intent on fomenting unhealthy attitudes in the city and republic. On the night of [8-]9 April the situation at the meeting has deteriorated sharply and has got out of control. Those at the meeting, some 8,000 people, are calling for a strike and civil disobedience. Slogans of a nationalistic and anti-Soviet character have appeared, calling for the end of Soviet power in Georgia, the creation of a provisional government and withdrawal from the USSR. Threats have been coming from the crowd to get even with the Communists. The extremists have blocked off all entrances to the square with lorries with slashed tyres and loaded with ballast.

2. Our unit's task, in conjunction with military unit 3219, is to conduct a special operation to oust the rioters, break up an anti-Soviet, anti-social gathering and clear the square in front of Government House. The crowd is to be pushed down Rustaveli Avenue in the direction of Republic Square. Subsequently all approaches to the square are to be blocked off, and public access to the square is to be

---

180 See the account in Brown, *Gorbachev Factor*, pp. 264–67.

prevented. . .

6. PR-73 rubber bullets are to be used at the discretion of the senior operational head. The use of rubber bullets against women and children is forbidden. The armoured personnel carrier BTR-60PB should be used by the group clearing the square for their effects on the crowd's morale. Fire engines are to be on hand behind the group clearing the square so that their hoses can be used, at the discretion of the senior operational head, in case of serious deterioration in the situation. The use of water cannons against women and children is forbidden.

Commander of the operative group of military unit 3419, Lieutenant-Colonel A.M. Baklanov
Chief-of-Staff of the unit operative group, Major A.N. Kleymenov

[Source: A. Sobchak, *Tblisskiy sindrom, ili Krovavoe voskresen´e 1989 goda* (Moscow 1993), pp. 223–24.]

While the troops were explicitly ordered not to fire live rounds, at some point in the chain of command they were empowered to use both tear gas and lethally sharpened spades as weapons. Twenty demonstrators were killed and as many as 5,000 injured. Gorbachev and Shevardnadze expressed horror at what had happened, and Patiashvili was promptly removed as First Secretary. At the Congress, an investigative commission was set up under the chairmanship of A. Sobchak, the radical mayor of Leningrad, whose membership of the Inter-Regional Group gave him credibility among critics of the Kremlin. The Commission roundly condemned the Georgian party leadership and the brutal measures taken by the units involved.

Document 250 | **From the conclusions of the Commission of the Presidium of the USSR Supreme Soviet on events in Tbilisi on 9 April 1989**

. . . 2. The Bureau of the CC of the Communist Party of Georgia and its First Secretary exceeded their authority in taking the decision to conduct the operation and appointing its head. . .

4. Sending in companies of the paratroop regiment must be considered a gross mistake. . . .

6. There were breaches of the regulations concerning the use of the tear gas 'Cheremukha'. As for the CS gas K-51, its use is illegal. The use of such substances and trench-digging shovels was not reported to the head of the operation or the MVD of the USSR.

[Source: A. Sobchak, *Tblisskiy sindrom, ili Krovavoe voskresen´e 1989 goda* (Moscow 1993), pp. 199–200.]

However, despite the steps taken by Gorbachev to repudiate what had happened, nothing could undo the shock to Georgian opinion created by this violent action, which was made all the more horrific by the number of women among the victims. The massacre had a disastrous impact on the standing of the Communist Party within Georgia and also gave a major boost to the already strong popular support for nationalism. Both the unity and the authority of the CPSU, key components of the approach that had contained such tensions for so long, lay in ruins.

In republics where local passions ran high enough to trigger popular demonstrations under the impetus of glasnost and democratization, the local party leaders were confronted by a grave dilemma. If they stood idly by, their authority dissipated and non-communist leaders gathered credibility. If they tried to crush the unrest with force, they stoked up further passion and could not count on Moscow's backing. They thus faced a growing temptation to shift their own primary allegiance and seek to undercut the Popular Fronts now emerging in every minority republic by championing the nationalist cause themselves. Gorbachev was horrified when, belatedly, he began to realize the very real prospect that minority nationalism would threaten the unity of the USSR. Yet the logic of his democratization programme had already committed him to establish what would prove to be the ideal mechanism to give momentum even to the weakest emergent nationalist movements: contested elections within each republic.

The competitive elections to the Congress of People's Deputies of March 1989 were to be followed early in 1990 by equivalent elections to local soviets and to the Supreme Soviet of each of the Union Republics. Nothing could have been more effective in turning the republican Popular Fronts into fully fledged nationalist parties challenging communist power. Where those movements were most vigorous, the pressure on the republic's communist leaders to shift their allegiance and try to compete for nationalist support became all but irresistible. In Lithuania, confronted by a Popular Front (*Sajūdis*) which was gaining support by the day through its nationalist clamour, local communist party leaders in desperation declared their organization independent of the CPSU in December 1989 and turned it into a Lithuanian social–democratic party. Gorbachev's attempt the following month to persuade them to reconsider failed dismally. Elsewhere, the ties of authority that had bound party officials to Moscow were frayed and loosened, and the significance of party membership became increasingly blurred. The critical fault-line lay now between those whose allegiance continued to be to the CPSU and those, whether still formally within the CPSU or not, who were more interested in pressing the claims and extending the autonomy of their own republic.[181]

---

181 See Beissinger, *Nationalist Mobilization*, for the gathering momentum of nationalism.

Soviet moves to thwart Lithuanian independence

In March, when the elections duly took place, the lead was again taken in the Baltic, where candidates sponsored by the Popular Fronts emerged with overall control of the new legislatures. It became clear in Lithuania that as soon as the new Supreme Soviet convened, the triumphant leaders of *Sajūdis* intended to declare the republic independent. Frantically Gorbachev and his colleagues tried to forestall that outcome. A range of measures was drawn up by four key figures from the Secretariat and Politburo to bring to bear every sanction, short of force, available to them—constitutional, legal, political and economic—to dissuade the Lithuanians.

Document 251 | Note on urgent measures to prevent Lithuania leaving the USSR from A.N. Girenko, Yu.D. Maslyukov, V.A. Medvedev, and G.P. Razumovsky to the CC of the CPSU

5 March 1990

Top secret

There are reasons to believe that a decision will be taken at the first session of the newly elected Supreme Soviet of the Lithuanian SSR to form an independent Lithuanian state.

Separatist forces are trying their best to push through the adoption of this decision by convening a session before the 3rd Extraordinary [session of the] Congress of People's Deputies of the USSR begins.

In accordance with the CPSU CC Politburo's resolution on *Urgent measures in relation to the deteriorating situation in the Lithuanian SSR* certain preparatory work has been done to counteract the separatist tendencies in Lithuania. It would appear to be essential over the next few weeks to implement the set of measures envisaged in that resolution, along with some additional measures demanded by the extraordinary nature of the situation which is developing in the Lithuanian SSR.

A draft list of these urgent measures and resolutions of the CPSU CC on this question is attached.

CPSU CC resolution *On urgent measures to prevent Lithuania leaving the USSR*
6 March 1990

Top secret

Confirm the list of urgent measures on this matter (attached).
CC Secretary

On item 10 of Minute No. 181
List of urgent measures to prevent Lithuania leaving the USSR
1. Publish in *Izvestiya* materials on the intentions of separatist forces in Lithuania and

the potential economic and other consequences of a decision on Lithuania leaving the USSR.

Before 6 March.

Comrades A.S. Kapto, I.D. Laptev, A.A. Sazonov, A.I. Milyukov, V.G. Komplektov.

2. Adopt a Declaration of the Supreme Soviet of the USSR on Lithuania's proposed secession from the USSR.

After confirmation of the agenda of the first session of the new Supreme Soviet of the Lithuanian SSR, the decree of the Supreme Soviet of the Estonian SSR of 12 November 1989 on *A historical and legal assessment of the events of 1940 in Estonia* and that of the Supreme Soviet of the Lithuanian SSR of 7 February 1990 on *The Soviet–German pacts of 1939 and the removal of their consequences for Lithuania* are to be considered as a matter of urgency at the 3rd session of the Supreme Soviet of the USSR. An estimation is to be given of the legislative acts and decrees of the government of the Lithuanian SSR and their conformity with the Constitution of the USSR and international pacts on human rights.

Comrades A.I. Luk'yanov, E.M. Primakov, G.P. Razumovsky, A.N. Girenko, R.N. Nishanov.

3. Adopt and publish (on the day of confirmation of the agenda of the first session of the new Supreme Soviet of the Lithuanian SSR) a declaration of the Council of Ministers of the USSR on measures to defend the interests of the USSR (of USSR citizens and of All-Union organizations) in the territory of Lithuania, in connection with the proposed adoption of the decision on creating an independent Lithuanian state.

Comrades N.N. Slyun'kov, Yu.D. Maslyukov, G.P. Razumovsky.

4. Consider measures to defend USSR property, located in the territory of the Lithuanian SSR, and make appropriate proposals.

Before 10 March.

Comrades Yu.D. Maslyukov, V.P. Mozhin, A.S. Pavlov.

5. Consider the question of submitting a proposal to the 3rd Extraordinary [session of the] Congress of People's Deputies of the USSR suspending the operation of Article 72 of the USSR Constitution until the adoption of a USSR law on the procedure for the secession of Union Republics from the USSR.

Before 12 March.

Comrades A.I. Luk'yanov, E.M. Primakov, R.N. Nishanov.

6. Organize a series of media events (a 'round table' on Central TV and a number of articles in the press—following a special plan) on those economic and other negative consequences for the population of the Lithuanian SSR which would result from the hasty adoption of separatist decisions on that republic's secession from the USSR.

Before 12 March.

Comrades A.S. Kapto, A.A. Sazonov, A.I. Milyukov, A.S. Pavlov, V.S. Babichev.

7. Consider in addition the political situation which might arise for a provisional CC of the CPSU of Lithuania (on the platform of the CPSU) in the event of a decision on Lithuania's secession from the USSR.

Before 12 March.

Comrades G.P. Razumovsky, V.M. Falin, N.E. Kruchina.

[Sources: TsKhSD, fond 5, opis' 102, delo 1330, pp. 30–34; *Istoricheskiy arkhiv*, No. 1, 1992, pp. 3–5.]

Moscow's threats and blandishments, and the promise of new legislation defining a legal procedure by which a Union Republic might eventually exercise the right to secession (to which successive Constitutions had paid lip service, most recently in Article 72 of the 1977 Constitution), succeeded in stalling Lithuania's attempted breakaway. But by then the party, the prime political mechanism which had bound the Union together and subordinated each republic to Moscow, was rapidly imploding. In the course of 1989–90, Popular Fronts took off, if with widely varying degrees of success, in each minority republic. There was popular protest against the monopoly power of the CPSU in the RSFSR, including a giant demonstration in Moscow itself. By February, the growing unpopularity and dysfunction of the CPSU had reached the point where Gorbachev judged it no longer politic to defend Article 6. The party leadership accepted that the formation of opposition parties should become legal throughout the USSR and itself repudiated the guaranteed 'leading role' of the CPSU. Article 6 was formally repealed at the third session of the People's Congress (12–20 March), a devastating blow to the prestige and authority of the party and the most dramatic expression of the erosion it had suffered since 1988. The fourth of the pillars on which communist rule had rested since the Great Patriotic War was crumbling away.

As it did so, Gorbachev accelerated the shift he had already begun to make regarding his own authority, placing less emphasis on the party and more on the state. The plainer it became that the CPSU could no longer confer effective power and was becoming a positive obstacle to sustaining legitimacy, the more urgent it became to establish his position within the context of the emergent new Constitution. Without stepping down from the party leadership, he, together with his advisers, drew up legislation, to be enacted by the March 1990 session of the Congress, creating a new post of Executive President.[182] Unlike the long-established honorific post of President of the Supreme Soviet, the Executive President was to be the active head of the

---

182 On the changing formal role of the presidency, see S. White, G. Gill, D. Slider, *The Politics of Transition: Shaping a Post-Soviet Future* (Cambridge 1993), pp. 60–78.

All-Union government, in a manner somewhat analogous to the president of the USA or France. He was to choose the Prime Minister, chair what became two Councils responsible for security and for relations between the republics, and control the main lines of policy. The authority of the post would flow not from the party but from the people, and in future it would be filled by direct and competitive popular election. In the interim, however, given the gravity of the multifaceted crisis—social, economic, political and constitutional—now gripping the country, the Congress would itself immediately elect the first incumbent. Gorbachev was nominated, there was no rival candidate and, although a significant minority voted against and almost as many again abstained, he was duly elected.

Document 252 | **From the report of the chairman of the Monitoring Commission on the Election of M.S. Gorbachev as the USSR President at the 3rd Congress of People's Deputies of the USSR**

15 March 1990

. . . The total number of people's deputies is 2,245. The number of people's deputies who received a ballot paper was exactly 2,000. On opening the ballot boxes 1,878 ballot papers were found, of which 54 were invalid.

The votes were distributed as follows: for the candidate for President—1,329; against—495.

Thus, comrade Mikhail Sergeevich Gorbachev is elected President of the USSR. Gorbachev received the votes of 59.2% of the total number of people's deputies, 66.45% of those who received ballot papers and 70.76% of those who took part in the voting.

[Source: *Izvestiya*, 17 March 1990.]

Yet the move did little to shore up Gorbachev's real power. It could have succeeded only if his new post, the battery of emergency powers assigned to it by the Congress, and the orders and decrees he issued in its name had commanded assent among civil and military officials, among the newly elected republican governments, and among the population at large. But they failed to do so. For all the initial excitement it had engendered, the Congress itself, elected twelve tumultuous months earlier, was by now widely lampooned as a chaotic talking-shop. The clash with Lithuania was only the most dramatic case of a 'war of laws' rumbling across the country. The Supreme Soviets of one Union Republic after another proclaimed their republics' 'sovereignty' (though not independence) and, reversing the core principle of the federation, declared All-Union legislation invalid unless confirmed by the local legislature.[183] And the one device which might conceivably have strengthened All-Union political allegiance at the expense of national political allegiance and arrested the flow of legitimacy from central to republican authorities was left untried by the decision not to hold an immediate, All-Union election to the new post of Executive President.

Russian nationalism

Moreover, the Union Republic elections of March 1990, in addition to providing the ideal context for mobilizing minority nationalism, also gave form to the nationalist movement which was to prove fatal to the USSR and CPSU alike: that of the Russian majority.[184] The political appeal of Russian nationalism was much more complex than that of minority nationalism.[185] Major obstacles stood in the way of it becoming the basis for a political movement challenging the authority of the CPSU or threatening the unity of the USSR. Russian national consciousness, it is true, was firmly enough embedded, and Russians shared their own version of many of the grievances fuelling minority nationalism—from the repression of non-communist traditions, cultural practices and religion, to economic shortfalls and damage to the environment. But most Russians unambiguously regarded the USSR rather than the RSFSR as their homeland, and 25 million of them lived outside the RSFSR in the other fourteen Union Republics. The CPSU had been, and still was, so manifestly dominated by Russians that for Russians to present it as a foreign oppressor, as minority nationalists were now so effectively doing, was very difficult. Many of the connotations of Russian nationalism—its association with authoritarianism, with Stalin, with the *Zhdanovshchina*, with anti-Semitism—rendered it suspect among would-be democrats. It was not easy to associate Russian nationalism with the cause of democracy, as non-Russian nationalists, however speciously, were so successfully doing with their own brands. For loyalists to the CPSU and the

---

183 For the view that it was of crucial importance that the Soviet Constitution recognized the notional sovereignty of the Union Republics, however vague and inoperative that sovereignty had hitherto been, see E.W. Walker, *Dissolution: Sovereignty and the Breakup of the Soviet Union* (Lanham, MD, 2003).

184 The emergence and the fragility of Russia's new parties is closely analysed in M. Urban, V. Igrunov and S. Mitrokhin, *The Rebirth of Politics in Russia* (Cambridge 1997).

185 See G. Hosking, *Russia and the Russians: From Earliest Times to 2001* (London 2001), for an analysis which provides a long-term historical perspective on the tensions embedded in appeals to Russian nationalism, and Y.M. Brudny, *Reinventing Russia: Russian Nationalism and the Soviet State, 1953–1991* (Cambridge, MA, 1998), on the Soviet regime's sponsorship of Russian nationalism in the decades before perestroika.

USSR, it made little sense to envisage the RSFSR demanding sovereignty, let alone independence. Yet when Gorbachev's reforms triggered competitive elections for a new RSFSR legislature—unlike the smaller republics, the giant Russian republic was to have its own Congress of People's Deputies, which would then elect a standing Supreme Soviet—the political struggle that ensued echoed that in the other republics.

Party traditionalists, implicitly critical of the extent to which perestroika had shaken the old order, were pitted against a 'Democratic Russia' bloc, which brought together reformist communist and anti-communist candidates united in wanting perestroika to go much further. And both sides made play of Russian nationalist themes. The traditionalists promised to create a distinctively Russian section of the CPSU to champion the RSFSR and resist damaging All-Union reforms. The Democratic Russia bloc promised to use the new Russian legislature, and the government it would appoint, as a base from which to accelerate the pace of reform within the RSFSR. While traditionalists held on to much of the countryside, the 'democrats' won about one-third of the seats, performing particularly well in the cities.[186] When the Congress met and proceeded to select the Supreme Soviet from among its members, there was a tense struggle over the election of its Chairman. Voting was almost equally split between Yeltsin, backed by the 'democrats', and I. Polozkov, emerging as a leading critic of the radicalism of perestroika. After two inconclusive ballots, Polozkov stepped down and, in the third, Yeltsin carried enough uncommitted deputies to defeat the candidate closest to Gorbachev, the incumbent head of the Russian Council of Ministers, A.V. Vlasov, as well as a third, independent, candidate, V. Tsoy.

Document 253 | **From the transcript of the Congress of People's Deputies of the RSFSR on the election of B.N. Yeltsin as Chairman of the Supreme Soviet of Russia**

29 May 1990

Report of the Electoral Commission of the Congress of People's Deputies of the RSFSR on the results of the secret ballot for Chairman of the Supreme Soviet of the RSFSR for 29 May 1990.

In accordance with the Provisional Regulations of the Congress of People's Deputies and the Supreme Soviet of the RSFSR, the Electoral Commission has counted the votes cast, and reports as follows:

The candidatures of the following People's Deputies of the RSFSR appeared on the ballot paper for the secret ballot for Chairman of the Supreme Soviet of the RSFSR:

---

186 Urban, Igrunov and Mitrokhin, *Rebirth of Politics*, pp. 172–200.

Aleksandr Vladimirovich Vlasov

Boris Nikolaevich Yeltsin

Valentin Tsoy

The total number of People's Deputies of the RSFSR is 1,060.

The number of People's Deputies of the RSFSR who received ballot papers was 1,038.

On opening the ballot-boxes 1,038 papers were found.

1 ballot paper was invalid.

The votes cast were distributed as follows:

Vlasov, Aleksandr Vladimirovich, 467 for, 570 against.

Yeltsin, Boris Nikolaevich, 535 for, 502 against.

Tsoy, Valentin, 22 for, 1,026 against.

Thus, People's Deputy Boris Nikolaevich Yeltsin is elected Chairman of the Supreme Soviet of the RSFSR.

[Source: *Sovetskaya Rossiya*, 31 May 1990.]

The immediate sequel was a declaration of the sovereignty of the RSFSR by the Russian Congress. All-Union legislation and taxation would be dependent on approval by the legislature and executive of the RSFSR. If implemented, this move would mean that the writ and authority of the All-Union Congress and President would become conditional and in a sense subordinate in the republic that constituted 75 per cent of the country's territory.

The Russian elections accelerated the internal fracturing of the CPSU, along both territorial and ideological lines. The RSFSR had suddenly emerged as a meaningful, indeed critical, polity in its own right. The spectacle of its government slipping into the hands of radical reformers added urgency to calls from those who opposed Yeltsin, whether traditionalists or supporters of Gorbachev, for the foundation of a Russian Communist Party (RCP) within the CPSU. This, they hoped, would provide a new political vehicle to halt Yeltsin and his allies. The founding Congress of the RCP took place in June 1990. The election for the post of First Secretary was fought between two of the men whom Yeltsin had just defeated, Polozkov and Vlasov. Polozkov's victory reflected the generally conservative hue of the new organization and its increasingly hostile attitude towards Gorbachev and the destabilization he had engendered.

Ideological divisions, too, moved towards a climax. Earlier in the year, reformers in the party who were frustrated by Gorbachev's compromises and rejected outright the traditionalism epitomized by Polozkov had formed a 'Democratic Platform'. Its aim was in essence to transform the CPSU into an All-Union party committed to pluralism and parliamentary government. In the run-up to the Twenty-Eighth Congress of the CPSU, due in July 1990, its leaders drew up a range of drastic proposals to that end. These were epitomized by the following draft motion for the CPSU to repent for its 'colossal guilt before the country and the people', and to renounce outright the land, buildings and wealth it had acquired in its seven decades of domination.

Document 254 | **From a draft motion on party property for the 28th Congress of the CPSU put forward by the 'Democratic Platform of the CPSU'**

July 1990

In its more than seventy years in power, the CPSU has proclaimed the good of the people and serving their interests to be its supreme aims. Over this period the CPSU has accumulated immense wealth in property and money.

In the information supplied to Congress delegates on the Party budget, the total volume of funds under the control of local Party bodies on 1 January 1990 amounted to 2.3 billion rubles. The total value of the CPSU's holdings is not given. The reserve financial fund amounts to 4.9 billion rubles.

The information provided reveals the real source for replenishing the CPSU's wealth today—income from its monopolized publishing activities. In 1990 alone, income from the profits of Party publishing houses to the CPSU budget will come to 1.076 billion rubles.

Owing to the CPSU's privileged allocation of funds and quotas, the real purchasing power of the CPSU ruble is higher than that of the country's citizens and their organizations. Thus, in 1989 the CPSU exchanged 44 million rubles for foreign currency and the plan for 1990 is to exchange 29 million.

For decades the CPSU has made use of state lands, buildings and other property without ever paying any rent. CPSU income, including that from its productive and publishing activities, is tax-free.

The value, and often also the historical and cultural worth, of buildings and other property which, over the period the Party has been in power, have been transferred free of charge to the Party by state bodies formed by the Party has also reached significant proportions.

Over the past years the sums thus taken from the people amount to many billions of rubles.

This Congress considers that the time has come for communists to move on from making declarations about the responsibility of the CPSU to a recognition of their colossal guilt towards the country and people for the current state of things, to repent and demonstrate this responsibility in practice. This includes responsibility for taking resources away from the people.

This Congress considers it essential that these resources be returned to the people, to which end the CPSU should renounce its property in favour of the Soviets of People's Deputies.

In keeping with the above, this Congress resolves that:

1. All of the CPSU's property, including buildings, structures, enterprises, publishing houses and financial means (excluding members' subscriptions received in the last three months), should become state and communal property, and that the right to manage this property should be transferred to the Soviets of People's Deputies. . .

4. Soviets of People's Deputies at all levels, managers of factories and organizations, and work collectives should be asked to give all possible assistance in finding employment for redundant Party staff.

[Source: *Argumenty i fakty*, No. 31 (512), 4–10 August 1990.]

Yeltsin's resignation from the CPSU

When the Congress itself met, there was deadlock.[187] Gorbachev was re-elected General Secretary, but his record and his proposals for a formal break from exclusive commitment to Marxism–Leninism came in for bitter criticism from traditionalists without going far enough to satisfy supporters of the Democratic Platform. No overall consensus on either ideology or policy could be agreed. The leader of the Democratic Platform, V. Shostakovsky, announced that they would presently withdraw from the party. And Yeltsin headed a number of prominent 'democrats' who resigned immediately. The manner in which he did so underlined the shift in power. He could not, he said, be bound by instructions from the party: his duty was to the Russian legislature and electorate.

Document 255 | **Boris Yeltsin's announcement of his resignation at the 28th Congress of the CPSU**

12 July 1990

In view of my election as Chairman of the Supreme Soviet of the RSFSR, of my enormous responsibility to the people of Russia and of the country's transition to a multi-party society, I cannot carry out only the CPSU's decisions. As head of the Republic's supreme legislative body, I must submit to the will of the people and their plenipotentiary representatives. Therefore, in accordance with the undertakings I

187 On the proceedings and politics of the Congress, see E.A. Rees (ed.), *The Soviet Communist Party in Disarray: The XXVIII Congress of the Communist Party of the Soviet Union* (Basingstoke 1992).

gave in the pre-election period, I announce my resignation from the CPSU in order to have a greater opportunity to influence the activities of the Soviets effectively. I am willing to work with all parties and sociopolitical organizations in the Republic.

[Source: *Izvestiya*, 13 July 1990.]

The decomposition of the CPSU

During the second half of the year, members of the Democratic Platform set up a new party, the Republican Party of Russia, with a view to merging with the newly formed Social–Democratic Party. The RCP, meanwhile, struggled unsuccessfully to find a firm footing and to articulate a viable socioeconomic programme.[188] The leadership was unable to resist pressure to accept formally the emergence of a multi-party system, the end of the *nomenklatura* system, and some form of market economy. And yet much of their time and energy went into looking back regretfully at the certainties of the past. The following extract from a speech in January by Polozkov to the CPSU leadership captures their ideological impasse. He wielded the traditional Marxist–Leninist schema, in which it was the CPSU, not the supposed 'democrats', who represented the authentic left of the political spectrum. Standing at the head of the working class, the party was beset by right-wing, bourgeois, reactionary enemies who, aided and abetted by inter-national capital, were whipping up disorder and ethnic conflict to seize power. In a revealing phrase, he bemoaned the disappearance of the party's 'monopoly of glasnost'. But after venting his anger at the loss of the party's power, he could not disguise his own bemusement. In place of the tradi-tional assertion that the party offered historically authenticated scientific guidance, he found himself worrying that the party had 'nowhere to call and lead the workers to'.

Document 256 | **From an address by I.K. Polozkov, First Secretary of the CC of the CP of the RSFSR, to a joint plenary meeting of the CC and CCC of the CPSU**

January 1991

First: It is now clear to everybody that the perestroika, conceived and launched by the Party and people in 1985 to renew socialism. . . extend democracy and improve the people's welfare has not taken place.

---

188 For a lucid account of the party's fracturing and implosion, see G. Gill, *The Collapse of a Single-party System: The Disintegration of the Communist Party of the Soviet Union* (Cambridge 1994), pp. 144–73.

The so-called democrats have managed to alter the aims of perestroika and seize the initiative from our Party. Society is at a crossroads. The people are being deprived of their past, their present is crumbling and nobody has yet said anything sensible about what the future holds.

We must admit that the CPSU did not spot the beginnings of the degeneration of perestroika in time, and allowed the process to gather momentum. It took a while for the Party to realize that it was abandoning its historical destiny—defending the interests of working people, that it was being taught meekly to accept the entrepreneurial class that was being artificially implanted at the expense of working people, and that a social base for political parties and movements remote from socialist aims was being created.

By counterposing human against class interests, and by giving priority to worldwide values, we have done a disservice to that socialist idea to which the CPSU reaffirmed its loyalty at the XXVIII Congress. The dialectical unity of class and humanity was broken. We all know that nobody has ever expressed human interests better than the working class.

Second: The liberals, or, to put it more precisely, the Right (or just reactionaries) have now thrown off the masks of democrats. They have proclaimed anti-Communism as their ideology and are bringing together the heirs of the overthrown classes, nationalists, dealers in the shadow economy—all those constrained by Soviet power.

Our pseudo-democrats are flouting the Constitution, whipping up ethnic conflicts and ignoring the elementary standards of democracy and morality. International capital is eagerly supporting the anti-Communist movement, is assisting in every way to extend its political base, helping to consolidate its material basis and genuflecting in various ways to its leaders.

And, as has already been said, all this is being done under the banner of saving perestroika, defending it from the conservatives and now even from the President and newly formed Cabinet.

The democrats are using their favourite weapons. Slander, calumny, forgery, blackmail—all are being used against those who try to stand against them or tell the people the truth. . .

Third: There can no longer be any question of a multi-party system in our country. There is the CPSU, defending socialist perestroika, and there are leaders of small political groups, all of whom in the final analysis have the same political physiognomy—anti-Communism. These groups are consolidating and coming together to fight the CPSU and seize power.

There is no glasnost. If the CPSU once enjoyed a monopoly of glasnost, now this monopoly belongs to those lined up against it. It is they who are having a corrupting influence on social consciousness.

We are now learning from real life, not from pamphlets, what bourgeois ways and morality are and what unscrupulous ways and means can be employed when it is a question of power.

. . . As has already been said here, we think we should develop our theoretical work. But we have proclaimed that we are going towards a humane, democratic socialism, haven't we? What does that mean? Where are we taking people? What sort of society would it be? If we do not provide some answers, we have nothing around which to rally the Party, and nowhere to call and lead the workers to.

[Source: *Pravda*, 4 February 1991.]

The party's retreat was on all fronts. By early 1991, at the centre, its General Secretary had ceased to look to the Politburo, Central Committee or Secretariat as the primary decision-making bodies or source of his own legitimacy and power, and looked instead to the newly formed executive presidency. In the Baltic, Georgia, Armenia, Moldova and the RSFSR, non-CPSU governments had come to office. The party's influence in soviets, the state hierarchy, the army and economic ministries was rapidly dwindling, and even where it retained power locally, obedience to Moscow broke down. Membership, having continued to rise into 1989, now went into dizzying decline as morale plummeted, and with it the payment of membership fees and the market for party newspapers and other publications. Its income collapsed and governments and soviets in anti-CPSU hands began to confiscate its property. By spring 1991, its expenditure exceeded its income so far that the huge subsidies now needed by every republican party organization were becoming impossible: bankruptcy loomed. The following extracts from a resolution passed in the summer reflected its desperate plight: the Central Committee apparatus of the once mighty Communist Party was told to find ways of shoring up its income by forming joint-stock companies, small-scale enterprises and working with foreign partners, while republican and regional bodies were enjoined to look to their own salvation.

Document 257 | From a CPSU CC Politburo resolution on the party's financial problems

11 July 1991

Secret

1. The CCs of the Communist Parties of the union republics and the republic, *kray*, and *oblast'* Party committees are granted the right independently to deal with questions of productive and economic activity, where this does not conflict with their political work. This can include the creation, reorganization and liquidation, according to agreed procedure, of enterprises and self-financing organizations.

It is established that the property managed by the CCs of the Communist Parties of the union republics and the republic, *kray*, and *oblast'* Party committees and institutions may be transferred by them for use or full economic management, or may be used for investment in newly founded enterprises and self-financing organizations, while retaining overall Party ownership rights. However, the alienation of Party land and buildings may take place only with the agreement of the owner.

2. In order to carry out the decisions of the January 1991 united plenary session of the CPSU CC and Central Control Commission, the CCs of the Communist Parties of the union republics are to take practical steps in 1991–1992 to reduce Party budget deficits consistently and switch to self-financing through developing productive economic activities and the efficient use of the resources allotted to them for this purpose.

To this end Party mass-media outlets are to extend their publishing activities, and their participation in productive and economic activity.

Income from productive and economic activity is to be used to fulfil the Party's official tasks, as well as for charitable purposes. . .

4. A fund for financing productive and economic activity is to be created, using part of the insurance reserve of the Party's cash funds for this purpose.

Action: The CPSU CC administrative section is to allot up to 400 million rubles to finance certain highly efficient projects and proposals from Party bodies, institutions and organizations, chosen on a competitive basis, taking account of their economic and legal expertise. In these cases funds are to be allotted in the form of interest-bearing credits, the interest rate to be determined depending on the term, the amount lent, and the economic effectiveness of the project.

5. In its economic activities the CPSU CC administrative section is to employ modern organizational and legal economic forms (joint-stock companies, small-scale enterprises, reliable foreign partners, etc.).

Action: Concrete proposals are to be worked out and put forward for setting up where necessary Party enterprises and firms, funds and other economic or social structures through which the management of Party property can be effected.

The operational aspects of the most important questions of productive and economic activity are to devolve upon comrades Shenin, Luchinsky, Manaenkov, Veselkov and Kruchina.

M.S. Gorbachev, General Secretary of the CC of the CPSU
This document is to be returned to the protocol sector of the CPSU CC General Department within three months.

[Source: *Istoricheskiy arkhiv*, No. 1, 1992, pp. 7–8.]

22

The Break-up of the USSR

By the winter of 1990–91, each of the four pillars on which the postwar Soviet regime rested was in ruins. The international status of the USSR had shrivelled along with the disappearance of the Socialist Commonwealth, and the notion of imminent 'imperialist' aggression had evaporated. The main-stays of the Soviet command economy had snapped, and both output and welfare provision were in decline. Marxism–Leninism had proved helpless before the intellectual and cultural forces unleashed by glasnost, and its monopoly claims had been abandoned by the party leader himself. The legit-imacy of the CPSU had been dealt a body blow both by All-Union and by republican elections. The governments that emerged, whether still proclaiming their loyalty to the CPSU or explicitly repudiating it, adopted the language and exploited the appeal of nationalism. The leaders both of the Union Republics and, increasingly, of the Autonomous Republics, proclaimed their own sovereignty. The drastic decline in the economic and financial power of the Soviet government was there for all to see as tax receipts were withheld at republican level or below, and regions, cities and individual enterprises began to defy the instructions of Moscow's central ministries. Its ability to call upon the ultimate sanction of coercive force became increasingly uncertain as one republican government after another appointed its own local KGB chieftain, issued orders forbidding its nationals to serve outside its own republican territory, and in some cases even began to form its own military units and 'national guards'. It does not follow that nationalist momentum within the constituent republics of the USSR made its fragmentation inevitable. It remained difficult for contemporaries, whether within or outside the USSR, to imagine the vast multinational state disappearing from the scene. Yet many of the established bonds which had held the Union together—international security, the command economy, the dominant ideology and the political system—had lost their purchase. And the year 1991 saw the dénouement ensue with breathtaking speed.

Gorbachev's retreat

Late in 1990, Gorbachev took steps to shore up his position among those in the party, the central ministries, the KGB and the army who were alarmed at the threat to the unity of the USSR. He replaced several relatively liberal ministers with markedly more conservative figures, and his condemnation of minority nationalism and 'extremism' threatening Soviet interests became much more fierce.[189] In December, Shevardnadze dramatically resigned as Foreign Minister, warning that reactionary forces behind Gorbachev were poised to stage a coup against the peaceful and liberalizing tendencies of perestroika. The following month, in apparent confirmation of Shevardnadze's warning, units loyal to Moscow made a show of force against nationalist self-assertion in Lithuania and Latvia, the most violent move coming on the night of 12/13 January when Soviet troops seized the television station in the Lithuanian capital, Vilnius, and fourteen people were killed. Gorbachev's own role remains contentious: he appears to have quickly drawn back from the resort to force but only after helping to foster the climate in which the frustration of the local Russian minority and of the Soviet military boiled over. Most perplexing for him was the public reaction in Russia, where vocal opinion was incensed at the resort to violence and strongly sympathetic to Baltic nationalism. Yeltsin swiftly aligned himself with this position. He flew to the Estonian capital, Tallinn, met the leaders of the three Baltic republics, and roundly condemned the Soviet government. In the following appeal he called upon Russian soldiers serving in the Soviet army in the Baltic republics to defy orders, claiming that a decree by the Russian Congress of People's Deputies a month earlier rendered their use outside the RSFSR unlawful.

| Document 258 | From an address by Boris Yeltsin, Chairman of the RSFSR Supreme Soviet, on military action in Lithuania |

13 January 1991

Soldiers, sergeants and officers! Fellow citizens called up into the army in the territory of the Russian Federation but now in the Baltic States!

Today, when our country is suffering an economic and political crisis and society's

---

189 For a detailed account of Gorbachev's apparent 'turn to the right', see G.M. Hahn, *Russia's Revolution from Above, 1985–2000: Reform, Transition and Revolution in the Fall of the Soviet Communist Regime* (New Brunswick, NJ, 2002).

healthy forces are seeking lawful and constitutional ways out of the difficult situation which has developed, you may be called upon to act against lawfully constituted state bodies and against a peaceful civilian population defending their democratic achievements.

You may also be told that order will be restored in society with your help. But can breaching the Constitution and the law really be seen as restoring order? It is towards precisely this that you are being pushed by those who are trying to solve political problems by armed force.

. . . Can you really consent to the role they have assigned to you?

I direct your attention to the fact that to send conscripts called up in the Russian Federation outside the borders of the Republic to participate in tasks not covered by Article 29 of the Constitution of the RSFSR goes against the decree of the Extraordinary Congress of People's Deputies of the RSFSR, adopted on 11 December 1990, and is therefore unlawful.

[Source: *Rossiya*, No. 3, 1991.]

Gorbachev appears to have been taken aback by the fury with which the action in Vilnius was met and, following further violence by special Soviet units a week later, this time in the Latvian capital, Riga, he explicitly disassociated himself from the resort to force. In the ensuing weeks his efforts were focused on securing a form of democratic mandate and on mobilizing support for upholding the unity of the USSR by calling a referendum on the issue. He had first mooted the idea in December 1990, following the publication of a draft of the new Union Treaty on which work had been proceeding. The new Treaty was designed to appease the demands of Union Republics while preserving significant power for the All-Union authorities, and, once endorsed, to set the stamp on a reformed USSR. He now proposed that the entire Soviet electorate be invited to endorse 'the maintenance of the USSR as a renewed federation of equal, sovereign republics'.

The referendum on the maintenance of the USSR

On the face of it, the referendum held on 17 March was a qualified success for Gorbachev. True, six of the fifteen Union Republics—Estonia, Latvia and Lithuania in the Baltic, Georgia and Armenia in the Caucasus, and Moldova—refused even to take part in the vote, the first four of these having organized separate referenda in which there was overwhelming support for outright independence. But the combined population of the six constituted only just over 7 per cent of the Soviet population as a whole, and in the rest of the country, a large majority of those who voted endorsed the preservation of the USSR. The vote gave the lie to the notion that in Russia, Ukraine, Belorussia, the five Central Asian republics and Azerbaijan there was unstoppable popular demand for the dissolution of the USSR in favour of independent nation-states. The following official announcement put a positive gloss on the results.

Document 259 | **From the USSR Supreme Soviet's resolution *On the Results of the USSR Referendum of 17 March 1991***

21 March 1991

Having examined the report of the Central Referendum Commission of the USSR on the results of the first referendum in the country's history, held on 17 March 1991, on the question of retaining the USSR as a renewed federation of equal sovereign republics in which the human rights and freedoms of people from all ethnic groups are fully guaranteed, the Supreme Soviet of the USSR notes the high level of activity and social responsibility of those who took part in the voting.

According to preliminary data 147 million people took part in the nationwide referendum. 112 million, i.e., 76% of those who took part, voted in favour of retaining the Union of Soviet Socialist Republics. Thus, the majority of citizens felt that the fate of the country's peoples is indivisible and that only by combined effort can they successfully solve the questions of economic, social and cultural development. Support was given to the position of the IV Congress of People's Deputies of the USSR and the Supreme Soviet of the USSR on retaining the USSR on the basis of democratic reforms.

Despite the fact that the authorities in a number of republics (Georgia, Lithuania, Moldova, Latvia, Armenia and Estonia) did not implement the decisions of the IV Congress of People's Deputies of the USSR and the Supreme Soviet of the USSR on holding a referendum, that citizens' rights were infringed, that moral pressure was put on them and that polling stations were blockaded, more than 2 million Soviet citizens living in these republics expressed their will and said 'yes' to the USSR. The Supreme Soviet of the USSR considers such a show of citizenship an act of courage and patriotism. The Supreme Soviet of the USSR condemns the use of power by these authorities, to the detriment of human rights, and under slogans of national sovereignty and democracy.

The Supreme Soviet of the USSR resolves:

1. The state bodies of the USSR and the Republics are to be guided in their practical activities by the people's decision, taken in a referendum, in favour of a renewed Union of Soviet Socialist Republics, the decision being final and binding throughout the territory of the USSR.

2. On the basis of the results of the referendum, the President of the USSR, the Federation Council and Supreme Soviets of the Republics are advised to work more

energetically on completing the drafting of a new Union Treaty, so that it can be signed as soon as possible. At the same time work on a new draft Constitution of the USSR must be speeded up. . .

[Source: *Izvestiya*, 22 March, 1991.]

Yeltsin's popular election as Russian President

In itself, however, the referendum made only a marginal impact on the balance of power between Gorbachev and republican leaders. For one thing, the authorities in six of the nine participating Union Republics had posed additional questions alongside the issue of perpetuating the USSR, and had elicited large majorities in favour of enhanced autonomy for the Union Republics. In Russia, the electorate had also endorsed the establishment of a directly elected Presidency of the RSFSR. Given Yeltsin's domination of the Russian political scene, there was no doubt that once the RSFSR Congress had approved the proposal, he would secure a popular legitimacy that would contrast sharply with the tarnished source of Gorbachev's authority, and would give him a measure of independence from the RSFSR legislature. Further weakening Gorbachev's position was the outbreak of a massive wave of miners' strikes shortly after the referendum, triggered in part by price rises of the kind the Soviet leadership had so long resisted. Yeltsin reaped the benefit of his refusal since coming to head the government of the RSFSR to back a coherent budget, sanction price rises or implement an economic reform package. Miners' leaders in Russia demanded both that Gorbachev should resign and that responsibility for the coalfields should be transferred from the Soviet government to that of the RSFSR.

Gorbachev was thus in no position to impose a new Union Treaty on the nine prospective member republics. On the contrary, he found himself forced to respond to the demands of their respective governments that the draft be amended to shift more power, and notably economic power, away from the centre. It was only on this basis that in April he secured the consent of the leaders of the nine to the so-called 'nine-plus-one agreement'. In retrospect, it is true, the ill-fated federation that was proposed, to be renamed the Union of Soviet Sovereign Republics, appears a political project of considerable significance. But at the time what was most striking was the reduction in the role of the centre. And the shift in the balance of power was underlined in unmistakable terms when elections to the new Presidency of the RSFSR were held in June. Yeltsin inflicted a humiliating defeat on his opponents, securing 57 per cent of the vote, with his nearest rival, Gorbachev's former Prime Minister, Ryzhkov, receiving 17 per cent. Just how low the stock of the Soviet establishment had fallen was shown by the derisory 3.7 per cent of the vote for the traditionalist General A. Makashov and 3.2 per cent for Gorbachev's own preferred candidate, V. Boldin. Both trailed well behind the remaining candidate, V. Zhirinovsky, whose outspoken nationalist, authoritarian, populist and eccentric rhetoric saw him rise rapidly from obscurity.

The August putsch

The following month Yeltsin used his new executive authority to ban the party from activity in all state bodies and enterprises within the RSFSR. Frustration among traditionalists and the more conservative of Gorbachev's ministers reached crisis point. Towards the end of July, they learned that Gorbachev had agreed with Yeltsin that, following the signing of the new Union Treaty, scheduled for 20 August, he would dismiss key figures known to oppose the proposed new order, including Kryuchkov, the KGB chief; V. Pavlov, the prime minister; and D. Yazov, the defence minister. It was on the very eve of the ceremonial signing of the new treaty that a group of officials within the government who were determined to halt the dissolution of central power and of Soviet unity took action. Unable to persuade Gorbachev to sanction their plans, they placed him under house arrest in the Crimea, where he was on holiday, and declared him temporarily too ill to carry out his duties as President. They proceeded to proclaim a state of emergency and the transfer of executive authority into the hands of an eight-man State Emergency Committee nominally headed by G. Yanaev, the uninspiring and low-profile official whom Gorbachev had the previous winter appointed to the new post of Vice-President.

Document 260 | The declaration of a state of emergency

18 August 1991

In view of the inability of Mikhail Sergeevich Gorbachev to carry out the duties of USSR President for health reasons and the transfer of the powers of USSR President to the USSR Vice-President, Gennadiy Ivanovich Yanaev, in accordance with Article 127(7) of the Constitution of the USSR;

In order to overcome the profound and all-round crisis, the political, ethnic and civil confrontations, the chaos and anarchy threatening the lives and safety of Soviet citizens, the sovereignty, territorial integrity, freedom and independence of our Fatherland;

Proceeding from the results of the all-national referendum on retaining the Union of Soviet Socialist Republics;

Guided by the vitally important interests of the people of our Motherland, of all Soviet people,

We declare that:

1. In accordance with Article 127(3) of the Constitution of the USSR and Article 2 of the USSR law *On the Legal Regime of a State of Emergency*, to meet the demands of broad strata of the population to take the most decisive measures to obviate society sliding into a national catastrophe, and to maintain law and order, from 04.00 Moscow time 19 August 1991 we declare a six-month state of emergency in certain parts of the USSR.

2. We confirm that the Constitution and laws of the USSR are to have unconditional supremacy throughout the USSR.

3. To govern the country and effectively implement the state of emergency, a State Committee for the State of Emergency in the USSR (GKChP) has been formed. Its members are as follows: O.D. Baklanov, First Deputy Chairman of the USSR Defence Council; V.A. Kryuchkov, Chairman of the USSR KGB; V.S. Pavlov, USSR Prime Minister; B.K. Pugo, USSR Minister of Internal Affairs; V.A. Starodubtsev, chairman of the USSR Peasant Union; A.I. Tizyakov, President of the USSR Association of State Enterprises and Industrial, Building, Transport and Communication Sites; D.T. Yazov, USSR Minister of Defence; and G.I. Yanaev, Vice-President of the USSR.

4. We confirm that the decisions of the USSR GKChP are binding on all state and administrative bodies, civil servants and citizens throughout the USSR.

G. Yanaev

V. Pavlov

O. Baklanov

[Source: *Pravda*, 20 August 1991.]

The leaders of what became known as the 'August putsch' denounced the incipient dissolution of the USSR. The referendum on the future of the USSR, and opinion polls at the time and later, suggest that a substantial proportion of the population, particularly in the nine major republics, had some sympathy for the aims of the Emergency Committee. Potentially, at least, there was a willingness to see if an alternative leadership could halt economic decline and what seemed mounting political chaos. Even among younger Soviet citizens, whose general attitude to the rapid breakdown of the traditional Soviet order was mostly positive, initial reactions were thoroughly divided.

Document 261 | Recollections of participants in the events of 19–21 August 1991

Dmitriy Gurevich, 22, a student: On the morning of 19 August I was asleep. It was the vacation. Some acquaintances rang to say Gorbachev had been removed. I asked them to stop messing around and let me rest. More calls. I switched on the TV. *Swan Lake* on every channel. I liked the content of the GKChP's first documents. I thought that people had been found who would restore order in the country, and that Yeltsin had already been arrested, a case was being prepared against him, and that maybe he would end up against a wall. I took everything very seriously, thinking it was a real coup. Now I think the events of 19–21 August were just a show.

Aleksey Rezaev, 31, an artist: For me nothing really happened on the morning of 19 August. Moreover, when I heard that politically active people who promised to tackle corruption and brigandage were taking power, I thought, 'At last we're going to have some order in this country.' It was hard to make sense of what was really happening. After I'd read Yeltsin's *Address*, I realized there'd been a coup. I also realized I couldn't remain indifferent. Once I had worked that out, I decided I must get out in the streets. Then I did a series of posters, *Before and after the coup*.

Vladimir Savin, from Nizhniy Tagil: On the evening of 21 August we managed to organize a meeting outside the Contemporary cinema. We had only learned the truth about what was happening in Moscow, St Petersburg and Ekaterinburg thanks to contacts with democratic organizations in our *oblast'* centre.

Aleksandr Vyshintsev, 79, war veteran: I was passing through Moscow. When I heard about the coup on the radio, I was really incensed. I fired a salvo, like I would have done at the front, and headed for Red Square. I, a former marine, felt ashamed that soldiers were embroiled in such a dirty deed.

Oleg Kokotov, 17, an anarchist: Once the shock was over, by the evening we were strengthening our barricade and then looked for petrol to make petrol bombs. There were gunshots during the night. On the whole, relations between people were very warm. I acquitted myself fairly well on the barricades and made new friends, but I am ashamed I was defending the government. I'm sure I became just a puppet in a political game and was taking part in some grand show.

[Source: *V avguste 91-go. Rossiya glazami ochevidtsev* (Moscow and St Petersburg 1993), pp. 201–10.]

Whatever the potential level of support for their goals, the Emergency Committee proved entirely incapable of gaining public confidence in their ability to achieve them. A part of the problem lay in their rhetoric. They rightly judged that traditional Soviet discourse had been so drained of credibility that to fall back upon it would only weaken their case. They made no reference to the collapse of the Socialist Commonwealth, to the planned economy or to Marxism–Leninism. Even the CPSU was not mentioned. Yet this silence did little to aid their cause. On the one hand, it did nothing to dissuade those who reacted against them that they intended to reverse the reforms of the Gorbachev years, to 'turn the clock backwards'. On the other, they could find no alternative language, narrative or vision of the future with which to legitimize their intervention.

Nor did they seem sure of the specific steps they would take once in power. They condemned the fanning of minority nationalist passion, and the way successive republican governments seized illegal sovereignty and proceeded to privilege the titular majority, thereby overnight turning others into embattled minorities or even foreigners within the republic in which they had hitherto lived peacefully. They denounced the disruption of the economy, the sharp fall in living standards, the rise in prices, and the threat to the established right to work and to social welfare. They pointed to rising levels of crime and the decadence for which they blamed unbounded glasnost, 'the propaganda of sex and violence. . . the octopus of crime and glaring immorality'. But on every issue—diplomatic, military, constitutional, economic, social, ideological—they sounded tentative, opportunist, ill-prepared. They would start a 'nationwide discussion'; they 'favoured' this; they would 'support' that; they would welcome constructive ideas from anybody. And the dishevelled, nervous impression they made on television underlined the hesitancy of their 'Appeal to the Soviet People'.

Document 262 | The Emergency Committee's Appeal to the Soviet People

19 August 1991

Fellow countrymen! Citizens of the Soviet Union!

At this grave, critical hour for the fate of the fatherland and of our peoples, we appeal to you! A mortal danger threatens our great homeland! For a number of reasons, the policy of reforms begun at the initiative of M.S. Gorbachev and conceived of as a means of ensuring the dynamic development of the country and the democratisation of the life of society has reached an impasse. The initial enthusiasm and hopes have given way to unbelief, apathy and despair. The authorities at all levels have lost the trust of the population. In the life of society, political intrigue has supplanted concern for the fate of the fatherland and the citizen. Malicious mocking of all state institutions is being propagated. In essence, the country has become ungovernable.

Taking advantage of the liberties that have been granted and trampling the shoots of democracy, which have just emerged, extremist forces have come into being and embarked on a course aimed at the liquidation of the Soviet Union, the break-up of the state and the seizure of power at any cost. The results of the nationwide referendum on the unity of the fatherland have been trampled. The cynical exploitation of national feelings is only a screen for satisfying ambitions. . .

The crisis of power has had a catastrophic effect on the economy. The chaotic, ungoverned slide toward a market has caused an explosion of selfishness—regional, departmental, group and personal. The war of laws and the encouragement of centrifugal tendencies have brought about the destruction of a unified national–economic mechanism that took shape over decades. The result is a sharp fall off in the standard of living for the over-whelming majority of Soviet people and the flourishing of speculation and the shadow economy. . .

All the democratic institutions created through the expression of the people's will are losing their authority and effectiveness before our very eyes. This is the result of purposeful actions by those who, blatantly flouting the USSR Basic-Law, are staging an unconstitutional coup, to all intents and purposes, and longing for unbridled personal dictatorship. . .

An offensive against the rights of the working people is under way. The rights to work, education, health care, housing and recreation have been called in question.

Even people's basic personal safety is increasingly under threat. Crime is growing at a rapid rate and is becoming organised and politicised. The country is sinking into an abyss of violence and lawlessness. Never before in the country's history has the propaganda of sex and violence gained such wide scope, jeopardising the health lives of future generations. Millions of people are demanding that measures be taken against the octopus of crime and glaring immorality. . .

The State Committee for the State of Emergency in the USSR is fully aware of the depth of the crisis that has struck our country; it is assuming responsibility for the fate of the homeland, and it is fully resolved to take very serious measures to bring the state and society out of crisis as quickly as possible.

We promise to conduct a wide-ranging, nationwide discussion of the draft of a new Union Treaty. Everyone will have the right and opportunity to think about this highly important act in a calm atmosphere and to make up his mind about it, for the fate of numerous peoples of our great homeland will depend on what the Union will be like.

We intend immediately to restore legality and law and order to put an end to bloodshed, to declare a merciless war against the criminal world, and to eradicate shameful phenomena that discredit our society and degrade Soviet citizens. . .

We favour truly democratic processes and a consistent policy of reforms leading to the renewal of our homeland and to its economic and social prosperity, which will enable it to take a worthy place in the world community of nations.

The country's development should not be built on a fall-off in the population's living standard. In a healthy society, continual improvement in the well-being of all citizens will become the norm.

In the process of developing a mixed national economy, we will support private enterprise, providing it with the necessary possibilities for developing production and the service sphere.

Our primary concern will be solving the food and housing problems. All available forces will be mobilised for the satisfaction of these very urgent requirements of the people.

We call on workers, peasants, the working intelligentsia and all Soviet people to restore labour discipline and order in the shortest possible time and to raise the level of production, so as then to move resolutely forward. Our life, the future of our children and grandchildren and the fate of the fatherland will depend on this. . .

For centuries, our multinational people have been filled with pride in their homeland: we have not been ashamed of our patriotic feelings, and we consider it natural and legitimate to raise present and future generations of citizens of our great power in this spirit. . .

We call on all citizens of the Soviet Union to recognise their duty to the homeland and provide every kind of support to the State Committee for the State of Emergency in the USSR and to efforts to bring the country out of crisis.

Constructive proposals from public-political organisations, labour collectives and citizens will be gratefully accepted as a manifestation of their patriotic readiness to participate actively in the restoration of a centuries-old friendship in the single family of fraternal peoples and in the revival of the fatherland.

The State Committee for the State of Emergency in the USSR

[Source: *Current Digest of the Soviet Press*, Vol. XLIII, No. 33 (18 September 1991), pp. 2–4.]

It quickly became plain that the State of Emergency Committee could not count on the loyalty either of the army or of much of the state apparatus. Those military units which mobilized acted without conviction, and the reluctance to spill blood ran all the way to General Yazov at the defence ministry. Even the KGB leadership found its control of the police apparatus uncertain and orders to arrest prominent radicals went unheeded. The Committee was endorsed by more conservative republican leaders—notably in Belorussia, Azerbaijan, Tadzhikistan and Uzbekistan—but across much of the country its authority was never established. Moreover, in Leningrad and above all Moscow the attempted putsch provoked large-scale counter-demonstrations: the White House, seat of the Russian Supreme Soviet, was surrounded by crowds defying the expected attempt by the Emergency Committee to use force to storm it. Resistance was personified by Yeltsin, who immediately denounced the Committee, threatening any official of the RSFSR who acted on its orders with criminal prosecution.

Document 263 | **The decree of the President of the RSFSR declaring the State Committee for the State of Emergency unconstitutional**

19 August 1991

In connection with the actions of a group of individuals styling themselves the so-called State Committee for the State of Emergency I decree as follows:

1. The Committee's declaration is to be considered unconstitutional and its organizers' actions classed as a coup d'état, which is nothing other than a crime against the state.

2. Any decision taken in the name of the so-called State Committee for the State of Emergency is to be considered unlawful and without validity in the territory of the RSFSR. Throughout the Russian Federation the legally elected authorities, in the form of the President, the Chairman of the Supreme Soviet, the Chairman of the Council of Ministers, and all state and local authorities, are continuing to operate.

3. Actions by civil servants who implement the said Committee's decisions will be subject to the Criminal Code of the RSFSR and will be liable to legal proceedings.

This decree comes into force from the moment it is signed.

B. Yeltsin

[Source: *Ural'skiy rabochiy*, 20 August 1991.]

Bold though the leaders of the RSFSR were in resisting the coup, the terms in which they couched successive appeals for popular resistance and moral support from the west reflected uncertainty over public reactions, and the acute paradoxes inherent in the situation. In a manner quite unlike their attitude hitherto, Yeltsin and his colleagues now emphasized Gorbachev's legitimate authority. In the following address, published in those newspapers which defied the Emergency Committee, they assured the public that they were working to preserve the USSR; they portrayed themselves as champions of Soviet security and international prestige; they even demanded an emergency session of the Soviet Congress of People's Deputies whose authority till now they had been working so assiduously to undermine.

Document 264 | **Address by the political leadership of the RSFSR to the citizens of Russia**

19 August 1991

During the night of 18–19 August 1991 the lawfully elected President of the country was removed from office.

Whatever reasons may be advanced to justify this removal, we are dealing with a rightist, reactionary and anti-constitutional coup. Despite all the trials and tribulations the people are going through, the democratic process in the country is becoming more entrenched and more irreversible. The peoples of Russia are becoming masters of their own fate and the uncontrolled rights of non-constitutional bodies, including Party bodies, have been substantially curtailed. The leadership of Russia has taken a firm position on the Union Treaty in trying to maintain the unity of the Soviet Union and the unity of Russia. Our position on this question has allowed us significantly to accelerate the preparation of this Treaty, co-ordinate with all the Republics and fix a date for its signing—20 August this year. Such a course of events has embittered the reactionary forces, prompting them to irresponsible adventurist attempts to solve the most complex political and economic problems by means of force. There have already been other attempts to carry out a coup.

We believed and still believe that these sorts of forcible methods are unacceptable. It discredits the USSR in the eyes of the world, undermines our prestige in the world community and returns us to the time of the Cold War and the isolation of the Soviet Union from the world community.

All of this has obliged us to declare the so-called Committee which has taken power unlawful. Consequently, we declare all this Committee's decisions and edicts unlawful.

We are certain that local authorities will unswervingly adhere to the constitutional laws and decrees of the President of the RSFSR.

We call upon the citizens of Russia to give a worthy reply to the putschists and demand the country be returned to normal constitutional development.

Gorbachev, the President of the country, *must* be allowed to speak to the people.

We demand the immediate convening of an Extraordinary Congress of People's Deputies of the USSR. We are absolutely convinced that our fellow citizens will not give their approval to lawlessness and arbitrary rule or to putschists who have lost all shame or conscience.

We call upon servicemen to show a high level of civic duty and not to take part in this reactionary coup.

Until these demands are fulfilled we call for an indefinite general strike.

We have no doubt that the world community will give an objective assessment of this cynical attempt at a right-wing coup.

B. Yeltsin, President of the RSFSR
I. Silaev, Chairman of the Council of Ministers of the RSFSR
R. Khasbulatov, Acting Chairman of the Supreme Soviet of the RSFSR
Arkhangel'skoe, midnight, 19 August 1991

[Source: *Ural'skiy rabochiy*, 20 August 1991.]

At the same time, making precisely the connection Yanaev and his colleagues sought to avoid, Yeltsin attacked the State Committee as essentially a front for the CPSU. With heavy irony, he accused the party of playing the role in the coup which the Soviet Constitution had so long assigned to it in Soviet society—of being its 'organizing and inspirational force'.

Document 265 | From Boris Yeltsin's appeal of 20 August 1991

A coup took place on 19 August. It is blindingly obvious that the date was not fortuitous: it was the last day before the signing of the new Union Treaty. A treaty which, despite all its compromises, was to put an end to the absolute power of the CPSU and the military–industrial complex.

I listen to the coup organizers speak and am astounded: how low can one sink! Yesterday they were stigmatizing the leaders of Russia for supposedly not wanting to sign the Union Treaty, while today they are trying to convince the people that our wish to sign it is apparently directed against the renewal of the Union.

In objective terms the new Union Treaty was going to deprive virtually every one of the coup organizers of their opportunities. That is the secret of the conspiracy. That is the main motivation of its participants. All their blather about the fate of the Fatherland is little more than a game to conceal their own selfish interests.

I had a reason for mentioning the CPSU. Let us not close our eyes to this: this very party is 'the organizing and inspirational force' behind the coup. The Committee's decrees have abolished all parties except the Communist Party. All newspapers except Communist ones have been banned. Is that not so? I am sure the time will come when the top people in the CPSU will disown participation in this evil deed against the people. But it will hardly succeed in using demagoguery to hide what lies at the heart of its activities—fighting the people to preserve its privileges.

I want to declare yet again in no uncertain terms that all that has happened in the last ttwenty-four hours has been no less than a coup d'état, and that its leaders are no less than state criminals.

Boris Yeltsin, President of the Russian Federation
20 August 1991

[Source: *Obshchaya gazeta*, 21 August 1991.]

Given the threatening tone of the Emergency Committee, the announcement of a curfew, and the scale of what was at stake, the attempted coup gave rise to remarkably little violence. In Moscow just three deaths arose directly from the emergency, on the night of 20 August, and while protesters saw those killed as victims of the coup plotters, the following account by

Zhirinovsky captures, in his eccentric way, the verdict of many that much blame lay with supporters of Yeltsin.

Document 266 | Verdict on August 1991 by V.V. Zhirinovsky (LDPR leader)

1993

August 1991 in Moscow was awful. Armoured personnel carriers were going under the bridge along Kalinin Avenue, and a crowd of furious, half-drunk Muscovites stopped one, dragged out the driver and were trying to set fire to it. Wasn't this barbarous behaviour? Even if deploying troops was in some way unjustified and in some way barbarous, it was even more barbarous to attack the troops, to try to beat up tank or APC drivers and commit violence against them. The troops would just have driven on. Three Muscovites wouldn't have died, if there hadn't been such an artificial clash and attempts to provoke and whip up hatred. These lads, the tank drivers, had entered Moscow and stationed themselves in specific places. They weren't shooting, they weren't threatening anybody, they just climbed out of their tanks, bought ice-creams and chatted with the girls. Children and adults were climbing onto the tanks—these were our lads, it was our army. And it was out of this that they were trying to provoke hostile actions and whip up a major conflict. And the final result was that there were victims. But it wasn't the GKChP [State Emergency Committee] that did this, but the 'Democratic Russia' people, certain adventurist forces who wanted to make the situation worse.

[Source: V.V. Zhirinovsky, *Posledniy brosok na yug* (Moscow 1993), pp. 109–10.]

By the following day, 21 August, the State Emergency Committee was in disarray. Although workers' protest was patchy and those who reacted most vigorously against the coup were dismayed by the extent of popular indifference, visible resistance and hostile demonstrations and declarations were sufficient to destroy the resolve of Yanaev and his colleagues. Pugo, the nominated Interior Minister, committed suicide and the coup collapsed.

The banning of the CPSU in Russia

Gorbachev was swiftly brought back to Moscow. But far from returning in triumph, the coup and its abject defeat rendered him almost helpless. Despite his refusal to support the coup, he was subjected to public humiliation by Yeltsin. Were not Yanaev and his fellow plotters men handpicked and appointed by Gorbachev himself? And had not Gorbachev signally failed to condemn the party for its patent support for the coup? Before Gorbachev's very eyes, Yeltsin signed a decree banning the activities of the CPSU throughout the territory of the RSFSR.

Document 267 | The President of the RSFSR's decree *On Halting the Activity of the Communist Party of the RSFS.*

23 August 1991

The Communist Party of the RSFSR, operating in the territory of the RSFSR but not officially registered, supported the so-called State Committee for the State of Emergency in the USSR, which staged a coup d'état and forcibly removed the President of the USSR from office. In several regions of the RSFSR, with the direct participation of republic, *kray* and *oblast'* organs of the RSFSR CP, emergency committees and commissions were formed, which is a gross infringement of the USSR Law *On public associations.*

Organs of the RSFSR CP in republics, *kraya* and *oblasti* have meddled on more than one occasion in legal proceedings and have been hindering the implementation of the President of the RSFSR's decree *On stopping the activities of the organizational structures of political parties and mass public movements in state bodies, institutions and organizations of the RSFSR.*

On the basis of the above I decree as follows:

1. The RSFSR Ministry of Internal Affairs and Office of the Public Prosecutor of the RSFSR are to look into the facts of the anti-constitutional activities of the Communist Party of the RSFSR. The corresponding materials will be sent for judicial scrutiny.

2. Until a final judicial decision has been reached on the unconstitutional activities of the CP of the RSFSR, all activity on the part of bodies and organizations of the Communist Party of the RSFSR is to cease.

3. The Ministry of Internal Affairs of the RSFSR is to ensure the safekeeping of the property and funds of the Communist Party of the RSFSR until a final judicial decision is made.

4. The Central Bank of the RSFSR is to ensure that all expenditures from accounts of organs and organizations of the CP of the RSFSR cease until instructed otherwise.

5. The Office of the Public Prosecutor of the RSFSR is to ensure compliance with this decree.

6. This decree comes into force the moment it is signed.

B.N. Yeltsin, President of the RSFSR

[Source: *Rossiyskaya gazeta,* 27 December 1991.]

Gorbachev immediately resigned as General Secretary and urged the Central Committee to dissolve itself. Over the subsequent weeks, he replaced the many senior officials implicated in the coup with much more liberal figures. But by now the Soviet government, its All-Union institutions, its administrative apparatus, and the KGB itself were in a tailspin. Yeltsin and his entourage began to take over parts of the Kremlin itself. Little more than a fortnight after his return to Moscow, Gorbachev found himself compelled to recognize the complete independence of the Baltic republics.

Document 268 | **'The State Council of the USSR has recognized the independence of Latvia, Lithuania and Estonia'—TASS communiqué on the first sitting of the USSR State Council on 6 September 1991**

As its first item on 6 September the State Council of the USSR, chaired by M.S. Gorbachev, has recognized the independence of the Latvian republic, the Lithuanian republic and the Estonian republic.

B.D. Pankin, the USSR Foreign Minister, speaking at the Press Centre of the USSR Foreign Ministry, made the following statement on the same day, 'The decision was adopted unanimously, having taken into account the concrete historical and political circumstances preceding the entry of these republics into the USSR. At the same time it was decided to hold the talks stipulated by the Congress of People's Deputies of the USSR with the aforementioned republics on a whole variety of questions connected with civil rights and the economic, political, defence, humanitarian and other interests of these republics and the USSR.'

[Source: *Pravda*, 7 September 1991.]

During October and November, Gorbachev brought some of his best-known allies of his early years back to office, including Shevardnadze as Foreign Minister. He continued to strive for the survival of some form of Union, however drastically reduced the powers reserved to the centre might be. But he was now widely disdained, both by those who despised the crumbling old order and by those who regretted its passing. The mechanism by which he had come to power, the Communist Party, lay in ruins, and he had never secured a direct democratic mandate. Without Yeltsin's support, he was impotent to resist the disintegration of the USSR. One republic after another declared outright independence, and the death knell for even the most residual form of Union was sounded on 1 December when a referendum in Ukraine, by far the largest Union Republic outside Russia, yielded a massive 90 per cent majority for independence. Yeltsin and the Ukrainian President L. Kravchuk flew to Minsk and in place of the USSR proclaimed the formation of a loose and ill-defined 'Commonwealth of Independent States' (CIS).

Document 269 | **The joint declaration of the heads of state of Russia, Belarus and Ukraine on a Commonwealth of Independent States, 8 December 1991**

We, the leaders of the Republic of Belarus, the RSFSR and Ukraine,
– noting that talks on the preparation of a new Union Treaty have reached a deadlock and that the objective process of republics leaving the USSR and forming independent states has become a reality;
– stating that the centre's short-sighted policy has led to a profound economic and political crisis, to the collapse of production and a catastrophic decline in the living standards of virtually every stratum of society;
– taking into account the growth of social tension in many areas of the former USSR, which has led to inter-ethnic conflicts costing many human lives;
– realizing our responsibility to our peoples and the world community and the urgent need for political and economic reform,

announce the formation of the Commonwealth of Independent States, regarding which the parties signed the agreement on 8 December 1991.

The Commonwealth of Independent States, comprising the Republic of Belarus, the RSFSR and Ukraine, is open to all the member states of the USSR and to any other state, sharing the goals and principles of this agreement.

The member states of the Commonwealth intend to pursue a policy of strengthening international peace and security. They guarantee the implementation of the international obligations devolving upon them from the former USSR and will ensure a unified control over nuclear weapons and their non-proliferation.

S. Shushkevich, Chairman of the Supreme Soviet of the Republic of Belarus
B. Yeltsin, President of the RSFSR
L. Kravchuk, President of Ukraine
Minsk, 8 December 1991

[Source: *Rossiyskaya gazeta*, 10 December 1991.]

Gorbachev went through the motions of protesting the wisdom and the legality of the declaration. But he was no longer in a position either to threaten or cajole republican leaders. His plaintive speculation that he 'would not rule out' a further referendum underlined how little leverage remained to him.

Document 270 | **Response by M.S. Gorbachev, President of the USSR, to the declaration on a Commonwealth of States**

9 December 1991

In Minsk on 8 December 1991 the leaders of Belarus, the RSFSR and Ukraine concluded an agreement on the formation of the Commonwealth of Independent States.

For me, as the country's president, the main criterion in evaluating the document is how far it meets the security needs of the citizens, the tasks of overcoming the present crisis, the maintenance of statehood and the continuation of democratic reforms.

This agreement does have some positive aspects.

The Ukrainian leadership, which has not recently been involved in the Treaty process, did take part in it.

The document emphasizes the need for the creation of a single economic space functioning according to agreed principles with a single currency and financial and banking system. It expresses a readiness to co-operate in the fields of science, education, culture and elsewhere. It sets out a definite formula for co-operation in the military-strategic sphere.

However, this document is of such significance, it has such a profound effect on the interests of the peoples of our country and of the world community, that it deserves very close political and legal scrutiny.

The following is in any case obvious to me. The agreement openly declares that the USSR has ceased to exist. Undoubtedly, each republic does have the right to secede from the union, but the fate of a multinational state cannot be decided by the will of the leaders of three republics. This question should be decided only by constitutional methods with the participation of all the sovereign states and with account being taken of their peoples' will.

Declaring that All-Union legal norms are no longer in force is also unlawful and dangerous and can only increase the chaos and anarchy in society.

The speed with which this document has appeared is bewildering. It was not discussed either by the people or the Supreme Soviets of the republics in whose name it has been signed. Moreover, this has happened at the very moment when the parliaments of the republics were discussing the draft treaty on a Union of Sovereign States devised by the USSR State Council.

In the current situation, I am profoundly convinced, it is vital that all the Supreme Soviets of the republics and the Supreme Soviet of the USSR discuss both the draft treaty on a Union of Sovereign States and the agreement concluded in Minsk. In so far as the agreement proposes another form of statehood, which is within the competence of the Congress of People's Deputies of the USSR, it is vital to convene a Congress. Moreover, I would not exclude holding a national referendum (plebiscite) on this matter.

M. Gorbachev

[Source: *Izvestiya*, 10 December 1991.]

He was unable to mobilize any significant constituency, and within days he accepted that the Commonwealth, with virtually no institutional structure binding it together, would replace the USSR and that he would step down. On 21 December the leaders of all the Union Republics bar those of Georgia and the Baltic endorsed the Minsk initiative, joined the CIS, and proclaimed that the USSR had ceased to exist.

Document 271 | The Alma-Ata declaration

21 December 1991

The independent states
– the Azerbaijani Republic, the Republic of Armenia, the Republic of Belarus, the Republic of Kazakhstan, the Republic of Kyrgyzstan, the Republic of Moldova, the Russian Federation (RSFSR), the Republics of Tadzhikistan and Turkmenistan, the Republics of Uzbekistan and Ukraine,
– in striving to form democratic states based on the rule of law, relations among which will develop on the basis of the mutual recognition of and respect for state sovereignty and sovereign equality, the inalienable right of self-determination, the principles of equality and non-interference in internal affairs, the repudiation of the use of force or the threat of forcible, economic or any other forms of pressure, the peaceful settling of disputes, respect for human rights and freedoms, including those of national minorities, and the conscientious implementation of obligations and other universally recognized principles and standards of international law;
– in recognizing and respecting each other's territorial integrity and existing borders;
– believing that strengthening existing historical ties of friendship, good neighbourliness and mutually beneficial co-operation meets the fundamental interests of the peoples, and serves the cause of peace and security;
– in realizing their responsibility for the maintenance of civil peace and inter-ethnic accord;
– as adherents of the aims and principles of the agreement on the creation of the Commonwealth of Independent States,

declare as follows:

The Commonwealth's participants will interact according to the principle of equality via co-ordinating bodies formed on the basis of parity and functioning as determined by agreements between the participants in the Commonwealth, which is neither a state nor a supra-state body.

To ensure strategic stability and security, a unified command over military–strategic forces and a unified control over nuclear weapons will be retained; the parties will respect each other's desire to achieve the status of a nuclear-free and/or neutral state.

The Commonwealth of Independent States is open for other states to join it, with the agreement of all its participants. These may be other member-states of the former USSR or other states sharing the aims and principles of the Commonwealth.

Adherence to collaboration is affirmed by the formation and development of a common economic space with pan-European and Eurasian markets.

With the formation of the Commonwealth of Independent States the Union of Soviet Socialist Republics ceases to exist.

In accordance with their constitutional procedures the member-states of the Commonwealth guarantee to fulfil the international obligations which flow from the pacts and agreements of the former USSR.

The member-states of the Commonwealth undertake unswervingly to abide by the principles of this declaration.

For the Azerbaijani Republic—A. Mutalibov
For the Republic of Armenia—L. Ter-Petrosyan
For the Republic of Belarus—S. Shushkevich
For the Republic of Kazakhstan—N. Nazarbaev
For the Republic of Kyrgyzstan—A. Akaev
For the Republic of Moldova—M. Snegur
For the Russian Federation (RSFSR)—B. Yeltsin
For the Republic of Tadzhikistan—R. Nabiev
For Turkmenistan—S. Niyazov
For the Republic of Uzbekistan—I. Karimov
For Ukraine—L. Kravchuk
Alma–Ata 21 December 1991

[Source: *Izvestiya*, 21 December 1991.]

Gorbachev's resignation

Four days later, in a televised speech with which he would later proudly open his memoirs, Gorbachev announced his resignation.[190] In doing so, he brought the curtain down on the three-quarter-century-long history of the

---

190 Gorbachev, *Memoirs*, pp. xxvi–xxix.

Soviet Union. He did not try to mobilize support for its continuation, nor did he predict its resurrection. But he lamented the break-up of the country and what he described as 'a great civilization'. And after listing what he regarded as the achievements—political, social, economic and cultural—that had flowed from the reforms he had launched six years earlier, he called on the heirs of the USSR to see it 'reborn as a new, modern and worthy life'.

Document 272 | From Gorbachev's television broadcast resigning as President of the USSR, 25 December 1991

Dear fellow countrymen and fellow citizens,

Owing to the situation resulting from the formation of the Commonwealth of Independent States I am ceasing my activity as President of the USSR. I have taken this decision as a matter of principle.

I have firmly supported the self-reliance and independence of the peoples and the sovereignty of the republics, but also the preservation of the Union and the integrity of the country.

Events have taken a different turn. The tendency towards dismembering the country and separating the states has prevailed, with which I cannot agree.

Even after the meeting in Alma-Ata and the decisions taken there my position on this question has not changed.

Moreover, I am convinced that such momentous decisions should have been taken on the basis of the exercise of the will of the people.

Nevertheless, I shall do everything in my power to make sure that the agreements signed there lead to real social accord and make getting out of the crisis and the reform process easier.

Speaking to you for the last time as President of the USSR, I think it is necessary to give my assessment of what has happened since 1985. . .

— The totalitarian system which made it impossible for the country to flourish and prosper has been liquidated.

— We have broken through onto the path of democratic reforms. Free elections, freedom of the press, religious freedoms, representative government organs and a multi-party system have become a reality. Human rights are recognized as a supreme principle.

— Movement towards a mixed economy has begun with the affirmation of the equality of all forms of property. . .

We are living in a new world:

— The Cold War is over and the arms race and senseless militarization of the country which deformed our economy, social consciousness and morality have stopped. The threat of world war has been removed.

— We have opened up to the world and have rejected intervention in others' affairs and the use of troops beyond our borders.

– We have become one of the main bastions for the restructuring of contemporary civilization along peaceful and democratic lines.

– Peoples and nations have achieved genuine freedom of choice in their paths to self-determination.

All these changes have required immense effort and involved fierce struggles against the growing resistance of the forces of the old, the outdated and the reactionary—the former Party-state structures, the economic apparatus, not to mention our own habits, ideological prejudices, and our reductionist and dependent psychology. These changes have come up against our intolerance, low level of political culture and fear of change. . .

I think it is vitally important to preserve the democratic achievements of recent years. We have suffered to achieve them through our whole history and our tragic experience. . .

I leave my post with foreboding. However, I also leave it with hope and trust in you, your wisdom and resilience. We are the heirs of a great civilization, and it is now up to each and everyone of us to ensure that it is reborn as a new, modern and worthy life. . . I am convinced that, sooner or later, our common efforts will bear fruit and our peoples will live in a prosperous and democratic society.

[Source: *Rossiyskaya gazeta*, 27 December, 1991.]

Documents

53. 'Damn the one who thought up this war!'—from the 1941–1942 diary of Mariya Dmitrievna Yarushok (née Arbatskaya), student at the Leningrad Mining Institute

54. Ol'ga Berggol'ts recalls the first performance of Shostakovich's 7th Symphony during the siege of Leningrad

55. '. . . Stalin will be evacuated tomorrow or later, depending on the situation'—State Defence Committee decree *On the Evacuation of the Capital of the USSR, Moscow*

56. V.P. Stavsky: '. . . the guards have been wearing down and striking the enemy'

57. K. Rokossovsky: 'Fighting near Moscow, you have to think *Berlin*'—from the memoirs of P.I. Troyanovsky

58. 'In this war may you be inspired by the courageous example of our great fore-bears—Aleksandr Nevsky, Dmitriy Donskoy. . .'—from I.V. Stalin's speech to a Red Army parade on Red Square

59. 'The Army has stopped retreating and has been pummelling the enemy for about 20 days now. . .'—from a report to I.V. Stalin by K.D. Golubev, commander of the 43rd Army

60. 'Our conceited and arrogant adversary was planning to spend the winter in the heated buildings of Moscow and Leningrad. . .'—from Supreme GHQ's Order No. 0428

61. 'The Germans were with us for only four days. . .'—from a transcript of school-children in 1941 talking about the war

62. '. . . I just could not comprehend how in our day and age such bestial murders of totally innocent Christians could be committed in a holy cathedral. . .'—from a report to the Patriarchate of Moscow

63. 'Yes, Dad, I'm the slave of a German baron, too. . .'—from a letter by a victim of the German occupation

64. The use of foreigners and POWs as forced labour by Nazi Germany 1941–1944

65. 'This is what we're avenging, fighting and dying for!'—from a letter by I.I. Shapiro, correspondent of a divisional newspaper, to her fellow students

66. '. . . Perhaps laying these 'typhoid mines' would work!'—from E.A. Dolmatovsky's notebook

9.   The Home Front, Legitimacy and the Economic War Effort

67. 'Aircraft are starting to be produced when we still don't have windows or roofs'—from the memoirs of the designer A.S. Yakovlev

68. '. . . together let's defeat the enemy'—machine gunner R. Usmanov to steel worker N. Bazetov

69. 'I promise to make steel only by high-speed methods'—steel worker Bazetov to machine gunner Usmanov

70. On the mobilization of the able-bodied urban population for work in industry and construction in wartime—from the decree of the Supreme Soviet of the USSR

Part Three: Stabilization and Stagnation (1945–1985)

13. The Cold War

15. The One-Party State

Dramatis Personae:
Biographical Index

Abakumov, Viktor Semenovich (1908–54). Soviet politician and secret policeman. Worker from 1924, joined CPSU 1930, in OGPU/NKVD from 1932. Close to Beria, organized repressions in Rostov from 1938. Noted for sadism. Headed SMERSH from 1943. Supreme Soviet Deputy from 1946. Fabricated 'Leningrad Case' 1950. Rival of Beria after war, arrested 1951. Tried and shot 1954. | 216, 299–300, 302

Adenauer, Konrad (1876–1967). German politician, mayor of Cologne before 1933. Formed Christian Democrats after war, West German Chancellor 1949–63. | 214

Adzhubey, Aleksey Ivanovich (1924–93). Journalist and CPSU functionary. N.S. Khrushchev's son-in-law. Chief editor of *Komsomol'skaya pravda* 1957–59, and *Izvestiya* 1959–64. On CPSU CC 1961–64. Removed from posts and CC with fall of Khrushchev. Wrote memoirs. | 337

Afanas'ev. Kiln operator at vacuum glass institute, 1968. | 350

Akbarov. Red Army orderly, Germany, 1945. | 149

Akhmadulina, Bella (Izabella) Akhmatovna (b. 1937). Poet, translator, essayist. Poems first published 1962. Visited Georgia 1970, began translating Georgian literature into Russian. Still publishing. | 338

Akhmatova (Gorenko), Anna Andreevna (1889–1966). Poet, translator. Began writing poems in childhood. 1910 married poet N.S. Gumilev. First anthology, *Evening*, published 1912. After 1917 worked in library, continued publishing. Son Lev in camps from 1930s. Criticized 1946 and banned from publishing, worked as translator to 1960s. | 329–31, 344–45

Aleksandr (Tolstopyatov, Anatoliy Mikhaylovich) (d. 1945). Churchman. Bishop of Molotov 1943, took part in September 1943 Church Council. | 162.

Aleksiy (Palitsyn, Vasiliy Mikhaylovich) (d. 1952). Churchman. Served in Volokalamsk 1941–42, Archbishop of Kuybyshev 1943. Took part in September 1943 Church Council. | 162

Aleksiy (Sergeev, Viktor Mikhaylovich) (1898–1968). Churchman. Served in

Vologda 1937, Vladimir 1938–39, Ufa 1942. In 1943 Archbishop of Ryazan'.
Took part in September 1943 Church Council. | 162

Aleksiy (Simansky, Sergey Vladimirovich) (1877–1970). Churchman. Took
monastic vows 1902. From 1927 favoured working with Soviet authorities.
1943–45 Metropolitan of Leningrad and Novgorod. Remained in Leningrad
during blockade. Worked for the Church's Defence and Peace Fund. From 1945
Patriarch of Moscow and All-Russia. | 152–53, 162

Alexander I (Romanov, Aleksandr Pavlovich) (1777–1825). Russian emperor from
1801. Relatively liberal reformer in early years of reign. Annexed eastern
Georgia, Finland, Bessarabia, Azerbaijan and the Duchy of Warsaw to Russia
1801–15. | 21

Alexander II (Romanov, Aleksandr Nikolaevich) (1818–81). Russian emperor from
1855. Noted for reforms: abolition of serfdom (1861), universities (1863), legal
system (1864), local government (1864, 1870), the army (1874), etc. Assassinated
by *Narodnaya volya* revolutionaries, 1881. | 21

Amin, Hafizullah (1929–79). Afghan Marxist politician. Studied in USA in 1960s.
Among founders of People's Democratic Party of Afghanistan 1965, and leaders
of Khalqi faction. Among organizers of April 1978 coup which put PDPA in
power. Overthrew former Khalqi colleague Taraki September 1979, became
President. Requested Soviet help in quashing rebellions. Overthrown and killed
in Soviet invasion December 1979. | 242–46

Andersen, Major R. US U-2 pilot, shot down over USSR, 1962. | 226

Andreev, Andrey Andreevich (1895–1971). Soviet politician. Metalworker,
Bolshevik from 1914, participant in October 1917 rising in Petrograd. Thereafter
held numerous party and trade-union posts. In 1931 deputy chair of Sovnarkom,
People's Commissar of Worker-Peasant Inspectorate, chair of CPSU CCC.
| 262, 264, 270

Andreeva, Nina Aleksandrovna (b. 1938). Politician, chemistry lecturer. Acquired
notoriety for anti-perestroika article in 1988. Formed Unity for Leninism and
Communist Ideals group 1989, Bolshevik Platform in CPSU 1990. From
November 1991 General Secretary of All-Union Communist Party of
Bolsheviks. | 392–93

Andrey (Komarov, Anatoliy Andreevich) (1879–1955). Churchman, took holy vows
1923. In Astrakhan' 1929–39. In 1943 Archbishop of Kazan', took part in
September 1943 Church Council. | 162

Andronov. Senior technician at automatic equipment research institute, 1968. | 350

Andronov, Nikolay Ivanovich (b. 1929). Artist, painter, representative of 'severe style'
in Russian art 1950s and 1960s. Took part in discussions between CPSU and
cultural figures 1962–63. Awarded State Prize 1979. | 338

Andropov, Yuriy Vladimirovich (1914–84). Soviet politician. 1936–44 in Komsomol
work, 1944–57 in diplomatic and CPSU work. Ambassador to Hungary,
1953–57. From 1957 section-head and, from 1962, Secretary of CC of CPSU.

Babajan. Afghan Lieutentant-General, co-ordinated with Soviet troops in invasion of Afghanistan, December 1979. | 247

Babichev, V.S. 1st deputy head of the CPSU CC cadres party-building section, 1990. | 427

Babitsky, Konstantin Iosifovich (1929–93). Linguist, human rights activist. Exiled for participation in demonstration against Soviet invasion of Czechoslovakia 1968, and lost post at Academy of Sciences' Russian Language Institute. | 350–51

Babushkin, Yasha (Yakov) L′vovich (1913–44). Studied in Leningrad, worked for Leningrad Radio Committee from 1937. Remained during blockade, initiated performance and broadcast of Shostakovich's 7th Symphony by Radio Orchestra. Dismissed from radio 1943, conscripted, died at front. | 101

Baeva, Tat′yana Aleksandrovna (b. 1947). Human rights campaigner, demonstrated in Moscow 1968 against invasion of Czechoslovakia. | 352

Bagirov, Mir Dzhafar Abbasovich (1896–1956). Soviet Azerbaijani party functionary and secret policeman. Bolshevik from 1917. Red Army political worker in civil war. 1921–27 and 1929–30 head of Azerbaijani Cheka/GPU, Azerbaijani commissar for internal affairs. Close colleague of L.P. Beria. 1st Secretary of Azerbaijani CP 1933–53. CPSU CC candidate 1934–39, full member 1939–53. Supreme Soviet Deputy from 1937. CPSU CC Presidium candidate 1953. Demoted, arrested 1954, tried and shot 1956. | 303

Baklanov, A.M. Lieutentant-Colonel, military commander of suppression of Tbilisi riots, 1989. | 424

Baklanov, Oleg Dmitrievich (b. 1932). Soviet politician. Electrical engineer, in CPSU from 1953. In Ministry of Machine-Building from 1976, minister 1983–88. On CPSU CC 1986–91, CC Secretary 1988–91. Candidate of Technical Sciences. Hero of Socialist Labour 1976, Lenin Prize 1982. People's Deputy in 1989. Member of GKChP, August 1991, amnestied 1994, later in Russo-Ukrainian trade apparatus. | 445

Balygeev. Collective farmer near Novgorod, 1946. | 294

Basov, A.V. CPSU functionary, on CC 1961–76, Secretary of Rostov *oblast′* CPSU 1962. | 275, 278

Batu Khan (c. 1205–55). Mongol ruler, founder of Blue Horde. Subdued most of European Russia 1237–39. | 71

Baybakov, Nikolay Konstantinovich (b. 1911). In CPSU from 1939. 1937–55 in oil industry, commissar of oil production 1944–46. Head of RSFSR Gosplan from 1957, USSR Gosplan from 1965. On CPSU CC 1952–61 and 1966–90. Retired 1988. | 251–53

Bazetov, Nurulla Kh. (1907–79). Steelworker. Pioneer of high-speed steel founding in WWII. Initiated the 'Front brigades' at the Verkh-Isetsk works near Sverdlovsk. | 117–19

Belakhov. Head of USSR Navy Commissariat political administration, 1941. | 73

Bell. Writer mentioned by Rostropovich. | 357

Belyakov. Fitter at Central Design-22, Penza, 1945. | 164

Belyutin, Eliy Mikhaylovich (b. 1925). Artist, leading figure in 'unofficial' school. Organized Manezh exhibition 1962, attacked by Khrushchev. Took part in CPSU–cultural figures talks 1962–63. | 338

Beneš, Edvard (1884–1948). Czechoslovak socialist politician, foreign minister 1918–35, President 1935–38 and 1945–48. Resisted communist takeover, resigned, died of natural causes. | 200

Berggol'ts, Ol'ga Fedorovna (1910–75). Writer, poet and broadcaster. Arrested 1937, pardoned 1939. In Leningrad during siege. Broadcast on radio, spoke at factories and to troops. Published in national and local press. In CPSU from 1940. | 100–01

Beria, Lavrentiy Pavlovich (1899–1953). Politician and secret policeman. In Transcaucasus Cheka and GPU 1921–34, head from 1931. In party work 1931–38. 1938–46 and March–June 1953 Minister of Internal Affairs, and 1941–46 deputy chairman of CPC. From 1946 deputy chairman, and March–June 1953 1st deputy chairman of Council of Ministers. Member of Politburo from 1946. Marshal of the Soviet Union in 1945. Awarded Hero of Socialist Labour 1953. Dismissed and arrested, June 1953, executed December. | 13–15, 53–54, 61, 92, 102, 125, 171, 182–83, 185–88, 193, 197, 216, 299–305

Berzin, Jan Karlovich (Ķusis, Pēteris) (1889–1938). Soviet security agent. In RSDRP from 1905. Served hard labour 1907–09 for killing policeman. Conscripted in WWI, deserted, worked in factory. Petrograd Bolshevik in 1917. Organized Soviet government security from December 1917. Deputy commissar of internal affairs in Soviet Latvia 1919. In Red Army intelligence from 1920, headed it 1924–35 and 1937. In Spain 1936–37. From 1932 also head of GULAG system in Far East. Arrested and shot 1938. | 54

Bilák, Vasil (b. 1917). Czechoslovak communist politician. In party from 1945, on its CC 1954–89, Secretary and Presidium member 1955–68. Prominent among the conservative wing of Czechoslovak communism 1968, appealed for Soviet intervention. | 232

Bochkov, A.I. Worker near Novgorod, 1946. | 294

Bogoraz (Bogoraz-Brukhman), Larisa Iosifovna (b. 1929). Philologist, human rights activist. Protested against invasion of Czechoslovakia 1968, exiled 5 years. One-time wife of Yu. Daniel'. Continued human rights activism, helped publish *Chronicle of Current Events*, chaired renewed Moscow Helsinki Group 1989–94. | 348, 350–51

Boky, A. Signatory to protest letter, 1967. | 346

Boldin, Valeriy Ivanovich (1935–2006). CPSU functionary, worked in CC apparatus from 1961. Gorbachev's assistant from 1985, CC member from 1988. Charged with assisting putsch August 1991, imprisoned. Wrote anti-Gorbachev memoirs after release. | 444

Bol'shakov, Georgiy Nikitovich. Soviet diplomat and colonel in Soviet intelligence 1962. In USSR Washington embassy as press advisor and head of Washington

chairman of Moscow city EC. CPSU CC candidate 1934–39, full member 1939–61, on Politburo/Presidium 1946–58. Deputy chair of USSR Sovnarkom 1938–44; 1938–45 head of State Bank. In front military councils during WWII, on State Defence Committee from 1944, USSR armed forces minister 1947–49 and 1953–55. Made USSR Marshal. Khrushchev ally to 1956, then in 'anti-party group'. | 217, 299–300, 303

Bylinsky, I. Chairman of the Belorussia Sovnarkom, 1942. | 191

Cajander, Aimo Kaarlo (1870–1943). Finnish botanist, academic and liberal politician. Professor of forestry 1911–34, head of Finnish forests and parks service 1934–43. Prime Minister 1922, 1924 and 1937–39 until winter war. | 21–22, 26

Carter, James Earl, Jr. (Jimmy) (b. 1924). US Democratic politician. Governor of Georgia from 1970, US President 1977–81. | 241, 247

Castro Ruz, Fidel (b. 1927). Cuban politician and revolutionary leader. Organized rebellions 1953 and 1956, then guerrilla war. Took power 1 January 1959. Reoriented Cuba towards USSR in response to US hostility, allowed Soviet nuclear missiles to be stationed on Cuba 1962. Major recipient of Soviet aid until 1991. | 225–28

Catherine II (née Sophia Augusta Frederika von Anhalt-Zerbst) (1729–96). Empress of Russia 1762–96. Her reign was marked by great territorial expansion, more freedom for nobles, and the extension of serfdom. | 369

Černík, Oldřich (1921–94). Czechoslovak communist politician and economic administrator. CP CC Secretary 1956–60, energy minister 1960–63, deputy government head and chair of state planning commission 1963–68, head of government 1968–70. On CP CC 1958–70, Presidium 1966–70. Associated with CP reformist wing 1968. Removed from all posts 1970, expelled from CP 1971. | 234

Chamberlain, Arthur Neville (1869–1940). British Conservative politician, Prime Minister 1937–40. | 18, 32

Charles XII (1682–1718). King of Sweden from 1697. Fought Northern War (1700–21) against Russia and others to defend Swedish control of Baltic. | 71

Chaykovsky, Boris Aleksandrovich (1925–96). Composer, studied at Moscow Conservatoire. Wrote concert and film music, noted for intellectualism and restrained style. | 357

Chebrikov, Viktor Mikhaylovich (1923–99). Politician and secret policeman. In Red Army in WWII. Joined CPSU 1944, functionary from 1951. Joined KGB 1967, deputy chairman 1968–82, chairman 1982–89. CPSU CC candidate 1971–81, full member 1981–89, Politburo member 1985–89. | 392, 396, 405, 423

Chernenko, Konstantin Ustinovich (1911–85). CPSU functionary, joined party 1931. Party worker in Krasnoyarsk 1933–44. Propaganda head in Moldova 1948–56, met Brezhnev, thereafter shadowed his career. CPSU CC candidate 1966–71, member 1971–85. Politburo candidate 1977–78, full member from 1978. Headed CPSU CC general section 1965–82. General Secretary February

1984–March 1985, chairman of USSR Supreme Soviet Presidium April 1984–March 1985. | 195, 197, 251–52, 291, 319, 375, 383

Chernichenko, Yuriy Dmitrievich (b. 1929). Writer on agrarian themes, politician. Published in *Novyy mir* 1960s. Now leader of the Peasant Party of Russia. | 345

Cherny, Sasha (Glikberg, Aleksandr Mikhaylovich) (1880–1932). Poet, satirical writer. First published 1904. Wrote satires on reactionaries and faint-hearted liberals, increasingly sarcastic and pessimistic. Served in WWI. Emigrated 1920. Published collections of short stories, poems and children's stories. | 357

Chorążyczewska, Bronisława (1924–?). Polish schoolgirl in Sarny, 1940. | 11–13

Chukovsky, Korney Ivanovich (Korneychukov, Nikolay Vasil'evich) (1882–1969). Writer, critic, translator and journalist. Wrote many children's works, including *Doktor Aybolit*. | 172

Churchill, Sir Winston Leonard Spencer (1874–1965). British Conservative politician, Prime Minister 1940–45 and 1951–55. | 201, 203–06

Clair, René (Chomette, René-Lucien) (1898–1981). Pioneer of French cinema, filmmaker from 1924. Elected to Académie Française 1962. | 354

Cripps, Sir Richard Stafford (1889–1952). British Labour politician. Solicitor-General in 1931, ambassador to USSR 1940–42, Minister for Aircraft Production 1942–45, President of Board of Trade 1945–47, Chancellor of Exchequer 1947–50. | 52, 68.

Dan (Gurvich), Fedor Il'ich (1871–1947). Doctor and politician. Menshevik from 1903. RSDRP CC member from 1905, leading Menshevik in 1st, 2nd and 4th Dumas. In 1917 on Menshevik CC, EC of Petrograd Soviet and VTsIK. Opened 2nd Soviet congress October 1917. From end of 1917 led Mensheviks along with Yu.O. Martov. Imprisoned 1921–22, then exiled. Led Menshevik delegation abroad, one of editors of *Sotsialisticheskiy vestnik*. Died in USA. | 136–37

Daniel', Yuliy Markovich (1925–88). Writer, poet, translator. Fought in WWII. Defendant in notorious trial 1965–66 with co-author Sinyavsky for publishing a work in the west, under pseudonym 'Nikolay Arzhak'. In prison and camps 1965–70. Remained in USSR. Published legally shortly before death. | 340–42

Davidovich, Irina Modestovna (1911–86). Actress in Sverdlovsk Drama Theatre 1940–48. One of a group of touring artistes giving concerts for Red Army in 1943. Also worked in military hospital in 1942. | 156

Davydov. Major of state security, Penza *oblast'*, 1943. | 178

Davydov, E.N. (1920–44). Student at Sverdlov University 1938–42. Sergeant on Leningrad front. Killed in action. | 159

Dekanozov, Vladimir Georgievich (1898–1953). Soviet politician and secret policeman. In Red Army 1918, joined RKP(b) 1920. In Azerbaijani Cheka from 1921, associated with Beria. Made career in Caucasus 1920s and 1930s. On USSR Supreme Soviet 1937–50, on CPSU CC 1941–52. Ambassador to Germany November 1940–June 1941. Failed to discern Nazi war plans. After fall of Beria in 1953 arrested and shot. | 53–54

Delone, Vadim Nikolaevich (1947–83). Poet, human rights campaigner. Arrested 1967 for demonstrating in defence of dissident A. Ginzburg. Sentenced to 3 years in camps for demonstrating against invasion of Czechoslovakia 1968. Emigrated 1975. | 350–51

Demichev, Petr Nilovich (b. 1918). Soviet party and state functionary. In Red Army 1937–44, in CPSU from 1939, Moscow party worker from 1945. 1st Secretary of CPSU Moscow committee 1959–60, of Moscow city committee from 1960. Administrator for USSR Council of Ministers 1958–59. On CPSU CC 1961–89, CC Secretary 1961–74. Politburo candidate 1964–88. USSR Minister of Culture 1974–86. | 252

Dimitriy (Gradusov) (1881–1956). Bishop of Ul'yanovsk, took part in Church Council September 1943. | 162

Dimitrov, Georgi (1882–1949). Bulgarian communist leader. Secretary of Bulgarian printers' union 1901. Joined Bulgarian Workers' Social-Democratic Party 1902, in its left wing (Tesnyaki) from 1903, on faction CC from 1909, faction became Bulgarian CP 1919. Secretary of general workers' union 1909–23, in Bulgarian parliament 1913–23. From 1920s in Comintern apparatus. Acquitted in Reichstag fire trial 1934, moved to USSR. General Secretary of Comintern 1935–43. Headed Bulgarian government from 1946, Bulgarian CP from 1948. | 211

Djilas, Milovan (1911–97). Yugoslav communist politician, joined CP 1932, on CC from 1938, Politburo from 1940. Commanded partisan resistance in Montenegro and Bosnia in WWII. Vice-President after war, negotiated with Stalin in 1948. Became critical of Yugoslav socialism, expelled from CC 1954, broke with party. Developed theory of 'new class' of rulers in communist states. Served two terms in prison 1950s and 1960s. | 207, 211

Dobrynin, Anatoliy Fedorovich (b. 1919). Soviet politician and diplomat. In foreign ministry from 1946. Advisor at Washington embassy 1952–55, assistant to USSR foreign minister 1955–57, UN deputy General Secretary 1957–60, ambassador to USA from 1962. CPSU CC candidate 1966–71, full member from 1971, CC Secretary 1986–88, advisor on foreign affairs to top leadership, now consultant to Russian foreign ministry. | 226

Doenitz, Karl (1891–1980). German Admiral, joined navy 1911. In WWII Commander of Submarines, Naval Commander -in-Chief from 1943. President of Germany for 20 days after Hitler's suicide. Served 10 years for war crimes 1946–56. | 150

Dolgikh, Vladimir Ivanovich (b. 1924). Mining engineer and politician. In CPSU from 1942. Served in Red Army ranks 1943–45. From 1958 chief engineer and director of Noril'sk metallurgical combine. 1st Secretary of Krasnoyarsk CP from 1969. On CPSU CC 1971–89. CC Secretary from 1972, headed CC heavy industry department 1976–84. Candidate Politburo member 1982–88. | 252

Dolmatovsky, Evgeniy Aronovich (1915–94). Writer, poet, songwriter. Worked on

Moscow Metro 1930s. First published 1934. Front-line war-correspondent WWII. Won prizes for his writing after war. | 114, 146–47, 149–50

Donskoy, Dmitriy Ivanovich (1350–89). Grand Duke of Muscovy 1359–89, of Vladimir 1362–89, and of Novgorod 1363–89. Mobilized great armies, fought and manoeuvred for ascendancy of Muscovy over neighbouring principalities. Defeated Tatar horde of Mamay 1380, but obliged to pay tribute to Golden Horde under Toktamysh after 1382. Regarded as Russian national hero. | 71–72, 105, 160

Dorosh, Efim Yakovlevich (1908–72). Writer and literary critic, noted for choice of agrarian themes. | 345

Dorozhkina, E.I. Collective farm worker, near Novgorod, 1946. | 294

Dovzhenko, Aleksandr Petrovich (1894–1956). Playwright and film producer. Among founders of Soviet cinematography. | 172

Dremlyuga, Vladimir Aleksandrovich (b. 1940). Worker, dissident in 1960s. In camps to 1974 for protesting against invasion of Czechoslovakia 1968. Emigrated 1974. | 350–51

Dubček, Alexander (1921–92). Czechoslovak communist leader. Born in Slovak communist family, lived 1929–38 in USSR. Joined Czechoslovak CP 1938, fought in underground against Nazis, in Slovak national uprising 1944. On CPCz CC from 1962. 1st Secretary of CC from January 1968, initiated 'Prague Spring' programme of liberalization, ended by Soviet invasion August 1968. Forced to reverse policies, 1969 removed from leadership, 1970 expelled from CP. End of 1989 elected chairman of Czechoslovak Federal Assembly. 1992 headed Slovak Social-Democratic Party. Died after car crash. | 231–32, 234, 236, 350–51

Dubchenko, G.V. Writer of letter complaining about exile of Solzhenitsyn, 1974. | 361–62

Dudintsev, Vladimir Dmitrievich (1918–98). Writer and journalist. First published 1933. His *Not by Bread Alone* (1956) very successful but not liked by authorities. 1963–87 unable to publish. Won State Prize 1988 for *White Clothes*. | 336

Dzhamilev, Mustafa (Cemiloglu, Mustafa; from 1991 Kirimoglu, Mustafa Abdulcemil) (b. 1943). Leader of Crimean Tatar national movement, Soviet human rights activist. Deported to Uzbekistan 1944. Joined national movement 1961. Sacked, imprisoned six times, expelled from institutes for views and activities. Imprisoned 1966 for refusing military service, on release joined with wider human rights movements. Among first Tatars to return to Crimea 1980s. From 1991 Chairman of Crimean Tatar National Mejlis, People's Deputy of Ukraine from 1998. | 352

Efimov. Former GULAG inmate decorated in Red Army, 1944. | 126

Egolin, Aleksandr Mikhaylovich (1896–1959). Specialist on literature and CPSU functionary. In 1943–44 headed the CPSU CC section for literature and deputy head of the propaganda section. Appointed editor of *Zvezda* 1946. Corresponding member of the USSR Academy of Sciences from 1946. | 331

Elevferiy (Vorontsov, Veniamin Aleksandrovich) (d. 1959). Churchman, Bishop of

Rostov 1943, took part in September 1943 Church Council. | 162

Eliasberg, Karl Il'ich (1907–78). Conductor. Chief conductor of Leningrad Radio Symphony Orchestra 1937–50. 1941–45 headed orchestra of musicians remaining in Leningrad, gave first performance of Shostakovich's 7th Symphony 1942. | 101

Elkin, S. Chief engineer at Novocherkassk Locomotive Works, 1962. | 278

Emel'kina, Nadezhda Pavlovna (b. 1946). Human rights activist in 1960s and 1970s. Married to V.A. Krasin. Political prisoner 1971–73. Emigrated to USA 1975. | 352

Engels, Friedrich (1820–95). German socialist theoretician, economist and historian, collaborator with Karl Marx. | 210, 224, 327

Erkko, Eljas (1895–1965). Finnish newspaperman and politician. Publisher of *Helsingin Sanomat* and other papers 1927–65, Finnish foreign minister 1938–39. | 26

Erokhin. Worker at factory No. 5, Penza, 1945. | 164

Evtushenko, Evgeniy Aleksandrovich (b. 1932). Poet, writer, performer, first published 1955. By 1960s had achieved world renown. Poems have strong social and political content, while remaining officially acceptable. | 336–39

Fadeev (Bulyga), Aleksandr Aleksandrovich (1901–56). Writer and Soviet politician. Joined RKP(b) 1918, fought and wounded in civil war. First published 1923 (*Against the Current*), from 1926 one of leaders of RAPP, then Writers' Union. Theoretician of 'socialist realism'. General Secretary of Writers' Union 1946–54. On CPSU CC from 1939. Supreme Soviet Deputy 1946–56. Denounced other writers. Became alcoholic, committed suicide. | 335–36

Falin, Valentin Mikhaylovich (b. 1926). Studied international relations after WWII, worked at Soviet Control Commission in Berlin. Then at foreign ministry information department and CPSU CC international department. In foreign ministry again from 1959, became section head. Ambassador to W. Germany 1970s, then in CPSU apparatus and on *Izvestiya*. Headed Novosti Press Agency from 1986. Head of CPSU CC international department from 1988. From 1992 at foreign policy institute in Germany. | 428

Faynberg, Viktor Isaakovich (b. 1931). Dissident. Demonstrated against invasion of Czechoslovakia 1968, in psychiatric hospital 1968–73. Emigrated 1974. | 349–50

Fedin, Konstantin Aleksandrovich (1892–1977). Writer. Studied commerce, but took to literature, first published 1913. Interned in Germany in WWI. From 1918 worked in education commissariat and in press. Wrote novels, plays, reportages. Lived abroad 1928–34. | 172

Fedorov, Vasiliy Dmitrievich (1918–84). Poet and critic. Wrote on pastoral themes, and in praise of Soviet man. Won State Prize 1979. | 338

Fedorovsky. Khar'kov University lecturer, 1944. | 170–71

Fierlinger, Zdeněk (1891–1976). Czechoslovak politician, social-democratic Prime Minister of Czechoslovakia 1945–46, joined communists. | 200

Firsov, Vladimir Ivanovich (b. 1937). Soviet Russian poet noted for patriotic themes, editor of *Rossiyane*. | 338

Firsova-Ageeva, M.F. Organizer of religious procession in Nikolo–Azyasi, 1943. | 178

Fomin, V. Military historian, eye-witness to events in Hungary, 1956. | 220–22

Gabay, Il'ya Yankelevich (1935–73). Poet, teacher, linguist, human rights campaigner. Imprisoned 1967, in camps 1969–72. Committed suicide. | 348, 352

Gaysumov, A. Spiritual leader in Checheno-Ingushetia, 1944. | 187

Georgadze, Mikhail Porfir'evich (1912–82). Soviet state and party functionary. Worked in agriculture from 1929, tractor driver, brigade leader. Engineer and administrator in agriculture commissariat/ministry 1941–51. In CPSU from 1942. In charge of machine-tractor stations in Georgia 1951–53, Georgian agriculture minister 1953–54, 2nd Secretary of Georgian CP 1954–56, 1st deputy chairman of Georgian Council of Ministers 1956–57. Secretary of the USSR Supreme Soviet Presidium from 1957. Candidate CC member 1966–82. | 311

Gerő, Ernő (1898–1980). Hungarian communist politician. Held numerous government posts after 1945, party General Secretary July–October 1956. | 219–20

Gierek, Edward (1913–2001). Polish communist politician, party First Secretary 1970–80. Led overambitious industrialization project. Replaced after legalizing Solidarność. | 249

Girenko, Andrey Nikolaevich (b. 1936). Mining engineer and party functionary. In Komsomol work in native Krivoy Rog from 1962, headed Ukrainian Komsomol 1970s, then in Ukrainian CP apparatus. CPSU CC candidate 1981–89, full member and CC Secretary 1989–91. USSR People's Deputy 1989–91. Leading figure in industrialists' organization since 1992. | 426–27

Glazunov, Il'ya Sergeevich (b. 1930). Painter, illustrator, architect, stage designer. First exhibited 1957. Noted for portraiture, and for Russian national themes in his work. Took part in CPSU-cultural figures talks 1962–63. Rector of Russian Academy of Painting, Sculpture and Architecture from 1987. | 338

Goebbels, Josef Paul (1897–1945). Nazi propaganda minister. Took part in *Barbarossa* planning. Committed suicide in May 1945. | 149

Gogol, Nikolay Vasil'evich (1809–52). Author, playwright, critic. Most famous for plays *Government Inspector* (1835) and *Dead Souls* (1842). Increasingly mystical and conservative in final years. | 335, 341, 361–62

Golikov, Filipp Ivanovich (1900–80). Professional soldier. In Red Army and RKP(b) from 1918. Held various command and political posts 1920s and 1930s. Commanded 6th Army in 1939, occupied eastern Poland. Deputy Chief-of-Staff and head of Red Army intelligence 1940–41. Failed to warn of impending German attack. Held various commands in WWII. In charge of repatriating Soviet citizens 1944–45. On CPSU Central Revision Committee 1941–52, CC 1961–66. | 48–49, 54

Golubev, Konstantin Dmitrievich (1896–1956). Professional soldier and secret policeman. In Red Army from 1918, RKP(b) from 1919. Commanded regiment in civil war. Commanded 10th, 13th and 43rd armies in WWII. At GHQ from 1944, active in SMERSH. Deputy head of repatriation section, involved in forcible repatriation of Soviet citizens after war. Lectured at GHQ military academy from 1949, sacked as Beria accomplice 1953. | 106

Gomułka, Władysław (1905–82). Polish communist politician, in party from 1926. Imprisoned as 'rightist' 1951–54, made party First Secretary after 1956 disorders. Removed 1970. | 205, 210–11, 219–20

Gorbachev, Mikhail Sergeevich (b.1931). Soviet statesman and politician. In CPSU from 1952. 2nd, then 1st Secretary of Stavropol' *oblast'* CPSU committee 1968–70. Secretary of CC of CPSU 1978–85. General Secretary 1985–91. People's Deputy 1989–90. Chairman of Supreme Soviet 1989–90. President of USSR 1990–91. Now heads Gorbachev Foundation and a small social-democratic party. | 4, 192, 267
—and democratization | 400–01, 405, 408–09, 411–13
—and disintegration of CPSU | 432, 434, 438, 440
—economic reforms | 283, 285, 383–89
—and glasnost | 391–96
—and ideology | 397–98
—initial reforms | 373, 375
—and international relations | 376–82
—and nationalism | 414, 416, 418–19, 423–26, 431, 440–43
—and repudiation of Stalinism | 13, 298, 301, 396, 414
—as USSR President | 428–29, 444, 450–51, 455–61
—and Yeltsin | 401–05, 451–55

Gorbanevskaya, Natal'ya Evgen'evna (b. 1936). Poet, writer, human rights activist. Took part in demonstration against invasion of Czechoslovakia 1968. Arrested 1970, spent year undergoing compulsory psychiatric treatment. Emigrated 1975. | 348, 350, 352

Gorbatov, Boris Leont'evich (1908–54). Writer and journalist. Worked as front-line *Pravda* correspondent during war. Noted for patriotic themes. | 146

Gorelov, L.N. Lieutenant-General. Main Soviet military advisor in Kabul 1979. | 243–44

Gorkin, Aleksandr Fedorovich (1897–1988). CPSU and state functionary. Bolshevik from 1916. In Tver' town soviet 1917–19, in Red Army 1919–20, then in local and central party apparatus. Secretary of Presidium of USSR TsIK and Supreme Soviet 1937–53, Supreme Soviet Deputy 1937–74. CPSU CC candidate 1939–52, on Central Revision Committee 1952–76. Chair of USSR Supreme Court 1957–72, involved in rehabilitations. | 60

Gorky, Maksim (Peshkov, Aleksey Maksimovich) (1868–1936). Writer, political activist. Orphaned in childhood. In Narodnik circles from 1884. Engaged in revolutionary propaganda. Published short stories and plays from 1890s. Associated with social-democrats 1900s, financed newspapers, raised funds. In Italy 1906–13. Internationalist in WWI, 1917 founded *Novaya zhizn'*. Very critical of Bolsheviks 1917–18, then more favourable. In Italy 1921–33, then returned to USSR. Head of Writers' Union from 1934. | 333

Gottwald, Klement (1896–1953). Czechoslovak communist politician. In socialist youth movement before WWI. In 1920s Czechoslovak CP functionary in Slovakia, then Prague. General Secretary from 1929. In USSR 1939–45. From 1945 CP chairman, chairman of National Front, acting head of government. President of Republic from 1948. | 205, 211

Gracheva, A. Schoolgirl in 1942. | 109

Granin (German), Daniil Aleksandrovich (b. 1919). Writer, with particular interest in history and scientific intelligentsia. Took part in defence of Leningrad. One of the authors of *The Siege Book* (1977–81). Interviewed A.N. Kosygin at end of 1970s. | 92–93, 95

Grigorenko, Petr Grigor'evich (1907–87). Professional soldier, prominent dissident. Joined CPSU 1927, Red Army 1931. Fought in WWII, gained rank of Colonel. 1945–61 taught at Frunze Military Academy. Major-General in 1959. Demanded democratization of CPSU 1961, criticized and sent to Far East. Organized dissident-communist group 1963. Interned in psychiatric hospital 1964–65, 1970–74. Defended demonstrators against invasion of Czechoslovakia 1968. Headed Moscow Helsinki group from 1975. Allowed to travel to USA 1977, deprived of citizenship. Converted to Orthodoxy. | 352

Grigoriy (Chukov, Nikolay Kirillovich) (1870–1955). Churchman. Involved in church education 1890s and 1900s. Rector of Petrozavodsk seminary from 1911. In Petrograd from 1918. Monk from 1942. Archbishop of Saratov and Stalingrad 1942. Took part in September 1943 Church Council. Held various other archbishoprics. | 162

Grishin, Viktor Vasil'evich (b. 1914). CPSU and trade-union functionary. In CPSU from 1939, worked for it from 1941, in Serpukhov to 1950; Moscow *oblast'* committee to 1956. Head of Soviet trade unions 1956–67. 1st Secretary of Moscow city CPSU 1967–85. On CC 1952–86, Politburo candidate 1961–71, full member 1971–86. | 252, 349

Gromyko, Andrey Andreevich (1909–89). Politician and diplomat. In CPSU from 1931. At Academy of Sciences' Institute of Economics to 1939, then foreign affairs commissariat. Counsellor at Soviet embassy in USA from 1939, ambassador from 1943. Headed Soviet delegation at San Francisco conference 1945. First Soviet permanent representative at UN from 1946. Ambassador to UK 1952–53. 1st deputy foreign minister 1949–52 and 1953–57. USSR foreign minister 1957–85. CPSU CC candidate 1952–56, full member 1956–89, on Politburo 1973–88. Supreme Soviet Deputy 1946–50 and 1958–89. 1985–88 chaired its Presidium. | 245, 251–52, 376

Gurevich, Dmitriy. In 1991: 22-year-old student. | 446

Gurvich, A.S. (1897–1962). Literary critic, denounced as 'cosmopolitan', 1949. | 334

Gusev, V. Colonel in Soviet intelligence, head of German section, 1941. | 48

Hasanov, Osman. Village head of Kouş, Crimea, 1942. | 180

Hensel, H. Struve. US Assistant Navy Secretary 1945. | 215

Hitler, Adolf (1889–1945). German Nazi party leader, Chancellor and dictator 1933–45. | 1, 3–5, 9, 15, 39, 43–49, 54, 57–58, 64–65, 67–69, 71, 74–75, 89, 101, 103, 106, 108, 123, 129–30, 135–39, 142, 147, 149–50, 169, 172, 191–92, 204, 291

Ho Chi Minh (Nguyen Tat Thanh) (1890–1969), Vietnamese communist and nationalist leader, fought against French colonial rule and US occupation of South Vietnam. | 215

Hoxha, Enver (1908–85). Albanian communist and nationalist leader, founder of Albanian Party of Labour, ruler from 1944. Broke with Yugoslavs 1948, USSR 1961, and China 1978. | 199, 218

Ignat'ev, Semen Denisovich (1904–83). CPSU functionary, secret policeman. In Cheka 1920; CPSU from 1928. On Central Revision Committee from 1939, on CC 1952–61, Presidium 1952–56, CC Secretary 1952–53. USSR Minister of State Security 1951–53. 1st Secretary of Bashkir (1953–57) and Tatar (1957–60) *oblast'* CPSU committees. | 303

Ignatov, Nikolay Grigor'evich (1901–66). CPSU functionary, secret policeman. Red Guard 1917, in Red Army from 1918, in Cheka-GPU 1921–32. In CPSU from 1924. Party worker from 1934, mainly in *oblast'* committees. CC candidate 1939–41. On CC 1952–66. CC Secretary and USSR procurement minister 1952–53. On CC Presidium 1957–61. Held other high government and Supreme Soviet posts. | 304

Il'ichev, Leonid Fedorovich (1906–90). CPSU functionary, ideologist. In CPSU from 1924. Komsomol worker 1920s, lecturer and party worker in N. Caucasus 1930s. Then worked on CPSU press. Chief editor of *Izvestiya* 1944–48, of *Pravda* 1951–52. In CPSU CC propaganda department. CPSU CC candidate 1952–56 and 1981–90, full member 1961–66; on Central Revision Committee 1956–61 and 1966–81. Head of CPSU CC ideological commission 1962; chief ideologist under Khrushchev. Organized meeting with cultural figures 1962. | 275, 337–38

Il'inykh. Trade-school teacher, decorated communist, killed by peasant bandits, Chelyabinsk, 1946. | 261

Indra, Alois (1921–90). Czechoslovak communist politician and functionary. Joined party 1937. Postwar held various party and state positions. On party CC from 1968, Presidium 1971–89. Advocated Soviet intervention 1968. | 232

Ioann (Bratolyubov, Sergey Vasil'evich) (1882–1968). Churchman, Archbishop of Sarapul 1943. Took part in September 1943 Church Council. | 162

Ioann (Sokolov, Ivan Aleksandrovich) (d. 1968). Churchman. Served in Orekhovo–Zuevo, Bryansk, Vologda and Arkhangel'sk 1928–39. In 1943 Archbishop of

Yaroslavl' and Rostov, took part in September 1943 Church Council. Metropolitan of Kiev 1944–64. | 162

Isaev, Evgeniy (Georgiy) Aleksandrovich (b. 1926). Poet and translator. Took part in CPSU–cultural figures talks 1962–63. | 338

Ivanov. Red Army lieutenant, 1941. | 104

Ivanov, B.S. Lieutenant-General, representative of the USSR KGB in Kabul, 1979. | 243–44

Ivanov, F.I. School teacher near Novgorod, 1946. | 294

Ivanov, L. Writer published in *Novyy mir*. 345

Jagodziński. Head postmaster in Sarny, 1940. | 12

Jaruzelski, Wojciech (b. 1923). Polish professional soldier and communist politician. Deported to USSR 1939, joined Soviet-sponsored First Polish Army, took part in liberation of Warsaw and taking of Berlin at end of WWII. Joined CP 1947, defence minister from 1968. From 1981 Prime Minister and party 1st Secretary, declared martial law December 1981, banned free trade union *Solidarność*. Resigned as Poland's leader 1990. | 249–55

Kádár (Csermanek), János (1912–89). Hungarian communist politician. In Nagy's government October 1956, became party leader after Soviet invasion. | 219–20

Kaganovich, Lazar' Moyseevich (1893–1991). Soviet politician. Worker, Bolshevik in Ukraine from 1911. In 1917 worked in trade unions, soviets and Bolshevik military organization. After October held several party, state and trade-union posts. On CC from 1924, 1925–28 head of Ukrainian CP. Stalin loyalist. Headed Moscow party from 1930, organized construction of Metro etc. Associated with 'anti-party' group plotting against Khrushchev 1957. Demoted to head of asbestos trust 1957–59, thereafter pensioner. | 102, 303, 313–14

Kalinin, Mikhail Ivanovich (1875–1946). Of peasant origin, became Petersburg factory worker, social-democrat from 1898, Bolshevik from 1903. Participated in February and October 1917 events in Petrograd. From 1919 chairman of VTsIK, nominal head of state, retained this position until 1946. Cultivated simple, approachable image. | 60

Kaminskaya, Dina Isaakovna (b. 1919). Lawyer, one of the first to take up legal defence of dissidents. Banned from taking part in political trials. Emigrated following house search, 1977. | 350–51

Kania, Stanisław (b. 1927). Polish communist politician. In Polish Workers' Party/United Workers' Party from 1945. On CC from 1968, CC Secretary 1971–80, on Political Bureau 1975–81. Party leader 1980–81. | 249–51

Kapek, Antonin (1922–90). Czechoslovak communist politician. In engineering industry to 1968, then Prague party chief 1969–88. On Czechoslovak CP CC 1958–89. Among opponents of Prague Spring who appealed for Soviet intervention 1968. Expelled from CP 1990, committed suicide. | 232

Kapitonov, Ivan Vasil'evich (1915–2002). CPSU functionary. In CPSU from 1939, party worker from 1941. Held positions as Moscow city and *oblast'* 1st Secretary.

Kapto, Aleksandr Semenovich (b. 1933). Writer, politician, sociologist, diplomat. On CPSU CC 1981–91. One-time Soviet ambassasdor to Cuba, Russian ambassador to North Korea. Since 1992 in Russian Academy of Sciences, specialist on UNESCO. | 427

Kapustin, Yakov Fedorovich (1904–50). CPSU functionary. Factory worker from 1923, studied production of steam turbines in England 1935–36. CPSU organizer from 1938, Secretary of Leningrad CPSU city committee 1940–45, 2nd Secretary 1945–49. Arrested in 'Leningrad Case' 1949, charged with spying for UK, shot 1950. | 301

Kardelj, Edvard (1910–79). Yugoslav communist leader and ideologist. Joined Yugoslav communist youth 1926, CP 1932. In Lenin School, Moscow, 1930s. On CP CC from 1937. In Tito's partisan administration in WWII, then in government. Held various government and state posts, including foreign minister 1948–53. | 207, 209–10

Karimov, Islam Abduganievich (b. 1938). Soviet and Uzbek politician. Worked in Uzbek Gosplan 1966–83, Uzbek finance minister 1983–86. 1989–91 1st Secretary of Uzbek CP. President of Uzbekistan from 1990, directly elected end of 1991, term renewed twice. | 459

Karmal, Babrak (1929–96). Afghan communist politician. Among founders of People's Democratic Party of Afghanistan, 1965, head of its *Parcham* faction. Installed in power in Kabul after Soviet overthrow of Hafizullah Amin December 1979. Removed 1986. Died in exile in Russia. | 366

Karpov. Leader of peasant bands, Chelyabinsk, 1946. | 261

Kassil', Lev Abramovich (1905–70). Writer and journalist. Studied aerodynamics at Moscow University, turned to literature 1925. Worked on children's journal *Pioner*, turned particularly to writing for children. Worked 9 years on *Izvestiya*. | 172

Kazaris, Boris Mikhaylovich. Variety performer, Sverdlovsk, entertained troops 1943. | 156

Kemmetov. Balkar émigré brought in by Germans, 1942. | 185

Kennan, George Frost (1904–2005). US diplomat and historian. In US Moscow mission 1944–46, sent 'Long Telegram' to US advocating 'containment'. | 201

Kennedy, John Fitzgerald (1917–63). US Democratic politician, President 1961–63. Assassinated. | 225–28

Kennedy, Robert (1925–68). Brother of J.F. Kennedy, Attorney-General in his administration. | 226

Khasbulatov, Ruslan Imranovich (b. 1942). Russian Chechen politician, economist. Tutor, then professor at Plekhanov Institute since 1978. Elected from Grozny to RSFSR Supreme Soviet 1990. Deputy to Yeltsin as chairman 1990–91, acting chairman following Yeltsin's election as Russian President 1991. Active in opposing GKChP August 1991. Defended parliament against Yeltsin 1993,

Kogan, Samuil Genrikhovich. Variety performer, Sverdlovsk, entertained troops 1943. | 156

Kokotov, Oleg. In 1991: 17-year-old anarchist. | 446

Kolchina, T.E. Organizer of religious procession in Nikolo–Azyasi, 1943. | 178

Kolder, Drahomir (1925–72). Czechoslovak communist. Party functionary from 1946, CC sector head 1954–58, headed North Moravian party organization 1958–62. On CC from 1961. Called for Soviet intervention 1968. | 232

Kolobov, L. Red Army platoon commander in Germany, 1945. | 148

Komplektov, Viktor Georgievich (b. 1932). In CPSU from 1962. Studied foreign relations, worked in Ministry of Foreign Affairs from 1955. Many years in USSR Washington embassy, expert on US affairs. Deputy foreign minister from 1982. On CPSU Central Revision Committee from 1986. | 427

Konev, Ivan Stepanovich (1897–73). Professional soldier, in army from 1916, joined Red Army and RKP(b) 1918, fought in civil war. Held various commands, especially in the Far East 1920s and 1930s. Colonel-General in WWII, commanded 19th Army, and various western fronts. From 1944 USSR Marshal. Involved in operations to take Prague and Berlin. Commanded Soviet troops in Austria from 1945. Commander-in-Chief of land forces, 1946–50, 1955–56. Deputy armed forces minister from 1946, 1st deputy defence minister 1955–60. Headed tribunal to try Beria et al. 1953, headed suppression of Hungarian rising 1956. | 139, 222

Kosmodem'yanskaya, Zoya Anatol'evna (1923–41). Komsomol member from 1938, joined partisans 1941, captured and executed by Germans. Made Hero of the Soviet Union and subject of cult. | 334

Kosterin, Aleksey Evgrafovich (1896–1968). Writer and journalist, Bolshevik from 1916, in GULAG 1938–55, brother executed 1938. Assisted Crimean Tatars' national movement. Resigned from CPSU over invasion of Czechoslovakia. | 348

Kostov, Traicho (1897–1949). Bulgarian communist leader, Vice-Premier after war, accused of 'Titoism', executed after show trial. | 211

Kosygin, Aleksey Nikolaevich (1904–80). Soviet politician, joined CPSU 1927. In Red Army 1919–21. In co-op and industrial work to 1938, then chairman of Leningrad Soviet. On CPSU CC from 1939. Supervised Leningrad evacuation in WWII. Deputy chairman of Council of Ministers 1940–60. Chairman of Council of Ministers 1964–80. On Politburo 1948–52 and 1960–80. Most noted for attempted economic reforms in 1960s aimed at boosting incentives. | 92–93, 197, 230–32, 280, 283–84, 286, 322, 340, 386

Kovalev, Sergey Adamovich (b. 1930). Biophysicist, human rights activist, politician. Opposed Lysenko's pseudoscience 1950s. Dissident in 1968, joined Initiative Group to Defend Human Rights in the USSR 1969, involved in *samizdat*. Sentenced 1975 to 7 years in camp and 3 years' exile. Resumed political activity during perestroika. Russian People's Deputy 1990–93, elected to State Duma 1993, 1995, for 'Russia's Choice' party. Critic of Kremlin policy in Chechnya. | 352

Kozlov, Frol Romanovich (1908–65). Soviet politician. Factory worker from 1923, joined CPSU 1926. Full-time CPSU functionary from 1940 in Izhevsk and Kuybyshev, from 1949 in Leningrad, 1st city Secretary in 1952. On CPSU CC 1952–65. Khrushchev deputy. On CC Presidium 1957–64, chairman of RSFSR Council of Ministers 1958. | 274–75, 280

Krasin, Viktor Aleksandrovich (b.1929). Economist, human rights activist. In camps under Stalin. Among founders of Initiative Group to Defend Human Rights in the USSR 1969. Arrested 1972, exiled. Emigrated 1975, returned to Russia 1991. | 348, 352

Kravchuk, Leonid Makarovich (b. 1934). Soviet and Ukrainian politician, economist. On staff of Chernovitsk *oblast'* CPSU committee 1960–67. 1970–88 in CP Ukrainian CC apparatus, head of propaganda. On Ukrainian CP Politburo 1990–91, on CPSU CC 1990–91, left CPSU 19 August 1991. 1990–91 chairman of Supreme Rada of Ukraine, directly elected President of Ukraine 1 December 1991–94. Now among leaders of United Social-Democratic Party of Ukraine. | 455–56, 459

Krebs, Hans (1898–1945). German career officer, joined army 1914. Military attaché in Moscow 1936–39. Infantry General on Eastern Front in WWII. Chief of army General Staff April 1945. | 149

Kruchina, Nikolay Efimovich (1928–91). CPSU functionary, deputy head of CPSU CC agriculture and food industry section 1978–83. On CPSU Central Revision Committee 1966–71, CC candidate 1971–76, full member 1976–91. Committed suicide after failure of GKChP coup 1991. | 428, 438

Krupska, Tereska, Polish schoolgirl from Sarny deported to Russia, 1940. | 12

Krupski. Pole from Sarny deported to Russia, 1940. | 12

Krymov (Beklemishev), Yu.S. (1908–41). Writer and front-line war-correspondent. Killed while covering a retreat. His bayoneted and blood-soaked letter was found in his shirt pocket. | 80–81, 83

Kryuchkov. Candidate CPSU member, killed by peasant bandits, Chelyabinsk, 1946. | 261

Kryuchkov, Vladimir Aleksandrovich (b. 1924). Soviet politician, lawyer, diplomat, secret policeman. Studied law after wartime factory work. In CPSU from 1944. From 1946 in Stalingrad procurator's office. In foreign ministry from 1955, in USSR Budapest embassy 1955–59. Then in CC apparatus. Assistant to Yu. Andropov in KGB from 1967. 1978–88 in charge of foreign espionage. From 1988 KGB chairman. GKChP initiator and leader August 1991. | 396, 444–45

Kulagin, G.A. Chief mechanic of Leningrad engineering factory, 1941. | 90

Kulemin, Vasiliy Lavrent'evich (1921–62). Poet and writer. Fought in WWII. Then worked on *Komsomol'skaya pravda* and *Smena*, published several anthologies of poems. | 338

Kulikov, Viktor Georgievich (b. 1921). Soviet and Russian soldier and politician. In Red Army from 1939, CPSU from 1942. Fought in WWII, commanded tank

Likovenkov. Secretary of the Krasnaya Presnya (Moscow) CPSU district committee, 1945. | 174

Limonov. Leader of peasant bandits, Chelyabinsk, 1946. | 261

Litvinov, Maksim Maksimovich (Wallach, Max) (1876–1951). Soviet politician and diplomat. In RSDRP from 1898, Bolshevik. In exile 1907–18. In Foreign Affairs commissariat from 1918, commissar 1930–39. Headed Soviet anti-fascist foreign policy, replaced by Molotov. | 5

Litvinov, Pavel Mikhaylovich (b. 1940). Physicist, involved in human rights movement and *samizdat* publication. In internal exile to 1973 for demonstrating against invasion of Czechoslovakia. Emigrated 1974. | 348–52

Lobanov, P.V. Arkhangel'sk transport section CPSU Secretary 1941. | 84

Lopatin, P.G. Head of Soviet espionage group near Minsk, 1943. | 138

Luchinsky, Petr Kirillovich (b. 1940). Soviet and Moldovan politician. In CPSU and Komsomol work from 1960; 1st Secretary of Moldovan Komsomol 1967–71, in Moldovan CP CC apparatus to 1978. In CPSU CC apparatus 1978–86, 2nd Secretary of Tajik CP 1986–89, 1st Secretary of Moldovan CP 1989–91. CPSU CC candidate 1986–90, member 1990–91, on Politburo 1990–91. Moldovan ambassador to Russia 1992–93, chairman of Moldovan parliament 1993–96, President of Moldova 1996–2001. | 438

Luka (Voyno-Yasenetsky, Valentin Feliksovich) (1877–1961). Churchman, doctor. With Red Cross in Russo-Japanese war 1904–05, then zemstvo doctor to 1917. Involved in establishing Tashkent University 1920, professor of medicine. Became monk 1923. Combined ecclesiastical duties with work as surgeon 1920s and 1930s. Archbishop of Krasnoyarsk from 1942. Took part in September 1943 Church Council. Held various other archbishoprics, gave up surgery 1940s as eyesight failed. | 162

Lukov, Leonid Davidovich (1909–63). Film producer, People's Artist of the RSFSR 1957. First major film *A Great Life* (1940); sequel to that film criticized by Zhdanov 1946. | 331

Luk'yanov, Anatoliy Ivanovich (b. 1930). Soviet lawyer and politician. In CPSU from 1955. Worked in legal commissions of Council of Ministers and Supreme Soviet Presidium, head of latter's secretariat 1977–83. On CPSU Central Revision Committee from 1981, CC from 1986. Chairman of USSR Supreme Soviet, 1990–91. Connected with August 1991 coup, imprisoned, later amnestied. | 427

Makashov, Al'bert Mikhaylovich (b. 1938). Professional soldier, politician. In Soviet Army 1950–91. Major-General from 1979. Elected People's Deputy 1989. Dismissed from army for supporting GKChP. CPRF CC member from 1993. Imprisoned 1993–94 after failure of anti-Yeltsin rising. Duma Deputy from 1995. Noted for extreme nationalist and anti-Semitic statements. | 444

Malenkov, Georgiy Maksimilianovich (1902–88). Soviet party and state functionary. Began party work in 1925. Secretary of CC 1939–46 and 1948–53. 1946–53 and 1955–57 Deputy chairman and 1953–55 chairman of the Council of Ministers, as well as Minister for Power Stations 1955–57. Hero of Socialist Labour 1943. In minor posts from 1957. | 39, 61, 73, 92, 197, 216–17, 219, 264–65, 271, 280, 301–04, 307, 312–14, 334–35

Malinin, Mikhail Sergeevich (1899–1960). Army General. Chief-of-Staff on various fronts in WWII, thereafter worked at General Staff; 1st deputy chief 1952–60. | 221

Malyshev. State farm worker near Novgorod, 1946. | 294

Manaenkov, Yuriy Alekseevich (b. 1936). In CPSU from 1960. Journalist from 1958, party career from 1962 in Tambov *oblast'*. From 1984 1st Secretary of Lipetsk *oblast'* CPSU. On CPSU CC from 1986. Responsible for CPSU CC economic activities 1991. | 438

Mao Zedong (1893–1976). Chinese communist leader. Led Chinese communists on Long March 1930s, proclaimed People's Republic of China 1949. | 214, 218

Mar, Danka. Polish villager in Sarny in 1940. | 12

Markov, Georgiy Mokeevich (1911–91). Journalist and politician. Komsomol functionary from 1927, edited magazines and papers in Novosibirsk and Omsk 1931–38. War-correspondent in WWII. From 1956 Secretary, from 1971 1st Secretary, and 1986–89 board chairman of USSR Writers' Union. 1966–71 on CPSU Central Revision Committee, from 1971 on CPSU CC. | 354

Markus, B. Guards' captain and deputy commander of political section. Secretary of Komsomol committee in an architectural institute until 1941. Called up in July 1941. | 141–42

Marshall, George C. (1880–1959). US professional soldier and politician. Chief-of-Staff during WWII, Secretary of State from 1947. Creator of European Recovery ('Marshall') Plan. | 205–06

Marx, Karl (1818–83). German socialist economist, sociologist, philosopher. Ideological inspirer of social-democratic and communist movements. | 4, 83, 210, 224, 327–28

Maslov. Senior Lieutenant, Red Army, 1941. | 103–04

Maslyukov, Yuriy Dmitrievich (b. 1937). In CPSU from 1966. Worked in engineering industry, then in defence ministry and planning. 1982 1st deputy chairman of Gosplan, chairman 1988. 1985 deputy chairman of USSR Council of Ministers, 1988 1st Deputy. On CC from 1986, Politburo candidate from 1988. Supreme Soviet Deputy. | 426–27

Matrosov. Former GULAG inmate decorated in Red Army, 1944. | 126

Mauriac, François (1885–1970). French novelist and journalist. Elected to Académie Française 1933, won Nobel Prize for Literature 1952. | 357

Mayakovsky, Vladimir Vladimirovich (1893–1930). Poet and political activist. Bolshevik from 1908, imprisoned 1909, began writing poetry, abandoned politics. At art college 1911–14, involved with futurists, later with Gorky. Welcomed October revolution, worked for ROSTA press agency producing posters 1919–22, wrote for newspapers, involved in literary groups LEF and New LEF

1920s. Disillusionment and personal problems led to suicide. | 339

Medvedev, Roy Aleksandrovich (b. 1925). Historian, journalist and political activist. CPSU member 1959–69, expelled for writing critique of Stalinism *Let History Judge*. Thereafter dissident, widely published in west. Gorbachev supporter, restored to CPSU 1989. | 360

Medvedev, Vadim Andreevich (b. 1929). CPSU functionary. In CPSU from 1952. Lectured in Leningrad 1951–68, then in CP work. 1970s headed Leningrad CPSU city committee. On CPSU Central Revision Committee 1976–86, CC 1986–91, Politburo 1988–91. Rector of CPSU CC Academy of Social Sciences 1978–83, Chair of CC Ideological Commission 1988–91. People's Deputy 1989–91. From 1992 in Gorbachev Foundation. | 426

Mekhlis, Lev Zakharovich (1889–1953). Soviet state functionary. In Jewish socialist group Poalei-Zion 1907–10. In army in WWI, joined RKP(b) 1918. In Red Army and Soviet work from 1919. Assistant to Stalin 1924–30. Editor of *Pravda* from 1930. As head of Red Army Political Administration from 1937 responsible for massive purge. Noted for insisting on party pre-eminence in military during war and denunciations of 'enemies'. Retired 1950. | 77, 83, 106

Mel'nikov, Leonid Georgievich (1906–81). CPSU functionary. Factory worker from 1920, Komsomol Secretary 1924–28, joined CPSU 1928. CPSU functionary from 1937, in Ukraine and Kazakhstan. 1949–53 1st Secretary of Ukrainian CP. USSR Supreme Soviet Deputy 1941–54, 1958–62, 1966–81; Presidium member 1950–54. On CPSU CC full member 1952–56, candidate 1956–61. CC Presidium full member 1952–53. Ambassador to Romania from 1953. Thereafter in secondary government posts. | 303

Merkulov, Vsevolod Nikolaevich (1895–1953). Soviet secret policeman and politician. Conscripted 1916, ensign. In Cheka in Transcaucasus from 1921, worked in its apparatus. In CPSU from 1925. 1931–34 assistant to Beria, Secretary of CPSU Transcaucasus *kray* committee. USSR Supreme Soviet Deputy 1937–50. From end of 1938 1st deputy commissar at NKVD and head of NKVD Main Administration of State Security. Noted for cruelty and use of torture. 1940 directed massacre of Polish officer prisoners. From 1943 USSR People's Commissar of State Security, replaced by Abakumov 1946. Arrested and shot 1953. | 15, 171–72

Merzoev, Aleksandr. Red Army soldier in Germany, 1945. | 148

Mesnyaev, Aleksey Petrovich. Honoured Artist of the USSR, variety performance director, Sverdlovsk, entertained troops 1943. | 156

Mezhevalov, Gennadiy Vasil'evich. In 1942: 14-year-old schoolboy keen to join Red Army. | 137

Mikhalkov, Sergey Vladimirovich (b. 1913). Writer, poet, playwright, lyricist, Writers' Union functionary, public figure. First published 1928. In USSR Writers' Union from 1937. Wrote words to Soviet national anthem 1944 (with G. El'-Registan) and 1977, and to Russian national anthem 2001. In CPSU from

1950. 1970–92 chairman of board of RSFSR Writers' Union and Secretary of board of USSR Writers' Union. Served on numerous literature prize juries. | 354

Mikhaylov, Nikolay Aleksandrovich (1906–82). CPSU functionary, diplomat. Industrial worker 1922–31. In CPSU from 1930. Then in CPSU apparatus. Edited *Komsomol'skaya pravda* 1937–38. 1st Secretary of Komsomol CC 1938–52. On CPSU CC 1939–66, CC Orgburo 1939–52. Promoted by Stalin 1952 to CC Presidium, CC Secretary and head of propaganda, lost these positions 1953. 1953–54 Moscow CPSU committee 1st Secretary; from 1954 ambassador to Poland, 1955–60 culture minister, then ambassador to Indonesia. | 303

Mikheev. Colonel, commander of the tank division of the Novocherkassk garrison, 1962. | 275

Mikheev, Filipp Egorovich (1902–50). CPSU functionary, in party from 1926, administrator of Leningrad *oblast'* and city CPSU committees, arrested 1949 in 'Leningrad Case', shot 1950. | 301

Mikoyan, Anastas Ivanovich (1895–1978). Armenian revolutionary, Bolshevik from 1915. Only survivor of 27 Baku commissars arrested 1918. Held numerous Soviet government posts, especially in economy and trade. After death of Stalin, loyal supporter of Khrushchev to 1964. Deputy or 1st deputy chairman of Council of Ministers 1937–64. On CPSU CC 1923–76, on Politburo 1935–66. | 61, 227–28, 274–75, 302–03

Milyukov, Anatoliy Illarionovich. In CPSU CC economic section 1974–85, its deputy head 1987–91. Since 1993 in private banking. | 427

Minin, Kuz'ma Minich (d. 1616). Russian national hero. Nizhniy Novgorod trader and local chief. Organized troops with D.M. Pozharsky and defeated Poles near Moscow 1612. | 105

Minina (née Tokmacheva), T.V. (b. 1923). Student at Urals University 1940–45, then teacher of Russian language and literature. | 129–30

Misztelanka, Wiesia. Pole from Sarny deported to Russia, 1940. | 12

Molaev, S. Chairman of Sovnarkom of Chechen-Ingush ASSR, 1944. | 186–87

Molotov (Skryabin), Vyacheslav Mikhaylovich (1890–1986). Soviet politician. Bolshevik from 1906, in Petrograd early 1917, led party work there before Lenin's return. Took part in October seizure of power, thereafter in party and state work. On CPSU CC 1921–57. CC Secretary 1921–30, chair of Sovnarkom 1930–41, foreign commissar/minister 1939–49 and 1953–56. Loyal Stalinist, defeated by Khrushchev 1957. Ambassador to Mongolia 1957–60. Expelled from CPSU 1962, readmitted 1984. | 5–8, 10, 13, 16–18, 22–25, 27–29, 33, 35, 40–41, 43–44, 52, 57–58, 61, 78, 92, 102, 156, 162, 169, 197, 209–11, 216, 302–03, 312–14, 337, 415

Mozhaev, Boris Andreevich (1923–96). Writer and screenwriter, noted for his rural themes. | 345

Mozhin, V.P. Economist, 1st deputy head of CPSU CC socio-economic section, 1990. | 427

Mutalibov, Ayaz Niyazi Oğlı (b. 1938). Soviet and Azerbaijani politician. Worked in electrical goods industry 1959–77, then in CPSU work. Azerbaijani minister for local industry from 1979, head of Azerbaijani Gosplan, deputy chairman of Council of Ministers 1982–89. 1989–91 Chairman of Azerbaijani Council of Ministers, 1990–91 1st Secretary of Azerbaijani CP, President of republic, 1990–92. Fled to Moscow 1992. | 459

Nabiev, Rakhmon (1930–93). Soviet and Tajik politician. Tajik agriculture minister 1971–73, chairman of Tajik Council of Ministers 1973–82, 1st Secretary of Tajik CP 1982–86. On CPSU Central Revision Committee 1981–86. September 1991 chairman of Tajik Supreme Soviet; President, November 1991–September 1992. | 459

Nagy, Ferenc (1903–79). Hungarian politician, among founders of Smallholders' Party 1930, party leader after end of WWII. Emigrated to USA. | 205

Nagy, Imre (1896–1958). Hungarian communist leader. POW in Russia in WWI, joined Bolsheviks and Red Army. In Hungarian Soviet government 1919, then underground worker for Hungarian CP. In USSR 1929–44. Held various government posts 1944–55 in Hungary, out of favour 1949–51 and 1955–56. Appointed Prime Minister 23 October 1956 during Hungarian rising, fled to Yugoslav embassy 4 November following Soviet invasion. Captured by Soviet forces, executed after secret trial 1958. | 219–21

Napoleon (Napoleone di Buonaparte) (1769–1821). French military leader, proclaimed Emperor 1804. Led disastrous campaign against Russia 1812. | 58, 71

Nasedkin, Viktor Grigor'evich (1905–50). Secret policeman, work camp administrator. In Red Army from 1920, Cheka from 1921. In transport section of OGPU/NKVD 1920s and 1930s. Joined CPSU 1937. From 1939 deputy head of NKVD economic administration, 1941–47 head of NKVD GULAG system, intensified exploitation of slave labour. Dismissed 1948. | 125–27

Nazarbaev, Nursultan Abishevich (b. 1940). Soviet and Kazakh politician. In CPSU from 1962. 1960–69 worked in construction and engineering, then party career. From 1979 Secretary Kazakh CP CC. From 1984 chairman of Kazakhstan Council of Ministers. 1981–86 on CPSU Central Revision Committee, on CPSU CC from 1986. Deputy to Supreme Soviets of USSR and Kazakhstan to 1991. Since 1991 leader of independent Kazakhstan. | 459

Neizvestny, Ernst Iosifovich (b. 1925). Sculptor and illustrator. Clashed famously with Khrushchev, later commissioned by Khrushchev to sculpt his gravestone. In emigration since 1976. | 337–39

Nekrasov, Nikolay Aleksandrovich (1821–77). Writer and poet. Worked on *Otechestvennye zapiski* from 1841, editor of *Sovremennik* 1847–66. Associated with democratic and revolutionary writers, wrote poems with pronounced social content. | 361–62

Nevsky, Aleksandr Yaroslavich (ca. 1220–1263). Prince, military leader, Russian national hero. Ruled Novgorod 5 years from 1236, defeated Swedes 1240. Most famous for defeating Teutonic knights on frozen Lake Chudskoe 1242. | 71–72, 105

Nicholas I (Romanov, Nikolay Petrovich) (1796–1855). Emperor of Russia 1825–55, succeeded brother Alexander I. Noted for conservative views, suppressed Decembrist rising on assuming power (1825), Polish rising (1830–31) and Hungarian national movement (1848). Reign ended in fiasco of Crimean War (1853–56). | 21, 361

Nicholas II (Romanov, Nikolay Aleksandrovich) (1868–1918). Emperor of Russia 1894–1917. Powers limited after 1905, abdicated March 1917, shot with family in Urals 17 July 1918. | 21

Nikiforova. Collective farmer, Molotov *oblast'*, 1948. | 263–64

Nikolaeva, M. School teacher, wrote critical letter to Khrushchev, 1956. | 269–70

Nikolay (Yarushevich, Boris Dorofeevich) (1892–1961). Churchman. In charge of monasteries 1920s and 1930s, Metropolitan of Kiev and Galicia 1941–44. Took part in September 1943 Church Council. 1946–60 in charge of external relations and publishing, Moscow Patriarchate. | 162

Nikonov, Pavel Fedorovich (b. 1930). Artist, painter, leading exponent of 'severe style', introduced elements of avant-garde into official exhibitions 1960s and 1970s. Took part in CPSU–cultural figures talks 1962–63. | 338

Nikulin, Lev Veniaminovich (Ol'konitsky, Lev Vladimirovich) (1891–1967). Writer and screenwriter. First published 1910. Studied in Paris 1911–12, where wrote first screenplay. In emigration in Berlin from 1920, later returned to USSR. Wrote novels praising Soviet secret services. In CPSU from 1940. | 173

Nilin, Pavel Filippovich (1908–81). Writer and journalist. Published short stories and newspaper articles 1930s, front-line *Pravda* correspondent in WWII. Screenwriter on *A Great Life* (1940 and 1946), second film script criticized in CPSU resolution 1946. Continued writing until 1970s. | 331

Nishanov, Rafik Nishanovich (b. 1926). Soviet Uzbek politician. CPSU functionary from 1951. Secretary of Uzbek CP CC from 1963, 1st Secretary 1988–89. In diplomatic work from 1970, Uzbek SSR foreign minister from 1985. Chairman of Soviet of Nationalities of USSR Supreme Soviet 1989–91. | 427

Niyazov, Saparmurad Ataevich (b. 1940). Soviet and Turkmen politician. In CPSU from 1962. In Turkmen CP apparatus from 1970, 1st Secretary of Ashkhabad city CPSU committee from 1980. In CPSU CC central apparatus from 1984. From 1985 chairman of Council of Ministers of Turkmenistan and 1st Secretary of Turkmen CP. Since 1991 leader of independent Turkmenistan, creator of homespun ideology *Rukhnama*. | 459

Novikov, Aleksandr Aleksandrovich (1900–76). Army and air force officer. In Red Army from 1919, in RKP(b) from 1920. Moved to air force 1933. Chief-of-staff, then commander, of Leningrad district air force from 1938. Commander of Soviet air force from 1942, defence commissar for air force 1942–43. USSR Supreme Soviet Deputy from 1946. Arrested 1946 after Stalin heard US planes were better than Soviet ones. Imprisoned, amnestied 1953, returned to air force. | 300

Novobranets, V.A. (1907–84). Lieutenant-Colonel. Head of Information Section of Red Army General Staff reconnaissance division 1940–41. | 48, 53–54

Novotný, Antonín (1904–75). Czechoslovak communist politician, party General Secretary 1953–68, Czechoslovak President 1958–68. | 231

Okudzhava, Bulat Shalvovich (1924–97). Poet, writer, songwriter. Fought in WWII until wounded, published first poems while at front. Began recording songs in 1950s. Took part in CPSU–cultural figures talks 1962–63. Published poems in 1960s, novels in 1970s. | 338

Oleshko. Major-General, head of Novocherkassk garrison, 1962. | 276

Osadchiy. Colonel, head of political department of 37th army, Red Army, 1942. | 184

Otstavnoy. Former GULAG inmate decorated in Red Army, 1944. | 126

Ovechkin, Valentin Vladimirovich (1904–68). Writer and journalist. Chaired agri-cultural commune 1925–31. In CPSU from 1929, party worker and journalist in 1930s. Many writings had a rural theme. Won various awards in the USSR for his work. | 344–45

Paasikivi, Juho Kusti (1870–1956). Finnish statesman. Prime Minister 1918 and 1944–46, President 1946–56. Led Finnish delegation concluding peace with RSFSR 1920, and as government minister concluded peace with USSR 1940. Ambassador to Sweden 1936–39, to USSR 1940–41. Headed private bank 1941–44, opposed war against USSR. In unofficial peace talks with USSR February–March 1944. Postwar foreign policy stressed friendly relations with USSR. | 22, 24, 33, 35

Paletskis (Paleckis), Justas (1899–1980). Lithuanian and Soviet politician and jour-nalist. Worked with Lithuanian CP from 1931, imprisoned 1939. Headed 'People's Government' after Soviet invasion June 1940, Chairman of Presidium of Lithuanian Supreme Soviet 1940–67, held numerous other Soviet and CPSU posts. Retired 1970. | 42

Pankin, Boris Dmitrievich (b. 1931). Journalist, diplomat and politician. One-time chief editor of *Komsomol'skaya pravda*. Diplomat from 1982, in Sweden, then Czechoslovakia. USSR foreign minister August–November 1991, Soviet ambas-sador to UK from November 1991. 1994 gave up diplomatic work, wrote biographical novel. | 455

Pasternak, Boris Leonidovich (1890–1960). Noted poet and writer. Studied music and philosophy in youth at Moscow and Marburg. In 1920s close to Mayakovsky, wrote poems and novels. In 1930s produced mainly translations. In 1950s worked on celebrated *Doctor Zhivago*, condemned in USSR, awarded Nobel Prize for Literature. | 94, 332, 336–40, 344–45, 353, 356–57, 361, 391

Patiashvili, Dzhumber Il'ich (b. 1939). Georgian and Soviet politician. Worked in Komsomol, then in Georgian CP, 1st Secretary 1985–89. Now heads opposition group 'Ertoba' in Georgian parliament. | 423

Paulus, Friedrich (1890–1957). German professional soldier from 1910. Commanded 6th Army at Stalingrad. Captured by Soviet forces, made anti-Nazi radio broadcasts. Witness for prosecution at Nuremberg. Imprisoned in USSR to 1953, then worked as police inspector in GDR. | 136–37

Pavlov, A.S. Head of the state-legal department of the CPSU CC, 1990. | 427

Pavlov, Dmitriy Grigor'evich (1897–1941). Professional soldier. In CPSU from 1919, CC candidate member from 1939. General from 1941, headed troops in Belorussia in June 1941. Accused of panic and cowardice after the Nazi attack, executed. Rehabilitated 1956. | 77

Pavlov, Valentin Sergeevich (b. 1937). Soviet economist and politician. In finance ministry 1966–79, in Gosplan from 1979. Chaired USSR prices committee from 1986, 1st deputy finance minister 1986–89, finance minister 1989–91, USSR Prime Minister 1991. In GKChP August 1991, amnestied 1994. Now president of Chasprombank, financial consultant and businessman. | 444–45

Pawlakówna, Stasia, Polish villager in Sarny, 1940. | 12

Pegov, Nikolay Mikhaylovich (1905–91). Soviet politician and diplomat. Industrial worker in 1920s, joined CPSU 1930. Managed silk factory 1930s. From 1938 CPSU functionary in Far East, 1st Secretary of Primor'e *kray* committee 1938–47. On CPSU CC 1939–86. USSR Supreme Soviet Deputy 1941–50, 1953–58, 1978–84. From 1952 CC Secretary, 1952–53 Presidium candidate member. Ambassador to Iran 1956–63, Algeria 1964–67, India 1967–73. Deputy foreign minister 1973–75. | 306, 311

Pel'she, Arvid Yanovich (1899–1983). Soviet Latvian politician. Bolshevik from 1915. On Petrograd Soviet 1917. 1918–29 in Cheka and political work in Red Army. In Kazakhstan from 1931. From 1941 Secretary of Latvian CP CC, 1st Secretary 1960–66. On CPSU CC from 1961, Politburo from 1966 until death. | 252

Peredreev, Anatoliy Konstantinovich (1934–87). Poet, noted for traditionalism in his art. | 338

Pervukhin, Mikhail Georgievich (1904–78). CPSU functionary and industrial manager. In RKP(b) from 1919, held various party and Komsomol posts. In power industry from 1929. From 1938 1st deputy heavy industry commissar. Headed power and chemical industry commissariats/ministries 1940s and 1950s. Held various top government jobs 1953–57. On CPSU CC 1939–61, Presidium 1952–57. Sided with 'anti-party group' 1957, demoted. | 303

Petrenko, N.M. Former deputy chairman of L'vov *oblast'* executive committee, 1943. | 140

Petrov. Engineer at agricultural research institute, Moscow, 1968. | 350

Petrovsky, Leonid Petrovich. Human rights campaigner, opposed rehabilitation of Stalinism and invasion of Czechoslovakia, 1960s. | 346, 352

Petukhov, B. Chairman of Krasnodar *kray* executive committee, 1957. | 269

Piłsudski, Józef Klemens (1867–1935). Polish politician and military leader. In revolutionary and nationalist politics from 1880s. Arrested 1887 for plotting to assassinate Alexander III, exiled to Siberia to 1892. Joined Polish Socialist Party 1893. Main orientation against Russia; worked with Japan and Austria-Hungary 1900s. Head of state and armed forces in Poland from end of 1918. Fought war against Soviet Russia 1919–20. Military and political strongman of Poland from 1926 until death. | 251, 254

Pitirim (Sviridov, Petr Petrovich). Churchman, in 1943 Bishop of Kursk. Took part in September 1943 Church Council. | 162, 177

Platonov (Klimentov), Andrey Platonovich (1899–1951). Writer, published in USSR from 1920s, war-correspondent with *Krasnaya zvezda* 1942–45. Fell from favour 1946 for work *The Ivanov Family*, published in *Novyy mir* 1946. | 345

Pliev, Issa Aleksandrovich (1903–79). Soviet career soldier, in Red Army from 1922. Advisor to Mongolian army 1936–38. Commanded cavalry in WWII. 1955–58 1st Deputy; from 1958 commander of troops of North Caucasus military district. General from 1962. Commanded troops in suppression of Novocherkassk rising 1962. CPSU CC candidate 1961–66. From 1968 inspector at Ministry of Defence. | 275, 279

Plyushch, Leonid Ivanovich (b. 1939). Ukrainian mathematician, dissident from 1960s, expelled to west 1976. | 352

Pod"yapol'sky, Grigoriy Sergeevich (1926–76). Poet, human rights activist. Dissident from 1965, involved in Human Rights Committee etc. | 352

Polikarpov, Dmitriy Alekseevich (1905–65). Organization Secretary of the Writers' Union, 1944–46. | 171–72

Polozkov, Ivan Kuz'mich (b. 1935). CPSU functionary, in party work from 1962 in localities until 1980, in CC apparatus 1980–85, 1st Secretary of Krasnodar *kray* CPSU from 1985. 1st Secretary of RSFSR CP CC 1990–91. USSR People's Deputy 1989–91, RSFSR People's Deputy to 1993. | 431–32, 435

Polyansky, Dmitriy Stepanovich (b. 1917). Soviet politician. From 1932 worked on state farm, studied agriculture. In CPSU from 1939, Komsomol worker. Worked in CPSU CC apparatus from 1945. In Crimea 1949–55. On CPSU CC 1956–76, CC Presidium 1960–66, Politburo 1966–76. Secretary of Krasnodar CPSU *kray* committee from 1957. Chairman of RSFSR Council of Ministers from 1958, deputy chairman and 1st deputy chairman of USSR Council of Ministers 1962–73. Ambassador to Japan 1976–82, Norway 1982–87. | 269, 275

Ponimatkin. Worker at factory No. 50, Penza, 1945. | 164

Ponomarenko, Panteleymon Kondrat'evich (1902–84). Soviet politician. Joined Red Army 1918. Komsomol worker from 1922. In CPSU from 1925. In CPSU CC apparatus from 1937, 1st Secretary of Belorussian CP CC 1938–47. On CPSU CC 1939–61. Partisan leader WWII. Led postwar campaign of arrests in Belorussia. On USSR Supreme Soviet Presidium 1941–46, 1950–51 and 1954–58. CPSU CC Presidium candidate member 1952–53, full member 1953–56. Ambassador to Poland 1955–57, India and Nepal 1957–59,

Netherlands 1959–61. Thereafter party school lecturer. | 190–91, 303–04

Ponomarev, Boris Nikolaevich (1905–95). CPSU ideologist and functionary. Joined Red Army and RKP(b) 1919, fought in civil war. From 1920 in Komsomol and CPSU apparatus. From 1930s concerned with CPSU history. In Comintern apparatus 1936–43. 1944–46 deputy head of CPSU international information department, 1946–49 in *Sovinformburo*. 1948–55 deputy head of CPSU CC foreign political commission, head from 1955. CPSU CC candidate member from 1952, full member from 1956. Candidate Politburo member 1972–86. | 243–44, 252

Popkov, Petr Sergeevich (1903–50). Soviet politican. Worked as joiner 1920s. In CPSU from 1925. Political career advanced in 1930s—from 1938 deputy chairman, from 1939 chairman of Leningrad Soviet. CPSU CC candidate member from 1939, in charge of wartime evacuation, Leningrad. 1st Secretary of Leningrad *oblast'* and city CPSU committees 1946–49, arrested in 'Leningrad Case' 1949, shot 1950. | 301

Popov, Georgiy Mikhaylovich (1906–68). Soviet politician and industrial manager. Joined CPSU 1926, Komsomol functionary 1925–28, at Central Labour Institute from 1928. 2nd Secretary of Moscow city CPSU from 1938, chair of Moscow Soviet EC 1944–50. 1st Secretary of Moscow city and *oblast'* CPSU committees 1945–49. 1949–51 Minister of Urban Economy, 1951 Minister of Agricultural Machine-Building. 1951–53 director of 'Frunze' aircraft factory, ambassador to Poland 1953–54, then back in aviation industry. | 173

Popov, Markian Mikhaylovich (1902–69). Professional soldier, in Red Army from 1920, RKP(b) from 1921. Colonel-General, front commander 1941–45, commanded Bryansk front June–October 1943. | 139

Pospelov, Petr Nikolaevich (1898–1979). CPSU functionary. Bolshevik from 1916, in Bolshevik underground, Chelyabinsk, 1918–19. Worked in CPSU CC propaganda department from 1924. On CPSU Control Commission from 1930, on *Pravda* editorial board 1931–34. Active party publicist from 1930s. On CPSU CC 1939–71, USSR Supreme Soviet Deputy 1946–66. Chief editor of *Pravda* 1940–49. Among authors of *Short Course* CPSU history (1938). CPSU CC Secretary 1953–60, candidate for CC Presidium 1957–61, director of Institute of Marxism-Leninism 1961–67. Prepared materials for Khrushchev's 'secret speech' 1956. | 303

Potapova, O.A. Organizer of religious procession in Nikolo–Azyasi, 1943. | 178

Pozharsky, Dmitriy Mikhaylovich (1578–1642). Russian national hero. Served at court during 'time of troubles'. Defeated Poles near Kolomna 1608. Invited by K.M. Minin to Nizhniy Novgorod, raised army there and defeated Poles near Moscow. Prominent in installing Romanov line on throne 1613. | 105

Pribylov, V. Head of agricultural administration, Krasnodar *kray*, 1957. | 269

Primakov, Evgeniy Maksimovich (b. 1929). Soviet and Russian politician, journalist, orientalist academic. Worked in radio and television 1953–62. In CPSU from

1959. *Pravda* foreign correspondent 1962–70. 1970–77 deputy director, from 1985 director, of Institute of World Economy and International Relations; from 1977 director of Institute of Oriental Studies. CPSU CC candidate 1986–89, full member 1989–90, Politburo candidate 1989–90. On USSR Presidential Council 1990–91. Deputy chairman of KGB September–October 1991, then in charge of USSR and Russian foreign espionage 1991–96. Russian foreign minister 1996–98, Prime Minister 1998–99. State Duma Deputy. | 427

Prishchepa, Sergey Ignat'evich. Variety performer, Sverdlovsk, entertained troops 1943. | 156

Prokof'ev, Aleksandr Andreevich (1900–71). Poet, born into peasant family. In Red Army 1919–30. First published 1927. Many poems have pastoral and national themes. Worked in political administration on Leningrad front in WWII. Took part in cultural discussions with CPSU leadership 1962. | 338–39

Prokof'ev, Sergey Sergeevich (1891–1953). Composer, concert pianist, studied at St Petersburg Conservatoire 1904–14. Debut performance 1908. Lived abroad 1918–36. Compositions include 8 operas, 7 ballets and 7 symphonies. Denounced as 'bourgeois formalist' 1948 and first wife arrested. Obliged to recant. Died of stroke shortly thereafter. | 332, 357

Proskurin. Foreman at factory No. 744, Penza, 1945. | 164

Pugo, Boris Karlovich (1937–91). Soviet Latvian politician. Komsomol functionary from 1961, joined CPSU 1963, held party posts in Latvia. Headed Latvian KGB from 1980, 1st Secretary of Latvian CP 1984–88. On CPSU CC 1986–90. USSR Minister of Internal Affairs 1990–91. Member of GKChP August 1991, shot himself following collapse of putsch. | 445, 453

Pushkin, Aleksandr Sergeevich (1799–1837). Poet, journalist, historian and public servant, regarded as founder of literary Russian. In state service in St Petersburg from 1818, in literary circles. Exiled to south 1820–24 for political epigrams. Close to Decembrists, but not participant in rising 1825. Most noted for *Eugene Onegin, Boris Godunov, Ruslan and Ludmilla*. Fatally wounded in duel. | 338, 341

Puzanov, Aleksandr Mikhaylovich (1906–98). State functionary and diplomat. In CPSU from 1925. In state control apparatus from 1933—deputy commissar for state control 1943–44. Kuybyshev CPSU head from 1946. On CPSU CC 1952–76. Chairman of RSFSR Council of Ministers 1952–56, 1st Deputy 1956–57. Ambassador to North Korea (to 1962), Yugoslavia (1962–67), Bulgaria (1967–72), Afghanistan (1972–79). In foreign ministry apparatus 1979–80, then retired. | 243–44

Rákosi, Mátyás (1892–1971). Hungarian communist politician, General Secretary of party 1945–56, Premier 1952–53 and 1955–56. In USSR from 1956 until death. | 219

Razumovsky, Georgiy Petrovich (b. 1936). In CPSU and CPSU functionary from 1961, made career in Krasnodar, 1st Secretary of *kray* committee from 1983. On CPSU CC 1986–90. Involved particularly in cadres work. | 426–28

Reagan, Ronald Wilson (1911–2004). US actor and Republican politician. Governor of California from 1966, US President 1981–1989. Noted for conservatism and anti-communism. | 255, 381

Reichenau, Walther von (1884–1942). German career officer, joined army 1902. Became Nazi 1932. Made Field Marshall 1940. Commanded 6th Army in invasion of USSR. Noted for harshness and anti-Semitism. Died of heart attack. | 301

Repkin. Private soldier, defended state buildings in Novocherkassk, 1962. | 276

Rezaev, Aleksey. In 1991: 31-year-old artist, active against GKChP. | 446

Ribbentrop, Joachim (1893–1946). German Foreign Minister 1938–45. Sentenced to death at Nuremberg for war crimes. | 5–8, 16–19, 40, 44, 64, 415

Rodionov, Igor' Nikolaevich (b. 1936). Professional soldier, noted disciplinarian. Commanded 40th army in Afghanistan in 1980s, Transcaucasia Military District 1988–89, violently suppressed Tbilisi disorders 1989. Headed General Staff Academy 1989–96. Defence Minister 1996–97, sacked for incompetence. Now State Duma Deputy, extreme anti-Semite. | 423

Rodionov, Mikhail Ivanovich (1907–50). CPSU functionary, in Komsomol and party posts in Gorky *oblast'* from 1927. Chairman of Gorky *oblast'* executive committee from 1939, 1st Secretary of *oblast'* and city CPSU committees 1940–46. On CPSU CC from 1941, on Orgburo 1946–49. Arrested 1949 in 'Leningrad Case', shot 1950. | 301

Rokossovsky, Konstantin Konstantinovich (1896–1968). Professional soldier. Fought in WWI, joined Red Guard 1917, Red Army 1918, RKP(b) 1919. Fought in civil war. Held various commands. Arrested 1937, refused to admit guilt, imprisoned in Noril'sk. Released 1940 to lead troops in WWII. Commander at battle of Moscow and on Bryansk, Stalingrad, Central and Belorussian fronts. Marshal of the Soviet Union 1941. Appointed Commander of Polish forces and deputy chairman, Polish Council of Ministers, in 1949 on Soviet insistence. Returned to USSR 1956, deputy defence minister to 1962. | 104–05, 139

Romanov, Ya.S. Civil war veteran, CPSU member in 1941. | 84

Roosevelt, Franklin Delano (1882–1945). US Democratic politician, President 1933–45. | 69–70, 144, 166, 168, 201

Rostropovich, Mstislav Leopol'dovich (b. 1927). Cellist, pianist and conductor. Solo cellist at Moscow Philharmonia from 1946, professor at both Moscow and Leningrad Conservatoires 1960–74. Great popularizer of Shostakovich. Since 1974 has appeared with world's greatest orchestras. Emigrated with wife G.P. Vishnevskaya following political pressure 1978. Awards, prizes and Soviet citizenship revoked, restored 1990. | 356, 358, 363–64

Rozhdestvensky, Robert Ivanovich (1932–94). Poet, first published 1950, published actively in 1960s. | 339

Ruch'ev (Krivoshchekov), Boris Aleksandrovich (1913–73). Poet. First worked in construction of Magnitogorsk 1920s and 1930s; wrote poems lauding socialist

Schulenburg, Friedrich Werner von (1875–1944). German ambassador to Moscow 1934–41. Involved in anti-Hitler conspiracy of July 1944, tried and executed. | 6, 16, 44, 47, 57–58

Sedlyarova, Aleksandra. All-Union variety performance award winner, entertained troops, Sverdlovsk, 1943. | 156

Seligeev. Khar'kov university lecturer, 1944. | 171

Sel'vinsky, Il'ya L'vovich (1899–1968). Writer, playwright, poet. Leading figure in constructivist school 1920s. Wandered in youth, held wide variety of jobs. Plays and poems noted for historical and political themes. Published actively until death. | 172

Semichastny, Vladimir Efimovich (1924–2001). CPSU functionary and secret policeman. In CPSU from 1944. Held various party positions. Chairman of KGB 1961–67, involved in removal of Khrushchev 1964. | 277

Semochkin, A.S. Lieutenant-Colonel. Former adjutant of G.K. Zhukov. Arrested 1946 at same time as A.A. Novikov, accused of military conspiracy, implicated Zhukov. | 300

Sergiy (Grishin, Aleksey) (1889–1943). Churchman, monk from 1911. Army priest in WWI. Held various bishoprics in 1920s, Archbishop from 1930. From 1942 Archbishop of Gorky and Arzamas. Took part in September 1943 Church Council. | 162

Sergiy (Stragorodsky, Ivan Nikolaevich) (1867–1944). Churchman. Took part in Church Councils 1917–18, 1943. 1917–23 Metropolitan of Vladimir and Shuya. Renovationist 1922–23, recanted 1924. Metropolitan of Nizhniy Novgorod and Arzamas from 1924. Metropolitan of Moscow and Kolomna from 1934. Patriarchal *locum tenens* from 1937, Patriarch of All-Russia 1943–44. | 71–73, 101, 110, 159–62

Serov, Ivan Aleksandrovich (1905–90). Soldier and secret policeman. In CPSU 1926–65. In Red Army 1920s and 1930s, NKVD from 1939. NKVD head in Ukraine 1939–41, then deputy commissar of state security. Involved in Katyn' massacre 1940, and mass deportations 1944. On CPSU CC: candidate 1941–56, full member 1956–61. From 1954 KGB chairman, directed KGB operation in Hungary 1956. Mobilized Khrushchev's supporters against 'anti-party group' 1957. Headed intelligence at GHQ from 1958. Sacked 1963 following spy scandal. Expelled from CPSU for corruption. | 222

Serzhantov. Former GULAG inmate decorated in Red Army, 1944. | 126

Shaginyan, Marietta Sergeevna (1888–1982). Writer. Studied in St Petersburg, in literary-philosophical circles before WWI. Welcomed October revolution. Prolific novelist and essayist from 1913 onwards. Noted for writings on Lenin. Corresponding member of Armenian Academy of Sciences from 1950. Hero of Socialist Labour 1976. Joined CPSU 1942. | 173–74

Shapiro, I.I. (b. 1922). Sverdlovsk University student 1941–43, later Lieutenant, worked on divisional front-line newspaper *Stalinets* 1943–45. Later worked in radio. | 113

Shaposhnikov, Boris Mikhaylovich (1882–1945). Professional soldier and military theoretician. Colonel in WWI. Volunteered for Red Army 1918. Held various commands 1920s and 1930s. In CPSU from 1930, candidate CC member 1939–45. Head of GHQ 1937–40 and 1941–42. Removed from commanding positions 1943. | 78–79

Shaposhnikov, M.K. First deputy commander of troops in North Caucasus district, 1962. | 278

Sharkov. Wounded by peasant bandits, Chelyabinsk, 1946. | 261

Shatalin, Nikolay Nikolaevich (1904–84). CPSU functionary. Komsomol worker and teacher from 1922, in CPSU from 1925. Combined party and teaching work to 1938. CPSU CC worker 1938–44, then in Baltics establishing Soviet rule. On CPSU Central Revision Committee 1939–52, CC candidate 1952, full member 1953–56, CC Secretary 1953–55. Then in minor jobs, retired 1960. | 303

Shchedrin, Rodion Konstantinovich (b. 1932). Composer and pianist. Author of numerous operas, orchestral works and piano pieces. Has made wide use of themes from Russian folklore. 1962–63 took part in CPSU–cultural figures talks. | 338

Shcherbakov, Aleksandr Sergeevich (1901–45). CPSU functionary. Factory worker from 1912, joined RKP(b) 1918. Komsomol worker during civil war and 1920s, from 1932 in central CPSU apparatus. From 1934 1st Secretary of Writers' Union. From 1939 on CPSU CC and CC Orgburo, from 1941 CC Secretary and Politburo candidate. From 1942 head of army political administration, deputy defence commissar 1942–43, head of war propaganda council. Drank himself to death. | 102, 177

Shchipachev, Stepan Petrovich (1899–1979). Poet. Orphaned as child, worked as village labourer. In Red Army 1919–31 as soldier and political worker. Published poems in leaflets and local papers, in collections from 1923. Worked on front-line papers in WWII. | 338

Shelepin, Aleksandr Nikolaevich (1918–94). Soviet politician, in CPSU from 1940. Komsomol functionary from 1940, mobilized members for partisan brigades. Komsomol CC Secretary from 1943, 1st Secretary 1952–58. On CPSU CC 1952–76, Politburo 1964–75, Supreme Soviet 1954–79. Chairman of KGB 1958–61. Main organizer of Khrushchev's dismissal 1964. Head of Soviet trade unions from 1967. | 275, 339

Shenin, Oleg Semenovich (b. 1937). Soviet and Russian politician. Worked in engineering and construction to 1974. In CPSU from 1962. Party functionary in Krasnoyarsk *kray* 1974–90, chaired Krasnoyarsk Soviet of People's Deputies. CPSU CC advisor in Afghanistan 1980–81. USSR People's Deputy 1989–91. On Politburo 1990–91. Involved with GKChP. Remains prominent in Russian communist-patriotic politics. | 438

Shepilov, Dmitriy Timofeevich (1905–95). Soviet politician. In CPSU 1926–62 and 1976–82. Held variety of legal, academic and CPSU posts 1920s and 1930s. In army political and propaganda work 1940s. Editorial worker on *Pravda* 1946–47, chief editor 1952–56. On CPSU CC 1952–57, CC Secretary 1955–57, candidate Presidium member. Foreign minister 1956–57. Supported 'anti-party group', lost all top positions 1957. Expelled from CPSU for factionalism 1962. Worked in archive administration 1960–82. | 312, 314

Shevardnadze, Eduard Amvrosievich (b. 1928). Soviet and Georgian politician. Komsomol worker from 1946, in CPSU 1948–91. Komsomol career to 1961, then Georgian CP functionary. 1964–68 1st deputy minister, then minister for public order, 1968–72 Georgian minister for internal affairs. 1st Secretary of Georgian CP 1972–85. On CPSU CC 1976–91, Politburo candidate 1978–85, full member 1985–90. USSR foreign minister 1985–91. President of Georgia 1992–2004. | 267, 423–24, 440, 455

Shkiryatov, Matvey Fedorovich (1883–1954). Soviet politician, Bolshevik from 1906. On Moscow and Tula Soviet ECs 1917. On CPSU CC (with breaks) from 1921. Worked in party control apparatus. Loyal supporter of Stalin. | 302

Shklovsky, Viktor Borisovich (1893–1984). Writer, historian, critic, literary theorist. In army in WWI, then in Red Army. Escaped temporarily to Finland 1922 to avoid testifying in SR show trial. Acquainted and worked with leading figures in arts from 1920s. Major work: biography of L.N. Tolstoy (1963). | 172

Shkvartsev, Aleksandr A. Lecturer, diplomat. Lecturer at Moscow Textile Institute, appointed Soviet ambassador to Germany September 1939, replaced by Dekanozov 1940, returned to MTI. | 16

Shlyapnikov, Aleksandr Gavrilovich (1885–1937). In RSDRP from early 1900s, strike leader, union organizer. On Bolshevik CC from 1915, liaised with leaders and foreign socialists. Headed Petrograd Bolsheviks February 1917. Held state, party and trade-union posts after October. Headed 'workers' opposition' 1921, thereafter out of favour. Wrote histories of revolutionary movement. Arrested and exiled 1930s, shot 1937. | 346

Shlyapnikov, I. Son of A.G. Shlyapnikov. | 346

Shokmanov. Balkar émigré brought in by Germans, 1942. | 185

Sholokhov, Mikhail Aleksandrovich (1905–84). Writer, from peasant family. Enthusiastic supporter of revolution from early years. First published 1923. Most famous for multi-part works *Quiet Flows the Don* (for which awarded Nobel Prize for Literature 1965) and *Virgin Soil Upturned*. Took consistently pro-CPSU line, denounced dissenters. | 342–43, 356

Shostakovich, Dmitriy Dmitrievich (1906–75). Composer, pianist. Criticized 1936 in *Pravda* for *Lady Macbeth of Mtsensk,* marking start of campaign against 'formalism'. From 1937 taught at Leningrad Conservatoire, in Leningrad to October 1941, composed 7th (Leningrad) Symphony, first performed 1942. Criticized again for 'formalism' 1948, but also awarded Stalin Prize and others. From 1960 in CPSU, 1st Secretary of RSFSR Composers' Union. | 100–01, 332, 357

Shostakovsky Vyacheslav Nikolaevich (b. 1937). Soviet and Russian politician. In

CPSU from 1961, Komsomol worker 1960s and 1970s. Headed CPSU Higher Party School 1986–90. Joined CPSU 'Democratic Platform' January 1990, left CPSU October 1990, formed Republican Party. Subsequently involved in 'Democratic Alternative' and 'Yabloko'. | 434

Shtemenko, Sergey Matveevich (1907–76). Professional soldier. Son of peasant, volunteered for Red Army 1926. In CPSU from 1930. In 1939 commander of tank battalion in invasion of eastern Poland. In General Staff from 1941, from 1943 headed its operational division. From 1946 deputy chief, from 1948 chief of General Staff. Deputy armed forces minister 1948–52. CPSU CC candidate 1952–56. Fell from favour under Khrushchev. General from 1968. | 300

Shushkevich, Stanislav Stanislavovich (b. 1934). Soviet and Belorussian politician, physicist. In CPSU 1968–May 1991. In faculty of nuclear physics at Belorussian State University 1969–86, pro-rector for science 1986–90. USSR People's Deputy from 1989, on Belorussian Supreme Soviet from 1990, chairman September 1991–January 1994. After 1991 opposed closer links with Russia. Lost presidential elections 1994. | 456, 459

Shvernik, Nikolay Mikhaylovich (1888–1970). Soviet politician. Bolshevik from 1905. In leadership of Petersburg metalworkers' union 1910–11. On factory committees and soviet in Samara 1917–18. In trade-union work from 1921. On CPSU CC from 1925, held diverse leading CC and trade-union jobs. On CC Presidium: candidate 1952–53, full member 1957–66. 1950s involved in mass rehabilitations of people repressed in 1930s. Supreme Soviet Deputy 1937–66, chaired its Presidium 1946–53. | 303

Sidorova. Surgeon at Hospital No. 16, Moscow, 1968. | 350

Silaev, Ivan Stepanovich (b. 1930). Soviet and Russian politician. Worked in aviation industry 1954–74. In CPSU 1959–91. 1974–77 Deputy, 1977–80 1st Deputy, 1981–85 USSR Minister of Aviation Production. Deputy chairman of USSR Council of Ministers 1985–90, chairman of the RSFSR Council of Ministers 1990–91. Defended RSFSR sovereignty against GKChP 1991, but broke with Yeltsin over pace of reform. After 1991 in diplomatic work, member of 'Kedr'—Russian ecological party—since 1995. | 451

Simonov, A. Correspondence course teacher, Novocherkassk, 1962. | 279

Simonov, Konstantin (Kirill) Mikhaylovich (1915–79). Poet, writer, playwright. Front-line war-correspondent from 1939. In CPSU from 1942. Won 6 Stalin Prizes. Edited *Znamya* 1944–46; *Krasnaya zvezda* from 1946; *Novyy mir* 1946–50 and 1954–58. Secretary of USSR Writers' Union 1954–59 and 1967–79. Candidate and member of CPSU CC 1952–56. | 66

Sinyavsky, Andrey Donatovich (1925–97). Writer, dissident, defendant in notorious trial 1965–66 with co-author Daniel' for publishing a work in the west, under pseudonym 'Abram Tertz'. Sentenced to 7 years, emigrated to France 1973. | 340–42

Slyun'kov, Nikolay Nikitovich (b. 1929). Soviet economic manager and party/state functionary. In tractor production, Minsk, 1950–72. 1st Secretary of Minsk city CPSU 1972–74; deputy chairman of USSR Gosplan 1974–83. 1st Secretary of Belorussian CP from 1983. On CPSU CC 1986–90, Politburo candidate 1986–87, full member 1987–90. USSR People's Deputy from 1989, retired 1990. | 427

Smetona, Antanas (1874–1944). Lithuanian nationalist politician, academic and journalist. Chaired Lithuanian State Council 1917–19, first President of Lithuania 1919–20. 1920s taught at Kaunas University, active in nationalist politics. Organised coup at end of 1926, authoritarian President of Lithuania 1926–40. Deposed by Soviet invasion, fled to Germany, died in USA. | 40–41

Smrkovský, Josef (1911–74). Czechoslovak communist politician. Young communist functionary from early 1930s, in Czechoslovak CP from 1933. In communist resistance to Nazis in WWII. On Czechoslovak CP CC 1945–51. Repressed 1951, fully rehabilitated 1963. On CP CC 1966–69, on Presidium 1968–69. Supporter of Prague Spring democratization. From 1969 removed from positions, expelled from CP 1970. | 234

Snegur, Mircea Ion (b. 1940). Moldovan politician. CPSU member 1964–90. Agronomist 1960s, in Moldovan Agriculture Ministry 1970s, CPSU functionary 1980s, 1985–89 headed Moldovan CP CC, then chair of Moldovan Supreme Soviet. President of independent Moldova 1991–96. | 459

Sobchak, Anatoliy Aleksandrovich (1937–2000). Politician, lawyer, academic, author. Teacher of law 1965–89. Chaired commission investigating Tbilisi events of 9 April 1989. USSR People's Deputy 1989–91. Mayor of Leningrad/St Petersburg June 1991–96. Headed Democratic Reform Movement lists for State Duma elections 1993, not elected. Accused of corruption 1998. | 424

Sobolev, Aleksey. Russian Orthodox priest, Vereya, 1940s. | 110

Sofronov, A.I. (1886–1935). Poet, playwright and writer. | 338

Sokolovsky, Vasiliy Danilovich (1897–1968). Professional soldier. Joined Red Army 1918. In Turkestan 1920s, suppressing *basmachi* guerrillas. In CPSU from 1931. In WWII Chief-of-Staff, commander etc. on the Western Front. Helped plan counter-offensive near Moscow, and operation to take Berlin. 1946–49 commanded Soviet troops in eastern Germany. 1st deputy defence minister 1949–60. 1952–60 head of GHQ. Supreme Soviet Deputy from 1946. 1952–61 full, 1961–68 candidate CPSU CC member. | 139

Solomentsev, Mikhail Sergeevich (b. 1913). CPSU functionary. In CPSU from 1940. Factory worker to 1954, then party worker in Chelyabinsk *oblast'* committee to 1959. In Kazakhstan: 1st Secretary of Karaganda *oblast'* committee 1959–62, 2nd Secretary of Kazakh CP CC 1962–64. On CPSU CC 1961–89, Politburo candidate 1971–83, full member 1983–88. On USSR Supreme Soviet 1958–89, RSFSR Supreme Soviet 1967–89. Chairman of RSFSR Council of Ministers 1971–83, then headed Party Control Committee until retirement 1988. | 252

Solzhenitsyn, Aleksandr Isaevich (b. 1918). Writer, historian, publicist, teacher. Fought in WWII, decorated. Arrested 1945 for negative remarks about Stalin, in camps to 1956. *One Day in the Life of Ivan Denisovich* published in *Novyy mir* 1962, worked on *GULAG Archipelago* and *Red Wheel* series etc. After publication in West, excluded from Writers' Union 1969. Awarded Nobel Prize for Literature, 1970. Arrested and expelled from USSR 1974. Returned to Russia 1994. | 337–39, 353–58, 360–64, 391

Sorokovoy, Aleksey. Steelworker, WWII. | 117

Stalin (Dzhugashvili), Iosif Vissarionovich (1878–1953). Soviet leader. Georgian social-democrat from 1898, Bolshevik from 1903. Active in Caucasus RSDRP, and in 1905–07 events. From March 1917 in Petrograd. Involved in October seizure of power, first Commissar for Nationalities. CPSU General Secretary from 1922. Made this the key party post, eliminated rivals, personal dictator of USSR until his death.

—and annexations 1939–40 | 40, 42–44
—approves Katyn' massacre 1940 | 13–14
—and Asia | 215
—and Church | 159–60, 176, 329
—and Comintern | 165–66
—conduct of war | 76–85, 87, 90–93, 97, 102–03, 105–08, 126, 131–35, 138–40, 192–93
—death | 198–99, 215–16, 219, 264, 271
—and Eastern Europe | 200, 205–12, 216, 221–22
—economic policies | 265, 267, 270, 386
—final years | 195, 197–99, 219, 258, 264, 292–304, 344, 371
—and Finnish War | 20, 32, 36
—historical appraisal of | 391, 394, 396
—legacy | 255, 257, 286, 302–06, 317, 328, 340, 346, 360, 414, 430
—and national minorities | 179, 182, 185–87
—and Nazi attack 1941 | 46–54, 57–59, 61, 63–66
—and pact with Germany 1939 | 5–8, 16, 18, 415–16
—popular attitudes towards | 117–18, 170, 178
—repudiated by Khrushchev | 218, 222, 308–10, 312, 316, 321, 335
—and run-up to war | 1, 3
—and Trotsky | 74–75
—and victory | 150, 152–54, 159
—and west | 67–69, 142–45, 147–48, 166–68, 301–02

Starikov, D. Literary critic, took part in CPSU–cultural figures talks, 1962–63. | 338

Starodubtsev, Vasiliy Aleksandrovich (b. 1931). Soviet politician and agronomist. From 1947 worked on collective farm, in mines, chairman of Novomoskovskoe collective farm 1964–97. Chairman of RSFSR Collective Farm Council from 1986, from 1990 headed USSR Peasant Union and Russian Agrarian Union.

GKChP leader August 1991, arrested, released on health grounds 1992. Now on CPRF CC and leadership of National-Patriotic Union of Russia. | 445

Stavsky (Kirpichnikov), Vladimir Petrovich (1900–43). Writer, journalist, war-correspondent. In CPSU from 1918. Wrote widely for central newspapers. Secretary of RAPP 1928–33, general secretary of Writers' Union 1936–41, chief editor of *Novyy mir* 1937–43, Supreme Soviet Deputy from 1937. From 1941 front-line war-correspondent for *Pravda*. Killed at the front. | 103

Stefan (Protsenko, Stefan Maksimovich) (1889–1960). Churchman. Took holy orders 1922. Bishop of Chernigov and Kozel'sk 1932–36. Archbishop of Ufa from 1942. Took part in September 1943 Church Council. 1944 Archbishop of Poltava and Kremenchug, 1945 Archbishop of Khar'kov. Metropolitan from 1959. | 162

Stepakov, V.I. CPSU functionary. On Central Revision Committee 1961–66, on CC 1966–81. In early 1960s section head with responsibility for ideology, RSFSR agriculture, etc. One-time chief editor of *Izvestiya*. At Novocherkassk in 1962. | 275

Strong, Anna Louise (1885–1970). American socialist journalist. Wrote for US trade-union press 1910s, Moscow correspondent for International News Service from early 1920s. Travelled widely round Europe and China. Helped found *Moscow News* 1930. Wrote numerous books of reportage on her travels. Observed the elections to the Lithuanian Seima on 14 July 1940, which she described in her *Lithuania's New Way*. Expelled from USSR in 1949 for 'espionage'. Moved to China 1958, firm supporter of Mao. Joined Red Guard 1966–69. | 41–42

Suchkov, Boris Leonidovich (1917–74). Specialist on German literature. Organizer and first head of Foreign Literature Publishing House 1946. Arrested with wife 1947 on charge of spying for USA, spent 7 years in camps. Wife never returned. Resumed academic work. Corresponding member of Academy of Sciences and Director of Gorky Institute of World Literature 1968–74. | 354

Susanin, Petr. Red Army soldier in 1943. E.P. Susanina's father. | 111–12

Susanina, E.P. (1928–43?). Soviet schoolgirl whose letter described her forced labour at the hands of the Nazis. Committed suicide. | 111–12

Suslov, Mikhail Andreevich (1902–82). Soviet politician. In Komsomol from 1920, RKP(b) from 1931. CPSU functionary from 1931. Secretary and 2nd Secretary of Rostov *oblast'* committee 1937–39. 1st Secretary of Stavropol' *oblast'* and city party committee 1939–44. Chairman of CC bureau in Lithuania 1944–46. Worked in CC offices 1946 and became Secretary in 1947. On CPSU CC from 1941, Politburo 1952–53 and 1955–82. Hero of Socialist Labour 1962 and 1972. | 252, 255, 320–21, 355, 376

Suvorov, Aleksandr Vasil'evich (1730–1800). Russian national military hero. Professional soldier from age 17. Favourite of Catherine II. Rose from Colonel, in 1762 to Field-Marshal 1794. Took part in Russo-Turkish wars, suppression of Pugachev rising 1773–75 and suppression of Polish rising 1794. | 105

Sven, Sarra. International award-winning dancer, Sverdlovsk, entertained troops 1943. | 156

Švestka, Oldřich (1922–83). Czechoslovak communist politician and journalist. Chief editor of *Rudé Právo* 1945–68 and from 1975. Chief editor of *Tribuna* 1969–71. On the CC from 1962, secretariat member from 1970. Among those who requested Soviet intervention 1968. | 232

Tanner, Väinö Alfred (1881–1966). Finnish politician. Chairman of Finnish Social-Democratic Party 1919–26 and 1957–63. Prime Minister 1926–27, Foreign Minister 1939–40. | 22, 24

Taraki, Nur Mohammed (1917–79). Afghan poet, writer and communist leader. First contacts with Indian communists in Bombay 1930s, learnt English. Held various jobs with Afghan administration 1940s and 1950s. 1965 founded People's Democratic Party of Afghanistan with Babrak Karmal and others. Leader of PDPA Khalqi faction. (Karmal led Parchami faction.) Pro-communist army officers' coup April 1978 put Taraki and PDPA in power. Khalqi faction split September 1979, Taraki overthrown, killed October 1979. | 242–45

Tarkovsky, Andrey Arsen'evich (1932–86). Film producer, most noted for film *Andrey Rublev* (1966). From 1982 obliged to work abroad. | 357

Tarnov, Sergey Kuz'mich (d. 1942). Turner in Moscow engineering works until 1941. Private 1941–42. Killed in action. | 120

Temushkin, Oleg Petrovich. Assistant USSR Procurator General, state prosecutor in Daniel' and Sinyavsky trial 1965–66. Author of many books on Soviet legal theory and practice. | 341

Ter-Petrosyan, Levon (b. 1945). Armenian scholar and politician. Born in Syria, moved with family to Armenia 1946. In 1970s worked in Armenian literary institute. Late 1980s involved in Armenian national movement over Nagorno-Karabakh, briefly arrested. Elected to Armenian SSR Supreme Soviet 1989, its chairman from 1990. Head of Armenian All-National Movement. 1991 elected President of Armenia, re-elected 1996, lost power 1998. | 459

Tereshchenko. Professor, Khar'kov University, 1944. | 171

Ternovsky, Leonard Borisovich (1933–2006). Doctor, human rights campaigner. Signed protests 1968, in 1970s active against abuse of psychiatry for political repression. Imprisoned for 3 years 1980. Rehabilitated 1991. | 252

Teterin, M.V. (d. 1940). Soviet soldier in Finland, 1939–40. | 30

Timoshenko, Semen Konstantinovich (1895–1970). Professional soldier and politician. Served in WWI, joined Red Guard 1917 and Red Army 1918. Held various commands in civil war, got to know Stalin. Joined RKP(b) 1919. On CC 1939–52. Led occupation of eastern Poland 1939, commanded NW Front against Finland 1939–40. Defence Commissar 1940–July 1941, accelerated war preparations. Commander-in-Chief of Western and SW sectors 1941–42. Commander of Western, SW, Stalingrad and NW Fronts 1941–43. | 32, 36, 39, 49, 52, 61, 78

Tito (Broz, Josip) (1892–1980). Yugoslav communist leader. POW in Russia in

WWI, joined Bolsheviks 1917, fought with Red Army. Joined Yugoslav CP 1920 in Croatia, worked in Comintern apparatus 1930s. Headed anti-Nazi partisans 1941–45, Yugoslav CP and government from 1945. Broke with Stalin 1948, from 1950s actively 'non-aligned'. | 199, 206–11, 216–19, 301

Tizyakov, Aleksandr Ivanovich (b. 1926). Soviet politician and industrialist. Followed dual career in Komsomol/CPSU and engineering from 1950. Chief engineer of factory from 1976, director of 'Kalinin' machinery factory from 1988. Headed All-Union Association of State Enterprises 1990. On GKChP August 1991, amnestied 1994, now involved in manufacturing and insurance. | 445

Torstensen. TV director at Central Television studio in 1968, critical of invasion of Czechoslovakia. | 350

Trotsky (Bronshteyn), Lev Davidovich (1879–1940). Revolutionary from end of 1890s, joined RSDRP. Briefly headed 1st Petrograd Soviet 1905. Joined Bolsheviks 1917. September 1917 chairman of Petrograd Soviet. Played key role in October seizure of power. War commissar 1918–24, founder of Red Army. On Politburo 1919–26. Expelled from CPSU 1927, deported 1929. Founded 'Fourth International' from his supporters 1938, assassinated 1940. | 74

Troyanovsky, Pavel Ivanovich. War-correspondent. On *Krasnaya zvezda* in WWII, Lieutentant-General, Red Army political officer. Wrote memoirs of war *On Eight Fronts*. | 104–05

Trubin, Nikolay Semenovich (b. 1931). Lawyer. Worked in local procurators' offices, in USSR Procuracy. 1976–78 consultant to the Cuban Procuracy. Then RSFSR deputy, then Procurator General. In 1991 Procurator General of USSR and RSFSR. Legal consultant from 1992. | 374–77

Truman, Harry S. (1884–1972). US Democratic politician, President 1945–53. Pursued foreign policy of 'containing' communism. | 201, 205, 213

Tsaruk, Aleksey. Frontline CPSU bureau Secretary, 1941. | 81

Tsoy, Valentin Evgen'evich (b. 1952). Businessman and politician. Worked as stockbreeder and in poultry production 1970s and 1980s. In CPSU from 1974. Formed co-operatives and businesses linked to agriculture. RSFSR People's Deputy from 1990, stood as independent for post of chairman of RSFSR Supreme Soviet. In KPRF 1994–95, expelled for standing for election in Khabarovsk against official KPRF candidate. | 431–32

Tukhachevsky, Mikhail Ivanovich (1893–1937). Professional soldier, Lieutentant in WWI. In RKP(b) and Red Army, successful against Kolchak, Denikin, Kronstadt and Tambov rebellions, failed in Poland. Worked on military theory and modernization of Red Army 1920s and 1930s. Made Marshal of USSR 1937. Arrested and shot 1937. | 346

Tukharinov, Yuriy Vladimirovich (1927–98). Professional soldier, Lieutenant-General in 1979, formed 40th Army to invade Afghanistan, headed force until 1980. | 247

Tupikov, Vasiliy Ivanovich (1901–41). Major-General, Soviet military attaché and intelligence agent in Berlin 1941. | 53–54

Bishop of Kalinin 1941, Archbishop of Kalinin and Smolensk 1943. Took part in September 1943 Church Council. | 162

Vatutin, Nikolay Fedorovich (1901–44). Professional soldier. General from 1943. Peasant's son, joined Red Army 1920, RKP(b) 1921. Held various commands 1920s and 1930s. In WWII headed HQ of NW Front, commanded troops on the Voronezh, SW (Stalingrad) and 1st Ukrainian Fronts. Fatally wounded by Ukrainian nationalist forces. | 139

Vavilov, Yu. Protester against rehabilitation of Stalin, 1967. | 346

Veniamin (Fedchenkov, Ivan Afanas'evich (1880–1961). Orthodox churchman. Took monastic vows 1907. In Church Council of 1917–18. Bishop to the army and navy in south Russia 1919–20, evacuated from Crimea. In Yugoslavia, Czechoslovakia and Paris 1920s and 1930s. From 1933 Metropolitan of Aleutians and North America, from 1934 representative of Moscow Patriarchate in North America. Returned to USSR 1947, held various church posts. | 164–65

Veniamin (Tikhonitsky, Veniamin Mikhaylovich) (1869–1957). Churchman. Bishop of Kirov and Slobodskoy from 1942. Took part in September 1943 Church Council. Archbishop from 1945. | 162

Veselkov, G.G. Politician and economist. Responsible for CPSU CC economic activities, 1991. | 438

Vishnevskaya, Galina Pavlovna (b. 1926). Soprano opera-singer. Honoured Artiste of the RSFSR in 1955. First sang in operetta in Leningrad in 1944. Soloist at Bolshoi 1952–74. Many highly successful world-tours. Exiled with husband M. Rostropovich 1974 for human rights activities, awards revoked, but restored 1990. | 356–57, 363–65

Vishnevskaya, Yuliya Iosifovna (b. 1949) Poet, writer, human rights campaigner from 1965, emigrated to Germany 1971. | 352

Vlasov, Aleksandr Vladimirovich (b. 1932). In CPSU from 1956, on staff from 1961. CC candidate member from 1976, full member 1981–91. Politburo candidate from 1988. USSR Minister of Internal Affairs from 1986. Chairman of RSFSR Council of Ministers 1988–90, lost to Yeltsin in elections for chairman of RSFSR Supreme Soviet. | 431–32

Vlasov, Andrey Andreevich (1901–46). Professional soldier. In Red Army from 1920. Held various commands 1920s and 1930s. In CPSU from 1930. Military advisor to Kuomintang, China, 1938–39. Lieutentant-General from 1941. Held various commands until captured by Germans 11 July 1942. Offered to collaborate with Wehrmacht, forming Russian Liberation Army from Soviet POWs. Captured by Soviet forces 1945, tried, hanged 1946. | 191–92, 362

Voionmaa, Väinö (1869–1947). Finnish social-democratic politician and academic. Historian, professor, active teetotaller. Founder of Workers' Educational Association in Finland. Foreign Minister 1926–27 and 1938. Participant in peace talks with USSR March 1940. | 33, 35

Vorob'ev, N. Took part in 1962–63 talks between CPSU leaders and cultural figures. | 338

Voronkov, Konstantin Vasil'evich (1911–84). Organizing Secretary of USSR Writers' Union, 1970. | 354

Voronov, Nikolay Nikolaevich (1899–68). Professional soldier. Joined Red Army 1918, RKP(b) 1919. Head of Leningrad Artillery School from 1930. In Spain 1936–37 head of Red Army artillery 1937–40 and from 1941. Head of anti-aircraft defence and deputy defence commissar in WWII. Commander of Soviet artillery from 1946. USSR Supreme Soviet Deputy 1946–50. Lost positions in purge of military 1950. | 92

Voroshilov, Kliment Efremovich (1881–1969). Soviet military and political leader. Factory worker from 1895, joined Bolsheviks 1904, strike leader in 1905. Arrested several times. Factory worker in Petrograd February 1917, from March in party and soviet work in Lugansk (later Voroshilovgrad). Active in civil war. On RKP(b) CC from 1921, Politburo from 1925. Promoted in Red Army and state by Stalin. Demoted in WWII. Sided with 'anti-party group' of Molotov etc. 1956–57, then recanted. Off CPSU CC 1961, back on 1966–69. | 13, 32, 36, 39, 42, 61, 78, 90, 303, 306, 311

Voznesensky, Andrey Andreevich (b. 1933). Poet, writer, first published in 1958. Took part in discussions with CPSU leaders 1962–63. | 336, 339

Voznesensky, Nikolay Alekseevich (1903–50). Soviet state and political figure. In RKP(b) from 1919, party worker from 1924. In economic apparatus from 1934, in Leningrad economic and city administration 1935–37. Deputy head of Gosplan from 1937, head from 1938. On CPSU CC from 1939, candidate for Politburo from 1941, member 1947–49. Deputy chairman of Council of People's Commissars/Ministers 1939–41 and from 1942. Arrested 1949 in fabrication of 'Leningrad Case', shot 1950. | 39, 60, 301

Vyshinsky, Andrey Yanuar'evich (1883–1954). Soviet politician, jurist, academic, diplomat. Menshevik from 1903, joined RKP(b) 1920. Worked in Food Commissariat 1919–23, also lectured in Moscow. Supreme Court Procurator 1923–25. Rector of Moscow State University 1925–28. Involved in all major show trials from 1928, prosecutor in 1936–38 trials. On CPSU CC from 1939. 1940–46 1st deputy commissar for foreign affairs, deputy foreign minister 1946–49, foreign minister 1949–53. Thereafter USSR representative at UN. | 215

Vyshintsev, Aleksandr. War veteran, 79-year-old protester in 1991. | 446

Walden, Karl Rudolf (1878–1946). Finnish soldier and politician. Rose rapidly in 1918 on 'White' side, Commander-in-Chief of Finnish army by end of 1918. War Minister 1918–19. Major-General from 1919. Defence minister 1940–44. Signed peace treaty with USSR 1940. | 33, 35

Wałęsa, Lech (b. 1943). Polish trade unionist and politician. Led shipyard strikes in Gdańsk 1980, headed Solidarność trade union. President of Poland 1990–95. | 249

Weidling, Helmuth Otto Ludwig (1891–1955). German career officer, joined army 1911. General in WWII, appointed military commander of Berlin April 1945. Surrendered Berlin to Soviet forces. Died in Soviet captivity. | 149–50

Wojtyła, Karol Józef (Pope John Paul II) (1920–2005). Polish churchman, appointed Cardinal 1967, Pope 1978. | 248

Yakir, Iona Emmanuilovich (1896–1937). Politician and soldier. Bolshevik from 1917, in Red Army from 1918. In 1920s held important posts in Ukraine, trained in Germany 1928–29. Arrested and executed 1937. | 346

Yakir, Irina Petrovna (1948–99). Human rights campaigner from 1960s. Daughter of P.I. Yakir. | 352

Yakir, Petr Ionovich (1923–82). Historian, human rights activist. First sent to camps age 14 as son of Iona Yakir, sentenced on false treason charge 1937. Spent 17 years in camps and prisons. In human rights movement 1960s and 1970s. | 346, 348, 352, 359

Yakobson, Anatoliy Aleksandrovich (1935–78). Historian, teacher, literature specialist, human rights campaigner. Opposed invasion of Czechoslovakia 1968, editor of *Chronicle of Current Events* from 1969. Emigrated to Israel 1973. Committed suicide when mentally ill. | 352

Yakovlev, Aleksandr Nikolaevich (1923–2005). Politician, academic and diplomat. Fought in WWII, seriously wounded. Worked in CPSU CC apparatus from 1950s, studied in USA 1958–59, head of CPSU propaganda department 1969–73 and from 1985. Ambassador to Canada 1973–83. On CPSU CC from 1986, Politburo from 1987. Close colleague of Gorbachev. From 1992 headed commission for rehabilitating victims of repression, and Democracy ('Yakovlev') Foundation. Head of state TV 1993–95. | 394, 414–15

Yakovlev, Aleksandr Sergeevich (1906–89). Soviet aircraft designer. Chief aircraft designer from 1935, designed most bombers used by USSR in WWII. Made Colonel-General of air force in 1946. In Academy of Sciences from 1976. Hero of Socialist Labour 1940 and 1957. | 116

Yanaev, Gennadiy Ivanovich (b. 1937). Soviet politician and functionary. Joined CPSU 1962, followed Komsomol career, then in youth and international friendship organizations. International secretary of Soviet trade unions 1986–89, from 1990 chairman of Soviet trade unions. On CPSU CC and Politburo 1990–91. Vice-President of USSR from January 1991, GKChP leader and Acting President 19–21 August 1991. Arrested following collapse of putsch. Amnestied 1994. | 444–45, 452–53

Yandarov, A.G. Spiritual leader in Checheno-Ingushetia, 1944. | 187

Yaroshevskaya, Vera. Student at Leningrad Mining Institute, 1941. | 99

Yarushok (née Arbatskaya), Mariya Dmitrievna (b. 1921). Student at the Leningrad Mining Institute 1940–47, then worked in Noril'sk and Leningrad. | 96–100

Yazov, Dmitriy Timofeevich (b. 1923). Soviet soldier and politician. In army from 1941, CPSU from 1944. Fought in WWII, then held various commands. Deputy

Minister of Defence from mid 1980s, Minister from 1987. Marshal of the USSR from 1990. On CPSU CC from 1987. Member of GKChP August 1991. Following amnesty not involved in politics, consultant at General Staff Academy. | 444–45, 449

Yeltsin, Boris Nikolaevich (b. 1931). Soviet and Russian politician. In CPSU 1961–90. 1976–85 1st Secretary of Sverdlovsk *oblast'* committee. On CC from 1981, Politburo candidate member 1986–88. Secretary of CC 1985–86. 1st Secretary of Moscow city party committee 1985–87. USSR People's Deputy from 1989. Chairman of Supreme Soviet of RSFSR from 1990. President of RSFSR from 1991. | 400–09, 418, 431–32, 434–35, 440, 443–44, 446, 449–56, 459

Yrjö-Koskinen, Aarno Armas Sakari (1885–1951). Finnish politician and diplomat. Foreign minister 1931–32, representative in Moscow 1939. | 22–24

Yusupov, Usman Yusupovich (1900–66). Soviet Uzbek politician, son of farm labourer. Started work as shepherd, then in cotton factory. In CPSU from 1926, Secretary of Uzbek CP CC from 1929, 1st Secretary 1937–50. Oversaw destruction of Uzbek CP old guard 1937–39. On CPSU CC 1939–56, on USSR Supreme Soviet Presidium 1938–50. Developed Uzbekistan as cotton republic. USSR Minister for Cotton Production 1950–55. Chairman of Uzbek Council of Ministers 1953–55. Demoted. | 183

Yuzovsky, Iosif (Yuzef) Il'ich (1902–64). Noted literary and theatre critic, denounced as part of anti-Semitic campaign 1949. | 333–34

Zakhar'in, A.I. Chief engineer at Leningrad engineering factory, 1941. | 90

Zamula, V.M. Chairman of Novocherkassk city executive committee, 1962. | 275

Zamyatin, Leonid Mitrofanovich (b. 1922). Diplomat and state functionary. In CPSU from 1944, on CC 1976–91. In Ministry of Foreign Affairs from 1946, in Soviet delegations to UN, IAEA. General director of TASS 1970–78, head of CPSU CC information section 1978–86, ambassador to UK 1986–91. | 251

Zanadvorov, Vladislav Leonidovich (1914–42). Writer, poet and geologist. Called up in WWII, killed at Stalingrad. | 155–56

Zanlavskaya, Tat'yana Ivanovna (b. 1927) Sociologist and economist. Noted as author of paper on Soviet social and economic ills ('Novosibirsk Report') 1983. | 286–88

Zatvornitsky, Vladimir Andreevich (b. 1929) Building worker and politician. Builders' brigade leader in Moscow from 1955. CPSU member from 1958. On CPSU CC 1981–90. Honoured Builder of the USSR. | 403–04

Zbarsky, Feliks-Lev Borisovich. Artist and animator. Took part in talks with leading CPSU figures 1962–63. Emigrated 1970s. | 338

Zemlyanichenko. Chairman of Sverdlovsk city executive committee, 1955. | 307

Zhavoronkov. Wounded by peasant bandits, Chelyabinsk, 1946. | 261

Zhdanov, Andrey Aleksandrovich (1896–1948). Soviet politician, in revolutionary movement from 1912, RSDRP(b) from 1915. In soldiers' soviets 1917. Soviet and party leader in Tver' 1918–24, Nizhniy Novgorod 1924–34, Leningrad from 1934. Close ally of Stalin. On CPSU CC from 1927. During war member of

North Western and Leningrad Military Council. Made Colonel-General in 1944. Secured party control over culture after war. | 33, 35, 39, 171–72, 206–07, 292, 300–01, 329, 333, 335

Zhigarev, Pavel Fedorovich (1900–63). Professional soldier, in Red Army from 1919, air force from 1925. Served in China 1937–38. Deputy head of air force from 1940, Commander-in-Chief 1941–42, then commander of Far Eastern forces. Head of air force again from 1949. Deputy from 1953, 1st deputy defence minister 1955–57. Headed air force academy in Kalinin 1959–63. | 92

Zhirinovsky, Vladimir Vol'fovich (b. 1946). Russian politician. Worked in international department of Soviet peace committee 1972–75, trade-union school for foreign students 1975–77, foreign section of justice ministry 1977–83, legal consultant to Mir publisher 1983–90. Founded Liberal-Democratic Party 1990. Stood as presidential candidate in Russia three times. Duma Deputy since 1993. Political positions very changeable, but consistently neither liberal nor democratic. | 444, 453

Zhukov. Radio commentator. | 362

Zhukov, Georgiy Konstantinovich (1896–1974). Marshal of the Soviet Union. Hero of Soviet Union 1939, 1944, 1945 and 1956. Joined Russian Army 1915, fought in WWI. Joined Red Army in 1918 and fought in civil war 1918–20. In 1939 defeated Japanese at Khalkin-Gol, Mongolia. From June 1940 commander of Kiev special military district. January–June 1941 Chief of General Staff and deputy PC for Defence. Commander of Leningrad Front at beginning of war. Commanded Western Front in defence of Moscow (1941–42). From August 1942 deputy PC for Defence and deputy Supreme Commander-in-Chief. Present at German surrender on 8 May 1945. 1955–57 Minister of Defence. Candidate and member of Presidium of CC of CPSU 1956–57. Deputy of Supreme Soviet 1941–58. | 48–52, 78–79, 90, 102, 104, 139, 147, 150, 299–300, 314–15

Zhutovsky, Boris Iosifovich (b. 1932). Artist, book illustrator and designer. Paintings denounced by Khrushchev when he closed the *30 Years of the Moscow Academy of Art* exhibition 1962. Took part in meetings between government and artists 1962–63. | 337–39

Zorich. Member of Krasnaya Presnya (Moscow) CPSU organization, 1945. | 174

Zoshchenko, Mikhail Mikhaylovich (1895–1958). Writer, satirist, translator. Conscripted 1915, in Red Army 1918–19. Began writing 1920, published short stories, and many articles in Leningrad papers, *Krokodil*, etc. Also in radio and theatre. Denounced by Zhdanov 1946, excluded from Writers' Union to 1953. | 172, 329–31, 345

Zverev, Arseniy Grigor'evich (1900–69). Soviet economist and politician. Son of peasant. Joined RKP(b) and Red Army 1919. Then in party and state work. Trained at Finance Commissariat, 1920s. USSR Supreme Soviet Deputy 1937–50 and 1954–62. On CPSU CC 1939–61. 1937 deputy commissar, from 1938 commissar/minister of finance. Organized finance of war effort. Retired 1960. | 265

General Index

Place Index